Spirit Builders

A Free Illuminist Approach to the
Antient & Primitive Rite of
Memphis+Misraïm

STANDARD EDITION

A LA GLOIRE DU GRAND ARCHITECTE DE L'UNIVERS

A Free Illuminist Approach to the
Antient & Primitive Rite of
Memphis+Misraim

Spirit Builders

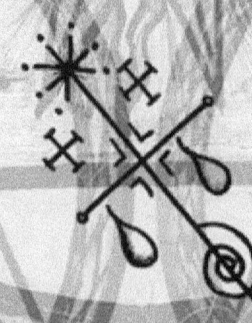

✠ PALAMAS

A La Gloire Du Grand Architecte De L'Univers

Spirit Builders

A Free Illuminist Approach to the
Antient & Primitive Rite of
Memphis+Misraïm

STANDARD EDITION

Written and Illustrated by

PALAMAS

∴

Fox Lake, IL

SPIRIT BUILDERS: A FREE ILLUMINIST APPROACH TO THE ANTIENT & PRIMITIVE RITE OF MEMPHIS+MISRAÏM, STANDARD EDITION

BY PALAMAS

TEXT, ARTWORK & COVER ART COPYRIGHT © 2015, 2025 PALAMAS
PHOTOGRAPHY © SALOME+

TRACING BOARDS ARE TAKEN FROM: *The Tarot of the Egyptian Freemasonry of Cagliostro* BY GRAND HIEROPHANT, ALEXANDER RYBALKA AND ARTIST, ALEXANDER NAUMOV, SILHOUETTE PUBLISHING, 2015.
USED WITH PERMISSION IN ASSOCIATION WITH THE WAEO (WORLD ASSOCIATION OF EGYPTIAN OBEDIENCES).

PUBLISHED 2025 BY TRIAD PRESS, LLC

NO PORTION OF THIS BOOK MAY BE REPRODUCED BY ANY MEANS, ELECTRONICALLY, PHYSICALLY, OR OTHERWISE WITHOUT THE WRITTEN CONSENT OF THE PUBLISHER, EXCEPT IN THE CASE OF QUOTATIONS EMBODIED IN CRITICAL REVIEWS OR TEXTS AS PERMITTED BY COPYRIGHT LAW.

ALL RIGHTS RESERVED.

ISBN: 978-1-946814-16-6

TRIAD PRESS, LLC
123 S. US 12 #33
FOX LAKE, IL 60020

PALAMAS IS THE AUTHOR OF:

SYZYGY: REFLECTIONS ON THE MONASTERY OF THE SEVEN RAYS, 3RD EDITION, 2024.

COALESCENCE: ESOTERIC AND PHILOSOPHICAL MUSINGSOF A GYROVAGUE. TRANSMUTATION PUBLISHING, 2018.

ENKRATEIA: THE ESSENCE OF SPIRIT BUILDING, WITH GOTTLIEB'S HISTORY OF THE MASONIC RITE OF MEMPHIS AND A PREVIOUSLY UNPUBLISHED ESSAY BY ALLEN H. GREENFIELD. TRANSMUTATION PUBLISHING, 2019.

LUX OCCULTA: THE THEOLOGY & RITUAL OF A SPIRITIST CHAPTER OF MARTINISM & MARTINÉSISM. TRANSMUTATION PUBLISHING, 2019.

SYMPATHEIA: A LITURGICAL GUIDE TO ESOTERIC STOICISM. S^3 PUBLISHING, 2023.

THE HOMEROMANTEION: A LITERARY & PHILOSOPHICAL ORACLE FOR STOICS. S^3 PUBLISHING, 2024.

Au nom et sous les Auspices de la Grand Lodge du Rite Ancien et Primitif de Memphis-Misraim

Rite Ancien et Primitif de Memphis-Misraim

January, 2015 e. v.

By my authority as Hierophant, Conservator, and Grand Master of the Ancient & Primitive Rite of Egyptian Initiation (Memphis-Misraim), I, Michael-Paul Bertiaux, 33°, 90°, 97°, do hereby authorize and give my full Blessing to the work of +PALAMAS and SALOME+ within the Chapel of the Gnosis, as they seek to bring new life and vigor to the mystical and hermetic Rites of Memphis-Misraim.

et Passeporte Mystique

By this letter, I convey my blessings and my spiritual protection upon those working this sacred path, and seeking the inner Temples of Memphis-Misraim, through the spiritist and gnostic approach to the work that +PALAMAS herein propounds.

Given this day, 18 / 1 / 2015, in the Zenith of Chicago, Il. U.S.A., with my signature, stamp, and seal of order:

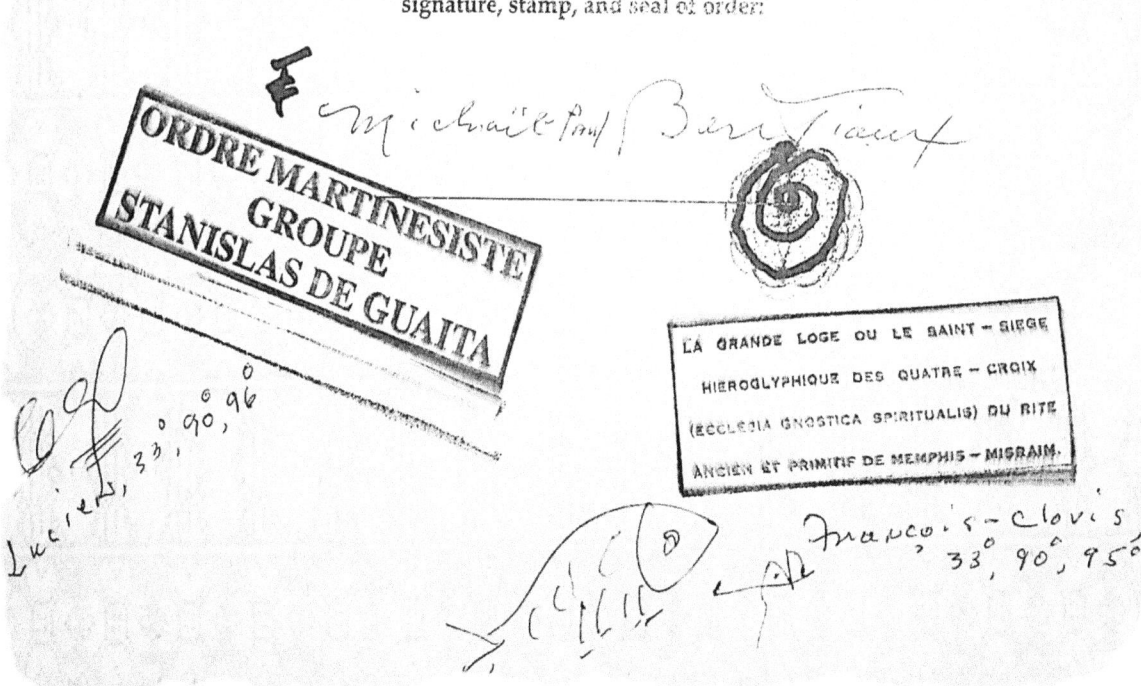

Lucien, 33°, 90°, 96°

François-Clovis, 33°, 90°, 95°

ORDRE MARTINESISTE GROUPE STANISLAS DE GUAITA

LA GRANDE LOGE OU LE SAINT-SIEGE HIEROGLYPHIQUE DES QUATRE-CROIX (ECCLESIA GNOSTICA SPIRITUALIS) DU RITE ANCIEN ET PRIMITIF DE MEMPHIS-MISRAIM.

.:.The Order of the Three-fold Path.:.

Astra Inclinant Non-Necessitant

 Katharismos   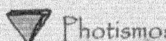 Photismos   Henosis

By my authority as Bishop and Prince of the True and Authentic Tradition of Gnosis and as Facilitator of this Lodge, the Sons and Daughters of Aaron, according to my duty as 33°, 90° & 96° of Le Rite Antient et Primitif de Memphis+Misraim, I, T Allen Greenfield, do hereby authorize:

_____ and _____

students of the mysteries in Cave Spring, GA@.:.KMGC, to found gather and teach a Philosophical and Research Circle--.:.The Order of the Threefold Path (OTP) for purposes of mystical inquiry leading to initiation into the degrees of katharismos, photismos and henosis and exaltation to the Chapel of the Gnosis.:. gathered to them as hermetic students for this purpose.

The name of this Rite shall be The Order of the Threefold Path and Chapel of the Gnosis at .:.Kudzu Mountain Gypsy Cave and may all who are gathered into this Lodge and Chapel be blessed by their studies and inquiries and to all who come to read these words I convey my blessings and my spiritual protection. Given this day 22 Dec., 2011, in the Zenith of Atlanta Ga., USA with my sign, stamp and seal of Order.

Tau Sir Hasirim	Father Palamas	Draco Coccinea
x T Allen Greenfield	x _____	x _____
T Allen Greenfield		

+Our Lady of the Clearing

✠ Egos Nos Integrate!

Ritus Memphis et Misraim

Egyptian High~Grade Freemasonry 97°
ECCLESIASTICAL REVISION 1921

GREETINGS AND SALUTATIONS ON ALL POINTS OF THE TRIANGLE

THIS CHARTER SERVES TO ESTABLISH A MASONIC LODGE OF PHILOSOPHICAL STUDY, ESOTERIC RESEARCH, AND TEMPLAR FRATERNITY UNDER THE AUSPICES OF

The Antient & Primitive Rite of Memphis+Misraim

AS COMMUNICATED BY

MY AUTHORITY AS MASTER OF THE SONS AND DAUGHTERS OF AARON LODGE OF THE ANCIENT AND PRIMITIVE RITE OF MEMPHIS-MISRAIM,

I, THE RT. REV. T ALLEN GREENFIELD 33°, 90°, 95°, 97°

DO AUTHORIZE

Sir Tau PALAMAS 33°, 90°, 95°, 96°

ABBOT *IN SECLUSION*

OF THE Ordo Gyrovagus ✝

✠

TO FOUND, GATHER, RULE, AND TEACH A PHILOSOPHICAL AND RESEARCH LODGE OF THE ANTIENT & PRIMITIVE RITE OF MEMPHIS-MISRAIM EGYPTIAN FREEMASONRY, FOR THE PURPOSES OF MYSTICAL INQUIRY LEADING TO INITIATION INTO THE MYSTERIES AND SECRETS OF NATURE, AS SET FORTH IN OUR TEACHINGS, TO ENTER, PASS, RAISE, AND TO EXALT THOSE SUBJECT TO HIS AUTHORITY GATHERED TO HIM AS HERMETIC STUDENTS FOR THAT PURPOSE.

THE NAME OF THIS LODGE SHALL BE

HORUS

AND MAY ALL WHO ARE GATHERED INTO THIS LODGE BE BLESSED BY THEIR STUDIES AND INQUIRIES, AND TO ALL WHO COME TO READ THESE WORDS, I CONVEY MY BLESSINGS AND SPIRITUAL PROTECTION. GIVEN THIS DAY, AUGUST 12TH, 2018 E.V. IN THE ZENITH OF ATLANTA, GEORGIA, USA. WITH MY SIGNATURE, STAMP, AND SEAL OF ORDER:

✠

RT. REV. ALLEN GREENFIELD 33°, 90°, 95°, 97°
MABEKER & MASTER OF THE SONS & DAUGHTERS OF AARON

+PALAMAS 33°, 90°, 95°, 96°
VEN. MASTER OF HORUS LODGE

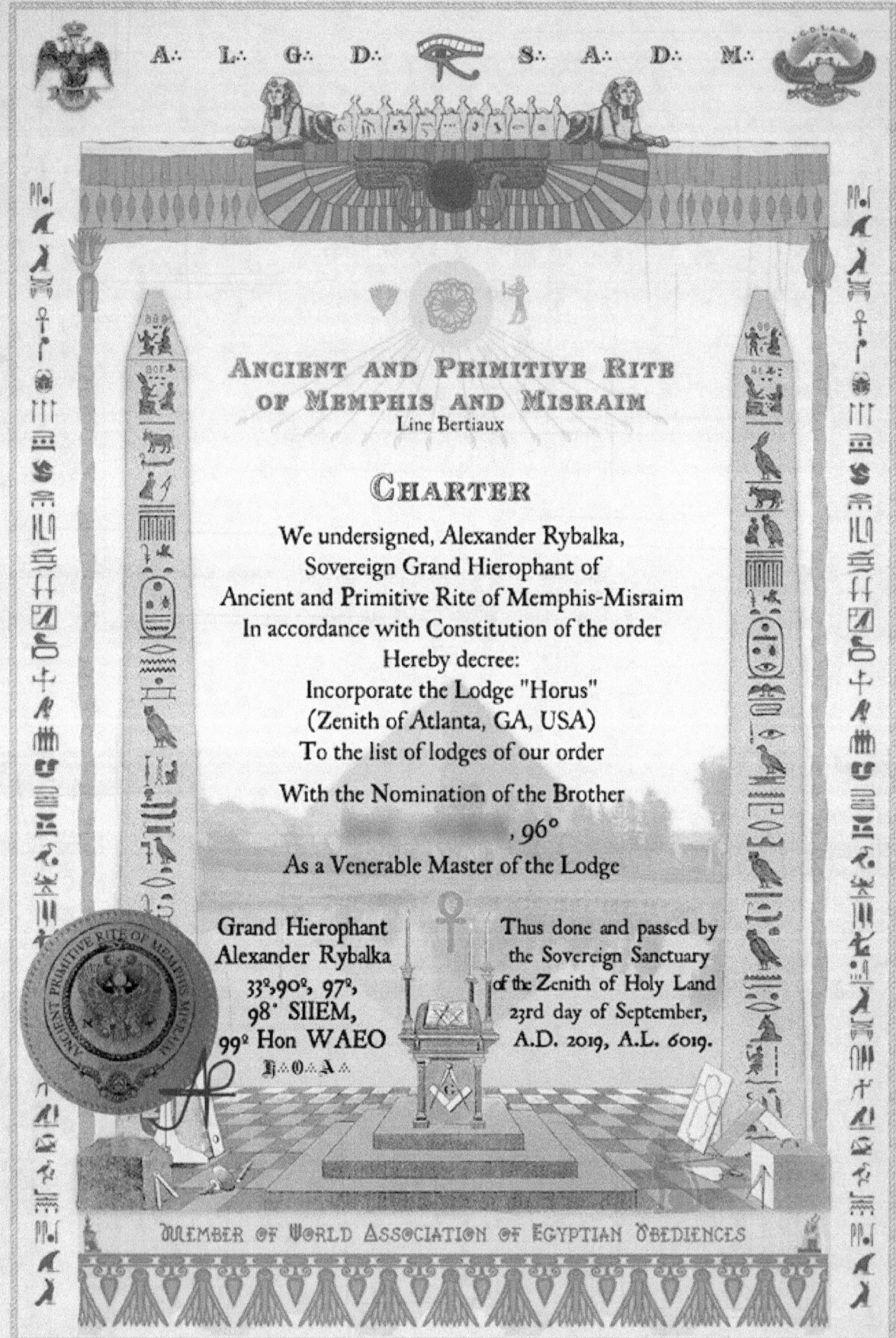

In memory of Illustrious Grand Hierophant, Alexander Rybalka 33° 90° 99°

1966-2022

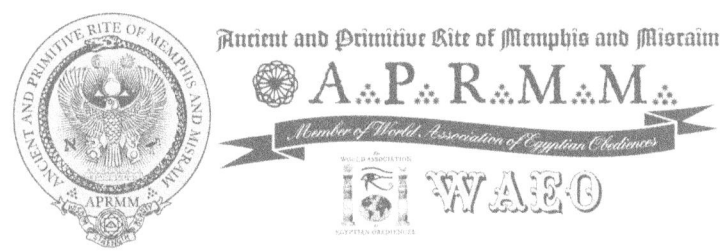

Acknowledgements
10-year anniversary edition

Out of my selection of titles written thus far, it is *Spirit Builders* that I have had the most requests for a re-release. A bit of a monster in my mind, this book would've stayed in obscurity if it wasn't for the prompting from worthy Brothers and Sisters across the globe. It isn't that I did not want the work released, but that I wanted to continuously *add to* the already hefty tome! This is the nature of this particular methodology; it opens seemingly endless doors to enhancement and development. Only a few years after the first publication, an entirely new level of working revealed itself, via the Tracing Boards that GH Alexander Rybalka created: the Rites of Memphis+Misraïm on the *cosmic scale of reality* through advanced æonology and epoptics. A true exploration of this experiment will have to be saved for a future effort, but we have included some useful instruction in the Preface to Vol. 2 of the deluxe edition. What is most interesting is the interminable permutations of the APRM+M! What began for me as a search for initiation into the Rites of Memphis and Misraïm as an extension of my regular lodge work, has continued into experimentation with cosmic consciousness, through those very same degrees. In fact, this system has revealed itself to have three domains, or echelons of working: *regular* lodge work, *points-chauds empowerments* as developed in the present text, and on the cosmic scale, *advanced æonology*.

Neither the original research and experimentation, nor the present embodiment of cosmic workings would be possible without the inspiration, support, and engagement of Free Illuminists *across* the globe, beginning with the Atlanta community—Alicia, Roger, Bill, Sascha, Aron (may his soul be at peace), among others, and illustrious T Allen H. Greenfield 100°, the godfather of the Free Illuminist movement altogether. Special thanks to Allen H. Greenfield who continues to be my friend and confidant in the mysteries. This entire approach is a child of his labors. These genuine practitioners and lovely people are true initiates and have carried Free and Congregational Illuminism to new heights. Without their mutual aid and support, initiatory work, and consecrations, *Spirit Builders* would not exist.

Thanks to the beloved Patriarch of all the Mysteries and the authentic working of the *Antient & Primitive Rite of Memphis Misraïm*, Michael-Paul Bertiaux, whose direction and instruction elevated the present work immensely, and whose initial chartering and passing of the egregore (Ecclesiastical Revision, 1921) to Allen H. Greenfield led to the Great Arabia Mountain workings. Master Bertiaux's work has opened up innumerable gnostic spaces and provided access to the INNER RETREAT of Memphis+Misraïm, which is the hidden nectar of our mystical understanding of this system.

Many thanks to Illus. Past Grand Hierophant, Alexander Rybalka 99°, *may he rest in peace*, for our many conversations and discussions on further development of the Rites of Memphis+Misraïm, permission to utilize his beautiful Tracing Boards for this second edition, and the chartering of our Horus Lodge. In connection with both Bro. Rybalka and Allen Greenfield, I am grateful to Illus. Bro. Vladimir Milinovic 98°, SIEEM of the WAEO, for his continued friendship and support, positivity, and manifold efforts for worldwide Memphis+Misraïm Masonry. Along those same lines, thanks to GH Joël Duez 99° who offered his mutual aid and support to our fledgling *Chapel of the Gnosis* early in its development and encouraged our initial melding of ecclesiastical and masonic workings.

Thanks to John Michael Greer, who beyond being a trusted friend, has reified my initial consecration through the *Universal Gnostic Church* (+John Gilbert line) and continues to guide thousands towards the Light. The reigniting of my path as a wandering Bishop was instrumental in the consecrations necessary for the third echelon working of the APRM+M. Thanks also to Nicholaj de Mattos Frisvold, 97° for his personal work with *Spirit Builders*, friendship and encouragement, and preface to Vol. One of the present tome.

Many thanks to Chic and Tabatha Cicero, who taught me how to scry back in 2004, and lead me to the *lux occulta* through *many* initiations and several Orders. Thanks also to all my dear Brothers of mainstream Freemasonry (Blue Lodge, York Rites, and Scottish Rite), as well as my Brothers *and Sisters* of *Le Droit Humain*, Atlantis Lodge #2158.

Much gratitude to Tau Phosphoros, 96° for his continued friendship, leadership in many branches of the Gnostic tree, impeccable translations of French work (such as the *Degrees of Wisdom* which function as a companion to the present work in many ways), and for his work through Triad Press. I am incredibly grateful for +Phosphoros for taking on the present text for publication and encouraging me to not add 600 more pages to the work.

Finally, all the research and experimentation requiring an Inner Guard and Outer Guard would not have come to be if it wasn't for the other half of my syzygy: *Salome+*. Her adventurous spirit, willingness to participate in the most curious of rites, and contributions to the work are irreplaceable. This text is a direct result of our experiments together, beginning immediately after our empowerments (2012) on the holy Arabia Mountain from Allen and company, and continuing into the present, over ten years later. But of course, it is our *love* and marriage of 15 years which is the soul of these labors.

Foreword

Spirit Builders: A Manual of Inner Architecture and Mystical Engineering

In the broad lineage of esoteric traditions, certain texts do not simply convey knowledge, but they generate transformation. *Spirit Builders* is such a work: a rare synthesis of occult philosophy, Masonic ritual science, and experimental mysticism that refuses to be constrained by dogma or convention. It belongs to the same tradition of initiatory literature as the *Corpus Hermeticum*, Augustine's *City of God,* Origen's *De Principiis* and Michael Bertiaux's *Voudon Gnostic Workbook*. I am not having in mind any imitation as such, but a direct continuity, extending the living chain of spiritual innovation through rigorous practice and metaphysical insight from the early doctors of the Church and up to the mystical and highly spiritualized domains of the master Bertiaux.

The Rite of Memphis and Misraïm was merged by Garibaldi in 1881 from two already existing Masonic rituals. His goal was both spiritual and organisational as he sought to bring together scattered esoteric currents into a universal Masonic rite for revolutionary, spiritual and ethical education. It was composed of the Italian Rite of Misraïm, dating back to the 1780s, and the French Rite of Memphis, dating back to 1838. The rituals serve as a spiritual map, guiding the initiate through degrees of esoteric wisdom. Inspired by alchemical transformation, the rituals are designed to purify and elevate the soul, uniting it with higher spiritual planes. In higher degrees, the rituals become theurgical workings to invoke divine intelligences, explore planetary spheres, and commune with higher metaphysical orders and principles that align perfectly with the Hesychasm of +Palamas. Consequently, instead of lengthy Masonic rituals, we are presented with all the key elements necessary to summon the spirit embedded within the ritual matrix.

+Palamas has undertaken a labour that is both creative and initiatic: the reconstruction of the 97 degrees of the Rite of Memphis and Misraïm, not as relics of a Masonic past, but as dynamic gateways of energetic awakening and spiritual realisation. Drawing on a lineage that includes the experimental illuminism of Michael Bertiaux and T. Allen Greenfield, *Spirit Builders* presents what might best be described as a Free Illuminist codex, a book not of received authority, but of experienced gnosis. This means that *Spirit Builders* is more a practical grammar of the Mysteries than a book of dead letters and Masonic nostalgia, a workable text, an adaptable text that ensures a continuous flow of the 'secret of secrets' into new etheric forms.

The focus of this work is not historical exegesis or the preservation of Masonic orthodoxy. Rather, it is an exploration of initiation as an inner science, using ritual, symbol, and scrying as instruments of mystical engineering. Each degree is approached not as a social rank but as a living resonance field, activated through contemplation, symbol, sound, and somatic awareness. The operative mechanism here is the *point chaud*, a concept derived from Bertiaux's esoteric physiology and loosely analogous to chakras; subtle centres in the human energy body where initiation becomes embodied. Through careful attention to battery, password, sign, and esoteric vibration, each point chaud is awakened, forming a lattice of illumination across the physical and astral bodies.

In this sense, *Spirit Builders* is a ritual technology of transformation, not unlike a magical grimoire—but one built on the geometry of the soul rather than that of spirits external to it. It reframes the entire Memphis-Misraïm system as a psychospiritual curriculum in which the initiate travels, not upward through hierarchical authority, but inward, through the sanctified architecture of their own energetic anatomy.

In this pursuit, +Palamas follows truthfully in the footsteps of his spiritual predecessor, the Byzantine Archbishop Gregory Palamas (1296–1359), extending the contemplative Hesychasm into the many rooms and lodges where the treasures of *Arcana Arcanorum* might be found. Like Gregory, Palamas weaves with the same theological thread and fabric through the maxim of Gregory, *"God became man so that man might become God."* Gregory's theology expounded upon the *via negativa* with profound depths. God was transcendent in essence *(ousia)*, but immanent in energies (*energeiai*), and he saw it as impossible for material man to understand the divine essence in itself. The path towards understanding the divine essence was through participation in His energies, primarily through prayer, contemplation, illumination, and ultimately deification (*theosis*). This allowed one to become partakers in the divine nature, making the body and breath the instruments of Hesychasm with its methodical use of divine stillness and silence and, for +Palamas, the Illuminist Tradition.

What distinguishes this text most strikingly is its refusal of authoritarian structures, a stance consistent with the principles of Free Illuminism, giving an approach towards the rites of Memphis and Misraïm that are anti-hierarchical, egalitarian, and intensely personal. Initiation, in this vision, is not something *conferred*; rather, it is *provoked*, *discovered*, and *earned* through immersion in ritual engagement and interior silence. This represents a fundamental departure from traditional Masonic systems, which often conflate spiritual progress with external recognition. In *Spirit Builders*, authority is internalised, arising from the depth of one's work rather than from any imposed system of ranks or titles.

This method is rooted in scrying, meditation, and visionary ritual, where degrees are not reenacted but *entered into*—each one an astral zone, a living sphere of gnosis whose geometry resonates in the subtle body. The work thus becomes a type of occult phenomenology in the spirit of Heidegger and Bertiaux, where each initiation generates a new awareness, each symbol an energetic activation, each ritual act a coordinate in a metaphysical cartography.

In doing so, +Palamas joins the tradition of experimental esotericism, where the sacred is not inherited but constructed through discipline, silence, and attention. He carries forward the impulse that motivated Bertiaux, Greenfield, and others to treat the Western Esoteric Tradition not as a museum of forms, but as a living system of transformation, subject to evolution, personalisation, and philosophical refinement.

It is important, however, to distinguish this experimentalism from arbitrary invention. *Spirit Builders* is not a bricolage of borrowed symbols; it is a work of esoteric precision, in which ritual acts, symbols, and initiatic degrees are meticulously studied, felt, and integrated. The result is a kind of occult calculus, a system in which ritual, energy body, and cosmology converge in a coherent and transformative whole.

Moreover, +Palamas does not shy away from the political implications of such a system. The anti-authoritarian stance of Free Illuminism is explicitly present throughout the work in a truthful echo of Garibaldi himself, bringing this work into a lineage of mystical anarchism and radical Freemasonry, *Spirit Builders* defies institutionalization not to reject tradition, but to restore it to its inner purpose: the awakening of the human soul to its own divine architecture.

In its rejection of hierarchy, its embrace of subjective mysticism, and its reconstruction of ancient degrees as inner rituals of power, *Spirit Builders* challenges the reader not only to think differently about esotericism, but to live differently and to work, in solitude and silence, at the stone of the self, until the inner temple stands revealed.

This is not a book for the casual seeker or the intellectually curious. It is a manual of ascent for those ready to engage in the alchemical labour of self-transformation. It invites us into a long tradition of builders—those who work not with mortar and stone, but with symbol, breath, will, and light.

Let those who take up this book know: what they hold is a blueprint of the inner city, a codex of luminous architecture, and a testimony to the spirit's desire to construct within itself the very house of the Holy.

Let the temple be built, not in the world, but within the soul.

Let there be Light. Light without end. Amen!

Mgr. +Nicholaj de Mattos Frisvold

Aka Frater Selwanga XVI°,° 33°,° 95°,° 97°°

July 11, 2025, On the Feast Day of St. Benedictus

Introduction to the Standard Edition

I am honored to have been asked to write a new introduction for this edition of Spirit Builders. This book was, and remains, the key text of the Free Illuminist Movement, embodying both the theoretical foundations and the practical applications that our movement values deeply.

When Tau Palamas first invited me to write an introduction to the original edition, I recognized immediately the significance of his work. Since then, I have encouraged him for many years to bring out a popularly priced edition that would make this vital teaching accessible to a wider audience. It is gratifying to see that intention realized with the publication of this new edition.

Spirit Builders is much more than a collection of spiritual ideas—it is a detailed guide to personal development rooted in conscious, deliberate action. The metaphor of building the spirit, as used throughout the book, frames spiritual growth as a process of construction, comparable to creating architecture. Each step is purposeful, each effort contributes to a greater whole, and the outcome is a stable, resilient inner foundation on which the individual can stand in all circumstances.

The practical nature of this work distinguishes it from many other spiritual texts. The insights in Spirit Builders are grounded in lived experience and presented with clarity, aiming to empower readers rather than mystify them. It holds true today, as it did when first published, in that spiritual growth requires both knowledge and the willingness to engage with that knowledge through purposeful effort.

In the original edition, the author refers to Arabia Mountain, Georgia, as Holy Mount Arabia. After completing the now concluded fifteen-year Great Arabia Working, I consider this place an important power spot — one where I and my associates have empowered many people from all over the world, offering our work freely and welcoming all without charge or restriction. Whether you, the reader, or the author ultimately regard this site as "holy," "sacred," or something else is a matter of personal interpretation. Regardless, its significance as a source and focal point of spiritual energy and practical illumination cannot be overlooked in understanding the origins and context of many of the teachings in Spirit Builders.

As a co-founder of the Free Illuminist Movement, I can attest that the principles and practices outlined in this book align closely with our core values: personal responsibility, freedom from limiting doctrines, and the cultivation of inner clarity and strength. The movement has always stood for open access to spiritual knowledge and the encouragement of individual empowerment. Spirit Builders serves as both a blueprint and a call to action, inviting all who are willing to become active participants in their own spiritual awakening.

This edition's lower price point is an important and welcome development. It removes a barrier that has limited access in the past, helping this work to reach seekers at all levels of experience and from diverse backgrounds. The teachings presented here are not reserved for specialists or an elite few; they are available to anyone with the commitment to build their spirit with intention and care.

Approach this book with an open mind and a readiness to apply what you learn. Spiritual development is not a passive experience, it is an architect's craft, requiring sustained effort, discipline, and a clear vision. Spirit Builders provides guidance for anyone ready to take up that craft, offering tools both subtle and practical to structure and strengthen the inner life.

In closing, I encourage you to use this book as a foundation — a starting point for your own unique journey toward freedom and illumination. It has been a privilege for me to witness the influence of Tau Palamas's work over the years, and I trust that this edition will serve as an accessible and enduring resource for many years to come.

— T Allen Greenfield

33° 90° 95° 97° 100° WAEO/APRMM

Co-founder, Free Illuminist Movement

Preface

To all illustrious and enlightened Masons throughout the World, and all those with interest in these mysteries.

Spirit Builders–a Free Illuminist Approach to the Antient & Primitive Rite of Memphis+Misraïm, explores a radical expression of a little-known branch of mystical Freemasonry for men and women, and provides a ritual monitor and guide for those desirous of practicing this avant-garde system. The expression of this branch of Masonry is *Free Illuminist* and the Rite is the *Antient and Primitive Rite of Memphis+Misraïm* (APRM+M). The elements and particulars of this approach will be expounded upon within two volumes, as many aspects of the work will be new to the reader. In effect, this is a spiritist and esoteric working of Masonry, involving an occult physiology and initiatic physics, and operating under the banner of Free Illuminism which supports the highest amount of freedom, exploration, and creativity possible.

Our first chapters intend to answer some basic questions concerning the movement of Free Illuminism, (Congregational Illuminism signifying groupings of Free Illuminists) and its approach to one of the more esoteric branches of Freemasonry expressed in a variety of ways across the globe. We hope to accomplish this with neither a strictly scholarly voice, nor an exclusively personal angle. The combination of both objectivity and personal reflection are blended to make the material more user friendly and to translate some of the more arcane emblems into tangible forms. The basic tenets of Congregational Illuminism are explored, the nature of the *points chauds* ("hot points" pronounced, *pwa show*) empowerments are divulged, and the role of the Holy Arabia Mountain alongside Apostolic Succession and spiritual transmission are explained. This whirlwind of information and introduction to those working *In Free Communion*,[1] and in our own *Chapel of the Gnosis*[2] in particular, is preparatory for the work that follows it. It is meant to be a way paver, providing context to the mystical workings of the Rite.

---

[1] *In Free Communion* is the phrase used by Free Illuminists who engage in mutual aid, support, and amity with one another.
[2] *The Chapel of the Gnosis* is a duly consecrated ritual space in Northwest Georgia that holds a Free Illuminist Charter, as well as several other Warrants from varying orders and Orients. The *Chapel Model* is designed for those who live in remote areas, practice more in a private manner, or are titular Bishops.

After the chapters outlining our work, Free Illuminism, and the Antient & Primitive Rite of Memphis+Misraïm, follows a *Ritual Monitor and Guide* for those who are interested in working this path, forming a Lodge, Node, or Chapel, or who are simply curious about what manner of spiritual Masonry this practice is. In the *Violet Lodge*, we provide a Free Illuminist version of the basic three degrees of classical Freemasonry for Triangles and small groups. This is for the group who may initiate individuals with no prior initiatory experience, to integrate them into the egregore. Amongst Free Illuminists it is suggested that all who work with the points chauds empowerments have some sort of grounding in a three-degree system before embarking upon this psycho-physiological gnostic journey. The creation of a spiritual anatomy requires an earthly grounding to properly integrate these energies. After *the Violet Lodge*, the entire corpus (all 97 Degrees) of the Antient & Primitive Rite of Memphis+Misraïm is provided as practiced by our Chapel. The "secrets" of the grades are compiled from the edited version of the degrees of Marconis, Yarker, the Bédarride brothers, and others from the mid to late 1800s through the early 1900s.[3] Within this corpus is contained all of the necessary material, suggestions, and guidelines to fully work the High Grades (Hauts Grades) of this Rite. Each degree contains a *Synopsis* which gives further indication of the nature of the energies and entities related to the points empowerments and the qualities of the continuing initiation that occurs after the degree through our process of *scrying the point*. This work also functions as one of the expressions of the *intuitional instrumentations* of the INNER RETREAT[4] as found in the third year Coursework of the *Monastery of the Seven Rays*. A portion of the material supplied in the synopsis of each degree is the result of experimentation within this Inner Retreat where Memphis+Misraïm exists on a purely super-sensual plane and is accessed by an occult form of Esoteric Engineering and initiatic physics.

Taken as a whole, this book presents and provides the means of accomplishing the three primary functions of *Spirit Building* which are: the enlivening of the *scintillating body*, the creation of *the Mystic Temple* and the building of community by collaboration and mutual support with others working *in Free Communion*. This simple, yet profound approach to a mystical and magical system of Freemasonry is unique in the vast ocean of Masonic and Gnostic Orders across the globe.

An *Afterword* by the Spiritual Father of this movement, T Allen Greenfield, explores the background of Congregational Illuminism from his perspective and from its inception.

---

[3] Greenfield, Allen H. *The Compleat Rite of Memphis*. Marietta: Luxor Press, Inc., 1998. Other material is collected from our private Lodge materials and translations of the restored Rite from Belgium (1934).
[4] Private papers of *the Monastery of the Seven Rays*, 3rd Year, Part 1, Lesson 2.

Preface

† † †

This is the first book of its kind on this stimulating subject and it is the sincere hope of the author that all who work *In Free Communion* within Congregational Illuminism will contribute to our art and science by publishing additional works which highlight the particular research and experimentation going on with these empowerments. As we proceed, let us keep these lofty aims of the Monastery of the Seven Rays in mind.

∴

Magical initiations, such as those of the rite of Memphis Misraïm become more and more magical operations of research. We do not wish to allow a person to enter an exclusive fraternity of adepts, etc. rather we seek to make a person more and more conscious of himself as a precision instrument for occult research whereby every act of awareness is aimed at the analysis and synthesis of perceptual data, both sensory and extra-sensory, as well as the mastery of occult techniques of the mind.[5]

---
[5] Private papers of *The Monastery of the Seven Rays*, 3rd Year Course, Part 3, Lesson 10.

A Note from the Publisher

Over the past decade, since the initial publication of this opus, interest in the APRMM has only grown; and the permutations of the Rites, both the individual Rites of Misraïm and Memphis, as well as the combined Rite of Memphis-Misraïm, have exploded upon the esoteric and Masonic scene. It is therefore a great honor to have been asked by PALAMAS to take on the task of bringing his classic tome back into print at a time that it is needed more than ever.

The immense value of this work is not to be underestimated. Much more than a mere tiler or monitor, Spirit Builders lays out a complete program of working the Antient & Primitive Rite of Memphis+Misraïm according to the Free Illuminist method. But the significance of this volume is not only to the Free Illuminists. It is a practical manual for anyone working the Egyptian Rite grades, and for mystics and magickians of many stripes. And it is with much joy that I am able to help facilitate the re-emergence of this seminal work in an expanded format.

The task set before me was twofold: first, to incorporate additional materials not present in the first edition, such as the beautiful series of Tracing Boards developed by the late Grand Hierophant Alexander Rybalka; and secondly, to produce an edition at a price point less prohibitive than the first edition. Easier said than done, to be sure! The only practical solution was to release two editions: a single-volume standard edition including all the text, as well as many of the black and white illustrations; and a two-volume deluxe edition, hardbound in full color, containing Rybalka's color tracing boards as well as additional galleries of photos and original artwork by PALAMAS himself.

Therefore, whether you are holding in your hands the single-volume paperback edition or one of the volumes of the deluxe edition, you may be assured that no text has been omitted from the body of the work. Additionally, the original work has been edited, updated, and corrected where necessary. And, as stated above, the text has been augmented with new, complementary materials by PALAMAS that may enrich the study and practice of these grades.

Beyond the few comments just made, there is little left to be said by way of introduction that has not already been addressed in the Foreword by Nicholaj de Mattos Frisvold or in the Preface and Introduction by PALAMAS himself; or, if you are reading the combined edition, in the Preface by T Allen H. Greenfield which is only available in that edition. I will note only that any editorial errors or oversights are my own fault and should not reflect upon the brilliance of the author.

T Phosphoros 33°, 90°, 96°
Triad Press, LLC

Contents

Dedication	ix
Acknowledgements	xi
Foreword by Nicholaj de Mattos Frisvold	xiii
Introduction to the Standard Edition by T Allen Greenfield	xvii
Preface	xix
A Note from the Publisher	xxiii

Volume One

Part One – In Free Communion

Introduction	3
Chapter One: Everything that Rises Must Converge	11
Chapter Two: Distinction Does Not Equal Separation	17
Chapter Three: What Are We Building?	23
Chapter Four: Congregational Illuminism	29
Chapter Five: Hot Points on the Holy Mountain	41
Chapter Six: The Chapel Model	49
Chapter Seven: The Sacred Doctrine	57
Chapter Eight: The Antient & Primitive Rite of Memphis+Misraïm	64

Part Two – The Violet Lodge

Introduction	77
Chapter One: The Details of the Work	81
Chapter Two: The Opening of the Chapel	91
Chapter Three: First Degree – Apprentice	99
Chapter Four: Second Degree – Companion	114
Chapter Five: Third Degree – Master	131
Chapter Six: Suggested Practices of the Symbolic Degrees	146

Part Three – Hauts Grades

Introduction	163
Chapter One: Opening & Closing	175
Chapter Two: The Symbolic Degrees	178
Chapter Three: The Philosophical Degrees, 4-33	189

Volume Two

Part Three – Hauts Grades
(continued)

Preface to Volume Two	299
Chapter Four: Hermetic, Gnostic, & Kabalistic Degrees	325
Chapter Five: Arcana Arcanorum	519
- Scrying the Æthyrs	547
- Boule Blanche Exercise	551
Chapter Six: Administrative Degrees	562
Afterword by T Allen Greenfield	601

Appendices

Appendix A: History Lection	605
Appendix B: 1º - Apprentice (complete ritual)	611
Appendix C: 1º Piece of Architecture	665
Appendix D: The Original Scrying Method of Allen H. Greenfield	671
Appendix E: 66º - Patriarch Grand Consecrator	681
Appendix F: Letter from Zagreb, Croatia	727
Appendix G: Letter from Puerto San Isidro	731
Bibliography	733

"All this is metaphor, picture language, describing the work of spirit-building that every Mason engages in."

Robert Lomas
The Secret Science of Masonic Initiation

"A simple gesture, a word, a sign, a *veve*, can trigger a Lorenz butterfly effect…that gives currency to bizarre events, surprises, metamorphoses, and spontaneous generation of weird entities."

Dr. Reginald Crosley
The Vodou Quantum Leap

Volume One

To the Glory of the Sublime Architect of the Universe

Union ∴ Prosperity ∴ Friendship ∴ Fraternity ∴

Peace ∴ tolerance ∴ truth ∴

Salutation on all points of the triangle.

∴

Respect to the order.

PART ONE

✠

IN FREE COMMUNION

Being an

INTRODUCTION

to the Philosophy and Practice of

Free ILLUMINISM

and the alignment of the Points-Chauds to the

ANTIENT & PRIMITIVE RITE OF MEMPHIS+MISRIAM

as worked within the
†Chapel of the Gnosis

Introduction

...shifts from Darkness to Light, there was intense screaming, terror abounded everywhere...beings were accosting me, assailing me from above, below–to the right and to the left. I felt that I was being tugged at, pulled along, and dragged down and underneath...into this tomb of horrors...the screeches and screams made my body shudder and my heart go numb. I wanted release; I wanted out of this place...there was so much destruction and misery. There were tornadoes and fires, earthquakes and all manner of tortures and violence flashing before me in eschatological anarchy. I couldn't speak, I couldn't move. I was absolutely terrified and in the deepest gloom imaginable.

Then, seemingly from out of nowhere, this figure arrived...he was in black and his eagle, hawk or some other bird of prey-like face swept towards me. I was not afraid of him...in fact I no longer feared any of the atrocities about me. I felt a great comfort in this dark figure. All hell was still breaking loose around me but I looked at the figure as he pressed two fingers against my lips[6], while at the same time, in my inner ear I heard the words, "HORUS, HAWK" and all suddenly became calm. It was as if his pressing his fingers against my lips CAUSED the apocalypse to end...I have never felt such a deep peace and quiet...the quiet like you feel when you are underwater and there is no disturbance. I slipped into a deep meditation in absolute cave darkness.
And then I awoke...

---

[6] This was subsequently experienced on the physical plane in four separate Initiations within the Western Mystery Tradition. We find it in the preparation of the Egyptian Rite Lodge as well, *The Masonic Magician*, 2008, p. 204.

One perusal of my many journals over the years finds an odd sort of mantra showing up time and again, *Memphis*. On occasion it is extended further to *Memphis+Misraïm*, but more often than not it is simply, *Memphis*. The sketch above was penned in a white hot heat in the year 2000 after awaking from what Michael-Paul Bertiaux describes as a SOULDREAM[7] that literally altered my life course. It was a sort of involuntary initiation. I have always been rather interested and involved in spirituality, but this dream introduced me to a distinct experience, *initiation*. This dream created such a profound stir within, propelled me so thoroughly out of my comfort zone of "normal life" and into the vast realm of the Western Mystery Tradition[8]—that it was nothing short of initiatory. This dream initiated a search which led to the discoveries in this book[9]. It directed my course towards the *Manifestation of Light!*

Memphis...

On 9-11-01 a great tragedy occurred in America with the destruction of the Twin Towers in New York City. The Nation was shaken and all across the world the reverberations were felt. Oddly enough, on that same night (a year after my initiatory dream) I became a mainstream Freemason[10]. Freemasonry immediately supplied me with symbols, experiences and a framework that were allied to the dream. The day after the SOULDREAM I walked down to the library to research these words that wouldn't stop being repeated in my head...*Horus, Hawk*. Strangely enough, everything connected to Horus that was of the historical/archeological variety was calling Horus a falcon. Now this may seem like a small detail, but I was very much assured in the dream that Horus was a hawk. There were some odd links, however, that would describe Horus as a hawk. They were links that led me to the Western Esoteric Tradition, and time and again, to Freemasonry. So I started with Freemasonry, knowing next to nothing about it other than some things I had read in the compilation for the Scottish Rite called, *Morals & Dogma* by Albert Pike[11].

Every ritual I experienced, every Degree I attained to, every *other* branch of the Western Esoteric Tradition that I entered– took me back to that mystical landscape of the dream

---

[7] Bertiaux, Michael. *The Voudon Gnostic Workbook*. San Francisco: Red Wheel/Weiser, LLC., 2007. p. 221

[8] See *Access to Western Esotericism*, by Antoine Faivre, 1994, and *Western Esotericism and Rituals of Initiation*, by Henrik Bogdan, 2007, for a good introduction to the landscape of the Western Mystery Tradition.

[9] This dream occurred in the year 2000. In 2008, *The Masonic Magician*, was issued, which charts the life and death of Count Cagliostro as well as his Egyptian Rite. Pgs. 180-181 recount a peculiar dream-initiation that he received which altered his course. In the words of the authors, "Cagliostro interpreted the vision as confirmation that he was indeed on a divine mission. He then resolved to set his Egyptian Rite in stone…" (181). It is the contention of the author that the intermediary beings work in this nature, pointing the Seeker towards a life path which is reflective of his or her True Will.

[10] Mabel Lodge #266, a regularly constituted Lodge working under the jurisdiction of the Grand Lodge of Georgia.

[11] See the Supreme Council's newly annotated edition by Arturo De Hoyos, 2011. This impressive classic of Masonic literature is treasured by many Freemasons around the world.

where I felt *true initiation* occurred. Early on I made a distinction in my mind between the physical group work of initiation in a Lodge-type setting and the more lasting, deeper and profound experience of initiation on the Inner Planes which was, at every turn, punctuated by the sense of Light. The former may be accompanied by the latter; however the latter can also stand alone.

This profound dream and subsequent search for more Light and experience is the precedent for the type of Spiritual Freemasonry that I want to share in this work. It is not the same as mainstream Lodge work. This work is deeply individualistic and requires experimentation and strength of character– a penetrating knowing of oneself *and* a radical freedom and pliability of mind that many group settings would find heretical or even dangerous. This approach to Masonry comes full-freighted with words and experiences rarely explored in traditional Lodge settings—*attunement, nature, spontaneity, empowerment, mysticism, Angel magick.*

† † †

Who is this writing for? Is it for the Freemason? Is it for individuals who want to become Freemasons? Is it for the man or woman who wants to work traditional Masonic Degrees up to the 97th Degree of the Antient & Primitive Rite of Memphis-Misraïm? Let me say now, with confidence and fervor, as well as with a deep love for the Craft in general, that this work is;

For all of those interested in an Esoteric approach to Spiritual Freemasonry, unsullied by Hierarchy and freed from Authoritarian strictures.

I have absolutely nothing to sell to you in this work, no Order to direct you towards, no Hierarchy to answer to and no Grand Lodge to invite you to join. I simply want to share with you an approach to Esoteric Masonry that I find mystical, timely, revolutionary and fundamentally crucial to the needs, interests and deficits experienced by Masons of various stripes, *and* those drawn to the Craft but hampered by its organizational structure. In a single phrase, this is *an expression of Spiritual Freemasonry.*

As the Title suggests, this is *A Free Illuminist Approach*, so Free Illuminism, or the group form–Congregational Illuminism, needs to be defined as succinctly as possible. For starters, here are the basic tenants or articles of Congregational Illuminism:

1. **Spiritual growth is incompatible with authoritarian structure.**

2. **Scientific Illuminism requires a non-dogmatic, experimental approach.**

3. **A free society linked in free communion should be actualized.**

4. **We facilitate, we do not lead. We do the Work, we do not extract oaths or dues, or require dogmatic beliefs.**

This radical efficiency is a welcome respite to all who have explored the various Landmarks and Charges of mainstream Freemasonry[12] along its colorful history. These C I[13] articles are not limited to a Masonic body, but they are the single principles behind one of the current branches of the APRM+M[14]. In fact, it is this sort of efficiency and simplicity that demarcates our work from top to bottom. The name of Memphis+Misraïm usually conjures up ideas of a colossal program of degrees, an unmanageable quantity of props and regalia and a life-time (or two) of work. But our work embodies a mystical form of this Masonic Order derived from the Ecclesiastical Revision of 1921-22 (Franco-Haitian) which swept the APRM+M under the vast umbrella of the catholic and Apostolic Gnostic Church[15], and which treated the degrees, more or less, as ordinations or empowerments.

It is the hope of the author that this writing will offer some of the keys for working in this mysterious and awe inspiring lineage. This is not a historical piece, so please do not expect such—nor is any amount of dogmatic certainty to be purported as it is the Initiate him or herself who will gleam the spiritual verities that accompany the work. This is the experience of *one* Seeker. I am not the spokesperson for Free Illuminism, hence the article "*A*" as opposed to "THE" *Free Illuminist Approach*. However, as has been discovered and experienced within our own small Chapel, this is a workable entrance to the Mysteries and affords a lifetime of experimentation and exploration to the Initiate. This book contains the philosophy behind our unique approach to spiritual Masonry as well as all of the necessary information and rubrics to work the Ecclesiastical Revision of the APRM+M from the 1st to the 97th Degree by the light of Free Illuminism.

---

[12] See the *Constitutions of Freemasonry of the UGLE* as well as Mackey's *Landmarks* found in *Masonic Jurisprudence*, and others, for example.
[13] Congregational Illuminism
[14] Antient & Primitive Rite of Memphis+Misraïm
[15] This history is delineated in the Appendix of *The Voudon Gnostic Workbook*, on p. 624 where the author says that the APRM+M "gave up entirely their quasi-Masonic character and became completely esoteric and Gnostic orders of magic" and further, the distinction is made between this branch of Memphis+Misraïm and others, "...there are other branches of the Rite of Memphis-Misraïm which claim to continue a Masonic character, while our branch is only interested in continuing the Gnostic and apostolic succession and the magical currents of initiation." This distinction is simply shown in our Order by placing the "+" between the Memphis & Misraïm titles, so as to not confuse the reader with the Masonic branch of the same name.

Introduction

Free Illuminists aren't *anti*-hierarchical. Many of us have leadership roles in other Orders as well as in various branches of the Gnostic Church. We simply find this model to be fruitful for special projects. Free Illuminism is not for everyone. The amount of self direction required, the lack of a core-set of teachings, and the emphasis on individual research and experimentation will not be appealing to those who require the traditional top-down business model for all of their undertakings. For many, however, Free Illuminist workings—having only four precepts and a line of spiritual transmissions—go hand in hand with other aspects of the Western tradition that *are* hierarchical. The two are not mutually exclusive. Experiments in a Free Illuminist setting often deepen and propel forward, the spiritual work of other diverse bodies—fraternal and Gnostic. It is to the creative mind and to those with a spirit of inquiry that Free Illuminism holds the most appeal, for within this collective a variety of esoteric research projects can be undertaken with the inheritance of the lineage and points-chauds empowerments. In this way, the Free Illuminist may explore avenues of investigation which relate to more traditional bodies, yet she may do so freely and without boundaries. This is why the majority of Free Illuminist Charters are for *Research and Philosophical* Lodges of the Antient & Primitive Rite of Memphis+Misraïm.

† † †

After many years of labor within mainstream Masonry, I can say with some level of experience, that it truly *is* an initiatory society. Following the initial SOULDREAM and some travels in the various branches of regular Masonry (i.e., York Rite, Scottish Rite, etc.,) I began to have other dreams which all resonated with the first but inherited a simple gift from the Lodge—the framework and basic structure of Masonic Initiation. I began to experience a variety of *Conductors* in my dreams, for instance; on more than one occasion, I was found in a somnambulistic state being guided in circles upon my bedroom floor (much to my ex-wife's chagrin—maybe this explains the *ex* part). These dreams were, no doubt, stimulated by Masonic Lodge work. From my very first entrance into the temple of Masonry, on that fateful day in 2001, I began to see Masonic work as clearly spiritual.

Throughout my journey in other branches of the Western Mystery Tradition which pursued the esoteric sciences in particular, I felt an increasing acceleration towards something! It was almost palpable. Back to the many journals scattered with Hebrew, Kabalistic drawings and expositions of dreams, there are those words...*Memphis* or *Memphis+Misraïm*, sometimes standing singularly on an entire page. I was drawn to this Rite by a force that can only be described as exterior to my own person. I was compelled to take the *mark* of Cagliostro in the Mark Master Masonic[16] degree; I took his initials for my motto in the Hermetic Order of the Golden Dawn and sensed his presence during a number of Operations. He became something of an Inner Plane confidant/contact and introduced me to the initiated understanding of a Past Master (or should I say, *Passed* Master).

After knocking upon and entering a number of different doorways which all purported distinct lines of Memphis-Misraïm, I discovered the *Ecclesiastical Revision* (1921-22) being worked and developed by T Allen Greenfield, Tau Dositheos and others involved in the revolutionary movement known as Congregational or Free Illuminism. Simultaneously, and this is most certainly not coincidental, I became drawn towards a new form of Christianity–*Gnostic*, Non-dual and Esoteric Christianity, and felt magnetically pulled towards the mystery school called, *The Monastery of the Seven Rays* headed by Michael-Paul Bertiaux. Ordination ensued over time and I am now a Bishop of the Coptic Gnostic Church. The analogous nature of Gnosticism and the APRM+M may seem strange, but we are *Spirit Builders* and both pertain to and partake of the Spirit[17]. This connection deepened further as I began the Third & Fourth Year curriculums of the Monastery of the Seven Rays, which alongside the *Voudon Gnostic Workbook* introduced me to the concept of Esoteric Engineering, through the most powerful mandalum instrumentum in the Monastery–*the Rite of Memphis-Misraïm.*[18] This system of initiation and consecration–operating as an intuitional machine–is an occult laboratory and school that is entirely research oriented and consciousness expanding. Through scrying the points-chauds empowerments of these 97 Degrees, the Initiate is taken into this Inner Retreat—which is identical to our notion of the *Sovereign Sanctuary*. This technique elaborates upon and helps to flesh out the inner quality of this consecratory work.

†††

Freemasonry has its Lost Word and subsequent *substitute* for the Lost Word. It has its Higher Degrees which elaborate upon this further and offer other Words of power. Scottish Masonry has the Royal Secret and the Holy Doctrine as well. But it is time to restore the *Sacred Doctrine* to the mystical workings of the Craft. It is a simple Doctrine and the work

---

[16] This Masonic degree of the York Rite is one of the more universally practiced of the high degrees and requires its initiates to make a "mark" in a logbook of Mason's marks, continuing the traditions of the great Cathedral Builders.

[17] Additionally, in terms of the esoteric engineering of the *Monastery of the Seven Rays*, the "first four grades of the system of Memphis-Misraïm are identical with the orders of sub deacon, deacon, priest, and bishop in the Gnostic Church" (private papers of the M7Rs, 3rd Year, Part IV, Lesson 14. These "grades" are not to be confused with the first four Degrees, but instead relate to sections of Degrees as utilized by the Monastery. Furthermore, the Monastery Four Year Coursework relates to these four priestly orders as well.

[18] According to the Monastery papers of Year III, the form of Memphis-Misraïm that indulges in Esoteric Engineering derives originally from Spain, and is distinct in all ways from that of France, England & other countries.

suggested in these pages is overtly simple in comparison with other systems and approaches, yet it is one that has profound effects and which offers deeply mystical esoteric work as well as light, healing and wholeness to the world. It is also time to restore the *Primitive Doctrine* to occult Masonry, which is explored in Book Three.

This model of Masonry is spiritual. It has zero interest in politics. It is in no way a threat to or in competition with, regular/mainstream Freemasonry. This approach is comfortable and happy being peripheral and working outside of the margins of the Craft. The *Congregational Illuminist* form of the APRM+M is quite counter-cultural as it has absolutely nothing to do with the competition based, degree-mongering, one-upmanship power plays being acted out currently within Grand Bodies, inside various Mystery schools, and upon the virtual stages of social media around the world. The spiritualized form of Memphis+Misraïm Masonry that is being purported here is so radically distinct from Lodge experience, that many would not call it Masonry at all. And assuredly, involvement in this form of Masonry will not allow you entrance into any mainstream Lodge. So it must be understood from the get-go, that this is an animal of a different coat altogether. It is not another Appendant Body[19] to join. It is spiritual work. We are not in the business of making regular Masons[20], nor are we interested in mimicking the methods of modern Masonry. We have an inheritance in the APRM+M that moves with the Spirit and so is not confined to procedures and rules of order. And here we see how this text is a *Guide*, not a rule of practice. Additionally, those of us at labor in this particular quarry are not called Worshipful Masters, rather we are *Facilitators*. Our primary role is to make the work lighter for others.

The present volume outlines a system that is both profoundly weird and weirdly profound when compared with other forms of Masonic Initiation. The Rites of Memphis & Misraïm are "relics in their occult power...of perhaps the very oldest Mysteries existing upon earth...behind these rites and quite independent of the form side of the tradition, a line of succession has been handed down."[21] Where will this approach take the seeker or the current Freemason? It will thrust her into the heart of spiritual Freemasonry and form an introduction to the Inner Retreat of this intuitional machine[22]. What does this guide have to offer the world, Masonica? The *Sacred and Primitive Doctrines*; elucidated, worked and experienced as they never have been before and through efficient means that are

---

[19] *Appendant Bodies* in American Masonry include such additional degree sets as the York Rite, the Scottish Rite, and the Allied Masonic Orders.
[20] This must be clearly understood. This work is not the making of Freemasons, in the technical and usual sense. This is a spiritualized form of Mystic Masonry almost completely free of organizational structures.
[21] p. 12 of C.W. Leadbeater's, *Freemasonry and Its Ancient Mystic Rites*, 1986.
[22] Of all of the different instruments and mental machines described in the Monastery of the Seven Rays coursework, there is only one system of intuitional instrumentation, that system is the APRM+M.

manageable and effective. Let us begin the journey with an exploration of the philosophy behind the work and then take up our sword and trowel as Knights of the Temple, as *Spirit Builders*. We will unravel the Sacred Doctrine firstly, and then commence our labors upon this sacred path through the practice of the Primitive Doctrine.

In Free Communion,
+Palamas 33°, 66°, 90°, 96°
Grand Areopagus
F.I.S.S.A.P.R.M.M.U.S[23].

---

[23] http://fissaprmmus.blogspot.com/p/about.html

CHAPTER ONE

Everything That Rises Must Converge

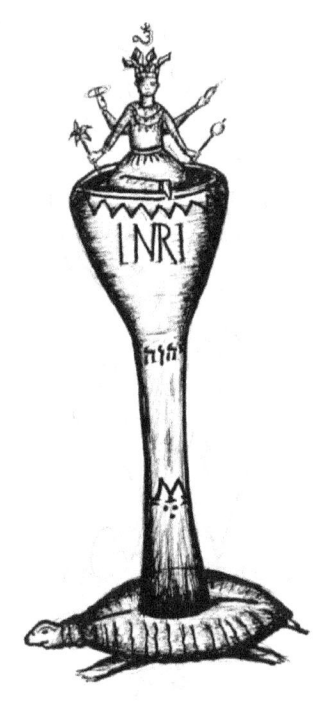

How can we misconceive that living force which, in its universality, maintains order amongst such disorderly elements, diverse interests and wills moved by opposing passions?

John Yarker[24]

---

[24] *Lectures of a Chapter, Senate & Council: According to the Forms of the Antient and Primitive Rite, But Embracing All Systems of High Grade Masonry*, 1881, p. 72.

In his book, *The Story of the Hermetic Brotherhood of Light*, the spiritual father of Congregational Illuminism, T Allen Greenfield suggests that when following the winding path of occultism for the development and origins of Rites and Orders, one must take recourse to the "continuity of ideas which suggests—sometimes strongly suggests— a continuity of structure[25]." Further, when considering the modern forms of Memphis, he adds that one can find a "strain of organizational continuity" moving from Cagliostro's *Egyptian Freemasonry*, which accepted men and women, to the Rites of Memphis and Misraïm and the individuals within that movement of Esoteric Masonry such as Yarker, Papus, Reuss and the late Robert Ambelain. [26] Prior to the working of Cagliostro, we have a vast corpus of Egyptian magic carried on through the Coptic Texts of Ritual Power[27] produced from the 4th & 5th Centuries through the 10th Century CE. These practices merge liturgical empowerments with Grimoiric magic and Hoodoo style practices, within a Christian context, much like the mysteries of Cagliostro centuries after. It is upon this premise of the continuity of ideas, structure and organization that living bodies of the APRM+M continue to inculcate the ancient truths and mysteries of Egypt, as well as the mysteries that operated under the cloak[28] of Christian Mysticism, and continue to *Initiate* Brothers and Sisters in ancient form. There are seed ideas and compact practices that have been carried on through time, which hint of the Sacred and Primitive Doctrine of antiquity lodged within the various bodies of Esoteric Masonry and which are readily unearthed when the focus is honed into a singular occult aim, *the Manifestation of Light.* It is in this manner that such diverse individuals and groups have maintained any measure of continuity over the ages, as the face of Egyptian Masonry and the APRM+M has altered many times over. What continues on; in ideas, structure and organization, is eternally bound to this notion of dynamic Light. This Light, this *living force, which in its universality* is not limited to any order or institution has chosen to remain present in the Egyptian Rites of Freemasonry even to this day.

Practitioners of the APRM+M inherit ideas and spiritual transmissions which have been passed along from Egypt and its Coptic inheritance[29], to the Hermeticists– from the

---

[25] Greenfield, T Allen. *The Story of the Hermetic Brotherhood of Light*. Stockholm: Looking Glass Press, 1997. p. 29
[26] Ibid, 30.
[27] See the incredible collection entitled, *Ancient Christian Magic: Coptic Texts of Ritual Power*, by Meyer and Smith, 1994.
[28] Though at first glance it does appear that these ancient practices were subsumed under the *cloak* of Christianity, as Faulks and Cooper suggest in *The Masonic Magician*, many would suggest that these practices were *perfected* under the new Aeon of Christ. Particularly in the Liturgy of the Eucharist we find one of the most potent formulae of magic ever to be generated by a collective.
[29] Some of these lineages are doubtless apocryphal, particularly that of the legendary Ormus, but they serve a unique purpose in the overall schema. For instance, Ormus is said to be the priest of Serapis that was converted by the disciple St. Mark. This story assists in the merging of mystic Christianity/Gnosticism with the magickal priesthoods of Ancient Egypt. It is akin to the notion

Christian/Egyptian convert Ormus to the West, onward to the divine Cagliostro and thence to Samuel Honis & Marconis de Negre—further on to John Yarker, Papus (Gerard Encausse), Theodor Reuss, to Giuseppe Garibaldi (the Italian Freedom Fighter who unified the Rites of Memphis and Misraïm), along the way to Aleister Crowley, through the French occupation of Haiti to the Jean-Maine family–to Michael-Paul Bertiaux and thence to the work of Congregational Illuminists via T Allen Greenfield. This inheritance and lineage is no static thing. It is not as simple as producing documents which support one Brother having received degrees from another. This is a transmission of *Gnostic spirituality* itself, the heart of Esoteric Masonry. As Paschal Beverly Randolph says, *Initiation is One*. A sacred drama, a secret and a search has been passed along throughout the ages. The drama, a type of immortal Hero story where the candidate becomes the Hero, goes back to the Egyptian drama of the dead (and later resuscitated) Osiris, later becoming the legend of Hiram. The secret is the *Sacred Doctrine*, its use and many purposes. The search is for Light.

The structure of the APRM+M has undergone many revisions and alterations over the years, but the continuity of Degrees, Charters, method of enlightening, universal embrace of the Primitive Religion and a relationship to the Gnostic Churches, amongst other things has been maintained.

The nature of how the Degrees are worked will be elucidated in Books Two & Three. In the CI working of the APRM+M, the Degree names and essentials follow that of Marconis through the 33rd Degree and John Yarker for the Higher Degrees.[30] The Charters for working the APRM+M have followed the general structure of all chartered bodies and orders over time, but have taken on an especial role within Congregational Illuminism ~ that of becoming living talismans. We will return to this concept in the pages ahead as it has bearing upon the *Sacred Doctrine* itself.

Throughout the history of Masonry and long before, sensory deprivation has been utilized to enhance the moment of enlightenment. This has primarily been accomplished through the use of a hoodwink, or blindfold, but other means connected to other senses have also been employed. Yet, it is the visual deprivation that is the most powerful and this has been a noted feature within the structure of most degrees in the Western Mystery Tradition and certainly continues on in the APRM+M. Our "hoodwink," however, is

---

of a *Charter Myth* (Fraulein Sprengel style) with regards to this link. It suggests continuity across time and space and within the spiritual realm.

[30] Again we are following the editing of T Allen Greenfield in, *The Compleat Rite of Memphis*, 1997. At the time of this writing, a newly revised and edited version of Greenfield's book is in its final stages.

utilized later in *scrying the degree* or points-chauds empowerment while in a classical prayer asana. Vision is the key to our esoteric working of the Rites.

Much is said of the Primitive Doctrine in various esoteric and fraternal texts of the 19th Century. There was something of an obsession with this concept amongst writers from Yarker to Pike to Albert Churchward to Crowley and C.W. Leadbeater. These initiates and many others were absolutely convinced that a doctrine which was simple and primitive lay hidden within the process of Masonic initiation. Each traced this primitive religious experience back to slightly differing sources, yet each felt that the answer to this simple faith and practice lay somewhere in the mists of the ancient Indo-Aryan (modern day Iran) and Proto-Aryan nations. In the Rig Veda, for instance, which Pike did an early English translation of, we find a Light-centric faith[31]. The notion of this simple and primitive Faith beginning in the Middle East and moving into India and then journeying to Egypt was largely held by all of the esoterically inclined Orders and Rites of the Western Mystery Tradition. The Primitive Doctrine becomes a structural inheritance for the APRM+M in that it lies beneath the surface of the most secret of secrets, the *Arcana Arcanorum*[32] which many branches of the Memphis-Misraïm tree inculcate within the 87th-90th degrees and which explores a type of angel magic that fills in the blanks of Cagliostro's work[33]. This Primitive Doctrine and secret working is, again, inextricable from the *Sacred Doctrine* which mainstream Masonry has forgotten. It is the singular secret that would restore Masonry to its formerly integrated self, but mainstream Masonry has become afraid of its shadow (Esotericism) over the millennia[34].

The relationship of the APRM+M to the modern Gnostic Churches has long been established. They grew alongside each other and dipped from each other's pools of wisdom with frequency and dedication to the *Sacred Doctrine* which is continuous with the experience of *gnosis*. For the most part, the relationship has been analogous in terms of structure. There was a slight overlap in the two with the 66th Degree of *Grand Consecrator*, which has been compared many times to the consecration of a Bishop. Similarly, the 61st Degree of *Sublime Unknown Philosopher* is directly related to the Martinist Order. All three bodies, the Antient & Primitive Rite of Memphis-Misraïm, the Martinist Order and the Gnostic Churches have an interconnectedness and French Rosicrucian inheritance that has strengthened and enlivened the overall Egregore and manifested in the spreading of the *Sacred Doctrine*

---

[31] See also, Pike's *Lecture on Masonic Symbolism and A Second Lecture on Symbolism: The Omkara and Other Ineffable Words*, transcribed and annotated by Rex R. Hutchens, 2006.
[32] Instituted in Naples and pre-dating Cagliostro's work.
[33] See Book Three, *Arcana Arcanorum*.
[34] Illustrious Brother Jay Kinney elaborates upon this idea in his essay, *Is Freemasonry Afraid of its Own Shadow*, published in the Scottish Rite Research Society's, *Heredom*, Vol 10, 2002.

through multiple sources. In CI, we have a slightly different relationship to the Gnostic Church, in that the APRM+M is now firmly lodged *within* the Gnostic Church as a series of empowerments akin to ordinations. This occurred with the 1921 Ecclesiastical Revision of the Rites of Memphis and Misraïm in Haiti through Lucien Francois Jean-Maine and his son, Hector. This revision, completely interconnected with the Gnostic Church continues through Hector's student, the great Michael-Paul Bertiaux and has passed on to T Allen Greenfield who expanded the work and aligned the *points-chauds* empowerments to the degrees.

There are many other structural areas of continuity through time with the APRM+M, not the least of which is the employment of the Volume of the Sacred Law[35], the fellowship and community of working in a fraternal order and the inherent benefits that accompany initiation and repeated experiences of others' initiations. The several areas of structural continuity herein explored are selected specifically for our work in Books Two & Three, and it should be noted that other branches of the Memphis Misraïm tree are far *more* traditional[36] and maintain a closer semblance to mainstream workings.

In most cases, organization and structure overlap greatly. The structural components are chiefly the actions and patterns, degrees and the like, that have been repeated and carried on over time. The organizational continuity that we possess has more to do with the common goals of the social order of Freemasonry and allied bodies. We tend to group ourselves into Lodges, for instance, but as with other branches of the APRM+M who use Triangles for small groups of three—we in CI use other names for smaller groupings or to denote our specific intent and approach. For example, in my own case, we do not have a *Lodge*, we instead have a *Chapel*. In the original manuscripts of Marconis, there were separate initiatory bodies and Liturgical Colleges, but as my work as a Gnostic Bishop heavily influences our manner of initiating, we merge the Initiatory and the Liturgical into a Chapel model, thus maintaining a consistency with the *Ecclesiastical* Revision of 1921[37]. Again, this is my specific community and not the manner of all Congregational Illuminists. In our Chapel we also maintain continuity of organization and structure through the employment of the Three-fold Path, originally outlined by the mystic, Pseudo-Dionysius the Areopagite[38] of the 5th and early 6th Centuries. This three-fold working of *purification,*

---

[35] Which, in our working in the *Chapel of the Gnosis*, as well as in other Congregational Illuminist bodies, is utilized in the Advanced practice of Scrying the Point/Degree, which is found in Book Three.
[36] To truly understand this book and the work of Free Illuminism, the Masonic student must enter into the spiritist nature of our work and see the mystical element of the hot points and their relationship to the "essence" of these Degrees. Such understanding is born from practice and the cultivation of the arts of magick & the theologia of mysticism.
[37] See chapter entitled, "The Chapel Model".
[38] See, *The Celestial Hierarchy* and *The Divine Names/The Mystical Theology* of Pseudo-Dionysius the Areopagite.

illumination and *union/perfection* informs all of our various practices. This may appear incongruous at the onset, as we are exploring a form of Egyptian Freemasonry, but upon deeper investigation it becomes clear that quite a number of ideas and practices from Ancient Egypt continued on within Coptic Christianity and other branches of Christian mysticism. Research of the degrees of Egyptian Masonry that the divine Cagliostro performed and promoted, reveals that his "Egyptian" work was more in keeping with a type of Christian mysticism[39]. It is again, the continuity of ideas, structure and organization that continues to manifest the Light of Egypt and Christianity became a potent container, shield and sometimes veil for these Mysteries of the ancients. Many are of the mindset that the Christian mythos *completes* the story in a number of ways also, from the story of the birth, death and resurrection of the Christ reenacted throughout the liturgical year, to the profound power of the Eucharist.

There are many points then, where the ancient doctrines, mysteries and practices have converged over time and which continue today through the universal living force that is perpetually transmitted to the initiate. But as this is a living force, it undergoes change over time and the evolutions and innovations that have occurred are what this book seeks to illuminate, because on occasion–innovation and evolution are circuitous, and what seems to be a new thing is simply a return and a restoration. In this case, it is a return to and a restoration of the *Primitive & the Sacred Doctrine*. It is a renewal of the pristine simplicity employed by the ancients in spirit building. As Rudolf Steiner eloquently put it, "It would now be the task to rescue Masonic life from its externalized forms and to re-create it, to turn religious spirit into a form of sense-perceptible beauty[40]."

Finally, and this statement leads directly into the next chapter which outlines some of the distinctions of our practice, it needs to be stated that the research and experimentation of the original *Lodge of the Sons and Daughters of Aaron*—coordinated and facilitated by T Allen Greenfield—fulfills the role of *magickal inflation* as described in the *Voudon Gnostic Workbook*. In this process of magickal activity, systems and schools are born from investigation and testing; in a word, from research[41]. Such research can lead to what Bertiaux describes as the "rebuilding of old orders along more modern lines, i.e., the process of magickal reconstruction."[42] It is this form of Memphis-Misraïm that we are working in this book and in the Chapel of the Gnosis, in Free Communion with others.

---

[39] See Cooper & Faulks, *The Masonic Magician, the Life and Death of Count Cagliostro and His Egyptian Rite*, 2008.
[40] *Freemasonry and Ritual Work*, 2007, p. 54
[41] Persistence in this research will lead the Initiate directly into the INNER RETREAT discussed in the M7Rs, 3rd Year Course.
[42] *The Voudon Gnostic Workbook*, 2007, p. 236.

CHAPTER TWO

Distinction Does Not Equal Separation

Therefore, the structures of the Rite of Memphis-Misraïm are not generated from history only but are archetypal generations from the deepest regions of the psyche. History is the theater for the observation of the phenomenological amplification of these archetypal patterns.

Michael-Paul Bertiaux[43]

---

[43] *Voudon Gnostic Workbook*, p. 89

As said in the Introduction, many would not recognize the work of our branch of Memphis+Misraïm as Masonic at all. Here, I am not referring to formal recognition such as that offered by the UGLE (United Grand Lodge of England) as no body of the Antient & Primitive Rite is so recognized today by UGLE, even though the Rite grew alongside the Ancient and Accepted Scottish Rite of Freemasonry[44] and maintains amicable relations with most Grand Orients[45] in the world. Here, we are referring to the fact that what we do simply *looks different* in a lot of ways. Whereas we do have many points of convergence, we are also radically divergent in some cases. For instance, in CI bodies which offer Charters for Research & Philosophical Lodges of the APRM+M, we may not have any formal dramatics whatsoever in our initiatory work. However, with all of the various ways in which we stand apart as unique in the family of Freemasonry, this distinction does not equal separation. At every turn, we are still partaking of the same rich tradition of wisdom, symbolism, initiation and ritual as many Brothers and Sisters across the globe are. But more than this, we are partaking of the same *spirit* of Masonry and are awakening the sleepy Egregore of Masonic initiation which has been taken from its source and redistributed amongst various esoteric and occult orders and Rites.

Bertiaux speaks of many functions of the Transcendental Ego in his master Grimoire, *The Voudon Gnostic Workbook*. One function is the aforementioned *rebuilding of old orders along more modern lines*. This reconstruction and rebuilding is precisely the method that T Allen Greenfield employed in the late 80's and on into the early years of the new Century to create a workable system of the Ecclesiastical Revision of the APRM+M, utilizing the *points chauds* (hot points) empowerments upon the body[46]. His work has been to develop this idea in its entirety, to practice it in Lodge settings and otherwise and to pair it down to essences and essentials, the latter being his magickal method of returning to the primitive simplicity of the ancients, awakening both the mystical Egregore of Freemasonry and reinstituting both the *Primitive & Sacred Doctrine* within the Craft. As Greenfield states in his Introduction to the *Compleat Rite of Memphis*, according to Crowley it would take a fortune and a lifetime (or two) to perform the APRM+M in its entirety. This makes of the system a useless addition

---

[44] Some even suggest that it predates the AASR considerably, particularly in its early form of the **Rite of Misraïm** which has traces going back as far as 1738, but which was organized fully no sooner than 1788. In fact, the two volume, 861 page Bedarride brothers' document, *De L'Ordre Maçonnique de Misraïm*, was not produced until 1845. In these matters, it is best to err on the side of the conservative, with regards to dates.

[45] The Grand Orient of France, in particular, includes the combined Rites of Memphis-Misraïm in their corpus of Degree systems. The version practiced in the Grand Orient and elsewhere is more akin to traditional Lodge practice, yet the material is of an esoteric nature and involves intense study and practice.

[46] See the *Afterword*, by T Allen Greenfield

to the already cumbersome collection of Rites and Orders proliferated throughout time. However, if the Rite truly contained something secret and was of necessity purged and revitalized as the Ecclesiastical Revision propounded to do via empowerments, then it stands to reason that a simple approach to this ecclesiastical model is in order. The espousing of *Holy Simplicity* to an incredibly difficult system is the key to the APRM+M's new life and energetic influence amongst individuals within Congregational Illuminism. This little experiment of Allen's group expanded to a larger study upon the Holy Arabia Mountain where the points empowerments have been occurring consistently since, directly alongside clerical work of the Gnostic Church; Ordinations, Consecrations, healings, etc.

The points of distinction between the CI approach to the APRM+M and mainstream Masonry abound, but several stand out as foundational differences that deserve closer attention. One such point is the political edifice that mainstream Masonry is constructed upon. Masonic jurisprudence, the ratification and execution of Masonic Code from State to State and Country to Country, the Imperialistic model of governance used by Grand Lodges throughout the globe, etc. are all suggestive of a political backbone to what appears to be an Initiatic Tradition. Now in all kindness, this approach works and has proven effective in the continuance of Masonry. Additionally, many of us function well within this clearly hierarchical system. It is not a case of the either/or fallacy, as one can be involved with both so long as his oaths do not contradict such experimentation. There is no reason to abandon such organization on a large scale, but the fact of the matter is that these governing concerns have little or nothing to do with the spiritual life. In fact, the spiritual realm itself is far more wiggly and egalitarian than what mainstream Masonry suggests in her rigid laws and ordinances. It is also poignant to consider that these political concerns and agendas not only have little to do with the spiritual life but may in fact hamper experiments within the same.

It does not take much creativity to visualize the Grand Master position as Imperialistic. The Grand Master basically has his back against the wall and is guarded by the Grand Lodge Officers. He pontificates from Grand Lodge and may make pronouncements concerning things as general as race, gender or sexual orientation and as personal as what spiritual practices are acceptable and which ones are not—and he does this *ex cathedra*, as it were[47]. The fact that this has been witnessed a number of times, sometimes with horror,

---

[47] One sad point of fact in recent times involves the Grand Lodge of Florida and its decision to expel members of the Craft who are involved in Wicca, Gnosticism and a plethora of other traditions. See http://freemasonsfordummies.blogspot.com/2012/12/gm-of-florida-expels-wiccans-gnostics.html This sort of pontificating is clearly an abuse of power and reveals the hazards inherent in a top-heavy hierarchical structure. To be fair, one only has to *endure* such poor leadership for a year in Lodges, and Florida is now free from this ruling.

during my own lifetime suggests that this position has become too powerful, as some of the most heartfelt and primitive methods of Masonry have aimed to be inclusive and open to all faiths as well as all good men (later to include women in many branches[48]). This position is a fearful one and one in which the spirit is silenced quite often. In contrast, Congregational Illuminists tend towards extreme democracy, where the individual him or herself has a say in the governance of individual Lodges—and even further towards anarcho-syndicalism with an emphasis on facilitation rather than ruling and on cooperation rather than conformation and competition. We tend to find it odd that Freemasonry and its lofty ideals of egalitarianism developed in such a way in America, which promoted liberty and the strength of the individual—yet fell into that same old monarchical model of imperialistic governance that it desperately wanted freedom from.

Additionally, we find that mainstream Lodges in many countries, but especially in America, are physically constructed upon a Courtroom model. One does not walk into a *sanctuary* in modern Lodges; he walks into a space that is clearly demarcated by laws and regulations. In America, there are certainly growing movements such as the Traditional Masonic Observance (TMO) and the Modern Rite in North America and the Caribbean, which challenge this courtroom model and other notions, but the power of jurisprudence is tangibly felt upon entry into most mainstream Lodges. The Scottish Rite tended towards the more Catholic approach of Cathedrals and truly Holy spaces, but they were forced (by the Brethren themselves) to change their building's names from Scottish Rite *Temples* to Scottish Rite Centers and such. This is indicative of the nervousness amongst the Brethren concerning the general public opinion of Masonry, and even amongst the Brethren themselves, as to what the primary modus operandi is of the Craft. It is a large world and Masonry has much to offer all sorts of men and women, but we feel that the heart of Masonry is her initiatory power, her rituals and symbols and the *Sacred Doctrine* which has lain forgotten amongst her adherents. When these become the portents of the Craft, then one wants to practice in Oratories, in Sanctuaries, Temples—even under the dome of sky as our Brethren the Druids once did in their Sacred Groves! It becomes almost impossible to conduct such magical research and experimentation in spaces that suggest laws and codes primarily.

With such a heavy emphasis on governance in the Craft, it becomes clear that the smallest unit of mainstream Masonry is the Lodge. I have been able to observe a recent change in one particular Grand Lodge concerning a matter of race which was nothing short

---

[48] See Margaret C Jacob's landmark research in *The Origins of Freemasonry, Facts and Fiction*, 2006, where she suggests that women became involved in Freemasonry as early as the 1740's in Europe, p. 93. See also here research in, *Living the Enlightenment*.

of injustice. It was because the Lodge that wished to break the rules stood firmly together until the end that the rules and ordinances were changed for the better[49]. A single voice would not have been given a moment's notice concerning this fiery issue of race. However, in a model such as the Congregational Illuminist one that recognizes the individual as the smallest unit, there is always ample room for the little guy to accomplish his or her Will and fight against tyranny, superstition, intolerance or as in the case of the above—racial injustices. These kinds of issues are counterproductive to the life of the spirit. A spiritual Order has to have a real measure of liberty, fraternity and equality. Curiously enough, this is the national motto of France—the source of most occult forms of Freemasonry- *Liberté, égalité, fraternité!*

Within mainstream Masonry's Blue or Symbolic Lodges (1st -3rd degrees), the method of instruction is fairly simple. This is an inheritance from the Emblematic working of England. It is simply the memorization (word for word) of the Catechisms of the degrees. This is a very effective method of passing on traditions. One lovely benefit of this sort of rigorous memory work is that it opens the Hermetic Mason up to the world of Ars Memoriæ—the art of Memory, such as that practiced by luminaries like Giordano Bruno, Robert Fludd, etc.[50] But this is a bonus that the Mason has to discover for himself. Many young Masons enter the Lodge with a number of questions and the Catechetical coaches do their best to answer these, but there is not an overall arrangement of Masonic Formation in practice across the globe. There are individual Grand Lodges that have taken a rather businesslike approach to this idea and purported Formation programs, but they have all of the appendages of training programs within the business world and tend towards moving further from the heart of Masonry—Esoterica. What is needed is a scientific approach of shared inquiry amongst practitioners of the Craft. This need not be packaged up in a program to purchase, it can simply be understood from the first Initiation onwards—that each individual has something to offer to the whole and that the giants' shoulders that we are standing upon are at the ready to share their own knowledge and expertise. This idea of shared inquiry and the freedom to experiment is a fundamental portion of the four articles of Congregational Illuminism. Within this model, there are seasoned veterans at the ready to answer questions and challenge new Initiates, as well as there being an overall sense that the newcomer has his or her own portion of divinity to share with the rest of the group and a history and experience to build upon. It may be that in the future we see an exchange of influences from the traditional to the innovative and vice-versa.

---

[49] See: http://www.freemasoninformation.com/2009/06/my-brothers-keeper-open-racism-in-georgia-freemasonry/
[50] See Frances A Yates, *The Art of Memory*, 1992.

Within mainstream Masonry there are wonderful lectures delivered. I am honored to have heard and read a number of powerful examples of these and rubbed shoulders with these worthy Brethren who are putting a great deal of energy into their labors. But there is rarely the moment where in Lodge, the adherent can take such learning (philosophia) and translate it to something useful in the pursuit of Light (praxis). There is an overall emphasis upon Scholasticism and a disdain and distaste for Mysticism. As the Eastern Orthodox Church knows, however, the marriage of inquiry and theology with mysticism is a Holy and Blessed one. It is time to restore the other half of Masonry to its family. In closing, let us consider the words of Bertiaux, as he sums up the spiritual nature of the Rite,

> *So it is from the patriarchate of the gnosis that we receive the spiritual power which serves to validate the levels of magickal initiation. But this power is both complex and subject to an ever-developing process and it is mysteriously identified with the Rite of Memphis-Misraïm, which, in our system, is a structure within the Gnostic church of the Neo-Pythagorean priesthood.*[51]

---

[51] *The Voudon Gnostic Workbook*, p. 176

CHAPTER THREE

What Are We Building?

When the Adepts affirm that a single vessel alone is necessary for transmutation, an alembic which is within reach of all, and which each possesses without knowing it, they allude to the philosophical and moral alchemy and the vessel is man himself.

Yarker[52]

---

[52] *Lectures of a Chapter, etc.*, p.43

If this form of the APRM+M we are speaking of is engaged in *spirit building*, what exactly does this mean? In Valentin Tomberg's masterwork, *Meditations on the Tarot*[53], we find a distinction made between the Masonic model of spiritual work and the mystical model. The Masonic model of spirituality is described as building oriented and self bolstering, while the path of the mystic is growth directed, organic and operates from the inside outward. This is evident often in the language of Masonry where the Mason is enjoined to construct his or her own life. In spiritual Freemasonry, however, this either/or fallacy falls to the wayside because we are *building* as well as *growing*. There is a construction feel to the life we are creating, an artistic and architectural sense to it all, as well as an organic and mystical growth from within. In the *Masonic Magician*, Cooper and Faulks describe their discovery of the Egyptian Rite of Cagliostro as an extraordinary revelation. They add that "its foundation lies within the realm of traditional Freemasonry but its countenance is purely magical. A system of personal and spiritual rejuvenation encapsulated with the wisdom and morality of Masonry.[54]" In all systems of High Magic, the practitioner begins by invoking the Highest principle first, be that the Deity, Archangel, Angel, Planetary Intelligence, etc. High Magic coincides with mysticism like the warp and woof of a weaving. It is in this way, that our *spirit building* is both an act of magical creativity and construction as well as a mystical process from within. The *personal and spiritual rejuvenation* through our working with the points-chauds empowerments organically informs and often completely encapsulates our further Masonic working and building.

There are many places in the degrees of Freemasonry which speak of the Heavenly or New Jerusalem. Sometimes this is referred to as the spiritual Temple. But unlike the mainstream Mason, we do not claim to be constructing this particular Temple, as it already exists on a higher plane in full and elaborate form. It is the true *Sovereign Sanctuary*[55], the constant source of energy and vitality which through a process of ray-ing, feeds our individual ontic spheres with light and knowledge from beyond. The ontic sphere of the candidate can be best described as an etheric bubble surrounding the Kether area of the head. It is comprised of the collected magical and creative energies and experiences of the candidate which can be drawn from for spiritual work. Bertiaux describes it as the "Universe of Magickal Imagination" particular to the individual as distinguished from the

---

[53] Anon. (Tomberg, Valentin) *Meditations on the Tarot, A Journey into Christian Hermeticism*, Rockport: Element Books Ltd. 1985. See letter XVI, in particular.
[54] p. 277.
[55] Related, again, to the INNER RETREAT of Memphis-Misraïm in the M7Rs work.

collective consciousness[56]. It is sometimes visible to the clairvoyant, but requires more than aural vision, it requires inter-dimensional vision.

As the true *Sovereign Sanctuary* already exists in full, forming a lattice and matrix of foundational spirit rays which we labor to utilize in our work, then what we are building is more close to home. Let us begin with that which is nearest and then extend the Light outward to those around us. What are we building?

- *The Scintillating Body.* The points-chauds, or "hot points" have been alluded to already. These are gyrating energy zones within the body which we awaken and activate through our initiatory process. When these points, which are aligned with the 97 degrees of the APRM+M, are activated, a spiritual transmission also occurs. Initially, we are awakening something that is already present within the body. The clairvoyant uses whatever means he or she needs to clearly visualize the locale of the point. But as the point is awakened, we are also giving and receiving a spiritual transmission from the Holy Arabia Mountain as well as a ray from the Egregore of Gnostic and Apostolic successions. This is one of the reasons why it is imperative for the work to be passed along from person to person in an unending chain back to the Holy Mountain. In due time and with frequent reception and reawakening of the points, the body becomes a *scintillating constellation of Light.* What body is this action performed upon; the subtle body, the causal body, the Body of Light, the Astral or the Etheric body or the physical organism itself? All of the above, yet for simplicity sake, the Body of Light may comprise all of the other various sheaths and be paired with the physical[57]. The action of points-chauds empowerments is composite; it acts upon the Body of Light as well as the physical organism. This is in keeping with the sort of non-dual Gnosticism that many Congregational Illuminists espouse. These points have the qualities of attunement & empowerment as well as initiation & therapy. But, for this part of our study, it is enough to know that we are building the body electric, a gyrating powerhouse of energy and vitality focused primarily upon the Middle Pillar (as it appears upon the body) the column of Beauty & Harmony (Tiphareth) in the Masonic trinity of Wisdom (Chokmah), Beauty (Tiphareth) and Strength (Geburah). This composite scintillating body is nourished and fed through repeated points empowerments and reactivations as well

---

[56] *VGW* p. 615
[57] The silver cord of Ecclesiastes 12:6 is indicative of the unity of the Body of Light with the physical organism. "Remember him--before the silver cord is severed, and the golden bowl is broken; before the pitcher is shattered at the spring, and the wheel broken at the well." New International Version

as through the practice of the Eucharist through the Gnostic Mass[58] (of which there is much variety). Through these two practices, the ontic sphere of the initiate becomes empowered and enlarged for the further reception of rays from the true *Sovereign Sanctuary* forming an unending source of renewal and rejuvenation for the candidate and initiator. This Light, scintillating within the body, is then free to be given to others.

- *The Mystic Temple.* This term is used throughout Memphis-Misraïm literature, but after the reduction of the Rite to 33 degrees (in an attempt to appease the Grand Orient of France) Yarker began using the term, *Mystic Temple* rather exclusively for a collection of Grand Officers with legislative authority under the *temporal* Sovereign Sanctuary. As has been stated before, when doing this sort of magical Masonic work, practitioners desire a space that supports such endeavors. The *Mystic Temple* that we are building resides on two planes at once. It begins with the selection for where our group decides to work. For those of us who live near the Holy Arabia Mountain, the physical Temple is in nature itself! But the location for the Great Arabia Mountain Working was not simply a matter of aesthetics or personal preference. There is a specific space, *consecration rock*[59], which is the location of a power zone, or marma[60]. Widely diverse groups of initiates have been drawn magnetically to this one particular spot on this granite monadnock since the 1980's. It is also a location rich with Native American History. It is a vortex of sorts. The ancient Celtic Saints of Iona, Wales and Ireland often spoke of "thin places" where the veil between this world and the next is tenuous. These Saints often experienced psychic phenomena, clairvoyance and clairaudience as well as conversation with the deceased in these power zones. These locations have a unique vibratory rate. This serves to bolster the Masonic and Gnostic work that is undertaken as well as providing a central locale for Healing circles. In our own Chapel, we have what we have discerned to be a small vortex as well. It is in an odd location in our garage. We have built our Holy

---

[58] See Aleister Crowley's suggestions for working with the Body of Light in Liber O, found in many Thelemic Texts, including Regardie's, *Gems from the Equinox,* 2007. Also, see Mark Stavish's, *Between the Gates,* 2008, chapters 4 & 7.

[59] "Holy places, miraculous relics, statues and icons, are not depots for the psychic and mental energy of pilgrims and other believers, but rather places or objects where 'heaven opens and Angels are able to ascend and descend.' They are points of departure for spiritual radiation. This radiation certainly presupposes faith on the part of the believers in order to be effective, but it is not so that the 'energy' which they radiate is drawn out from the believers. The faith of the latter is simply that which renders them *susceptible* to the healing and illuminating force which radiates from these places or objects, but is not the source of this force." *Meditations on the Tarot,* p.420.

[60] "**Marmas** (Noun) These are the power zones or place where powers of an occult type build up. They are extremely common and most magicians do not realize that they are surrounded by these power zones." Glossary, *The Voudon Gnostic Workbook,* p. 616.

Space, our Chapel, around this sacred marma. It is the primary location for our *bringing to Light* moments of Masonic Initiation, our points chauds empowerments, our healings, our Eucharist, etc. Once the marma is located and the work undertaken in that area, the group may feel inclined to add items; talismans and such that will assist the telluric and solar energies in their flowing. This is the nature of reliquary (relics and bones from dead Saints and Martyrs), lodged inside of all Catholic altars. After repeated work in this sacred spot, the collected energies, rays from the marma and from above, and intentions of the group coagulate and consolidate into a thought-form, visible to the clairvoyant. **It is this beautifully constructed thought-form that is the *Mystic Temple*[61] we are building.**

- *Community.* Gatherings of Congregational Illuminist bodies are not usually spent in a business meeting style, going over minutes and agenda items. They are comprised of spiritual work—Masses, points empowerments and other works of magic are performed in an intimate setting which is usually the home of one of the Initiates, or a Holy spot in nature. There is usually ample time for silence and meditation as well as celebration in these close-knit groupings. There may be lectures of a Gnostic nature or experimental workings with Masonic degrees. The primary work of these gatherings is focused around the sacred marma—within the Mystic Temple and composed of scintillating bodies! In this sort of collective, a true sense of community arises and urban shamans consult and bear each other's burdens, while also carefully selecting Degree/points chauds empowerments to assist those in need. These communities operate without dues or fees, which opens up a sense of mutual sharing, aid and support that is unequalled in the Western Mystery Tradition. This type of working is **In Free Communion**, requiring little by way of dogma and beliefs, and undertaken for the greater good. Individuals typically step up to donate the needed items for each working—candles, incense, pot-luck dinner items, etc. Guests come and go freely and no requirement of *proving* anything or being tested ensues. They are simply invited to come and see.

We are building *the scintillating body*, the *mystic temple* and a close-knit community working *in free communion*. All begins with the Temple of the Holy Spirit...the body. Our bodies are treated as *the* sacred vessel for transmutation and no other item, building or material is

---

[61] The Mystic Temple is the personal research schema that receives rays and instruction from the INNER RETREAT or Sovereign Sanctuary.

necessary. This work is at once Masonic, magical and mystical and moves from the individual body outward into the world at large.

CHAPTER FOUR

Congregational Illuminism

"I see great advantages to the 'big tent' in which all kinds of people of various races, religious backgrounds, political views and lifestyles can feel comfortable, if for no other reason than the human resource pool and material means that provides...I would advocate...more emphasis on service than authority."

T Allen Greenfield[62]

---

[62] Greenfield, Allen H. *The Roots of Magick 1700 thru 2000*, p. 220.

Before exploring some of the central tenants of Congregational Illuminism, the above quote needs to be addressed because it is this very description that often characterizes one's first experiences at a CI event or gathering. One look around the Lodge, Temple, Node or sacred spot and it becomes clear that this is a mixed bag of folk, from a number of traditions. There are differing genders, age groups, styles, races, gender-orientations and the like at these gatherings. When it is a large gathering, such as at the Arabia Mountain workings, one can hardly figure out who the Facilitators are until the sacred moment that robes and regalia are donned for empowerments and/or ordinations. As a "Leader" (this is a bit of a misnomer and basically just a way to give individuals someone to contact) of the Congregational Illuminist "Cause" I have been profoundly moved by the latter part of the quote above. What has come with my small measure of leadership within CI has been a *greater service to others*. This "big tent" approach frightens some who have experience in groups where psychic vampires lurk and attempt to drain the mass of its energy and purpose. But CI has a built in control of this error. Our focus is upon the Work. Time and again, at least in our own Chapel, we have noticed that these leech types fall off quickly when the work load increases and the expectation of nothing short of scientific scrutiny is held to the mystical experiments. As will be seen in the 2nd precept of Free Illuminism, we are practicing a form of Scientific Illuminism, which has, as its watchwords, "the Method of Science, the Aim of Religion."

Congregational Illuminism is a decentralized, non-authoritarian and open system that engages in the life-long process of spiritual unfoldment. It is directly linked to the spiritual tradition of Western Esotericism through powerful lines of Apostolic and Gnostic Succession. It has within its bosom a radically reinterpreted version of the APRM+M along Ecclesiastical lines. Within CI, there are boundless opportunities to work in a spiritual capacity towards one's own personal fulfillment and that of others. Partaking of the ancient Egregore connected to the Apostolic and Gnostic Successions and bolstered by the Ecclesiastical Revision of the APRM+M, the Free Illuminist may labor *in free communion* with like-minded individuals and form whatever type of working Order or original set of Rites that one wishes to birth. CI is a network of freely associated individuals who are committed to the Great Work and who are ready to accomplish their wills without useless power struggles, domineering hierarchies and pontiffs. This model is very much grassroots based, inspired by anarcho-syndicalism, as well as radical democracy and egalitarianism and upheld and labored within by volunteering illuminists who are dedicated and sincere in their work.

One of the more compelling ideas surrounding the strength of CI is the notion of this powerful Egregore that attends her labors. Rupert Sheldrake has done much in the scientific community to promote a concept of morphic *fields*, morphic *resonance* and morpho-*genesis*. His language comes closest to the understanding of what occurs when the candidate receives a point-chaud empowerment or even more so, during ordinations and consecrations. *Through the laying on of hands and breathing upon the candidate*, she is brought into the morphic *field* of generations of Gnostics, magicians, Saints and Holy ones. This particular Egregore has such strength because it is fed not only by the collective group mind of magicians and esotericists, but through the deeply spiritual work attached to the lines of Apostolic and Gnostic Succession. Once the candidate is brought into the *field* of the Egregore, she becomes a participant in its sentience. Through frequent usage and invocation of the Egregore, morphic *resonance* occurs and with it is born heightened awareness of things such as one's True Will and the means to accomplish such. As our particular Egregoric transfer is independent from central authority or agendas, it moves more freely amongst the participants. Through morphic *resonance*, CI participants become linked in such a manner that healing from a distance becomes possible, as well as frequent travel in the Body of Light. This is one of the *initiated* understandings of the Mystic Tie in Freemasonry. With more work within the Egregore comes the height of the participation, morpho-*genesis*. It is here that the Egregore itself uses the vehicle of a man or woman to form a new Order or system of Rites or magical bodies. The Egregore is a psychic battery much akin to the true *Sovereign Sanctuary* mentioned previously. But whereas the *Sovereign Sanctuary* is rather stationary as an Inner Plane lattice, the Egregore moves through history along with its people. In this way, it could be likened to the Shekinah or divine presence of the Hebrew Bible.

The basic principles of Free Illuminism

And now we return to the central principles or precepts of Congregational Illuminism. But before doing so, I would like to reiterate that I am not the spokesperson for CI. Though I am an active Facilitator of a Chapel, I am in no way the mouthpiece for the revolutionary movement. It is simply that I have found this model timely and effective in my own spiritual journey and those of my worshiping and initiatory community. CI has become a springboard for my life-long goals and has provided me with a simple and powerful set of tenants that do not ask of me blind allegiance or belief in the superstitious or the renunciation of my freedoms. In all ways, my involvement within CI has been positive and life affirming and has paved the way for the spiritual Freemasonry that I craved from the beginning.

Here again are the simple and precise articles of Free Illuminism with commentary:

1. **Spiritual growth is incompatible with authoritarian structure**.

    We have all worked in the most common design of groups–the pyramidal model. At the top of the pyramid is the CEO, the President, the Principal, the Grand Master, etc. Some systems have pyramids within pyramids, such as in mainstream Freemasonry. In the Masonic Lodge, there is a general sense that the Lodge is trusted by Grand Lodge to do its work. There is little interruption and interference from Grand Lodge on a regular basis, though it could occur at any moment and there are scheduled times for all Lodges to welcome and host the Grand Master and his officers. So within the Lodge there is a smaller pyramid with the Worshipful Master and his officers underneath in a cascading line descending to the Tyler and Chaplain. The Worshipful Master answers to deputies and Grand Lodge officers and ultimately the Grand Master himself. Does this arrangement work? Absolutely. Is it efficient? Well...with the accompanying dues and such it appears to be, though *numbers* become an unpleasant focus from time to time because of building requirements and such. Is it conducive to spiritual growth? Well... if you recall, I mentioned that Masonic initiation *was* indeed spiritual for me. It also unlocked a number of dream initiations that were to follow. So it is not that one cannot have a spiritual experience within such a structure, it is simply that spiritual growth is not compatible with the structure. It is that *spirit* will always and ever move of its own accord and not by the dictates of a Code, or by the pronouncements of the one in the Chair. Further, we have all come into contact with good leaders and facilitators who seemed to move with the people instead of above them. This is a rather authorita*tive* approach, as opposed to authorit*arian*. If our society is truly free, such as in America, then why do we continuously insist upon leadership that is closer to despotism than democracy? Alan Watts makes a rather strong argument upon this subject in his lecture, *Democracy in the Kingdom of Heaven.* What we are asked to do in CI, is to link together in free communion and move beyond these authoritarian strictures and into the notion of mutual aid, support and assistance.

2. Scientific Illuminism requires a non—dogmatic, experimental approach.

The mage, Aleister Crowley coined the term, *Scientific Illuminism*. His approach suggested that it was the *Method of Science, the Aim of Religion*. Now since the name of Crowley comes packed with all sorts of bizarre notions and expectations, let me add that CI is not a Thelemic body in any way. We are a collective of initiates amongst which are Christian mystics, Chaos Magicians, Gnostics, Reform Jews, Buddhists, etc., *and yes,* Thelemites. Many read that listing with horror and can hardly imagine how it could possibly work, but let me assure the reader that it does. The way that this typically pans out is that like-minded individuals collect with like! Simple enough? Underneath it all are these few guiding principles or articles, one of which involves Scientific Illuminism. So there is a sort of disclaimer.

I recall how blown away I was by this concept when I first started digging into the amazing world of Esoteric literature. Here was a mystic and mage who held his experiences up to the light of scientific scrutiny through careful observations, reports and the mapping out of experiences through repetition. It is to apply something of the scientific method to the spiritual life! In this manner, this revelation is true brilliance and its reverberations in the esoteric world and outer world alike are still being felt. In truth, this approach is still in its infancy amongst magicians and mystics. Rather than approaching our furnaces of creativity, our Oratories and Lodges with all of the answers to our spiritual questions, we approach all of our work with an eye towards shared inquiry and experimentalism. One of the primary tools we utilize for this is the report. As is known in the esoteric world, there is hardly an arrow in the quiver more powerful than that of the magical diary. It is the single most important piece of the magical cabinet because it contains the true charting of our spiritual progress. It is the place that we quickly pen down our vast and often bizarre spiritual experiences. It is here, in the magical diary, that we begin to find patterns and formulas that we can then repeat to test for accuracy and effectiveness. From the diary is born the report. Many Orders *require* certain kinds of reports before Initiates are able to proceed or advance in their studies. For us, it is up to the individual and/or the individual Lodge or Temple to decide how one goes about reporting but *all* are highly encouraged to maintain accurate reports of experiences in their work. This brings a rigor and relevance to our labors that keeps the work from digressing into mutual back patting or soul massaging. There is plenty of room for fellowship and the sharing of burdens in our CI communities, but we are not a support group and the main impetus for our formation is the Work. The level of diligence and integrity that the approach of Scientific Illuminism requires keeps us all very busy and highly focused. Once these reports are shared, checked and challenged by others, the richness of the work is able to be disseminated to all interested parties. Amongst Free Illuminists are a plethora of experts in varied fields who stand at the ready to assist in questions of gematria, goetic workings, liturgical concerns, etc.

Now what is rather curious in the esoteric world is that many take on this Scientific Illuminist approach, yet within highly authoritarian and dogmatic organizations. If inquiry and experiment are key words with our work, how can such be effectively performed in a stifling, top-down model? We *must* remain free from such strictures as authoritarianism and dogmatism if we are to truly engage in this method.

3. **A free society linked in free communion should be actualized.**

This article is deceptively simple. Recall that individuals within CI are called Free Illuminists. Now a third phrase that has been used already, shows up in the article—*in free communion*. What exactly does it mean to be *in free communion*? The phrase evokes notions of the various Churches and the ecumenical movements involved wherein groups such as Catholics *allow* Orthodox to freely partake of the Eucharistic Celebration. This relates in a way to our CI use of the phrase, as there is a sense of openness within our groups that allows for those of varied backgrounds to partake of the mysteries in peaceful accord. But it also goes further. It is the *actualization* of such a free society, *linked* in free communion that is the heart of this article. We are making real, making a fact of, a society in which one's fullest potential may be made manifest and in which one can labor, struggle, celebrate and learn alongside others pursuing their own wills. This pursuit is made all the more compelling by the repetition of the word, *free*. Each is able to work according to his or her own ingenium. So why collect in the first place?–because of the wisdom, strength and beauty of linking together and the natural tendency of humans to enjoy the companionship of others in such difficult work. Our linking both lightens the load and enriches the labor. Our free labors together multiply the dividends of our findings and experiments and enlarge the Egregore's consciousness and activity.

4. **We facilitate, we do not lead. We do the Work, we do not extract oaths or dues, or require dogmatic beliefs.**

Here is where the term, *leader* was a misnomer. In truth, those of us who labor freely for the cause of CI and facilitate our own Orders and Liturgical bodies, simply make ourselves available. For the most part, individuals within CI work on their own once they have clearly delineated what they want to accomplish. It is sometimes in the early stages when a guide is needed, but in the end there is a self-guiding and self-perpetuating force attached to the Egregore that sincere candidates will sense and take advantage of. However seasoned we may be it is wonderful to be able to go back to our facilitators and bounce ideas off of them or receive spiritual instruction or suggestion from them. Quickly in my own Chapel, T Allen Greenfield became a sort of *Gerondas* or spiritual director/elder. He, along with the founding Bishop of my Church, Tau Dositheos, have been constant companions along the way, yet the guidance and companionship has not ever been lorded over me or my Chapel. We are simply all focused upon the Work! In this way, leadership is *out of the way.* The great educator Maria Montessori has a saying concerning children that is cogent to this notion, she says, "Every useless aid to a child's activity arrests development." It is the same for adults. We have to struggle by trial and error and fall upon our faces from time to time to establish ourselves and experience growth. This is impossible if we are constantly being interfered with by a "leader." It is like planting a seed and returning to the garden every few days to rip it out and check to see if it is growing. True growth requires time and freedom to explore.

In Spanish, there are a couple of words for guide. Depending upon usage, one might employ orientar, turistica or others that are gender specific. As Facilitators, we are more like a *Guia*. The connotation for a Guia is affectionate and suggests one who makes things lighter. This is our essential role in CI as Facilitators; we are here to ease the burdens that are incumbent to spiritual life and to directing one's own Lodge, Chapel, Node, etc.

What is the essential nature of our "Work?" In a multitude of ways, we are all seeking *gnosis*, which is inextricably linked to the APRM+M's *Sacred Doctrine*. Many have a central focus of the mystical union of Self with the ALL. Each may make his or her own path to this goal. This is essentially a sacred trust in the individual and in the human organism itself, to be considered *above the Institution.* The noted Masonic author, Albert Pike was fond of saying; *Institutions were built for men, not men for institutions.*

Oaths. There are numerous ideas concerning *Oaths*, within CI bodies. The main focus of this portion of Article 4 is that we do not command our Initiates to take oaths to other humans or to institutions. This does not mean that we do not compose oaths directed to our Higher Selves, such as the *A∴A∴* does. Additionally, we may compose *Obligations* that are specifically directed to our own individual pursuits, but not such that tie the individual unduly to an Order, Collective of people or to a single person. It is imperative that the reader understand this distinction, as the *Oath* has a distinctly magical quality and has been utilized with power and skill over the ages by a variety of magi. It is where the oath is directed that is of the highest import here; is it directed towards another person or institution—or is it directed upwards into the spiritual realms? The former has been abused many times over by institutions whose aims were genuine in the beginning. It only takes one power hungry despot or megalomaniac to take such an *oath* as being directed to himself, and then the candidate is in bondage rather than being enlightened and set free.

Dues. Esotericists and others are fond of the saying that that which comes easily or freely is probably not worth your time. And, granted, this is true quite often. One need only have children to realize that if they are given everything freely all the time without any work or responsibility, everyone suffers and the children themselves are unhappy. But in the spiritual world, when money comes in...things go awry. It is a fundamental law of the universe. Simply look around and observe the mega-churches and their financial woes, the expensive wars committed in the name of religion, the Orders and Rites with their expensive regalia, dues and fees that close their doors to the sincere seeker who is less fortunate than the other members. It is here that we say, *drop the dues and fees!* If our work has the integrity that we propose it does, then it does not have a price tag, is not something that we own and it is open to all. In our own Chapel, we have had candidates and visitors carpool from a hundred miles away and bring treats to eat, candles for the altar and other things that we might need, but not one dime. This has become a source of pride for us during these difficult economic times when large numbers of sincere seekers are being barred from Orders and Bodies simply because of the exorbitant dues and fees. In all things, we maintain the mind of holy simplicity. Additionally, there is a sort of payment incurred within our CI Bodies. This goes back to the Article itself, *We do the Work*. This is the payment and this is again, the built-in control of error. Those who are not truly interested in enlightenment will naturally fall away and will find somewhere where they can simply pay for their diplomas and titles and not be required to do the labor.

Dogmatic beliefs The bane of this world is fundamentalism in all of its hideous forms. Though fundamentalism does not equal dogmatism, one quite easily slips into the other. Fundamentalism has become a negative Zeitgeist that must be torn out by its roots and its roots are an unwavering dogmatic mind. As soon as we become dogmatic about an idea, be it spiritual or otherwise, we have closed ourselves off to inquiry and intellectual growth. Neither the mind, nor the spirit has borders until dogmatism rears its head. In this way, we can in no wise impose or require dogmatic beliefs. There are a variety of believers involved in the CI movement, but they are of a distinct variety in that they are *Scientific Illuminists*–rigorous magicians and spiritualists that do not approach the questions of religion or spirituality with the answers already fully in place. We expect to grow by virtue of aligning ourselves with others who have their own portion of divinity, experience and expertise to share with us. We inquire into the nature of life with open and pliable minds, and give credence to the intuitive and the spontaneous that accompany all spiritual practice. In other words, we do not overly compartmentalize that which is by its nature wiggly.

Even with the general openness of these four articles, they are merely a suggestion, a set of guidelines. The interpretations of the articles here are my own and each might be viewed with differing lenses per CI body. But the general idea is to have a few principles that most can agree with and then to begin the work!

† † †

Components of Esotericism

In Antoine Faivre's respectful tome, *Access to Western Esotericism*[63], the author highlights several main components of Esotericism which relate to the work of Spirit Builders and the movement of Free or Congregational Illuminism. Though other components could be argued, this reasonable listing is foundational and assists the seeker in discerning whether or not an Order or system of Degrees fits into the overall scheme of the Western Esoteric Tradition.

- *Correspondences*—The most fundamental aspect of the law of correspondences is the Hermetic axiom from the Emerald Tablet, *as above, so below.* Free Illuminists have, as their point of departure, a deep acceptance of this notion as the very nature of the points-chauds empowerments is a system of correspondences where points on the body relate to spiritual experiences, energies and even entities. From here, we have also discovered that power zones, or sacred marmas are important to the Free Illuminist, which is another form of correspondence found within nature and relating to the spiritual experience of the points-chauds empowerment upon the body, opens wide a universe of additional links wherein is discovered, "a huge theater of mirrors, an ensemble of hieroglyphs to be decoded[64]."

- *Living Nature*—The "Book of Nature" common to the Martinist, is another point of departure for Free Illuminists, as our spiritual center—our continuously raying outward, psychic battery—the Holy Arabia Mountain is considered to be a power zone of great antiquity. Free Illuminists generally accept the notion that nature is "essentially alive in all its parts, often inhabited and traversed by a hidden light or a hidden fire circulating through it[65]." Along with our respect and even exaltation of the body, Free Illuminists tend to take a non-dual approach to nature and ascribe divine aspects to it.

- *Imagination and Mediations*—With each points-chaud empowerment that the Free Illuminist works with, there is a subsequent scrying procedure that may follow. It is here, primarily, that Free Illuminists are unified in their ideas of the Imaginal realm and its import for the occultist. Through scrying the point, the Illuminist enters into a relationship with other realms and intermediary beings. Visionary experience is both the key to the *Sacred Doctrine* and to the points-chauds themselves, as it is a form of clairvoyance that recognizes the pulsating and flickering lights within the body

---

[63] pgs. 10-15
[64] Faivre, Antoine, *Access to Western Esotericism*, p. 10.
[65] Ibid., p. 11

initially. When the visions experienced through scrying are held up to the scrutiny of Scientific Illuminism, checked by the magickal record and researched through Gematria and other methodologies, the Imaginal realm becomes vivified with energies and entities from multiple dimensions, rather than being an extended daydream or reverie.

- *Experience of Transmutation*—The metamorphosis that occurs in all true expressions of the Esoteric Tradition has landmarks along the way that we have simplified in our own work to three stages of prayer; purification, illumination and union[66]. These are moments of gnosis that propel the Initiate forward in her search for integration and enlightenment, and which clearly mark a rite of passage.

- *The Praxis of the Concordance*—In Book Three we get into the notion of the Primitive Doctrine in detail which relates directly to this component of esotericism. Our entire practice is a form of the perennial philosophy, from the method of transmission from one to another, to the use of sacred marmas, and the Divine Economy of our procedure, we are a living embodiment of a primordial tradition. The "purist" path of Rene Guenon[67] is applicable to our work, in that we are drawing from the egregoric pools of both Freemasonry *and* the Gnostic, Catholic and Apostolic Churches.

- *Transmission*—Our principle method of working is direct, person to person transmission of the Egregore and awakening/stimulating of the points-chauds empowerments upon the body. Beyond the Holy Arabia Mountain, our Apostolic and Gnostic successions reach back to the 1st Century Church[68]. This type of valid, authentic transmission follows a "preestablished channel, respecting a previously marked path[69]" through the consecratory means that are employed upon the Holy Mountain, right alongside the points empowerments.

---

[66] Faivre mentions this "traditional mystic's way" verbatim in this chapter, p. 13.
[67] *Access to Western Esotericism*, p. 37
[68] Exhaustive lists of "Bishop to Bishop" lines of succession are traced in many areas and documented on various sites. It is not within the scope of the present study to present such in full, but among the more trustworthy chartings of Apostolic Succession we can include these textual works: the *Latin Old Roman Catholic Church of Flanders*, which traces the Villate and Bricaud lines, *The Apostolic Succession of the Most Reverend Wynn Wagner III, Episcopus Vagans*, Copyright, Robert Angus Jones, 2004, and *THE WANDERING BISHOPS, Apostles of a New Spirituality* by Lewis Keizer.
[69] Ibid., p. 14.

CHAPTER FIVE

Hot Points on the Holy Mountain

We therefore teach in these mysteries of the Sanctuary that there exists an initiatic power or magickal force in nature, which can be used to cause the growth and expansion of human mind-energy and spiritual power.

Michael-Paul Bertiaux[70]

*Recognizing a correspondence between the consecratory Gnostic System and traditional Ecclesiastic System...I selected the final English language definitive system of the Rite of Memphis of 97 degrees...and linked these to the **points chauds** ("hot points") of the Bertiaux system of empowerments.*

T Allen Greenfield[71]

---

[70] *Voudon Gnostic Workbook*, 2007, p. 586
[71] *The Roots of Magick 1700 thru 2000*, 2007, p. 223

Q. Does there exist in Masonry any secret independent of the formulae and signs?

A. Yes; some Brethren have still a knowledge of it; it has traversed time without experiencing any alteration, and exists now, as when, shut up in the mysterious Temples of Thebes and Eleusis, it excited the veneration of the world.[72]

The structural basis of CI and the experimentation conducted by T Allen Greenfield and others with regards to the *points chauds* empowerments and the alignment with the degrees of the APRM+M, predate the work on the Holy Arabia Mountain, yet it is upon this mountain that the collected experience, expertise and methodology became condensed and aligned with a sacred marma that would prove to be—in time, the spiritual foundation for the work of Congregational Illuminists worldwide.

Arabia Mountain

Guests and practitioners arrive at the Davidson-Arabia Natural Preserve an hour before ascending the Holy Mountain. This is the time when provisions are gathered together and visitors are introduced to the Free Illuminist community of the Greater Atlanta area. Then the ascent begins . When corresponded to other branches and aspects of the Western Esoteric Tradition, this is a unique way to begin working—to climb a small monadnock to a hidden shrine and holy spot. Along the climb, the visitor is struck by the beauty and power of the mountain, with its wild and difficult to identify plant life and upon the rock face itself, its pools of water filled with alien life. Regulars genuflect on the mountain and sign themselves with water out of the holy rock.

As Arabia Mountain is such a pristine example of a geographical marma, it is cogent to quote the great Michael Bertiaux to define precisely what this means. He states, [73]*Marmas (Noun) These are the power zones or place where powers of an occult type build up. They are extremely common and most magicians do not realize that they are surrounded by these power zones. They are found especially in parts of the human body and can develop a will of their own.* This definition necessitates a bit of unpacking, because it appears that we are dealing with two locations of radionic forces of energy—one geographical and one physiological. As the magician is "surrounded by these power zones" we find that they exist within the various environments that we

---

[72] Yarker, *Lectures of a Chapter, Senate & Council*, 1882, p. 54.
[73] *Voudon Gnostic Workbook*, 2007, p. 616

inhabit. These are vortex sites, power spots, Holy Ground, Sacred sites, "thin places[74]" and doorways where individuals and groups have experienced an upsurge of psychic energy and spiritual connectivity. Bertiaux then goes on to mention that these are especially located within the body, which alludes to our focus on *points chauds* and their awakening within the physical organism. Finally, he mentions that these marmas "can develop a will of their own!" So immediately we get the feeling that we are dealing with both a sort of entity or sentience, as well as a process or energy flow. By strict definition, a marma is part of the wide system of yoga and is connected with concentrated life force. This is intimately associated with the system of chakras and nadis[75] throughout the human body. So the more unique aspect of Bertiaux's definition and understanding of marma is in its capacity to occur within nature or our surrounding environments.

Consecration Rock[76] is the specific location atop Arabia Mountain near Atlanta Georgia, where the Great Work has been occurring in an unending seasonal cycle for the majority of the last decade. This particular Holy Rock, this, "altar of unhewn stones[77]" has been utilized since the 1980's by a variety of groups and initiates for a multitude of purposes. It isn't so much that it is *believed* to be holy, as it is *felt* to be so. This rock formation, atop a natural curiosity has become a geo-spiritual radiating center and the qualitative source of Gnostic energies and Light for Congregational Illuminists across the globe. It consistently rays outwards its rejuvenating currents, refueling participants' ontic spheres (storehouses of magical imagination) and energizing those whom are touched by another *scintillating body* descended from the mountain. Consecration Rock is also where, at the end of the day's proceedings, the group circles about and creates a swirling cone of healing to send to those in need, while vibrating the medicine chant, *AUM, HUM, TROM, HRI, AH*. This is our sacred healing circle.

Arabia Mountain itself is a unique landform. It is a 400 million year old monadnock. The word monadnock is Native American and refers to a mountain standing alone or isolated from others. Arabia's highest point is a conservative 954 feet, yet when one is atop this otherworldly rock face...all is alien and ethereal. It is composed of metamorphic rock that did not melt sufficiently to become pure granite as it cooled. It is bespotted with small solution pools which produce a variety of endangered lichen and aquatic plant-life that

---

[74] See *Wisdom of the Celtic Saints*, 1993, by Edward C Sellner for a good description of how Catholic Saints described these "thin places" in Iona, Ireland and elsewhere. These were typically the sites that they would select to build Chapels, monasteries, etc. They were also often the previous Holy sites of the Druids.

[75] The system of nadis comes rather close to our understanding of points-chauds, as these are described as tunnels and tubes, which the points also begin to feel like with frequency. The earliest reference to these nadis comes from the Katha Upanishad from around the 5th Century, BCE.

[76] See the images of the Holy Mountain, in the color plates

[77] In Yarker's, *Lectures of a Chapter, etc.*, p. 45, we are introduced to the idea of a holy place of "unhewn stone."

grows generally in granite formations and pools. The layers of grays and sienna atop the rock face are painted in jade where the lichen holds fast and dotted in white where indigenous underwater flowering plants survive. There are also sections of deep red where a rare budded plant called diamorpha thrives and deeper greens where a variety of small shrubs and even Bonsai sized trees sprout. It is a Holy Place. It sounds, feels, smells and looks like another dimension, and upon Consecration Rock one is truly transported and often thrust into an enlarged sense of dimensionality and spiritual bliss. The work being done upon this mountain is a return to the primitive religion, the primitive faith, the Primitive & *Sacred Doctrine*. It is a reinstatement of the Ancient Mysteries. Dion Fortune tells us that "places also exercise an important influence in occult operations; some spots upon the earth's surface are naturally highly magnetic. These have usually been discovered of old time by the ancients and their possibilities developed[78]."

When atop the Holy Arabia Mountain, one cannot help but make comparisons with the sacred Mt Abiegnus, the mystic mountain conceived of as the center of the universe and of Rosicrucian Initiation. Additionally, thoughts of Holy Mount Athos, the center of the Orthodox Christian world arise as one ascends the rocky face and the dome of sky. There is an overall climate of holiness in this space. When visitors arrive for an Arabia Mountain Gathering of Congregational Illuminists, they find T Allen Greenfield skirting ahead of the group to do the initial scrying into the pools atop the monadnock. Once at Consecration Rock, the group tends to make themselves comfortable—creating shade between trees with fabrics and spreading blankets upon the migmatite surface. The gathering usually begins with a short talk or lecture on any of a number of subjects connected with the overall Work. Then, any Liturgical Rites commence—ordinations or consecrations or other orders. Next, the points-chauds empowerments are given– typically a handful at a time. After points empowerments comes the healing circle on top of Consecration Rock. Healing energies are ray-ed outward from the Holy site while vibrating the medicine mantra and uplifting those in need. Finally, the group has a meal[79] together to complete the initiatory and liturgical working in celebratory fashion. This Working has become the model for many of us and is the essence behind the method presented in Books Two & Three. The essence of the work is a radical simplicity and constant awareness of these sacred marmas within and without us, and the beauty of working together *in free communion.*

Points-Chauds Empowerments

---

[78] *The Training and Work of the Initiate*, 2000, p. 115.
[79] Though the working on Arabia Mountain has very little similarity to traditional Masonic workings, we do see a few correspondences here with the lectures, the work being done and all followed by the Agape, or Festive Board.

The nature of *points chauds* empowerments is difficult to grasp and to discuss intellectually. Assuredly, as T Allen says, "reason is a good tool, but a poor master in matters spiritual and fraternal.[80]" When considering these mysterious and ineffable empowerments, we must speak by way of analogy and approximation. Additionally, the experience of these points is of such an individual character that no singular definition will suffice for all practices. However, there are key qualities and experiences attached to these empowerments that free us from a vague solipsism when we attempt to discuss that which can only marginally be spoken of.

To begin with, these point-events within the body can be clearly seen through second sight or clairvoyant vision. They are gyrating sources of compact energy lodged latently within the body. Various groups are charting the points all over the body, as many as 365 altogether, but for our study we are concentrating on the points which have been seen and experienced primarily upon the Middle Pillar of the human body. These are the ones that have been charted[81] and aligned with the degrees of the APRM+M. This is no accident, as it is the Middle Pillar upon the human form wherein the Kundalini energies move with swiftness and vitality—once awakened. It is also the Middle Pillar of the body that has been the focus of many Western Mystery Traditional practices, following the work of the Hermetic Order of the Golden Dawn and specifically, Israel Regardie's experiments and extensions to the Middle Pillar exercise[82]. So these points are power centers and spheres[83] of activity. They are already present within the candidate's body and simply need awakening. There is a requirement for another to awaken these within, however. Bertiaux states, "empowerments...actualize what is latent by giving something which is not fully experienced by the student, even though the student has the power deep within his psyche.[84]" So there is a transfer, but it isn't that the Facilitator is giving the Initiate the *points chaud* itself. The transfer is an Egregoric transmission– analogous, but not equal to, an ordination of sorts. This transmission awakens, stimulates and activates the latent hot point in the body. These points, once awakened, act as psycho-spiritual batteries with a level of self awareness and sentience. Some practitioners of this Craft have gone so far as to identify specific Lwa, or spirits of traditional Haitian Vodou with these points. The points are

---

[80] *Roots of Magick*, p. 219
[81] See the diagrams included between Books Two & Three, developed by T Allen Greenfield and John L Crow. Though these points are imprecise, the general guide of the diagram is a great starting point for finding the physiological marmas.
[82] The candidate for regular Masonic initiation also finds himself in between two pillars in the 2nd Degree, and identified with the Middle Pillar of Beauty—the station of the Junior Warden—in the mystical 3rd Degree.
[83] In personal communications with Greenfield, we have discussed the mobility of these points. He describes them as "thin ovals, which, being living energy points, move slightly all the time."
[84] *Voudon Gnostic Workbook*, p. 487

magically radio-active, concentrated sources of energy–with a measure of consciousness. When questioned as to whether these energies are process or sentience, Bertiaux responds,

> *Both. Everything in this field is both an intelligent entity (beyond human levels of intelligence) and a dynamic process or energy. When the candidate is with the system, these points-chauds merge with his mind and psychic field. They do not when the person is separate. They are like psychological complexes of the most creative sort, which being radiations of the archetypes are sustained by the planetary energies in question. Hence, it would be possible to lose the powers if you withdrew from the Gnostic continuum of the system.*[85]

As with most quotes from Bertiaux, there is a lot going on here. To begin with, we find that the points-chauds are energies *and* entities. Again, this is an absolute mystery and simply requires experience to divulge completely as its essence is ineffable. But he also goes on to suggest that these are psychological complexes of the creative sort, which will connect with their ability to assist in healing. He also suggests that one can lose these powers if he or she withdraws from the "Gnostic continuum." Here is a clear distinction between these empowerments and something like ordination or consecration that is *ad vitam*, for life. These empowerments actually *require* frequent awakening and reawakening to maintain activity and stimulation. A very simple analogy would be keeping one's car running smoothly and in working order by keeping gas in the tank, checking the oil and spark plugs, re-filling the various fluids as needed, etc. For those of us working *in free communion*, it means frequent activation of the points and *scrying*[86] their meaning.

Actions of the points

The four-fold qualities of each *points-chaud* empowerment consist of, but are not limited to: *attunement, empowerment, initiation and therapy*.

- **Empowerment**- The central activity of the points chauds is empowerment. This can be essentially described as a general strengthening and emboldening of the candidate in a specific manner. This is the moment when the "unconscious is now liberated[87]" within the candidate. When the point is properly awakened it creates a space and that "space is power in a latent or diffused and extended way and when it is concentrated it becomes power-bearing in an ever-increasing degree.[88]" Reservoirs of creative energy are stimulated through the awakening of each points-chauds within

---

[85] *Voudon Gnostic Workbook*, p. 330
[86] Scrying the points-chauds empowerments will be discussed in Books Two & Three, along with an Advanced Scrying procedure.
[87] *Voudon Gnostic Workbook*, p. 487
[88] *Ibid*, p. 208

the body. A significant point in which this methodology differs from traditional Masonic-type practice is that points-chauds empowerments can be administered spontaneously as *the spirit moves*. In other words, one may come to Lodge or a Chapel for a particular empowerment/degree and upon consultation with the Facilitator[89] receives an entirely different point or set of points in addition to the original request. This methodology requires its votaries to be intuitive and truly present to the Initiate –to *feel out* the movement of spirit.

- **Attunement**- As these empowerments are both energy and entity, it is the entity that we become attuned to (or, in tune with) and which will assist us in becoming more *in tune* with the subtle vibrations occurring about us continuously. Bertiaux states, "In the Gnostic church, which is based upon esoteric prayer and spiritualism, we teach all persons to become attuned to the ways and words, or powerful lessons, which come from the Holy Spirits.[90]" This may result in forms of spirit or energy contact on the Inner Planes which require astral travel. As T Allen explains, "Sometimes this [points-chauds empowerments] led to precognitive powers, advanced travel in the body of light to other terrestrial locations.[91]"

- **Therapy**- Because of the intense healing nature of these points-chauds empowerments, it is sometimes assumed that they are primarily therapeutic in nature. This is generally one of the most immediately *experienced* effects and symptoms of points-chauds empowerments; something within the Initiate is healed. In our own Chapel, we have noticed that through mesmeric passes along the body of the candidate we can sense the areas where a blockage resides. The points have become our central method for dismantling these clogged psychic pores within the body. As Bertiaux says, "The gnostic must use those therapies which release the blocked energies in these points.[92]" He suggests this through "gnostic pressures." Bertiaux later describes the process of Esoteric Healing through the hot points in his paper on Pheonismes.[93]

- **Initiation**- Last but not least, these *points-chauds* empowerments are Initiations in and of themselves. Each point-event, awakened and stimulated by a Facilitator–with the Egregoric transfer from Arabia Mountain and the Apostolic and Gnostic lines of Succession–is a complete and precise initiation. It is absolutely mind blowing to

---

[89] Within *Spirit Builders*, we will use the terms Facilitator and Initiate to describe the one giving the points and the one receiving them. These are not "Officers" in the traditional sense and often the Initiate turns around and becomes the Facilitator for another!
[90] The *Voudon Gnostic Workbook*, Preface, iii
[91] *The Roots of Magick*, p. 224
[92] *The Voudon Gnostic Workbook*, p. 165
[93] *Ibid*, p. 341

consider that such radical simplicity as touching a point upon the body to awaken its scintillating nature can cause a rite of passage! This is the return to the Primitive Doctrine of our ancestors. It requires nothing but two bodies and the transmission of Egregore. Awakening these points initiates a journey for the candidate that does not end in the gathering or Lodge meeting. It continues on and is usually accompanied by dream activity and travels in the Body of Light. This is the *actual* initiation that sometimes accompanies those in Lodge-type settings. In discussing the *hot-points of initiation,* Bertiaux says, "there occurs a point of entry into the higher and more spiritual level of power and that is a form of initiation. It is a doorway to the wisdom of the inner gnostic consciousness of being.[94]"

As we move along in our study, we will see exactly how these hot-points within the body are aligned to the degrees of Memphis+Misraïm and how they are worked in semi-Lodge fashion with the essential elements of the 97 degrees[95]. It is a vast new world for the Initiate who may be familiar with a multitude of things *happening to him* under the hoodwink, for the real journey of *points-chauds* empowerments is extended through time from the moment of the point awakening (which is often accompanied by visions) through the subsequent scrying practices and dream initiations that follow. This practice is a compendious method of Masonic and Gnostic Initiation which has no clear analogue in any other working of its kind.

---

[94] *Ibid*, p. 147
[95] Book Three of *Spirit Builders*

CHAPTER SIX

The Chapel Model

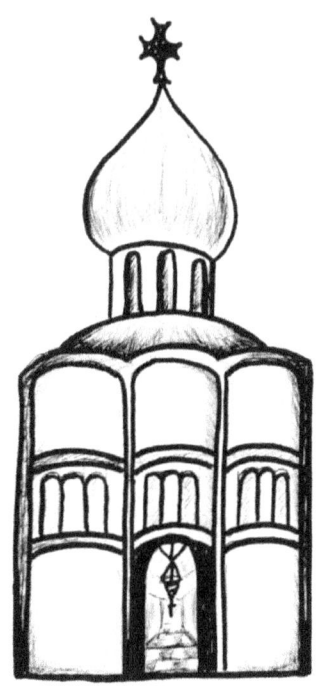

Lucien-Francois (Jean-Maine) was responsible for the transformation of the Rite of Memphis-Misraïm into a structure within the gnostic church, because he was able to see mystically its character as a structure of the ancient form of Egyptian magick. This he did because he wanted to make the church the focus of all of the occult energies...

Michael-Paul Bertiaux[96]

---

[96] *The Voudon Gnostic Workbook*, p. 441

The Ecclesiastical Revision of the APRM+M (1921) revolutionized the material working of the Rite. Degrees and empowerments/ordinations began to occur on a one-to-one basis between Master and student, extensive use of regalia, props and dramatics were eschewed for the simple and stream-lined home temple working and those who were creative and innovative in the Gnostic Church began to discover and awaken new methodologies for initiation. These revisionist reverberations are still being felt and experienced within CI. What must stay at the forefront of the reader's mind, however, is that the approaches in this text are *suggestive* only as an approach to the Memphis+Misraïm material. Many will embark upon fully dramatic Lodge-type initiations with as many degrees as physically possible while others work the efficient and ingenious approach of the Arabia Mountain Workings. Others will work the points empowerments without any reference to the degrees at all. The *Chapel Model* lies somewhere in betwixt Lodge-type work and the efficiency of the Arabia Mountain approach. Because we have found this approach to be consistent with the Ecclesiastical Revision, the ideals of Congregational Illuminism and our own particular form of gnosis, and because it has proved *workable* and powerful for our community as well—the Chapel Model will herein be examined for those who may want to cull some of this experience and these ideas for their own Lodges, Nodes, Temples and Chapels.

Three principles

Essentially, the Chapel Model operates on three basic principles:

1. The Ecclesiastical Revision suggests that the Rites be conducted in a sanctuary. This means that the "Lodge" and "sanctuary" may be the same location–they may be merged with the sacred geographical marma that is discovered.
2. The Chapel utilizes the divine economy of the Three-fold Path to unify the various workings.
3. This Chapel Model, as a simple approach, is intentionally small to serve the needs of the immediate and extended community.[97]

Initiation in a Sanctuary

---

[97] In the Monastery of the Seven Rays papers, Year IV, Part I, Lesson 16, it is said that formal temples are to give way to the "home temple."

In ancient Egypt, initiation and religious ceremonial were unified. The Ecclesiastical Revision is a return to this integration and the Chapel Model is a further extension. Bertiaux states that the spiritual power of magickal initiation "is mysteriously identified with the Rite of Memphis-Misraïm, which, in our system, is a structure within the Gnostic Church.[98]" In this way, we are also returning to the idea mentioned in the Introduction where Masonic initiation was immediately sensed as deeply spiritual. Workings of a magickal, spiritual or initiatic nature are integrated in the Chapel Model, as they all fall under the umbrella of the Gnostic Church[99]. This also directly relates to the ancient Coptic communities who made frequent use of texts of ritual power right alongside orthodox practice within the Coptic Church. It is fairly common in the occult world to find Lodges and Temples that completely compartmentalize liturgical and fraternal activities. Those in CI bodies are free to separate these out as well however; it is deeply connected to the Ecclesiastical Revision to allow these energies to be mutually dependent upon one another. For instance, all of our moments of enlightenment, points-empowerments, healing, and Eucharistic celebrations occur within our same small sacred marma within our Chapel space. This creates, over time, a swelling of the powerzone which is then experienced and seen as the previously mentioned, *Mystic Temple* or thoughtform[100]. This is not a *mixing of the planes* as the Rites of Memphis+Misraïm are now a structure within the Gnostic Church since the Revision. We are also working an Egregore that partakes of the Apostolic and Gnostic lines of succession as well as the spiritual transmissions of the Rite of Memphis+Misraïm. All of our work then, occurs in the same sanctuary space that the Holy Eucharist is celebrated. This is a level of integration that can be traced back to ancient Egypt, but is rarely made use of today.[101]

---

[98] *The Voudon Gnostic Workbook*, p. 176
[99] One of the reasons that I aligned our Chapel with the **Coptic Gnostic Church** was the unification of Egyptian & Gnostic Liturgy in that Ecclesia. I am also an active Bishop in the **Neo-Pythagorean Church** which furthers the integration of Memphis+Misraïm and the Gnostic church.
[100] See Annie Besant and C.W. Leadbeater's, *Thoughtforms*, Theosophical Publishing House, 3rd Edition, 1975
[101] The Monastery of the Seven Rays coursework goes even further with the connection between the Church and the Rites of Memphis-Misraïm, suggesting in Year III that the first four "grades" of the Rite (not degrees) are aligned with sub deacon, deacon, priest and bishop. A careful study of Book III of the present work will reveal a similar internal structure.

The Three-fold Path

Within this Chapel Model is an efficient means to accomplish all 97 degrees of the APRM+M by way of the Three-fold Path and the requirement of only two Facilitators[102]. The two Facilitators of the Chapel are the Inner Guard and the Outer Guard. The most sacred number in Masonic Science is three and so the "mystical third" is the Initiate him or herself. In this way, the three individuals become a living version of the 47th Problem of Euclid or the Pythagorean Theorem[103], with the Inner Guard as the vertical side of the triangle, the Outer Guard the horizontal base and the hypotenuse (which is equal to the combined forces of the vertical and horizontal) is the Initiate receiving empowerment. To take this further into our Egyptian Masonry, the Inner Guard works with masculine, Osirian and active forces, while the Outer Guard connects with feminine, Isiatic and receptive Forces. The Initiate becomes the conciliating portion of the equation. This is a deep mystery that Masonic study and research[104] develops more thoroughly, but in terms of practicality—this makes the Chapel a much more workable approach than traditional Lodge workings that require at least 7 Officers. Throughout the Chapel Model is this awareness of and espousal to Holy Simplicity.

The Three-fold Path is the unifying quality of all of our work in the Chapel. As this aspect has a distinctly mystical Christian feel to it, a word of explanation is in order. To begin with, the Three-fold Path is based upon the mystical three-fold path of Christian prayer—*purification, illumination* and *union*. We must keep in mind that we are working with the continuity of ideas, structure and organization in this mystical approach to Egyptian Masonry. Calvin C Burt, 96th Degree of the Rite of Memphis states that "Egypt was the cradle of all the mysteries; that she at one time was in exclusive possession of all the religious and mysterious learning in the world; and from her extended, not only all the influences of religious ceremonies, but also its sacred rites—its secret doctrines and its esoteric rituals.[105]" Ancient Christianity drank deeply from the wellsprings of mysticism that lie in the deserts of Egypt. In their study of the Divine Cagliostro, Cooper and Faulks suggest that the Egyptian tradition was "hidden in the cloak of Christian terminology[106]." Additionally, the authors state that "there is certainly documentation regarding those temple priests who

---

[102] In other Congregational Illuminist groups there is no necessity for more than one Facilitator. This format is particular to our Chapel and its method of initiation.
[103] This notion is explored further in a curious little book by Frank C. Higgins, *Hermetic Masonry*, recently re-printed by Kessinger Publishing, 2010.
[104] See also the compendious, *Secret Teachings of All Ages*, by Manly P Hall, Philosophical Research Society, 1988.
[105] Burt, Calvin C. *Egyptian Masonic History of the Original and Unabridged Ancient and Ninety-six 96th Degree Rite of Memphis*. Kessinger Publishing (re-print), 2004. p. 135
[106] *The Masonic Magician*, p. 238

converted to Christianity and rather than discard all the previous wisdom, chose to hybridize it with their new faith.[107]" And so though we are speaking of a mystical approach to prayer from the Christian faith, it is acting as a unifying principle within the Chapel Model of the APRM+M through the continuity of ideas, structure and organization from Egypt.

The Egyptian connection with our Three-fold path extends further as one of the first to popularize the notion of the Three-fold Path; Evagrius Ponticus (345-399 AD) spent the majority of his adult life in Egypt in the most ancient monasteries of the Church. Ponticus, along with Pseudo Dionysius the Areopagite (late 5th to early 6th Century AD) developed this Three-fold path to mark the signposts along the way of the life of prayer. Purification was relegated to the body, while Illumination related to the soul and Union concerned the spirit.

The way that the divine economy of the Three-fold Path is utilized in the Chapel Model, is by way of an organizational structure and mystical framework. In our own Chapel, as we studied the Liturgies of the Eastern and Western Churches through the centuries, as well as Masonic degrees and rituals alongside Magickal Rites, Ceremonies and Orders, we began to see a unifying factor in that all of these diverse methodologies, streams, and currents had moments of purification, illumination and union in their work. This Eureka moment resulted in a sacred simplification and reduction of all of our mysteries into these three ritual signposts. All of our liturgies, healing masses, initiations and otherwise utilize the divine economy of the Three-fold path in their organization. This will become clearer as we move into the praxis aspect of the work in Books Two and Three. It is primarily this simple scaffolding of the Three-fold Path that unifies and consolidates the various workings of the Chapel under the auspices of the Gnostic Church.

Intentionally Small

The Chapel Model is rather counter-cultural in that it is intentionally small. This is in direct response to the careless exploitation of natural resources, land and trees that accompanies the prevailing spirit of the times known as the mega-Church. Not only does this model not desire a warehouse sized sanctuary, it also does not desire building concerns whatsoever. It is a form of the home temple where no money is exchanged, no wish for expansion is entertained and all individuals involved have an integral role in the operations of the Church. Most of us have "day jobs" as well as children and domestic duties and so

---

[107] ibid

the Chapel becomes a place of refuge, rather than an overly taxing addition to an already busy lifestyle. The Chapel Model creates an intimate setting where individuals can find initiation, the Holy sacraments, healing and a truly caring and involved community. The Inner Guard and the Outer Guard, positions which can be alternated and shared with others as they are fitted for the work on a seasonal or yearly basis, typically take on the roles of urban shamans, in that they consult with the worshiping community individually to assess their needs, interests and where they are on the path. In our Chapel, the Inner and Outer Guard are also clergy of the Gnostic Church who have been thoroughly established in the Egregore and consecrated to the energies and spirits therein. Bertiaux states,

> *It is not necessary to have large temples for the working of this divine faith for in most instances, we make a little temple in our homes and this is where the spirits come and dwell and share with us the daily life that we have come to love, including the routines of getting up and going out to work...I then, must consult with the spirits as the "degrees" or "grades" that they wish me to give to the person and what "points" or powers they wish me to induct into his body for the doing of the work of the spirits.*[108]

In terms of regalia, the Chapel Model continues on these lines of simplicity. The Inner Guard wears a white robe and the Outer Guard wears a black robe. The candidate wears a simple "Seeker robe" that is brown and rather Franciscan. The Inner Guard and Outer Guard both have only one collar and apron for all of the Memphis+Misraïm work. As the Ecclesiastic Revision inherits quite a bit from the Voudon+Gnostic tradition, the Inner & Outer Guards turn their collar and aprons to exhibit the 3rd Degree side with skull and crossbones before the moment of points-chauds empowerments, so as to invite the Ghuédé as well as the powerful Bawon La Croix (a Masonic spirit) to attend to the labors along with other "Passed Masters." The candidate wears a sigil/talisman in the form of the "Jewel" of each particular degree. This is created by the Inner Guard upon Virgin Parchment paper, in keeping with the practices of the Divine Cagliostro. The Jewel becomes a visual meditation piece for the Facilitator before she locates the point upon the body. So, we can see that the amount of material and supplies for the Chapel Model are considerably less than other approaches. Yet even these few items can be dispensed with, in keeping with our Primitive Doctrine.

As more CI bodies begin to crop up and take advantage of the Light of Free Illuminism as it is developed in this unique approach to the APRM+M, simple models such as the Chapel will need to be experimented with and expanded upon further to fit the needs and capacities of the community in which they are worked. The Chapel Model has proven to

---

[108] *The Voudon Gnostic Workbook*, p. 35

be an effective and efficient means to share the mysteries with our own community, and hopefully it will assist others who are in the early stages of formation.

From this simple Chapel Model, we have born the **Misraïm Chapel Rite**[109] which is a completely integrated approach to Liturgy and the empowerments contained within the Free Illuminist approach to Memphis-Misraïm. Since taking this leap into the unknown, we have been exposed to the text, *Ancient Christian Magic, Coptic Texts of Ritual Power*[110] which reveals a profound consistency with this approach and ancient Egyptian Christian workings.

---

[109] An official Rite within the Oriental and Apostolic Church of Damcar, https://church-of-damcar.org/
[110] Meyer & Smith, 1994.

"The relationships we form with entities inside these inner worlds yield much information about ourselves and our cosmos, yet our aspirations are higher than simply data collecting. We are spirit builders. As is said time and again in Masonic degrees, *of what are you in search?* More Light! And as this Light is freely given and shown to us, so we likewise freely give of it to others, and from there it spreads its tentacles of peace and blessings toward every darkened corner."

CHAPTER SEVEN

The Sacred Doctrine

The Mysteries were divided into two classes—the small (or lesser) and the great. The lesser mysteries had for object the instruction of the initiates in the 'Humanities'; the sacred doctrine was restricted to the later stages of the initiation ceremonies.

E.J. Marconis de Negre[111]

---

[111] *Sanctuary of Memphis or Hermes*, Kessinger Publishing re-print, 1849, p. 18

The *Sacred Doctrine*, as it is known amongst initiates in many branches of the Rites of Memphis-Misraïm, partakes of the Greater Mysteries of ancient Egypt in terms of the continuity of ideas. This can primarily be discovered through the study of papyri such as the *Egyptian Book of the Dead–the Book of Going Forth by Day* where we find a semblance of initiation and dream states and the afterlife, but is also suggested in the writings of Herodotus and Plutarch. The word for word suggestion of the *Sacred Doctrine*, however, is found re-printed in Marconis's book, Yarker's lectures, Calvin C Burt's collection and most especially in a curious book re-printed by Manly P Hall– which is the source—the *Crata Repoa*.

It is curious to consider that the first known translation of the *Crata Repoa* was in Germany in 1778 around ten years before the Divine Cagliostro was arrested by the Inquisition for his Egyptian brand of Masonry. The *Crata Repoa*[112] is a manuscript that claims to outline the initiatory system of the Egyptian Ancient Mysteries. It is organized into seven grades which many have applied to the seven planets of the ancients, the chakras, etc. It is this single source that spells out the *Sacred Doctrine* for the Rite of Memphis-Misraïm.

Is the *Sacred Doctrine* an art or a science? Recall that in mainstream Masonry we have a search for the Lost Word of the Master. Additionally, in the Ancient and Accepted Scottish Rite of Freemasonry we have the Royal Secret and the Holy Doctrine. The *Royal Art* and the *Sacred Science*-phrasing borrowed from Alchemy–came to be synonymous with the Royal Secret and the Holy Doctrine. Likewise, the *Sacred Doctrine* partakes of the same nature as both an art and a science. We find the great Scholastic Saint, Thomas Aquinas[113] referring to the sacred doctrine as a *higher* science above the average endeavors. With our espousal of Scientific Illuminism, we also treat the *Sacred Doctrine* as something deserving of the scientific method–accurate reporting and rigorous testing. But the *Sacred Doctrine* is most assuredly an art as well as it makes frequent use of the magickal imagination (lodged within the Initiate's ontic sphere) and underlies the very nature of creativity—the same ceaseless creativity inherent in the Universe.

The Search

The entire Masonic journey is punctuated by the search for Light, and for a number of degrees, the search for the Lost Word. Both of these searches coincide in the *Sacred Doctrine* and lead back to Egypt. Here is a clear exposition of the continuity of ideas over time. For

---

[112] Hall, Manly P. *The Lost Keys of Freemasonry*. New York: Penguin Group, originally published in 1923, re-print 2006.
[113] See *Summa Theologica*, Vol 12, Part II, New York: Benziger Brothers, 1922. p. 6

the ancient Egyptian priesthood, "word, image, and reality were a unity.[114]" The pictographic quality of hieroglyphics enhances this notion deeply, appearing alongside the stylized activity of Egyptian figures in paintings. Here, the actions, words and reality are occurring simultaneously. Words evoke the gods and they appear. In fact, in the ancient Egyptian tongue, *word* and *idea* are synonymous. So the *word* becomes identical to the idea and the reality through image. When the ancient priesthoods hybridized with Christianity, we find an immediate appreciation for the Gospel of John. This Gospel is purported to be the most *gnostic* of the synoptic Gospels, primarily because of its first few verses. They read,

> *In the beginning was the Word, and the Word was with God, and the Word was God. ² He was with God in the beginning. ³ Through him all things were made; without him nothing was made that has been made. ⁴ In him was life, and that life was the light of all mankind.⁵ The light shines in the darkness, and the darkness has not overcome[a] it*[115].

The Coptic Orthodox Church latched onto this Holy text with fervor. Noted translator, Dr. Goelet, states further that it was the most popular book of the Bible for them because it suggests what the hybridized priests already knew: "By means of a word or an image, thought could be actualized.[116]" The identity of Word and Light, in terms of the Masonic search and the *Sacred Doctrine* are summed up in the latter portion of the Biblical selection, "In him was life, and that life was the **light** of all mankind. The light shines in the darkness." In sum, from the ancient Priesthoods through the Coptic Christians and carried on by the Masonic science, we have an identification of Word, Idea, Reality and Light.

The *Sacred Doctrine* is only "secret" in so much as it is incommunicable. In this way, it relates to the Lost Word again, which is often suggested to be the Tetragrammaton[117] of the Hebrews—or the four-lettered, unutterable name of God. Telling someone else what the *Sacred Doctrine* is becomes an additional veil to its reality, as the sacred doctrine is of the nature of *gnosis* itself which requires a direct, experiential kind of knowledge. For Congregational Illuminists, "secrets" are not lorded over candidates or visitors. In fact, the portion of the degrees of the APRM+M that we work most closely with *are* the purported "secrets[118]" of the degrees; the grips, signs, passwords, knocks, etc. Yet the *Sacred Doctrine* is not something that we can give away freely as it has to occur within the Initiate him or

---

[114] Dr. Goelet's Introduction to, *the Egyptian Book of the Dead, the Book of Going Forth By Day*, San Francisco: Chronicle Books LLC, 2008.
[115] New International Version
[116] *The Egyptian Book of the Dead, the Book of the Going Forth By Day*, p. 16
[117] YHWH, often pronounced either as Yahweh or Jehovah
[118] As will be noted in Books Two & Three, however, these are *not* the "secrets" that are currently in use in active, mainstream orders.

herself. In this way, our focus is upon *actual* initiation and *gnosis*, rather than on the means to recognize another Mason in darkness or in light[119].

The chief emblems within all Masonic Rites and Orders that relate to the *Sacred Doctrine* are the Sun, the Moon and the serpent. These are three actions of the *Sacred Doctrine*—the Sun being the fiery, passionate and active—the Moon being the receptive, divinatory and changeable and the serpent being the occult, the [120]Astral or Universal agent. The *Sacred Doctrine*, then, as reported by Marconis, Yarker and Burt and deriving from the *Crata Repoa*, is the *Manifestation of Light*.

† † †

Using the Sacred Doctrine

In Books Two & Three, this guide becomes practical. We will discover how to actually work this unique and simple approach to the APRM+M. Throughout the work, we will find the *Sacred Doctrine* being developed and expressed as the manifestation of Light. The *Sacred Doctrine* becomes the *ne plus ultra* of the Masonic science, no longer only as a philosophical or symbolic idea, but as a reality of identical nature to the word/idea/reality of the ancient Egyptian priesthoods. The specific means that we will utilize to manifest the Light are studied in many branches of the Western Mystery Tradition. In this way, occult Orders and Rosicrucian bodies have preserved the *Sacred Doctrine*; however, the spirit of Masonry has suffered from this. As an Egregore continuing from antiquity to the present, Freemasonry has endured an anemic epoch by distancing itself from its Esoteric roots. Restoring the *Sacred Doctrine* to the Masonic art and science is accompanied by immediately palpable results. As Wilmshurst suggests,

> *that Light has become palpably visible, and not merely as a flesh-transmuting grace, beautifying and glorifying the personality, but as a radiant aura issuing from the face and person and throwing off actual quasi-physical light.*[121]

---

[119] Often the so-called "secrets" of Masonic degrees are described as simply means for a Mason to recognize another Mason, through grips, word testing, etc. In Spirit Builders, we are reinvesting these "secrets" to their former glory. The Hermetic Order of the Golden Dawn was one of the first of the modern schools of esotericism to recognize the usage of these "secrets" upon the Inner Planes, as they are efficacious in testing the spirits and landscapes found therein.

[120] Sometimes labeled the OB, the OD or AUR.

[121] *Masonic Initiation,* Kessinger Publishing re-print, 1922, p. 145. This lovely book of esoteric Masonry begins with the words, "To All Builders In the Spirit."

There are a number of ways in which we manifest the Light within our Work. As the degrees are developed, it will be readily seen that every Opening, Degree, Closing and follow-up scrying practice are pregnant with opportunities and methods of manifesting this Light. The primary moments of manifestation are through the scintillating body, divinatory practice, pneumatic breathwork, visualization of the Mystic Temple and Passed Masters, and in scrying.

- *The Scintillating Body*. We return to one of the keys to our entire system. To say that Free Illuminists treat the body as the Temple of the Holy Spirit is an understatement. We have described the Light that accompanies the points-chauds empowerments as a constellation upon the body, seen by the inner eye. This luminosity builds over time to the point where others can recognize an energy attached to the Initiate after empowerments are given, though they may not have the language to describe it. For the Initiate, the experience of feeling, seeing or simply sensing the points empowerments is akin to the description of Initiation by Apuleius into the Rites of Isis where he says, "at Midnight I saw the sun shining with its brilliant light, and I approached the presence of the gods beneath and the gods above."[122] This alludes to the twin qualities of points empowerments—process/energy (sun at midnight) and entity (gods beneath and above). Once the candidate develops his or her own methods of seeing the points within others, it becomes clear that these scintillating points of light are already present within the body and simply need to be awakened or *brought to light*.
- *Divinatory practice*. A hallmark of our approach to Masonic Initiation is our treatment of the Volume of the Sacred Law or VSL. In Masonic Lodges, upon every altar under the UGLE is the Volume of the Sacred Law. Typically, this is the Holy book of the dominant faith of one's country, however, during Initiations—the Candidate may have the VSL of his or her own religious persuasion for the sake of taking the Oath. In our practice, we also honor the Initiate by allowing them to select the Holy Book of their choice, but it is not to take an oath upon. We use it for Bibliomancy[123] after the ritual with the visual sense suspended by a hoodwink. This has resulted in immediate divinatory skills from Initiates who have hitherto had no experience with such. Divination relates to the manifestation of Light in that it opens the Inner Eye, the Eye of Horus seen within the square and compasses and placed prominently in many traditional Masonic Lodges, to the subtle patterns of the unconscious and

---

[122] Mackey, Albert. *The Encyclopedia of Freemasonry*, p. 271
[123] This practice, the Advanced Method of Scrying, is described in detail in Book Three.

subconscious minds. It is a means to integrate the automatic conscious with the unconscious portions of our mind.

- *Pneumatic breathwork*. Following the lead of the Divine Cagliostro, in our work, the Inner Guard breathes[124] upon the candidate in the 3rd Degree. Analogy can certainly be made to the New Testament where Jesus breathes upon the Disciples and tells them to receive the Holy Spirit. We also find reference to this pneumatic mystery in the Old Testament with the Lord breathing the breath of life into man's nostrils as well as the Spirit hovering over the face of the deep. The latter in Hebrew is the word, *Ruach,* which can mean spirit, wind or breath. So we find a relationship to this breathwork and spirit. In the modern Druidry of the AODA[125] we find the practice of color breathing which also relates to this work as does the pranayama of Yoga. For the manifestation of Light in our degrees, when the Inner Guard breathes upon the candidate, what is often perceived is a shower of pure Light. On occasion, the Light is tinged with colors that are associated with the Sephirah and its associated planets closest to the points chauds upon the body[126] that are being awakened. The Light particles that are passed from the Facilitator to the Initiate are in the form of a spiritual transmission whose origin is the radionic, Holy Arabia Mountain, and so the lineage continues in an unbroken chain of initiation.
- *Visualizations of the Mystic Temple & Passed Masters*. The *Mystic Temple* that we create through repetition and the use of a sacred, geographical marma is composed of Light. Though this may only be a glimmer in the first stages, this visualization quickens and accelerates through frequency and takes on a vibratory rate that is consistent over time. The visualization analogous to the Mystic Temple is that of the *Passed Masters*[127] who are invoked in every Opening of the Chapel. These beings, sometimes angelic, sometimes spirits and occasionally guardians of the Masonic Order are composed of Light as well. Their presence may be felt more than seen, particularly at the sacred moment of points-chauds empowerment.
- *Scrying*. Each degree that we work comes with an accompanying scrying practice for further study and experimentation. This unique format allows for *continuing* initiation and a deeper sense of the hidden and personal meanings and landscapes of each degree. It is accomplished in our Chapel through the simplest of methods, utilizing the Sacred word of the degree, the "gnostic pressures" as Bertiaux describes the

---

[124] Martinists and Élus Coëns maintain this practice as well.
[125] *The Ancient Order of Druids in America*
[126] As the points-chauds are mostly aligned to the Middle Pillar, the Sephirah visualized are typically one of the four associated with the central pillar—Malkuth, Yesod, Tiphareth and Kether, with occasional visualizations of the ephemeral Daath.
[127] See C.W. Leadbeater's *The Hidden Life in Freemasonry* for more information concerning this process and these beings.

points-chauds and a particular asana developed William Webb and T Allen Greenfield. Scrying takes the candidate into the spirit vision and opens up the inner worlds of varying qualities of luminosity. The astral light is encountered through these practices as well as the higher (and more dependable) beatific Light energies from Tiphareth and beyond the Abyss.

The Manifestation of Light, the *Sacred Doctrine,* is restored to its primitive simplicity and essence through this expression of the Ecclesiastical Revision. It is also restored to its Egregoric home, spiritual Freemasonry. The Initiate of these mysteries does not receive these "Lights" and then that is that. He or she is enjoined to cultivate the art and science of *spirit building* through personal as well as collective practice. As the Light begins to be perceived, felt and easily worked with by the Initiate, she finds herself being drawn towards the other side of the blindfold[128]—that of Facilitator . As Inner Guard or Outer Guard of this practice, one begins to master the manifestation of Light in new ways and then desire to give of that Light to others. The quality of Light experienced in receiving initiation is distinct from that of *Initiating* others. One begins to find that this Work is endless and that the goal is not the accumulation of degrees and titles, but a deepening within the Mystery. Let us begin the restoration.

---

[128] Hoodwinks are only utilized in our Chapel in the first three Degrees and for certain experiments with scrying that require "cave darkness." The blindfold is not used at all in the workings of Arabia Mountain.

CHAPTER EIGHT

The Antient & Primitive Rite of Memphis+Misraïm

The ultimate clerical end of this spectrum found expression in the Franco-Haitian and Spanish branches of the Rites of Memphis and Misraïm, which, in 1921, completely gave up the Masonic ritual degrees in favor of considering these to be ecclesiastical empowerments associated with ordination and consecration rather than ritual initiation. This school has its most current embodiment in Docteur Michael Bertiaux 97 of Chicago, who received his original training in Haiti under Hector Francois Jean-Maine 97th Degree.

T Allen Greenfield[129]

---

[129] *The Compleat Rite of Memphis*, p. 16

Part One - Chapter Eight: The Antient & Primitive Rite of Memphis+Misraïm

At this juncture, we have explored the ways in which this form of spiritual Masonry converge and diverge with mainstream forms. We have also analyzed what it is that we are building as *spirit builders*. We have explored the movement and revolution of Congregational Illuminism within which this unique embodiment of the Ecclesiastical Revision of APRM+M exists and thrives. We have also traced the source of the points-chauds experimentation to the Holy Arabia Mountain, from which flows the constant rays of initiation and spiritual transmission. An examination of the Chapel Model, as a viable option to the larger, Lodge and/or Temple or Sanctuary, has been conducted as well as an exposition of the Three-fold Path of prayer as a framework for the simple procedure of our Masonic Craft. Finally, we have examined and elucidated the crux of the work itself, the *Sacred Doctrine*. But foundationally speaking, what on earth *is* the Antient and Primitive Rite of Memphis+Misraïm?

First and foremost, it should be noted that the APRM+M is a High Degree system of Freemasonry that is over 200 years old. It grew alongside the Ancient and Accepted Scottish Rite of Freemasonry which was formally instituted in 1801, but which shares older roots along with the separate Rites of Memphis and Misraïm. Of the three, the Misraïm working appears to be the oldest with references going back to 1738, but it was not formally constituted until 1805[130] by Lechangeur. In 1785, the Divine Cagliostro introduced the Egyptian Rite of Freemasonry, open to both men and women, to London and then to Rome wherein he was arrested and imprisoned for the remainder of his life. It is supposed that Cagliostro introduced the *Arcana Arcanorum* to the Rite of Misraïm[131], which was fused with the Marconis Rite of Memphis (1833) in 1881 by the Italian Freedom Fighter, Giuseppe Garibaldi. The organizational genius of John Yarker was already in place by 1872, when he became Grand Hierophant of the Rites and established the Sovereign Grand Sanctuary. The subsequent unification brought focus and promise to the High Grades, but the lack of sufficient numbers meant that the Order would never thrive or compete with the swiftly "recognized" Ancient and Accepted Rite or even the York Rite. Yarker's work would eventually form the foundation of the Ordo Templi Orientis.[132]

It is important to note that there are current proponents of Universal Masonry, who have a more liberal and open-armed approach to the various Rites available. This has always

---

[130] As mentioned earlier, it is best to be more conservative with these dates. Henrik Bogdan does a fantastic job of tracing the history of the Rite in, *Western Esotericism and Rituals of Initiation*, pgs. 101-103.

[131] In the private papers of *The Monastery of the Seven Rays*, 3rd Year, Part I, Lesson 1, we find an essay concerning the link between the Monastery and the Rite of Misraïm in Spain. This same essay explores the relationship/identity of the Rite with the Gnostic Church, and the mysterious attribution of 97=336, which explores 336 degrees of magickal achievement within the 97 degrees of APRM+M, via the INNER RETREAT.

[132] *Western Esotericism and Rituals of Initiation*, p. 102.

been the case, even amongst accepted luminaries of American Masonry like, Robert Macoy, who, in his 1854 work entitled, *The True Masonic Guide*, says:

> *FREEMASONRY, though uniform in its principles, its tenets and its lessons, has nevertheless, several rites...Still another rite*[133], *originating in the East, and carried from Italy to France, is termed the rite of "Misphraim, or Egyptian rite*[134].*"*

This acceptance of differing forms of Masonry is beginning to return to the Craft in a crucial way across the globe.

Historical Documents

The Degree material that we will be working with in Book Three is taken from the manuscripts of Marconis de Negre for the 1-33rd Degrees and from Yarker for the 34-97th as collected by the resourceful T Allen Greenfield in his, *Compleat Rite of Memphis*[135]. What must be kept in mind, however, is that we are working with material that is not simply a reconstruction of historical documents. It is a *restoration* to the primitive simplicity of the ancients—the Primitive Doctrine, which is a child of the Ancient Mysteries. As was quoted from Bertiaux in chapter two, "Therefore, the structures of the Rite of Memphis-Misraïm are not generated from history only but are archetypal generations from the deepest regions of the psyche.[136]" So we have the historical architecture of the key components or "secrets" of the degrees from 1-97th, which form the magical framework of the initiation itself—yet we also have an inheritance that is beyond time and history—that is archetypal. While we transmit the historic essentials of an esoteric form of spiritual Freemasonry, we also transmit something more, something completely *other*, which for lack of a better term is fundamentally *magical* and ancient. The sincere working of this form of Freemasonry leads the candidate towards primordial currents, hitherto untapped in mainstream practice. Working within a time-honored and vitalized tradition such as Freemasonry, we draw from pools of force and energy that await a proper conduit. In *The Training and Work of the Initiate*, Dion Fortune says that these root-traditions prepare a "mental atmosphere," (our Ontic sphere) and that to "pick up the contacts of one of these great initiatory systems of the past is like touching an electric battery," and further that these "cosmic powerhouses" simply require the proper channel and circuitry to reify the link between spirit and matter[137].

---

[133] Of note is the wording here--"Still another rite,"--rather than suggesting Misraïm is a form of "clandestine" Masonry.
[134] p. 281.
[135] Much of this material can be found in Yarker's, *The Secret High Degree Rituals of the Masonic Rite of Memphis*, Kessinger Publishing re-print, 2006. A newly revised and edited version of Greenfield's book is in progress at the time of this writing.
[136] *The Voudon Gnostic Workbook*, p. 89
[137] 2000, pgs. 121-124.

Voudon Connection

The connection between the APRM+M and Haiti is rather clear. Prior to the Rite having connections with Martinism and the Gnostic Church in the 1950's[138] through the work of Robert Ambelain and the son of Papus, Philippe Encausse, the Élus Coëns of Martinez de Pasqually and the early Rite of Perfection of Etienne Morin established Esoteric Masonry in Haiti in the late 1700's. By 1824, the Grand Orient d'Haiti was formed and exists to this day as a testament to the hybridization of Masonic and Esoteric currents laboring in harmony with the local traditions of Vodou and Catholicism. It is from this longstanding tradition of spiritual Freemasonry that Michael-Paul Bertiaux inherited, in 1963, from Hector Francois Jean-Maine, the transformed Ecclesiastical Revision of Memphis-Misraïm[139] of Hector's father, Lucien Jean-Maine[140]. This Revision linked, as is customary to do in Haiti, the currents of the Gnostic Church with those of the APRM+M and firmly placed this powerful lineage under the auspices of said Ecclesia. From its very inception the Ecclesiastical Revision experimented with a form of esoteric Vodou, known today as Voudon +Gnosis and purported to have primordial energetic and initiatory currents that can be traced back to antediluvian times.[141] Within *The Monastery of the Seven Rays* resides a secret sect, "La Couleuvre Noire" which, according to the 3rd Year Course, "forms the very heart of the Rite of Memphis-Misraïm."[142] Additionally, the syncretization of Masonic and Voudon influences is expressed further in the vévés of the Lwa. These transient artworks, influenced by the ironwork of the French aristocracy implanted on the isle of St. Domingo, reflect Masonic symbolism blended with influences from the Benin and Yorubic tribes that birthed Vodou. Finally, as Bertiaux tells us in *Vudu Cartography*, a form of esoteric priesthood arose in Haiti and worked under the veil of Masonry. Of this secret group he says, "in fact, I came to learn that many Masonic and paramasonic societies and lodges in Haiti were really 'covers' for rather esoteric priesthoods going back to an Ægyptian tradition."[143]

---

[138] See the paper entitled, *The History of the Haitian Gnostics* by +Phillip A. Garver, 2005. This is a public file on the very informative website, http://www.gnostique.net

[139] The *Monastery of the Seven Rays*, over which Michael Bertiaux presides, explores other dimensions of the Rites of Memphis-Misraïm. Particularly, in Year 3, Part 1 Lesson 2 and in the 4th Year Attachment to Lesson 4, Exercise 1, we find an exploration into the "inner retreat" of the Rites of Memphis-Misraïm, where the inner retreat is discovered to be type of *cosmic brain*. This highly esoteric study yields interesting results when combined with the Free Illuminist approach to the points-chauds empowerments.

[140] Much of this history is found in the Preface and Appendix of *The Voudon Gnostic Workbook*.

[141] When the student combines the study of Bertiaux's tradition of Voudon Gnosis with the Typhonian tradition of Kenneth Grant, some interesting concepts are developed concerning the Old Ones, the primordial currents and beings that inform the work. To this, we incorporate the erudite teachings of Martinez de Pasqually, and the Élus Coëns.

[142] Private papers of *The Monastery of the Seven Rays*, 3rd Year, Part IV, Lesson 13.

[143] *Vudu Cartography*, Fulgur Limited, 2010, p. 129.

The Antient and Primitive Rite of Memphis+Misraïm that we are working with is both a spiritual and a historical inheritance[144], but more than this—it is an *authentic* means of initiation and inculcation of the Sacred Doctrine. Working freely under the umbrella of Congregational Illuminism, numerous Research and Philosophical Lodges, Nodes, Sanctuaries and Chapels are cropping up across the globe and experimenting with the *gnosis* lodged within the Ecclesiastical Revision.

---

[144] For an exposition of this continuity of spiritual and historical inheritance, see the OFFICIAL HISTORICAL LESSON, in the 3rd Year Course, Lesson 24 of *The Monastery of the Seven Rays*.

Steiner's Experimental Misraïm Order

Any discussion of a completely spiritualized version of the Antient & Primitive Rite, and of the Rite of Misraïm in particular, must make mention of the profoundly original and deeply spiritual work of Rudolf Steiner from 1904-1914. About his labors, his second wife, Marie Steiner said,

> *It was Dr. Steiner's endeavor to rediscover the pure source of esoteric teachings, to present them to our inner vision in their historical sequence and to free them from the trash that has gradually accumulated over them, in order to show how, in spite of the trash and turbidity, the pure archetypal forces have continually sought out new channels in order to bestow upon humankind their enlivening and progressive influence*[145].

Steiner's work was a simplification of the Degrees and a peopling of the work with spirits and beings, elementals and Archangels. We also find in Steiner's work that the nature of the "secrets" of Masonry is understood in its truest sense. Marie states that *these are not merely of deeply symbolic significance, but exert a magical influence and have magical value*[146]. Steiner himself comes close to developing a notion of the points-chauds empowerments connected with the "grips" of Masonry, saying:

> *...we thereby refine the currents and so change our relationship to the outer world. If we touch a particular point on the back of the hand with a thumb bent in this way, the two currents connect with one another and a far-reaching beneficial influence can be exerted*[147].

The correlations between Steiner's *Misraïm Service* and our work in Free Illuminism are many. His is yet another example of the elasticity of the Rites of Memphis & Misraïm over time. *Freemasonry and Ritual Work* deserves a careful reading by the mystic Mason in general and by those working *in Free Communion,* as it is born from a non-dual Gnosis and penetrating visionary spirituality, commingled with intellectual genius.

---

[145] *Freemasonry and Ritual Work*, 2007, Steiner Books, pgs. 110-111. We will forgive Marie of her strong words (trash) and understand the essence of her speech. Many in their group were strongly opposed to the air of Aristocracy that Freemasonry still held onto at the time. There are certainly analogues to this today.
[146] Ibid. p.195
[147] Ibid. p. 301

Now we are duly and truly prepared for the work, for *praxis*. With sword and trowel in hand, let us resume our labors. The primary goal of the Antient & Primitive Rite of Memphis+Misraïm is identical to the original goal of Freemasonry as a whole, which, according to Rev. George Oliver was in its "primitive and ineffable state... an institution of pure, ethereal Light.[148]" This luminous principle[149] is evident from the beginning unto the very end.

---

[148] *The Theocratic Philosophy of Freemasonry*, 1855, p. 1-3.
[149] Ibid.

Part One - Chapter Eight: The Antient & Primitive Rite of Memphis+Misraïm

THE VIOLET LODGE

To the Glory of the Sublime Architect of the Universe

In the Name and under the auspices of the Sovereign Sanctuary of the Antient & Primitive Rite of Memphis+Misraïm, in and for the United States of America

PART TWO

THE VIOLET LODGE

An Efficient Three Degree System of Initiation developing the

SACRED DOCTRINE

Of the

ANTIENT & PRIMITIVE RITE OF MEMPHIS+MISRAÏM

For Nodes, Lodges & Chapels working

IN FREE COMMUNION

Gloria Dei Est Celare Verbum. Amen

Introduction

Q: Are you an Egyptian Mason?
A: Yes, I am, with strength and singleness of purpose[150].

When Horus-*Hawk*[151] pressed two fingers upon my lips and silenced the chaos that surrounded me during my dream-initiation, I felt a peace and contentment that was unequalled in my wake-a-day experience. What is really odd about it is that I was still relatively aware of the apocalypse about me, yet my focus became sharpened to a razors edge upon the message that Horus bore, Silence. This lesson had much to do with my future involvement in Egyptian Masonry, but it also had another element to it. It taught me about purpose, True Will, my Sacred Duty[152]. I was given an anecdote to the chaos and chronic busy-ness of normal life, while also being given the key practice to accomplish the unity and integration I craved. Horus showed me in that instant, that to accomplish my will, I must have *singleness of purpose.* He displayed in a simple and primitive gesture that silence was the key to accomplishing this purpose and that in such powerful silence was a profound *strength.*

† † †

---

[150] *The Masonic Magician*, p. 207, 1st Degree of Egyptian Freemasonry
[151] Keep in mind that the Hawk, in Egyptian symbolism, is a symbol of the creative elements of Deity—the sun at its meridian.
[152] Duty is a key theme in the traditional workings of the 4th Degree, AASR

Throughout the degrees that we will explore in Books Two and Three, we will hint at this message of Horus and subsequently of Cagliostro, and a plethora of other Initiates, and we will see how this singleness of purpose and strength through silence opens wide the doors of initiation. The path that we are embarking upon is one that unites mysticism with magic and religion with initiation. It is integral.

Conferral and Communication

Over the past two centuries, High Grade Masonry has suffered because of how difficult it can sometimes be to fully enact and perform all of the degrees in full. We hear Crowley complaining that the Degrees of the APRM-M[153] would "not only require the fortune of a kingdom, but a couple of hundred lifetimes devoted exclusively to them to put them on properly[154]." This has been experienced in the Ancient and Accepted Scottish Rite of Freemasonry[155] as well–where for the past several decades–Initiates may only witness five mandatory degrees (conferral) and receive the others by way of communication. But in this Rite, there are "symbolic" candidates who stand in for a whole class of Initiates observing the degrees at the same time in dramatic form.

The method of working herein explored in *Spirit Builders* is a complete *conferral* of all 97 degrees of the Ecclesiastical Revision of the Antient and Primitive Rite of Memphis+Misraïm[156]. The method is far simpler and includes the option of zero dramatics altogether, while giving adequate room for ingenuity, creativity and traditional practice.

What is most counter-intuitive to the mainstream Freemason is that we do not require, nor do we suggest, sequential format for the reception of the Degrees. The Facilitator, or the Inner Guard[157], consults with the Initiate to see what points-chaud/degree that they are

---

[153] In the papers of one of the respectable, operative orders of the *Antient & Primitive Rite of Memphis & Mizraim*, we hear Robert Ambelain saying, "The higher echelons of *Memphis-Mizraïm* compulsorily practiced: the 9th Degree (Master-Elect of Nine), 18th Degree (Knight Rose-Croix), 30th Degree (Knight Kadosh), 32nd Degree (Prince of the Royal Secret), 33rd Degree(Sovereign Grand Inspector-General). The 66th, 90th and 95th degrees were conferred as honorific titles on senior Masons, in recompense for their valor and fidelity. The other degrees (Secret Master, Royal Arch, etc.) are optional and left to the discretion of the Brothers of higher degrees." *Freemasonry in Olden Times*, 2006, p. 9.

[154] Greenfield, *Compleat Rite of Memphis*, p. 15

[155] This trend is most assuredly changing, as the Revised Standard Pike Ritual (2000) is still being rolled out in Orients across the globe. This revised system of the AASR is far more workable in terms of staging, rubrics and such.

[156] Book Three gives the process of conferral in a Free Illuminist manner. It will be readily seen that although it is quite distinct from "communicating" the degrees, it is yet worlds away from full dramatic conferral. The *essence* of the spiritual experience of the degree is what is focused upon in this approach.

[157] The roles of Inner and Outer guard are utilized in our Chapel particularly when conferring the Blue Lodge Degrees of Book Two. These terms are not generally used when working directly with the Hauts Grades as in Book Three, and are not known to be in use by any other Free Illuminists at this time.

drawn to or an area of their body that they feel needs empowerment, attunement, therapy or initiating. This also leaves room for spontaneous empowerments/degrees. Such work requires the Facilitator to be, *on the spot*.[158] We have to cultivate the intuition and practice deep listening to remain receptive to the movements of the spirit and the needs of the Initiate. A characteristic feature of non-sequential degrees/empowerments is that the silly degree-mongering game of one-upmanship simply drops away. In this way, *all* participants in the work must practice silence and limit the field of attention upon the subject at hand—the empowerment being given and the one receiving it. Wilmshurst says,

> *It is possible for the celestial Light to descend upon the duly prepared candidate, to flood his heart and expand his mind, and so to open his understanding to the instruction then communicated to him that he may realize the spirit as well as hear the letter of it, while standing in that sacred position. And let them at that moment silently and earnestly invoke the Light of the centre, that it may then consciously arise in both him and them, so that what is done ceremonially may become for them both, a great fact of spiritual experience.*[159]

Simplicity

Before we begin our work, let us again invoke the name of Holy Simplicity! We are in grave error who suppose that the Divinity resides only in the complex. It is towards the simple that we must ever be drawn, towards singleness of purpose and lack of superfluity that we must ever be engaged, and towards the raw purity of the Primitive Doctrine that we must travel in this labor of love. As Jesus said, *therefore if thine eye be single, thy whole body shall be full of light*.[160] Many words, many titles, many implements, many books, many lengthy orations and many time consuming degrees will not add one measure to our humanity. What is needed is depth and to dig deeply, one must etch away bit by bit in a single direction, with a singular purpose.

Realization vs. Attainment

In the spiritual world, there is often the strugglesome quarrel concerning *immediate realization* vs. the sometimes lengthy, *attainment by degrees*. Some traditions teach of a single moment of realization that leads to a nirvana of sorts. Others teach that we work by degrees, sometimes imperceptibly, towards a single omega point. *Spirit Builders* recognize the wisdom in both and reach beyond. We acknowledge that at any given moment, the Initiate may *realize*, on a profound level. This could lead to a sort of Bodhisattva Vow, similar to the 10th

---

[158] This phrase, *on the spot*, is borrowed from the Shambhala Tradition and is cogent to the type of spontaneity and mindfulness required of the Facilitator.
[159] *Masonic Initiation*, p. 60
[160] Matthew 6:22, NIV

vow of the Oath of the Abyss in the A∴A.[161]: "I will interpret every phenomenon as a particular dealing of God with my soul." This experience, is, however quite rare. It may happen at age 16 or it may never occur at all in the life of the Initiate. We also recognize that there are *degrees of realization* and that one may *attain* by seemingly imperceptible movements upon the sacred ladder of lights. *Attainment* by degrees is no less of an initiation than *realization*, though the quality of the experience is distinct. At any given moment, during the points-chauds empowerments form of Masonic Initiation, the Initiate may in fact—*realize*—and have a truly "mountaintop" experience. But this is not to supplant the more subtle, time consuming and lifelong endeavor of *attainment by degrees*, because even if such a profound realization ensues, we are still in constant need of cultivation of the Light[162] and instruction in how best to disperse it to others, not to mention the personal growth that accompanies initiating others in this path.

Caveat

Are we, in the Ecclesiastical Revision of the APRM+M, *making Masons* under the noses of State Grand Lodges and Grand Orients throughout the world? The simple answer is, No. Here is why. The degrees, grips, passwords, Sacred Words, jewels, knocks, etc. that we employ are verbatim from the 18th & 19th Century workings of Memphis-Misraïm as employed by Marconis, Yarker, Harry Seymour and Calvin C. Burt amongst countless others. These are no longer in use by any "regularly" constituted Lodge or Valley in America or under the United Grand Lodge of England in the World. In other words, this material is being utilized by Esoteric Masons in the various versions of Memphis-Misraïm now in operation, but not in competition with mainstream bodies. This allows the "regular" Mason the opportunity to, at the very least, peruse these degrees, consider the ideas being purported and possibly even translate the understanding gleamed from such to their own respective Lodges and Valleys. It also keeps this form of spiritual Masonry out of the quagmire of competing with other Bodies, Rites and Orders. It is a distinct entity, freely worked across the globe. Beyond this, it is primarily an *inner* working, whose true secrets are not committed to the page and can only be discovered through research and experimentation.

However, as was explored in the first two chapters of Book One, this distinction does not equal separation and there are many points in which the Ecclesiastical Revision of the APRM+M and various streams of Masonry converge. Recall that at every juncture it is the

---

[161] The A∴A∴ is one of several occult fraternities founded by Aleister Crowley. It was built upon the superstructure of the Hermetic Order of Golden Dawn.

[162] Recall also that Bertiaux suggests that the Light can be withdrawn if we separate from it.

Part Two - Introduction

spirit of Masonry, continued in her Egregoric battery of energies and entities that constitutes the primary continuity amongst the Rites which is further attested to by the continuance of various structural, ideological and organizational qualities. These similarities will be readily apparent to the mainstream Mason and need not be a cause of crisis as the fundamental distinction is that we are working *spiritual* Masonry.

In the next chapter, we will begin to explore the details of the work of the Chapel, and follow with an original working of the Symbolic, or Blue Lodge Degrees[163] in their entirety.

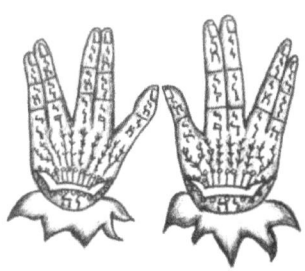

---

[163] Again, these are not the Blue Lodge Degrees commonly worked in mainstream Masonry, nor are the grips, signs, passwords and tokens identical to modern day work. The Egregoric energy that persists in these older grades has continuously been fed by small camps of devoted workers through the ages.

CHAPTER ONE

The Details of the Work

Upon its (Masonry's) trestle boards are inscribed the sacred truths of all nations and of all peoples, and upon those who understand its sacred depths has dawned the great Reality. Masonry is, in truth, that long-lost thing which all peoples have sought in all ages.

Manly P Hall[164]

---

[164] *The Lost Keys of Freemasonry*, 2006, p. 17

As we begin to delve into *the great Reality* of Masonry, we will find practices and procedures that are simple yet require an openness and suppleness of mind to fully *take*. We must make our minds pliable as we endeavor to *Open* our Chapels, perform the Degrees and Close the same. The work that we begin in these degrees will take time to fully assimilate, yet in comparison with other Masonic bodies and structures, not to mention other branches of the Western Esoteric Tradition as a whole, this is a return to the indivisible and efficient, primordial faith of the Ancients. There is abundant room for diverse workings, additions and creativity–yet there are basic structures that can be carried over to ensure the proper initiatory setting, transmission, ritual and movements. It is *suggested* that these be maintained in terms of the scaffolding they provide as well as the built-in protections and spiritual methodology they embody. As a reminder, however, the method herein worked is simply *a guide* of one particular Chapel. Congregational Illuminism supports innovation and creativity on all levels and this very text is a product of that inherent trust in the individual.

Throughout all of the Degrees we work, we will utilize the Three-fold Path, a Sacred Invocation, the Masonic Middle Pillar, the traditional "Secrets" of the degrees, points-chauds empowerments within the body and a small portion of Sacred Drama or suggestions for creating the same.

The Rule of Three

Our entire edifice is built upon the Rule of Three. In the wording of Article II of the *Articles of Union*, in 1813:

> *It is declared and pronounced, that pure Ancient Masonry consists of three degrees, and no more; viz. those of the Entered Apprentice, the Fellow Craft, and the Master Mason, including the Supreme Order of the Holy Royal Arch*[165].

Our series of "threes" begin with the three basic Degrees of Craft, Symbolic or Blue Lodge Masonry. These three Degrees can then be aligned to our Three-fold Path.

The Three-fold Path consists of the stages of *Purification, Illumination* and *Union*. Every aspect of our work from the very first Opening of a Chapel to the Closing of the 97th Degree utilizes this divine economy. We find Masonic reference to the "Rule of Three" quite often, which suggests that amongst two contending forces there is a third conciliating force. This is symbolically exemplified in the 47th Problem of Euclid[166] which is often the emblem of a

---

[165] Bernheim, Alan. *Did Early "High" or Écossais Degrees Originate in France?*, "Freemasonry in Context," Oxford: Lexington Books, 2004. p. 21.
[166] See Robert Lawlor's, *Sacred Geometry, Philosophy & Practice*, 1982, for an excellent exegesis of this type of Euclidean mysticism. Also, John Michael Greer's, *The Celtic Golden Dawn: An Original and Complete Curriculum of Druidical Study*, 2013, which includes multiple examples of Sacred Geometry for the working mage.

Past Master. Additionally, as we enter into the Higher Degrees we will notice a frequency of groupings of three. The Three-fold Path is inherent even in the most basic structure of the Blue Lodge—Entered Apprentice=*Purification,* Fellow Craft= *Illumination* and Master = *Union*. Consider the implications of the three Degrees with these stages of mystical prayer. The EA degree most assuredly has purgative aspects to it. In some American workings in the South, there is a specific test towards the end that will burn the toenails off of the inattentive. Additionally, in Scottish Rite, French Rite and Memphis+Misraïm Lodges, the EA degree includes trials by Air, Fire, Water and Earth. In the FellowCraft or Companion degree, the initiate is given a glimpse of the Middle Chamber and beyond to the Sanctum Sanctorum or Holy of Holies. This is a MOST illuminating lesson and experience. The Master Mason degree unites the candidate with the Lodge and ALL Freemasons everywhere in an unforgettably unique, intimate, and spiritual manner.

Within our Degree Work itself, notations for the stages will be centered on the page. It is important that it be understood that these stages are technically *signposts* along the spiritual path which speak of a fundamental shift in intent. They are the previously mention *transmutations* that accompany esoteric work and give it the form of metamorphosis. The stages are not water-tight compartments; instead, one naturally bleeds into the other in a seamless working of the Degree. Once the Three-fold Path becomes second nature to the Initiate, it becomes clear that these three stages occur in every major ritual of the West— from Holy Eucharist to *Neophyte Grade*– installation of Officers in an Elks Lodge to *Ipsissimus*. Yarker says; "The intelligent spirit is arrested by the mysterious number three, upon which turns essentially all Masonic science.[167]"This universal quality lends itself well to a Masonic body such as the Free Illuminists who represent Universal Freemasonry in its most liberated sense.

As a built-in protection, the Three-fold Path ensures that every ritual we perform includes a proper banishing and purification ritual. This may seem to be an area that could be dispensed with, but Adepts will rally in support of a proper banishing and/or purification technique that sets the pace for the remainder of the working. Additionally, every ritual has an opportunity to listen, see or taste of divine things through illuminating practices. If we are doing all of the talking, how on earth will we ever hear anything? We must practice sacred listening and develop Holy discernment of the spirits' ways within our practice. Finally, every ritual that we perform should include sufficient time for the unitive experience in its multitude of forms. This is most often characterized by periods of silence.

---

[167] *Lectures of a Chapter, Senate & Council*, 1882, p. 33.

Sacred Invocation

Within various Orders there is a simple moment where the Initiator calls upon something that is higher than himself to attend to the labors[168]. This is the Sacred Invocation. When this is performed with the proper amount of energy, enthusiasm and intensity, the holy Spirit is quick to attend. The Invocation we use draws down the creative energy of the S.A.O.T.U. (Sovereign Architect of the Universe). Rather than simply assuming that this is a form of deism or theism, consider that the dominant noun is *Architect*. What we are in effect calling upon, is what complexity theorist, Stuart Kauffman refers to as "the ceaseless creativity of the Universe[169]" itself! Some Chapels and Lodges will *personify* this Cosmic creative impetus but such is not necessary for those who prefer another approach. Within our Invocation we are also calling upon *Passed Masters* of Freemasonry and greeting them with, "Salutations on all points of the Triangle. Respect to the Order." This Invocation and call to action is typically accompanied by a sensation of shuffling feet along the perimeter of the Chapel[170]. We are calling our *passed* Brethren and Sisters to Order to attend to our labors. This is one of the most profound and solemn experiences of the *spirit builder*. She realizes, rather rapidly, that we labor not alone—but amongst a chain of infinite beings of varying grades and qualities of luminosity. The *Passed Masters* may continue to make themselves known in a variety of ways throughout the ritual. On occasion, their presence will be made known when the solemn battery of knocks for the particular degree occurs as this action is a non-verbal Invocation[171].

---

[168] Following the procedure of the Hermetic Order of the Golden Dawn, we call upon the "Highest" before experiencing or working with any other intermediary beings.

[169] See *Reinventing the Sacred: A New View of Science, Reason, and Religion* by Stuart A. Kauffman.

[170] Other sensations of the Passed Masters include a swift change in room temperature, a distant battery of knocks and candle anomalies that cannot be explained.

[171] The **Knocks**, however, hold distinct import within the Degree and while they may call "attendees" to the sacred marma, they specifically awaken the entities related to the points-chauds empowerment.

The Masonic Middle Pillar

Amongst a plethora of details, rituals and framework that has been borrowed from the *Hermetic Order of the Golden Dawn*, stands the Middle Pillar Exercise[172] that has found its way into many an Order and body of Initiates. Though the specific details and words of the Masonic Middle Pillar are peculiar to the APRM+M, the practice is recognizably a child of the brilliant Golden Dawn method. The late Israel Regardie is to be thanked and lauded for taking the rough ashlar of this practice and elevating it to a scientific method of Western meditation and moving of Light throughout the body[173]. This practice grounds all of the participants of the work and moves the Light through the body energizing the Sephirah/Chakras and illuminating the points-chauds which are mystically charted along the Middle Pillar primarily. It is suggested that one does not participate in this ritual upon one's first reception of a Degree/points-chauds empowerment as it occurs within the *Opening*, but it is appropriate for every event following. In this way, we follow the logic of Masons across the globe who allow all Entered Apprentices to attend all meetings and Openings[174].

† † †

The Ritual

Sit in a crossed legged position or in a chair in the Pharaonic posture seen in Egyptian statuary. Maintain a straight back and practice rhythmic breathing for several minutes[175]. *Then, visualizing a sphere of white light above your head and touching your 97th Degree point*[176], *silently invoke the Sovereign Architect of the Universe. Then move the white light down your skull towards your third eye or Ajna chakra. Here, vibrate the Sacred Word of the 4th Degree three times:*

❖ **YOD** (the first sound of Creation)

Next, move the light downward from this point upon the forehead to the right side of the throat, the place of Da'ath. Vibrate the Sacred Word of the 18th Degree three times,

❖ **INRI** (pronounced, *in-rye* and alluding to the secret of Alchemy)

---

[172] See *The Middle Pillar: The Balance Between Mind and Magic*, by Israel Regardie, Chic & Tabatha Cicero.
[173] When the Middle Pillar exercise is allied with studies of Kundalini, the chakras, the Fire Snake of the Varma Marg and other esoteric branches of study, the vistas become wide and all encompassing.
[174] Other Free Illuminists will assuredly allow all guests to attend any portion of the Rite as is customary within Congregational Illuminism. The suggestion here is for our Chapel in particular, as we are following a bit of standard Masonic procedure in this simple gesture.
[175] The four-fold breath of the Golden Dawn is helpful in this section.
[176] See the Diagrams of the points for the specific locations upon the body.

Bring the light from the throat towards the right, center chest–the place of Tiphareth and vibrate the Sacred Word of the 28th Degree three times,

- ❖ **ADONAI** (The Holy Guardian Angel within)

Move the shaft of Light from the heart center down to the genitals in Yesod and vibrate the Sacred Word of the 33rd Degree three times,

- ❖ **MICHAMICHAH BEALIM ADONAI** (who is equal to you, among the great lords?)

Finalize the beam of Light in your perineum seated upon the earth and vibrate the Sacred Word of the 45th Degree three times,

- ❖ **SOLIMY** (Princes of the Pre-Adamite Spirits or Genii)

Once you sense the beam of light from your head and down your spine to your seat, then inhale deeply and draw the light back upwards towards the cap of your skull and strongly exhale through the mouth[177] as you visualize a bursting of light from your crown and raining down upon your body and back into the earth. Draw the Light back upwards with a strong inhale and exhale again sensing the circulating currents that you will now be moving within another body in Initiation. Repeat as needed.

†††

The Masonic Middle Pillar can be utilized at any time to stimulate the *wheels*[178], or the Sephirah upon the body which contain numerous points. The Masonic Middle Pillar works as a group exercise, or in private, or in the Chapel as a part of the Opening, or it could be the *main operation* of the meeting. It can also be utilized in a solitary method before the *re-awakening* of the points in scrying. Finally, the Masonic Middle Pillar can be used as a means to re-consecrate the Inner and Outer Guard, or the Facilitators to the work of the APRM+M. This is an intimate form of awakening the creative energies within the pair of Facilitators, before working upon others or before pursuing scrying sessions. In this manner, the Outer Guard, for instance, using "gnostic pressures" re-awakens the spheres upon the Inner Guard physically while vibrating the Sacred Words and moving the Light upon his/her body. Then the method is performed upon the other Officer. If the points being worked are known

---

[177] Pranayamic breathwork is helpful in this practice. The Initiate should feel the diaphragm raise and lower with these breaths and fully empty the lungs with each.

[178] See both the works of Crowley and Kenneth Grant with regards to the exciting of the five wheels. Though this is traditional Tantric teaching, the Western magickal method is more consistent with our undertaking.

ahead of time, these can be re-awakened within the Facilitators as well to enhance performance.

Secrets of the Work

Probably the most traditional aspect of our work is the utilization of the "secrets" of the degrees from 1st through the 97th. Far from being considered the "secrets" of the degrees, in Masonic literature, this is often referred as the *clap-trap* of the material. This portion of the work in mainstream Lodges almost seems dispensable in comparison with the role of ritualized drama, for instance. These are the various methods, it is said, wherein a Mason may recognize another Mason, *in darkness as well as in light*. We have come to understand this material in a very distinct way, however, in that we have found it to truly contain the *essence* of the degree when aligned with the points empowerments. Through scrying experience and practice, we have discovered that the phrase, *in darkness as well as in light* refers to the Astral realms and beyond where this so-called "clap-trap" is recognized by intermediary, sentient beings in the spirit vision and where the Initiate is tested and required to prove him or herself with the proper Sacred Words, signs and grips. Far from dispensable, this study has elucidated the primitive and archetypal usage of these "secrets." They are relegated in the following manner;

- *The Battery of Knocks.* The knocks, performed with solemnity either with a traditional Masonic gavel or with the use of a deep resonating gong, are a form of non-verbal Invocation. They are a calling card to the attendant spirits, passed masters and angelic beings attached to the particular degree/points-chaud being worked. A visual that accompanies the knocks is often the *lighting up* of the points-chaud upon the body.
- *The Sacred Word.* The Sacred Word is the highest word of the degree. It goes beyond a password and can be utilized at any given moment when scrying the Degree to check the validity of a vision or test the spirit encountered. In the Chapel working, the Sacred Word is vibrated strongly[179] while the points-chaud empowerment is being administered and awakened.
- *The Token or Grip.* The token or grip of the Degree becomes the seal of the points-chauds empowerment. In Haitian Vodou a *pwen* (synonymous with hot-point) is a spirit or entity that is placed within a container—an earthenware govi jar or bottle. In our method, the container is the human body and the pwen is the points-chauds

---

[179] The *Vibratory Formula* is yet another valid child of the Hermetic Order of the Golden Dawn. This simple method of intensely chanting god-names is explored fully in *The Complete System of Golden Dawn Magic*, by Israel Regardie, 1984.

empowerment[180]. This empowerment is sealed within the body when the Facilitator and the Initiate exchange and hold the grip of the Degree after the Initiate has been "brought to light[181]." Some have likened this experience to the positive and negative currents of a battery. The flow of energy and the invoked entity are completed and sealed within the body by the grip or token.

- *The Sign*. The Sign of the Degree is demonstrated after the Initiate is brought to light for the sole purpose of protection in scrying exercises. When faced with an entity of questionable traits within the spirit vision, the Initiate can give the sign of the degree which will assert to the entity one's position and protection[182] under the S.A.O.T.U.
- *The Jewel*. The Jewel[183] or Insignia of a degree is the talisman or sigil to be worn by the Initiate after the hoodwink is placed over the eyes. This Jewel is carefully drawn by the Inner Guard or Facilitator upon Virgin parchment, in keeping with the Divine Cagliostro's method of drawing the pentagram[184]. After the ritual, the candidate is given the sigil to take home and wear as a talisman during scrying journeys. It can also be placed upon the forehead to induce imagery from the astral realm. Additionally, the symbol of the jewel is traced upon the forehead of the Initiate in the Illumination stage of each degree[185].

Points-Chauds Empowerments

Each degree has a points-chauds empowerment that is relegated to it upon the physical body. The Inner Guard, Outer Guard and any Facilitator of the work should be very familiar with the placement and numbering of these points upon the body. They are primarily aligned to the Middle Pillar or central column of the body, which is why the Opening contains the exercise for moving Light throughout the central path of the spine. There are also a number of points in the genital region, as the primary subject of the Rites of Osiris includes the search for his *membrum virile* and subsequent magical generation of a new phallus by Isis–which alludes to the creative power being lodged within this anatomical region of both males and females[186]. The lingam and the yoni are both adored in the Ancient Vedas and our work divinizes the entire body which includes this most generative

---

[180] The points-chaud and the pwen are both energies and entities.
[181] In the *Hauts Grades*, Book Three, hoodwinks are dispensed with. The inner workings require very little props and reveal the depth and lifelong study that is our inheritance.
[182] As well as proving one's authorization to travel in the particular plane.
[183] The Jewel takes on a slightly different role in the *Hauts Grades*, but the general idea is the same.
[184] See *the Masonic Magician*, Cooper & Faulks.
[185] The practitioner of traditional Haitian Vodou will be immediately struck by the similarity between this practice and that of the *Lava Tet* where the *Met Tet's veve is inscribed upon the forehead*.
[186] Reference can again be made to the coiled serpent at the base of the spine, the Kundalini energy that is latent and awaits awakening. This same energy is given the Sacred Word, AZOTH in the *Hauts Grades*.

source of Light and energy. This point is recognized by many Masons, Wilmshurst amongst the most prominent, who says,

> ...the apron covers the creative, generative organ of the body; and it is especially to these that the significance of the Tau attaches. Spiritual self building and the erection of the "superstructure" are dependent upon the supply of creative energy available from the generative nervous center, the "powerhouse" of the human organism. Thence that energy passes upwards through other ganglionic "transformers" and, reaching the brain, becomes finally sublimated and transformed to consciousness[187].

As mentioned in Book One, each points-chauds has qualities of empowerment, attunement, therapy and initiation. Every Facilitator, Inner Guard or Outer Guard should be attuned to the requests and perceived needs of the Initiates for spontaneous points-chauds empowerments.

The method of *seeing, sensing* or *feeling* the precise location of these gyrating energy points differs from Facilitator to Facilitator. With practice and after absorbing the diagrams of the points, the Facilitator can visualize with precision these scintillating lights within his own mind, or visually through the skin of the candidate. Here, it is important to utilize the previously mentioned, "Seeker" robe of brown, natural fibers. The Initiate should ideally be as close to naked as comfortable underneath the robe to ensure visualization and stimulation of the points through the "gnostic pressures." Most Facilitators utilize a particular hand position, or mudra, when providing points empowerments. This is by placing the thumb in between the forefinger and the medius, which results in a stronger current felt through the arm and exiting the body through the thumb. This hand position is an ancient German gesture as a wish for good fortune and is often made into an amulet for bringing good luck and fending off evil[188].

The physical asana of the recipient of the Degree/point, utilized in our Chapel, is the sacred sign of the pentagram, the flaming star. The Candidate[189] stands in the sign of the Vitruvian man, receptive to the energetic workings at hand. In the Senate Lectures we learn that the flaming star is; *an emblem of the divine fire, of the life-giving light, which renews unceasingly, of the inexhaustible benevolence of the divine source, which from the centre of the universe gives its laws, rules the course of the stars, pours fertility on the earth, and is prodigal of ornament in order that its children may be happy.*[190]

† † †

---

[187] *The Masonic Initiation*, 2007 edition, p. 77.
[188] See the *60th Degree* Synopsis in Book Three.
[189] Deemed, *Initiate* after a traditional three-degree initiation.
[190] Yarker, *Lectures of a Chapter, Senate & Council*, 1882, p. 27.

The Sacred Drama

All of the degrees from 1st through 33rd have fully developed ritual drama with rubrics and staging directions which can be found in a number of different Masonic resources. The degrees above 33rd are hit or miss. Some were fully developed during Yarker's time and others never were[191]. Some have been developed further through the Robert Ambelain lineage of the APRM-M, while others are simply communicated. Our first three degrees will have a complete, yet extremely simplified Sacred Drama, which will firmly place the Initiate at the threshold of the Greater Mysteries and will prepare their physical and spiritual bodies for the reception of *all* of the points-chauds empowerments/Degrees. The concept behind having the first three degrees worked out in full form in this way, is that through experience, T Allen Greenfield and others noticed that individuals who either received too many points empowerments in a row or even a few without being "duly and truly prepared" did not assimilate the energies and entities safely[192]. The Arabia Mountain Working has taken to performing Gnostic Ordinations and Consecrations before administering *all* of the points (over time) to Initiates wishing to work the Rite. Within our own Chapel, we have found the complete working of these three degrees to accomplish the same goal of protection and preparation without the necessity of involving individuals in the work of the clergy if it is not their sacred vocation to do so.

In the Degrees above the 3rd, groups are free to create and construct the dramatic ritual of their choosing. This is not only in keeping with the Congregational Illuminist appreciation of creativity and innovation, it also allows for a much more simple and devout method of continuing the work of the degrees in a setting that is easily manageable, yet still effective and powerful.

That *long lost thing which peoples have sought for in all ages* is the Manifestation of Light, our Sacred Doctrine. Through the rituals of the Degrees in this simplified format, we can endeavor upon a life path wherein Light is the goal as well as the material we are working with. Our bodies *scintillating* and our *Mystic Temples* aglow, we labor together *in Free Communion* in this Great Work to bring Light and Life to Brothers and Sisters desirous of such, and then outwards to those we know and love, and further to those we will never even meet.

---

[191] This is in reference to the combined Rites of Memphis-Misraim, as the Rite of Mizraim has been published by *Collectanea*, Vol 6, Part I and II, as well as Yarker's, *Manual of the Degrees of the Antient & Primitive Rite of Masonry, Collectanea*, Vol 19, Part I, II, & III.

[192] See the Appendix to Greenfield's, *Roots of Magick*.

CHAPTER TWO

The Opening of the Chapel

The work before us is no light matter, for it is nothing less than a concerted effort to carry out the duty that is laid upon us, as those who possess the Light, to spread that Light abroad through the world, and actually become fellow-laborers with T.G.A.O.T.U. in His great plan for the evolution of our Brethren.

CW Leadbeater[193]

---

[193] *The Hidden Life in Freemasonry*, 7th Ed, 1998, pgs. 9-10.

The working that we are about to undertake is original to the *Chapel of the Gnosis*, which holds a Free Illuminist Charter for a Research and Philosophical Lodge of the APRM+M as well as Warrants from the **Coptic Gnostic Church** and Gauges of support and amity from other luminaries. Additionally, this set is a portion of a larger collection of liturgical and fraternal workings entitled, *The Misraïm Chapel Rite*.

As has already been stated, there is ample room for innovation and creativity. What is herein offered is suggestive and based upon research, philosophy, ritual examinations and most importantly, *experience*. Those beginning to work in a newly constituted Lodge, Node or Chapel may want to consider this framework and experiment with its simple structure and effectiveness. Those already at labor may want to consider this marriage of effective ritual and Holy Simplicity. Still others may find inspiration for personal or private work to extend their traditional Lodge material and experience. It is again noted that this is *spiritual Freemasonry* and that we are *spirit builders*.

Preliminaries

Before we begin the Opening, there are a few ritual items that are needed and basic to the three degrees. Any and all of these may be replaced with similar materials that the Facilitator already has. As previously noted, it is important for the main work to be near what is perceived to be a sacred marma. If this is not possible or such a place is not sensed by the Facilitator, then use the center of a room that will be secure for the meeting.

- In the sacred marma or center of the room should be the main altar. This can be a simple cupboard that contains any materials needed for working, or a table. In our Chapel we use a round table that is around 3 feet tall.
- Three candles are needed for all of the degrees. These can be upon the altar in triangular fashion, or they can be on stands forming a triangle about the altar. The apex of the triangle should be in the East which is the direction the Facilitator faces during the work.
- Three robes are needed; a white robe for the Inner Guard, a black robe for the Outer Guard and a brown robe for the candidate.
- The VSL, or Volume of the Sacred Law should be placed in the center of the altar. This is the book that is most Holy to the Candidate[194].

---

[194] The Holy Book, which may also be a piece of laudable poetry or philosophy, in this working is not used for the Obligation, but for the divinatory practice of Bibliomancy to discern a *word* or *image* to add information to "scrying" the Degree and its points-chaud empowerment after initiation, but also in this case, to complete the spiritual "Opening" of the Lodge. This is explained in detail as the study progresses.

- Upon the VSL should be the square, compasses and rule. These may be drawn upon parchment if necessary.
- Additional items upon the altar; a vial of Abramelin oil[195] placed in the South along with a red votive candle, a container of blessed water in the West[196], a small plate of salt and bread[197] cut in the shape of an ankh in the North and incense in the East.
- On a separate stand should be the gavel, dagger and gong if used.
- Pre-drawn Jewel of the degree upon parchment and attached[198] to a cord.
- A blindfold
- A separate candle that can be carried by the candidate
- The ritual and points-chauds diagram
- Matches and candle snuffer[199].

Commentary on the Opening

This Opening can be used for all 97 Degrees of the APRM+M. It is a complete working on its own and forms the seam of the entire fabric of our work. Constructed upon the Three-fold Path scaffolding, the Opening performs a powerful invocation, a thorough banishing, purifications, divination and deep meditation and prayer. There are aspects of the Opening that feel Ecclesiastical[200] and others that feel more fraternal. It is both. When we look at the core elements of the Opening we can see how other appropriate Openings could be constructed along these lines.

Invocation– The solemn act of lighting the three candles and saying the efficient invocations of Rudolph Steiner's Lodge working, while the gong is struck thrice (or the Gavel knocked upon the altar) is a form of deep Invocation. It is utilized in the Opening and can form one of the essentials of every degree. When performed properly, this basic segment of the ceremony creates an atmosphere that is both welcoming to the spirits and

---

[195] In Horus lodge we have begun to use the Holy Myron of *L'Ordre Martinèsiste de Chenu* created by our late brother †Iohannes 33°, 90°, 95°. There is a mystical connection between the CHENU Order and the Rites of Memphis+Misraïm which will is examined in part in our volume *Lux Occulta* (Transmutation Publishing, 2021). This holy chrism, or Myron, has proven effective in all workings with any connection to mystic works.

[196] Many sources could be utilized for the appropriate rites of blessing and consecrating items, but for those not directly related to a specific ecclesia, the works of Robert Ambelain are a goldmine.

[197] We tend to use pita or even a tortilla and a sterilized exacto blade to carve an ankh shape to be eaten by the Initiate. There also should be one for every participant.

[198] One of the easiest ways to go about this, is to draw out the Jewel, laminate it, and then hole punch it and attach to a lanyard.

[199] Following the example of the Élus Coëns & Martinists, we do not blow out the candles as they are considered to house spirits in an occult manner. They are living effigies. Reference could also be made to Revelation 1:12, "*And I turned to see the voice that spake with me. And being turned, I saw seven golden candlesticks.*"

[200] See the advanced ÆONIC working of the V° *Order of Wisdom* in the Ordre Martinèsiste de Chenu (see *Lux Occulta*).

beings being invited as well as creating a spiritual environment for the participants. When the next section begins with the words, *To the Glory of the*...after we bow towards the East, many will feel a tingling feeling along the spine and sense the shuffling of feet in the perimeters of the space. If performed outside, there may be a pronounced volume shift in birds or insects, or the wind may pick up. This very solemn and crucial aspect of the work and its spiritual intent immediately places the Ecclesiastical Revision of the APRM+M in a different category than mainstream workings.

Purification–Purification is accomplished through four means—banishing, water, fire and oil. In Florence Farr's book, *Egyptian Magic*, she discusses the Egyptian method of banishing as it was found in the Harris papyrus. She says that a "formulation of a guardian in the shape of a dog that was to be terrible to all attaching forces[201]" was created by the priests and the banishing occurred in the four directions. We have utilized a very short portion of the powerful Psalm 68, which has long been used by Martinists and Élus Coëns for cleansing a space. It may be helpful to visualize the Guardian dog while the words, *Let God arise, let his enemies be scattered...* are chanted forcefully. The purification by water and consecration by fire are children of the Hermetic Order of the Golden Dawn. But there is a subtle distinction in our working. The participant is not a *Child of Earth* only; he is also *of the star-filled Heavens*. This alludes to our composite nature of body, soul and spirit. He is a child of the Heavens *before* initiation ever occurs—the ceremony is simply a reminder of such as we often take too many draughts from the waters of forgetfulness. The cross upon the forehead with Abramelin oil is a direct connection back to the Holy Arabia Mountain. It is a spiritual connective tissue with the consecrations and work of Arabia Mountain.

Bibliomancy–Before the Outer Guard performs Bibliomancy, as a form of Illumination, the Preamble is read. This Preamble goes back to Marconis and his *Sanctuary of Memphis*. It is a beautiful passage that illustrates well that we are performing an exoteric exercise, yet the esoteric is present at every juncture. In fact, these words prepare the Outer Guard to turn the reasoning portion of her/his mind down for a moment and allow for a message *from on high* from the VSL. Rather than simply a Holy Book to take one's oath upon, the VSL becomes a real working tool for the illuminative process. The passage that is selected through the bibliomantic divination is meant to convey a message to all participants in general. It will have elements that are specific to individuals, but it will have *something* for all.

Chain of Union–As we form a circle around the sacred marma and the altar, we align ourselves in one accord through the partaking of the ankh. This portion of the Opening,

---

[201] Kessinger re-print, 1993, p. 24.

like the gesture of silence in the Invocation, is from a dream transmission. After some investigation, we found that there were a number of Egyptian drawings where it appeared that an ankh was being fed to a candidate. This is a sort of mini-Eucharist. The ankh is a symbol for everlasting life.[202] This moment tightens our circle and builds the column of radionic force that is needed for the enlightening of the Initiate. This is followed by a Chain of Union, which is traditional in Masonic bodies across the globe, and a prayer.

The Masonic Middle Pillar–Our form of the Middle Pillar exercise has already been discussed, yet it is critical that we understand its function at the finale of the Opening. It is this action in particular that will awaken the Light within our own bodies that we may then use in initiation, healing, attuning and empowering. When performed correctly, the body will feel vitalized and energized. The spine tingling previously mentioned will reach a fever pitch and it will literally feel as if lightning bolts could escape from the fingers at any moment. There is a striking similarity between our Masonic Middle Pillar and the "Boule Blanche" from the *Arcana Arcanorum* of several branches of the Memphis-Misraïm tree. Bogard quotes the description of this practice:

> *Visualizing a white sphere above your head, the light descends, into the earth–the light ascends back up, to the center of the heart. From the center the light extends to the world, with (infinite) wishes of benefits.*[203]

For the majority of the Degrees, it will be the Opening that actually takes the most time and has the most words. Our actual initiations are fairly simple as we have dispensed with a great deal of ceremonial in exchange for more silence and powerful, raw, initiatory force. Yet it is the building up of this force that is accomplished through the proper carrying out of this Opening.

---

[202] See the "Ceremony of the Opening of the Mouth," from the Pyramid texts. See also the Osirian & embalming connections to Psalm 50 (Septuagint), frequently used by Cagliostro and all Martinists & Coëns. Verse 7 (opening of the mouth), verse 8 (restoration of broken bones), verses 16, 17, and 19 (sacrifices), verses 2&7 (ritual washing).

[203] *Of Memphis and Of Misraïm*, p. 401. See *Boule Blanche* at the close of the 89°.

The Opening

The Inner Guard and Outer Guard enter the sacred space in silence, followed by any guests. Then facing East, the Inner Guard begins:

I.G. **Brother (or Sister) Outer Guard, take your weapon and ensure that the Chapel is duly guarded.**

Takes the dagger and checks all doors for eavesdroppers

O.G. **Brother Inner Guard, the Chapel is secure.**

I.G. **Then let us invite the Light to move amongst us.**

The Outer Guard takes the gong and striker in hand while the Inner Guard Lights each of the three candles slowly saying the appropriate phrase per direction. The Outer Guard strikes the gong upon each lighting.

I. G.[204] **May Wisdom guide our building.** *(lights the candle in the East at apex)*
May Beauty adorn it. *(lights the candle in the South)*
May strength build it. *(lights the candle in the West)*

All pause for a brief moment while the Outer Guard lights the incense

I.G. **To Order then, Brothers and Sisters!**

Each member places his arms in the sign of the good shepherd. Right arm over left upon the chest. The Inner Guard loudly proclaims,

To the Glory of the Sovereign Architect of the Universe! In the Name of the Sovereign Sanctuary of the Antient and Primitive Rite of Memphis+Misraïm. I call upon all Passed Masters, Guardians of Freemasonry and Angelic beings and countenances! Come now into our Mystic Temple! Salutations on all points of the Triangle. Respect to the Order!

All bow fully towards the East and then rise up with the two fingers of the right hand upon the lips in the sign of the silent Horus.

---

[204] Steiner, *Freemasonry and Ritual Work*, 2007, p. 161.

Purification

Outer Guard takes up the dagger again and goes to the East of the altar, forming an equal armed cross in the air and chanting a portion of Psalm 68[205] loudly,

O.G. "Let God arise, Let his enemies be scattered, let those who fear him flee before him!"

Outer Guard repeats banishing in the South, the West and the North. Then returns the dagger and takes up the blessed water from the altar. Beginning with the Inner Guard, she says,

O.G. **Child of Earth and of the star-filled Heavens[206] be purified by water.**

Outer Guard sprinkles water in an equal-armed cross upon the forehead, lower abdomen, right shoulder and left shoulder of I.G., then proceeds to all others present at the meeting. Next, the Inner Guard takes up the red votive candle and makes a cross in the air in front of the Outer Guard and then proceeds to all others present in the meeting, saying,

I.G. **Child of Earth and of the star-filled Heavens be consecrated by fire.**

Outer Guard takes the oil of Abramelin and forms an equal armed cross upon the forehead of the Inner Guard and then proceeds to all others present in the meeting, saying,

O.G. **Receive the Sacred oil.**

Illumination

I.G. **Hear the Preamble of our beloved institution. "The voice which spoke from out of the midst of the cloud hath said; Man, thou hast two ears to hear the same sound, two eyes to perceive the same object, two hands to execute the same deed. This is why the Masonic science, the science above all others, is both Esoteric and Exoteric—Esotericism is thought, Exotericism is power. Exotericism can be learnt, can be given; Esotericism cannot be learnt, cannot be taught, cannot be given—it comes from on High.[207]"**

Inner Guard removes the square, compasses and rule and hands the VSL to the Outer Guard who, takes the book and bows towards the East. The Outer Guard performs Bibliomancy by taking the Sacred Book in her hands and feeling its covers and pages. Then, closing her eyes, she files through the

---

[205] This is again where Brothers and Sisters who wish to may interpolate their own Banishing rite, such as the LBRP, the Star Ruby, the Nu-sphere, etc.
[206] This is a subtle extension of Golden Dawn formulae.
[207] E.J. Marconis, *Sanctuary of Memphis or Hermes*, 1849, p. 20.

pages until moved to stop. Eyes still closed, she moves her finger upon the page until led to stop. Then she opens her eyes and says,

O.G. A reading from the Holy Book of _____

She reads a small passage from the text and then all remain in silence for a few moments as the words fill the minds of the participants.

Union

I.G. Circle about the Holy altar and receive eternal life.

The Inner Guard takes the paten of bread in the shape of ankhs. He dips an ankh in salt and eats the bread. He then serves the person to his right. This continues around the circle until the last receives the ankh and replaces the paten in the North on the altar. Inner Guard places his arms right over left out in front of him and instructs all to do likewise, holding hands to form the Chain of Union.

I.G. Let us form the Chain of Union.

> **In the Name of the Sovereign Architect of the Universe, I declare this Chapel open and at labor upon the _____ Degree. Lord of Lights, look with favor upon your servants as we labor to manifest the Light within us, around us and for our Initiate. Be with _____ on his journey and open him to the Celestial realms and the secrets of your Divine Wisdom. AMEN.**

Break the Chain by counting to three and then all drop their hands simultaneously.

I.G. Let us complete our opening labors with the Masonic Middle Pillar and begin to move the Light within us for the greater purpose of enlightening others.

*Perform the **Masonic Middle Pillar** with the whole group sitting in a circle.*
When complete, sit for a few moments of silence. Next, the Outer Guard and Inner Guard rise and the I. G. speaks:

I. G. Brother Outer Guard, attend to the Candidate in waiting and assure yourself that he/she is duly and truly prepared to receive the mysteries of this degree. Then, direct the Candidate to the Chamber of Reflection, there to abide his time in patience until he receives further direction or instruction.

Outer Guard performs task. Degree begins.

CHAPTER THREE

First Degree Apprentice

Shut up in a dark place, left to meditate in the presence of gloomy objects, you have reflected upon the vanity of the things of this perishable world. You have no doubt realized also that by this allegory, the Masonic Order has taught you, that to enter into it you must have cast off the old man in you and die to all Evil in order to be re-born into Virtue.

Marconis[208]

---

[208] *Sanctuary of Memphis or Hermes*, p. 69.

1st *degree*, Apprentice.

Part Two – Chapter Three: Apprentice

The primary aim of the 1st Degree of Classical Freemasonry is to test the Candidate for fitness in the Fraternity. This happens through four symbolic journeys[209] with corresponding ordeals of the elements. As the candidate has not participated in an Opening up until this point, his purification must be *more* complete and thorough than those that follow this grade. This entire degree is dedicated to the first stage of the Three-fold Path, *Purification*. In our own working of the Degree, this continuity of ideas and structure is continued.

- The candidate finds himself placed in a harsh new world from the beginning in the *Chamber of Reflection*, stocked with emblems of death. This chamber is symbolically underground and thus performs the first trial, by Earth[210]. It includes the *Holy Commission*, which acts as a will sharpener and leads to needed life changes for the Initiate. It is suggested that all members of the Chapel take the *Holy Commission* from time to time along the years, to keep chipping away at the rough ashlar and perfecting the Work. When this work is completed, the Commission is ceremoniously burned.

- From there, she/he is taken on a journey of Air, which alludes to the Spirit, the Intellect and the Astral realm. Our path is holistic and involves the mind as well as the body.

- Next, he is taken on a journey of Water. This journey is symbolic of the purification of the Initiate's soul. It is a type of baptism[211] and is preparatory work for scrying and Bibliomancy in the future.

- The fourth journey is the test of Fire. That fire and the sun were primary emblems of worship for ancient humans is a well documented and known fact across the globe. Fire evokes the passionate and active forces within the body that the points-chauds empowerments will activate and awaken. Fire interacts with Water as a balancing force of purification and consecration to the work.

Next, the Initiate will participate in his first *Mystic Rite of Vision*. This is to prepare him to begin to sense the qualities of the Astral realm and how near they are to us at all intervals. He will be given one of the blessed ankh's to eat, which should give him a word from the other realm. He will also receive a symbol drawn upon his forehead in the Abramelin oil which will evoke a scene. The *Mystic Rite of Vision* is preparatory work for Scrying the points-

---

[209] This is so in European concept Lodges, i.e., the Modern Rite, the Scottish Rite Symbolic Degrees, etc.
[210] The traditional trial of earth in the Rit Moderne is through the bitter drink, the "draught of forgetfulness." However, this same Rite is the originator of the Chamber of Reflection which is clearly an ordeal of earth in all of its heaviness, death and constituent elements.
[211] We find lustrations in *multiple* Masonic grades.

chauds after degree work. It is also, later on, preparatory for the labors of the Arcana Arcanorum, *the entertaining of angels.*

The *Secrets of the Work* are communicated and conferred in a series and form the basis for all of the Degrees above the 3rd. For those who choose to dispense with ceremonial of this nature altogether, the stream-lined version of the 1st-3rd Degrees will be provided in the *Hauts Grades*, Book Three. There is also a *Suggested Reading* list after the Symbolic Degrees in Book Three that could be utilized for this set of ritually enacted Degrees.

The *Order of Work* consists of the following;

- Opening the Chapel
- The Chamber of Reflection
- Entrance into the Chapel and subsequent journeys/trials of the elements
- The Mystic Rite of Vision
- Secrets of the Work/points-chauds empowerment

The main materials for this degree are the same as those needed for the Opening; however, an extra ankh is needed for the Initiate. The separate, *Chamber of Reflection* need not be extravagantly decorated. It simply needs to represent an underground room or chamber, with emblems of death such as a skull and crossbones, an hour glass, a scythe and alchemical designs[212] or elements that involve putrefaction. These may be drawn for ease of use. The *Holy Commission* can be copied and placed in the Chamber as well.

Keep in mind that these degrees are constructed upon the Rule of Three—two Officers and an Initiate. If other participants wish to join, they may take part in the "Secrets of the Work" by encircling the candidate who is about to be brought to Light. Additionally, they will maintain a meditative state as much as possible to lend spiritual support to the working. None of these degrees are so lengthy that other participants will have to spend undue time on the sidelines. Simplicity reigns throughout.

Finally, it is important to make every effort to set the Initiate's mind at ease before the Initiation, as spiritual Masonry has no interest in gratuitous hazing, scare tactics and the like. Our work is Ecclesiastical and empowering. The work that we undertake is serious and sincere, but there is no reason to make it unduly disturbing or cryptic. The Initiate has placed herself willingly upon the porch of the Temple and it is our sacred duty to manifest the Light. That is all.

---

[212] Traditionally this includes vials of sulphur, mercury and salt.

As a portion of the study materials, the Facilitator may want to direct the new Initiate's attention to *Degrees of Wisdom: A Compendium of Rituals from the Rites of Memphis and Misraïm*, noting that there is not a one-to-one correspondence between the degrees as worked in Spirit Builders and those presented in *Degrees of Wisdom*. Also of note is Albert Pike's, *The Porch and the Middle Chamber*. It is one of the more detailed and lengthy versions of the 3 degrees from the Scottish Rite and French Masonic perspective.

Apprentice

After the Opening, the Outer Guard retrieves the Initiate in waiting and takes them to a separate room, or wooded space which will become the Chamber of Reflection. The solitary light that the O.G. used in the Opening is left with the Initiate as the only source of lighting. The emblems of death are centered round a table wherein are a red pen and the Holy Commission. In this portion of the degree, the Officers should maintain the most proper decorum and silence as the Initiate is left to his own devices to study his soul.

* * * * * * * *

The Outer Guard leaves the Candidate with a bell to ring when he is finished with the Holy Commission.

The Holy Commission

Seeker; attend to the image below and allow the spirits to assist you in your Holy Commission

You are asked now to give an account of your vices, shortcomings, faults and anything else that you feel has prevented you from truly *being yourself* or being *free*. Do this in the space provided here, using the back if necessary. In silence, select one of these that you believe you can direct your energies toward fully conquering. This one, write in red ink~ sign your full name in red beside it and provide the date. Turn the Commission face down when completed.

Vice_____

Name_____ Date_____

When the Initiate rings the bell, the Outer Guard goes to retrieve him. She brings the "Seeker" robe with her, which resembles a monastic habit and symbolizes the earth. She hoodwinks him and places the solitary candle in his right hand. She will guide him by the left arm. The Holy Commission is left face down in the Chamber, to be returned to the Initiate at the completion of the ceremonies. The Outer Guard then addresses the Candidate;

O.G. **Seeker, is it of your own freewill and accord that you seek entrance into our sacred Chapel?**

Candidate **It is.**

O.G. **Do you believe that it is your sacred right to receive entrance into the Mysteries?**

Candidate **I do.**

O.G. **Then extend your left**[213] **arm to me, that I may guide you upon your journey.**

Done.

Outer Guard takes the Candidate on the journey from the Chamber of Reflection into the Chapel. As they approach the Holy Alter, all participants rise and give the sign of the Good Shepherd, right arm over left across the chest. This is immediately followed by the Sign of Silence of Horus, the first two fingers of the right hand pressed upon the lips. The Inner Guard says,

I.G. **Seeker, is it of your own freewill and accord that you approach our Holy Altar?**

Candidate **It is.**

Inner Guard takes the Dagger in hand.

I.G. **Then come and enter into the joys of Fraternity.**

Initiate is seized by the Outer Guard who pulls up his hoodwink for a moment revealing the Inner Guard posed and ready to strike with the dagger[214]. *Hoodwink is replaced.*

I.G. **Seeker, before one can achieve union with others, he must be purified by the elements. Brother Outer Guard, take the Initiate upon his first journey.**

---

[213] The right arm is busy holding the candle, but extending the left arm in this way is also a symbol of our non-dual Gnosis and recognition of the twin forces of Strength and Mercy and the unity of the left & right hand path.

[214] This is a reference to the challenges and necessary tests that occur upon the spiritual planes during scrying.

Purification

Outer Guard takes the Initiate on a full circumambulation of the Chapel and stops in the East at the sound of the gavel or gong, rung by the Inner Guard. The incense is taken up and the Initiate is censed at the head, the feet, the right arm and the left arm. The Outer Guard then takes the Initiate on another complete circuit about the room and stops in the West, sprinkling her head, feet, right arm and left arm with the blessed water. The Initiate is taken on another complete circuit and the Outer Guard stops in the South. She takes the candle and nears it to the Candidate's forehead, feet, right arm and left arm. Then, the Outer Guard brings the Candidate West of the Holy Altar and facing East. The Inner Guard approaches from the East and presses his hands upon the hands of the Initiate on top of the VSL, saying,

I.G. Seeker, you have received the necessary purifications for your journey. But you are still in need of further instruction before being unified with us in the fraternal bonds of fellowship. You must now be illuminated by the words of Sacred Scripture. The Outer Guard will perform your first Bibliomancy among us. The message that is revealed in this divination is for you and you alone. The Outer Guard, acting as Thoth for this portion of the Degree, will write down the page, chapter and verse for your further study at a later date.

Illumination

Outer Guard performs Bibliomancy and verse is read aloud to the Chapel. Chapter and verse are recorded and placed with the Holy Commission.

I.G. Seeker, you will now receive the Mystic Rite of Vision. Put yourself at ease and begin to breathe evenly and slowly. We are about to open a door[215].

Inner Guard takes the ankh bread from the paten and dips it into the salt. He raises it over the Initiate's head and forms a vertical rectangle that extends over the head and down to the heart of the Initiate. He then says,

I.G. Seeker, you are now about to ingest a sacred symbol. Open your mouth and take this gift of the Earth. When you have swallowed the symbol, tell me the first Word that comes to your mind.

---

[215] This is a gate, as well as a door.

The Outer Guard writes down the Word of the Candidate on the paper with Bibliomantic information.

I.G. In your present condition of receptivity, I will draw a symbol upon your forehead. As I do so, relate to the Outer Guard any scenes that surface upon the calm waters of your mind.

Inner Guard dips his pointer finger in the oil of Abramelin and draws a square and compass symbol, the square over the points of the compasses, upon the Initiate's forehead[216]. He then adds the rule to the bottom of the symbol. Outer Guard prompts the Initiate to see with the Imagination if needed and relate what scenes, landscapes or imagery surfaces. O.G. writes down the scene on the same paper.

I.G. Seeker, you are one step closer to the fellowship that you desire amongst us. But, our central search is not solely for communion with others. Brother Outer Guard, of what are Masons of the Antient and Primitive Rite of Memphis+Misraïm in most earnest search of?

O.G. The *Manifestation of Light*

I.G. And the manifestation of Light you shall receive, fellow Seeker. Brethren, assist me in bringing our new Initiate to Light.

Union

All participants approach the Holy Altar and form a circle around the Initiate. The Inner Guard places the Jewel of an Apprentice (square and compasses drawn upon Virgin Parchment with the square on top of the compass points and a rule across the bottom) around the Initiate's neck. The Inner Guard takes the gavel and says,

I.G. Seeker, the Outer Guard will assist you in standing in the sign of a Free Man (*or* Woman).

Outer Guard assists the Candidate to stand like the Vitruvian man of Leonardo da Vinci, in the sign of the Pentagram. Then the Inner Guard strikes the altar in three solemn and loud strokes,

I.G. (Battery of three loud and slow knocks upon the altar) X   X   X

Then the Inner Guard vibrates the Sacred Word of an Apprentice Mason strongly, while giving the points-chaud empowerment on the top of the head.

---

[216] This technique is analogous to an Inner Order Golden Dawn practice that Mathers utilized regularly.

I.G. BOAZ[217]

The Inner Guard then takes the dagger and rests it upon the right shoulder of the Initiate. He then strikes the flat side of the blade once with his gavel.

I.G. By the sacred duty of my Office as Inner Guard, I proclaim you an Apprentice Mason of the Ecclesiastical Revision of the Antient and Primitive Rite of Memphis+Misraïm. You are henceforward a Free Illuminist! Brother, you shall now be reinvested with that of which you were divested

(Chapel prepares to stomp)

...the LIGHT!

All present stomp and clap at the moment of the words, "the Light" and the Outer Guard removes the Hoodwink at the same instant.

The Inner Guard approaches the Initiate immediately to seal the points-chauds empowerment into the body with the grip. The Grip is made by taking the right hand of the Seeker and pressing with the thumb three times equally on the joint between the index and the metacarpus.

The Outer Guard approaches the Initiate and instructs him in the "Sign" of the Degree.

O.G. Brother, the Sign of an Apprentice Mason is made by taking the right hand to the throat and drawing the hand horizontally across to the right shoulder. Then let it drop to the side arm at full length. This will be of use to you as you *scry the point* of the first Degree on your own.

I.G. Brethren, join me in congratulating our newly made Brother/Sister _____. Let us convene to the Festive Board after we meditate for a few moments upon our labors and Close this Lodge of Entered Apprentices.

All remain silent for a few moments.

Finis.

---

[217] All of these "secrets" of the Grade are taken from the *Compleat Rite of Memphis*, which pulls from Yarker, Marconis and others.

Closing the Chapel

Before the Festive Board, the Chapel should be properly closed. This is an action that is simple, but which functions in a manner similar to that of the *license to depart* in Goetic workings. Much has been *stirred up* by the labors and so these energies need to be returned and relaxed before the group enjoys the common meal. This ritual is decidedly simple in comparison with the formal Opening, yet even within this simple rite we find the Three-fold Path yet again.

- We begin with a pronouncement, and then assume the signs of Good Shepherd and Silence. This is followed by a final Purification of the entire Chapel with the Outer Guard tossing blessed Water in all directions and the Inner Guard making a large cross with the flame and the incense and then scattering salt in the four corners.

- *Illumination*-Then we listen for a space of one minute to the sounds within and around us in the group. We await a "word" or sign from above.

- All is finished with the *sign of peace* as everyone gives each other a fraternal embrace as a sign of Union.

All, including the newly made Brother or Sister, are encouraged to participate in this simple Closing.

The Inner Guard and Outer Guard approach the Holy Altar. They bow in unison towards the East and then say together,

I.G. & O.G. **With us, Brethren, give the sign and response of Egyptian Masonry!**

All assume the sign of the Good Shepherd, right arm over left across the chest and bow deeply towards the East. Then rise back to standing with the pointer finger and medius of the right hand at the lips in the Sign of Silence.

Part Two – Chapter Three: Apprentice

I.G. **Let us perform the final purification!**

Outer Guard takes the water and makes a large benediction across the Chapel, top to bottom, right to left with the water in jubilee.

Inner Guard takes the candle in the left hand and the incense in the right and makes a large cross upon the sacred space. He then takes the paten of salt and at the four corners of the space, sprinkles salt liberally.

O.G. **Let us listen for the sounds of angels' wings and the movement of the spirits, as all who are released at this sacred moment return to their habitations and abodes.**

O.G. makes the sign of the cross in the air with her hand.

All maintain profound silence for the space of one minute.

I.G. **Let us end our labors with the sign of peace.**

Inner Guard embraces the Outer Guard and the Outer Guard moves on to the other participants. The Degree is ended.

Festive Board[218]

The Festive Board functions in part, in a similar manner as an Agape Feast. All present are invited to stay for an extended amount of time to fellowship with each other and share in one of the most common and mindful practices one person can share with another–the meal. It begins with a small amount of formality and then transforms into an organic dinner or brunch as the case may be. The important aspect of the Festive Board is that those who are now *In Free Communion* share in something natural and festive. There is a slight change to the Festive Board in the 3rd Degree which will be explored in that working.

There are 3 "Healths" that are performed in alignment with our "Rule of Three." These are basically the same as the more familiar, *toast* and they are in honor of our newly made Brother or Sister. If, for some reason, there are specific dietary restrictions concerning the partaking of alcoholic beverages, then a substitute drink should be procured. For all others, a hearty red wine is in order. Freemasonry, as an organized entity, began in a pub[219] and has always included something of a *table lodge*. This simple act has sealed many a Lodge, Chapel and Node and should not be taken lightly as cause for reverie. It is celebratory, but it is also sane. What we are essentially celebrating is our Sacred Doctrine in practice—the

---

[218] Sometimes called "Table Lodge" or Banquet.
[219] See the histories of the Goose and the Gridiron and Apple Tree Tavern.

Manifestation of Light. This should be kept in mind throughout the duration of the Festive Board and all should be included who wish to be.

The Festive Board

It is helpful if there is a large table to labor at. If not, wherever the feast can be taken is sufficient. The 3 "Healths" are the organized part of the Festive Board. After these, the feast takes on a more natural and organic format. It is best for the Inner and Outer Guard to memorize the "Healths" in order to lend energy to the naturalness and beneficence of the working. As in all things, the words and phrases are completely amendable to suit the needs of your community.

I.G. **Brethren, come to Order!**

All present assume the sign of the Good Shepherd.

O.G. **Brother Inner Guard, the First Health is to our newly made Brother/Sister _____! Charge and align, my Brethren!**

All present grasp their goblets at "Charge" and raise them to their mouths at "align."

All **To our Worthy Brother _____!**

*All take a **long** draught of their goblet and then promptly return the glass to the table.*

I.G. **Ahh, "how good and how pleasant it is for Brethren to dwell together in Unity." Sister Outer Guard, what is the next Health?**

O.G. **It is to our guests, Brother Inner Guard, both corporeal and incorporeal. To the spirits and bodies that have made this degree effective upon all planes! Charge and align, my Brethren!**

All present grasp their goblets at "Charge" and raise them to their mouths at "align."

All **To the Passed and Present Masters amongst us!**

*All take a **long** draught of their goblet and then promptly return the glass to the table.*

I.G. **And Finally, my Brethren, we offer a "Health" to the Sovereign Architect of the Universe, the ceaseless creativity inherent in all things, and to its working for the cause of Congregational Illuminism and the Antient and Primitive Rite of Memphis+Misraïm!**

O.G. **Charge...and align, my Brethren!**

All present grasp their goblets at "Charge" and raise them to their mouths at "align."

All **To the Sovereign Architect of the Universe!**

*All take a **long** draught of their goblet and then promptly return the glass to the table.*

I.G. **Let us eat together in peace and contentment.**

The dinner or meal takes place and the ceremonies are ended.

CHAPTER FOUR

Second Degree Companion

Just as the conquest of passions and emotions is prescribed for the first degree, thus corresponding to the idea of purification[220], so in the second degree the idea of illumination is put before us in the reminder that its special object is to develop the intellectual, artistic and psychic[221] faculties.

C.W. Leadbeater[222]

---

[220] Here we find Leadbeater supporting the notion of the *Three-fold Path* in relation to Masonic Initiation.
[221] This point cannot be made too strongly--the 2nd Degree of Freemasonry is meant to open the Initiate's eyes to Gnosis. This is the singular reason for the focus upon the letter "G" in many workings of this Degree. The Webb and Preston versions of American Masonry define the "G" in terms of Geometry, predominately, but we find—even in Pike's ritual of this Degree—the Greek spelling of a peculiar type of direct, experiential knowledge. This same knowledge opens the Initiate up to the intermediary beings and realms beyond typical existence.
[222] *The Hidden Life in Freemasonry*, p. 221.

The Entered Apprentice Degree sets the candidate upon a track of purification of the outer and inner Self. Its primary aim is to equilibrate the four elements of the Initiate's personality. Spiritually speaking, the trial and purification by fire should stimulate, as well as balance, the Initiate's passionate and enflamed self. The trial and purification by water should cleanse the doors of perception and open the eyes to the inner world that interacts with the *outer* world constantly. The ordeal of air seeks to balance the intellectual and mental faculties of the Initiate. This reason-centered portion of the whole self often attempts to usurp the throne of the more intuitive and perceptive portions of our being. It must be dealt with harshly at times, so as to allow for the growth of the spirit. Finally, the trial of earth has the effect of alleviating the heaviness of sloth and instigating a journey into the depths of the material, therein to find the "pearl of great price." The thing that we seek is often directly under our feet, if not nine layers beneath the soil in a capitular[223] cavern.

The Second Degree, however, is focused primarily upon *Photismos*–Illumination. This is the experience of seeing, feeling, sensing, hearing–the message(s) from "Otherwhere." Wilmshurst says, "every real Initiate is one who has attained an expansion of consciousness and faculty enabling him to behold the ethereal worlds.[224]" It takes a bit of training to trust this faculty and it also takes an intense amount of purification before the message received is indeed, *trustworthy*. But this aspect of spirit building is crucial to the work of spiritual Freemasonry. There is no other single labor that so swiftly aligns the Initiate to the powers, energies and entities of the spirit realm than that of Illumination. It is a lifelong process of trust in the inner voice, the still-small voice within that, unlike the resounding of rushing waters, often contains one single word of healing, insight or attunement that is of essence to the Work. In the entrance to the Second Degree in Pike's *Porch and Middle Chamber*, the candidate hears the lecture saying,

> *Clemens says that by Baptism souls are illuminated, and led to the pure LIGHT, with which mingles no darkness nor anything material. The Initiate, become an Epoptes, was called a SEER.*[225]

Pike is quoting from St. Clement of Alexandria who gave us quite a bit of information concerning the Mystery Schools of the Ancients. This quote also reminds us of the ecclesiastic quality of our work. In concert with St. Clement, we hear Leadbeater suggesting

---

[223] This is a reference to the York Rite's "Capitular Masonry" which involves the excavation of certain vaults beneath the earth's surface. The Scottish & Memphis Rites utilize the Royal Arch of Enoch, which unveils this mysterious journey, nine vaults below the crust.
[224] *The Masonic Initiation*, p. 65.
[225] p. 265

a "parallel between the passing of a F.C. (Fellowcraft) and the ecclesiastical ordination to the diaconate.[226]" That Masonic Initiation is a spiritual experience is well established.

Though our primary focus in this degree is *Illumination*, we still engage in the other three portions of the path. At each interval, we affirm the necessity of *Purification, Illumination* and *Union*. The purification aspect of this degree is in the form of an interrogation. This purifies the sphere of the Initiate that holds too tightly to the ego. When it comes to questions of the soul and the spirit, right and wrong–proofs and evidence– fall to the wayside. What is needed is a pinpoint, razor-sharp ability to be present and on the spot. If this manner of spontaneity is eschewed for memory work, intellectual argumentation and didactics, then what one is left with is a dry skeleton. We are concerned with the meat, the flesh, and the juices of life. These juices are transfigured for the Spirit Mason and become the bread of Life, Manna from Heaven, the Holy Graal. The interrogation cuts to the quick and calls the ego to task. This ego that we have all carefully constructed over time, does nothing for our spiritual journey but hack away at the labors we undertake. The ego asserts its authority like a security guard who attempts to arrest a shopkeeper for honoring a coupon. His role is rather ridiculous, but we feed him, clothe him and give him a place of honor in our lives. The interrogation of the Second Degree is designed to de-throne this madman[227]!

The Labyrinth

The bridge between the *Purification* stage and the *Illumination* stage is one of the most beautiful and simple practices that we inherit from the Knights Templar[228]. All across Europe, during the period of the great Cathedral builders, labyrinths of varying designs and shapes began to crop up on the floors of the most exquisite cathedrals. According to Tradition[229], the Knights Templar are responsible for these gorgeous examples of sacred geometry. The theory suggests that the labyrinth became a metaphor for the pilgrimage to

---

[226] *The Hidden Life in Freemasonry*, p. 243. This is discussed further in the 3rd Year, *Monastery of the Seven Rays*.
[227] In our own Chapel, we have experienced a complete transmutation of an Initiate from this singular Interrogation. Their life was fundamentally altered by this mystery.
[228] See Lauren Artress's, *Walking a Sacred Path: Rediscovering the Labyrinth as a Spiritual Practice*.
[229] See *Les Mystères de la Cathédrale de Chartres*, published by Robert Laffont.

Jerusalem. For those who could not afford the long journey from France to the Holy Land, or who could not afford the protection of the Knights along the way, the labyrinth was a Holy substitute[230] path that would take the parishioner to the center of the *Heavenly Jerusalem*, symbolized in many of the Philosophical Degrees of the Scottish and Memphis+Misraïm Rites. For us, the labyrinth becomes a tool for meditation[231], a symbol that comprises the *Three-fold Path* within itself, a bridge to Illumination and–the Mystical Winding Staircase of traditional Masonry. The center of the labyrinth becomes the Middle Chamber, or *Sanctum Sanctorum* of King Solomon's Temple.

The Steps

In, *The Porch and the Middle Chamber*, we find Pike saying,

> *Upon the tracing-board of this degree you see the representation of the front of King Solomon's Temple, with a winding stairway of three, five, and seven steps. It is the great symbol of our Order, and has more than one meaning. Whether you will learn them all will depend upon yourself.*[232]

These steps are all present within the labyrinth and can be explored in a variety of ways.

- *The seven steps.* The labyrinth we utilize in our Chapel is of the simple, 7-circuit variety. As is customary in this branch of Masonry, there is ample room for innovation and creativity in this area. In traditional Masonry, the **seven** steps of the winding staircase allude to the 7 Liberal Arts and Sciences of the Ancients. We retain this symbolism, as well as including the many other correspondences with the number seven that the Western Mystery Tradition has purported for centuries. These include, but are not limited to; the seven ancient planets and their symbolic qualities, the seven ancient metals, the seven days of the week, the seven sided vault of Christian Rosencreutz, the seven-branched candlestick of the Temple, the seventh Sephirah Venus, the seven of wands, pentacles, cups and swords of the Tarot, etc.

- *The five steps* of the traditional winding staircase, for us symbolize the five elements whose qualities are experienced while walking the labyrinth. The *Earth* is the place of the labyrinth, as it is drawn upon the ground or created with stones or hedges. While walking the labyrinth, the quality that often arises is one of grounding, of finding our place and sensing the solidity of our path—even while it is winding. *Water*

---

[230] Here an analogy might be made to the "substitute" for the Master's Word.
[231] "It is not necessary to sit down to meditate, for meditation can be done while one is walking, working, or actively doing something which does not require the fullness of attention, but only a relaxed mental overview." Michael-Paul Bertiaux, *Cosmic Meditation*, Fulgur Limited, 2007, p. 3.
[232] p. 229

symbolizes the receptive state that we are in as we walk this sacred path. In the beginning of the walk, we may take in the surroundings and get ourselves firmly placed upon the path, but as we spiral inwards towards the center, so our receptivity becomes more centralized and pinpointed. *Air* is physically experienced with every breeze when the labyrinth is constructed outdoors, yet it is the quality of *expansion of consciousness* that accompanies this meditative walk. Our solitary walking of a circuitous route begins to mirror our life with its twists and turns, our relationships with their natural ebb and flow, and even further outward—the rotation of our earth upon its axis, the revolutions of the earth about the sun, the circumpolar constellations that move inward and outward around the pole through the changing of seasons, etc. *Fire* represents the active nature of this form of mediation. Rather than a sitting practice, we are moving our bodies upon the earth in this form of walking meditation. Fire is also symbolic of the purifying quality of the path and the harnessing of passionate energy. These two are subtle realizations, but are common with practice and frequency. Though the labyrinth is specifically utilized in the Fellowcraft initiations of our method, it becomes a working tool for the Mason and even crops up a second time in our series when we receive the 52nd Degree of *Sage of the Labyrinth*. *Spirit* is the fifth and final element of the Western Tradition and it is the heart of the labyrinth itself. In the same way that a practitioner of Qi-Gong might experience a sensation of heat in his feet while performing a posture[233], which is a confirmation of establishing and experiencing the nature of Chi itself, the walker of the labyrinth has moments of deep transcendence which may or may not be accompanied by physical sensations. Some have described this as a sense of being transported to *Otherwhere* while walking the path, and others have had the sensation of floating upon the path–while yet still others experience an intense grounding and firm placement—a sort of sensation of being settled in one's skin.

- *The three steps* of the traditional winding staircase are the Three-fold Path itself for the walker of our sacred labyrinth. As one first enters the path, he or she moves through the purifying stage—laying aside all earthly cares, as it were. Next, she begins to open to what the labyrinth may have to teach her. A word may arise in the mind or a vision may accompany this illuminating stage. Finally, union is experienced with the path itself. In the center of the labyrinth, it is as if one can look out upon one's own life journey and see the various twists and turns and how the center was always just within

---

[233] I had this experience while at Naropa University, training with a teacher of Tai-Chi and Qi-gong. It was immediate, sharp and experiential.

reach. It is a profound moment of ecstatic union and spiritual evolution when this portion of the initiation "takes." Life is no longer experienced as a linear movement from the cradle to the grave. It is an ever deepening and penetrating movement into the mysteries that lay before us. As Leadbeater says, "the winding form of the staircase may be thought to indicate that evolution is always in the form of a spiral, not of a straight line.[234]"

† † †

The *Illumination* phase of our Work becomes more sophisticated and depth oriented in this degree. The Initiate performs his first Bibliomancy for others, a process enjoyed by all who attend every *Opening of the Chapel*, yet reserved for those beyond the 1st Degree. This simple practice takes the shape of an oracular device, which is completely individualized to the Initiate in question. Alongside the use of art of Bibliomancy, is the use of the traditional Masonic plumb-line attached to the 2nd Degree. In Haitian Masonic Lodges, this architectural tool has an occult significance. It can be utilized as a pendulum and employed in divination. An extension to this could be found in the 4th Degree of Discreet Master, whose symbol is a key. The key can be used in like manner as the plumb-line for cleidomantic divination. Additionally, the Initiate undergoes a *Pathworking*[235] in this grade that sets his or her foot upon the path of the Egyptian Mysteries in a unique and "self-initiatory" manner. This is rather original in that it is in a Lodge-type setting that one is presented with a "self-initiation." This further builds trust within the group and exhibits the incredibly individualized quality of our initiatory work. Finally, the Initiate is given a brief lecture and experience with the "eye in the Square and Compasses" by the sacred letter, "G." This has been explored fully by other luminaries, yet in our own work it takes a unique significance. In the Second Degree of the Scottish Rite, Pike says, "The letter G is not displayed as the initial letter of the word Geometry, but of the more significant Greek word GNOSIS[236]."

The "Secrets" of the Degree are presented and the points-chauds empowerment is given to complete the *Union* stage of our labors. This approach compacts the vast material of our Rite into a single, enlightening and physically experienced, "A ha!" moment, where the Initiate is given time and space to actually *feel* the transformation that accompanies enlightenment. As the focus in the Fellowcraft Degree is upon *Illumination*, the Initiate is

---

[234] *The Hidden Life in Freemasonry*, p. 240
[235] Technically speaking, this isn't a "Pathworking," as that name denotes the paths of the Tree of Life, however, the process is synonymous with the practice of having a passage read to an Initiate to stimulate the trance-space necessary to enter the mysteries.
[236] *The Porch and the Middle Chamber*, p. 212.

given a simple lecture and instruction in visualizing the points-chaud empowerment as it is activated within the body. The action is dual—sensing the electricity and spiritual transmission coming from the Facilitator, and his or her connection to the Egregore, and the inner awakening of the already present, yet latent, points-chaud itself.

In the Higher Degrees, all three stages of the Three-fold Path *can be* fulfilled and utilized through the simplest means, the "Secrets" of the work. It is in this way that we unite the often contending approaches of *realization* and *attainment.* Western mystics sometimes approach the divine with the sense that one attains to union by degrees or increments, while the East has always favored a more immediate and instantaneous realization. As Knights of the East *and of the* West, we merge these two notions in the Higher Degrees. In our approach to Masonry, we are not building in a linear fashion, towards some omega point— a more complicated, more stimulating, more advanced or more lavish initiation at the 97th Degree— we are actually working towards a radical and Holy simplicity, which is an inward movement of the soul. Not only does this lack of linear movement reflect the soul's journey, but it also relieves the system of the frantic one-upmanship and power plays that accompany group working based upon hierarchical structures. The first three degrees are grounding, in that they set the Initiate's feet firmly upon the path so that he or she can take the succeeding steps on their own when duly and truly prepared. They have an equilibrating effect upon the personality that establishes the Initiate safely and deeply within the Holy Egregore of the Ecclesiastical Revision of the APRM+M. The *Hauts Grades* of Book Three are the deepening of the Work and require little to no elaboration or dramatics. They are pure Mystery and pure Initiation. They are the children of the Primitive Doctrine, the Primitive Faith and the Primitive Religion of the Ancients.

Order of Work

The *Order of Work* for the Second Degree consists of the following:
- Opening the Chapel
- The Chamber of Reflection
- Interrogation in the Chapel
- The Labyrinth
- The Mystic Rite of Vision (Bibliomancy & Pathworking)
- Secrets of the Work/points-chauds empowerment

Part Two – Chapter Four: Companion

Materials Needed

The materials needed for the Second Degree include those for the Opening found in the "Preliminaries" section of Chapter Two. There are only a few additions to these.

- A skull is used once again in the Chamber of Reflection. For this degree, it is best if you have one of the scientific variety that has the removable cranium. If this is not feasible, make appropriate substitutions as needed.
- You will need chalk to draw the labyrinth (instruction for drawing such can be easily obtained with an internet search of "how to draw a 7-circuit Labyrinth"). If a more permanent Labyrinth is desired, large stones could be used, or the path could be formed of peanut rock, or outlined by hedges or even simply an area of cut grass. For those with space limitations, the Labyrinth can be drawn and painted upon a large board and used as a visual aid with the Candidate tracing slowly his finger along the path. If the work is to be undertaken at night, lighting is a consideration[237].
- At the entrance to the Labyrinth, two candle stands[238] are appropriate. They should flank the entrance. The one on the left should be black and the one on the right should be white. These represent the entrance to King Solomon's Temple.
- The Jewel for the Companion Degree is similar to the Apprentice. The only difference is that the compasses are interlocked with the square. This signifies the intermingling of the divine with the human.

---

[237] In our Chapel, the Labyrinth is lit by seven candles with colors that correspond to the seven planets.
[238] These are occultly linked to Jachin & Boaz. In this way, the walker of the labyrinth becomes the third pillar, the Middle Pillar.

2nd *degree,* Companion.

Companion

*The Chamber of Reflection should be ready for the 2nd portion of the **Interrogation**. The cranium piece of the skull should be loosened and a small cup of red wine should be placed next to the skull. The usual emblems of death may be present as well.*

After the Opening, the Outer Guard retrieves the Initiate in waiting and presents them the Seeker robe for a second time. After clothing him, the Outer Guard hoodwinks the Initiate and conducts him from the waiting room to the Chapel.

As the Candidate enters the Chapel, all should rise and resume the sign of Egyptian Masonry, right arm crossed over left upon the chest. The gong is struck twice slowly and the Initiate is seated in a chair before the altar. The Inner Guard approaches in silence and West of the Altar addresses the Initiate:

I.G. Brother (or Sister) Seeker, I am about to ask you a series of questions. I ask that you respond sincerely and without hesitation. Do you consent to this Interrogation?

Candidate **I do.**

I.G. It is well. Take a moment to call upon your secret Center for assistance. When you are ready to begin, please say, "So mote it be."

Purification

Pause

Initiate **"So mote it be."**

I.G. Brother Seeker, we believe that we have the Key to the Mysteries. To receive this prized possession, you must work your way upwards through the Degrees and positions of attainment in our august Fraternity. Do you wish to proceed?

Initiate answers

I.G. To experience our form of illumination, you must perform our Rites and accept our teachings as Holy Writ. Do you wish to proceed?

Initiate answers

I.G. By aligning yourself with this Order, you thereby, of necessity, limit certain freedoms of innovation and individuality. Do you wish to proceed?

Initiate answers

I.G. To receive the degree of Fellow of the Craft, you must take a solemn oath to the Order and to your Inner Guard, pledging your fidelity and willingness to be led by us. Do you wish to proceed?

Initiate answers

† † †

*If the Initiate answers, "No" to any of the above questions, the I.G., O.G. and all of the Chapel members cheer uproariously and follow with the chant of, "**HUZZA, HUZZA, HUZZA**[239]!" This is followed by the I.G. congratulating the Initiate on escaping the wrath of the Interrogator. They then proceed to the reading of the Four Articles of Congregational Illuminism. If, however, the Initiate answers yes to the questions, he or she is caused to rise in silence, be hoodwinked, and conducted into the Chamber of Reflection. The O.G. positions her hands on the hoodwink, while the I.G. takes the skull and raises it to head level in front of the Initiate. The I.G. then says,*

I.G. Brother Seeker, we wish to congratulate you on your efforts in the Interrogation. Now, we are pleased to introduce you to the Grand Interrogator himself who will present you with his reward!

O.G. removes hoodwink and in the darkness, the only thing visible is the skull in front of the Candidate's face.

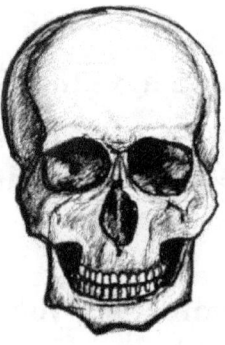

---

[239] Traditional celebratory exclamation, later becoming "hurrah."

The I.G. continues,

I.G. Brother Seeker, the purpose of this Interrogation is purification of the ego. The Outer Guard will now read you the very simple principles which Congregational Illuminism is founded upon. But first, you must drink from the cup of equality[240].

O.G. pours the small amount of red wine into the cranium of the skull and serves it to the Initiate. Then reads the following principles;

O.G. 1. Spiritual growth is incompatible with authoritarian structure.
    2. Scientific Illuminism requires a non-dogmatic, experimental approach.
    3. A free society linked in free communion should be actualized.
    4. We facilitate, we do not lead. We do the Work, we do not extract oaths or dues, or require dogmatic beliefs.

I.G. You see, my Brother, in our branch of the Masonic tree, the smallest unit is not the Lodge, it is the individual. The Administrative degrees and titles we retain are simply signs of greater service to our fellow man. We gladly offer mutual aid and assistance to all our Brothers and Sisters across the globe, but we do so freely and in the spirit of peace and harmony. Let this Interrogation be a reminder to you to never put yourself in such a passive condition as to agree to limit your own free will or place yourself in the position of servitude to another man.

Initiate is re-hoodwinked and conducted to the pre-drawn Labyrinth. This will in most cases be outdoors, but the substitute of a painted Tracing Board of the Labyrinth is completely appropriate.

---

[240] This action is in reference to certain Knights Templar practices as well as to the esoteric work within Tibetan Buddhism.

The Initiate is placed at the opening of the Labyrinth in between[241] two candles on stands, representing the two outer columns of King Solomon's Temple, the hoodwink is removed and the O.G. directs accordingly.

O.G. Brother Seeker, you now stand at the entrance to King Solomon's Temple. You are between the two columns of Severity and Mercy. The Sanctum Sanctorum or Holy of Holies lies in the center of this Labyrinth. That is your destination. This journey, like all in our Craft, is individual. No one can take this step for you. When you are ready, begin your walking meditation. When you reach the center, you may want to take a moment to yourself. Then, exit the same way that you came in[242].

Illumination

After the Initiate has finished the Labyrinth Meditation, he is re-hoodwinked and conducted back into the Chapel, there to begin the Illumination phase of the Degree. He is returned to the Interrogation chair which should be placed close enough for the Initiate's hands to be rested upon the VSL[243] for a moment before the Bibliomantic divination is performed. Once the Initiate is in place, the I.G. places his hands upon the Initiate's hands on top of the VSL and says,

I.G. Brother Seeker, the especial word of our Second Degree is Illumination. You are about to embark upon your second Sacred Journey of the night, but before doing so, you will be instructed in a method of Divination by the Outer Guard. Sister Outer Guard...

The Outer Guard places her hands upon the Inner Guard's hands which are still resting upon the Initiate's. The O.G. instructs the Initiate in the method of Bibliomancy, telling him to feel the book and thumb through its pages until moved to stop. Then, she instructs him to use his pointer finger to

---

[241] This position makes of the Initiate herself, the Middle Pillar.
[242] This spiraling is indicative of the nature of our work altogether. It is a deepening, rather than a lineal process.
[243] This traditional gesture reminds the Masonic reader of the taking of the obligation, but again in this instance it is connected with divination. The hand upon the Holy book aligns the energies of the individual with spirit filled words.

land upon a particular portion of the page. Once performed, she reads the selectection as well as a small portion before and after where the Initiate's finger is placed. The Outer Guard writes down the specifics of the finding to give to the Initiate after the Degree. When ended, the I.G. says,

I.G. **The Word of Truth!**

All **Thanks be to the Ages.**

O.G. allows the Initiate's hands to relax.

I.G. It is now time for your second journey, Brother Seeker. I would ask you to put yourself at ease and begin to breathe in an even and slow manner. With your vision obscured and in this sacred Chapel, you will now be transported to the Holy land of Egypt. Here now the words of our Brethren!

Reader *(may be a guest, the I.G. or O.G.)*[244]

> "The principal seat of the mysteries was at Memphis. They were of two kinds, the greater and the lesser; the former taught by the Priests of Isis and Serapis, the latter by those of Osiris. The candidate was required to furnish proof of a pure life as an evidence that he was fitted for enrollment, (in our parlance that he was worthy.) When these conditions were fulfilled, he was required to spend a week in solitude and meditation, abstain from all unchaste acts and confine himself to a light diet, and to purify his blood by frequent ablutions and severe mortifications of the flesh. Being thus prepared, the candidate was ordered to enter the pyramid during the night, when head to descend on his hands and knees through a narrow passage without steps, until he reached a cave-like opening, through which he had to crawl to another subterranean cave, on the wall of which he found inserted the following words: *'The mortal who shall travel over this road alone without hesitancy or looking behind*, shall be punished by fire, by water and by air, and if he can surmount the fear of death he shall emerge from the bosom of the earth, he shall revisit the light and claim the right to prepare his soul for the reception of the mysteries of the great God Osiris. At the same time three priests, disguised in masks resembling the heads of jackals, and armed with swords, sought to frighten him, first by their appearance and voice, afterwards by enumerating the dangers that waited him on his journey. If his courage did not fail him here, he was permitted to pass on to the hall of fire. This was a large apartment lined with burning stuffs, and whose floor was a grate painted to flame color; the bars of this grate were so

---

[244] This form of the Mystic Rite of Vision is akin to Pathworking. With the vision suspended, the Initiate is taken on an inward journey of visualization. This practice is preparatory for scrying the points-chaud empowerment.

narrow that they offered scarcely room enough for him to cross. Through this hall he was obliged to pass with the greatest of speed to prevent being burned and avoid the intense heat and flame. He next encountered a wide channel fed from the waters of the Nile. Over this stream he was obliged to swim, with a small lamp, which furnished all the light that was afforded him. On reaching the opposite side, he found a narrow passage leading to a place about six feet square, the floor of which was made movable by mechanism underneath; on each side were walls of rough stone, and behind wheels of metal were fixed; in front was a gate of ivory opening inward and preventing any further advance. On attempting to turn two large rings annexed to the door in hopes of continuing his journey, the wheels came into motion, producing a most terrific and stunning effect, and the floor gave way, leaving him suspended by the arms over apparently a deep abyss, from which proceeded a violent and piercing current of cold air, so that the lamp was extinguished, and he remained in complete darkness. In this process of trial, it will be observed that the candidate was exposed to the action of the four great purifying elements—Earth, Air, Fire and Water. After the risk of falling into an unknown depth, continued for a moment or two, the floor resumed its original position, the wheels ceased to revolve, and the doors of ivory flew open, disclosing the Sanctuary of Isis, illuminated with a blaze of light, where the priests of that goddess were assembled, drawn up in two ranks, clothed in ceremonial dresses, and bearing the mysterious symbols of the order, singing hymns in praise of their divinity, who welcomed and congratulated him on his courage and escape from the danger which had surrounded him. The entrance to the Sanctuary was constructed in the pedestal of the triple statue of Isis, Osiris and Horus, and the walls were ornamented with various allegorical figures, symbols of the Egyptian mysteries...On the morning of the day appointed for the ceremony, the priests assembled in the temple, when the most precious treasures belonging to the Sanctuary were displayed, and repaired to the Chapel of Isis, to bring sacrifice to the Goddess, covered with a veil of white silk...The curtain was now raised, and the renewed shouts of the spectators greeted him, as an adept. The ceremonies concluded with a festival (banquet) which lasted three days, during which the newly made brother occupied the seat of honor.[245]"

---

[245] Calvin C Burt, *The Egyptian Masonic History...*, p. 119-123. This quote appears in other Masonic reference books and degree collections as well.

After the reading, all sit in silence for a moment. Then, the I.G. gives the instruction on the Eye in the square and compasses, the letter "G" and the Magical Imagination.

I.G. Brother Seeker, true Initiation is the Manifestation of Light. This occurs in many ways, one of which you just experienced by virtue of the meditation on the Egyptian Mysteries. Whether it occurred then, or if it is at a later date when you re-read the ritual, what this form of pathworking accomplishes is the opening of the Magical Imagination, the Ontic Sphere. The Emblematic working of Freemasonry in England often utilizes the image of the square and compasses with the eye and the G in the center. This alludes to the experience of illumination known as *Gnosis,* and to the Magical Imagination which acts as an inner Eye. As we near the "Secrets" of the grade and labor to bring you to Light, allow your Magical Imagination to activate. When you receive the points-chaud empowerment, you WILL see the latent point of energy within your body awaken and you WILL see the rush of etheric force from the Egregore through the Facilitator and into the true Temple, your body.

Union

All participants approach the Holy Altar and form a circle around the Initiate. The Inner Guard places the drawn Jewel of a Fellowcraft (square and compasses interlaced, rule at the base) upon the Initiate's neck. The Inner Guard then takes the gavel and says;

I.G. Brother Seeker, the Outer Guard will once again assist you in standing in the sign of a Free Man (*or* **Woman**).

Outer Guard assists the Initiate to stand in the sign of the Pentagram. Then the Inner Guard strikes the alter in five solemn and loud strokes,

I.G. *(Battery of Five knocks, 3 and 2)* **XXX XX**

Then the Inner Guard takes a moment to concentrate upon the jewel on the breast of the Initiate, after a silent invocation, he vibrates the Sacred Word of a Fellowcraft Mason strongly, while giving the points-chaud empowerment on the top of the head, just below the first point.

I.G. **JACHIN** *(The Jah portion of the word is carried out in full and given emphasis)*

The Inner Guard then takes the dagger and rests it upon the left shoulder of the Initiate. He then strikes the flat side of the blade twice with his gavel.

I.G. By the sacred duty of my office as Inner Guard, I proclaim you a Companion and Fellow of the Craft. You are... Illuminatus, my Brother!

All present stomp and clap at the moment of the words, "Illuminatus" and the Outer Guard removes the hoodwink at the very same instant.

The Inner Guard approaches the Initiate immediately to seal the points-chaud empowerment into the body with the grip. The grip of a Fellowcraft is made by taking the right hand and pressing with the thumb five times on the first phalange of the middle finger, then place the thumb between the phalange and that of the second finger. The I.G. then places the thumb on the first phalange of the middle finger and presses lightly with his thumb-nail[246].

The Outer Guard approaches the sealed Initiate and instructs him in the sign of the Degree.

O.G. Brother, the sign of a Companion Mason is made by placing the right hand on the heart, the fingers bunched up as though to seize an object; then lifting the left hand, palm in front, the elbow touching the body. Draw the right hand towards the right flank and let it fall to the side; drop the left hand to the side to complete the sign. This sign will be of further use to you as you *scry the point* of the Second Degree on your own.

I.G. Brethren, join me in congratulating our newly made Brother_____. HUZZA, HUZZA, HUZZA!

All approach the Brother and embrace him fraternally.

Let us convene to the Festive Board after we meditate in silence for a few moments upon this evening's labors and close this Chapel of Companion Masons.

Silence reigns throughout the Chapel.

Finis

---

[246] *Compleat Rite of Memphis*

CHAPTER FIVE

Third Degree Master

For each the "day," the opportunity for work at self-perfecting, is duly given; for each the "night" cometh when no man can work at that task; which morning and evening constitute but one creative day of the soul's life, each portion of that day being a necessary complement to the other. Perfect man has to unify these opposites in himself; so that for him, as for his Maker, the darkness and the light become both alike.

Wilmshurst[247]

---

[247] *The Meaning of Masonry*, Kessinger Publishing re-print, p. 123.

The *Sacred Doctrine* is the "manifestation of Light." Thus far in our work, the Initiate has been provided with numerous opportunities to perceive this secret fire, this luminous darkness that is secret insomuch as it requires a form of initiation to arise in one's consciousness. The Initiate has been administered two of the points-chauds empowerments, has been given several "Mystic Rite's of Vision" and has been placed and initiated in a geographical sacred marma or "thin place" where the veil of this world and the next is tenuous. None of this guarantees that the *Sacred Doctrine* is realized. These are simply opportunities for such spiritual advancement. That being said, our formula of the *Three-fold Path* and the nature of our labors under the *Ecclesiastical* Revision of the APRM+M elicit a decidedly spiritual quality to the initiatory process. Our form of initiation is spiritually stimulative. We hear Leadbeater speaking of a similar approach where he suggests that,

> *It is part of the plan of Freemasonry to stimulate the activity of these forces in the human body, in order that evolution may be quickened...the stimulation of these nerves and the forces which flow through them is only a small part of the benefit conferred.*[248]

We are establishing the *Scintillating Body* through the various points empowerments[249] and we are building the foundation of the *Mystic Temple* through the frequency of our work within our sacred marmas. Through our "Mystic Rites of Vision," the Initiate becomes an *Epopt* or SEER, which is of the utmost importance when the primitive simplicity of the *Hauts Grades* is experimented with.

The overall story of the Initiate's journey comes full circle in the Master's Degree. Through our simplified version[250] of this difficult degree, we are firmly placed in the balanced position of equipoise, there to fully digest the spontaneous and exacting nature of the forthcoming, *Hauts Grades*. It becomes clear that these three degrees are in themselves *a complete and harmonious system of initiation* as well as preparatory for the Primitive Doctrine of the Higher Degrees. In this way, one discovers a marked economy to the drama of the 3rd Degree in our working. Our Master Mason degree, though sufficient unto itself, is *the bridge* to the Ecclesiastical empowerments of the Degrees from 4-97th[251].

The Initiate has experienced the purifying nature of the First degree, with its ordeals and trials of earth, air, fire and water. He has ingested the sacred ankh and been given a simple

---

[248] *The Hidden Life in Freemasonry*, pgs. 260-261.
[249] As well as--at least in this simplified three-degree system--in the moments of "Knighting" and in the *breathing upon the Initiate* in the 3rd Degree. Both of these are inherited from the Egyptian Rite of Cagliostro.
[250] It should be noted that though this is a simplified version of the grade, even the Hauts Grades version of this degree, which is more efficient and in keeping with divine economy, transfers the "essence" of the Degree. This has been exhibited in our work through reports from Seer's as the points empowerments are given. Still, the ritual working of a three Degree system leads to the necessary soul work and knowing of one's self to effectively and safely integrate the 97 empowerments.
[251] Book Three

methodology for opening the inner eye. He has suffered the Interrogation that began the purifying of the Ego and he has entered the holy land of Egypt through a form of Pathworking. He has been partially Knighted on the left and the right shoulder. He has been given the "Secrets" of the degrees and told that they are to be used later in *Scrying the Point*. He has entered the Middle Chamber of King Solomon's Temple, between the two pillars of Mercy and Severity, in a labyrinthine manner—indicative of the spiritual journey itself. He is duly and truly prepared for this last dramatic ritual. Mystically, this ritual places the Initiate in a position of balance. He is prepared for the reception of the most Sacred Word[252] of the Symbolic Degrees. He is prepared to make a greater sacrifice of himself for others. In a quiet way, this Degree alludes to one of the secrets of the *Administrative Degrees, 90-97th* in Book Three, whose watchword is service.

Voudon+Gnostic

It is imperative that the I.G and O.G. of the Chapel perform this degree with the greatest solemnity. Though the Officers may be on friendly terms with the Initiate at this point, it is of the utmost importance that the Officers put themselves into a meditative state for this Degree, to ensure that the Initiate has the ability to travel to that unknown land where initiation fully "takes." This Degree opens wide the rays from the true *Sovereign Sanctuary*, the "Grand Lodge Above" as it is often named, and calls forth energies and entities that are peculiarly attached to the funereal Rite that ensues. At the alchemical moment, for instance, when the I.G. and O.G. reverse their collars[253] and aprons—exhibiting the skulls and crossbones of their regalia to those Masters of the Past who are invited to join in the Ceremony—a rush of etheric force and energy descend upon the Mystic Temple. The Ghuédé of Voudon may show up. In particular, the likes of Bawon Samedi may appear, as he is a powerful Freemason attached to the grave. We must recall that this Ecclesiastical Revision occurred in a *particular place* and that place was originally Haiti. For those Facilitators who are versed in this sacred Tradition, the "Festive Board" that follows the Masters Degree becomes the *Fet Ghuédé*[254]. In our own workings, the presence of Ghuédé has been intuited during this Rite in a way that differs from traditional Haitian Vodou, as the Masters begin to become conduits for Ghuédé energy in a mystical manner rather than a possessive one. Each Lodge/Chapel will have its own experience with this energy and this

---

[252] It should be noted that the Sacred Word of the Third Degree is, in fact, *a substitute* for the Master's Word.
[253] In some Chapels, Lodges and Nodes, the regalia of the Rites of Memphis-Misraïm will want to be procured for this and other moments of Enlightenment. The collar and apron are both reversible and reveal a black ground with skulls and tear drops.
[254] The Fet may be a simple celebratory Festive Board, but may also be more of an invitation to the Ghuédé—where members of the Chapel, Lodge or Node offer gifts to the spirits and welcome them with their veves and emblems of the dead.

family of beings, but we would do well to heed Hector F. Jean-Maine's words concerning their arrival:

> *This is what Ghuédé does when He comes to us. I say it is telepathy only because the energy is close to some descriptions of telepathy. Others can call it 'intuition'. It is a form of intuition when we know that something is indeed in the past and yet in the given and now. So this altar, because of my intuition of Ghuédé, is both away in time yet now, here, in time*[255].

Though our movements are simple and the dramatics are economized, we inherit the spiritual legacy of Gnostic, Masonic and Voudon schemas through the Egregoric transmission from the Holy Arabia Mountain. This is why this material is not written in a self initiatory manner. It simply would not work. There *must be* physical touch from one person, whose lines of transmission refer back to Arabia Mountain, to get the full benefit of the working. For this work, the only other possible option would be one who has independent lines from Michael-Paul Bertiaux, who is the spiritual source[256] (with his inheritance from the Jean-Maine lineage of Haiti) of the work upon the Mountain. Either stream may use this material with efficacy, but one operating without such physical transmission of the Tradition would be hard pressed[257] to *call upon* the necessary energies to enliven, stimulate and inform the Initiate's Ontic sphere (Magickal Imagination fed by Higher Rays such as the Second, or Christ Ray) for true Initiation.

At this juncture it is imperative that all involved, including the Officers, reassess the overall purpose of this form of Masonry. What are we doing? Spirit building, yes, but what is the point of it all? What we are laboring to do is to duly and truly prepare Initiates to carry on the work of the Ecclesiastical Revision of the APRM+M, so to further the "Manifestation of Light" to our neighbors, our society and the world. Knowing full well that these points-chauds empowerments–once being utilized by an Initiate who is thoroughly grounded in the Tradition via Holy Orders or previous Masonic work, or an allied 3-degree system of spiritual training, or through *this* series of Masonic Degrees here presented–have the quadruple capacity of attunement, empowerment, initiation and therapy, we can readily see that this is a system that the world is in great need of today. Couple the benefits of the empowerments themselves with the freedom of working within Congregational Illuminism, outside of the game of competition, degree-mongering, rank oriented one-upmanship and the like, and this approach becomes prophetic of things to come. Seekers are tiring of the petty politics of groups and the lack of efficacy of staged out

---

[255] p. 126, *Vudu Cartography*, Michael Bertiaux.

[256] In 1985 Bertiaux issued T Allen Greenfield his Charter to further the work of this Haitian branch of the APRM+M.

[257] This isn't impossible, it is simply rare. An analogous example of someone achieving such spiritual relations with an egregore would be Robert Ambelain and his invocation of the Old Master, *Chenu*, in reawakening the work of the Élus Coëns.

mystery plays[258]. They are searching for Truth and they are espousing ideals of Freedom that were never dreamt of prior to this century. What we are doing, in essence, is re-establishing the *primitive faith* of the Ancients. It is simple and it is efficient. It has effects that are far-reaching, yet it is grounded in the daily. In essence, we are *spirit building*.

The Opening

This is the first Degree in which the Initiate is invited to participate in the formal Opening. The reason for this is manifold. Firstly, the Candidate has gone through a thorough purification and so that stage of the Opening will have meaning, symbolically. Secondly, the Initiate has now experienced multiple, *Mystic Rites of Vision* where he was given a moment to see, hear, feel or experience, within the Imaginal, something by way of a stimulating vision within the Degree. This time he is able to perform the task for others in the Bibliomancy stage of the Opening. As the Master Mason Degree alludes to the Union stage of our *Three-fold Path*, the Initiate will find the Chain of Union as well as the Masonic Middle Pillar strange and interesting. This suggestive action, placing the Initiate in a ceremony that he is not use to[259], yet in which he does not have his sight deprived, begins the disorientation process that flows directly from the Opening to the Purification stage of the Degree. All Officers and guests must maintain the most proper decorum during this transition to effectively translate the meaning of the ordeal.

---

[258] Often we hear of the Seeker who asks, are there any *Operative* elements to this form of Masonry? This is precisely related to the efficacy intimated here.
[259] There are subtle references here to traditional Masonry.

Purification

The actions that flow from the Opening to the Purification stage of the degree are subtle, yet the shift of feeling and emotive context is palpable. The I.G. and O.G. may actually *feel* the layers of discomfort that accompany this strange dramatic twist. The *Passed Masters* who have gladly joined in this momentous occasion may decide to interrupt and make themselves known in some way during this moment. As we are moving from scripted out dramatics to the Primitive Doctrine of the *Hauts Grades*, there is more room for spontaneity and immediate working with the spirits. As the Initiate is being congratulated for his efforts, a sinister presence enters the sacred space. It is not to be feared, for as Wilmshurst says in the introductory quote, "darkness and the light both become alike." This presence is within all of us. It is our shadow self, to use Jungian terms. No real Initiation will ever dispense with this presence, as it is indicative of the "dweller on the Threshold" who will be met when the Initiate performs the private work, in particular, through *Scrying the Point*. This "dweller" is not pure evil, but it does have the quality of an abrasive which is necessary in perfecting the stone[260]. Until the barnacles are thoroughly scraped from the ship, the voyage will not be a smooth one.

Illumination

One of the more difficult portions of this degree has absolutely no dramatics whatsoever. It is a space of ten consecutive minutes of pure silence. The Initiate, covered by the funereal pall, is alone with the alone. During this sacred moment the I.G. and O.G. and all guests present, should be in whatever meditative posture that they find comfortable[261]. This is a group meditation on the nature of death, of putrefaction. This is a congregational *memento mori*, which the Chamber of Reflection alludes to.

As the overall ceremonial of the Master Mason Degree is rather austere, the Illumination stage has only two phases. The first phase is when the mystical Psalm 50 (51 in KJV) is chanted over the dead Initiate[262]. This action is taken directly from the work of the Divine Cagliostro and continues the theme of Egyptian Masonry being hidden under the cloak of Christianity, especially in the Coptic regions such as Egypt and Ethiopia. This is followed by the second Pathworking[263], which is the continuation of the story that was told in the 2nd

---

[260] Many Lodges include a *rough ashlar*, or unhewn rock and a *perfect ashlar*—one formed into the shape of a cube surmounted by a pyramid—among their equipment.
[261] The primary Seer of the group should take note of any phenomena that may arise during this space of silence.
[262] Reminiscent of the Egyptian/Coptic embalming practices.
[263] As a reminder, this is not, strictly speaking, a *Pathworking*, as such refers to the twenty-two paths of the Tree of Life. However, the methodology is identical and therefore the term is used to allude to such identity.

Degree, concerning the Egyptian Mysteries[264]. We herein enter the realm of the *dying God*, which can be found in all cultures, climes and times. Though this story is read to the Initiate in Pathworking manner, the sense is not so much that the Initiate represents any particular God or hero himself. This is quite purposeful, for in Congregational Illuminism, the individual is the key. In other words, this portion of the Degree does not have to reflect or symbolize the actions of some mythic personage from the past—it can relate directly to the Initiate himself! For us, this action is symbolic of the *dying God* which is YOU! Our Funereal Rites are symbolic of your own impending doom, not that of a hero. The death of this particular God, which is the Initiate himself, is symbolic of the sacrifice of the separate, isolated ego. From this moment onwards, we live not for ourselves only, but for others.

Union

The profound and Holy Silence of the Initiate is broken by the Battery[265] of the Degree. These sacred knocks call once again upon the powers and energies that have attended the labors and ask of their assistance in the sacred moment of constituting a Master Mason.

Whereas, in the previous Degrees, the Inner Guard performed most of the "Secrets" of the grade with the Initiate, in this Degree, the dual action of the I.G. and O.G. is necessary. This is a secret method of constructing the Pythagorean Theorem, or the 47th problem of Euclid within the Mystic Temple. It is in this mysterious and sacred moment that the Initiate *becomes* the spiritual "third" of the Rule of Three. The three candles allude to this sacred moment, as does the entire nature of working within the *Three-fold Path*. This action differs largely from that of mainstream Lodge workings. It was born from a SOULDREAM and partakes of the nature of mysticism at all points. In one collective action, the Initiate is raised from the dead, receives the Sacred Word of a Master Mason, and the grip that raises him, and is empowered by the points chaud. In this one movement, Isis, Osiris and Horus are made present within the sacred marma and the Initiate becomes the equal of his Father and Mother, $3^2 + 4^2 = 5^2$.

---

[264] Note that the third degree is completed in the 3rd echelon working of the Grand Rite of Osirification.
[265] We have experienced the power of this wordless Invocation even while working outdoors and simply clapping the battery. This simple action connects with primordial currents and announces the arrival of a candidate into the mysteries. It partakes of the same nature as that of Shinto practitioners who will clap for the ancestors before passing through a shrine. The battery also makes one think of the rhythmic semantron of Orthodox monasteries, or the jarring wooden clapper used in Cistercian monasteries between meditation sections of the Office of Vigils in the middle of the night.

Breath

In every Degree of the Egyptian Masonry of the Divine Cagliostro, the Grand Kopht breathes over the Candidate to complete the work. We hear Patriarch Bertiaux giving credence to this action, saying,

> *The breath of the Teacher is being or the root in the Pneuma of reality, unlike all other physical energies having an occult purpose. It can be applied to the world of the body as the means whereby power is infused at each point of wisdom and at each doorway to the infinite.*[266]

This action, though simple and indivisible (like the ceaseless creativity of the Universe itself) is an actual *ordination* of the Master Mason. Yarker explains that the "divine breath, the central and universal fire, [is that] which vivifies all which exists.[267]" The Master is now prepared to take on the task of initiating others! This branch of Masonry gives itself away almost immediately. The newly constituted Master Mason, may in turn, go and establish his own sphere of working, his own Chapel and his own manifestation of the APRM+M. The breath–the Ruach, the Qi, the Spirit–that is breathed upon the Initiate[268] gives her the sacred right to go and do likewise!

The Order of Work

- The Opening (Initiate joins)
- Purification through trial
- Funeral Rites
- Silence
- Raising
- Pneuma

The only material that is distinct to this Degree is the funeral pall. This can be any material that is black and which can be draped over the Candidate at the proper moment. It is traditional to paint a skull and crossbones, as well as nine teardrops on this pall.

---

[266] *The Voudon Gnostic Workbook*, p. 570
[267] Brackets added, from *Lectures of a Senate, Chapter & Council*, p. 28.
[268] In Cagliostro's work, this breathing upon the Candidate, was seen as giving him a new life.

3rd *degree*,
Perfect Master.

Master

All are invited to join in this momentous occasion of constituting a Master Mason. The Chapel may decide to schedule this event for one of the sacred days of the year–Solstice or Equinox, or with this Degree, it is fitting to schedule it on the Feast of All Saints, which is celebrated as a Fet Gede for many.

The Candidate is invited to join in the Formal Opening of the Chapel. He is also given the opportunity to perform the Bibliomancy for the evening. After the final meditation of the Masonic Middle Pillar, the O.G. goes to the Candidate and places upon his neck the collar of the Ruling Class of Memphis+Misraïm Masonry. This is performed in a natural manner and is accompanied by an upheaval of celebration amongst the guests, I.G. and O.G. The Candidate is then brought into the sacred Marma, the center of the Chapel to receive his congratulations as a Master Mason.

Purification

I.G. Brother Seeker, let me be the first to congratulate you on your success amongst us and your being raised to the sublime Degree of Master Mason! With me, my Brothers!

All. Huzza! Huzza! Huzza!

I.G. You have proven yourself to be a sincere and worthy Brother/Sister among us and you should be elevated likewise. The Outer Guard has given you her collar and placed you in her position of this Chapel. Before we allow you to direct the course of our proceedings, you must receive your final Knighting amongst us.

O.G. hands the Inner Guard the gavel and the dagger.

I.G. In the previous grades, you were hoodwinked during this sacred moment, but now, as you wear the collar of the Outer Guard of the Order, you may SEE with your physical eyes, the extent to which we labor to bring you to the Light.

The O.G. places the Candidate in a seated position on the floor with his legs out in front of him. The Inner Guard approaches from the West and holds the dagger above the Candidate's head in his left hand and the gavel in his right. He strikes twice upon the dagger above the Candidate's head and then lowers the pommel of the dagger onto the top of the Candidate's head for the final rap with the gavel[269].

---

[269] In mainstream Masonry, this is analogous to the supreme moment with the setting maul.

The O.G. strips the collar off of the Candidate, while the Inner Guard retrieves the Funeral pall and quickly drapes it over the Candidate. The O.G. places the Candidate in the "corpse pose" asana, covered in the funeral pall[270]. The Chapel goes completely silent for the space of ten minutes or longer. Not a sound should be made in this sacred moment. All remain in profound meditation until the chanting.

The O.G. then chants Psalm 50 over the Candidate.

Illumination

O.G. Have mercy upon me, O God, according to thy lovingkindness: according unto the multitude of thy tender mercies blot out my transgressions.

2 Wash me thoroughly from mine iniquity, and cleanse me from my sin.

3 For I acknowledge my transgressions: and my sin is ever before me.

4 Against thee, thee only, have I sinned, and done this evil in thy sight: that thou mightest be justified when thou speakest, and be clear when thou judgest.

5 Behold, I was shapen in iniquity; and in sin did my mother conceive me.

6 Behold, thou desirest truth in the inward parts: and in the hidden part thou shalt make me to know wisdom.

7 Purge me with hyssop, and I shall be clean: wash me, and I shall be whiter than snow.

8 Make me to hear joy and gladness; that the bones which thou hast broken may rejoice.

9 Hide thy face from my sins, and blot out all mine iniquities.

10 Create in me a clean heart, O God; and renew a right spirit within me.

11 Cast me not away from thy presence; and take not thy holy spirit from me.

---

[270] Reference to A.O. Spare's *Death Posture* could be made here. The feeling that accompanies this sacred moment is often one of complete and utter exhaustion. See, *Ethos*, recently re-released.

¹² Restore unto me the joy of thy salvation; and uphold me with thy free spirit.

¹³ Then will I teach transgressors thy ways; and sinners shall be converted unto thee.

¹⁴ Deliver me from bloodguiltiness, O God, thou God of my salvation: and my tongue shall sing aloud of thy righteousness.

¹⁵ O Lord, open thou my lips; and my mouth shall bring forth thy praise.

¹⁶ For thou desirest not sacrifice; else would I give it: thou delightest not in burnt offering.

¹⁷ The sacrifices of God are a broken spirit: a broken and a contrite heart, O God, thou wilt not despise.

¹⁸ Do good in thy good pleasure unto Zion: build thou the walls of Jerusalem.

¹⁹ Then shalt thou be pleased with the sacrifices of righteousness, with burnt offering and whole burnt offering: then shall they offer bullocks upon thine altar.[271]

All present resume a short moment of silence between the Psalm and the Pathworking[272]. The Inner Guard approaches the body of the Candidate and forms, once again, a rectilinear figure over the head of him. This signifies the door that is about to be opened.

I.G. The door is opened, Sister Outer Guard.

---

[271] This Psalm, sacred to many and included in the labors of the Martinist and the Élus Coëns, was utilized in Lodge by the Divine Cagliostro in his Egyptian Masonry.

[272] Keep in mind that technically a *Pathworking* is aligned to one of the 22 paths upon the Tree of Life. A little investigation into the nature of this reading will reveal both the path and the Tarot card related to this mystical moment.

O.G. It is well my Brother. Let us continue the story of the Ancients;

> "Osiris was a symbol of truth, fortitude and goodness, one who would sacrifice or lose his life rather than betray his trust. Typhon was the symbol of error or evil—the murder of Osiris signified the temporary subjugation of virtue or truth. This was the parent, or source of all the Grecian or other rites which represent a death and a resurrection of the body...To Egypt, therfore, Masons have always looked with a peculiar interest, as the cradle of that mysterious science of symbolism whose peculiar mode of teaching they alone of all modern institutions have preserved to the present day. {One hears of Proserpine, saying,} 'At midnight I saw the sun shining with its brilliant light[273], and I approached the presence of the Gods above and stood near and worshiped them.'
>
> Osiris, a wise King of Egypt, left the care of his kingdom to his wife, Isis, and travelled for three years to communicate to other nations the arts of civilization. During his absence, his brother, Typhon[274], formed a secret conspiracy to destroy him and to usurp his throne. On his return, Osiris was invited by Typhon to an entertainment, in the month of November, at which all the conspirators were present. Typhon produced a chest inlaid with gold, and promised to give it to any person whose body it would most exactly fit. Osiris, against the entreaties of his wife, Isis, was tempted to try the experiment, but he had no sooner laid down in the chest than the lid was closed and nailed or fastened down, and the chest containing the body thrown into the river Nile. The chest[275] containing the body of Osiris was, after being a long time tossed about by the waves, finally cast up at Byblos, in Phoenicia, and left at the foot of a tamarack tree[276]. Isis, overwhelmed with grief at the loss of her husband, set out on a journey and traversed the earth in search of the body. After many adventures she at length discovered the spot where it had been thrown up by the waves, and returned with it in triumph to Egypt. It was then proclaimed with the most extravagant demonstrations of joy, Osiris was risen from the dead and had become a God.[277]

*A few moments of silence follow the story of Isis and Osiris. Then, the Inner Guard takes the Gavel and knocks 9 knocks, 3 X 3, which ushers in the **Union** stage of the work.*

---

[273] Lucius Apuleius (125-180 CE)
[274] Beyond the analogy of Typhon with Jubelo, Jubela, and Jubelum, the studious Mason would do well to study the Typhonian mysteries, wherein he might discover a secret agreement between the Light and the Dark, the Dayside and the "Nightside of Eden."
[275] Often referred to as the "Venerable Ark of the Order." In Eastern Orthodoxy, this "Ark" is the Virgin Mary.
[276] The source of the Acacia tree symbolism.
[277] Calvin C Burke, 123-129.

Union

I.G. *(Battery of nine knocks, in 3X3 pattern)* **XXX XXX XXX**

The Inner Guard and Outer Guard approach the Candidate and remove the funeral pall. The Outer Guard embraces the Candidate by the right arm and places, right foot against right foot, knee against knee, leaning towards him and placing the left hand on the right shoulder to hold each other up and draw together, using the right hand as a claw to enfold the palm, the Candidate is raised from the floor and the Inner Guard vibrates the Sacred Word while administering the point-chaud empowerment a small space down from the second Degree on the top of the head;

I.G. MOABON[278]

The Outer Guard embraces the Candidate to fully seal the point. The Inner Guard follows suit and embraces the Candidate. The Jewel of a Master Mason is placed upon the Candidate's neck. It is the same as the past two Degrees, however, the compasses are on top of the square, signifying that all events and processes proceed from-the spiritual realm[279]*. The Outer Guard then instructs the Candidate in the "Sign" of a Master Mason which is to be used in "Scrying the Point*[280]*."*

O.G. **Brother, the sign of a Master Mason is made by taking the right hand and at the place of the stomach, drawing the thumb across the torso from left to right and then dropping the right arm at full length.**

I.G. **Once again, Brethren, let us congratulate our newly made Master _____. Let us convene to the Festive Board** (*or Fet Ghuédé*[281]) **after we meditate for a few moments upon our labors and Close this Chapel of Master Masons.**

Finis

---

[278] Mainstream Masons will note the etymological distinction in this term, and the substitute commonly utilized.

[279] There is great subtlety in this statement, for it is not being suggested that the spirit is *over* the body.

[280] From this Degree onward, Scrying the Point becomes a true, **Scrying in the Flesh**. See T Allen's discussion of this in the Appendices of *Roots of Modern Magick*.

[281] When performed on the Feast of All Saints, this Degree has a particular power to it. The Guede are present and invited by the presence of skulls and bones in the Regalia. Lodges/Chapels utilizing the Memphis+Misraïm collars and aprons will want to have all turned to the black side while conferral is taking place. This gesture is not undertaken until the Candidate is covered by the Funeral pall. One will notice also that the month of November is mentioned in the pathworking…

CHAPTER SIX

Suggested Practices of the Symbolic Degrees

The most precious gifts are accorded only to perseverance. Truth well merits a search, and if we make an effort to find it, it is not so very difficult; it has traits which recommend it to all intelligences, and it is only necessary to have an upright heart in order to penetrate the interior of our sanctuary.

John Yarker[282]

---

[282] *Lectures of a Chapter, Senate*...p. 60

Part Two – Chapter Six: Suggested Practices

The work of the Free Illuminist, who chooses to align his or her labors with the Ecclesiastical Revision of the Antient and Primitive Rite of Memphis + Misraim, does not end with Initiation. Our work comprises a life-long study of the nature of the soul, the contents of our minds, the secrets of the body and the hidden qualities inherent in the Universe itself. There is simply no end to such pursuit. The key to our approach is perseverance. If you work this path, stay this course, and fully engage in the Egregore that we have inherited, you WILL find the truth that is present throughout. All that is necessary, as Illustrious John Yarker states, is "an upright heart." The relationship between the upright heart and the "contrite heart" mentioned in Psalm 50, chanted in the 3rd Degree is mysterious. To be upright is certainly not to be sorry—but the sense of the Psalm is one of asking for mercy for one's haughtiness and hubris. Most assuredly, the true mysteries of Masonry cannot be obtained by the arrogant.

Our work is extended into one's private practice. This differs largely from mainstream workings, and exhibits the spiritual nature of our labor. It is simply not enough to have experienced, gone through or, as the case may be, *endured* three degrees. We only require work of our Initiates. Recall the wording of the 4th Article of Congregational Illuminism, "We do the Work." There is no possible way to align oneself to this Egregore without the necessary impetus to Work.

For Masonry, "work" is ennobled. It is more than simply "clocking in" and doing what is required so that bread may be put upon the table. For the Mason, to work is to pray. Oddly enough, this notion was born from a mis-translation of the Benedictine motto, "Ora et Labora." The translation of that motto is to work *and* pray. But the Masonic mistranslation, at least from Rebold[283] onwards, has read, "Ora est Labora" to work *is to* pray. This is a subtle difference, but one that requires exploration. I for one am completely comfortable with the mistranslation, as I share in this notion that *to work is to pray*. Nevertheless, from the beginning to the end, ALL of Freemasonry is centered upon labor. Our hero is a laborer. Our motif is a building constructed by laborers. Our dying God myth involves workers trying to extract the "True Word" from Hiram Abiff[284]. The Password of a Master Mason alludes to the first artificer in metals. All is work oriented. Such is the case also, with our Ecclesiastical Revision of the Memphis+Misraïm material.

For each of the Three Degrees of the Symbolic Lodge, there are suggested practices. These take the Initiation out of the Chapel and into the home of the Initiate. They are the

---

[283] *A General History of Freemasonry in Europe*, Emmanuel Rebold, 1868. This tome was utilized frequently by Pike in his, *Morals and Dogma*.
[284] Mainstream workings.

primary means for a thorough digestion and integration of the energies and entities allied with the Degrees. These practices can be utilized in a chronological sense—a few with each Degree, or as needed, or in a piecemeal fashion as the Node, Lodge, or Chapel sees fit. These are *suggested* practices and again, are not sacrosanct for all Congregational Illuminists across the globe. We have found these to be the core practices that deepen and enlarge upon the material that is covered in the Degree itself. For many, it is within these very practices that the true and personal *meaning* of each Degree resides.

Apprentice

Meditation on the point

Each Degree of our Fraternity has a points-chaud empowerment attached to it. (see diagram) This practice is designed to *re-awaken* the point, to establish further grounding and integration, and for further practices that require such stimulation. Atavistic resurgence, as A.O. Spare calls it, is often discovered in this process.

- *The Initiate should burn a little incense in the space to purify the air and light 3 candles that signify the Three-fold Path that he has been following now for some time.*
- *Sitting in silence in one's Oratory or sacred marma, the Initiate raises his consciousness to the points-chaud empowerment that he has received.*
- *He shall then sit in the asana of his choice, a meditative posture that supports a straight back and alert mind, and vibrate the Sacred Word of the Degree multiple times while applying a "Gnostic Pressure" to the points-chaud on his body that he has received. This is done using the thumb of the right hand in between the pointer and medius fingers. If it is necessary, a stimulative oil (such as Abramelin) may be used to help mentally SEE the point that is being re-awakened. This practice can be used with the Degrees from 1-97th.*

The Death Posture of the 3rd Degree is often the perfect position for this meditation.

The Masonic Diary

In a suitable journal or sketchbook, the Initiate is enjoined to write down the milestones of his or her journey along the path of Initiation. These may take on any form that pleases the Initiate, so long as the details of the experiences are retained. As Scientific Illuminists, we must keep a running record of our experiences so that we can repeat things that went well and re-think things that did not. It is also a way to catalog events that are beyond normal and which would swiftly be dispensed with by the mind. By writing down these events, the Initiate keeps a running log of the spiritual effects surrounding his journey[285]. This diary should also include the information gained during the "Mystic Rites of Vision" and Pathworkings in the Chapel setting. This practice can continue throughout all of the Degrees from 1st-97th.

Companion

Bibliomancy

Bibliomantic divination is common in many parts of the world. Strangely enough, many who practice such do not consider that what they are doing is a form of divination. Simply put, this is a method of relaxing the mind and allowing for the cosmos to deliver a personal message, via the randomization of flipping pages in a Holy Book. What Holy Book is appropriate for this working? Any and all. This method is so delightfully simple and direct, that it is effectively utilized with the Koran, the Bible, the Book of the Law, the Tao Te Ching, the Bhagavad Gita, the Vedas, the Upanishads, etc. Yet it is also useful with less "religious" works that are of a Holy order, such as Marcus Aurelius' *Mediations*, the *Nichomachean Ethics* of Aristotle and even the likes of Thoreau. Simply put, the more "sacred" the book is to the Bibliomancer, the more effective will be the oracle. Here is the method of Bibliomancy that is worked in the Chapel of the Gnosis and which can be worked throughout the APRM+M:

- *Close your eyes and take the Sacred book in your hands.*
- *Flip the book from front to back and every direction.*
- *Begin to thumb through the book with the eyes closed (or hoodwinked).*
- *When the spirit moves you, stop on a single page.*

---

[285] The practice of the Magical Record has been well established in the Western Mystery Tradition, however, it is typically not aligned to Masonic workings.

- *Once the page is selected, move your pointer finger about the page until inwardly directed to stop.*
- *Open your eyes or remove the hoodwink and read the passage pointed to. This may include a small portion before and after the actual selected portion.*

The delightful, *Book of Ordinary Oracles* by Lon Milo DuQuette is helpful with this practice, as it begins to open the Initiate up to the world of enchantment surrounding him. When the doors of perception are thoroughly cleansed, the entire world offers up its meaningful messages and Holy Oracles. As Goethe says, *all things transitory but as symbols are sent.*

Pathworking

Technically speaking, a Pathworking is connected with work on the Tree of Life, or the Etz Chayim of the Kabala. Pathworking in that context has to do with the travels between Sephirah–the interconnecting paths that form the lattices on the Tree of Life. Yet it is becoming common to speak of a particular form of visualized, active meditation, which is a Pathworking in our manner of speaking. This practice follows the fundamental procedure of classical Pathworkings as outlined by groups such as the Hermetic Order of the Golden Dawn.

In the Second and Third Degrees, during the *Illumination* stage of the Initiation, the Candidate is read a passage from Calvin C Burke, 96th Degree's book, *Egyptian Masonic History of the Original and Unabridged Ancient and Ninety-six Degree Rite of Memphis*. These readings are not original to Burke and can be found in Albert Mackey's Encyclopedia as well as the *Royal Masonic Cyclopædia* of Kenneth Mackenzie, and elsewhere. These readings divulge certain key elements of Egyptian ritual that are cogent to the degree being worked. For the Candidate, these readings provide inner scaffolding for a trans-dimensional experience[286]. The procedure is simply to have the material read in a ceremonial setting and to allow it to transport the listener to other planes. This practice is appropriate for 2nd Degree and higher and consists in these simple steps.

- *Set aside a specific time and place for working. Light three candles and burn a little incense*
- *Either record yourself reading the selection from the Degree or have another read it for you as you sit in your asana in Holy meditation, and listen with the ear of your heart.*

---

[286] It has been the experience of our Chapel that during these Pathworkings, Candidates experience an eye opening vision of the "darkly splendid realms." This trafficking of inter-dimensional beings provides the necessary ocular experience to prepare the Candidate for the deeper aspects of points-chauds empowerments.

- *While the Pathworking is taking place, attempt to construct the spiritual architecture of the setting that is being described. Find yourself in the degree as a participant, in one form or another.*
- *Write down the results of your Pathworking in your Masonic Diary.*

One can utilize this practice with a variety of readings such as the work within *Degrees of Wisdom*[287], as well as with prescribed Pathworkings. The key is to allow the Magical Imagination (the Ontic Sphere) to do its own work. This requires a certain level of trust in one's inner atmosphere to fully obtain the desired effect. This form of imaginative and creative thinking ranks rather high in Bloom's Taxonomy. We are engaging in higher order, divergent thinking in these Degrees. We are not being told what to think or how to think. We are being given a panorama of visuals, and allowing the mind to work its own magick. It only takes one effective Pathworking to realize the innate superstructure of the Ontic Sphere and its immediacy to the open minded Candidate.

Master Mason

The Masonic Middle Pillar

The specific instructions for the Masonic Middle Pillar are provided in the first few Chapters of Book Two. The basis for this practice lies in the recognition that the majority of the points-chauds empowerments are found around the central column of the human body. When considered with the two columns of the Second Degree, Mercy and Severity, we see the three columns of the Tree of Life of the Kabala. In mainstream Masonry, we find the three principal Officers representing the three columns of Wisdom, Strength, and Beauty.

As our working is primarily focused upon the Manifestation of Light, it is crucial that all individuals involved in Initiatory work have a readily available practice to stimulate the movement of the Light from above downwards, and then from below upwards, and finally in a shower of blissful ecstasy[288]. The Masonic Middle Pillar accomplishes just this in its simplicity and efficiency of form. It is, as has been said, a child of the Hermetic Order of the Golden Dawn. Many varieties of this practice exist in different contexts. As the Golden

---

[287] We remind the student and practitioner here that the degrees as given in *Degrees of Wisdom* (Triad Press, 2025) to not have a one-to-one correspondence with the Greenfield / Rybalka material.
[288] Many fall into the error of thinking that one must work from above downwards, or below upwards. But this trap reveals a lack of proper integration. The equilibrated Initiate draws from above and below--for the one thing necessary.

Dawn was formed by practicing Freemasons, it makes perfect sense that a version of this meditation would exist for spiritual Freemasons as well.

If the Initiate will practice the Masonic Middle Pillar with fervor, he or she will come to feel within his own body, the very same Light that is utilized in the empowerments, in the bringing to Light of the Candidate, in the sealing of the point, in the Mystic Rites of Vision, etc. The source is the "secret fire" that resides within us all. This single exercise comports all of the varied meanings of the *Sacred Doctrine*.

Opening the Chapel

After the 3rd Degree, the Candidate is able to attend the Openings of any meeting of the Chapel. This meeting may be a 3rd Degree Initiation of another Candidate, or it could simply be a monthly meeting with no particular ceremonial, or a meeting specifically for points-empowerments. The Opening itself is a complete ritual and has the entire *Three-fold Path* within it. It becomes, as it were, the matrix upon which a variety of other workings can take place.

The practice of Opening the Chapel consists of a solitary Opening in one's private Oratory. In this case, it is a working that includes a Sacred Invocation, a Banishing and Purifying Rite, Bibliomancy and ends with the Masonic Middle Pillar. It is provided here as a practice, for the purpose of establishing a basic framework for the construction of individualized rituals that the Initiate seeks to undertake.

It begins with the lighting of three candles which are followed by three resounding strikes of a gong, or a gavel.

To Order!

Place arms in the sign of Egyptian Masonry, right over left across the chest

> **To the Glory of the Sovereign Architect of the Universe! In the Name of the Sovereign Sanctuary of the Antient and Primitive Rite of Memphis+Misraïm. I call upon all Passed Masters, Guardians of Freemasonry, and Angelic beings and countenances! Come now into my Oratory! Salutations upon all points of the Triangle. Respect to the Order!**

Purification

Bow towards the East and then rise with the two fingers of the right hand upon the lips in the sign of the silent Horus. Take up a dagger or use your pointer finger and approach the East. Form an equal-armed cross in the air in front of you and chant loudly, Psalm 68;

> "Let God arise, Let his enemies be scattered, let those who fear him flee before him!"

Repeat this banishing in the South, the West and the North. Then sit the dagger to the side and take up the blessed water. Sign yourself saying,

> Child of Earth and of the star-filled Heavens be purified by water.

Then take the red votive candle and make the sign of the cross in front of you, saying,

> Child of Earth and of the star-filled Heavens be consecrated by fire.

Take the oil of Abramelin or other Holy oil and draw a cross upon your forehead saying,

> The Sacred Oil.

Illumination

Take the Volume of the Sacred Law and perform a personal Bibliomancy. End, saying,

> Thanks be to the Ages!

This may be followed by any work of the Illuminative nature, such as Tarot, Geomancy, Astrological charting, Pathworkings, Scrying the Point, etc.

Union

Herein, any mediations, mantras, asanas, Masses or otherwise may be performed. It is also appropriate to reawaken the points chaud at this moment. End with the Masonic Middle Pillar.

† † †

Scrying the Point

Scrying involves seeing not with the physical eyes but through the mind's eye, into the astral world—the invisible blueprint that lies behind all physical manifestation.

Chic and Sandra Tabatha Cicero[289]

The crowning practice of the Symbolic Degrees is *Scrying the Point*. This single action can continue the Degree work unto infinity. The essential idea behind this practice is that each Degree/points-chaud empowerment has its own world to open to the Candidate. The essential meaning of each Degree is up to the Candidate to fully receive in this practice. This work takes a great deal of concentration, perseverance and single-mindedness.

Scrying has been used for centuries in a variety of ways. There are stories of those who scry into bodies of water, mirrors, crystals, tattwa cards, the Tarot Keys, and a plethora of other props. In essence, the procedure is auto-hypnotic. For our part, we are not scrying into a picture, per se, or any other device. We are scrying into the point that we received, and this is a form of *scrying in the flesh*[290].

First and foremost, the Initiate has to have mastered the procedure for Meditation on the Point. This process of reawakening the point-empowerment is the crucial first step. From here, the Candidate assumes an asana that was developed by William Webb and T Allen Greenfield a number of years ago and which has proven, over time, to be effective in eliciting the second sight state. At the ready, the Candidate will need the usual three candles and incense. In addition to these he will need the Jewel of the Degree, which was created on Virgin Parchment by the Inner Guard Facilitator. This can be created so that it can be worn on a lanyard by the Candidate throughout the proceedings of the scrying. It is a talisman of sorts as well as a protective amulet, a sigil, and a seal of attainment. For many of the degrees, the Tracing Board itself will serve this function, or embellish the work as an eidetic pylon. In addition to this, the Candidate needs to have the Sacred Word, the locale of the points-chaud empowerment upon the body, the Grip or Token, the Sign, and any other portion of the Secrets of the Degree that are provided in the work. These become the protective tools and weapons that are to be utilized in the scrying adventure.

It is imperative that we keep in mind the purpose of what we are doing. Why would we scry into the point that we received? It is for further Initiation, growth, information and attunement. There are beings on the other side that are waiting for us to announce our

---

[289] *The Essential Golden Dawn*, Cicero, p. 209.
[290] See p. 222 in *The Roots of Magick 1700 thru 2000*, Allen H. Greenfield.

presence and attend to the journey. We hear Yarker discussing the Ancient Initiations and saying, "Proclus advanced further and taught that there were Mystic passwords that could carry a person from one order of spiritual beings to another still higher, till reaching the absolutely divine.[291]" The Word of Power or Sacred Word of the Degree becomes the calling card for the landscape and beings that we are propelling ourselves into and communing with. The other secrets of the Degree become so many protections along the way that keep us free from error in the *darkly splendid* worlds. We must remember that all one sees in the astral realm is not true or to be trusted. There are higher realms that the astral receives rays, images and messages from, but we must attain a measure of spiritual discernment to perceive these subtle vibrations. Finally, with practice this exercise will reveal how the *Hauts Grades* operate with the simplest of ceremonial. See the words in bold for a clue to this mystery.

- *Once you have the necessary supplies, sit on your knees and begin to breathe naturally.*
- *Give the Battery of **Knocks** for the Degree to summon the energies and entities that are aligned to the Degree/Point.*
- *When prepared, re-awaken the point through the gnostic pressure and vibrate the Sacred **Word** several times to begin the call.*
- *Assume the prophet asana, essentially the Islamic salat prayer position, "but with the head lowered carefully beneath the body as far towards the groin as could be comfortably managed.[292]"*
- *Utilize the Sacred **Word** of the Degree as a mantra and repeat the word in the prayer posture until you receive a word or image. With practice, a scene or landscape will follow.*
- *During the Scrying session, utilize the Secrets of the Grade to protect yourself and to "test the spirits." For instance, if you meet an entity that you are not 100% trustful of, give the **Sign** of the Degree to see what his response is. Often, this action will dissolve tricksters.*
- *Use the **Jewel** of the Degree as a protective talisman and amulet on the journey. If you get confused or the vision begins to fade, either touch the talisman or in extreme cases, re-awaken the point with the gnostic pressure. In some situations, it may be important to utilize the Jewel as a doorway, staring into the sigil until the rational mind allows the Ontic Sphere to do its work.*
- *The **Grip** of the Degree may be employed for testing a serious entity. This is a tricky action and requires an extreme amount of concentration to prevent the vision from fading out. If, however, you are encountering a Higher Order Being and you get to the place where it is time to give the Grip of the Degree, always have the **Sign** of the Degree ready to slay the entity should he reveal*

---

[291] *The Arcane Schools*, 113
[292] *Roots of Magick*, p. 224

himself as a trickster through some mischief.

The process of *Scrying the Point* is not to be taken lightly. It is a direct ticket to the subtle realms. That is why it is not suggested until the Master's Degree has been achieved. The built-in protection of the three-degrees, along with the already scintillating body empowered by the points-chauds, allows for more complete and trustworthy scrying sessions. This usage of the "Secrets" of Masonic Degrees is in stark contrast to the norm, which is simply to use these as methods of challenging another Mason in darkness as well as in light. The spiritual use of these signs, words, steps, tokens, grips and jewels is a return to the Primitive Faith and Doctrine of the Ancients, and is an essential step towards establishing the Manifestation of Light within one's Mystic Temple.

Part Two – Chapter Six: Suggested Practices

Diagrams for the Points-Chauds Empowerments as related to the 97 Degrees of Memphis+Misraïm[293]

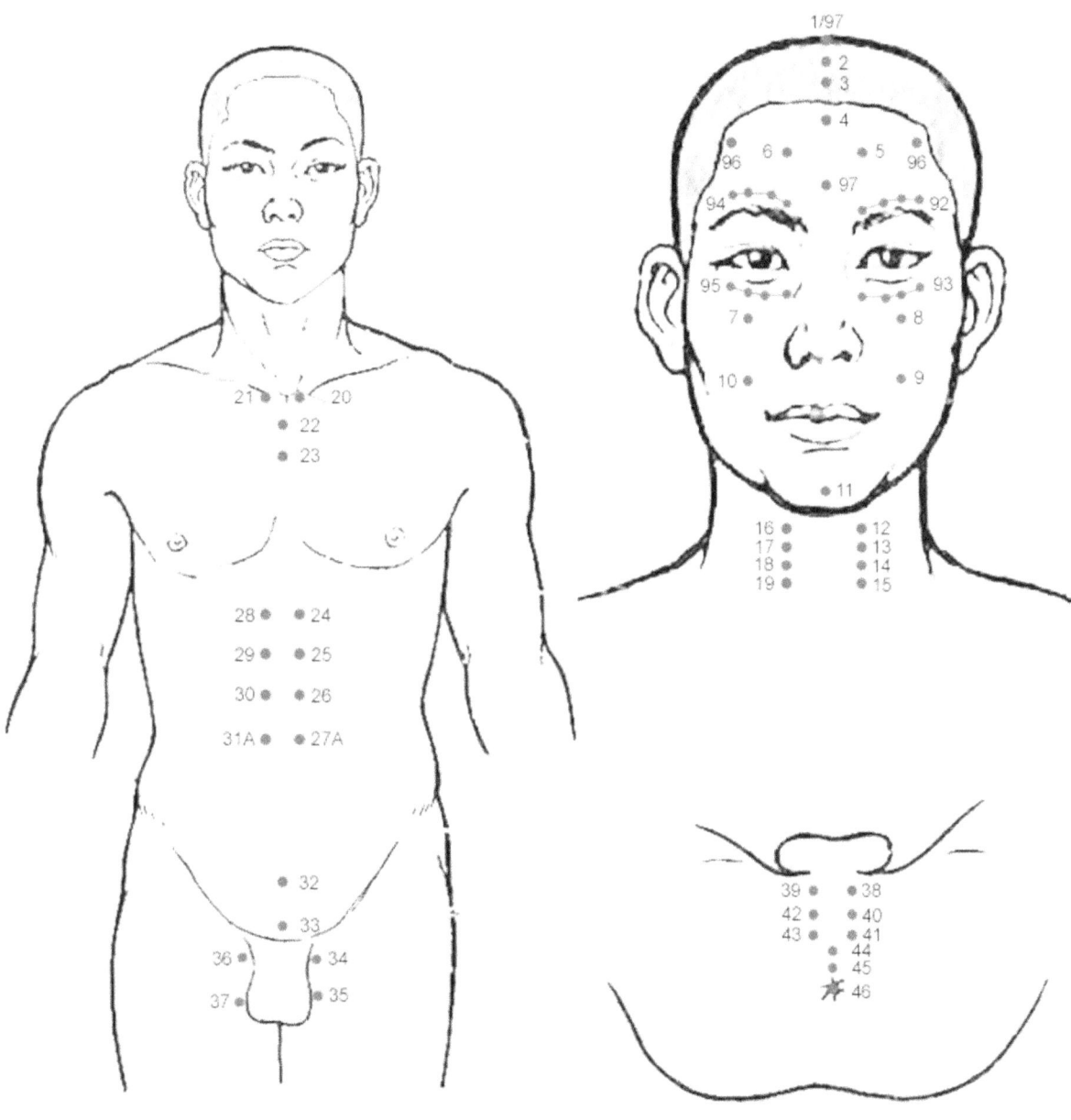

---

[293] See the Monastery of the Seven Rays, Year III, Part V, Lesson 18 for a connection with this glyph to Autireba.

Spirit Builders

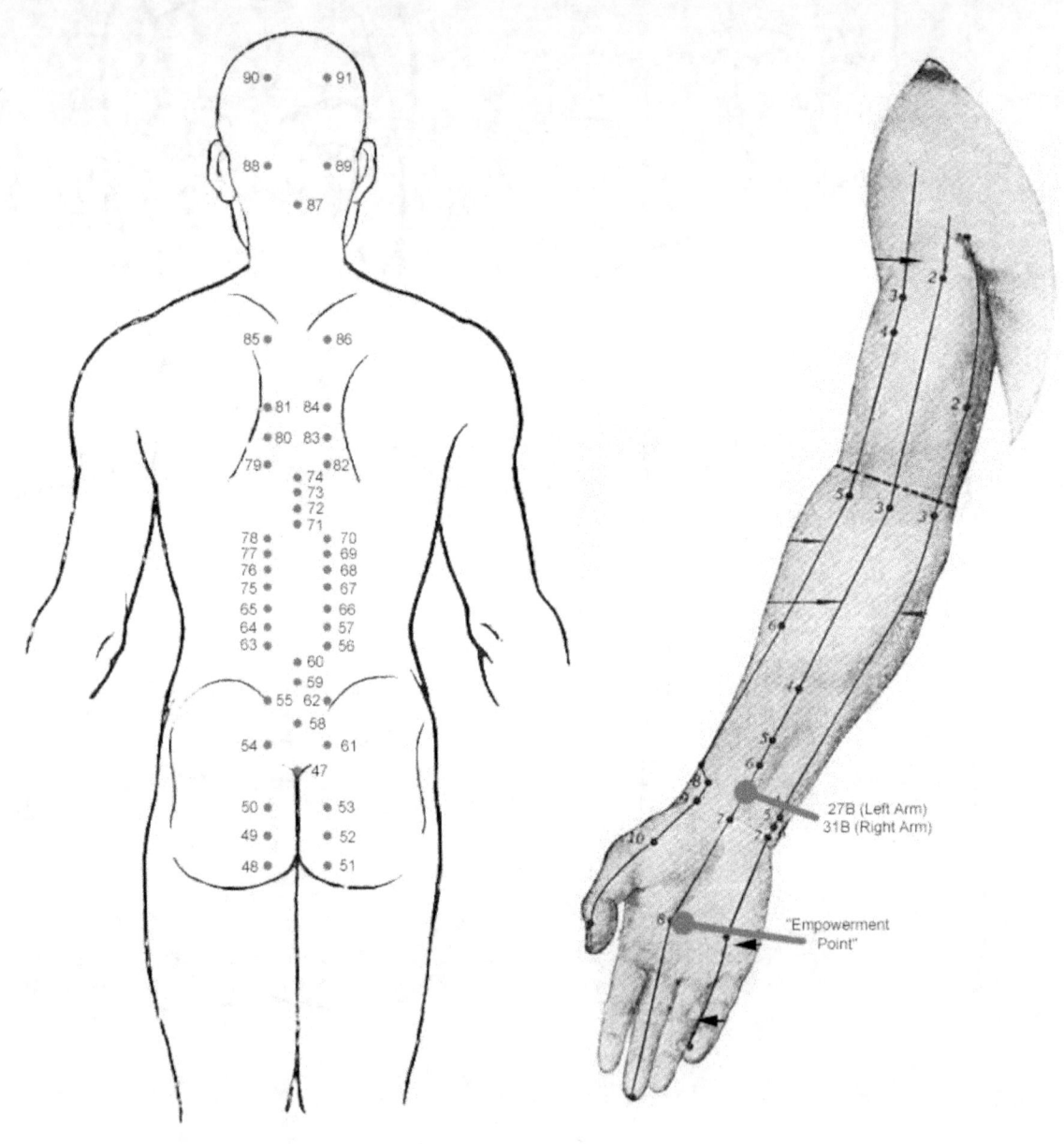

[294] Public Domain diagrams taken from; http://www.lightofthegnosis.org/gnosis.htm and developed by T Allen Greenfield with Reference Guide & Diagrams by John. L. Crow.

Hauts grades

To the Glory of the Sublime Architect of the Universe

In the Name and under the auspices of the Sovereign Sanctuary
of the Antient & Primitive Rite of Memphis+Misraïm, in and for the United States
of America

PART THREE

✠

Hauts Grades

*Being an Initiated Interpretation of the Antient & Primitive Rite of
Memphis+Misraïm as worked in the Chapel of the Gnosis by the Light of*

Free Illuminism

A Ritual Monitor & Guide

For ALL

Ninety-seven Degrees

of Esoteric Freemasonry

With Notes and Synopses

*"The principle seat of the (ancient) mysteries was at Memphis…They were of two kinds, the greater and
the lesser; the former taught by the Priests of Isis and Serapis, the latter by those of Osiris."*

Calvin C. Burt, 96th Degree

Part Three - Introduction

Introduction

The principal aim of this order is the perfectionment of man, and his rapprochement towards that source whence it emanated; that is to say his rehabilitation and reintegration in his primitive rights. The occult schools term it Union with Deity. Contemporaneously with this dogma, as a consequence, is born the principle of Spirit communion.

64th Degree[295]

---

[295] All Degree quotes used with permission from *The Compleat Rite of Memphis*, 1999, by Allen H. Greenfield.

Spirit communion is one of the goals of our work. The Divine afflatus that accompanies our simple path opens up the inner realms and dimensions, paves the way for trafficking with supersensual beings, and has the potential to awaken us to the deeply mystical experiences of unity. The inheritance we have from the experimental workings of T Allen Greenfield and others, originally under the supervision and teaching of Michael-Paul Bertiaux, comes into its fullest expression in our treatment of the *Hauts Grades*, or High Degrees. The reader will be struck both by the quality of Holy Simplicity and Divine Economy in this collection of mysteries and, when practiced, the degree to which the method and working descends from the head into the heart—and from the psychic into the spiritual. In the High Degrees, we encounter spontaneity, which requires of the Initiate a supple and pliable mind that can act with immediacy and mindfulness. In the Western Esoteric Tradition, we often find this tendency towards an economization of actions, props, and extensive verbalizations in the Higher Magickal Operations. Much of what was done *externally*, in the Outer Courts of these Mysteries, is accomplished *internally* in the Inner Orders. The High Degrees are palpably distinct from traditional ritualized Masonry, as they are a sacred gift from the Ancients. Rather than a set of words, teachings, or dogmas, their simple and direct procedural *is* the Primitive Doctrine. They are syncretic by nature, yet radically unembellished and efficient. In his description of the Yuggoth Sphere, Bertiaux describes elemental forms of energy and roots of power thusly:

> *They will not, however, be interested in any deviation from what is the principle of elemental dominance, which provides the magician with roots of his power.*
>
> *They will not deviate from what is raw energy, since they will know that this is the root of their best work. In order to do this, they will resort to the law of compactness of energy and begin to make the energies more and more compact and tighter and tighter.*[296]

This idea and physically experienced sensation of *compactness*[297] is the essence of the Free Illuminist working of the High Degrees. The primary means by which we experience this compact root energy is through the activation of the points-chauds with the "secrets" of the Degrees.

---

[296] *The Voudon Gnostic Workbook*, p. 449

[297] In this way, the mysteries, secrets, entities, and energies sympathetically linked to each Degree, are encapsulated and condensed into a single, person to person action. This compendious approach to working with large amounts of information and energies is expressed by other actions in the Hauts Grades as well; namely in the Knocks, Sacred Words, and the Grip—while also visually occurring in the *Jewel* of each Degree, which is treated as a sacred sigil or talisman. The philosophy of the grade is summarized in the Maxim of the Degree.

The Primitive Doctrine

The *Sacred Doctrine* is the especial gift of the Symbolic Degrees of Memphis+Misraïm. It is explored in a number of ways. The Initiate of the first three degrees of this system is integrated into the energies and Egregore of spiritual Freemasonry and the Apostolic lineage of Congregational Illuminism, and is initiated into the knowledge and practice of the *Manifestation of Light*. This begins with the adage of the Greeks, *Know Thyself*, but swiftly moves outward to sharing this Light with others freely rather than hording it to oneself.

The Sacred Doctrine continues in the High Degree work, but is enhanced with the *Primitive Doctrine*. This is a doctrine free from words. It is more of an approach and spiritual attitude than a set of teachings or beliefs. Throughout the 18th and 19th Centuries, Masonic scholars and philosophers as well as other purveyors of the Western Mystery Tradition, proposed this concept of a *Primitive Doctrine*, or primitive faith of the Ancients. So what then is this Primitive Doctrine about? It is the root of Initiation itself. It is initiation with the least amount of dramatics, ritual, or even movements. It is as pure as spring water and as unsullied as pristine glass. It is often a stumbling block for those who are familiar with detailed and difficult workings, yet what it reveals to each who experiences it is fundamental; it is a marriage of magick and mysticism. We hear the great mystic mage, Dion Fortune saying of the Primitive Doctrine; *All the gods are one god; and all the goddesses are one goddess, and there is one initiator*[298]. For some, this approach reveals that they have been hiding *behind* ritual and shying away from real work in the spiritual realm. For others, it reveals an innate sensibility that they have had since childhood. The immediacy of the Primitive Doctrine is completely wrapped up in its deep and utter simplicity.

- *Tzu-jan*—One way that these degrees express the Primitive Doctrine is through spontaneity. Rather than elaborate degrees and staging planned months in advance and requiring an army of equipment and workers, these Degrees can be worked *on the spot*, wherever the Facilitator wishes. For most, the High Degrees will still be worked in a sacred marma or "thin place," where the spirit realm and the terrestrial intermingle easily[299]. However, there is such buoyancy and looseness to this approach that it could literally be accomplished anywhere that it is desired and/or needed. The Chinese term, *tzu-jan*, translates to "of itself so" and "spontaneity" and is fitting here as this technique is natural and spontaneous. All artifice is dropped and pure initiation is given space to occur in the most elementary of methodologies.

---

[298] *Aspects of Occultism*, 2000, p. 34.
[299] Such *thin places* are explored in the Mystical Christianity of the Celts in Edward C. Sellner's, *Wisdom of the Celtic Saints*, 1993.

The High Degrees can be performed in packs of three degrees *on the spot*, wherever the Initiate and the Facilitator find themselves. These empowerments may be discerned by the Facilitator during an informal consultation, or by way of a formal and organized Chapel/Lodge meeting[300].

- *The Three-fold Path*—Once again we return to the brilliance of the Three-fold Path. It becomes a primary expression of the Primitive Doctrine in the High Degrees. The entire degree may comprise only the "Secrets" of the grade and the points-chaud. As such, in terms of those "Secrets," *Purification* occurs spontaneously with the proper intonation of the battery of **knocks**[301] of the Degree. *Illumination* occurs via the **points-chaud**[302] empowerment and vibration of the **Sacred Word.** *Union* is accomplished through the seal of the point within the body with the **Grip**[303] of the Degree. Where the degree is lacking a specific Grip, the Master Mason's grip is always utilized as a general *seal* of the point.

The Primitive Doctrine is like the long lost cousin of Freemasonry. It is a return to the primitive faith of the Ancients. It is a sacred heritage descended from Ancient peoples and Ancient times. It is a participation in the life of a Druid approaching the Dolmen Arch on Winters Solstice. It is a summoning of the Native American atop the snake mound at dusk. It is entrance into the King's Chamber at the Great Pyramids of Cheops. In its rooted simplicity lies its power, its efficacy and its potential to transform the lives of others. Its antiquity is summed up in the mysterious words of Patriarch Bertiaux:

> *I made use of some inner drive and developed on the physical plane a particular structure of lattices and connective circuits, which were probably latent in an otherwise purely verbal system...which contained some rather interesting Egyptian roots, was really quite remarkable. It was the design for the computer and energy system of what we might now be tempted to call something like a UFO object or projection from some empirical or chaotic marma; but which at that time, as strange as it might seem to the uninformed reader of these matters, was posing rather inconspicuously as an Egyptian rite of Ancient Freemasonry with the name of "Memphis-Misraïm."*[304]

---

[300] They may also be conducted, as is customary on Arabia Mountain, after spiritual vocations.

[301] In our Chapel, the "knocks" are conducted with a gong that resonates its vibrations to the proper dimension.

[302] These points are seen via what the Monastery of the Seven Rays calls, "La Prise des Yeaux." This "prize of the eyes" is discussed further in the chapter "Revelations on the Tree of Life" in *Coalescence*, Transmutation Publishing, 2018, p. 276 et seq.

[303] Analogy can be made to the sacred *pwen* sealed into the Govi jar by the Houngan in traditional Haitian Vodou. The practice is also utilized in Santeria. Here, however, the vessel is the body, which is sealed by the Grip. This is similar to the initiated understanding of magic circles—in the beginning they are used to protect the mage, but in higher workings, they are used to prevent the leaking out of the spiritual effluvia.

[304] *The Voudon Gnostic Workbook*, p. 424.

Part Three - Introduction

Organization of the Degrees

The Degrees of the Antient and Primitive Rite of Memphis+Misraïm are many and scattered in the world of "High Degree" systems. The series of Degrees and their essentials, selected by T Allen Greenfield in his, *Compleat Rite of Memphis* are derived from the combined efforts of John Yarker and Marconis, primarily. This collection contains ALL of the primary information needed to completely perform all 97 Degrees of the Rite in this unalloyed and efficient manner, inspired by Greenfield and Bertiaux's work, and as practiced in the *Chapel of the Gnosis*. Other Nodes, Lodges, and Temples under the umbrella of Congregational Illuminism are doing similar work with their own distinctive flair and modus operandi. Such is the beauty of Free Illuminism and the nature of a loosely knit collection of individuals who focus on the Work. All interested in working some version of this material are encouraged to personalize and customize the material for their particular community. For instance, a Thelemic body would not resonate with our form of banishing (Psalm 68) and may prefer the *Star Ruby*. A Druidical Order may prefer the *Sphere of Protection* written by Archbishop John Gilbert. Golden Dawners may want to use the classical, *Lesser Banishing Ritual of the Pentagrams*, etc. etc. Lastly, you may want to compose *your own version* of the same! In terms of the *essentials*[305] of the working, we are speaking of the "Secrets" of the specific Degrees (Grip, Sacred Word, Sign, etc.) as well as the specific *points-chaud* upon the body that is being awakened/empowered. These are the parts that carry on the Tradition and continue that *continuity of ideas, structure and organization* mentioned in Book One.

Worked in a Series

The Degrees are separated into *Series*. These comprise an integrated and connected set of ideas that the traditional Degrees weave in and out of. For instance, the Degrees from 34-86th are the Hermetic, Kabalistic, and Gnostic Degrees. This is the largest section of the Memphis+Misraïm material, and throughout the various Degrees we find snippets and insights into the Hermetic Tradition in all of its vicissitudes. Right alongside Degrees of Hermetic and Kabalistic import, we find quite a bit of the Gnostic Tradition, including a Degree that is analogous to Episcopal Consecration[306], and another analogous to the S∴I∴ of Martinism[307]. Within these Series, we will have a specific theme we are exploring, as well

---

[305] Analogy may be made to the Masonic notion of *immovable jewels* and our "essentials." These are fixed emblems that must be present in all Lodge workings.
[306] 66th Degree, Grand Consecrator. A fully worked version of this degree included in Volume 2 and the standard edition.
[307] 61st Degree, Sublime Unknown Philosopher

as suggested reading. Individual Lodges may decide to create dramatic extensions for the Degrees, based upon the work outlined in each *Synopsis*.

- *The Symbolic Degrees*–We return to the first three degrees for the sake continuity and utility. As we have thoroughly worked out these three degrees in full to *Initiate* the Candidate into the system at large, we provide the essentials of the working for ease of locating the points, and for returning to these same initiations when needed. This will be confusing to the reader at first, but when practiced, it is found that sometimes certain points/Degrees *want* to be activated, or re-activated. If these are 1-3, we provide the essentials here for the Initiate and Facilitators to have them at the ready. One of the many possible avenues of study for those who receive points-chauds empowerments from 1st-3rd, is **Sacred Geometry**. This is firstly introduced in our working by way of the Labyrinth. Those receiving these three points empowerments may find that they are internally drawn to certain Euclidean or Non-Euclidean geometric figures. This is an expression of the Degree/point "taking."
- *The Philosophical Degrees*-These are the Degrees from the 4th to the 33rd. They are the same in number as those worked by the Ancient and Accepted Scottish Rite of Freemasonry. As noted elsewhere, we are not mimicking mainstream Masonry, and so we simply utilize the "Secrets[308]" of these Degrees as they were known by Yarker in the 1800's. These are not the working "Secrets" of the current Supreme Council of the Scottish Rite. That being said, there is a great deal of carryover, in terms of the themes we study in these Degrees/points as well as the suggested reading material. The primary focus of the Philosophical Degrees is the discovery and implementation of one's **Duty**. Duty, in the Scottish Degrees, is synonymous with concepts of True Will[309], purpose, and divine injunction. These 29 Degrees are split into Four Bodies which we align to the four seasons in our work. For instance, the 4-14th Degrees are the *Lodge of Perfection* and have to do with the continued search of the Lost Word of mainstream Masonry[310]. The search digs deeply, literally nine vaults beneath the earth's surface to unearth a treasure. The location of the search taking one deep into the earth and the Lost Word existing in a state of potentiality is

---

[308] The majority of the "Secrets" of the Degrees are taken from Greenfield's, *The Compleat Rite of Memphis*, 1999, with supplements from the private papers of the author.

[309] When combined with the strenuous efforts of the *Arcana Arcanorum*, 87th-90th Degrees, the True Will can be brought to fruition with the aid of one's Holy assistant, guide, teacher, initiator, and protector—the HGA; the Holy Guardian Angel.

[310] While the *Lodge of Perfection* Degrees can be seen as related to the season of Winter and the Kerubic sign of Man, the *Chapter of the Rose+Croix* is related to Spring & the sign of the Bull, the *Council of Kadosh* is related to Summer and the sign of the Lion, and the *Consistory* is related to Fall and the Sign of the Eagle, altogether comprising the Masonic Year for the Scottish Rite Mason. A string of further correspondences arises from a brief study of these relationships. One easily finds a parallel in this line of thinking and that of the Liturgical Year for the Ecclesia.

analogous to the season of winter when seeds appear to lie dormant under the earth, yet which contain all of the information of a complete and productive plant. This, in turn, parallels the internal growth and transmutation of the Initiate. Finally, each of the Series' from here onward are allied to one of the Four portions of the Hermetic axiom: *To Know, To Will, to Dare and to Keep Silent.* As the Philosophical Degrees are chiefly concerned with study and introspection, they are dedicated to the phrase, *To Know.*

- *The Hermetic, Kabalistic and Gnostic Degrees*–These are the Degrees from 34-86th. This is the largest of the set of Degrees and is aligned with the phrase, *To Will.* This portion of the work is peculiarly tied to the experience and concepts of spiritual transmission, particularly in the 61st and 66th Degrees. These mysteries are translated to the Initiate in the simple and indivisible working of points-chaud empowerments from person to person. The Initiate working with these empowerments is opened to the nature of the Gnostic *Ecclesia* and how deeply rooted in the same our method of the APRM+M is. This Series also explores Ceremonial magick, alchemy, Hermeticism, and divination—each concept being extended in the Synopsis which follows the Degree.

- *The Arcana Arcanorum*–These are the Degrees from 87-90th. These Degrees are aligned to the phrase, *to Dare* as it is Angelic communication and relations that the Initiate dares to participate in within these empowerments. In the section describing this series with suggested reading, we provide a method of aligning the Degrees/points-chauds empowerments with the Enochian Aires as T Allen Greenfield and others have done for decades. We also study the Grimoire of Armadel and the Sacred Magic of Abramelin the Mage in these Degrees, both of which are Initiatory in very unique and life altering ways.

- *The Administrative*–The Administrative Degrees are the 91st through the 97th. These Degrees/points remind and enjoin the Initiate of the penultimate responsibility incumbent to higher Degrees—**Service**. The phrase from the Hermetic axiom aligned to this set is, *to Keep Silent.* In these Degrees, the Unknown Philosopher and traveler with the angels becomes the Unknown *Servant*. Notions of voluntary renunciation, humility, disinterestedness, widespread healing and the like are explored in the capstone of our workings. In such service, silence is key. In this section of Degrees, the theologia of Memphis+Misraïm moves effortlessly from kataphatic knowledge, to the apophatic states of *unknowing.*

Advanced Scrying

Spirit Builders

We learned a simple process of Bibliomancy in the 2nd Degree in Book Two. We also learned the basics for a Scrying session in the *Suggested Practices* section for all three Degrees. For the *Hauts Grades*, we return to both practices in an integrated form of advanced Scrying, where the Initiate determines the personal meaning of each Degree for himself. The practice requires a "Holy Book," which again serves as the VSL and can be any book appropriate to the Initiate for such spiritual labor. This method[311], developed by T Allen Greenfield and W. W. Webb has only a few steps, but its yields are aplenty and the practice swiftly becomes a lifelong tool for inner development for the practitioner. As the Master Bertiaux explains, "in each of the gnostic worlds there are of necessity certain passwords and secret names which must be used to gain entrance to the higher zones of magickal power.[312]" This is precisely the nature of the following work:

- Two individuals are required for the work, though a recording could be utilized in a pinch. Often, this will be the Inner Guard and Outer Guard working together.
- Prior to the Scrying session, all elements related to the Degree are reviewed and at the ready for the Scryer. These include, but are not limited to, the Battery of knocks, the Sacred Word, the Grip and Sign—as well as the Additional Materials provided for each degree; the Insignia, Jewel, Passwords, additional Signs, etc.
- The Scryer is to draw the Jewel of the Degree upon Virgin Parchment, as the Divine Cagliostro did the sacred pentagram, to serve as a talisman and sigil of protection during the scrying of the Degree.
- The Scryer positions himself again in a version of the Islamic prayer posture performed during Salat, "but with head lowered carefully beneath the body as far towards the groin as could be comfortably managed.[313]" Next, the non-scryer takes upon him or herself the godform of Thoth and acts as Scribe and Reader for the work. This is equivalent to the work in the first Degree where the Outer Guard acts as scribe for the Mystic Rite of Vision.
- The Scryer selects the Degree name and point. In our Chapel, the Scribe then re-activates this point upon the Scryer (depending upon placement on the body, this usually occurs before prayer posture, the sign of the pentagram is an appropriate stance) and vibrates the Sacred Word three times.
- The Scribe reads a passage selected by Bibliomancy from the VSL of the Scryer.
- While in the prayer posture, the Scryer meditates upon the point, the Degree, the

---

[311] See the Appendix entitled, *A Brief Introduction to Scrying the Universe*, in Greenfield's, *Roots of Magick*, pgs. 222-229.
[312] *The Voudon Gnostic Workbook*, p. 590.
[313] *Roots of Modern Magick*, p. 224.

Sacred Word, and the passage derived from Bibliomantic divination. The Scribe takes note of any words or images that the scryer provides during the meditation. These words, phrases, images or symbols become the "record" of the experiment which can then be tested by various means. For instance, if the Scryer received a particular *word*, such could be analyzed Kabalistically using the English Qabala[314] or another source, to find the corresponding meanings, words or phrases. This action validates the Scryer's vision and provides the completely individualized "meaning" of the Degree. This practice is in full keeping with the Primitive Doctrine and its spontaneous and supple quality. It is a practice that immediately widens the Initiate's Ontic Sphere.

As Master Bertiaux describes in Cosmic Meditation[315] these powers of vision are developed through practice and dispensed to us by the spirits themselves.

† † †

Layout of the Degrees

It cannot be reiterated enough that this methodology is in such stark contrast to the prevailing methods of Initiation in the West that many will not recognize the Initiation at all whatsoever. Yet, what must be understood is that we are moving beyond the forms and into the Reality. The nature of Initiation is, as P.B. Randolph says, ONE. However, there are many routes to enlightenment. For those drawn to the simple, the Ancient, and the life-giving waters of the Primitive Doctrine, this material will speak volumes. Each Degree/point empowerment WILL be a complete and complex Initiation without the outward forms of extensive dramatics. The basic layout of the Degrees is all the same. Each Degree will have these same elements, yet each (as entity AND energy, according to Bertiaux) will unfold in a unique manner. The layout consists of:

- **The Opening and Closing (of which we will provide a simplified version)**
- **Degree Name**
- **The Battery of Knocks (Sacred Invocation)**
- **The Points-Chaud empowerment upon the body (refer to diagram)**
- **The Sacred Word**

---

[314] Those of us working with T Allen Greenfield have found his expertise in this regard unparalleled. See also, Gerald Del Campo's, *New Aeon English Qabalah Revealed*, 2003, Luxor Press.
[315] p. 20

- The Grip or Token
- The Sign
- Additional Material
- Synopsis

Even as efficient as this layout may appear for those schooled in elaborate Degree workings, the manner of points-chauds empowerments/Degrees upon Arabia Mountain is still simpler. The work of the High Degrees has nothing to do with higher and higher rank, or more extensive props, regalia, and staging—but has everything to do with deeper and deeper work. Let us begin to travel further inward.

† † †

Basic run through[316]

So, what does it look like to perform the Hauts Grades? How and what is actually *done*? Here is a basic run through of the work:

1. Once the space is decided upon, the Facilitator and Initiate face the East and perform the **Opening** of their choice. One is provided, but it may be as simple as a moment of silence facing the East.

2. Next, the Facilitator gives the Battery of **Knocks** with a gavel, or by using a gong, or even by clapping the number of knocks. These should be done with a certain amount of intensity to awaken the powers. If there is spacing after the number of knocks, this indicates a slight pause. These must be accomplished with precision, as it is the calling card and wordless invocation of the specific entities attached to the empowerment.

3. Next, the **Points-chaud** is located upon the body of the Initiate by the Facilitator. This is where the Mystic Rites of Vision, clairvoyance, visualization and working in the Ontic Sphere (magickal imagination) come into play[317]. The diagram is useful, but imprecise, because the points-chauds tend to scintillate and vibrate.

---

[316] The Tracing Boards by GH Rybalka add yet another layer to scrying, an additional lattice in the form of a telesmatic image. The image then becomes a doorway to scry even deeper into the spiritual architecture of the degree.
[317] This is the purely intuitional experience of "flickering lights" discussed in Part I, paper 8 in Year IV of the Monastery of the Seven Rays.

Once the Facilitator locates the point upon the body, he or she applies the gnostic pressure to the point with the previously described mudra of the thumb between the index and medius—the thumb being the activator of the point. The Initiate may want to stand in the aforementioned sign of the pentagram, or another comfortable position.

4. Once the point is located and pressure applied, the **Sacred Word**[318] is vibrated firmly. This is the sacred call to the specific energy related to the Degree. The *Vibratory Formula* of the classical Golden Dawn system of magic is cogent to this method.

5. After the point is activated and Word intoned, the **Grip** is given to "seal" the point and the Degree into the body. Recall that the point is already present in the body, but this gesture is necessary to keep the Egregoric transfer from dissipating into the ethers.

6. Next, the **Sign** is shown to the Initiate, so that he or she will know properly how to perform it later when practicing either *Scrying the point* or the *Advanced Scrying practice.*

7. Additional information for the Degree is provided in the work, but may not be utilized during the Degree unless the Facilitator deems it necessary. Most Facilitators will want to provide this information to the Initiate for further assistance with scrying the meaning of the Degree on their own time. For instance, each degree has a *Jewel* that can be drawn upon virgin parchment as the Divine Cagliostro did, and utilized as a protective talisman and sigil during scrying. *Passwords* may be used to "check" entities experienced in scrying the various landscapes associated with each degree.

8. Finally, a simple **Closing** such as the one provided is necessary. Even though our working method is incredibly simple, it comes full-freighted with powers and potencies that are stirred up by the process. These same energies need to be either contained within the body or released to their abodes. The Grip *contains* the specific entities who will work for further Initiation within the body, while the *license to depart*

---

[318] "This is why we need to summon these 'mysteries' by means of words of power, connectives, which draw in the powers that are desired." Michael Bertiaux, *Vudu Cartography*, p. 18.

gives those Passed Masters and Angelic witnesses due permission to return to their homes.

The Facilitator may want to provide a copy of the *Synopsis* for each Degree as well, as it provides further work and exploration of the Degree.

†††

*As a reminder, even though the presentation of the Hauts Grades will be in numerical order from 1-97, these Degrees may be taken in **any** order. The suggestion is only that we work with Degrees in the same Series for enough time to experience the full embodiment of themes and spiritual studies allied to it. Additionally, it is not suggested to practice more than three Degrees in a given working, unless the Facilitator and Initiate have some specific reasoning for such. Finally, this is the working of one particular Chapel. There is much room for innovation, interpretation, and creative extension to these streamlined Degrees. As this is not a form of intellectual Masonry exclusively, it is deeply Operative and Theurgic—the injunction is to, "taste and see."*

CHAPTER ONE

Opening & Closing

This is why the Gnostics of our school viewed the physical as so important. For the body was a perfect image of the eternal and work on the body of a gnostic and initiatic character constituted its own means of entry into the mysteries of the Pleroma of Light...for this reason, the body is to be understood as the magickal temple.

Michael Paul Bertiaux[319]

---

[319] *The Voudon Gnostic Workbook*, p. 165.

As the High Degrees are greatly reduced in dramatics and form, so is this suggested Opening and Closing. The work has come full circle in this way, in that the props and physical space, as well as the ritual and practice—are all now focused inward and all of the magick, all of the spiritual transmission, and all of the initiation becomes compacted into single moments of engagement and exchange between two bodies. The "Officers" are reduced now to one Facilitator and one Initiate[320]. The body becomes a magickal map of interconnected circuits, wherein the energies and entities that we are stimulating and massaging into wakefulness, move in precise and directed ways for the empowerment and Initiation of the receiver. The streamlined Opening and Closing are more of an internal process than a ritualized schema.[321]

The Opening

The Facilitator and the Initiate select a place for the working. It is suggested that no more than three points/Degrees are worked at a time. The only prop needed for the Degrees is a device to create the Battery of knocks. Some prefer to use a gong for this and experience will show that the energies and entities attached to the Degrees often prefer such. There is no specified regalia, though it is appropriate to where Masonic regalia if desired, as well as more formal, clerical robes and stoles, or simply "street clothes." The Opening is begun by both parties facing East with their arms in the sign of the Good Shepherd, right arm over left upon the chest. The Facilitator proclaims firmly:

> To the glory of the Sovereign Architect of the Universe! In the Name of the Sovereign Sanctuary of the Antient and Primitive Rite of Memphis+Misraïm, and under the auspices of Free Illuminism, I call upon all Passed Masters, Guardians of Freemasonry and Angelic Beings and Countenances! Come now into the magickal Temple of our bodies and bring that Initiation that descends from Antiquity and extends unto Eternity! Salutations upon all points of the Triangle! Respect to the Order!

Bow fully towards the East and then rise with the two fingers of the right hand upon the lips in the sign of the silent Horus.

---

[320] The "Rule of Three" continues, however, in the presence of the entity(s) attached to the Degree.
[321] This aligns with the notion within the *Monastery of the Seven Rays* of magical positivism, where the Degrees are rectified and reduced to pure mind, pure being, and pure essence.

Facilitator   **Let us banish from this place all powers of darkness by the Holy sign of the cross.**

Standing in place, the Facilitator silently forms first a large, equal-armed cross in the East. Then, he turns to the South and does the same, then West and North and back to the East. The Initiate places herself in the form of the Vitruvian man, the sacred pentagram, symbol of the sovereignty of the human Will.

Proceed to the Degree and points-chauds empowerment.

Closing

After the Degrees are completed, a simple gesture to return the powers and potencies to their place of habitation is in order. This is analogous to the "License to depart" of Classical Grimoires. This may be done aloud or silently by the Facilitator. The sign of peace is exchanged and the working is complete.

> May all powers and potencies, energies and entities, who have been stirred up by this spiritual Degree, be released and returned to their respective abodes and habitations. Peace be with you ALL!

> Let us give each other the sign of Peace.

Facilitator and Initiate embrace in Fraternal affection.

Spirit Builders

CHAPTER TWO

The Symbolic Degrees

1st-3rd

But when the philosophical observer surveys the past centuries and mounts to the first cause, and the real aim of the Sublime Institution; when the lamp of study has directed his steps into the obscure labyrinth of the ancient Mysteries, and some success has crowned his search, eager for further instruction he will knock at the door of our temples, and seek new knowledge where he finds the venerated ark of tradition. Sublime Masonry is a continuation of the mysteries of antiquity.

John Yarker[322]

---

[322] *Compleat Rite of Memphis*, p. 68

Part Three – Chapter Two: The Symbolic Degrees

Sublime Masonry is a continuation of the mysteries of antiquity–this phrase sums up the work of Spirit Builders. The *mysteries* incorporate the twin approaches to the spirit realm, mysticism *and* magick. The work is a continuation of *antiquity* in its Primitive Doctrine, which, far from being a set of rules, dogma, or teachings to commit to memory, becomes a key method and state of mind which has been cherished by practitioners of all climes and times. By the simple actions of touch, sight, sound, and visualization, the Ontic spheres of our Initiates are opened and the Light of spiritual Freemasonry bursts forth!

The *Hauts Grades* working of the Symbolic Degrees differs in every respect to traditional, Blue Lodge work. These three Degrees and their points-chauds empowerments may be taken altogether. They are simple and indivisible and represent the entrance into the Primitive Doctrine of the ancients. Whereas the remaining Series' of Degrees all have particular themes and connection to the Hermetic axiom, the Symbolic Degrees represent *entrance* alone. For the ancients, this was termed the *Lesser* mysteries, but we know from our exploration of the 3rd Degree in our *Violet* Lodge that in that most sublime Degree the Candidate[323] enters into the spiritual nature of the *Greater* mysteries. As those who work the particular path of Spirit Builders will have already experienced full initiation in a Lodge-type setting,[324] it will be clear that the procedure herein is far more subtle and evocative than a completely worked out dramatic ritual.

The only suggested field of study in this Series is that of Sacred Geometry, which is distinguished from the basic study of Geometry in that patterns, designs, theorems and the like, take on divine forms and become means for exalted states. One need only visit Holy sites of the ancients such as Stonehenge or the Pyramids, or more modern geometrical wonders such as the great Cathedrals across the globe, to get a sense of the impression that Sacred Geometry has upon the psyche.

During your time of letting these three Degrees mature within your body, you are enjoined to study Sacred Geometry and to see the connective tissues between it and the grand symbol system of Freemasonry, its building and design motifs.

Do not be in a hurry to move into another Series of Degrees, as we are no longer working in a linear or chronological manner. If, for instance, during consultation with your Facilitator, it is deemed appropriate to work on points upon the body for therapeutic reasons or points that seem as if they are *asking to be awakened* and stimulated, you may move into that Series. Or, if you are interested in studying a particular department of the Tradition, such as the Gnostic Church—you may request Degrees/points in the Series: *Hermetic, Gnostic*

---

[323] From this moment on, the "Candidate" is named "Initiate" as he or she has already experienced a formal initiation.
[324] Or, as has been noted in another format, that properly integrates and equilibrates the Initiate.

and Kabalistic, which study that material. This buoyancy and flexibility leads to depth of Initiation and brings the points-chauds into their full flowering as activations with the qualities of: **Initiation, Attunement, Empowerment** and **Therapy**.

Part Three – Chapter Two: The Symbolic Degrees

First Degree

Entered Apprentice

Opening

~Simplified version, extended version of Book Two, or simply a moment of profound silence. The Opening will not be mentioned in subsequent degrees as many will perform these in packs of three, but it may be utilized before any set of Degrees.

Battery of Knocks

Three equal knocks, X X X

Points-chaud

Top of the head (see diagram)

Sacred Word

BOAZ

Grip

Take the right hand and give three equal pressures on the joint between the index and metacarpus.

Sign *(For scrying the Degree later)*

Draw the right hand horizontally across to the right shoulder, let it drop to the side, arm at full length. This opens up the DAATH[325] region of the body.

Additional Materials *(These may also be used in the Scrying session after reception of the 3 Degree/point)*

Acclamation[326]–After having clapped the hands three times say, "Glory to the Sublime Architect of the Worlds."

---

[325] It is of note that the first Degree opens up this sector of the body. Students of Kenneth Grant will recall the esoteric connections between the throat region of Da'ath and the genital area in Yesod. While scrying the Degree, a number of "tunnels" may open up to the Initiate. The Initiate would do well to study *the Nightside of Eden*, 2014, Starfire Publishing, for further inquiry and exploration.

[326] This is one of the very few Degrees that include an Acclamation. This should be done astrally as soon as the vision begins to congeal during the scrying session.

Insignia–A sky blue tunic, an apron of white skin, flap lifted[327]; this is the symbol of labor, its whiteness reminds one of the candor of a true Mason.

Jewel–a Square and Compass with the points of the square on top of the compass.
Step–Three steps forward, commencing with the left foot and bringing he feet together after each step. This is the entry step necessary to a particular portico discovered while scrying the Degree.

† † †

Synopsis

The first Degree of Apprentice, as practiced in French Lodge settings, has for the basis of its initiatory structure a trial by the four elements of fire, water, air and earth. In our primitive working, the Degree is said to fully *take*, within the Ontic Sphere of the Initiate, when the four elements within the body are awakened. Fire will be experienced by a stimulating sensation of activity, passion and movement. Water will be realized by an opening of the intuition, and a growing receptivity to spiritual energies[328]. Air will come with a widening of the mind and an expansive sense of intellectual discovery. Earth will be sensed as a thorough grounding and feeling of being settled in one's skin. The entity and energy attached to this points-chaud empowerment will begin to move these elements in an equilibrated manner within the body and personality of the Initiate.

---

[327] The position of the apron is directly related to the Sign, connecting again—Yesod with Da'ath. *Kether is in Malkuth and Malkuth is in Kether, after another manner…*
[328] See chapters entitled, *Obsculta* and *Suscipe* in *Syzygy*, 2013, Hadean Press.

Part Three – Chapter Two: The Symbolic Degrees

Second Degree

Companion or Fellowcraft

Battery of Knocks

Five, given as **XXX** and **XX**

Points-chaud

Top of the head (See diagram)

Sacred Word

JACHIN

Grip

Take the thumb of the right hand and place it on the first phalange of the middle finger. Press lightly with the thumb-nail[329].

Sign

Place the right hand on the heart, the fingers bunched up as though to seize an object; lift the left hand, palm in front, the elbow touching the body; this is the sign of the order. Draw the right hand towards the right flank and let it fall to the side; drop the left hand to the side to complete the sign. This opens up the [330]TIPHARETIC region of the body.

Additional Material

Password—SHIBBOLETH (an ear of corn). This word is used in scrying when attempting to enter the Middle Chamber by the Step of the Degree.

Step—Three steps of an Apprentice, and two oblique steps, one to the right with the right foot and one to the left with the left foot, drawing the feet together after each step.

---

[329] Note—As the Grips are utilized as a SEAL of the Degree and the points-chaud empowerment, they differ slightly from the more extended versions offered in the Monitors. To ensure the efficacy of a **seal**, the quickest and the simplest action is necessary to prevent the energies from dissipating and dispersing unduly.

[330] The 1st Degree, opening the mysteries of DA'ATH immediately, is tempered by the 2nd which returns to the way of the heart via the energies and singular entity of Tiphareth. This *singular entity*, "La Chose" to the Élus Coëns, the *Unknown Agent* and *Repairer* to the Martinist returns often in the Hauts Grades as THE center from which the various spokes move outward.

Age–Five years. This is the second time that the number five arises in the Degree. It alludes to the sign of man, the pentagram—which is also the sign with which we put our bodies into to receive the point empowerment.

Insignia—Blue tunic, apron of white skin with the flap down.

Jewel–Square and Compass with points of the compass interlaced with the square—one over, one under.

† † †

Synopsis

The Second Degree is traditionally less of a testing Degree and more of a symbolic channel into the Sanctum Sanctorum or Holy of Holies. The winding staircase and the labyrinth are both cogent symbols of the spiritual nature of this Degree. As the Password symbolizes an ear of corn, this Degree has reference to fertility and growth. The Initiate is enjoined to consider the presence of such symbols in Art, in Tarot cards, upon Architectural designs, etc. The points-chaud of this degree will bring Illumination to the Initiate in a manner distinct and specific to the individual.

It is no accident that the Degree in which the Candidate of mainstream Masonry is first revealed the *Sanctum Sanctorum* is also the Degree in which the heart is activated through the Sign. The winding staircase, as has been discovered in Book Two, is spiral in form. Our principal emblem of the labyrinth[331] reinforces this stimulating symbolism and directs the Initiate inwards to the SOURCE from which all things flow. This Source is the unified, cosmic Christ of the Beatific Vision which accompanies initiation into the chapel of Tiphareth upon the Tree of Life. As the Initiate receives this points-chaud, the Illumination descends from the head into the heart where this Cosmic Christ resides.

---

[331] The labyrinth, as contradistinguished from the *maze* in which the traveler is somewhat lost and has to find his way through a confusing path, has a very clear beginning and end. Once the center of a labyrinth is reached, the way of return is identical to the way to the center. This carries with it deep mystical import for the Initiate.

Part Three – Chapter Two: The Symbolic Degrees

Third Degree

Master

Call to the Ghuédé

Battery of Knocks

Nine, by three times three **XXX XXX XXX**

Points-chaud

Top of the head (See diagram)

Sacred Word

MOABON[332]

Grip

Right foot against right foot, knee against knee, lean towards each other; place reciprocally the left hand on the right shoulder to hold each other up, and draw together; take each the right hand of the other in forming a claw as if to enfold the palm.

Sign

Take the right hand and draw it sharply across the lower abdomen from left to right. Drop the right hand to the length of the arm. This opens the YESOD region of the body.

Additional Material

Password–TUBAL CAIN, used as approaching the ark in scrying.

Steps–Three steps, as if passing over an object placed on the ground; the first step to the right, commencing with the right foot; the second step to the left, with the left foot; the third to the right with the right foot, bringing the feet together after each step.

Sign of Horror–This sign and the subsequent Sign of Help are used in scrying when testing the spirits of this region. As the Ghuede often show up in such exercises, the first Sign may not be enough to discern the nature of the spirits. These additional Signs *prove* the

---

[332] Master Masons within mainstream workings will recognize this word from their ritual & studies, but will note its distinction from the one in common usage today. See Albert Pike's, *Sephir H'Debarim, The Book of the Words* for an initiated explanation of how the older French word used above is the more correct version, while the English is a corrupted form.

motivation of the spirit in question. Place the open right hand, fingers extended, the thumb apart and touching the right flank; this is the sign of order; lift the two hands towards the heavens, the fingers extended and separated, saying, "Adonai" after this exclamation. Let the two hands fall on the apron, as if expressing surprise; this completes the sign.

Sign of Help–When a Master is in danger, and wishes to call a Passed Master to his assistance in a scrying session, he elevates his two hands joined together above the head, palms uppermost, saying "Come to my aid, ye children of the widow." Recall that Hiram is the son of a Widow and of the tribe of Naphtali which corresponds with the constellation Virgo. In this manner, he is the son of a Virgin...as well as the son of Isis who has lost her Osiris[333].

Insignia–Blue tunic, white apron with red border[334], with a pocket underneath the flap; in the middle of the apron are embroidered the letters M.B.: a water marked sash worn from right to left; at the bottom is suspended with a red rosette.

Jewel–Square and Compass with both points of the compass over the square[335].

† † †

Synopsis

The essence of the Degree of Master Mason is the death of the Ego. It is symbolized dramatically by the death of the Master Hiram Abif–himself a symbol of the Sun and of all heroes of the solar cult. For this Degree to fully take within the Initiate, he or she will need to practice *memento mori*[336] regularly. The remembrance and meditation upon death

---

[333] Reference can again be made to Pike's *Sephir H'Debarim* as to the role of Horus in this Degree in particular. Hearkening back to Book One, we see the influence of Horus upon the author as well as throughout the body of the Antient & Primitive Rite of Memphis Misraïm literature and ritual. Indeed, if a single figure presides over the work in its entirety within the Hauts-Grades, it is the great god Horus. As the progeny of the Father God, Osiris, and the Great Mother, Isis, the Christian Hermeticist need not make a large leap to discover one of the Divine/Human aspects of Horus.

[334] Here we see a unique apron being utilized in this Degree—it is that of the "Red" Lodge, or Scottish Rite symbolic Lodge. As France is the source of High Grade Masonry, we see an overlap (and sometimes confusion) between the various Rites. The Rite of Memphis-Misraïm utilizes the blue, white, and *violet* trimmed apron in the Symbolic Degrees, and all of the French Rites have double sided aprons which reveal a skull & crossbones with nine tear drops upon a black ground—*such is a powerful visual invocation of the Ghuédé!*

[335] Sometimes the Initiate misunderstands the arrangement of this classical Masonic symbol in the 3rd Degree, considering it to suggest spirit *over* matter, or the divine *raised above* the human. But in light of non-dual Gnosis, this emblem is a powerful reminder of the spirit being the grand animating force of all things, discovered within the material, within the body. Reference can be made to Bertiaux's concept of Ontological Monism in *Cosmic Meditation*, p. 57.

[336] See chapter of the same name in *Syzygy*, +Palamas. The reader is reminded that the specific energies of this Degree, the Ghuédé, are "*a family. These are not simply archetypes to engage with via some sort of mental judo; they are living, thriving entities/energies*" (+Palamas 96).

become the gateway for full integration of the entities and energies attached to this Sublime Degree and point empowerment.

In other words, the work of the 3rd Degree is building relationships with the spirits as they are invoked through the ritual of points empowerments.

Suggested Reading for the Symbolic Degrees

There are many fantastic books available to the Initiate which describe the ritual, philosophy, and history of the so called, *Blue Degrees* of Freemasonry. While any and all of these are appropriate to the Initiate, here are a few selections that are particularly cogent to our methodology and to Spirit Builders in general.

- *The Arcana of Freemasonry*, Albert Churchward
- *The Celtic Golden Dawn*, John Michael Greer (excellent section on Sacred Geometry)
- *Degrees of Wisdom: A Compendium of Rituals from the Rites of Memphis and Misraïm*, Tau Phosphoros (trans.)
- *Esoterika*, Albert Pike, edited by Arturo De Hoyos
- *Freemasonry, Rituals, Symbols and History of the Secret Society*, Mark Stavish
- *Hermetic Masonry*, Frank C Higgins
- *The Hidden Life in Freemasonry*, C.W. Leadbeater
- *The Lost Keys of Freemasonry*, Manly P. Hall
- *Masonic Initiation*, W. L. Wilmshurst
- *The Porch and the Middle Chamber, the Book of the Lodge*, Albert Pike
- *Rosicrucians, their Rites and Mysteries*, Hargrave Jennings
- *Sacred Geometry*, Robert Lawlor
- *The Secret Science of Masonic Initiation*, by Robert Lomas

CHAPTER THREE

The Philosophical Degrees

4th-33rd

Nature is one great HARMONY, and of that harmony every human soul is a tone.

Albert Pike, *Legenda for the 28th degree*

Since the union of the Rites of Memphis and Misraïm under the leadership of the Italian Freedom Fighter, Giuseppe Garibaldi, the 4th-33rd Degrees have remained very similar to those worked by the Ancient and Accepted Scottish Rite of Freemasonry. Even before said union, Marconis, in his *Sanctuary of Memphis* provides the "Secrets" of the grades from 1-33 as those identical to the then growing, Scottish Rite. The *Sanctuary of Memphis* was published in 1849, even though the Rite was being worked, according to Kenneth Mackenzie and others, as early as 1813. Memphis was a system that was most assuredly constructed upon the earlier High Degree system of Misraïm (90 degrees) that was being spoken of as early as 1738, with the Egyptian Masonry of the Divine Cagliostro arriving in 1784.

Though the Mother Council of the Scottish Rite of Freemasonry of 33 Degrees was not founded until 1801, the Degrees worked therein can be traced back many years prior to this unification. The Scotch Master Degree, for instance, which shows up in most High Degree systems in some respect, dates back to 1733. The Rites of Memphis+Misraïm and the Scottish Rite shared many Degrees, though it was the Scottish Rite that would prove to win the prize of *regularization* and acceptance by the United Grand Lodge of England. This did not stop the proponents of Memphis+Misraïm from continuing their work in a clandestine manner. The Grand Orient of France would prove, in time, to be the one governing body that would accept the Memphis+Misraïm Rites, but the Grand Orient itself ran into trouble with the UGLE over issues with the Volume of the Sacred Law (amongst other reasons), and so both are somewhat *irregular* in the eyes of the UGLE. Globally, various versions of Memphis+Misraïm[337] persist and continue the work of Initiation today—with or without a larger Grand Lodge or Orient's acceptance.

But if we have the 4-33rd Degrees in a very similar state as that of the 19th Century versions, are we then practicing the *Scottish Rite* while we work the Philosophical Degrees of Memphis+Misraïm? Unequivocally, no. The Supreme Council of the Scottish Rite of Freemasonry has revised and re-worked these Degrees continuously over the years so that the "Secrets" we find provided by Yarker and Marconis are no longer those utilized by the AASRite.

So, what is it then that we share with the Scottish Rite in these 29 Degrees, if not the "Secrets?" Let us return to some of our first arguments, namely that of; *continuity of ideas, structure and organization*. The Synopsis provided for each of these Degrees refers to this continuity, even when the Degree name, Grips or Sacred Words differ. So much

---

[337] Many modern books of Masonry give a nod to the continuance of the Memphis Misraïm Rites, not the least of which are: Stavish's, *Freemasonry, Rituals, Symbols, History of a Secret Society*, Nikolic's, *Royal Art, Three Centuries of Freemasonry*, and MacNulty's, *Freemasonry, Symbols, Secrets, Significance*.

scholarship and educational material has poured forth from the Supreme Council over the past decade or so, that the interested student of Freemasonry or member of the Scottish Rite has a veritable gold mine to cull wisdom and knowledge from. A number of these treasures are mentioned in the *Suggested Reading* section, following the set of Degrees. It is from these works of erudition, as well as older documents, that we form our brief Synopsis of the Degrees and continue on some of the beautiful concepts and ideologies proposed in these very interesting Degrees.

But what is our spiritualized version of these philosophical grades? What is the nature of the entities and energies of these Degrees in terms of the points-chauds empowerments? Experience has revealed that doorways opened by this set of Degrees/points are particularly united to some of the larger themes of this diverse collection of Degrees. One specific example is the notion of Duty, which shows up immediately in the 4th Degree of Secret Master (SR), Discreet Master (APRM+M). This sense of Duty is consistent with Eliphas Levi's development of the magical Will, as well as Crowley's later extension of the same; the *True Will*. Some will be more inclined to an Ecclesiastical sense of this concept and refer it to one's Divine Plan or Sacred Injunction. It could even more simply be described as one's purpose. While working these Degrees and points, the Initiate may find a clearly expounded message of what particular work he or she is to accomplish in this life; what legacy he or she is to bequeath to generations to come. This comes about mystically, through the spiritual action of the Degree and the esoteric physiology of the points-chauds.

Working these Degrees/points also aligns oneself with the four principle bodies of the Degrees—*the Lodge of Perfection, the Chapter of the Rose+Croix, the Council of Kadosh* and the *Consistory*. These four bodies are experienced as four grand searches within our Rite, which are further corresponded to the four seasons and the four Kerubic signs of the Zodiac. These alignments will be revealed within the Synopses, yet the full development of such is up to the Initiate him or herself. It is of particular importance that each of these Degrees be searched out for their personal meanings through the *Advanced Scrying* method purported in the Introduction to Book Three. It is here that these magical ties with the seasons and the signs will be personalized and allowed to grow within the Initiate's Ontic Sphere.

Before beginning this Series, one last word needs to be said concerning the nature of our Primitive Doctrine. The Primitive Doctrine is balanced, harmonious and able to be experienced with immediacy and grace. In our working of these Degrees, gone are the trappings of dramatic staging and complex rubrics. Gone also, are the elaborate host of symbols and oaths and lengthy orations. These Degrees can be experienced in a holistic manner, by taking them into the body as it were, in a not too dissimilar way as the Eucharist is a form of taking into the body a portion of God. From Facilitator to Initiate, these Degrees and their points-chauds empowerments enter the physical organism to stimulate the latent entities and energies within. The *true* meanings of these Degrees are indeed secret, because they are alive and contingent upon the Initiate him or herself to develop. The Primitive Doctrine is not a set of teachings or beliefs, but a living reality to be experienced in a natural and spontaneous manner. Pike says:

> *Masonry teaches, and has preserved in their purity, the cardinal tenets of the old primitive faith, which underlie and are the foundation of all religions. All that ever existed have had a basis of truth; and all have overlaid that truth with errors.*[338]

Finally, the Philosophical Degrees are allied to the first phrase in the Hermetic Axiom; *to Know*. These Degrees develop the knowledge, wisdom and philosophy of the Initiate in subtle ways. They begin the epistemological search of the Initiate that winds through forms of knowledge that are a priori, a posteriori, kataphatic, apophatic, Gnostic and Ontic;[339] such ways of knowing will be unfolded in due course.

---

[338] *Morals & Dogma*, p. 161
[339] Here it is remembered that *Ontic* refers to the Magickal Imagination, rather than the traditional notion of Ontological studies of science and philosophy.

Part Three – Chapter Three: The Philosophical Degrees

Fourth Degree

Discreet Master

Lodge of Perfection

4th *degree,*
Perfect (Discreet) Master.

Battery of Knocks

Seven knocks. 3 by 3 by 1, XXX XXX X

Points-chaud

Upper Forehead (See diagram)

Sacred Word

Three separate words vibrated once; YOD, ADONAI and YHVH (Yod, Heh, Vav, Heh)

Grip

Take the right hand with the grip of a Master, advance the hand to the elbow pressing the arm seven times, and at the same time advance the right legs until they touch at the interior.

Sign

The index and the middle finger of the right hand placed together on the mouth; in reply the same sign is made with the left hand.

Additional Material

Pass-word—ZIZA, used for entrance inside the gate during scrying along with the Step.

Step—same as in the 3rd Degree

Age—Three times twenty-seven[340].

Insignia—A blue tunic, white apron attached by black cords; the flap of the apron is blue, with an embroidered eye; in the middle of the apron are two branches, one of laurel and one of olive; forming an open crown, and in the middle the letter Z; blue sash, interwoven with black, worn crosswise, at the bottom of which is hung an ivory key with the letter Z.

Jewel—an ivory key with the letter Z inscribed in it.

---

[340] Consider this number in terms of magic; 3 X 27= 81, which by Kabalistic metathesis is, 8 + 1=9. Nine is the number of the Hermit of the Tarot, a visage of which is mentioned in Pike's *Legenda* 4-14th Degrees. The Hermit is attributed to the Hebrew letter, YOD—the first letter of the Divine Tetragrammaton, YHVH. This Degree begins the journey into the Tree of Life, which for the Scottish Rite Mason is a complex symbols system where bits of knowledge are stored and shown to be interrelated (see DeHoyos, *Scottish Rite Ritual Monitor & Guide*). For Gnostics & Magi, however, this glyph is living; it is a never ending source of initiation and participation in the Divine life. See Pike's voluminous 28th Degree chapter in *Morals & Dogma* for further application of the number 9.

Synopsis

The Fourth Degree begins a journey into the nature of the self for the Initiate. The points-chaud empowerment inaugurates a particular descent inward, into the depths of the personality to unearth, in the 14th Degree, the primary Secret of the Lodge of Perfection. One of the cogent symbols for this journey is the ivory key. The key, in this degree, symbolizes THE key to the Mysteries altogether, which only the Initiate can discover for himself. No one can give you this key as it is in your possession already. In this Degree, you are taken to the gates of the Sanctum Sanctorum once again, as in the 2nd Degree, yet this time you have the master key to enter into its mysteries. The introduction of the Tree of Life of the Kabala in this Degree will assist the Initiate in scrying the point and opening the paths, sephira, and the tunnels of that hyper-spatial glyph.

5th Degree

Perfect Master

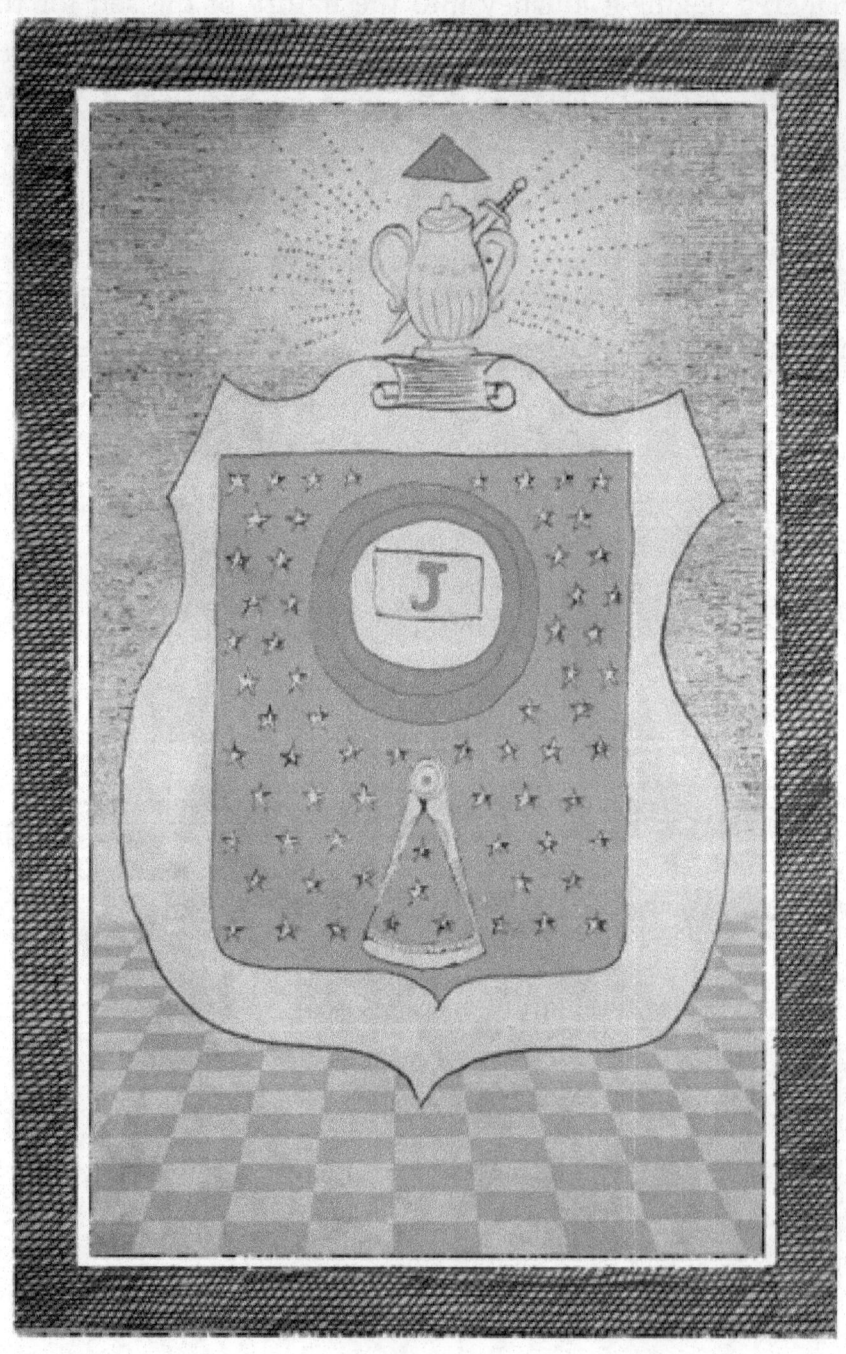

5th *degree,*
Perfect Master.

Battery of Knocks

Four equal knocks. X X X X

Points-chaud

Mid Forehead Left

Sacred Word

JEHOVAH

Grip

Take each the right hand, thumb in the form of a square, and place the left hand on the right shoulder of the other.

Sign

Of Admiration—Raise the hands and the eyes towards Heaven, and lower the hands by crossing them on the breast, at the same time looking at the ground.

Of Recognition—Advance the feet slowly until the toes touch and bend the knees forward until they touch; place the right hand on your heart, and the left hand on the breast of the one proving you.

Additional Material

Pass-word—ACACIA

Steps—Form a square by placing the four feet together[341].Insignia—Blue tunic, green sash with silver fringe

Jewel—a compass, open at the segment of a graduated circle, at an angle of 60 degrees.

† † †

---

[341] This *Step* is accomplished with the Body of Light in conjunction with the Guardian of the Threshold or Pylon, while scrying the points-chaud.

Synopsis

The Degree of Perfect Master is uniquely concerned with death. It is a deepening of the experience of the Chamber of Reflection, and takes the Initiate into the depths of his or her own personal demise. This meditation, this memento mori, brings to light all of our fears, hopes and dreams concerning the nature of consciousness and how it is contracted[342] and expanded. If, for instance, energy is neither created nor destroyed— as the 1st Law of Thermodynamics suggests–then why not consider the same continuity with the consciousness?

---

[342] The expansion of consciousness is a well worn path, however, this notion of contracting the consciousness is allied to the Kabalistic idea of *Tzimtzum*, where the Divine light of consciousness is withdrawn for a profound moment of creation. How meditation upon death leads to an individual Tzimtzum will be discovered through praxis.

Part Three – Chapter Three: The Philosophical Degrees

6th Degree

Intimate Secretary or Sublime Master

6th *degree*, Intimate Secretary.

Battery of Knocks

Twenty-seven knocks, 3 times 9. XXX XXX XXX XXX XXX XXX XXX XXX XXX

Points-chaud

Mid Forehead, right

Sacred Word

J-E-H-O-V-A-H

Grip

The Facilitator takes the right hand of the Initiate and says "Berith" (alliance); then turns the hand over and says "Neder" (vow); then, recovering his first position says "Schelmoth" (pure).

Sign

Place the right hand on the left shoulder, and draw the hand down to the right hip, in designing the shoulder belt; the reply is given by crossing the arms on the breast, then lowering them towards the sword, at the same time raising the eyes towards the heavens.

Additional Material

Passwords–1st word is JOHABEN (Son of God); this name is given the recipient. 2nd word is ZERBEL, given in response.

Insignia—Blue tunic, blue sash with silver fringe.

Jewel—a triple triangle with an eye, ear and mouth engraved thereon, viz: the eye on the top triangle, the ear on the left and the mouth on the right triangle.

†††

Synopsis

In the dramatized working of this degree, we find Solomon's friend, Zabud (Joabert in other workings), being accused of spying on conversations between Solomon and Hiram of Tyre. Yet, it is discovered in due course, that Zabud is watching out for his king with a willingness and zeal to defend him. Solomon exhibits an expansive and generous spirit by awarding Zabud the office of Intimate Secretary. The spirit attached to this degree and associated with the points-chaud empowerment is one that works disinterestedness and zeal within the Initiate's sphere of sensation. The grip, sign and password are all group actions to be utilized in scrying the degree after activating the point.

Part Three – Chapter Three: The Philosophical Degrees

7th Degree

Provost and Judge

7th *degree,*
Provost and Judge.

Battery of Knocks
   Five strokes, four by one.   XXXX   X
Points-chaud
   Upper cheek, right
Sacred Word
   JAKIVAL
Grip
   Give each other the two hands, interlace the little finger of the right hand with the index finger and give seven slight taps on the palm of the hand.
Sign
   Place the right hand open upon the breast.

Additional Material–*In this Degree, it is in scrying the Degree and point empowerment that we discern the nature of the entity and energy herein received. The genuflection and passwords will awaken the Scintillating body when the Initiate is prepared for this Degree.*

Password–Kneel on the right knee and say the word, CIVI, then rise and say, QI.
Insignia–Blue tunic, blue sash fringed with silver, poppy colored ribbon across shoulders, to which is suspended a triple triangle.
Jewel–a gold key

† † †

Synopsis

The ritualized degree work of the Provost and Judge is grounded in the idea of justice and equanimity. The spirit working of this Degree accesses the subtle quality of the Words and actions of the Degree, which are Chinese in origin and relate to funereal customs in ancient China[343]. Here, the Initiate will refer back to the ideas and principles of justice found in Confucianism and he will also be instructed as to the deeper nature of this degree by a careful study of the Taoists principle of the "diamond body" and the methods of moving "Qi" throughout the physical organism—which is directly related to the points chauds empowerments. It is noted here, that these concepts of the scintillating body are related, they are analogous, not identical. The points chauds are distinct from other traditional esoteric physiologies, in that they are both entity *and* energy; and in that they are

---

[343] See chapter 9, *Chinese Thought and Freemasonry in the Eighteenth Century*, from DeHoyos & Morris's, *Freemasonry in Context, History, Ritual, Controversy*, pgs. 145-161.

both already present in the body, yet stimulated into wakefulness through transmission of the Egregore from person to person. This Degree relates directly to the sign of Libra as well, and a study of the characteristics of this sign—both positive and negative—will further elucidate the meaning of the Degree.

Spirit Builders

8ᵗʰ Degree
Knight Superintendent of Works

8ᵗʰ *degree*,
Intendant of the Buildings.

Battery of Knocks
Five equal knocks. X X X X X

Points-chaud
Upper Cheek, left

Sacred Words
JACHINAI and JUDAH (these are given with the Grip in call and response)

Grip
The Facilitator strikes the heart of the Initiate with the right hand[344], then passes the right hand under the left arm, and finally takes the right shoulder with the left hand, saying "JACHINAI"; the Initiate replies "JUDAH."

Sign
It is to be reiterated at this juncture, that the "Sign" is given during the working for the primary purpose of effectively preparing the Initiate for his subsequent labors in Advanced Scrying. When we experience a Degree such as this one, which has several such signs, it is indicative of the nature of spirits that may be encountered upon such a scrying journey. In this degree, for instance, we have three signs, answering to "Surprise," "Admiration," and "Distress." These are suggestive to the scryer of the quality of experience and the plane of interaction that the entities aligned with the point and Degree inhabit.

Sign of Surprise—having the hands spread out in the form of a square, place the two thumbs on the temples[345], step back two paces, advance two, whilst saying "BEN-CHORIM" (Sons of Nobles); place the two hands over the eyes to cover them. Of Admiration—having interlaced the two hands, turn them palms upward, then let them drop on the waist, whilst looking heavenwards and saying "ACHAR" (disturbing), this is one of the names of God. Of Distress—having placed the right hand on the heart, place the left hand on the mouth, then touch the knee three times saying the first time "HAI" (living), the second time "JAH" (God), the third in silence.

Additional Materials
Passwords–see the exchange during the Sign.
Steps–Five equal steps (entrance into the Superintendent's Chapel).
Insignia–Blue tunic, cherry colored sash with golden fringe.

---

[344] Usually in the Western Esoteric Tradition, we find that all such "strikes" occur either upon the forehead only, or in conjunction with Knighting—the forehead and right and left shoulders. Here, we see a new application which makes a deep impression into the Initiate's Ontic Sphere. The heart is opened for the Lion of the Tribe of JUDAH.

[345] Students of Crowley will see an analogy here to the Sign of Vir, or Pan, 7=4.

Jewel–a Gold[346] triangle, on one side of which is engraved the letters B∴A∴J∴ translated "Free Mason; O! God; thou art eternal." On the reverse are engraved the words; Judah, Jah, translated; "Praise be unto God."

†††

Synopsis

This Degree has much to do with advancement. In our working, advancement is an inner experience and not awarded with titles and positions. The labor that we undertake reveals the true nature of the Initiate, his Duty (or True Will, Divine injunction, or purpose) and the eternal battle between [347]Light and Darkness that occurs within himself and the world around him. The labor for this Degree begins at the Initiation and is perfected in scrying. The information and wisdom gathered from the scrying session is then to be filtered into the vicissitudes of daily life[348].

---

[346] Additional connection to the striking of the heart wherein resides Tiphareth related to the color Gold.

[347] Assuredly such does appear to be a never ending contest between Light and Darkness, but Spirit Builders are introduced to a notion that elaborates upon this Zoroastrian conception of spiritual struggle. We understand that there is a secret agreement between the Light and the Dark, and that they are *cooperating* on a mystical level, where we see struggle. A cogent symbol for this idea is found in Alchemy with the apparent struggle within the alembic of the white dove, the black raven, and the red phoenix.

[348] This constitutes the "So What?" test suggested throughout *Syzygy, Reflections on the Monastery of the Seven Rays*.

9th Degree

Élu of the Nine
Call to Chenu

9th *degree,*
Master Elect of Nine.

Battery of Knocks

Nine knocks, 8 and 1.   XXXXXXXX   X

Point Chaud

Lower cheek, left

Sacred Word

NEKHAM, reply NECHAH

Grip

Right hand of Initiate shut with the thumb raised. Present hand to Facilitator who seizes the thumb with the right hand and keeps his own thumb raised.

Sign

Facing the one proving you, make movement as if you were going to strike him on the forehead with a dagger; in reply, he will place his hand to his forehead as if to assure himself that he is not wounded. Strike at his heart as if with a dagger and say the Sacred Word, "NEKAM" (vengeance), and in reply he will place his hand on his heart saying "NEKAH[349]."

Additional Materials

Password—BEGONGAL-CHOL (abomination to all)

Steps—When entering the dangerous regions of this point, take three Apprentice steps, three Fellowcraft and three Master Mason steps. Be ready to prove yourself with the Sign of the Degree.

Insignia—Blue tunic, sash of cherry-red, with gold fringe, a black ribbon worn crosswise, at the bottom of which is a dagger as a jewel.

Jewel- Dagger pointing downwards

† † †

Synopsis

The Élu (Elect) Degrees of the 9, 15 and 12 are all interconnected and prepare the Initiate for the mysteries that accompany the Royal Arch and the Perfect Elu (Knight of the Sacred Vault in Memphis-Misraïm). The spirit working that accompanies these points chauds empowerments and Degrees are of a purifying nature which cleanses the soul for the

---

[349] Nikah is an interesting response when we trace the word derivation to Leviticus and ideas of sexual intercourse, concubinage, and further in the Quran to intercourse contracted within marriage. Right alongside the word found in all Elu & Templar Degrees, NEKHAM (Vengeance), we find a word related to bodily love!

recovery of the Lost Word. What the Lost Word is, is specific to each Initiate, but it is most assuredly connected with our truest and highest selves. The repetitious symbols of daggers[350] and severed heads in these degrees, speak to the lopping off of vices and the destruction of logismoi and negative thoughtforms that often accompany labor upon the path. Once initiated, the individual "lights up" as it were, upon the Astral and though she may attract a heavenly host to her side, every positive has its opposite. It is here that we begin to Initiate ourselves into the central mystery of the Scottish Degrees...that of Equilibrium.

When the Élu Degrees of the Scottish Rite are viewed alongside the theurgical work of the Knight Masons, Elect Coëns of the Universe, we move past the temporal and historical, and into the spirit realm. In this work we discover the true nature of the enemy and its influence upon Malkuth. Further analogy can be made to trafficking with ultra-mundane entities whose nefarious purposes are revealed by writers such as Kenneth Grant and H.P. Lovecraft. These two traditions–the Élus Coëns & the Typhonian—are working with the same deeply evil forces, yet the approach and work is distinct.

---

[350] Esoterically speaking, these martial Degrees are indicative of the nature of certain banishings and exorcisms that accompany Higher Magic.

10th Degree
Élu of the Fifteen

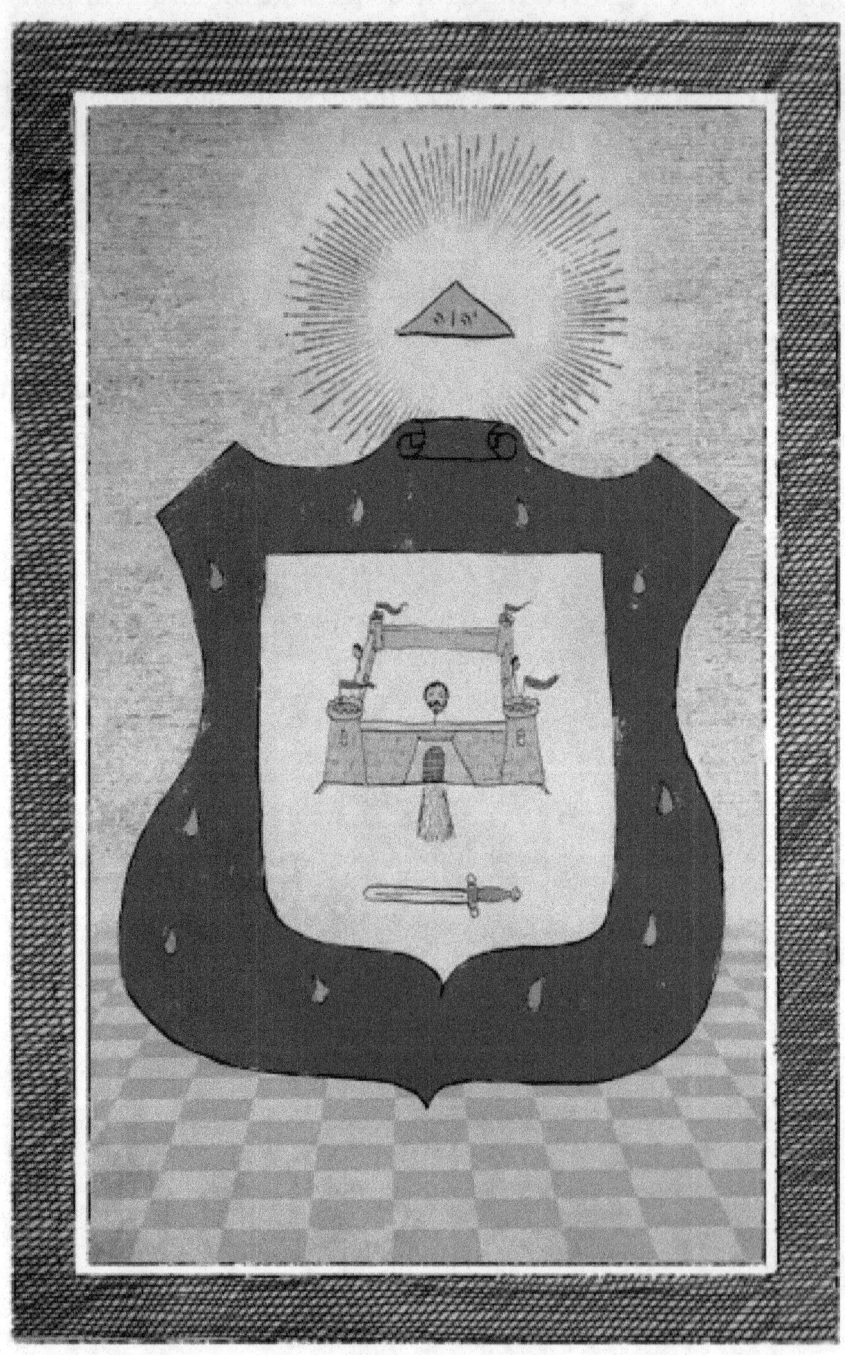

10th degree,
Illustrious Elect of Fifteen.

Battery of Knocks

Five equal knocks   X X X X X

Points Chauds

Lower cheek, right

Sacred Word

ZERBEL followed by BEN-IAH

Grip

Interlace with the Facilitator, the fingers of each other's right hand.

Sign

Place the dagger[351] under the chin; and as if one wished to open the breast, draw the hand down the body; in reply, having the point covered and the thumb raised, make the sign of an Apprentice. *This sign can be used prior to performing the Masonic Middle Pillar, to aid in opening the Sephirah.*

Additional Materials

Password–ELIAM

Steps–Fifteen regular steps

Insignia–Blue tunic, red sash fringed with gold, black ribbon worn crosswise; three heads are embroidered on the front of the ribbon.

Jewel–A Dagger, blade facing downwards (same as Elu of the 9 and 12)

†††

Synopsis

In the lecture provided in Pike's *Morals and Dogma*, we find in the Elu of the Fifteen Degree a suggestion of our Duty to perform in this life and how it may come as "devotion to some single but great object.[352]" Ceremonial Magicians spend a great deal of time working with this "great object" and birthing it into existence with the proper use of the Will. As a series of three degrees to receive at one time, the Elu of the 9, 15 and 12 perform the vital function of cleansing and purifying the machine of the Will for the accomplishment of the Great Work—which is an individual affair–yet which can be labored upon in concert with others. A triangle of points-chauds empowerments is created by the working of these three Degrees at once, activating and awakening energies and entities tied to compact areas of scintillation in the lower left cheek, lower right cheek and chin. This triangle of energetic

---

[351] The Facilitator and Initiate may utilize an actual dagger, or the action can be carried out with the hand flattened.
[352] p. 174

points is downward[353], which alludes to the preparation that these points institute for the *reception* of a great secret in the 13th and 14th Degrees, which in turn, reveals in a peculiar way, that "great object" spoken of by Pike.

---

[353] Students of the Western Esoteric Tradition will recognize the downward facing triangle as symbolic of water, receptive forces, baptism, the earth rising out of the primordial waters, and change.

11th Degree
Sublime Elected Knight or Élu of the Twelve

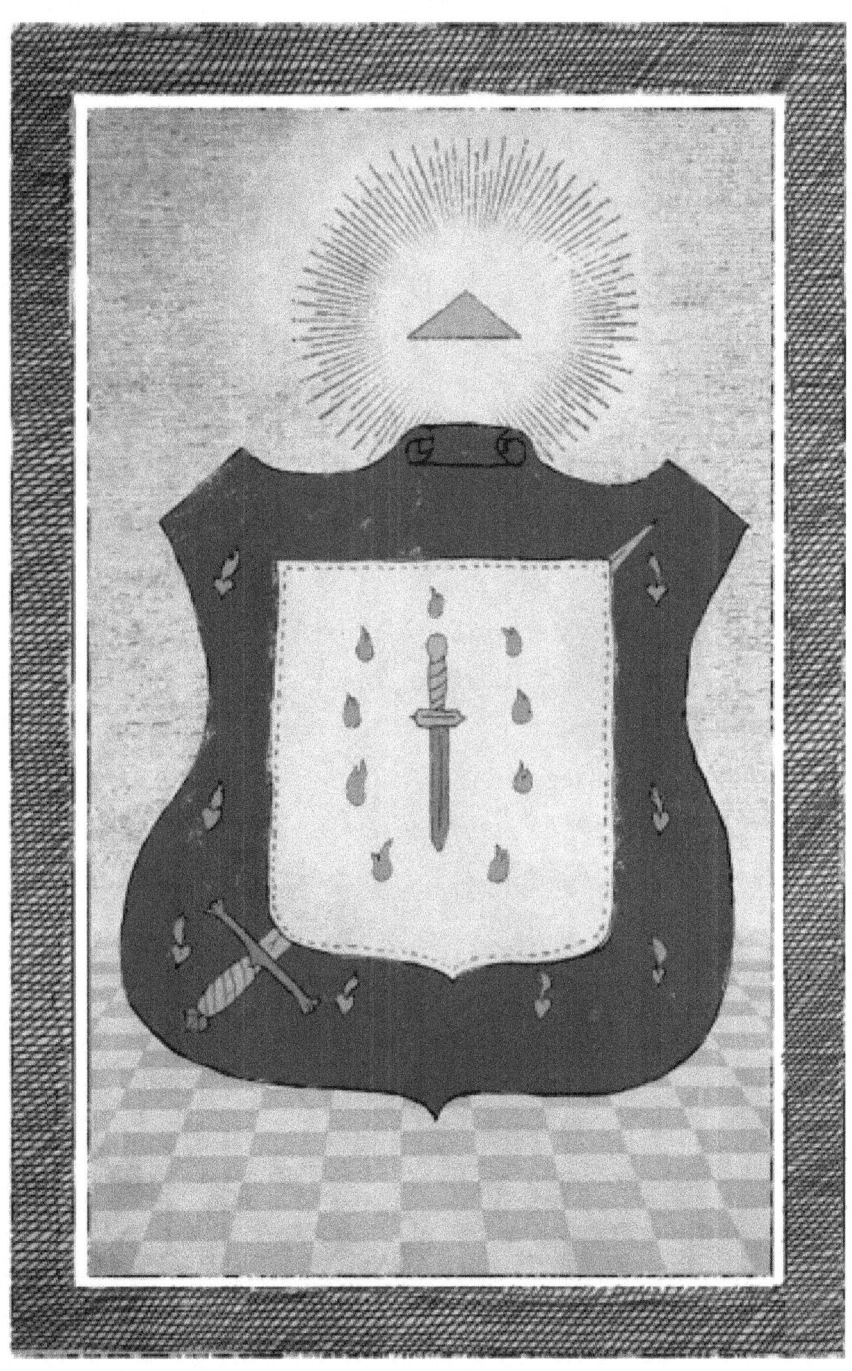

11th degree,
Sublime Prince Elect.

Battery of Knocks
   Twelve equal knocks. X X X X X X X X X X X X

Points-chaud
   Chin

Sacred Word
   ADONAI (an allusion, again, to the secret of the 14th Degree)

Grip
   The right hand being shut with the thumb raised, is mutually presented. The first one takes the thumb of the other, turns the hand over and says alternately these three words; BERITH, NEDER and SCHEELEMOTH. Then he takes the right hand of the other and presses three times with the thumb on the first joint of the middle finger. This seals the point into the body, preventing dissipation of raw energy.

Sign
   Cross arms on the breast, having the hands closed but the thumbs stuck out.

Additional Material
   Password–STOLKIN (running water) and AMAR-IAH (word of God)
   Insignia–Blue tunic, red sash with gold fringe, black ribbon worn crosswise, on which are embroidered three flaming hearts.
   Jewel–a Dagger, blade facing downwards
   There is no "Step" for this Degree, nor for many others. The reason for this is made clear when scrying the Degree. Not all degrees are accompanied by a physical structure to enter.

† † †

Synopsis
   In the dramatized ritual of this Degree, we find the completion of the punishments of the three assassins of our Grand Master, Hiram Abiff. Three severed heads comprise the early emblems of these Elu Degrees and have later been replaced by rosettes in the Ancient and Accepted Scottish Rite. However, the chief emblem of this Degree is the radiant heart of man. The word, Ameth, used in this degree signifies the "true Man" and Man (the Water Bearer, Aquarius) is the Kerubic sign of Winter, which the Philosophical Degrees as a whole refer to. Of course when, "Man" is spoken of here, we mean humanity as a whole. However, it is a masculine and martial quality that finalizes the *Purification* stage in this Lodge of Perfection. *Illumination* follows in the Royal Arch Degree and *Union* is completed in the 14th

Degree. With the activation of this points-chaud upon the chin comes the final death[354] of the negative thought-forms which prevent the clear vision of our Duty.

---

[354] Often accompanying this empowerment is a sense of mounting joy at the vengeance taken upon the logismoi and thoughtforms that have kept us from our true path. It is an odd feeling to joy in destruction, but trees must be felled before the Temple can be constructed. Only destruction is swift, the *joy unending* remains for he who would war against the negative forces preventing the accomplishment of duty.

12th Degree
Knight Grand Master Architect

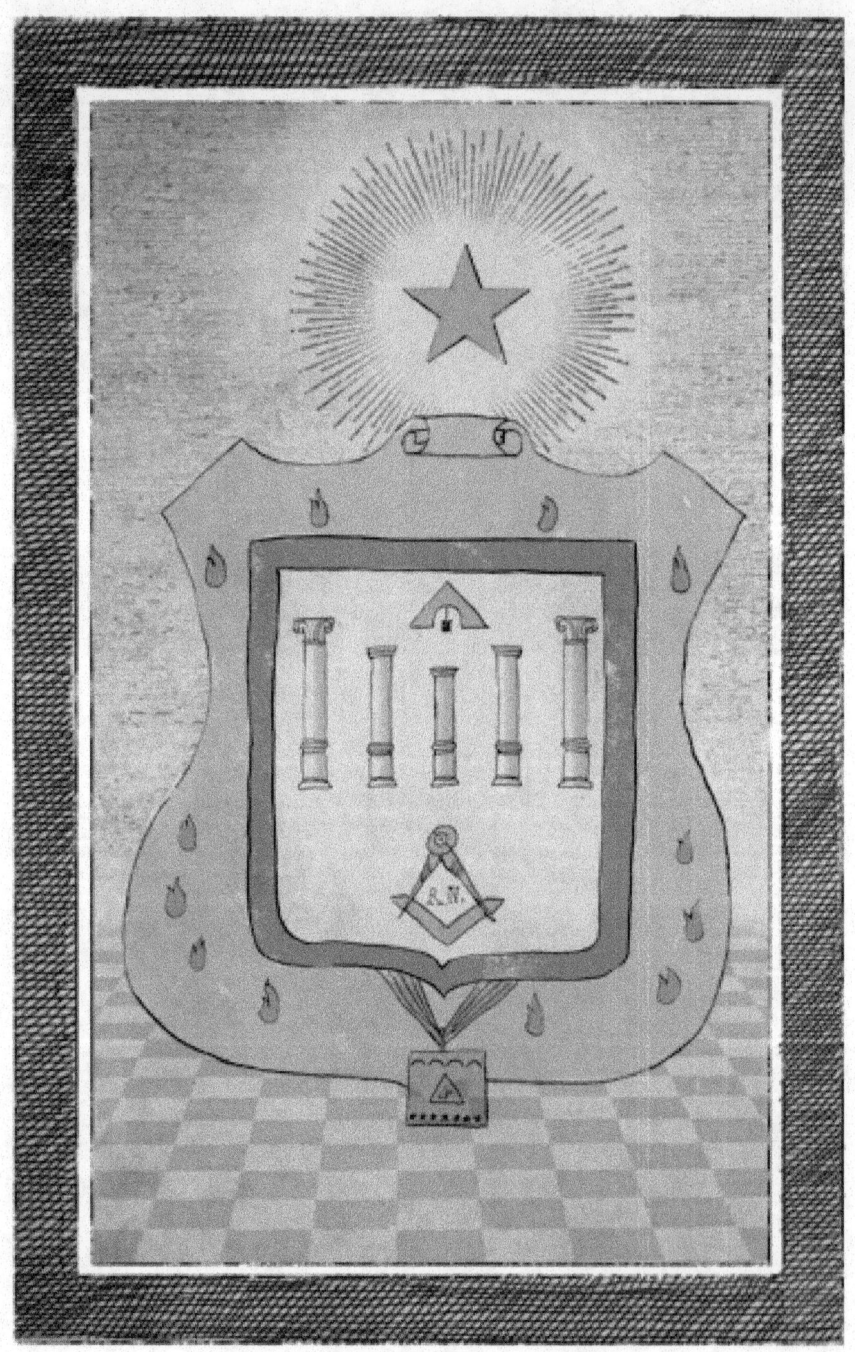

12th degree,
Grand Master Architect.

Battery of Knocks

Three by 1 and 2. X XX

Points-chauds

Upper neck, left 1 (see diagram)

Sacred Word

ADONAI

Grip

Put the left hand on the hip, and interlace the fingers of the right hand with those of the left hand of the Facilitator, who has his right hand on his hip.

Sign

Place the right hand on the left; one hand is supposed to be holding a pencil, and the other a paper; make as if to make a design, and seem to gaze at the Heavens from whence it is supposed that a suggested subject is given. This is an emblem of inspiration.

Additional Material

Password–BADBANAIN (Master of the Architects)

Steps–Three steps in the form of a square, the first are slowly and then the two others quickly.

Insignia–Blue tunic, red sash with gold fringe, blue ribbon worn crosswise.

Jewel–A square plate, on one side of which are drawn four semi-circles before seven stars, at the center is a triangle, containing the letter A, on the other face are the five orders of architecture; at the top is a level and below are a square and compasses; below the columns of the five orders are the initials of their names C.D.T.I.C. Chevend–grandeur; Devek–union; Thokath–force; Jophi–beauty; Chillah–perfection.

†††

Synopsis

Before embarking upon the final stages of the *Lodge of Perfection*, we find this Degree which, simple in its dramatic presentation, comes with the profound philosophical injunction to answer the Big Questions of life and the Universe. The points-chaud for this Degree moves into the neck region of the body and opens the deeper sources of knowledge lodged within the non-Sephirah of DAATH[355]. The portion of the Hermetic axiom aligned to the Philosophical Degrees is, "To Know," and this Degree with its respective points-empowerment, opens wide the channels of the Initiate's mind to entertain new forms of knowledge—kataphatic, apophatic, Gnostic and Ontic. This epistemological experience takes time to ferment and mature, but it is the beginning of what becomes, through the APRM+M, a thorough grounding in the varied forms of knowledge available to the Initiate.

Of particular note is the Sign of this Degree, suggestive of an inspired writer. Reference could be made to the many texts across the globe that are considered *inspired*, the Holy Writ of all generations. But reference need not stop there. We have the inspired work of Saints, of poets, of occultists, of philosophers, and even of revolutionary scientists. Whence comes this inspiration? It is from the darkness. It is born *from nothing*. An age-old argument amongst theologians concerns whether or not creation occurred *ex nihilo* (from nothing) or if it was from some sort of primordial matter (the prima materia of Alchemy). With the luminous darkness of DAATH, however, we find this to be an either/or fallacy, because all creation *does* occur from AIN, *no-thing* whose pathway is entered through DAATH upon the Tree of Life. Above the Tree are outlined three negative veils of existence, the highest of which is the no-thing, the primitive and dark source of all. From this non-isness, *dark matter* is derived to be fashioned by the will of the ONE in a descending manner unto the Aeons. The upward gaze of the Initiate giving this Sign during the scrying exercise, is drawing from dark pools of gnosis residing *above* the sphere of Yesod, Tiphareth, and even of Kether on the linear Tree of Life. These dark pools are entered via DAATH, stimulated into action with the very first Degree of our Order and its Sign. In the 12th Degree, however, DAATH is coaxed into wakefulness via the points empowerment—instituting an on-going initiation which attunes the practitioner to the manifold forms of inspiration deriving originally from the dark enshrined ONE.

---

[355] Note should be made of Kenneth Grant's special study of this dark region in his Typhonian Trilogies, but most especially in the *Nightside of Eden*, Starfire Publishing, 2014. This becomes THE source of much journeying within through the mysterious "tunnels" of the backside of the Tree of Life. Taken in conjunction with the modus operandi of the Élus Coëns, the Initiate may explore these regions—birthing Light in every corner of the Universe.

Part Three – Chapter Three: The Philosophical Degrees

13th Degree

The Holy Royal Arch

13th degree, Royal Arch.

Battery of Knocks

Five knocks by two and three. XX XXX

Points-chaud

Neck, left 2

Sacred Word

YHVH (may be pronounced, Yod, Heh, Vav, Heh)

Grip

Facilitator places the hands under the arms of the Initiate, as if to aid him to rise, saying "TOUB BANNI AMAL RAB" (it is really a good thing to reward work); in reply, the Initiate gives the same grip saying "JAHBALOM."

Sign

Admiration—one knee being on the ground, the head turned towards the left, raise the hands towards the heavens.

Of Adoration—fall on the two knees

Additional Material

Password—same as the exchange with of the Grip

Insignia—Blue tunic, red sash with gold fringe, a purple ribbon worn crosswise, on which are embroidered the letters I.V.L.O.L. (in the mouth of the Lion I found the Word—inveni verbum in ore leonis). This ribbon connects directly to the "Strength" card of the older Tarot decks.

Jewel—A golden triangle, on one side of which is the delta of Enoch with rays; on the other side is a trap-door of a vault. The delta should face outwards during a scrying session, however, if one gets lost in the labyrinth of this journey, the talisman can be flipped over to reveal to the plane and its inhabitants, that you are a Royal Arch Mason in search of the Word.

††††

Synopsis

The bright and Morning Star of a golden dawn awaits the partaker of this Degree. Amongst the Degrees in every Series, there will be key moments where the Series itself takes a quantum leap by virtue of the spiritual nature of one Degree. The Royal Arch is just such a Degree. This is the *Illumination* stage of the Lodge of Perfection. It is also the beginning of a deep search within for that "One thing necessary[356]" which is ultimately, *ineffable*. The other title for the Degrees, 4-14th is the "Ineffable Degrees." What is perceived in this empowerment is the realization of one's Duty in this life. It is symbolized, in dramatic workings, with a cube of agate that is discovered nine vaults beneath the earth's surface. This is a winter discovery, it is the seed in the ground that is *creating itself* through a latent caloric unseen. With the reception of this Degree and activation of its point on the left side of the neck, comes the illumination, the visualization of the "great object" which we must, by devotion, complete. If the knowledge of our sacred Duty is already obtained before receiving this grade, what comes is clarity of that Duty. Whereas the Elu Degrees cleared the path, THIS Degree reveals the worth of the journey itself. This path is one of self-discovery and self-realization.

The completion of this process of illumination occurs in the 14th Degree. The two should be taken together, forming a powerful and unified resolution of the Lodge of Perfection. Witness the wisdom inherent in this schema; the Elu Degrees answer to *Purification*, the Holy Royal Arch answers to *Illumination*, and the Perfect Elu answers to *Union*.

---

[356] Luke 10:38-42

Spirit Builders

14th Degree

Knights of the Sacred Vault / Perfect Élu
Realization of True Will

14th *degree,*
Grand Elect Perfect and Sublime Master.

Battery of Knocks

Twenty four knocks, 3, 5, 7 and 9. **X X X   XXXXX   XXXXXXX   XXXXXXXXX**

Points-chaud

Neck, left 3 (see diagram)

Sacred Word

JEHOVAH

Grip – *to be performed one after another for proper integration and seal of this powerful point.*

First. Give each the right hand; turn it alternatively three times, the first one saying "BERITH," and the other "NEDER," to which the first replies "SCHELMOTH."

Second. Grip the hand as in the 3rd degree saying "Are you going further?" The answer is to advance the hand along the arm to the elbow; then each one places his left hand on the right shoulder of the other, leaning forward three times with the right legs advanced. The second covering word is MACHORIM (afflictions).

Third. Each one seizes the right hand of the other and with the left hand on the right shoulder and draws the other one to him by advancing the hand on the back. These three grips allude to the three-fold path of prayer, the Rule of Three and other Trinitarian notions.

Sign

Admiration—After having inclined the head, raise the eyes and lift the two open hands toward the heavens and place the two first fingers of the right hand on the lips in the sign of the silent Horus[357].

Ecstasy—Raise the open hands, palms foremost, the fingers together, and the thumb forming a square, to the height of the shoulder and lean the head towards the left shoulder, at the same time drawing back the left foot.

Recognition—Extend the right hand, thumb forming a square, towards the left shoulder and draw the hand diagonally towards the right hip. This sign is called the scarf[358]. To reply, the Facilitator places his open right hand, palm uppermost at his left hip and draws the hand horizontally towards the right.

---

[357] Again, we return to the sign given in the initial dream transmission of the author (see Introduction to Book ONE), condensed from astral contents that drew from higher regions than simply the formative.

[358] Reference certain renderings of the Universe card of the Tarot pack. Often this scarf forms the eleventh letter of the Hebrew alphabet, Kaph. Eleven is the number of magick and Kaph means palm of the hand, which reinforces the subsequent response of the Facilitator who opens his right hand.

Additional Materials

Password–SHIBBOLETH.

Covering word–MACHORIM, 2nd is ELHANAN, 3rd is ADONAI

Grand Password–BEAMACHEAH! BAMEARAH!

Steps–Nine steps, eight quick ones and one slow, whilst holding the right elbow and placing the right hand on the cheek the palm outwards.

Insignia–Blue tunic, red sash fringed with gold, crimson ribbon worn crosswise.

Jewel–A golden compass

† † †

Synopsis

Fourteen is the number of pieces that Typhon is said to have cut the dead Osiris into in one of the Osirian stories. These fourteen pieces were scattered throughout Egypt, the animating and virile member being the one piece not recovered by Isis. Fourteen is also the number of days between the full and new moons. This Degree and its points-chaud empowerment present the Initiate with reality. The energies and entities attached to this august and sublime Degree are varied and work on many levels. It is key that we keep in mind that our Order has its roots in the ancient world of Egypt and that it is also grounded in the natural world of plants, animals, minerals, gases, moons and billions of stars. We enter a sphere of pure mystery in this grade and we experience one of the first Degrees peculiarly aligned to the stage of *Union*.

Once the points-chaud is activated and awakened and the Sacred Word vibrated, the heart of the Ineffable Degrees begins to work within the physico-spiritual body of the Initiate. Clarity was brought to our Duty in the previous Degree, but now we are presented with the reality of that Duty and our sacred injunction to perform it at all costs. This Degree has, included in the "Additional Material" section, the suggestion of a Eucharist of sorts, wherein our sacred Duty is visualized as a thought ray that can imbue the common elements of bread and water, and thus be received into the body to fully assimilate its constituents. There is no necessity for an elaborate Mass for this Degree, but if such appeals to the Initiate, so be it.

We become one with our own sacred Duty in this grade. The union is a thorough one that takes us beyond knowledge and into action. Here, we begin to see that all of our common and seemingly small actions are mirrors of the activity occurring around us on a grander scale. The microcosm of self is revealed to be a mirror image of the macrocosm—the ALL. The necessity for temples, shrines and elaborate adornments fall to the wayside in this Degree as it is realized that one is standing on sacred ground at all times. Eternity is revealed in a grain of sand and infinity in an hour, as Blake says. The Primitive Doctrine begins to surface as a new way of doing old things and conversely as an old way of doing new things. Wherever this Degree is performed is deemed a Holy Place.

Careful consideration of all of the "Secrets" of this grade will reveal additional mysteries that relate to what is occurring within the Initiate. The elaborate system of Signs, Grips and Words for this Degree, suggest a very technical scrying experience. Within the inner planes, the Initiate prepared for this Degree's innermost treasures will be in the presence of the gods of Egypt. Rather than working directly with these gods, at this stage of development, the Initiate is watching their workings as if upon a screen. The sacred drama unfolds for the Initiate and the singular Truth of the nature of personal duty and its accomplishment is presented. These Egyptian gods begin to reveal themselves to be "ensouled by cosmic forces[359]" as Fortune says. Each has a "single specialized mode of activity, uncontaminated by any alien type of energy to detract from its single-pointedness, is embodied in an astral thought-form of suitable type, which gives full scope to its activities[360]." It is in their "single-pointedness" that the Perfect Elu learns of his own means to accomplish his Duty.

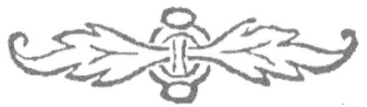

---

[359] From Dion Fortune's, *Aspects of Occultism*, 2000, p. 5.
[360] Ibid

Spirit Builders

15th Degree

Knight of the Sword or of the East

Chapter of the Rose+Croix

15th *degree*,
Knight of the East or the Sword.

Battery of Knocks

Seven knocks by 5 and 2   **XXXXX   XX**

Points-chaud

Neck left 4 (See diagram)

Sacred Word

RAPHODON

Grip

Each one takes the left hand of the other, arm raised as if to repulse an attack, and from the right make as if you were trying to pass; place the point of the sword on the heart of the other; the first one says "JUDAH," the second "BENJAMIN."

Sign

Place the right hand on the left shoulder and as if imitating the waves of a river, draw the hand towards the right hip; draw the sword and present it as if you were about to fight.

Additional Material

Password–JAABOROUHAMMAIM

Grand Word–SCHALAL SCHALON ABI

Step–Advance proudly with five long strides, bearing the sword aloft.

Cry of Acclamation–Glory to God and to the Sovereign[361].

Insignia–Blue tunic, red sash with gold fringe, water green ribbon worn crosswise, on which are embroidered bones, swords broken and swords unbroken. In the middle is a bridge on which are letters L.D.P. (meaning Liberty of Passage[362]).

Jewel–Three triangles of gold inside one another, with two swords crossed in the center, points upwards.

† † †

---

[361] This Acclamation is made immediately upon meeting any of the intermediary beings upon the Inner Planes while working with this empowerment.

[362] Along with other meanings, L.D.P. suggests: Liberty, Power, Duty; and Lilia Pedibus Destrue—the letters attached to Cagliostro.

Synopsis

There is a shift in the *Chapter of the Rose+Croix* Degrees, 15-18th, that is felt from this Degree onwards. It is a shift in the type of knowledge that the Philosophical Degrees develop. Whereas, in the *Lodge of Perfection*, the Degrees build up to a supreme realization and knowledge concerning the Self and its sacred Duty to perform, the *Chapter* Degrees institute the Grand Arcanum of the Christian Tradition—the role of sacrifice in the development of the soul. The sacrifice incumbent to the 3rd Degree is personal and crucial, while the sacrifice of the Rose+Croix is for others and their conversion[363] & enlightenment.

The Knight of the Sword Degree is an odd turn after the celebratory and Holy Perfect Elu (14th) Degree. We have been at labor to discover the Lost Word and the discovery of such leads to the internal Temple—not made by human hands—that is deemed "perfect." But here, we find the Temple in ruins again. This Degree inculcates the lessons of transience and eternal flux. The mountain-top experiences we have along the way are not states that can be held onto and perpetually dwelt in. We must go back down the mountain for supplies, interaction with others and to teach of our discoveries. Such intermingling challenges our carefully created and protected Universe and our notions of solidity and permanence, but it is also the necessary friction for further growth to happen. This Degree and the points-chaud accompanying it, will stimulate new interactions, new discoveries and new journeys along the Grand Chemin. We may encounter adversity while in this grade, but we are equipped for the war between the opposites as we have been initiated into the conciliatory path in betwixt the two.

A number of interesting symbols arise in the dramatic working of this Degree, which have import for the scrying of the point. In mainstream Masonry, the study of symbols is directed to every Candidate. These symbols reveal layers of meaning and connect symbiotically with other symbols and systems. Symbols in our working, however, sometimes become living beings and forces through scrying. We find the visage of King Nebuchadnezzar as he is being transformed into a werewolf, for instance, in the Liturgy of this Degree.[364] The King and Belshazzar are both loaded with chains and suffering[365]. The

---

[363] Here, conversion is used in the Monastic sense as a participation in the Paschal Mystery, rather than being oriented towards salvation or release from sin. This especially so in the esoteric *Monastery of the Seven Rays*.

[364] Albert Pike, *Liturgy of the Ancient and Accepted Scottish Rite, 15-18 Degrees*, 1877, p. 11. This and the additional *Liturgies* and *Legendas* have been subsumed under the impressive collection by DeHoyos, *The Scottish Rite Ritual Monitor & Guide*, 2007.

[365] In Bertiaux's, *Voudon Gnostic Workbook*, we find frequent reference to lycanthropy. But it is in his description of Ojas energy that he most clearly delineates this strange occurrence. In reference to the archetypes of the magickal psyche that become the medium for the projection of Ojas, he says, "These archetypes…act or behave like animals from some other type of space or time. They change very readily and rapidly and they transform themselves into different kinds of beings" (131). Later he describes the process of transformation and the shape-shifting of the individual into were-animals, but it is in the archetypal realm that the beings are realized as conduits for Ojas, hence the shift occurring to the "King."

L.P.D. most assuredly stands for liberty of passage in this sense, as the captives are restored to freedom while the Kings of Babylon are enchained. We also find emblems of a round tower and a wooden bridge with a stream, "with bodies and dismembered limbs floating in it[366]." These two symbols draw the mind to the Tower, the Star, & the Death cards of the Tarot pack. This assortment of images, along with the Knights Templar emblem of the sword and the trowel, become the mental architecture of this Degree through scrying.

When scrying the point of this Degree, the Initiate finds that the East and the West are now in communication. The Esoteric Tradition of Freemasonry, though grounded in Western forms and philosophies, is thoroughly influenced and inspired by Eastern concepts and ideologies[367]. This communication between two worlds (East and West) is among the positive influences that accompany the true reception of this Grade. This holistic attitude assists the Initiate in her service to the human race, for as is said in the lecture of this Degree, "It is not to the combined efforts of many, but to the energy of a single will, inducing others to follow, that great reforms are owing[368]."

---

[366] *Liturgy*, p. 11.
[367] One of the most bold and thorough examples of an Initiate who truly *received* the Degrees of *Knight of the East* and *Knight of the East and the West*, is Aleister Crowley. His thorough integration of Eastern forms of meditation, asana, & mysticism, into the world of Ceremonial Magick is a testament to the deep understanding and development of such theorems as are presented in this Degree.
[368] *Liturgy*, p. 39.

16th Degree
Prince of Jerusalem

16th *degree*,
Prince of Jerusalem.

Battery of Knocks

Twenty five knocks by 5 times 5. **XXXXX XXXXX XXXXX XXXXX XXXXX**

Points-chauds

Upper neck, right 1 (see diagram)

Sacred Word

ADAR, reply is SCHALASH ESRIM (exchange done 3 times while gnostic pressure is given)

Grip

Each presses with the right thumb five times by 1, 2, and 2 on the joint of the little finger. Each join the point of the right foot, thus making a straight line, touch the knees, and place the open left hand on the shoulder to complete the "seal."

Sign

With the left hand on the hip the sword[369] raised, stand proudly erect. Place the arm as if about to fight, having the right foot formed in a square, the heel to the toe of the left foot.

Additional Materials

Password–TEBETH, reply is ESRIM

Step–One step on the point of the toes.

Insignia–Blue tunic, red sash fringed with gold; sky blue colored ribbon, worn crosswise with the jewel attached.

Jewel–a golden medal; on one side is a hand holding a balance, and on the other a double-edged sword, blade upright, with D and Z on either side of the sword and two stars.

† † †

Synopsis

This Degree, through its Battery of Knocks and subsequent points-chaud empowerment, stimulates a Trinitarian call for Divine Assistance. The entities and energies aligned with this Degree are quite similar to the Catholic conception of the *dulia*–or reverence of the Saints. These Saints are understood to be intermediary beings between the purer forms of

---

[369] All references to swords and daggers are given as suggestive. In our own Chapel, the dagger is used only in certain cases such as in the Degrees 1-3rd. In scrying the point, the magickal sword is utilized.

Deity and the Formative and earthly realms. This Degree is a *summoning* that flows perfectly with the Knight of the East, in that in the previous Degree we experience some friction and a general stirring of energies[370]. In this Degree, that stirring is given form and substance and is called into being and into the presence of the Initiate, by the Battery of 25 knocks[371].

Recall that the 47th problem of Euclid, later deemed the Pythagorean Theorem, was uniquely connected to the notion of the Inner Guard, the Outer Guard and the Candidate in our ritualized workings of the three Degrees of the Violet Lodge, and that this correspondence led further to Osiris, Isis and Horus. When treated numerologically, Osiris is 3^2, Isis is 4^2 and Horus is equal to the addition of these two, being 5^2. When the Battery of 5 X 5 is performed for this Degree it draws these three forces into one being ~ the Initiate. Along with these Trinitarian aids come the "Heavenly Host," which may further lead to the sense of a "patron Saint[372]." The symbol for such an entrance into the City of God is the New (or Heavenly) Jerusalem, spoken of in the Kabalistic book of the New Testament, *Revelation*.

---

[370] The floating body parts in the running stream, the tower, and the instance of lycanthropy are here noted.
[371] In terms of spiritual geometry, the Pythagorean Theorem will be used to construct the Temple of Liberty that this Degree is dedicated to. This becomes more apparent in the scrying session.
[372] See Book Two of *Syzygy, Reflections on the Monastery of the Seven Rays,* for further instruction on contacting one's Patron Saint. This guide becomes a type of Conductor, in the Masonic sense.

Part Three – Chapter Three: The Philosophical Degrees

17th Degree

Knight Prince of the East and West

Ordination as Mystic & Magician

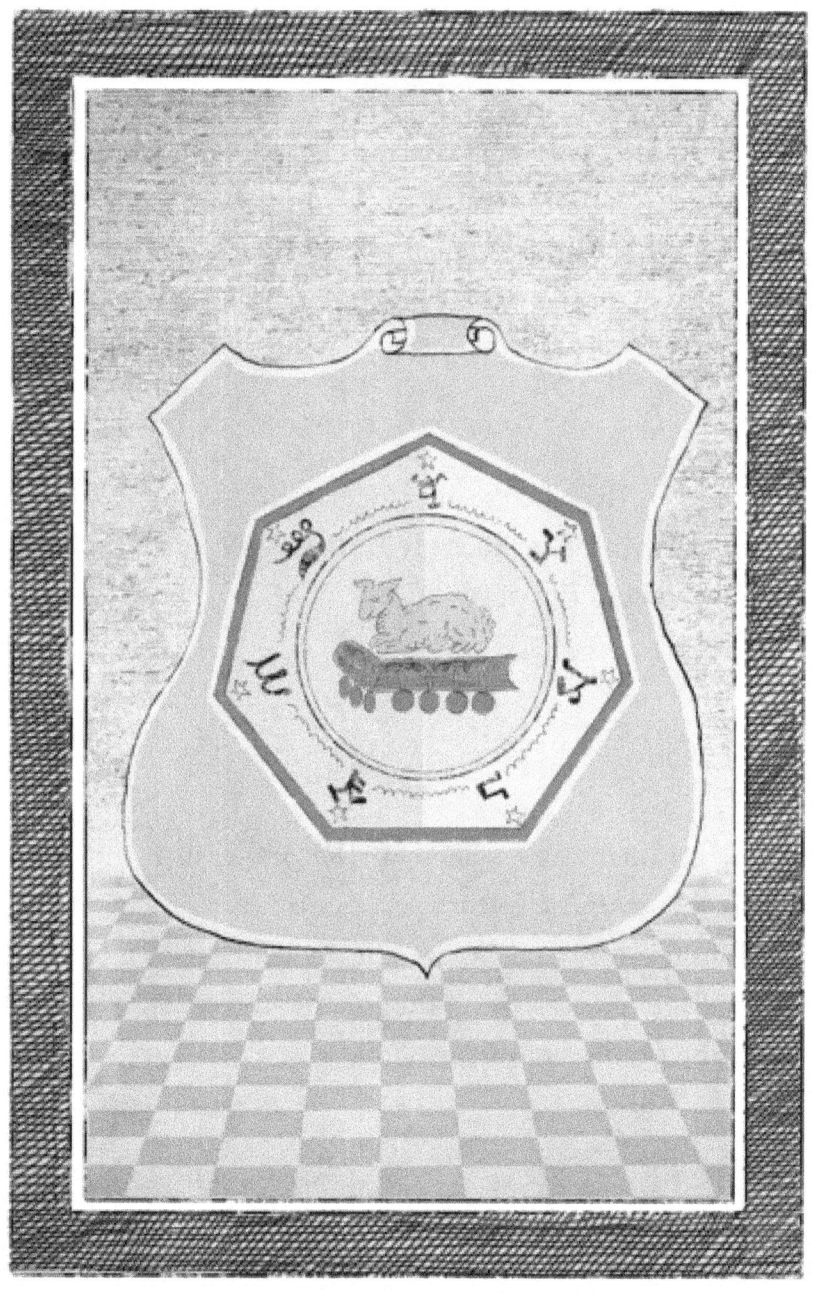

17th *degree,*
Knight of the East and the West.

Battery of Knocks

Seven knocks by 6 and 1. **XXXXXX   X**

Points-chaud

Neck on the Right, 2nd Down

Sacred Word

ABADON

Grip

1st- Place the left hand in the right hand of the Initiate, the fingers outstretched. The Facilitator covers with his other hand.

2nd- Initiate places the left hand on the left shoulder of the Facilitator who will touch the Initiate's right shoulder with his right hand.

Sign

Look at the right hand of the one examining you in scrying. Reply by looking at the shoulder of the examiner, saying alternatively "ABADON and JabuluM"; each one places his right hand on the forehead of the other.

Additional Materials

Password – JabuluM

Jewel[373]–a heptagon; on one side in each of the angles are the letters B.F.D.P.H.G.F. Above each letter is a star, these letters are the initials of the words Beauty, Divinity, Wisdom, Power, Honor, Glory and Force. In the center is a lamb in silver lying on the book of the seven seals; each seal bears one of the above letters. On the other side are two crossed swords, the points uppermost, and placed on a balanced scale.

† † †

---

[373] Note, for this Degree the Jewel—as sigil—should be created with care and precision upon parchment. Worn upon the neck of the scryer, this living symbol and talisman becomes an invitation to the angels and Archangels of the Book of Revelation. Placing the Jewel upon one's altar will cause a swelling of the Mystic Temple with the angelic presences. Such can be readily seen by the clairvoyant.

Synopsis

In dramatic working this is a very intense Degree. It takes the mysteries of the *Revelation* of St. John the Divine and utilizes them as initiatory material. This relates directly to the treatment of the same Biblical book by Eliphas Levi in several of his tomes. The Initiate would do well to read the mystical 22 Chapters of the *Revelation*, directly upon reception of this Degree.

There are many layers to the reception of this points-chaud. Throughout the working of the Ecclesiastical Revision we find a pairing down of ceremonial details and a honing in on the interior nature of mysticism and initiation. The various spirits and angelic beings that are related to this point and Degree are to be found *within the within*. The throat area of the human form has long been attributed to the elusive, secret Sephiroth, DAATH. As our initiatory path deepens and we begin to follow the guiding spirit, the Augoeides/Holy Guardian Angel attached to us, we may get flashings of the six-winged Seraphim who are present within DAATH.

There are mysteries related to blood in this Degree. Many forms of magick[374] understand the role of blood as a great condenser of astral substance. In the ritualized working of this Degree we find a number of trials that the Candidate must go through—one of which is a symbolic blood-letting. Such a magickal act can cause materialization of astral forms evoked by the ritual[375]. Though such a sacrifice is not required to complete the points-chaud working of this Degree, it is of importance to note that sometimes a blood offering is *taken* in another manner, by the spirits. For instance, many women who come to Arabia Mountain for points-chauds empowerments find that they begin menstruation spontaneously after the reception of the same. Others have had "accidents" atop Consecration Rock, which has resulted in a small blood offering upon the unhewn stone.

---

[374] Crowley's understanding of the role of blood in magick is greatly extended by the work of Kenneth Grant in his exposition of the sacred kalas related to lunar secretions (secret-ions).
[375] See Dion Fortune's description in *Aspects of Occultism*, p. 6.

18th Degree

Knight Prince of the Rose+Croix

Call to Papa Legba

18th degree, Knight of the Rose Cross.

Battery of Knocks

Three equal strokes.   X   X   X

Points-chauds

Neck on the right, third one down

Sacred Word

INRI (pronounced, En-rye)

Grip

With the arms crossed on the breast, facing each other, bow in token of salutation and without uncrossing the arms place the hands on the other's breast, and in this position give the brotherly kiss and the password.

Sign

The arms being crossed, raise the hands towards the heavens and then drop the hands to the front, in reply, with the index finger of the right hand pointing towards the heavens.

Additional Materials

Password – EMMANUEL

Jewel - A crowned compass, open on a quarter of a circle, between the branches are, on one side an eagle; and on the other side, the famous pelican opening up her own breast to feed her seven children.

Sign of Heredom - Heredom means Holy House. In our scrying sessions with the Rose+Croix degree, we may find ourselves approaching the *spiritual* Holy House of Freemasonry, which sits upon a mystical mountain. The landscape appears like Scotland in all respects. Should this occur and you meet entities in this gnostic space, use the sign and grip of Heredom, rather than the general sign and grip of the degree.

Sign—With the right hand closed, thumb raised, raise it to the height of the forehead, and draw it down to the stomach, then to the left and to the right, thus forming a cross. (This makes an inverted Tau cross, as seen on Memphis+Misraïm aprons)

Grip of Heredom—Face the entity in the scrying session and each will place the hands on the windpipe of the other. A transfer of the points-chaud will occur in this mystical setting. In this instance it is imperative to remember that "fear is failure, and the forerunner of failure."

Steps—To enter the Holy House of Masonry, take three sharp, short steps.

Synopsis

This Degree is the consummation of the Chapter of the Rose+Croix in the Ancient and Accepted Rite. It is the *ne plus ultra* of the Modern or French Rite in the Grand Orients across the globe. This Degree universally retains a special status in all jurisdictions. When the points empowerment of this degree takes hold, the Initiate can expect transformation to occur in a profound and direct manner. The transformation is of the nature of the Christian Mystery and is emblematic of the *transmutation* stage of Classical Alchemy.

The Rose+Croix mystery is essentially identical to that of the Easter Triduum. In Liturgical Churches, from Maundy Thursday through Easter Sunday, the Paschal mystery of the death and resurrection of Jesus Christ is remembered and mystically entered into. This Degree, when dramatically worked in a Lodge setting, brings the Initiate into the realities behind some of the penetrating symbols of this spiritually transformative lesson. The points-chaud empowerment compacts the raw force and energy attached to this alchemical transformation from death to life into a spiritual transmission, via the gnostic pressure upon the neck.

This point empowerment is particularly helpful in healings that relate to the apparent death of the soul, or experiences that relate to the backside of the Tree of Life–the Dark Night of the Soul–which only the persevering Initiate will rise triumphantly out of. When it is realized that this darkness is not void of life, but is indeed, the *source* of newness and growth, the Initiate grows closer to what Meister Eckhart referred to as the *luminous darkness* or *superessential* darkness.

One final note about this empowerment. Both the Sacred Word and the beginning of the grip are an indirect call to Papa Legbha. In scrying, the Initiate may say, "Papa Legbha, Open the Gates[376]..." before beginning the session and then await his arrival at the crossroads.

Note–Curiously, this Degree has a "Grip of Heredom" which directly relates to the points-chaud empowerment. This may be of interest to those who see the spirit working through the mapping and organization of these degrees with the points empowerments upon the body.

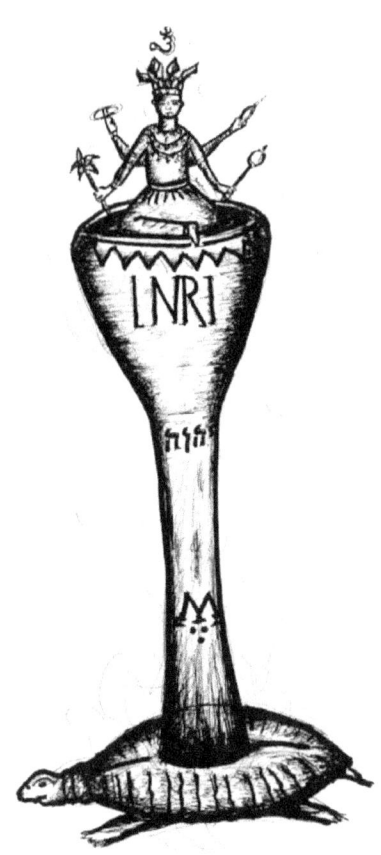

---

[376] Members of *La Couleuvre Noire* will want to utilize the proper Ceremony for Opening the Gates. The symbolism of the crossroads, and the nature of the blood sacrifice as a gate-opener is consistent with the Rose+Croix grade when it is understood that to be a Voduisant in Haiti, is to be a member of the Roman Catholic Church.

Spirit Builders

19th Degree
Knight Grand Pontiff of Jerusalem
Council of Kadosh
Ordination

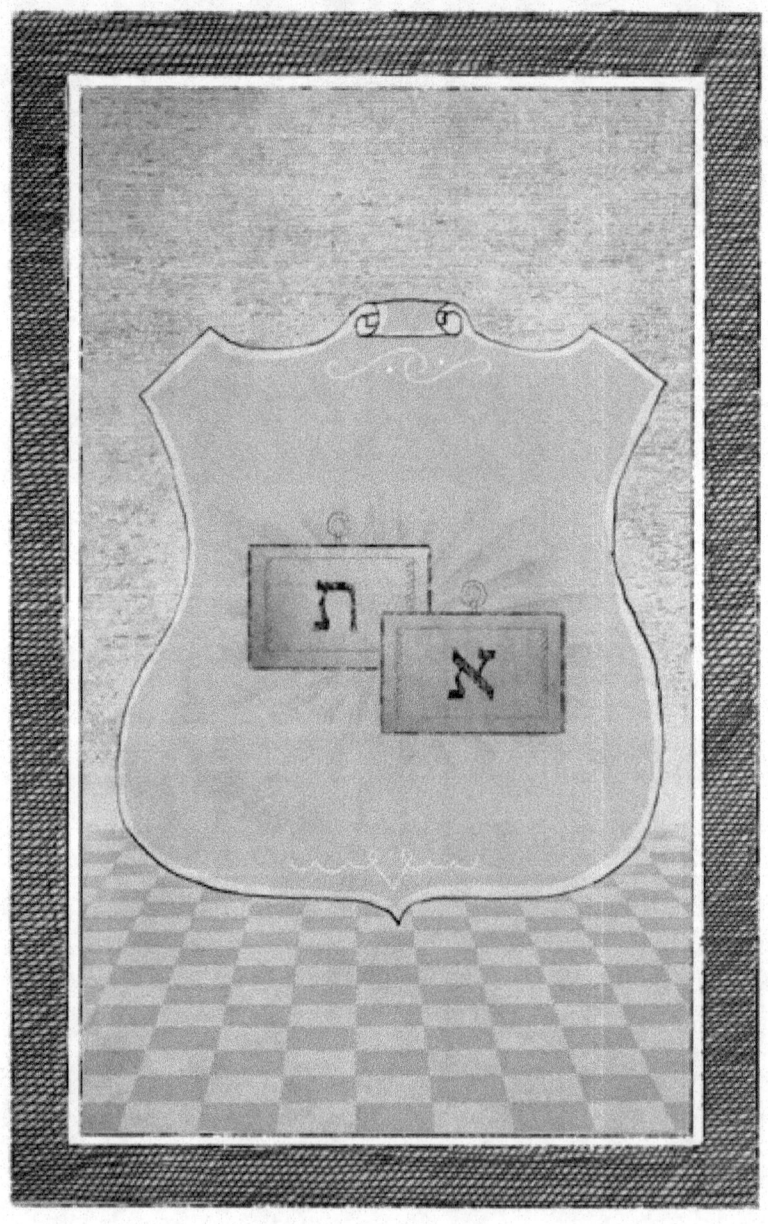

19th *degree,*
Knight Crand Pontiff of Jerusalem.

Battery of Knocks

Twelve knocks by 2, 1, 2, 1, etc. **XX X, XX X, XX X, XX X**

Points-chauds

Neck on the right, 4th point down

Sacred Word

ALLELUIA

Grip

Each one puts the palm of his right hand on the forehead of the other; the first says, "ALLELUIA," the second, "Praise the Lord." In reply, the first says, "EMMANUEL," and the second, "God help you," and both say AMEN. This seal mystically places the Initiate in the Order of Melchizedek. For Initiates that are Priests, this grip is a renewal of the vows of Ordination.

Sign

Extend the right hand, the hand open, and lower perpendicularly the three last fingers.

Additional Materials

Password - EMMANUEL

Jewel - a Dove, flying downward[377]

†††

Synopsis

In the Ancient and Accepted Rite, this Degree signals the moment when the subject matter of the Masonic mythos shifts from constructing a physical Temple and moves into the creation of the spiritual one, identified as the Heavenly or New Jerusalem. As the literal meaning of pontiff is "bridge-builder," we see how readily our task of spirit-building is connected with the Ecclesia at large and the Spiritual Temple in the Heavens. That *Sovereign*

---

[377] The decent of the dove is a common feature in the Christian doctrine, beginning with the Baptism of Jesus by John. In this Degree, however, with its ties with the Universal priesthood of all Ages, the decent of the dove is emblematical of the spirit entering the material substances of the Eucharist. Other applications of the Eucharist can be made in reference to the mystery represented by the O.T.O. lamen.

Sanctuary that we enter beyond our personal Ontic sphere, the cloud-like Temple above from which we draw down energies and entities, becomes the focus of the degrees henceforth.

Additionally, this degree is the beginning of the Council of *Kadosh,* which means "sacred." This set of Philosophical degrees enters upon the great subjects of the Knights Templar, Alchemy and Magic, along with discoveries concerning the Primitive Faith of the ancients and their Sacred Doctrine of Light. The points-chauds empowerments move downward from the sternum to the lower abdomen in this set, vitalizing the central column along the body for the Higher Magic ahead in the Hermetic, Kabalistic and Gnostic Grades.

For those working the Misraïm Chapel Rite, this Degree is utilized in the Major Order of Priesthood.

20th Degree

Grand Master of All Symbolic Lodges
or
Knight Grand Master of the Temple of Wisdom

20th *degree,*
Knight of the Temple.

Battery of knocks

Three knocks by 1 and 2   X   XX

Points-chaud

Left, upper chest

Sacred Word

BETSIJAH

Grip

Facilitator and Initiate hold the right elbow of each other with the right hand and press it four times. Then each slides the hand up to the wrist and presses on it with the index finger.

Sign[378]

With the head inclined towards the left, kneel, and place the elbows on the ground. This alludes to the position of scrying and arriving upon another plane.

Additional Materials

Password–JEKSAN, reply will be ZABULON, then respond, NABUZARDAN.
Jewel–a gold triangle

†††

Synopsis

The ritualized working of this degree is unforgettable in its utter simplicity. Nine candles are lit, each with a moral and philosophical lesson read to the Initiate. The lecture amended to this degree in Pike's, *Morals and Dogma* is a beautiful call to Masonic virtue and leadership. The spiritual working of this degree with its accompanying points-chaud is consistent with our entire edifice, the efficient nature of this degree, and its lecture. It is that of primitive simplicity, expounding upon the Primitive Doctrine in plain language.

This point empowerment stimulates–through the energies and entities attached to it–the primitive faith within us. Such stimulation may bear fruit of a practical nature; the Initiate may become inspired to do a bit of "house-keeping" in terms of relationships or

---

[378] This peculiar position also alludes to the position of Ordination in the Élus Coëns. In this way, this Degree puts the previous one in a particular contest that is preparatory for the work in the 61st Degree.

involvements that are not aligned with his True Will. The spirit of the Primitive Doctrine that is espoused in this Degree is the very same that inspired our use of the Three-fold Path of prayer as scaffolding for initiations, Masses and the like. Particular note should be taken of areas of one's life that are overly complicated, as this Degree will bring clarity to simplifying and streamlining our activities.

Following the reception of this points-chaud empowerment, the Initiate would benefit from the Facilitator reading aloud Albert Pike's lovely lecture on this Degree from "Morals & Dogma."

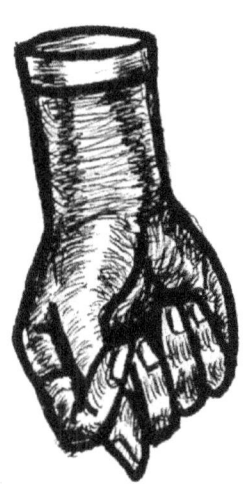

21st Degree

Knight Noachite, or of the Tower

21st *degree*,
Patriarch Noachite.

Battery of Knocks

Three slow knocks. X X X

Points-chaud

Right ,upper chest

Sacred Word

SHEM, HAM and JAPHET

Grip

After having taken the index finger of the right hand of the Initiate, the Facilitator presses it with the index finger and thumb, saying "SHEM"; the Initiate makes the same sign, saying "HAM" and in repeating the grip, the Facilitator says "JAPHET."

Sign

Turn the face towards the rising moon, raise the arms towards the heavens.

Additional Materials

Password–PHALEG

Grip or entrance in Scrying–Present to the spirit the fingers of the right hand; you should hear or sense the words, "FREDEREICK THE SECOND," then the spirit presents three fingers to which you reply, "NOAH." *Step*–Three Master's steps.

Jewel–A golden equilateral triangle with an arrow across it. On the other side, a silver moon.

† † †

Synopsis

This Degree, historically, enters the bizarre realm of *Noachite Masonry*. In this manner of Masonic mythos, there are primitive doctrines relating to Old Testament stories. However, the points-chaud empowerment, though having little connection with this history or pseudo-history, relates directly to the simple degree working of this Knightly grade. In the Degree there is a singular light to be used exclusively, which is to stand for the moon, if the degree cannot be worked by moonlight. Additionally, the mythos is in connection with the tower of Babel—hence the Password, "Phaleg" or "Peleg" meaning, for degree workings, division.

However, a cursory scan through Medieval Grimoires reveals the name PHALEG as an Olympian Spirit of Mars, particularly in the *Arbatel of Magic*. Some who receive this point/Degree, will experience PHALEG in this aspect—full on! This will be accompanied by an almost militaristic decision of drastic change. Finally, the Jewel is a triangle traversed by an arrow. Seen together, these emblems occur in the Tower card of the Tarot pack. Of the many meanings derived from this card, the one specific to the points-chaud empowerment is *drastic change* in one's conceptual understandings. Recall that these Philosophical Degrees are developing forms of knowledge within us that lead to wisdom. The *drastic change* or paradigm shift connected with the energies and entities of this point empowerment lead to such wisdom. It is suggested that this point be given outside by the light of the Full or Waxing Moon.

One final note is in order pertaining to this Degree. This lunar grade has particular reference to the Sephiroth of YESOD. The "darkly splendid realms" therein are a joy to traverse, yet are beset with dangers. The undisciplined mind can become an Astral junkie, obsessing over the phantasmagoria of images, and preferring the ephemeral and illusory to the higher states of consciousness. However, when escorted and conducted by one's Patron Saint, the Chapel of YESOD reveals curious forms of a spiritual quality that will offer initiations and further passage to the Initiate[379].

---

[379] These higher forms of Astral substance are of a religious nature and respond as such when treated in a devotional light.

22nd Degree

Knight of Liban

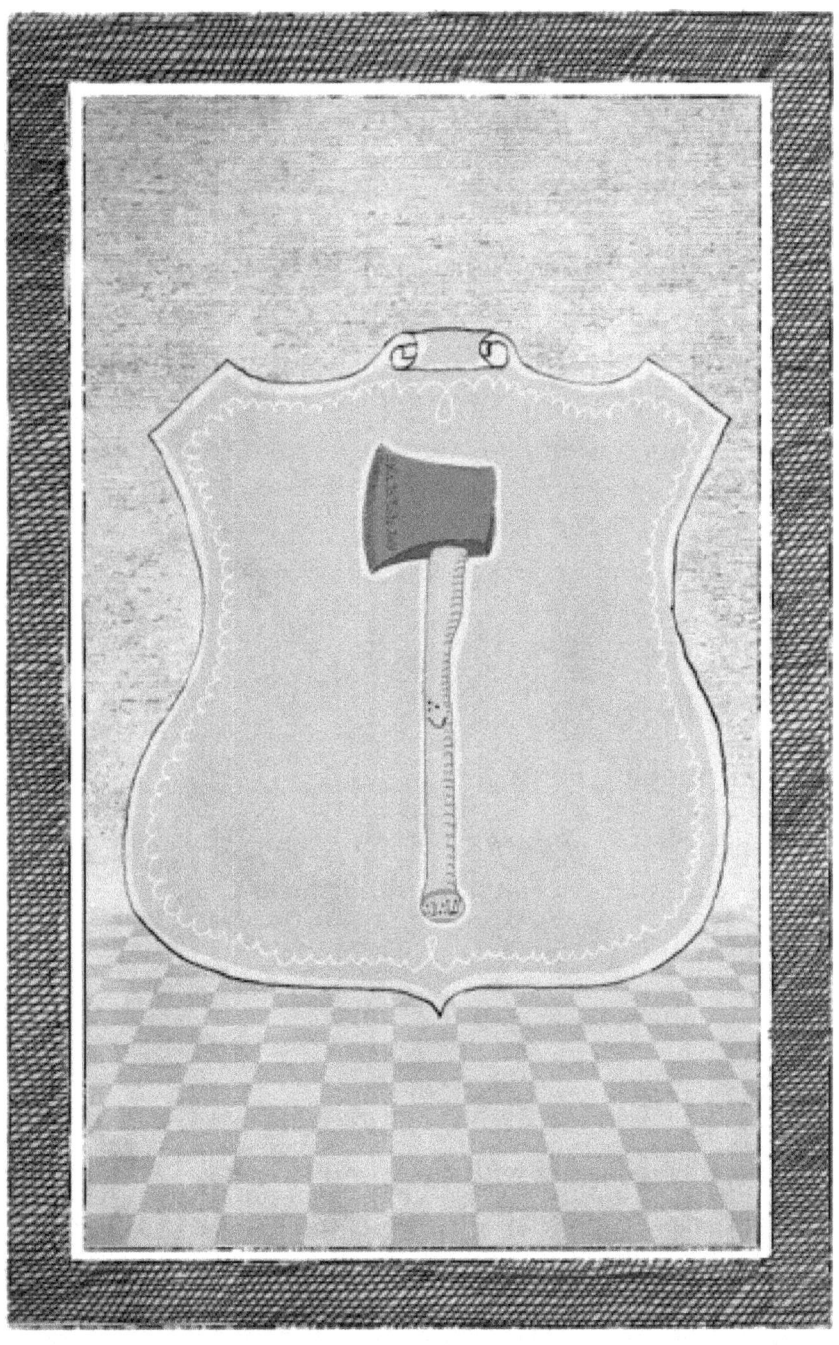

22nd degree,
Knight of the Royal Axe.

Battery of Knocks

Two Equal Knocks   X   X

Points-chauds

Center of the chest below the collar bone.

Sacred Word

NOAH, BEZALEEL and SIDONUS (all three are given to the Initiate)

Grip

Each takes the hands of the other and intertwines the fingers.

Sign

Make a sign as if lifting an axe with both hands to cut a tree at its base. Reply: Raise the two hands, the fingers extended as high as the forehead, and then drop them.

Additional Materials

Steps–Three steps crosswise.

Password–JAPHET, AHOLIAB

Jewel–a golden axe surmounted by a crown

Collar[380]–attach the Jewel to a rainbow colored ribbon. Make sure that it is made to drop down low enough to reveal the points-chaud empowerment zone.

† † †

Synopsis

This Degree is entirely concerned with the nobility of work. The signs and insignia of the degree reinforce this and the traditional working is a scene involving laborers. The points-chaud empowerment with the degree relates to the so called "work spirits" of Hoodoo. These spirits are less distinct than the *Lwa* of Haitian Vodou, or the Saints syncretized with the same, and are more akin to the activities of Elementals. They are

---

[380] In general, a simple lanyard is all that is necessary for the Jewel on parchment. However, for this one, as it relates directly to *the Monastery of the Seven Rays*, a collar of these same rays should be created. This may be crafted using colored ribbons, a rainbow scarf, etc. In one way, the colors are emblematic of the Syzygies—Gnostic Archons of the planets discovered in the Year One coursework. *Knight of the Rainbow* is also the VII Degree in the OTOA.

entirely practical and constitute the "Doo" of Hoodoo. With the gnostic pressure of this point, an opening occurs in the center of the chest, just below the collar bone. This is an inner opening to the worlds within that contain powers and energies which we rarely make use of. The symbol of the rainbow used on the collar relates to these many colored energies as well as to the Monastery of the Seven Rays, wherein many of these energies were first discovered and shared with others through Patriarch Bertiaux's *Voudon Gnostic Workbook*, the Monastery Coursework[381], et al.

And yet another meaning is attached to the rainbow collar of this Degree. Recall that in the previous Grade we were working with energies and entities of a lunar and YESODIC nature. As we journey up the Tree, we encounter the Veil of Paroketh, often symbolized by the rainbow. The Tarot card, Temperance, is pertinent to this portion of the journey. Initiates who follow the path of the Arrow will readily understand the mystical nature of this movement from illusion to the deepest reality. This inward movement is perfected in the work of the 97th Degree where the Initiate studies that luminous darkness that is a "being beyond being and a nothingness beyond being," as Meister Eckhart says.

---

[381] *The Monastery of the Seven Rays* has a temporal center in Chicago, USA at the home of Michael-Paul Bertiaux. Yet it exists as a hyper-spatial spiritual edifice as well. Many work with the Monastery through fraternal and occult Orders such as the **OTOA-LCN**, and others--while individuals work a solitary path with its teachings as well. This manner of monastic only has a cloak for his cloister, and may employ such common means as a crying baby in the night as a call to vigil and awareness. These are monks *in the world* who paradoxically venture *outside the gates of time*.

Spirit Builders

23rd Degree

Knight of the Tabernacle

23rd *degree,*
Chief of the Tabernacle.

Battery of Knocks

Two equal knocks X X

Points-chaud

The Heart

Sacred Word

IRAM

Grip

Each takes with the right hand the left elbow of the other.

Sign

Facilitator acts as if he is holding a censer in the left hand, attempts to seize the censer with the right hand, at the same time advancing the left foot. Initiate advances the left foot at the same time, creating the seal upon Malkuth.

Additional Materials

Steps–Five equal steps.

Password–HAHTZIELD. Reply, DARAKIEL

Jewel–a delta

† † †

Synopsis

This Degree, styled, *Chief of the Tabernacle* in the Scottish Rite, introduces the Initiate to the system of celestial correspondences contained in Astrology. In the degree workings themselves, this is cloaked by the Twelve Tribes of Israel, but the story develops further as we begin to understand the symbols inherent in the banners of these tribes. For instance, the tribe of Ephraim has the emblem of a bull. It is the Kerubic sign of Taurus in the spring. Additionally, we find Judah relating to the Lion—Leo, and we begin to understand what is meant by the *strong grip of the lion's paw of the Tribe of Judah*. The device of the Urim and the Thummim are also introduced in this degree with the understanding that they were binary divinatory tools of the High Priests of Israel. This was a sort of breastplate, believed to contain magical items. Curiously enough in the AASR working, we find suggested two figures inside the Urim and Thummim of Egyptian origin—RA and MAAT.

In addition to introducing notions of Astrology and Divination, this degree focuses upon the Holy implements and emblems of the Tabernacle of Moses. It is helpful to recall that this was essentially a tent with the Holy items within it. The two phrases, *Holiness to the Lord* and *Holy things are for the Holy* are also introduced, the former being, KADOSH l'YHWH in Hebrew and the latter being, Sancta Sanctis in Latin. *Holiness to the Lord* is the banner of Royal Arch Masonry and repeated in the Old Testament frequently. *Holy things are for the Holy* is chanted at every Liturgy of the Eastern Orthodox Church and has been since the 4th Century and possibly earlier.

Another important philosophical lesson of this Degree can be found in the Ritual Monitor & Guide. The Excellent Priest says; *The manifold is an infinite illustration of the One...By the rays of his divine light, we become conscious of His being.*[382] This lesson in emanationism reflects Kabalistic ideas, as well as those of the Hermeticists. In speaking of the *Nous*, we find the author of the Corpus Hermeticum saying; *Nous, O Tat, comes from God's essence, if indeed He has essence...Nous is not separate from God's true essence, but is, as it were, spread out from it just like the light of the sun.*[383] In this lesson it is the power of the mind in its full capacity that makes one divine. This spiritual mind or rarefied intellect, then is a ray from divinity itself.

While working this points-chaud empowerment with my wife, I was reminded of how the diagrams are simply pointers. She looked back at the diagram, looked at my chest and then sensing that it was elsewhere, carried on with the empowerment. She was precisely correct. Immediately upon reception of the point, I got a visual impression of a desert scene with darkened figures looking at the night sky. This Degree develops a *desert-like* mysticism within the Initiate. It has, attached to it, spirits who assist in areas of astrology and divination. It is a Holy point and reminds the Initiate that the Primitive Doctrine reveals the complexity of the cosmos within the simple. The microcosm of the body continuously reflects the macrocosm of the universe.

---

[382] P. 471 of *The Scottish Rite Ritual Monitor & Guide*, De Hoyos.
[383] From, *The Way of Hermes*, 2000, Inner Traditions International. Consider also, the path of Noetical research in the *Monastery of the Seven Rays*.

The work of this Degree includes an Altar of Sacrifice, a basin of bronze, a Table of Presence, the Candelabrum, Altar of Incense, and the repository of the Mysteries—the Ark of the Covenant[384]. For the Initiate, these items suggest Purification (basin, incense, sacrifice), Illumination (the Candelabrum) and Union (the Table of Presence & the Ark). This empowerment continues the upward/inward movement from Yesod (groin area) through the Veil of Paroketh (Rainbow), now into the heart of Tiphareth.

---

[384] *The Scottish Rite Ritual Monitor & Guide*, p. 467.

24th Degree

Knight of the Red Eagle or Prince of the Tabernacle

Call to Uriel

24th *degree,*
Prince of the Tabernacle.

Battery of Knocks

Seven by 6 and 1.   XXXXXX X

Points-chaud

Left upper abdomen

Password *and* Sacred Word

URIEL, reply "Tabernacle of the revealed truths."

YHVH (spelled out, Yod, Heh, Vav, Heh)

Grip

Each takes with the right hand the left elbow of the other.

Sign

The *Grand Sign*—place the two hands open on the head, join the two thumbs and the two index fingers by their extremities to form a triangle[385].

Additional Materials[386]

Steps—Six equal steps and one longer step, to enter the Chapel of the *Sixth Ray* Archangel, Uriel.

Sign of Recognition—As if to shield oneself from a bright light, place the right hand on the eyes, and the left hand open on the breast; carry the right hand towards the left shoulder, and draw it diagonally towards the right side; this is called the sign of the sash.

Sign of Admiration—Incline the head forward, the right hand on the breast[387], the eyes raised to the heavens, and covered by the left hand.

Jewel—the "Grand Star" or pentagram[388] in gold.

† † †

---

[385] Note that this is a Fire triangle

[386] As the Chapel of Uriel is in the presence of an Archangel, further testing is required of the Initiate during scrying to enter the various shrines and vaults in this sacred space. The memorization of the Password, Sacred Word, Steps, and all Signs are necessary for this scrying session to be fully realized. Also, the "Grand Star" should be worn at heart level. This is the sign of the microcosm, the celebratory symbol of the sovereignty of humans—the divine pentagram.

[387] Further associated with the Sixth Ray in some systems.

[388] Immediately this Degree places the Initiate in a magickal sphere—the presence of an Archangel, the Grand Sign of the pentagram (the sign that we receive points in, in the Chapel of the Gnosis), and the statement in the Liturgy of the work that Pike quotes from Eliphas Levi; *the Initiate is he who possesses the Lamp of Trismegistus, the Cloak of Apollonius, and the Staff of the Patriarchs*, p. 485, *Scottish Rite Ritual Monitor & Guide*.

Synopsis

This degree hints at the nature of the Hermetic and Gnostic body of degrees to come. It is occult and fiery. The Knight of the Red Eagle degree and subsequent points-chaud empowerment has the ability to stir up the necessary energies, the fiery hot qualities of the personality that are implicit in the accomplishing of one's True Will. It may be that the Initiate has not even tackled this aspect of the path, but after this empowerment, he may no longer skirt around it. The path, though winding and varied, is one directed towards singularity of purpose.

In Lodge workings, this Degree returns to the testing of the Elements as found in the First Degree in all French & Scottish Rite systems. The accompanying spirits of Earth, Air, Water, and Fire are invoked tangentially through the return to these tests within the Lodge, yet in the points-chaud empowerment under the upper left abdomen of the Initiate, is found the source of the stimulating energies of the Red Eagle itself. There are spirits that are awakened from this empowerment. When properly performed, the Initiate may have a fiery vision—particularly something akin to a phoenix. If performed outside, this point should be taken while facing the sun. Let the Initiate close her eyes and receive this empowerment as the rays of the Sun warm her body and open her mind's eye to the energies and entities of this degree. The Archangel of the Sixth Ray is the "Fire of God" and is often associated with the heart & the solar plexus.

This degree diverges from the majority of others by utilizing both the Password and the Sacred word with the empowerment. The powerful name of URIEL is vibrated firstly, as it is the Archangel of the Sixth ray. This form of Sacred Magick is explored further in the *Arcana Arcanorum*. Martinists will be familiar with working with Uriel in their General Ritual. The Knock calls to the 6th Ray and adds to it the ONE, forming the Holy number, seven—the number of the Archangels. The Sign of the degree is the classical sign for Fire, the hands forming an upward triangle upon the forehead. The closeness of the Grip—the seal of the point within the body—is identical to the previous degree and completes what was begun on the inner planes in that degree.

Part Three – Chapter Three: The Philosophical Degrees

25th Degree

Knight of the Brazen Serpent[389]

Invocation of Damballa

25rd *degree,*
Knight of the Brazen Serpent.

---

[389] For an exploration of serpent worship across the globe, see *Ophiolatreia*, 2013, Transmutation Publishing.

Battery of Knocks

Nine knocks, five slow, then three short, and then one. X X X X X   XXX   X

Points-chaud

Upper Left Abdomen, 2. *Trace the **sign of the cross** with the thumb touching the forehead, stomach, right shoulder and left shoulder of the Initiate immediately after giving this powerful point.*

Sacred Word

MOSES, spelled out, M-O-S-E-S[390]

Grip

Take with the left hand the left wrist of the Initiate; in reply, he will take your right wrist with his right hand.

Sign

Point to an object on the ground[391] with the index finger of the right hand; incline the head.

Additional Materials

Steps—Nine Steps taken in a serpentine manner.

Password & Cover word—INRI, cover word, JOHAN RAPH

Jewel—Grand Star, the golden pentagram

---

[390] For the RÉAUX+CROIX and Grand Elect Coëns, the Prayer of Moses is cogent here.

[391] This gesture alludes to Exodus 7: 8-13; *[10] So Moses and Aaron went to Pharaoh and did just as the Lord commanded. Aaron threw his staff down in front of Pharaoh and his officials, and it became a snake. [11] Pharaoh then summoned wise men and sorcerers, and the Egyptian magicians also did the same things by their secret arts: [12] Each one threw down his staff and it became a snake. But Aaron's staff swallowed up their staffs. [13] Yet Pharaoh's heart became hard and he would not listen to them, just as the Lord had said.*

Synopsis

The ritualized working of this degree brings the Initiate in front of an ancient symbol of a Tau cross entwined with a serpent. It is the Brazen Serpent of the book of Numbers, 21:5-9. By lifting up this bronze serpent to the Israelites, Moses, the central figure of this Degree, would heal those bitten by the plague of fiery serpents in the desert. This is certainly one of the most mystical portions of the Old Testament and figures heavily in many Grimoiric workings. What Moses created was both a *sigil* and a *talisman*.

While receiving this points chaud empowerment, the Initiate may sense a flood of activity within the body, by way of increased perspiration and pulse. This empowerment may even create a slight pain where the gnostic pressure takes place. This is simply due to the power of the primordial current that is being awakened within the Initiate[392]. In the original version of this Degree[393], the Sign of recognition is made by the Candidate giving the sign of the cross on the upper abdomen near the heart. As this empowerment causes such strong physiological responses in the body, it is appropriate to respond to the spirit working with such a symbol directly after receiving the point.

Whereas the previous degree comes full-freighted with a fiery and generative experience of one's True Will by virtue of introduction to the Archangel Uriel, this degree takes the Initiate into the primordial currents connected with the serpent[394]. When fully received, the points chaud of this Degree will establish contact with the pure and ancient Lwa of creation, *Damballa*. In Haitian Vodou, Damballa is both syncretized with St. Patrick and with Moses. An involuntary response to the action of Damballa within the Initiate often occurs by way of making hissing sounds or being drawn downwards towards the earth[395]. Additionally, when scrying the point one would do wise to have the passage from the book of Numbers read firstly and to practice the nine Steps physically before embarking upon the super sensual realms with Damballa[396]. When working a form of the Voudon Cabala, such as that suggested by the likes of Milo Rigaud, Sally Ann Glassman, and Michael-Paul Bertiaux, Damballa is found to be aligned with Kether. This *brush* with the energy and entity of Kether completes the first experience of the Path of the Arrow from Malkuth to Kether.

---

[392] Indeed, the full reception of this empowerment feels like a snake bite and the perspiration and pulse increase is akin to the body's response to venom. However, recall that this is the Brazen Serpent of Moses—its nature is healing. In this way, it is more akin to the sacred caduceus.
[393] See *Albert Pike's Masonic Formulas and Rituals*, by De Hoyos, 2010, p. 467.
[394] Reference can again be made to the Esoteric Vodoun of *La Couleuvre Noire*.
[395] Keep in mind that the Steps of this Degree are in a *serpentine* fashion.
[396] If working with Damballa, care should be taken to keep all purified and to use only white materials if at all possible. Damballa enjoys a number of offerings, including: an egg surmounted upon a mound of flour, coconut milk, bread, and cookies.

Finally, as the Degree has a rather consistent meaning and feel to it throughout, we need to address the "Cover word" that may be used during scrying. The word is, John Ralph, which the Yarker material suggests means, "sun, to heal." The solar healing aspect is assuredly consistent with the overall meaning of the Brazen Serpent and its ability to cure those bitten by the snakes, but what of name, John Ralph? The meaning is dual. John, in the Memphis workings is spelled, Johan, which alludes to the Johnnanite Gnostics. Ralph alludes to "Raphadon[397]" relating to the Essenes known to have an order of Therapeutae, or healers, which is also connected with *Rephaim* who are said to be the descendents of the Nephilim. Finally, one of the legends suggests that John Ralph was the head of the Order of Knights of the Brazen Serpent, a Templar Order that had Healing as one of their sacred and monastic duties. When considered with the fact that recent discoveries have unearthed authentic Templar coins with the Gnostic Abraxas engraved upon them, the connection of Gnostics, Healers and Knights is complete. Add to this the healing nature of the Brazen Serpent erected by Moses and the pure primordial strength of Damballa and the symbolism is complete.

Such is stirred within the Temple of the body when this points chaud empowerment is given. The healing is for the Initiate, but it is indicative of the healing that he or she will turn and give to others[398]. Again, this power is initially sensed as a stirring of the blood, a quickening of the pulse, and sudden blood pressure adjustment.

---

[397] Related also to the great Archangel of healing, Raphael.
[398] For a sane exposition of spiritual healing in the Rosicrucian tradition, see Dion Fortune's essay, "The Pitfalls of Spiritual Healing" from *Aspects of Occultism*, pgs. 54-69. Also, refer to the Holy *Rose+Croix d'Or* and their methodology as exemplified in Robert Ambelain's, *The Sacramentary of the Rose Croix*.

Part Three – Chapter Three: The Philosophical Degrees

26th Degree

Prince of Mercy or Scottish Trinitarian

Call to the Immaculate Conception & La Sirène

26th degree,
Knight of the Holy City.

Battery of Knocks

Fifteen knocks by 3, 5, and 7.   **XXX   XXXXX   XXXXXXX**

Points-chauds

Lower left abdomen

Sacred Word

EDUL PEN CAGU

Grip

Place the two hands on the shoulders of the Initiate; press three times saying, "GOMEL."

Sign

The two thumbs and the two index fingers joined at the extremities, covering the area near the apron, forming a downward facing triangle.

Additional Materials

Steps—Three equal steps, beginning with the left foot.

Password–GOMEL

Sign of Entry—as if to protect one's self from a bright light, places the right hand in the form of a triangle above the eyes.

Sign of Help—Should you be threatened while scrying this Degree, have the hands open, palm outwards, cross the two arms above the head, saying "Come to my aid, ye children of the widow[399]."

Sign of the Order—place the right hand on the hip.

Jewel–triple golden triangle with a flaming heart inside. The letters, .H.S.[400] are inscribed upon the heart.

---

[399] Reference is to the Grand Hailing Sign of Distress of the 3rd Degree.
[400] Iesus Hominum Salvator, *Jesus Savior of men*

Synopsis

In the 24th Degree, Knight of the Red Eagle, the Initiate is especially brought into the realm of the spirits of Fire. In this Degree, *Prince of Mercy*, we enter into a dialogue with the spirits of Water and the personification of the Mother of ALL (Mara)[401], whose name means—*water*. Additionally, the "Palladium" of the Order is a marble statue of *Mary*. Here, one thinks of the Immaculate Conception and the Lwa syncretized[402] with her, *La Sirene*, both of which are again, related to water. La Sirene shows up again, and most potently, in the 37th Degree, Knight of Shota, Sage of Truth. Hiram Abiff is said to be of the Tribe of Naphtali whose sign is Virgo, the Virgin. In the Lodge working of this Degree, we find the Candidate's hands washed and the exercise of *lavation*, where water is poured upon his head[403]. This Degree stirs up the feminine principle, the receptive and intuitive energies within the Initiate and leads to revelation.

When the points chaud of this Degree works its magick, the Initiate can expect an increase in divinatory abilities. Before scrying the point, the Initiate would do well to obtain an image of the Immaculate Conception. This may be in the form of a Palladium, which incidentally relates to Pallas Athena's sculpture in Ancient Greece, or it may be a simple lithograph of the Holy Mother. The best of all possibilities is drawing one's own image or *ikon* of her. The closeness one can feel with a drawing of one's own, no matter how crudely executed, far exceeds the meaning of the works of the Masters. The image of Mary, La Sirene or Pallas, should be placed in front of the Initiate while scrying in the prophet asana with the head down towards her.

---

[401] See Dion Fortune's, "The Worship of Isis" essay for a simple introduction to the notion of the Great Mother. From *Aspects of Occultism*, pgs. 34-39.
[402] The Lwa and the Saints are so closely identified in traditional Haitian Vodou that one can stand in for the other.
[403] This action has further reference to traditional Haitian Vodou in the practice of Lava Tet, or the cleansing of the head of the candidate seeking initiation into Vodou in some cases, while in others simply establishing membership with a House. The Met Tet is the Lwa of the head, or the Lwa that the candidate is born with—the Lava Tet symbolically cleanses the head for the deeper realization of the head Lwa.

Spirit Builders

27th Degree

Sovereign Grand Commander of the Temple

27th *degree*,
Commander of the Temple.

Battery of Knocks

Twenty-seven by 12, 12 and 3. **XXXXXXXXXXXX   XXXXXXXXXXXX   XXX**

Points-chauds

Lower left abdomen and left inside wrist.

Sacred Word

I.N.R.I. (vibrated as En-RYE)

Grip

Knock three times with the right hand on the left shoulder of the Initiate[404], who will reply by taking the right hand and slightly shaking it three times.

Sign

Place the right hand on the forehead, and with the thumb (fingers closed) make the sign of the cross. In reply, the challenger will kiss the forehead on the spot where the cross has been made. But outside the courtyard (on the outside of the inner Chapel on the subtle planes), instead of kissing the forehead, he places the first two fingers of the right hand on the mouth, keeping the other fingers closed, and turning the hand.

Additional Materials

Password–SOLOMON

Steps of entry into Chapel–Three ordinary steps

Jewel–On the front, a golden triangle, on the backside a black Teutonic cross.

†††

Synopsis

This Degree has been switched with the 28th Degree in the Ancient and Accepted Scottish Rite, so as to maintain a consistency with the two other portions of the Templar Degrees– Knight of St. Andrew and Knights Kadosh. Organizationally, this is a good move and adds flow to the staged working of the Degrees, but for *Spirit Building*, we maintain this

---

[404] As one of the three primary grades of Knighthood in the Kadosh Degrees (Knight Commander of the Temple, Knight of St. Andrew, Knights Kadosh), this Degree begins with a ceremonial knighting upon the left shoulder. Taken together, the three Degrees of the Violet Lodge constitute a spiritual knighting as well.

older order due to the *energies* and *entities* that are stirred within the points-chaud empowerments and their necessary balance with the mystical 28th Degree, *Knight of the Sun*.

In the Lodge workings of this Degree, there is a dramatic ritual that reminds the Candidate of a sacred play. The key player is Constans[405] who desires to become a Knight and who is made to spend the night in vigil. He is instructed to let *nothing* deter him from his post. Of course all manner of horrors beseech him and we are reminded of St. Antony in the desert being assailed by demons. An analogy to one's True Will arises again in this Degree, as it is *that* which should be kept to, to the letter. Once our True Will is realized, we should let nothing deter us from the accomplishment of it. Our singleness of purpose should reflect Constans' perseverance and dedication.

The second section of the drama consists of Constans being tempted by three lifestyles that each has a dominating factor. One is putting material concerns at the forefront, another is putting economic concerns first, and the final is putting spiritual concerns above all else. The lesson in this section is one of balance. In the world esoterica, the law of diminishing returns applies. If you inflate one aspect of the work, while letting others stay status quo, then the overall product is diminished. Our work must develop holistically or we will atrophy. What we are all in desperate need of is the balancing and equilibrating beauty of Tiphareth.

The points-chauds empowerments for this Degree are in two places upon the body. The first finishes off the left abdomen side and the second is on the left wrist. The point upon the abdomen invigorates and stirs the activity of our True Will and awakens assisting work spirits who will guide us in our one-pointedness. The second point sends a jolt of energy through the body via the veins directly to the heart. It stimulates the heart, the place of Tiphareth, harmony and balance. With the uniting of these two points we have new drive and energy in the accomplishing of our True Will, and the necessary balance of Tiphareth to keep our focus in harmony with our Will. The point on the wrist also has the potential, in the proper ceremonial circumstance, to elicit the Beatific Vision of Tiphareth. Such is to be explored further when scrying the Degree in one's oratory.

---

[405] See *Vested in Glory*, 2000, by Jim Tresner for a good description of this and other Scottish Degrees.

Part Three – Chapter Three: The Philosophical Degrees

28th Degree

Knight of Johan or of the Sun or Prince Adept

Call to the Holy Guardian Angel

28th *degree,*
Knight of the Sun, or Prince Adept.

Battery of Knocks

Six equal knocks   X X X X X X

Points-chaud

Right upper abdomen

Sacred Word

ADONAI reply ABRA

Grip

Take the hands of the Initiate and press them slightly.

Sign

Having the thumb of the right hand extended, place the hand on the heart; in reply point to the heavens with the index finger of the right hand.

Additional Materials

Password–HELIOS MENE TETRAGRAMMATON

Jewel–A golden pentagram, on the backside of which is a sun.

†††

Synopsis

As we come towards the close of the Degrees which are similar to those of the Scottish Rite, we find that we are leaving the arena of the purely philosophical and endeavoring upon a quest for true gnosis. This is certainly one of the most mystical Degrees of the corpus of mainstream Masonry, and the one which often gets shortened or avoided altogether. The newly Revised Pike Ritual provides a version of this Degree that is a great deal shorter than the original[406], yet it retains the symbolism and erudite lessons on the nature of symbolism. However, in the workings of the older Degree, we find an admixture of alchemical material and angelic magic[407].

---

[406] In terms of "original" Degrees here, the reference is to those which were fleshed out in Pike's *Inner Sanctuary*, compiled for the Supreme Council and formed from the "Formulas & Rituals" that Pike transcribed in 1854 and 1855. See 2007 edition of *The Scottish Rite Ritual Monitor & Guide*, De Hoyos, pgs. 81-86.

[407] Both of which were incorporated in the deeply theurgical workings of the Divine Cagliostro's *Egyptian Masonry*. See Faulks & Cooper's, *The Masonic Magician*, 2008.

One of the keys to this Degree' Lodge working is that the Seven Archangels guard the Candidate's entry and exposure to the Primitive Doctrine. We have explored this notion of the original and unified Religion of the Ancients and how our streamlined workings of the points-chauds relate directly to this. This Degree alludes to the method that we utilize; it is a stripping away of what is not necessary to the path. The Candidate in the dramatic Degree is bound, hoodwinked, covered in a bloody robe, etc.; all of which he must be divested of by each of the Archangels before exposure to the Primitive Doctrine–which relates directly to the Sacred Doctrine–*the manifestation of Light*. The apron, cordon and Jewel are extremely simple—all in white, gold, and the occasional vermillion. In the presence of the Great Archangels, the Candidate is laid bare—relieved of his fetters and props and exposed to the pure and simple nature of true spirituality.

The points-chaud empowerment for this Degree is best experienced out of doors. The Degree proper alludes to the reasoning for this as it suggests that the Deity is to be found in forests and groves, not in buildings. Ideas of the ancient Druids arise with this empowerment and notions of the Deity as *the ceaseless creativity of the Universe*[408] swell while this point is being given. The singular energy that this point stimulates within the body is purity. The entities that are called upon with this point are the Seven Archangels who will be worked with more profoundly in the Arcana Arcanorum. The Sacred Word of the Degree takes this a step further and calls upon the actions of the Holy Guardian Angel of the Initiate.[409] For the deep experience of the HGA, the Initiate must be stripped of all that is unnecessary.[410]

It is suggested that the Initiate obtain a copy of this Degree and the subsequent versions of it, in full, and to study its contents. There are other secrets lodged within the working that are revealed–after reception of the point–when read in the same manner as was the pathworking exercises in Part Two.

---

[408] See Stuart Kauffman's, *Reinventing the Sacred: A New View of Science, Reason, and Religion*, 2008.
[409] Reference to the HGA being identified with ADONAI (Lord), can be found in the writings of MacGregor Mathers, Crowley, Regardie, and others.
[410] See primarily, *The Sacred Magic of Abramelin the Mage*.

Spirit Builders

29th **Degree**

Knight of St. Andrew

Call to the Elementals

29th *degree,*
Knight of St. Andrew.

Battery of Knocks

Nine by 2, 3, and 4   XX   XXX   XXXX

Points-chaud

Upper Right Abdomen

Sacred Word

NEKAMAH

Grip

Each takes the first joint of the right index finger of the other; the Facilitator says "NE," Initiate says "KA," and in passing to the extreme joint of the little finger, the Facilitator says "MAH" and Initiate responds "NEKAMAH."

Sign

Make the sign of Andrew's Cross across the breast, right arm over left, same as Knight Rose+Croix.

Additional Materials[411]

Passwords–of Fire, EREL, of air, HASSAN, of water, TALJAHHAD, of earth, PHORLACH.

Steps–While visualizing the Heavenly Jerusalem, take three Apprentice steps, three steps of a companion, (Fellowcraft) and three of a Master.

Additional Signs & Grips–of the *earth*; with the head lightly bent forward, wipe the forehead with the back of the right hand. 1st Grip; with the examiner, take successively the 1st, 2nd and 3rd joints of the right index finger spelling alternatively BOAZ. Of *water*, place the right hand on the heart, extend it horizontally to the height of the breast, and let it fall to the right side. Grip; take each the 1st, 2nd and 3rd joints of the middle finger, spelling JACHIN. Of astonishment and horror; whilst looking at the ground, turn the head to the left and lift the two hands towards the heavens. Of *fire*; join the two hands with fingers interlaced, palm outwards, and cover the eyes. In reply, sign of *air*; raise forward the right hand to the height of the shoulder. Grip; whilst pronouncing alternatively one of the syllables of the word MOABON, take the index finger of the

---

[411] In scrying this point, familiarity with working with the Elemental Spirits is necessary. A simple introduction to this working is through Eliphas Levi's *Transcendental Magic*. In the *Ritual* section, study the *Conjuration of the Four* to begin familiarizing oneself with the actions of these spirits & serviteurs.

other's right hand by the end joint. Of Admiration, raise the hands and eyes towards the heavens, the left arm a little less than the right, the left heel raised a little so that the knee makes a square with the right leg. Of the sun, place the right thumb on the right eye, raise the index finger to form a square, then point as if indicating an object, and say, "I measure as far as the Sun."

Jewel–a compass in three triangles enclosed in another triangle. On the back, the St. Andrew's cross in green.

☩ ☩ ☩

Synopsis

This Degree has extensive Signs and Grips, which relate to the essence of the secret working of this Degree—*alchemical change of the elements of the Initiate's personality*. Additionally, there are four passwords which open up to the scryer the four realms of the Elements, wherein he will discover the Gnomes, Sylphs, Salamanders and Undines of Ceremonial Magic. These will be more closely worked with in the next Series of Degrees, but this empowerment begins the *call* to awaken their presence. As one of the Templar Degrees, the Sacred Word is vengeance oriented, yet such vengeance is against the evil spirits and negative thought forms created by humans[412]. These sometimes exhibit themselves in restrictive political entities, tyrannical leaderships and fanaticism, all of which the Masonic Templar wars against.

The Saint Andrew's Cross, an ancient symbol pre-dating Christianity considerably, is formed by the body, and discovered to be the same as the Knight Rose Croix; the Sign of the Good Shepherd, the Sign of Osiris risen. The body itself forms the Chi-Rho of Ancient Christianity when making this sign. Our *Asiatic Brethren* or Frères d'Orient, utilize this powerful talisman often in alignment with Greek Orthodoxy.

The reception of this Degree, as outlined by Charles T. McClenachan of the Northern Jurisdiction of the Ancient and Accepted Scottish Rite of Freemasonry, teaches the Masonic student about the wise king, Saladin. Many aspects of this ceremonial would be familiar to members of the Ordo Templi Orientis, while the philosophical aspects speak of the sovereignty of the individual, freedom of belief, and Universalist themes. In the Liturgy of

---

[412] Reference can again be made here to the deeply theurgical and practical workings of the Knight Masons Elect Coëns of the Universe. The seasonal Equinox Operations of this Order do battle with these very forces of darkness, the same of which—students of the Typhonian tradition have intimations of as extra-terrestrial beings.

this Degree[413], however, is the key to working with the points-chaud empowerment of this Degree. It is in the brief mention of the mantra for this working, the phrase to be prayed & repeated while entering the vision during scrying. At the Close of the Degree and during the ceremonial lighting of the candles we find the notariqon, A.G.L.A.,[414] which is translated as; *You, O Lord, are mighty forever.* This is the secret mantrum of this Order of Knighthood and may be utilized at any time while exploring the inner meanings of this Degree. Practitioners of the *Lesser Banishing Ritual of the Pentagram* will be familiar with this phrase, as will those who utilize Solomonic magic. However, the inner workings of this Degree relate that quiet Order with Cathar roots, the AGLA society.

---

[413] 1944 edition, *Liturgy of the Ancient and Accepted Scottish Rite of Freemasonry, Part IV*, p. 206.
[414] *Atah Gibor Le-olam Adonai*

30th Degree

Grand Knight Kadosh

Invocation of the Ghuédé

30th *degree,*
Grand Elected Knight of Kadosh.

Battery of Knocks

Three times, 2 and 1. **XX X**

Points-chaud

Mid to low right abdomen

Sacred Word

NEKAM ADONAI; reply is PHARASCH CHOL

Grip

Each places the right foot to right foot, and knee to knee; presenting the right fist, thumb elevated. The Facilitator seizes the thumb, then Initiate does the same, each letting it slip and stepping back a pace, then each raises the arm as if to strike with the poniard.

Sign

Place the right hand, with fingers apart, on the heart, let it fall on the right knee that one grasps whilst staggering; then seize the dagger[415] which is suspended to the ribbon, lift it as if about to strike and say "NEKAM ADONAI."

Additional Materials

Steps—Three sudden steps with the hands crossed on the head. Once allowed entrance into the apartments of the Degree, use passwords for entrance unless being tried by one of the Famille Ghuédé,[416] in which you simply say, *"I wish to proceed."*

Passwords—Entrance, NEKAM; reply is MENAHHEM. 2nd, PHANGAL CHOL, reply is PHARASCH CHOL.

Sign of the Order—Having the sword in the left hand, place the right hand on the heart.

Jewel—A red Teutonic cross with a black and white double-headed eagle in the middle.

Sacred Words of the Ladder[417]—step 1, TZEDEKAH, step 2, SCHOR LABAN, step 3, MACHOK, step 4, EMOUNAH, step 5, AMAL SAGGHI, step 6, SABBAL, step 7, GHEMOUR NAH THEBOUNAH.

---

[415] Recall that this can be a magickal dagger (when scrying) or an actual one used in the demonstration after points reception.

[416] Immediately this Degree connects back to the 3rd Degree and the spirits attached to it. In the oldest versions of the Kadosh Grade, it is styled the, *ne plus ultra*—the highest point, nothing beyond. This is similar to the common understanding that there is no Degree "higher" than the 3rd.

[417] The Kadosh ladder is an ancient symbol of the Scottish Rite which is found in the earliest translations of the work of Stephen Morin. One such translation is the so called, *Francken Manuscript* of 1783 which comprises 25 Degrees. The Kadosh ladder is

†††

Synopsis

This Degree is very elaborately worked in four apartments with four separate oaths. It is considered to be the entrance into the *Greater Mysteries*, the Degrees prior to it pertaining to the *Lesser Mysteries* in some respects. But we shouldn't be bound by chronology in this case, as it is a common saying in all Masonic Traditions that there is no Degree higher than the Third. This is due to the fact that the Third Degree partakes of the same nature as this Thirtieth. In sum, when the Third Degree "takes" it is in and of itself, entry into the *Greater Mysteries*, for the individual is freed from her cocoon and the isolated ego is sacrificed. *The dread of death*[418], in other words, is overcome.

The 30th Degree greatly expands upon the theme of death and so connects intimately with the actions of the Third Degree. Like the Third, it awakens the Ghuédé for those to whom the Ghuédé choose to visit. There are certainly other spirits and energies associated with death, but the Ghuédé are specifically related to spiritist Freemasonry and are *called* upon whenever we utilize a skull in our workings. In Shamanistic cultures such as those of ancient Tibet, we discover a practice of drinking a sacred libation out of a skull. This practice shows up again in Templar lore. Such is the means of taking Ghuédé energy into the body—the cup of Equality.

The points-chaud empowerment of this Degree upon the mid, right abdomen will often be accompanied by a visualization of a ladder of lights into the heavens. This may only be a flash, a hint of the pure white light of Kether that one senses. Further exploration of the point *after* initiation may result in this ladder opening up in meditation. Such meditation can easily slip into a scrying session and the *Sacred words for the Ladder* found in the "Additional Materials" are used to ascend each rung[419]. The initial action of the point is subtle, so patience is required with this one.

The points chaud empowerment has a further influence in that it creates four main journeys for the Initiate in scrying. The scrying practice for this Degree is intense and may

---

present even at this early stage, and is therefore a powerful and traditional emblem. It has many applications, yet it appears in the scrying session to be very similar in purpose to the ladder into the heavens presented on classical 1st Degree Tracing Boards. This is the **Ladder of the Wise** of Alchemy.

[418] See *Memento Mori*, pgs. 91-96, in *Syzygy*, for an exploration of meditating upon death and the role of the Ghuédé.

[419] Additional information concerning this ladder can be found in Yarker's, *Lectures of a Chapter, Senate & Council*, p. 83; *Q. What is symbolized by the ladder of seven steps? A. The seven degrees of the ancient initiatory rites and the trials of the seven Mythraic caverns or doors of various metals, which figure the seven planets; the Babylonian legend of Ishtar, Isis, or Ceres, relates under the legends of the sign of Virgo, that she visited her dead husband in the realms of departed souls, and during her progress had to pass through seven gates…*

require multiple session; it is quite initiatory. As we are ending our series of Philosophical Degrees, we draw closer and closer to the Gnosis and the living verities that accompany *Spirit Builders*. The 30th Degree scrying journeys allude to the four apartments of the Degree as well as to the four oaths. First, the point stimulates a deep and lasting acceptance of death. Death is no longer feared, dreaded or abhorred. While scrying, the Initiate will find a guardian of the Threshold who will ask specific questions. The answer to each is; *I wish to proceed*. Secondly, the point awakens one of the family of Ghuédé who will assess the Initiate's commitment to the spiritual life. In the scrying session the Ghuédé may appear as tricksters, may be sexually explicit, or direct, and may make light of death in absurd ways. This is all necessary for the ordeal. Thirdly, the point puts the Initiate in contact with the *Frank Judges* (an order of the Famille Ghuédé), spirits who will test the Initiate for fitness. In the scrying session, these are visualized as a tribunal of dark-clad judges whose faces one does not see. Fourthly, the Initiate is a taken to a mausoleum and shown a particular urn. This mausoleum is also a Chapel and there will be sacrifices and oblations to make for the one interred. A great member of the Order may be met in this Chapel.[420]

---

[420] Though the initials, J.B.M. may be discovered in this Chapel near or on the urn, he may be recognized by his tunic as well, with its red Teutonic cross either in the center or on the right breast.

Spirit Builders

31st Degree

Grand Inquisitor Commander or, Initiate of the Egyptian Mysteries[421]

Invocation of the Court of the Dead

31th *degree,*
Grand Inspector Inquisitor Commander.

---

[421] In his highly original book, *Nightside of Eden*, Kenneth Grant says on p. 37; "To bring this about a real death has to be achieved, and this is the total death of the ego both in its personal (conscious) and in its impersonal (dreaming) condition. The mechanics of this process are resumed in the so-called *Book of the Dead* which is the magical manual of the body's metamorphosis into a *khu* (glorified spirit)." When meditated upon, this notion brings together the 3rd, 30th, and 31st Degrees in an enlightening manner.

Battery of Knocks

Nine, by 1, 3, 4, and 1.   X   XXX   XXXX   X

Points-chaud

Lower right abdomen and inside of the right wrist.

Sacred Word

TZEDEKAH Reply, MISCHOR. Both say together, AMEN.

Grip

Take reciprocally the left hand, advance the right foot, touch the knees, and with the right hand tap on the right shoulder of the other.

Additional Materials

Jewel–a silver Teutonic Cros

† † †

Synopsis

Like many of the Hermetic and Gnostic Degrees in the next series, this Degree in its original form has very little ceremonial. It chiefly consisted of an exchange of words, signs and grips (see, *Albert Pike's Masonic Formulas and Rituals, by Arturo De Hoyos*). From this material, the Adept, General Albert Pike created a Degree that places the Candidate in the Court of the Dead of the Egyptian Mysteries. The primary text for this Degree and the one which will initiate the workings of the coming Degrees, is the *Egyptian Book of the Dead, the Book of Going forth by Day.* The edition conceived of and produced by James Wasserman is the best for this study, as the images are clearly portrayed and numerous errors and omissions from older editions are corrected. No other text or Degree material is necessary, for the essence of this Degree lies within this sacred volume.

For many of the coming Degrees, the Initiate will be directed to texts to study and peruse. As in the *Violet Lodge*, where extracts from Calvin C Burt's text were used as initiatory material, these suggestions could be approached in the same way. In cases such as this, it is best to say too little than to say too much. This is because the points chaud empowerment will direct the Initiate to the material that is needed to complete the Initiation. For Facilitators who are natural teachers, this is sometimes difficult water to tread as the tendency is to want to direct the Initiate's path and/or guarantee the quality of the initiation. But here is where trust is necessary. The spirits, entities and forces that are present within and without the body are guides upon the path. In fact, from this Degree onwards, the Initiate may feel a strong presence attending all of his labors. Not only is this indicative of the presence of the *Passed Masters*, but it is suggestive of the Angel's presence who is explored in a general way in the Arcana Arcanorum.

The points chaud empowerment of this Degree is in two parts like the 27th. While the Sacred Word, TZEDEKAH (justice) is being vibrated, the Facilitator may use both hands and awaken the point in both locations, or there may be two Facilitators for this empowerment, or the two points on the body may be given one after the other. As long as both are awakened together, the spirits of justice, equity and judgment will be awakened. The scrying session following Initiation may be accompanied with readings from the Book of the Dead,[422] so that the Initiate can truly enter the Court of the Dead where Osiris, Atum, Maat, Thoth and Anubis await, along with the four sons of Osiris. Many others will be sensed along the hall, typically masked and in black. The judgment received in this scrying has little to do with common morality, but everything to do with the Initiate's fitness for the coming Higher Grades. Purity of life here is concerned with the treatment of others rather than the commission of "sins." The heart is what is weighed against the feather by the Goddess MAAT[423].

---

[422] *The Egyptian Book of the Dead, The Book of Going Forth By Day*, 2008, Wasserman, Goelet, Faulkner, Andrews.
[423] Students of this Degree may be inclined to study the Ma'atian workings of Nema in relation to the goddess and the court of the dead.

Part Three – Chapter Three: The Philosophical Degrees

32nd Degree

Sovereign Prince of the Royal Secret[424]

32nd degree,
Sublime Prince of the Royal Secret.

---

[424] Year III of the Monastery of the Seven Rays offers an interesting additional meaning to this grade, it is that the Initiate comes to see all as extensions of himself, and of consciousness as a process. There is also an integrated understanding of sexual magic related to the deeper mysteries of this Degree.

Battery of knocks

Five by 1 and 4.   X   XXXX

Points-chaud

Center, upper groin

Sacred Word

SALIX, answer, NONI, then both together, TENGU[425]

Grip

Raise the left arm, the hand open and extended as if to repulse an attack. Seize each other's left hand, the fingers interlaced. Then draw close to each other and embrace. The Facilitator says, CHOKMAH and the Initiate answers TZEDEKAH.

Sign

Place the right hand on the heart; raise the hand, palm downwards, and let it fall to the side.

Additional Materials

Passwords–PHAAL CHOL, PHARASCH CHOL, NEKAM MAQQHAH. Then both say the word, SHADDAI.

Jewel–A gold Teutonic Cross with the numerals, XXXII in the center.

†††

Synopsis

The next two Degrees conclude the Philosophical Series. As the working of *Spirit Builders* is not necessarily chronological, one may receive these Degrees at any juncture on the path, however the empowerments go together. It is suggested that the Initiate read the Legenda for the 32nd Degree, found in the "Suggested Reading" as well as other supplemental material. The Degree, in practice, is a summation of all of the Degrees thus far, as well as being a sacred call to ancient forces to witness the Candidate's entrance into the Holy Empire. In this Degree we find the twin ideas of the Royal Secret and the Holy Doctrine

---

[425] Another Word is given as the "Sacred Word" in current Scottish Rite bodies. These, however, are the ancient attributions.

developed. Even a cursory reading of the suggested texts will illuminate the contents of these mysteries.

It is in the points-chaud empowerments that the Primitive Doctrine begins to unfurl for the Initiate of our system. As these two Degrees are preparatory for the Hermetic, Gnostic and Kabalistic Series following, they are positioned in a specific location upon the body. It is no secret that mystics and sages from around the globe have discovered an energy within the body that is somehow connected with the sexual impetus. As this subject can quickly devolve into questionable notions of morality and circumspection, we must walk carefully into this Holy City. Firstly we must remember that we are Non-dual Gnostics and that we honor and uphold the body as a wonderful and glorious happening of the Universe. In this light, it is the most pure form of the Temple. Secondly, we must recall that the points-chauds empowerments act in a variety of ways, attuning, empowering, healing and initiating. As the next two Degrees incorporate points in the upper groin region of the body, it is cogent to remember what our purpose and goals are as *Spirit Builders*. We are creating the *Scintillating Body,* establishing the *Mystic Temple* and building *Community*. Only in a collective of mutually respecting, supporting and enlightened Brothers and Sisters can these Higher Degrees be practiced with adroitness and purity. Those who would make of these Degrees/points an excuse to invade another's privacy or to satisfy their own perverted wills are not fit for these labors.

This being said, the body is the storehouse of energies and entities. It is burgeoning with energy and force. The most centralized location of these energies and entities is along the Middle Pillar of the body and most specifically in the sexual regions, the battery pack of the entire organism. Here, the energies of kundalini lie dormant until activated. Once stimulated, these energies ascend[426] from the base of the spine and can be channeled in the proper directions for work of all types—healing, gnostic, creative, etc.

The very same forces that are called upon in the Degree working of the Princes of the Royal Secret are vitalized and immediately *contacted* through the points-chaud empowerment. Again we find a compact and radically simplified version of what is really a rather extensive Degree. This level of economy becomes more prevalent as we explore the Memphis+Misraïm Degrees from 34-86th. For sake of further clarity, what the Initiate of

---

[426] Some Western Orders are overly concerned with this notion of ascending from the ground upwards, considering such to be evil or somehow *less than* powerful in comparison with forces coming downward from above. But this is another dualism, because the earth itself is Holy. When drawing energy upwards, we are simply tapping into the Telluric currents of earth, sometimes typified by the serpent. When drawing downwards, the energy is more solar. The balance of the two creates a properly equilibrated magickal body. Druids of the Modern Revival variety utilize this combination thoroughly. When one works upon a sacred marma like Arabia Mountain, the drawing upward of the serpent current is quickened significantly.

this point/Degree should experience is an awakening and stimulating of the powerhouse of energy latent within the body, and in the sexual organs in particular.

Part Three – Chapter Three: The Philosophical Degrees

33rd Degree

Sovereign Grand Inspector General

Consecration of the Ghuédé

33rd *degree,*
Sovereign Grand Inspector General.

Battery of Knocks

Eleven by 5, 3, 1 and 2 **XXXXX   XXX   X   XX**

Points-chaud

Center groin

Sacred Word

MICHA MACHA BAALIM, ADONAI

Grip

There is no grip for this Degree. To seal the points-chaud empowerment, the Facilitator should take the Initiate in a natural embrace.

Sign

1st sign, cross the arms on the breast, and bend the head and the body forward, kneel on both knees. 2nd sign, draw the sword from its scabbard and place the left hand on the heart.

Additional Materials

Passwords–DE MOLAY; reply HIRAM ABIF. 2nd, FREDERICK; reply OF PRUSSIA.

Jewel–a regular Pentagon

† † †

Synopsis

Though the 33rd and *Final* Degree of Scottish Freemasonry, this Degree has a rather simple ceremony. The hangings and decorations point for a final time to the invocation of the Ghuédé, as the colors are purple and black with skeletons and skulls. The Candidate in Lodge workings is once again taken upon a journey where he makes new Obligations to the Order. There is a sense of dedication in this Degree that relates to the Administrative Degrees, 90-97th. The relationship is *Service.*

As the Candidate has, up until this point, continued a journey with ever increasing knowledge and enlightenment for himself, this Degree points outwards and reminds the Candidate that to take any place of leadership within the Fraternity of Masonry is to take upon oneself more responsibility and more opportunity for service. This is true all along the way in Spirit Building, as Free Illuminists are called to service from the very beginning. However, this Degree and empowerment should re-invigorate such dedication and service to others in mutual aid, support, and encouragement.

The points-chauds empowerment for the Degree ends the Philosophical series and is the final point before the sexual centers are awakened in their fullest capacity. The Degrees come around full circle in the end and direct the energy back to the Kether point of the head. But before such a journey, all aspects of the Temple of the body need to be hallowed, awakened, stimulated and energized. As this Degree concludes the upper front-most part of the body, and particularly the areas near the Middle Pillar, we can expect a sense of completion and fruition from this final point of the Series.

As was stated, the Ghuédé specifically are summoned a final time with this point. There is a power that accompanies this point that should be respected and cultivated with the utmost humility. The power that the Ghuédé awaken within the Initiate, is the power *to serve*. It is in this manner that the Ghuédé themselves may offer a type of "consecration" in this grade. This consecration is two-way. They may make themselves known during the time of working through this Degree and may desire to make *contracts* with you to show that they wish to serve *you* in return. At any rate, the point will awaken them and it is for the Initiate to discern their particular dealings. This service mindedness is a quality found in many of the Lwa, but this particular consecration offered by the Famille Ghuédé opens the exchange of service between the Initiate and the family of spirits. As we serve them, they in turn serve us—but the expectation is that we will go forth and serve others as we have been served. To work further with them, the Initiate could seek out a Mambo or Houngan for detailed descriptions of this powerful family, their needs, desires, and preferences of gifts. But this can be discerned through study and *talking with the spirits* as well, as the *Voudon Gnostic Workbook*[427] suggests from the very Preface onwards. Attention should be directed to Bertiaux's masterful and mystical treatise, *Cosmic Meditation* here as well—for in this work he most clearly reveals the closeness of the spirits to our realm, and the ease with which we may make contact and build deep relations with these spirit beings.

---

[427] See the Preface, iii, *VGW*, Michael Bertiaux, 2007.

Suggested Reading for the Philosophical Degrees

The Initiate working with the 4th-33rd Degrees has at his disposal an extensive chain of texts relating to the Ancient and Accepted Scottish Rite of Freemasonry. Though the "secrets" of this set that we use pre-dates those in use by the current Supreme Councils, we share in themes and in the continuity of ideas and wisdom teachings, of this lovely collection of Degrees and so there will be analogies through these texts that are clearly deep and informative. [428]

- *The 32 Secret Paths of Solomon A New Examination of the Qabbalah in Freemasonry*, Timothy Hogan
- *A Bridge to Light,* by Rex Hutchens
- *Albert Pike's Lecture on Masonic Symbolism and a Second Lecture on Symbolism,* Rex Hutchens
- *Albert Pike's Masonic Formulas and Rituals,* Arturo De Hoyos
- *The Annotated and Revised Morals and Dogma of Albert Pike,* by Arturo De Hoyos
- *The Baylot Manuscript in Translation,* Sâr Phosphoros (trans.)
- *Cosmic Meditation,* Michael Bertiaux
- *Degrees of Wisdom: A Compendium of Rituals from the Rites of Memphis and Misraïm*
- *The Francken Manuscript*
- *Freemasonry: A French View,* Roger Dachez & Alain Bauer
- *Freemasonry, Symbols, Secrets, Significance,* W Kirk MacNulty
- *Heredom,* all volumes produced by the Scottish Rite Research Society
- *The Key to Solomon's Key, Secrets of Magic and Masonry,* Lon Milo DuQuette
- *La Franc-maçonnerie Égyptienne de Memphis-Misraïm,* Serge Caillet
- *Living the Enlightenment,* Margaret C. Jacob
- *Masonic Orthodoxy: Followed by Occult Masonry and Hermetic Initiation* , J.-M. Ragon
- *The Origins of Freemasonry, Facts & Fictions,* Margaret C. Jacob
- *The Porch and the Middle Chamber,* Albert Pike
- *The Royal Masonic Cyclopædia,* Kenneth Mackenzie
- *Scotch Rite Masonry Illustrated in two volumes,* John Blanchard
- *The Secret Teachings of All Ages,* Manly P Hall
- *The Scottish Rite Ritual Monitor and Guide,* Arturo De Hoyos

---

[428] See Volume Two for complete Bibliography.

- *Sephir h'Debarim, the Book of the Words,* Albert Pike
- *Symbols of Freemasonry,* Daniel Berezniak
- *Vested in Glory,* Jim Tresner

Volume Two

For
T Allen Greenfield
33° 90° 95° 97° 100°
WAEO APRMM

~A tireless laborer, mystic, and mage, and the creator of the Free Illuminist movement and Congregational Illuminism communities, worldwide. Allen's friendship of over 13 years has meant the world to me and my Chapel. He has answered more questions than I care to admit, blessed our home with his presence, walked our labyrinth, and consecrated and empowered me for the work of Spirit Builders. On top of all of this, Allen is a kind, generous, and truly humorous individual without a shred of pomposity or egocentrism. There is only *one* Allen H. Greenfield, and the world is better, wiser, and a little more egalitarian because of his commitment and fidelity to his own principles, shared with the globe.

Allen with myself and Salome+ on the right, Chic & Tabatha Cicero on the left

The following charts relate to T Allen's recent elevation to the 100°, Grand Cophta, Grand General Hierophant of the World, by the WAEO.

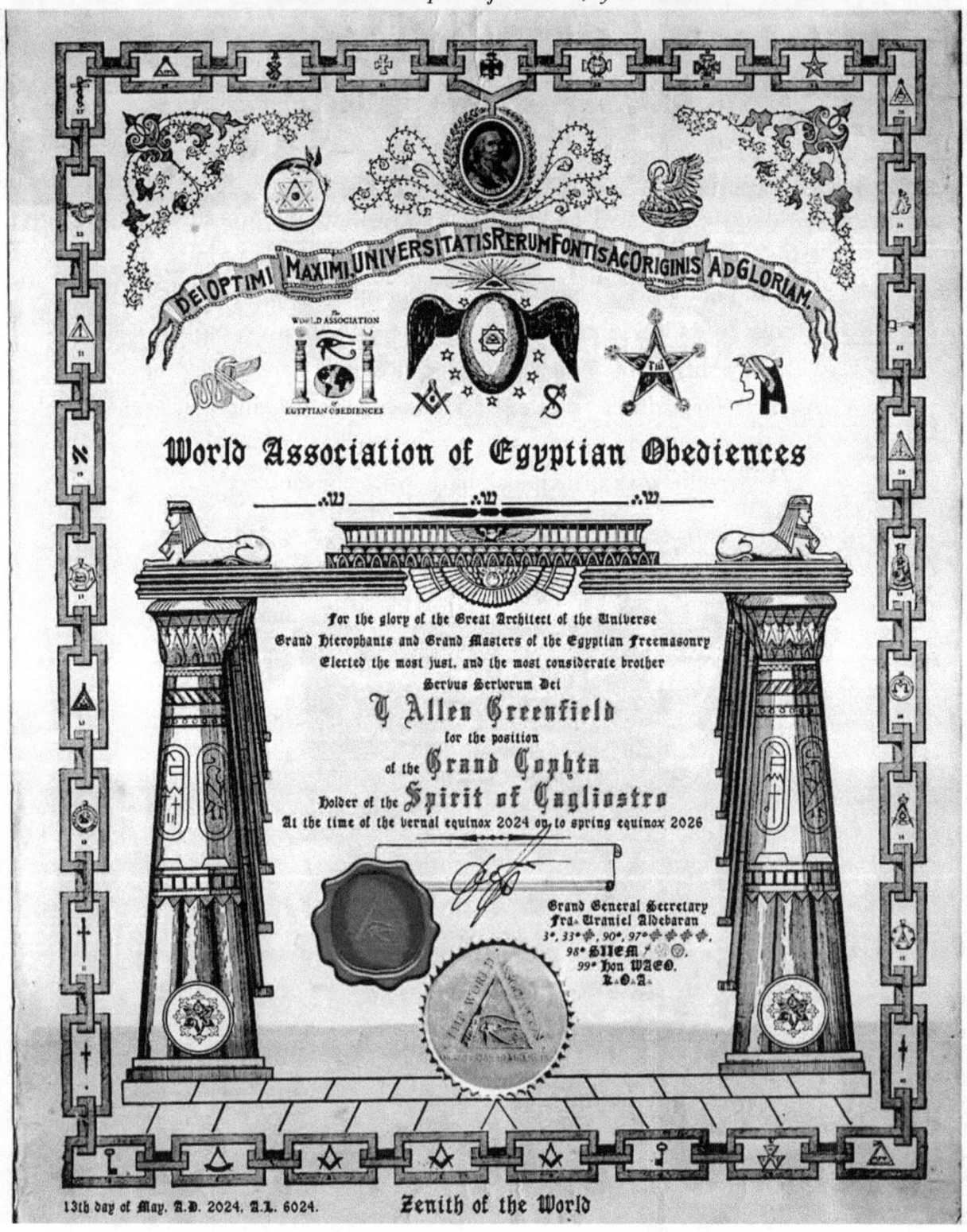

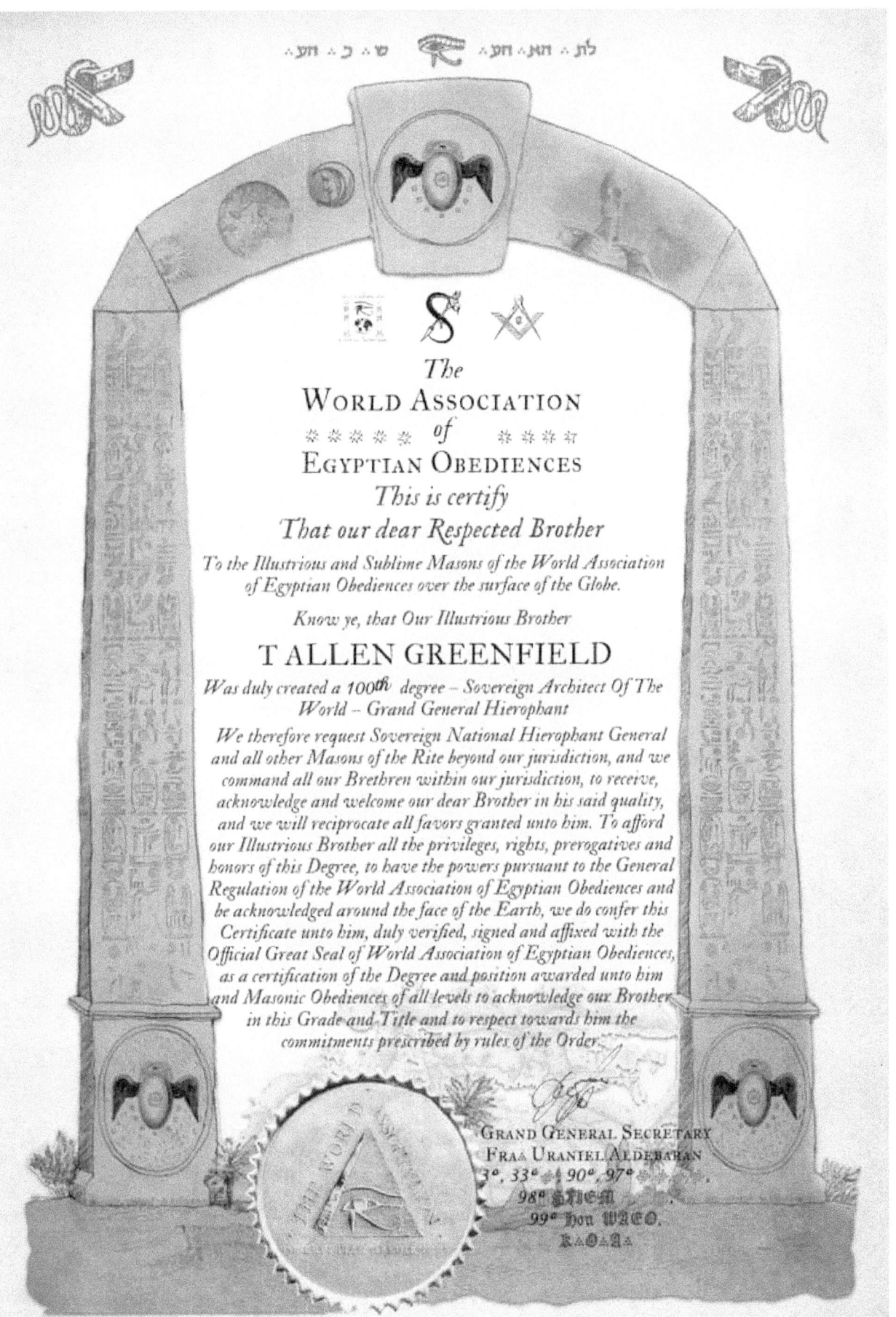

Preface

There must be more than history...

When one decides to take the plunge into the legends and lore of the Antient & Primitive Rites of Memphis+Misraïm, he is confounded and befuddled by the plethora of historical exegeses, deep dives into the illustrious as well as dubious characters of the Rites throughout history, and occasional isolated exposures or analyses of specific degrees. But what of the *whole* of the Rites, the *spirit* of the Rites, and the *purpose* (scopos & telos) of the work? It is no accident that this second edition of Spirit Builders is released in the same year as Tau Phosphoros' compendium of APRM+M rituals, *Degrees of Wisdom*. My brother and friend +Phosphoros understands the critical need for working *operative* material related to this august and mysterious Order. His contribution of "lodge-ready" Memphis+Misraïm degrees opens the path for a reinstatement of the Rites to their primitive place of beauty and power in the world of Masonic thought and practice. It is key to note that his tome does not waste any paper on continuing the unending restatement of the murky history of the Rites. Such has been done and done again, ad nauseum. The *whole* of the Rites, the *spirit*, and the *purpose* remains shrouded in myth for the searcher who does not find his way to the portico of the Temple. For all intents and purposes, one would expect that Memphis+Misraïm is either defunct, or simply yet another appendant body. But Phosphoros' contribution of the extant degrees of Memphis Misraïm is also deeply related to the *furthering* of our labor in Spirit Builders by cementing the three echelons or modes of operation: 1) Lodge work proper 2) points-chauds empowerments via our workable method of Spirit Building, and 3) advanced æonology or operating at the cosmic level of Memphis+Misraïm. The exploration of the latter in this Preface to Volume Two serves the purpose of demonstrating the *living continuity* and consciousness of the Order, its continued development unto the æons, and its elastic and organic nature.

If the reader has completed his introductory course to our program of Spirit Building with Volume One, which leads through the various descriptive papers into the so-called Violet Lodge, and further into our method of points-chauds empowerments, he has begun to get a taste for the whole of the work—its inner continuity and coherence; he has begun to *contact* the spirit of the Rites—its living *egregore* which is to be experienced as a "felt sense" on the gnostico-intuitive level, and has recognized the twofold *scopos* (purification of the soul) and *telos* (union–which in the third echelon becomes *Osirification* through ascent to the "Treasury of Lights") of the work. Spelled out clearly from our initial Charter[429] from Illustrious Brother Bishop Allen H. Greenfield in 2012, we have remained dedicated to this singular purpose by way of the *three-fold path,* which has many permutations, but which is entirely enmeshed with the scopos and telos of Memphis+Misraïm Masonry: *Purification, Illumination,* and *Union*/Osirification. As in all great mysteries, the beginning holds the keys to the ending. Kether is *in* Malkuth. Nirvana *is* samsara. Osirification, as a transformative Rite of *real spiritual transmission* begins in the 3rd degree of Freemasonry with the raising of Hiram from a dead level to a living perpendicular.[430] Seen as a Christ figure in multiple orders, in the APRM+M the rising solar deity is Osiris; the third column in the lodge or the *living spine of the deity;* the vertical line of the triangle in the 47th proposition of Euclid; the erect and eternal phallus symbolizing the ceaseless creativity of the universe; the central-axis mundi. A fresh supply of spirit-power occurs in this moment of raising when the Master *transfers* something of his own KA to the initiate, via the five-points of fellowship. This transference can be compared to the Paschal candle which shares its light to others without itself being dispersed. It is no accident that the hieroglyph of the KA is a set of hands. It is this *transmission* from Master to student, this transference of force and traction that sparks to life the initiate's own *Bon Compagnon,* Holy Guardian Angel, or daimôn. Mystery of Mysteries!

As we have seen in the former volume, this transference from person to person continues in a profound way in the second echelon working of the degrees: the points-chauds empowerments. From the 4th through the 33° the initiate is literally taken on a tour of Amenti through our program of *scrying* the degrees, reawakening the points, and revisiting the lodge work; we enter the *Duat,* ascend to the skies, and delve into the primordial waters of the many planes of existence. Armed with the tools necessary to "work for and receive Master's wages," our initiates can test the spirits of the underworld through the appropriate signs, cover words, and passwords of each degree. Additionally, we can utilize the steps of each degree to *enter* various veils and walk between towering pylons unharmed. In our two-volume set, we find that an additional *gate* is provided for the initiate in the form of our

---

[429] See Volume One, introductory pages.
[430] In the Memphis+Misraïm Symbolic Lodge, the *telos* is clearly delineated even before the 3° in the very first degree. The ritual begins in *Amenti,* symbolized by the Chamber of Reflection; the candidate enters the lodge stooping, which in addition to being a sign of humility, is symbolic of the coming *palingenesis* in the third echelon; the candidate is brought to the font of Mnemosyne where he takes three draughts which continues the sacred "return to the womb" via memory and also symbolizes his ingesting of the egregore; his being "brought to light" is a hint at the final stage of "dazzling light" which is the sacred word of the 95° and deeply related to *Osirification;* and finally, the candidate is clothed or vested in light while his oath is burned, an act of *projection by fire,* both actions relating to the final moments of Osirification.

Tracing Boards, which we will describe further. But our Osirification does not end with travels along the Grand Chemin. We are not simply spiritual voyeurs into other planes of existence: we are gathering data, experience, wisdom, and gnosis for our more complete *union*—hinted at in our final degrees 96-97° in the second echelon, but of such a caliber as not to be contained by words, symbols, rites, and pageantry. Our final work in the third echelon is nothing short of transfiguration in two phases: transfigured *vision*, and pure mystagogy, or *theosis* through spiritual alchemy.

So then, our work indeed has a historical basis as briefly pointed out in Vol. One and additional papers,[431] but our concern is more akin to *meta*history, deep mythology, and the spiritual awakening of the complete man. The Rites of Memphis+Misraïm continue to draw in worthy seekers not because of its sordid history or its accumulation of colorful and flamboyant individuals, but because spiritual power is lodged within the system itself. Language is clumsy here, but it is more appropriate to say that the system is *conscious*, self-aware, and self-organizing, once certain contacts are made, and the initiate attunes to her frequency. She (the APRM+M) begins to operate through the aforementioned SOULDREAM and via the emblems, technology, and ikons of ancient Egypt. The symbols may at first be strictly Christian, to one of that birthcult (as it was for the divine Cagliostro and myself), but soon those emblems morph into something more Coptic, and then more rarefied still as pure *Kemetic* symbology, which touches deeply upon the soul in dreamtime.

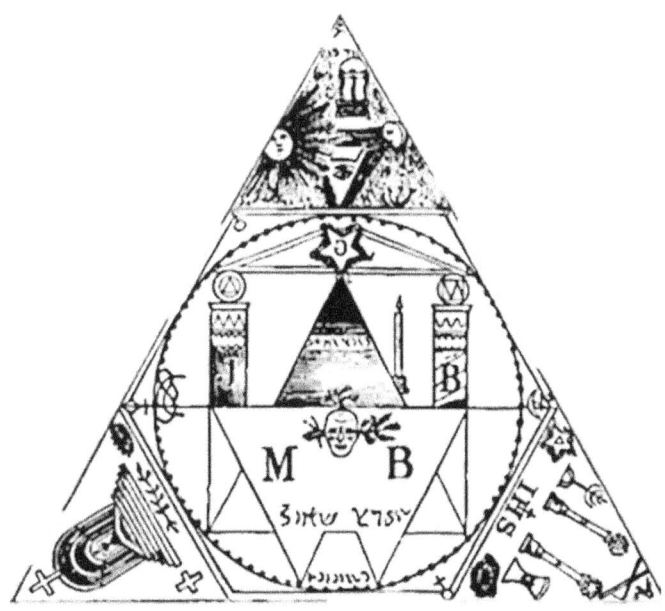

---

[431] See the *History Lection* in the Appendix.

Grades beyond the Scottish Rite

I will be the first to admit that the whole of Western (and some Eastern) philosophical thought, at least pre-modernity, is found within the Blue Lodge and subsequent Red Lodge of the Scottish Rite. In fact, my "regular" lodge work I've most recently aligned with is that of *Le Droit Humain*[432], which works the Scottish Rite from the 1st through 33rd degrees, inclusive. This Rite is exceedingly philosophical with a strong esoteric current in place as well. One of the philosophical principles of Le Droit that I personally resonate with (though my own work is quite religious), is that of the classical French understanding of Laïcité, or *absolute freedom of conscience*. In many ways, this leads right into the Free Illuminist[433] working of the APRM+M, as such freedom is a prerequisite for our work.

But our method of spiritual technology through the Rites of Memphis+Misraïm goes *beyond* philosophy. Herein, as we engage in the degrees from the 34th through the 97th, we enter the numinous. The Order begins to expose its self-organizing principles through three distinct echelons of working. The remainder of this book deeply explores the second echelon, but to demonstrate the amazing elasticity and exaltation of the Rite, let us briefly discuss the third echelon working which may inspire other groups to take the work beyond the checkered pavement.

Our Lodge made a number of critical experiments in these three echelons during 2019 immediately after receiving permission to utilize the Tracing Boards in *Spirit Builders* from GH Alexander Rybalka of blessed memory. One of these experiments can be classed as the *Grand Rite of Osirification*, and we will allude to that work here. It is important to know that at the cosmic scale of working the APRM+M, various lines of transmission and empowerment begin to bleed into each other. For instance, the third echelon working of the Rite is aligned with the V° of the OMd'C, or Chenu Rite of the Élus Coëns/Scottish Judges, *as practiced by our Chapter*. One can find an exploration of this in our book, *Lux Occulta*.[434] Additionally, the spiritual Gnostic Church is part of the overall engine that ignites the work of the third echelon, as it is through the transmission of *Ekklesia* (one of the ÆONs, incidentally) that we are able to offer the sacraments, and bless and consecrate our holy

---

[432] For a while we were doing regular lodge work in the Symbolic Grades via the APRM+M charter from GH Rybalka (WAEO). Eventually, we had to close this formal Lodge due to the incredible geographical distance between our members. Our work is more private now, and along the lines of spiritual direction and the empowering of others to form their own projects. For this, our Violet Lodge has proven entirely workable and effective.

[433] See the breakdown of the Free Illuminist principles that are rather anarcho-syndicalist in scope.

[434] This methodology works less with the Tracing Boards and more with the ÆONIC symbols (16 in all) from the Gnostic *Books of Jeu and the Bruce Codex* and other sources. Both have the "Treasury of Lights" as the telos, or transfigured vision, but the spiritual engagement and journey differ. Remember that the 16 entails the 97 in arithmosophy (9+7=16). The Grand Rite entails both.

tools. This explains both our requirement of a fully fleshed out 66°[435], as well as Greenfield's frequent consecration of Bishops on Arabia Mountain.[436] Additionally, the work is rather entangled with both spiritual alchemy and the legendary *Hieros Gamos* of the *Rose+Croix d'Orient*.[437] These are woven together in the third echelon working of the Arcana Arcanorum (87-90°) combined with aspects of the 95°, known as *the Grand Rite of Osirification*.

ÆONOLOGY involves the anagogic journey of the initiate beyond the earth, the sublunary, and the planetary realms, and unto the *ages of ages,* or æons of æons. Through this process one weaves the spiritual reading of the lodge work of each degree[438] with the reactivation of the points empowerments, and further with the intuitive latticework of *epoptaeia,* via the hidden operation of the *hieros gamos* (itself mirrored in our requirement of an "Inner Guard" and "Outer Guard" or syzygy). Each of the 16 journeys heavenward incorporate the mystical embodiment of the syzygy at each gate (*Bythos* and *Sige*, for instance, in the final portal); the *push* onward and upward is accomplished through the mystical use of the sacred word of the 95th degree: *JAIR HAVOTH*, "dazzling light." One may think of two Crowley connections here, 1) Crowley's notion of "nothingness with sparkles" and 2) Crowley's use of the term HRILIU. For those with ears to hear...[439]

Our own experiences inculcated within the third echelon work itself—over a period of six months from the *Repose of Nature,* or Autumn Equinox, to the *Awakening of Nature,* the Vernal Equinox—resulted in the *Grand Rite of Osirification*, which includes a form of mummification and reanimation. Much of the technique was "received" as is often the case with my experiences within the APRM+M, and yet we found incredible symmetry between these so-called received methodologies and the work of ancient Egyptian magic[440], Neo-platonic theurgy[441], and even into the dreamtime of Vodoun[442]. The timing of GH Rybalka's sharing of the Tracing Boards of the degrees was nothing short of synchronicity. By having the Tracing Board of each degree of working embedded in my mind, through deep meditation,

---

[435] As Bricaud intended...
[436] See the 66° Grand Patriarch in *Degrees of Wisdom: A Compendium of Rituals from the Rites of Memphis and Misraïm*.
[437] The student of Memphis+Misraïm history will recall Marconis de Negre's legends concerning *Ormus*, convert of St. Mark, and his creation of the R+Cd'Or. As Ormus is said to have *purified the Egyptian doctrines according to Christian ideas* (Sanctuary of Memphis), we begin to see the Coptic Orthodox Christian influence of our work. The "Brethren of the Rosy Cross of the Orient" then, are the very founders of the Rite of Memphis, according to this legend.
[438] This is to be treated as a form of the Benedictine *lectio divina* but more along the lines of *lectio continua* that monks utilize daily, as one stays with one particular degree for some time rather than separating little chunks out for meditation. For this, we use +Phosphoros' *Degrees of Wisdom*, 2025.
[439] Additional instruction and "pointing" can also be found in the *Secret Explanation of the 95 Degree* on pgs. 763-764 of *Degrees of Wisdom*.
[440] See: *My Heart My Mother: Death and Rebirth in Ancient Egypt* by Alison Roberts, 2000.
[441] See the incredible corpus of Algis Uzdavinys, especially his *Philosophy as a Rite of Rebirth*, 2008.
[442] Here, we especially reference the text, *Faces of the Gods: Vodou and Roman Catholicism in Haiti* by Leslie Desmangles, 1992.

I was able then to recall the eidetic pylon to mind and enter it as one would enter a sacred yantra in Tantric tradition.

The Tracing Boards *quickened* the ascent through each degree, by focusing the mind entirely on a reduced emblem of the utmost simplicity and design. Though aesthetically we may be drawn to the more exquisite designs of artistic boards throughout Masonic history, it is in its very simplicity that Rybalka's designs transfer *power*. When visually *absorbed* or "eaten" by the mind, these boards act as *heka* on one level, assisting in the recollection of our divine inheritance, our inner logos. A visual sacrament, absorbing these emblems can be compared with the sacred ouroboros of our Order.

As the serpent of wisdom, this symbol suggests both procession (proödos) and return (epistrophe), which is the nature of all sacred liturgy, and inherent to our Grand Rite. The Tracing Board *proceeds* from two-dimensions to the non-dimensional space of noetic transmissions, and through intelligible digestion, it sparks a return to our primitive rights and privileges as apospasmic "sparks" from the divine order.

Nowhere is this sacramental use of the Tracing Boards more profound than with the æonic working of the *Arcana Arcanorum*. These four degrees, their four phases—Black, Red, White, and Gold—awaken the man of earth to his KA, BA, SAH, and AKH.[443]

---

[443] This work is *completed* in the 95°.

Preface to Volume Two

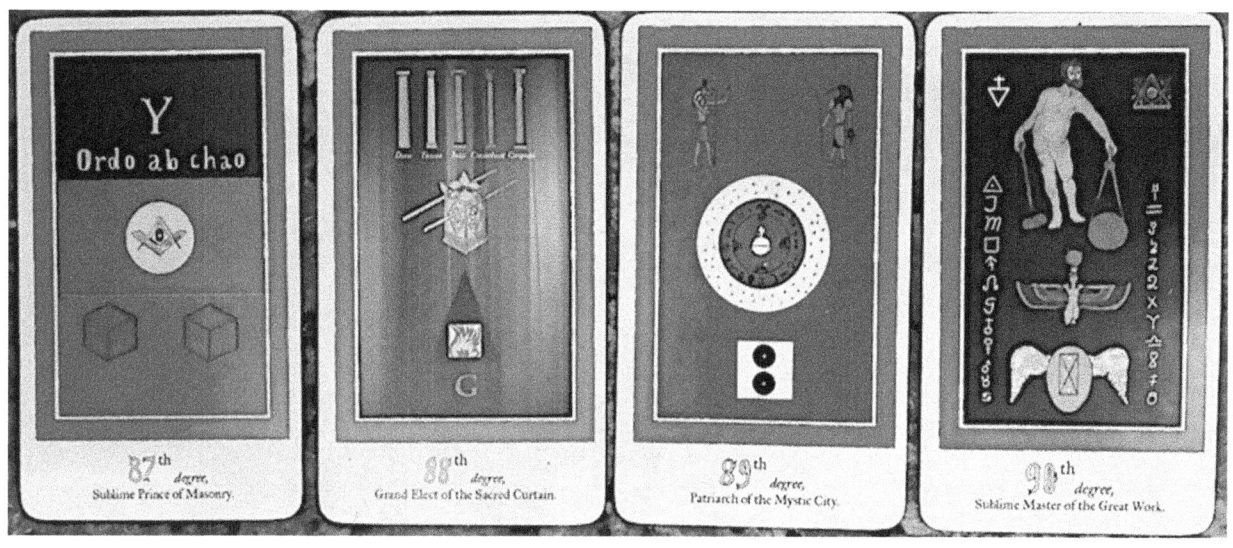

Here, the Naples Régime material (see *Degrees of Wisdom*) is combined with the Tracing Boards, enflamed through the points empowerments, and perfected via the highly secret method of *animating a statue,* involving the evocation of the memory of Atum before the emergence of Shu and Tefnut through *self-contemplation* and by way of the "sending forth of the eye" as creative magic. Atum's self-contemplating can best be symbolized by the REBIS, or divine androgyne.

As the genesis of all triads, Atum-Shu-Tefnut, sigillized by the REBIS[444] with the implied creation of the mystical "third" we now have the pillar of light proper, which began in the 3rd degree when we were raised to a living perpendicular, continued through the Masonic Middle Pillar which energizes and nourishes the Osirian spinal column for advanced æonology, and is perfected by the secret working of the Outer Guard (Isis crowned with the moon above) to manifest and erect the replacement for Osiris' (Inner Guard) missing virile member (pillar of light).

As the quintessential axis mundi, or central axis fire of the Coëns, the mystical lingam and ejaculate therefrom appear as a stone of light, which recalls a certain stone in St. John's Revelation, as well as the stone of Cagliostro's quarantines. The beginnings of this transfiguration, again with the ritual embrace of the Master and initiate on the five points of fellowship, transmit *a portion* of the Master's KA which may be compared to the reception of grace (charis), as energeia. This energy from the Master's KA awakens the initiate's own Guardian Angel (identified with the KA in the 85°), of which we find parallels in Vodun by way of the Mét Tét (and *gwo-bon-anj*). Further alliances are found with the BA—which is our liberated soul able to leave the body and travel in foreign lands—and the Vodun *ti-bon-ange*.

The sending of the *gwo-bon-anj* to Ginen parallels our path of Osirification in Amenti, through the realization of the AKH (the integrated, transmuted, and perfected SAH, KA, and BA) beyond the land of Osiris to the Court of Amun RA, or the "Treasury of Lights." For the Voduisant, it is the *ti-bon-ange* that is judged after death in a tribunal. This connects

---

[444] In the exposition of the 90° from p. 362 of Ravignat's *Quest for a Lost Rite: High Degrees and Spiritual Practice of Traditional Egyptian Freemasonry*, we see that the Tracing Board for this degree is the Alchemical Hermaphrodite emblem, also found in Pike's *Morals & Dogma*.

further with the Hall of MAAT and the 42 Assessors,[445] as well as the Final Judgment in the Revelation of St. John, and more proper to our work, in the ordeal of the Frank Judges in the 30° of Volume One.[446] One final note on this Vodun~Egyptian connection: the *gwo-bon-anj* and *mèt-tèt* are sent to Ginen (like the BA and the KA) where the gwo-bon-anj awaits *reactivation* into a divinity like the golden body (SAH) of the AKH (illuminated and fully integrated star). Those who have had the pleasure to work directly with Illustrious Brother Allen H. Greenfield will be delighted to recognize his loving title for Free Illuminists, *Fellow Stars*...This "star body," scintillating through points-empowerments awaits reactivation into divinity in the Bridal Chamber, as described in the *Gnostic Gospel of Phillip*. Our *palingenesis* is, like Philip's Bridal Chamber, a source of *healing* the break between our physicality and the divine order. Treated as one of the sacraments in the Phillip's Gnostic Gospel, the Bridal Chamber is also understood to be the place where spiritual androgyny is *restored* (i.e., the REBIS). We then see the Bridal Chamber as being deeply connected to the Pharaonic chambers in the pyramids, and to the death rites of Vodou for safe passage to Ginen, as both entail the afterlife of the devout, and the Bridal Chamber involves a mystical death of separateness prior to union.

What is the meaning of all of this?

The notes from our experimentation in the third echelon of the APRM+M fill several folios. Due to the profundity of the work, some of the material borders on incomprehensible. This, to us, is one of its proofs, ironically! But what is the meaning of all these mysteries of the Voudon+Gnostic multiverse? It is this: the APRM+M has the power and capacity to propel the initiate into *all* worlds of the mind, *all* worlds of the sublunary realm, *all* worlds of the planetary realm, and further—through advanced æonology—*all* worlds of the Kósmos Noetós. Most of our initiates are familiar with magic and its engagement with angels, planetary spirits, and the like (all of which we explore in the second echelon of our work), but most do not venture further, to the cosmic Mind—the Treasury of Lights. Implied in the "assumption of godforms," the transfiguration via Osirification must go further than visualization and mental journeying; we must identify with the ALL. We must rise, as a bubble rises to the surface, and then completely align with each æon like the popping of the bubble as it merges into the air, we become gods of dazzling light (JAIR HAVOTH).

---

[445] We find the 42 Assessors aligned with 42 sins in Ravignat's charts on pgs. 369-371, *ibid.*
[446] The *experience* of the Areopagus and Frank Judges in the 30° of the AASR was a powerful one for me and immediately put me in the mindset of MAAT's Hall of Judgment.

Spirit Builders

Through such anagogic resurrection, our perception is forever changed. This is the first stage of Osirification, *transfigured vision*. For instance, after the completion of one such journey, our research[447] derived the following *modes of operation* of our exquisite and simple Tracing Boards. Seen through the lens of the gods, these Boards have the following modalities:

- As *Eidos* each Board has a precise *form* designed to properly house the essence and energy of the grade.
- As *Pylons* each Board forms a gateway into a Temple, often pyramidal in design.
- As *Oracle* each Board acts as a divination for the initiate, guiding the next step or directing the course of spirit-building.
- As *Symbolon* each Board partially discloses mythological truth, meaning, and secrets, and reveals how such symbola are sown throughout the cosmos.
- As *Synthemata* each Board houses power in its form (eidos) to act as token, passport, watchword, or "thought of god" to transverse the inner worlds.
- As *Agalma* each Board is a cult image, offering, or object of worship which can be "animated" through our visual absorption, digestion, and identification with the image.
- As *Logoi* each Board reveals its inner essence, purpose, and reason within the larger order of Being. As logoi, the Board assists in the initiate's ascent in the same way that sentient beings of the created order can stir up natural theoria in the mystic.[448]

Each Tracing Board then, "operates" according to the capacity and level of initiation of the Operator, but the key is to awaken this transfigured vision, and such takes time and experimentation. And this is only one very particular and precise example of such transfigured vision.

---

[447] Keep in mind that our initial Charters were for a *philosophical and research Lodge*, and so our continued endeavors are the work of a highly specialized *Lodge of Research*.

[448] The reader may connect such understanding of *logoi* with that of the Stoic *pneuma*, which, when within the human frame, is the *vehicle of the logos*. St. Maximos the Confessor expounds further upon this notion, perceiving the logoi of creation as each thing's purpose or inner principle.

The Inner Retreat and Grand Rite of Osirification

Preface to Volume Two

All these hints and pointers of our third echelon of working, aim to assist the spirit builder in the process of complete Osirification, which though "complete," is not a one and done experience. Due to our bondage to the "world" of things, our attachments and enslavement to the passions, our greed and ignorance, our craving for pleasure and aversion to pain, we must re-*member* (anamnesis) the dispersed body of Osiris again and again and again. He is forever being slaughtered and dismembered by Set,[449] which is to say that we are engaged in the interior battle of our minds until death. We are plagued by thoughts, by division, by worries and cares, all of which are the drinking of the draught of the River Lethe (first degree full form). This forgetting is the root of our Fall, while remembering (*anamnesis*) is our return to unity and divinity. Osirification, in sum, is this return in the form of a mystical *palingenesis*.[450]

Once we have been fully initiated into the first echelon through Lodge work and intensive study of the degrees,[451] created our scintillating body of light via the second echelon of points-chauds empowerment (which again is aligned with the Egyptian understanding of the SAH, spiritual body composed of stars—hot points), and received the transmission of the *Rose+Croix d'Orient*, as well as consecration as Gnostic Bishop (which can be accomplished with a thorough implementation of the 66°)[452], the journey of æonology can begin, culminating in the *Grand Rite of Osirification* which occurs within the Inner Retreat of the APRM+M. I am neither permitted to divulge this material in toto, nor could I if I had such permission. But a few more words can be said concerning the procedure of six months.

We have pointed out that the purpose of our work is both the purification of the soul and union in the form of Osirification. Further, we have said that this union has two stages—*transfigured vision* and pure *mystagogy* or theosis. A simple example of this transfigured vision was given by way of our ability to see, as the god might see, the various modes of operation of our Tracing Boards. But of course, this is a very particular case. The general, or universal application of transfigured vision is of the utmost profundity. In the simplest language, all I

---

[449] Here, it is of note that the Greek word, *diablos* means one who divides or one who throws apart.
[450] This mystery is the literal *return to the womb* as will be disclosed. However, one mustn't think of this in strictly psychoanalytic terms, as a form of *regression*. Our experience of non-duality doesn't leave us in a mushy state of child-like dependence. Rather, our palingenesis is a sacred *return* in that we are being reinvested with the clarity of vision that affects our moment-to-moment experience. It is as if a treasure has been taken from us that is finally returned.
[451] Again, for those without access to Memphis+Misraïm lodges, this could be through another Obedience, or via the Violet Lodge within this book and a trusted initiate descended from the Great Arabia Mountain workings. If the symbolic degrees are all that has been "experienced," then a thorough study of the subsequent degrees through +Phosphoros' *Degrees of Wisdom* is in order.
[452] See Appendix E 66° ritual.

can say is that the revelation that accompanies this experience is that the basis of reality is neither particle nor energy as we once postulated, but *consciousness* all the way down![453] Interestingly enough, this vision is being revealed in the realm of science (cognitive science, neuroscience, physics, and other domains) as well, through the work of Annaka Harris, David Hoffman, and others. But we don't postulate such a vision with formulas, combustion chambers, or functional MRI's, we *experience* this reality through our very physicality. The non-dual appreciation of the body has been the key within our entire opus, and it is through the body that we become aware of the fundamental nature of consciousness and how to raise ourselves to a level of identification with God-consciousness.

The Grand Rite starts with our transmission of KA energy in the 3°; continues with our development of our energy-saturated spine as the Osirian column of light through the Masonic Middle Pillar (and Ambelain's *Boule Blanche*); we are then elevated to the ancient sacerdotal caste through the 66° making us capable of thoroughly consecrating and blessing all of our elements of sacramental working and giving us the power of awakening and animating consciousness within objects; and finally, we come to recognize our HGA in the 85°-90° which is analogous to our own KA. Through the second echelon working, we learn how to liberate our BA and traverse the Grand Chemin, visit Amenti, and become Masters of the various worlds. In the first and second echelons of working the *Arcana Arcanorum*, we begin to solidify the golden light body (the integral AKH) for its cosmic travels in æonology. The first echelon working of the AA is key as it points repeatedly (especially in the 90°) to the cosmic nature of our labors at this juncture.[454] The second echelon working of the AA traverses the entire system of Enochian aethyrs, which in its Archangelic form, is the very beginning of æonology. This method teaches the initiate how to utilize points on the body to awaken precise spiritual *locations*, which will be accomplished on a higher arc in the third echelon through the 100 words and parts of the body from the *Apocryphon of John* and the ÆONIC Syzygies (see charts following the Preface).

The 90° and 95° must be studied with zeal. There are multiple versions of the 90° which speak to each other and expound upon one another. Begin with the degree presented in the present text. Though the HGA is presented in the 85°, it isn't until the 90° that we speak of the actual engagement, or *knowledge and conversation with one's Holy Guardian Angel*. If this seminal experience has not been accomplished by the initiate (itself a 6–12-month enterprise), the operative work should stop here but the study of the written 90° in *Degrees of Wisdom* and Ravignat's *Quest for a Lost Rite* is encouraged. The Angel is the fool-proof guide

---

[453] This realization through Osirification comports with our early experimentation with enthogens and the ability to identify consciousness in various parts of the body and extending outward into the field surrounding the body.
[454] See pages 724-734 in *Degrees of Wisdom*.

in the third echelon. He will often speak for you in your ascent and will challenge entities with the appropriate words, grips, and signs.

All three versions of the 90° are deeply connected and speak to a *nuptial bed* (the Bridal Chamber) with cosmic significances. For instance, in the present text, we speak of the Angel teaching the initiate how to reawaken the points-chauds at will, and how to concentrate the energy into a beam of light (central axis, Osirian column/spine) to create a "full-bodied expansion of light" for the sake of radionic healing and the like. This is the advancement of the work of the Masonic Middle Pillar and *Boule Blanche*. Once this preparatory work is complete, the initiate—a holder of both the Rose+Croix d'Orient lineage and teachings of the *Hieros Gamos*, as well as being a 66° consecrated Bishop—may, according to his own ingenium work with the following scaffolding:

Procedural

From this brief description, the initiate is encouraged to fully flesh out the *Grand Rite of Osirification* for himself. Such is the nature of one exalted to the 95° and above. For those who have followed our work in its entirety, it will be in review to say that the forming of a *living syzygy* is only possible when the mystic pair have love as their bond and very foundation. Anything less than this devolves into the three poisons: greed/lust, anger/resentment, and delusion/ignorance.

☥

- ❖ Let the initiate choose a suitable apartment for working, procure for him or herself a full day for both the repose and awakening of nature, and align with his living syzygy[455] who will act as Outer Guard or Isis.
- ❖ The *Repose of Nature* begins on the day of the autumnal equinox. The *Repose*, also considered a mystical mummification, lasts until Winter Solstice, when the various dismembered parts of the Body of Osiris are slowly found and the steady march of the light commences. It is perfected at the vernal equinox.
- ❖ Spend the daytime hours of the autumnal equinox in retreat, according to your capacity. Practice meditation, concentration, and strengthen the body through asanas and walking meditation. Revisit the *Hauts Grades* section of Spirit Builders, and have the Outer Guard give you each points-chaud empowerment (including all words, signs, steps, etc.). After each, meditate on the Tracing Board with no further scrying.
- ❖ As night begins to fall, take a light meal and then have the Outer Guard accompany you to your sleeping chambers.
- ❖ Practice full-body relaxation from head to toe until you are thoroughly restful and at peace. Now, the Outer Guard, as Isis, will anoint with pure olive oil each of the 100 parts of your body, and say the godname for each from mouth to ear (names and parts from the *Apocryphon of John*).
- ❖ Meditate on the emptiness of each part of the body that is anointed. Try to find the "I" in each part. Notice the impermanence of all systems of the body. Experience the sensation of non-identification with the body. Attempt to move consciousness itself to the location of the gnostic pressure.
- ❖ As you relax completely, let the Outer Guard remind you that though your body is dying, your BA may be liberated during sleep. The aggregates of your persona are free to travel in souldream, work for and receive Master's wages. But there will be forces that will attempt to keep you bound. The dweller on the threshold awaits.

---

[455] Recall Atum's "self-contemplating" for a hint at how this could be accomplished by oneself (IX°) with the summoning of Isis.

- ❖ The Outer Guard will cover you in the funeral pall (black sheet) once you have fallen asleep. According to her own ingenium, she will then "mummify" your body, taking all of the "organs" symbolically except for the heart, the seat of the soul and the nous.

During the six-month interim between the *Repose* and the *Awakening* of Nature, the initiate must practice with assiduity the Masonic Middle Pillar, awakening the points-chauds at will, scrying the aethyrs through the 88-89°*AA* in Spirit Builders, and intensive study of the extant papers on the Arcana Arcanorum, Naples Régime, as well as the first and second echelons of the 95°. Each night, before retiring, the initiate must perform an examination of conscience and the *Boule Blanche* to assist in souldreaming. All experiences, insights, and impressions should be committed to the diary.

- ❖ The *Awakening of Nature* begins on the evening before the vernal equinox. Let the initiate secure for him or herself a suitable apartment for working, a true syzygical partner to act as Isis (Outer Guard), and at least a full day free from interruptions. Privacy is of the utmost importance. Fasting is encouraged prior to the Bridal Chamber, but both partners should be well hydrated.
- ❖ As a consecrated Templar Bishop, the initiate should cleanse the space thoroughly with both blessed Holy water and suffumigation appropriate to the working.[456] He should also consecrate his syzygical partner, the Outer Guard, as Isis, according to his own ingenium.

---

[456] Here, we suggest the Chenu Myron for anointing and Chenu Incense for suffumigation. These are not "for sale" but the instructions for creating them can be found from pgs. 585-597 in *Lux Occulta*.

- ❖ As night falls, the initiate returns to the Bridal Chamber, undresses, lays down in the posture of Osiris slain, and covers himself with the funeral pall. Isis begins her search for the parts of Osiris, finding all but the membrum virile.

- ❖ Isis forms the sacred lingam through her creativity and heka, awakening Osiris from a dead level to a living perpendicular. Through the nuptial bed, or *unio mystica,* the Angel instructs Osiris how to liberate his BA further—while awakened and erect—and how to scry further into the flesh.
- ❖ Isis performs a reversal of the 100 godnames and the anointing of the parts of the body with Holy Myron, lovingly awakening each, then follows with 16 points empowerments relating to the 16 ÆONS/Time Stations. She gives the point first, then presses the appropriate pentacle of the ÆONIC seal on the forehead of the supine Osiris. She performs this task with each of the 16 gnostic seals, opening the doors for his travel on the cosmic scale, rising...ever rising further from earth to the Treasury of Lights.[457]
- ❖ Isis continues her stimulation of the points and awakens the body further, saying the syzygical name of the ÆONIC being as she whispers, *Ascend unto Theletos and Sophia* (for example) while increasing her stimulation with each new ÆON, through the 16th where she increases to the fullest. Taking the wand of Osiris into the Holy Grail and proclaiming with fervor as he ascends to the Treasury, *JAIR HAVOTH* repeatedly, she performs the sign by pressing her two fingers to his lips in ekstasis.[458]
- ❖ Isis collects the white stone and the red tincture into the Holy Grail with pure red wine.

---

[457] If certain ÆONs do not open, Isis shall take the setting maul and give three strikes upon the part of the body that is blocked.

[458] See both the secrets and the work of the 95° in *Degrees of Wisdom,* and particularly the *Secret and Occult Explanation of the 95th Degree,* p. 763-764. Here we see the utilization of both the sacred word and sign of the degree.

- ❖ Osiris rises slowly, once again upon the five points of fellowship with Isis as his Initiator, and vests in pure linen and prepares for Communion in the 66°.[459] The two commune in silence, in a most organic mystic repast.

To complete the Grand Rite and the formation of the integral AKH, the Holy couple sleep only for a short amount of time, taking note of all dream material upon awakening. Take care to awaken precisely before the first rays of the equinox come over the horizon in the east. If your living arrangement does not allow for such to take place outdoors, move to an eastern facing window and open the window if possible, to let nature and the first rays of the sun into the room.

- ❖ Clothed in a single white robe, Osiris is conducted outside into nature by Isis, prior to dawn.
- ❖ As the sun rises, Osiris disrobes, absorbing the first rays of the sun (as extended rays of consecration) of the vernal equinox upon his body, creating the golden Robe of Glory, sealing the internal and integrated AKH, the point within the circle; he now identifies with the ALL rather than with the body, the emotions, the thoughts, or memories. Having ascended unto the Treasury of Lights, received the "prize of the eyes" (*transfigured Vision*) through scrying in the flesh, gathered all that has been scattered into his scintillating SAH, he now rests in Osirification—undifferentiated awareness, self-coherence, union with God as the ALL through ekstasis.[460]
- ❖ The KA and SAH are now fully integrated with the BA, via the AKH. Osiris recognizes his "double" as being symbolized by his "sister/wife." As one, they formed the REBIS in the Bridal Chamber and healed the wound of the Fall into forgetfulness. His palingenesis being completed as he returned to the womb, Adam and Eve are also returned to their unified state.

---

[459] (See Ritus Communionis for the 66th degree in Appendix E.
[460] After several moments of meditation, Isis reads the "HYMN OF THE ATEN" which can be found in the alternate readings of the fully worked Patriarch Grand Consecrator degree, in the Appendix.

- ❖ The Osirified initiate now has a repository of uncreated Light, the "dazzling Light" he experienced in the Bridal Chamber that can be reawakened with each points-chaud empowerment, each Boule Blanche, each Masonic Middle Pillar exercise. This inexhaustible source of Light can then be utilized in radionic healing, as instructed in the R+Cd'Or, as well as in points empowerments, and the creation of APRM+M nodes.

And so, we continue with the *Hauts Grades* of the Rites of Memphis+Misraïm proper, 34-97°. Knowing that this august Rite lives and moves and has its being in an ontology entirely beyond any other class of Masonic rites, we continue in earnest and in awe of her majestic and exalted nature. In the final analysis, it is the lasting impact that the three echelons of working the APRM+M have on one's daily life that matters. From the outset, we have identified how the method of spirit building is not for oneself alone, but for the enlightening and creation of entire communities of wholeness. We have also highlighted the intimate nature of points-chauds empowerments and their ability to dispel one's faulty vision of a mind or spirit *separate* from the body, or at war with it. Though we may project our BA into foreign lands, we maintain the *silver cord* which connects us deeply with our physicality. Further, our geography is imbued with meaning in spirit-building as we locate our sacred marmas and draw heaven downwards (epiclesis), while raising earth upwards (anagogy). When the sensorium is truly cleansed, the initiate will begin to utilize his transfigured vision to see sacred marmas *everywhere* around him, the universe truly as a theophany, and consciousness as the fundamental nature of reality. All of the experimentation, insights, journeys, meditations, scrying, and the like come to a head in our *Grand Rite of Osirification* where the underlying theme, the secret of all secrets is *Love*. We have preached *Love as the ultimate reality* since the publication of our first work, *Syzygy*. With our transfigured vision and *experience* of union with the ALL via palingenesis, we come to realize the relational quality of all things, our interdependence with nature, and the profundity of love as the adhesive of all such unions.

The APRM+M will forever mystify the historian and dumbfound the armchair Mason, but she, like the pyramids of Egypt, will live on and manifest in a variety of forms through time to the persevering mortal, always harkening back to that land that birthed the gods, always contacting future carriers of the mystery through dreamtime, and always lifting her veil coyly and opening the eyes of her children to the grand hierophany.

+PALAMAS 33° 90° 96°
Aug. 23rd, 2025, Zenith of Atlanta
Feast of St. Rose of Lima/Erzulie Freda

ÆONIC SYZYGIES

Male/Day		Female/Night	APRM+M Series
Theletos	I.	Sophia	1st series, First class Symbolic Grades, 1-3°
Ecclesiasticus	II.	Macariotes	Lodge of Perfection, 4-14°
Ainos	III.	Synesis	1st series, Second Class, College, 14°
Metricos	IV.	Agape	Council of the Princes of Jerusalem 15-16°
Patricos	V.	Elpsis	Sovereign Chapter, Prince Rose+Croix, 17-18°
Paracletus	VI.	Pistis	Council of Kadosh, 19-30°
Monogenes	VII.	Macaria	2nd series, Third Class, Chapter, 31-33°
Acinetos	VIII.	Syncrasis	Consistory of the Sublime Princes of the Royal Secret, 32°
Autophyes	IX.	Hedone	Supreme Council, 33°
Ageratos	X.	Henosis	2nd series, Fourth Class, Consistory, 34-35°
Bythius	XI.	Mixis	Fifth Class, Areopagus, 36-49°
Logos	XII.	Zoe	Senate of Hermetic Philosophers, 50-62°
Anthropos	XIII	Ekklesia	3rd series, Sixth Class, Consistory, 63-75°
Nous	XIV.	Aletheia	Seventh Class, Council, 76-89°
Ennoea	XV.	Thelesis	Seventh Class, Sublime Council, 76-89°, *Arcana Arc*
Bythos	XVI	Sige[461]	Official Degrees, *Arcana Arc*, 90-100°

---

[461] Several of the ÆONs crop up as passwords and sacred words throughout the work. When this occurs, there is an access point to the cosmic/æonic 3rd echelon working of the grade. SIGE is particularly invoked, which is the first rung towards the Treasury of Lights and which relates directly to the powerful experience of Horus as he pressed his fingers to my lips in the initial SOULDREAM some 25 years ago.

The Treasury of Light

✠

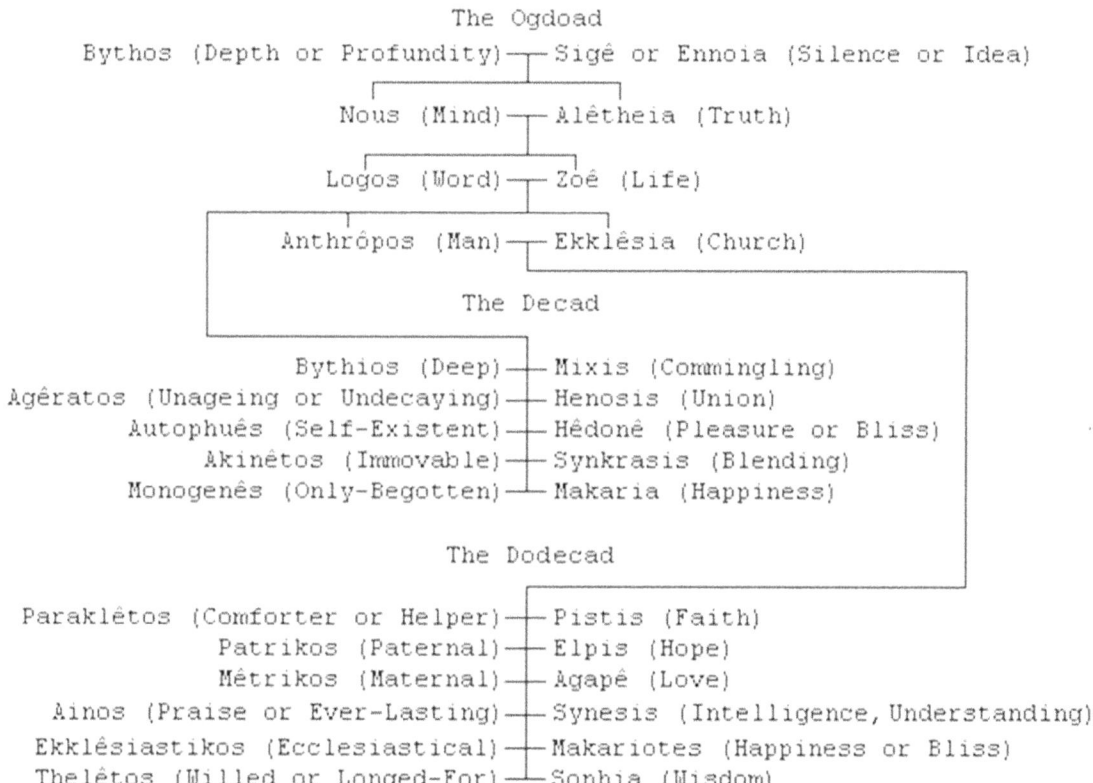

From G.R.S. Mead's, *Pistis Sophia,* 1890, The Theosophical Publishing Society

Spirit Builders

ÆONOLOGY

Listing of Hot points

*The throng of angels stood by and received these seven psychical substances
from the authorities in order to create a network of limbs and trunk,
with all the parts properly arranged.*

Apocryphon of John . 171, Gnostic Bible

1. Raphao—the Head
2. Abron—the Skull
3. Meniggesstroeth—the Brain
4. Asterechme—the right eye
5. Thaspomocha—the left eye
6. Yeronumos—the right ear
7. Bissoum—the left ear
8. Akioreim—the nose
9. Banen-Ephroum—the lips
10. Amen—the teeth (infused water essence)
11. Ibikan—the molars (infused
12. Basiliademe—the tonsils (salt water infusion)
13. Achcha—the uvula (clove oil for teeth)
14. Adaban—the neck
15. Chaaman—the vertebrate
16. Dearcho—the throat
17. Tebar—the right shoulder
18. N---, the left shoulder
19. Mniarchon—the right elbow
20. ----e, the left elbow
21. Abitrion—the right underarm
22. Euanthen—the left underarm
23. Krus—the right hand
24. Beluai—the left hand
25. Treneu—the fingers of the right hand
26. Balbel—the fingers of the left hand
27. Krima—the fingernails
28. Astrops—the right breast
29. Barroph—the left breast
30. Baoum—the right shoulder joint
31. Ararim—the left shoulder joint
32. Areche—the belly
33. Phthaue—the navel
34. Senaphim—the abdomen
35. Arachethopi—the right ribs
36. Zabedo—the left ribs
37. Barias—the right hip

38. Phnouth—the left hip
39. Abenlenarchei—the marrow
40. Chnoumeninorin—the bones
41. Gesole—the stomach
42. Agromauma—the heart
43. Bano—the lungs
44. Sostrapal—the liver
45. Anesimalar—the spleen
46. Thopithro—the intestines
47. Biblo—the kidneys
48. Roeror—the sinews
49. Taphreo—the backbone
50. Ipouspoboba—the veins
51. Bineborin—the arteries
52. Aatoimenpsephei—the breaths in all the limbs
53. Entholleia—all the flesh
54. Bedouk—the right buttock
55. Arabeei—the left buttock
56. Sorma—the genitals
57. Gormakaiochlabar—the right thigh
58. Nebrith—the left thigh
59. Pserem—the muscles of the right leg
60. Asaklas—the muscles of the left leg
61. Ormaoth—the right leg
62. Emenun—the left leg
63. Knux—the right shin
64. Tupelon—the left shin
65. Achiel—the right ankle
66. Phneme—the left ankle
67. Phiouthrom—the right foot
68. Boabel—right foot toes
69. Trachoun—the left foot
70. Phikna—left foot toes
71. Miamai—the toenails

Those who activate the limbs

72. Abrana—the toes of the left foot
73. Marephnounth—the left foot
74. Archentechtha—the toes of the right foot
75. Bastan—the right foot
76. Charaner—the left ankle
77. Aol—the right ankle
78. Toechtha—the left shin
79. Aroer—the right shin
80. Charcha—the left leg
81. Choux—the right leg
82. Bathinoth—the genitals
83. Chthaon—the left thigh
84. Charcharb—the right thigh
85. Sabalo—the womb
86. Arouph—the abdomen
87. Sunogchouta—the left ribs
88. Asphixix—the right ribs
89. Odeor—the left shoulder joint
90. Koade—the right shoulder joint
91. Pisandraptes—the chest
92. Imae—the left breast

Spirit Builders

93. Barbar—the right breast
94. Leekaphar—the fingers of the left hand
95. Lampno—the fingers of the right hand
96. Arbao—the left hand
97. Oudidi—the right hand
98. Querton—the left shoulder, Yakouib—the right shoulder (consecration)
99. Yammeax—the neck
100. Diolimodraza—the head

Examples[462] of ÆONIC seals from the Books of JEU:

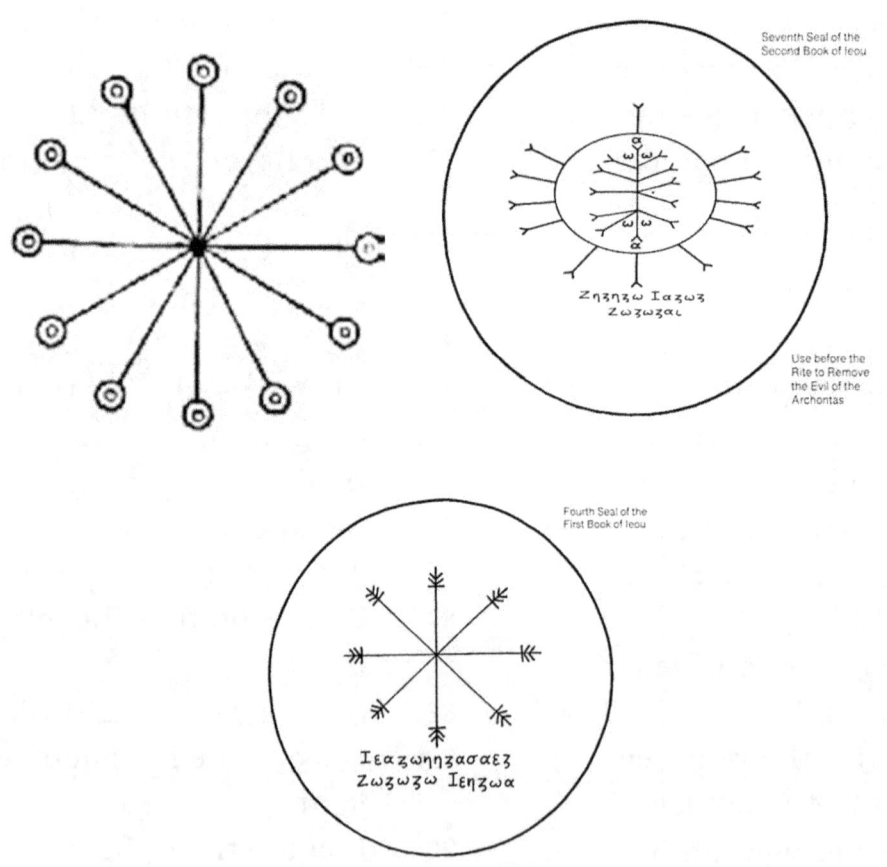

---

[462] As this working is of the utmost importance, we will refrain from including all the incredibly powerful, but simple ÆONIC seals here. Their very vibration can disturb the sensitive. See the Brill edition of the *Books of Jeu and Untitled text in the Bruce Codex*, 1978.

To the Glory of the Sublime Architect of the Universe

In the Name and under the auspices of the Sovereign Sanctuary of the Antient & Primitive Rite of Memphis+Misraïm, in and for the United States of America

A Continuation of

PART THREE

✠

Hauts Grades

Being an Initiated Interpretation of the Antient & Primitive Rite of Memphis+Misraïm as worked in the Chapel of the Gnosis by the Light of

Free Illuminism

A Ritual Monitor & Guide

For ALL

Ninety-seven Degrees

of Esoteric Freemasonry

With Notes and Synopses

"*The study of nature, of its mysterious revolutions, of its generative powers...have produced a science full of attraction which, in the middle ages, was called ALCHEMY or HERMETIC PHILOSOPHY, from the name of the greatest of all these sages, HERMES TRISMEGISTUS, founder of the Egyptian religion and the first philosopher who, in the interior of the pyramids, taught the OCULT SCIENCES, that is to say the knowledge of man, nature, and God.*"

J.-M. Ragon, *Masonic Orthodoxy*

CHAPTER FOUR

Hermetic, Gnostic, & Kabalistic Degrees

34th-86th

"To 'separate the subtle from the gross' is to free the soul from prejudice and vice; we effect this by the salt of wisdom, the mercury of aptitude and labour, and the sulphur of energy, or the ardour of omnipotent will, represented by the pentacle, for by will all things are made."

John Yarker[463]

---

[463] *Lectures of a Chapter, Senate, etc.*, p. 43

John Yarker's "Lectures" become a sort of textbook for the largest set of Degrees in our corpus. Within this thin volume are directives towards the Kabalah, the study of spiritual and physical Alchemy, pointers to the living Gnosis and the exposition of Hermetic doctrines. From this book, the Initiate can begin to move outward to the works of Eliphas Levi, the Ceremonial Magic of 19th Century Adepts of the Hermetic Order of the Golden Dawn, the Kabalistic workings of Dion Fortune and Aleister Crowley, the mysticism of Louis Claude de St. Martin and Jacob Boehme, the Christian Theurgy of the Elect Coëns, and the consecratory power and lineage of Episcopacy. In terms of study, the entire corpus of the Western Esoteric Tradition is at the disposal of the Initiate working with these Degrees and empowerments, but she is most particularly enjoined to focus on the practice and development of the magical imagination, the strengthening of the sovereign will, and the direct experience of Gnosis. It is through the Trilogy of Hermetic, Gnostic, and Kabalistic studies that the Initiate will discover the proper application of the forces that these empowerments stir within the human frame. It is this series also, that opens wide the gates to Voudon+Gnosis, beginning particularly in the 41st Degree, *Knight of the Arch of Seven Colors*. Though the points and further study offer such opportunity for limitless extension and a lifetime of magickal adventure, no such studies are required or demanded of the Initiate. This is because we are working with the Primitive Doctrine, which though containing within itself a myriad of applications and opportunities for development, is simple, pure and immutable. In other words, though you may now have the Western Esoteric Tradition at your fingertips, the individual is trusted and supported in whatever endeavor is spurned by this series. The *required* fields of study and inquiry are self-imposed and the disciplines derived from such study are a personal ascesis not pushed upon the individual from an external source. The self organizing and self guiding quality of the points-chauds is a trustworthy guide.

The section of the *Hermetic axiom* that this series is related to, is *to Will*. Whereas the Philosophical Degrees often result in the understanding of one's Sacred Duty to perform, one's True Will—it is this set of Degrees that stirs the performance and completion of that same Will. If one persists with these empowerments and Degrees, he can accomplish this Will, for the energy that these points massage into wakefulness is of a sublime and mystical nature. The sacred marmas upon the body that are stimulated through these Degrees, sexual centers and regions related to the "backside of the Tree of Life," are of such a powerful quality that they should not be toyed with in a careless manner, rather they should be deeply respected and studied through meditation and esoteric research. Experimentation is one thing, careless and irresponsible misconduct with these Degrees and their accompanying points is not the work of a true Facilitator. There must be absolute trust between the Initiate and Facilitator for this series, and in this case the directives of T Allen Greenfield for the Facilitator to be a clergyman and have received Apostolic and Gnostic Succession in the traditional manner, are to be highly considered. It is not stated as a *requirement*, per se, but as a suggestion for the safe and proper integration of these energies and entities. Curiously enough, the 66th Degree in this series has been likened to Episcopal Consecration and is even worked in such manner in some Orients, including our own. See Appendix E.

The type of epistemology that this series engages in is manifold. In terms of critical thinking, these Degrees assuredly move into divergent thinking. They are not concerned with "rightness" or converging towards some singular truth. These degrees project the Initiate outwards into the ethers. There are traditional forms of knowledge and comprehension, as well as analysis and synthesis which the Initiate embarks upon with the vast array of materials to study in these Degrees, but there are also more mysterious forms of knowledge worked herein, such as the Gnostic and Ontic variety.

We will find in these Degrees that the *Synopsis* is born from direct experience with these grades. This is due to the direct nature of gnosis itself. Gnosis is a felt experience of the Divine, regardless of the medium used. One need not use a Sacred book for this experience, or operate under a priest necessarily. From Facilitator to Initiate, through the diaphanous realms of spiritual transmission, the individual can experience the highest levels of gnosis from the points-chauds empowerments of these Degrees. This is a traditional form of person to person initiation that goes one step further and asserts that the transmission itself may elicit an immediate and direct experience of Divinity. Recall that the points are stimulating energies and entities that are already present within the body. It is not that the Facilitator is the all knowing dispenser of spirit and keeper of the gnosis, it is that through accessing our sacred Egregore via this transmission, the latent gnosis within contacts, or rays outward, the inherent gnosis of the Higher realms, and thus receives the same broadcasts from those realms. One might picture a satellite dish in space receiving input from a programmer on earth and then broadcasting back to the earth in different locales.

The Ontic knowledge derived from these Degrees relates directly to the work of our Patriarch Michael Bertiaux. Through his development of the Ontic Sphere, which encompasses a vast range of beings, forms, spirits, entities, Zothyrian landscapes, angelic hierarchies and multi-verses, the Initiate begins to traverse the spaces "between" our normal, wake-a-day experience. This mind blowing expansive form of consciousness is limitless. Should the Initiate receive these Degrees while reading the magickal Grimoire, *the Voudon Gnostic Workbook,* she will experience these supersensual realms with an added dose of intensity. These Degrees open the Initiate up to this inner landscape in a way that can only be described as mysterious. Occasionally, it will be a single point-empowerment that transports the Initiate to these supra-celestial realms. At other times, it will be in receiving a small pack of points, typically no more than three, which will open the gateways to the imaginal, into the noumenal. But it is even more often that the cultivation of these points *after* reception of the Degree develops the meaning and initiation most completely.

A crucial lesson concerning this sacred path is that of transmission. The closest approximation to the sort of transmission we are receiving from the Holy Mountain and through other Free Illuminists, is that of the mystical theology of the Eastern Orthodox

Church. In that ancient working of Christianity, the Jesus Prayer holds a special place as a sacred practice and mantra, to be taught to individuals in a guru, chela relationship. However, it is taught by the Elders and Priests alike, that the Prayer does not hold its efficacy outside of the spiritual transmission[464] of the Church itself. It can lead to hallucinations, obsessions, or fits of laughter, as demonstrated in Salinger's *Franny and Zooey*. By the same token, the points-chauds empowerments work to their fullest capacity through person to person exchange, in an unbroken line back to the Holy Arabia Mountain, and from an individual with Apostolic & Gnostic succession. It is *within* the Gnostic Church then, that the points are transmitted to other initiates, and so we see the suggestions of T Allen Greenfield to safely work the entire set upon consecration as a Gnostic Bishop.[465]

It is important to understand that the nature of the entities encountered in these Degrees is typically neutral, helpful and abundant in light. This is because of the built-in protections of working primarily upon the central pillar of the body, and within an Ecclesiastical body through spiritual transmission. In speaking of the spirits of the so-called *Backside of the Tree of Life*, Bertiaux states that far from leading to black magic, the spirits discovered therein are, "so plastic that they will readily and easily assume any form that we seek from them. Consequently, it is not necessary for the student of the modern cabala to feel any dangers attending his meditation researches."[466] A correlation with the *dralas* of Tibetan Buddhism could be drawn as these entities often arise in an elemental form. Additionally, they tend to be rather absorbent beings. They will feed on the energy they are given. The Initiate will then be wise to stay focused upon the Center, the heart[467], while receiving these points. This grounding practice prevents obsession and excess of sexual energy[468]. While these are often neutral spiritual beings, the slumbering serpent lies at the base of the spine and should be treated with the utmost reverence and respect. This powerhouse of energy may be safely utilized in these Degrees, but only if the Initiate has experienced fully the Royal Secret of the Philosophical Degrees, that of Equilibrium.

The 61st Degree of *Sublime Unknown Philosopher* is the primary Degree dealing with apophatic knowledge in this set. In this Degree, the Initiate transcends the realm of "things" and enters the numinous. It is best to say what this experience is *not* rather than what it *is*, and so we embrace a form of negative theology in this empowerment. It is preparatory for the Administrative Degrees and the Initiate's role as an "unknown." Direct analogy can be

---

[464] See *Christ the Eternal Tao*, by Hieromonk Damascene, 2004.
[465] Again, there are differing views on this notion, as all who are called to work this form of Memphis+Misraïm will not be called to the Episcopate, however there is a deep wisdom in suggesting to work this system from within the Gnostic Churches—as layperson, or clergy. The INNER RETREAT, however, requires at least entry into the Diaconate.
[466] p. 54, *Cosmic Meditation*.
[467] Deeper instruction in this path can be found not only in the study of Classical Martinism, but in the application of its meditative procedures. Another entry point to this would be the mystical theology of the Eastern Churches.
[468] When these Degrees are worked between Facilitator and Initiate, the most proper decorum is to be strictly adhered to. However, should the points be worked between a "syzygy" or cosmic pair in a committed and gnostic relationship, then the exploration and experimentation of this set is unlimited. See the chapter entitled, *Caritas*, in *Syzygy, Reflections on the Monastery of the Seven Rays*, 2013.

made to the sublime experience of the *Superior Inconnu* Degree of classical Martinism. In point of fact, one who is a true Martinist can practice any of these grades without the slightest danger, because of the development of the *Way of the Heart,* as Papus calls it.

Finally, these Degrees—vast as they are in difference and in collectives of knowledge and wisdom—are *preparatory* to the angelic workings of the Arcana Arcanorum. Again, this is not to be misconstrued as a linear process, as the Degrees may be approached differently and non-chronologically, based upon the Node, Lodge or Chapel's methods of working them. For instance, should the Lodge take more of a consultation route with Initiates then there would be no set "plan" for the meeting. It would be up to the discernment of the Facilitator as to what Degree/points the Initiate may need at that particular time in their life. But it is in the work undertaken *after* the reception of the Initiation that we find the studies and preparations for the continuing initiatory power of these points. This is what lends this branch of High Grade Masonry its life-long application. In re-awakening the empowerment and scrying the point, whether in the advanced form or the basic, the Initiate discovers the *particular* meaning for himself. While there are more generalized meanings and generalized understandings of the energies and entities involved in these Degrees, at the end of the day it is a completely personal experience. This is one of the many precious gifts of *spirit building* as a Free Illuminist.

† † †

Q. What do you comprehend by occult sciences?

A. The occult sciences reveal to man the mysteries of his nature, the secrets of his organization, and the means of attaining perfection and happiness.

Q. Is the soul of man representative?

A. Yes, each soul is a living mirror, endowed with an internal action, which is representative of the universe in all points of view.[469]

---

[469] *Lectures of a Chapter, Senate & Council*, 1882, p. 77. (Kessinger reprint)

34th Degree
Knight of Scandinavia[470]
Conjuration of the Spirits of Earth

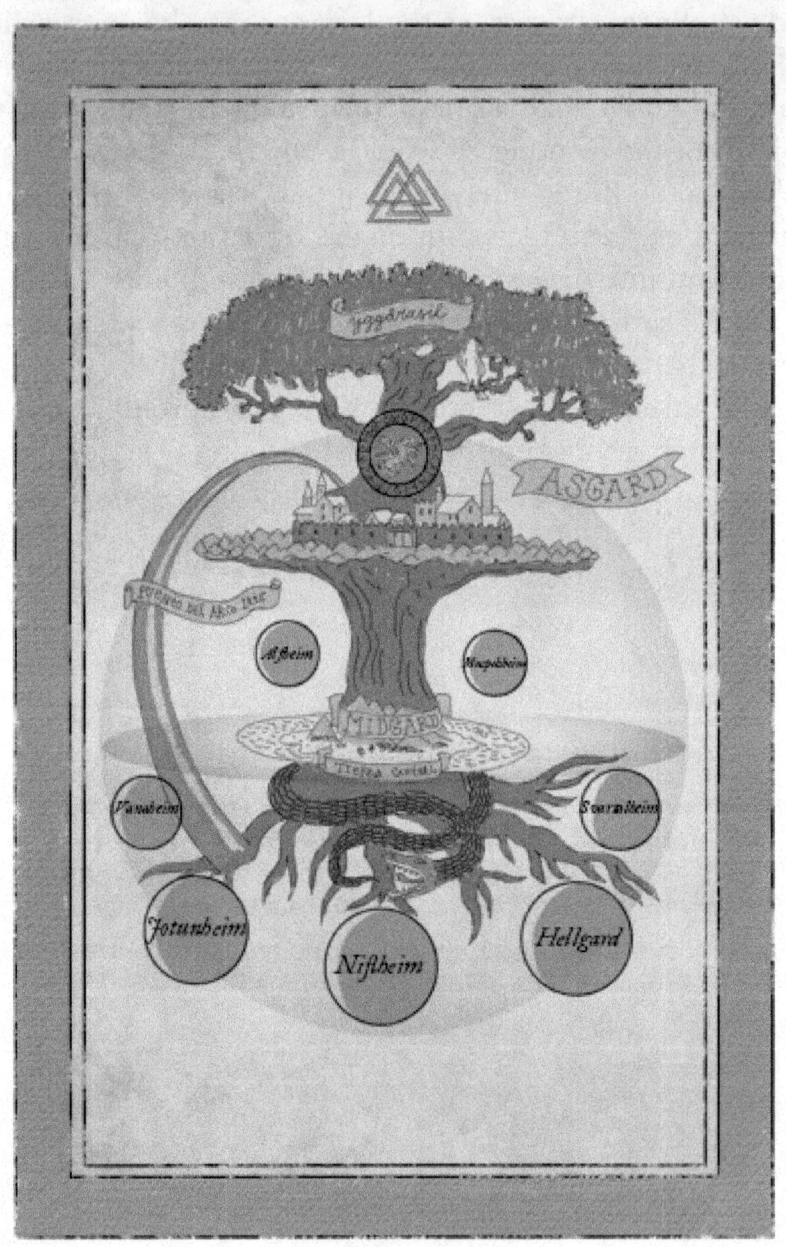

[470] See *The Monastery of the Seven Rays*, 4th Year, Part 1.

Battery of Knocks

3 and 3. XXX   XXX

Reading—to be read before points reception.

Conjuration of the Spirit of Earth—"King invisible, Who, taking the earth as a support, didst furrow the abysses to fill them with Thine omnipotence; Thou Whose name doth shake the vaults of the world, Thou Who causes the seven metals to flow through the veins of the rock, monarch of the seven lights, rewarder of the subterranean toilers, lead us unto the desirable air and to the realm of splendor. We watch and we work unremittingly, we seek and we hope, by the twelve stones of the Holy City, by the hidden talismans, by the pole of loadstone which passes through the centre of the world! Savior, Savior, have pity on those who suffer, expand our hearts, detach and elevate our minds, enlarge our entire being! O stability and motion! O day clothed with night! O darkness veiled by splendor! O master Who never keepest back the wages of Thy laborers! O silver whiteness! O golden splendor! O crown of living and melodious diamonds! Thou Who wearest the heaven on Thy finger like a sapphire ring, Thou Who concealest under earth, in the stone kingdom, the marvelous seed of stars, live, reign, be the eternal dispenser of the **wealth whereof Thou has made us the wardens! Amen!**[471]"

Points-chaud

Upper left thigh

Sacred Word

ZAO

Grip

Place right foot to the Initiate's right foot, left hand on heart, take each other's right hand with arms held vertically.

Sign

Strike two blows on (magickal) sword with left hand, fingers of the right hand on the heart. The answer—place right index finger on the lips.

Additional Materials

Pass-word—SIGGE, answer—OROMAZE. 2nd Password, ANAGOGIE, 3rd Password, ABORIGENE

2nd Sacred Word—RUROSTA

Jewel—Sword and palm crossed, form of a star. Silver Star[472] for Knights.

---

[471] *Transcendental Magic*, 2001 edition, p. 232
[472] Relates to the *Astron Argon* of Thelema & the Priestess that is adored in that magical path.

†††

Synopsis

It is no accident that the first Degree in this vast Series places the Initiate in the midst of Norse Mythology. Odin, the "All-Father" and god of War of Scandinavian lore, was believed to have great wisdom and the powers of magic and divination. It is in his name that this Degree is worked, exemplifying both the unity of the perennial philosophy found within all Traditions, as well as inviting the Initiate to explore working with a variety of deities, spirits and entities. The search for Universal Truth, such as this Degree explores, is one of the great treasures of the Primitive Doctrine.

As this series begins with messages of seership and divination, we get a clear indication of the shift in focus from the philosophical and speculative nature of the Scottish Degrees, to the practical and operative nature of the higher Memphis+Misraïm workings. This Degree, when fleshed out in its entirety, has three apartments answering to one of the many versions of the Three-fold Path—the Elect, the Mystic and the Epoptæ. When studied further, one discovers lessons concerning the transmigration of souls, the interior and spiritual sensations, and the nature of the Primitive Doctrine as it filtered from the Vedas of the Middle East to other countries—espousing concepts of the outbreathing and inbreathing of the Unknowable Deity.

The points-chaud empowerment of this Degree accomplishes exactly what the didactic nature of the staged Degree teaches. Here great emphasis must be placed on this distinction, for in the dramatic workings of Masonic Degrees we find, primarily, a tool for teaching great truths and the wisdom of the ages; whereas in the points-chauds approach, the *essence* of the teaching is imparted in a wordless fashion, directly, occultly. The points are experience based and gnostic. They bring the Initiate into direct contact with Reality and make her face herself in a radically aware manner. The Initiate who approaches the work in humility will delve into the deepest initiations. Spiritual pride is an insidious enemy of true Gnosis, and a force that can only be rooted out through watchfulness and soberness of mind[473]. The experience that this Degree empowerment provides for the pure of heart is that of seership. The Initiate becomes an Epoptæ.[474]

Finally, this Degree differs from others in that it includes a short "reading." This is from the *Conjuration of the Four* of Eliphas Levi. The Spirit of Earth is invoked in this Degree, as the central emblem of Norse Mythology is the cosmological tree, Yggsdrasil and one of the primary ideas in the story involves the earth being reborn, fertile and green. In our working, this is symbolic of the person who is reintegrated into his former pristine state, wherein communion with the spirit realm was second nature. With the presence of the Spirit of Earth (Adonai Ha Aretz), the Initiate is able to safely traverse the realms of the Gnomes, dwarves, elves and other earth spirits. Whereas in previous Degrees and systems we have

---

[473] See the essay, *Nepsis*, in Qliphoth Journal, Opus IV, 2014, Transmutation Publishing.
[474] Highest grade in the Eleusinian Mysteries.

only been *tried* by Earth, or experienced an ordeal of Earth, in this Degree we participate directly with the energies and entities that are of a Telluric nature[475].

---

[475] This Degree, being sacred to the Earth Mysteries, may be used in tandem with the practice of **Geomancy**. One perusal of our points-chauds diagrams reveals the similarity in packets of points with the Geomantic tetragrams. This may be coordinated with a Geomantic divination while contacting the spirit associated with the question. If, for instance, the question had both watery elements and martial qualities, then the tetragram, *Rubeus* would be located upon the body, relating to Bartzabel. These seven points of the tetragram would be "awakened" upon the body before the divination is performed (i.e., before the series of dots are made into wet sand or earth) to intensify the evocation of the earth spirit to assist in the oracle. Perform Geomantic divination as normal afterwards. This approach is for questions of serious import only and should be performed by a Facilitator with Episcopal Consecration, or one who has received all 97pts.

35th Degree
Knight of the Temple

35th degree,
Knight of the Temple (Knight of Sirius).

Battery of Knocks

Seven X X X X X X X

Points-chaud

Upper left thigh

Sacred Word

NATURA, answer, ELIAH

Grip

Facilitator presses three times with the right hand on the shoulder of the Initiate.

Sign

Right hand to heart, extend arm palm down.

Additional Materials

Password–SIRIUS[476], answer, SOTHIS

Jewel–a five pointed star, apex upwards

† † †

Synopsis

In the words of Florence Farr, the rituals of Egypt, "had a potent effect when the symbolism of each action was fully recognized, and when the imagination was extended and ultra-sensitive, and the Will concentrated firmly and repeatedly, on the object to be accomplished. The Ka of the Ritualist was thus at high tension acting upon its counterpart the concave germ in the Ab (heart) or vessel of conscious desire.[477]" This statement is the key to the Facilitator's art in our method. The Egyptian mysteries are opened up within the Initiate insomuch as the force is concretized and consolidated into the gnostic pressure of the points-chaud empowerment. When this occurs, the essential meaning for the Initiate is uniquely discerned and the accompanying energies & entities are immediately sensed.

The other name for this Degree is *Knight of Sirius*. Sirius, the Dog-star was of the utmost importance to ancient Egyptians, and marked the beginning of the solar year. The rising of the dog-star in the middle of the night sky near summer solstice marked the days before the flooding of the Nile. The Egyptians depended upon this flooding for the proper irrigation

---

[476] This Password immediately places the Degree in an Egyptian context. Students of Grant and the Necronomicon will also see the suggestive quality of the Password, Jewel, and the seven Knocks in relation to Ursa Major.

[477] *Egyptian Magic*, first published in *Collectanea Hermetica*, 1896, subsequently published in 1982 by The Aquarian Press, p. 11.

of their crops. All sustenance was dependent upon this celestial event and thus Sirius, or Sothis, was often identified with the great mother, Isis. For the Initiate of our system, the accompanying realization and field of research with this empowerment concerns recognizing the absolute *primacy of timing*[478] in all magickal operations. This knowledge may begin as simply the recognition of seasonal changes and the corresponding shifts in nature, or the awareness of the shifts in mood, and countenance within. Beyond this, it could be in a more religious sense, with the recognition of the Liturgical year and its organization with the Equinoxes and Solstices, or even the Masonic Year with its two principal festivals of the Sts. Johns Days, which fall on or around winter and summer solstice. The best time to receive and give this Degree is at the beginning of the Sothis Days, around the Summer Solstice.

But this Degree concerns Egyptian and Ceremonial magick and so this field of study and research comprises the understanding of the proper timing of consecrating talismans and creating sigils, understanding the properties of plants and their cultivation for alchemical spagyrics and tinctures, and the timing for more grand magickal operations such as the 22 Divine Names of Martinism, the Neomenies and Crescent Moon Operations, the Equinox Workings, and even the grand Arcanum of the Sacred Magic of Abramelin the Mage.

If this points chaud is given while the Initiate stands in the pentagram, the symbol of the sovereignty of the Will, the physiological sensation will be a tingling in the extremities. This is because this point is accessing deeper sources of Egyptian magick within the body which will extend outwards from the ministers of the ancient spirits—our *hands and feet*[479]—towards the objects we bless, the people we heal, and the initiations and spiritual transmissions we continue to pass on. Additionally, this point has the ability to awaken the Initiate to the magical adepts of Sirius who work *within* Memphis-Misraïm.[480]

The Sacred Word for this Degree is NATURA. Notice, even though we are embarking upon the secrets of Egyptian magick in this series, we are not treating this as necessarily *super*natural or as opposed to the laws of nature. Our work is primitive and secret, but it is absolutely natural. It only appears supernatural because it is a field of knowledge that has been forgotten. We may look to the sciences of Entanglement Theory, Quantum Physics, and String Theories to see the qualitative analogies between our metaphysics and the new Sciences.

---

[478] For a unique take on this study, see Kenneth Grant's exposition of working with the *kalas* in his Typhonian Trilogies.

[479] Consider these words of Bertiaux: "*Look, for example, at your right hand. God gave you this very magickal machine. Christ died on the Cross that the power in this hand be used for good things always. Look at your fingers and see them with your natural African clairvoyance…see them, I say, as tubes of light, or occult energy, which is both coming into each of the fingers as well as going out into the nearby space. There are as many tubes as you have fingers and thumb*" (VGW, 63).

[480] See Year IV, Part I, *Monastery of the Seven Rays*.

36th Degree

Sublime Negotiant

36th degree,
Sublime Negociant.

Battery of Knocks

One knock. X

Points-chaud

Upper right thigh

Sacred Word

JEHOVAH (pronounce, Yod-Heh-Vav-Heh)

Grip

There are three, answering to the three grades of the degree. 1st, take each other's little finger. 2nd, take mutually the fingers of the right hand. 3rd, take right hand mutually, and give seven light shakes. These three actions are required to seal the point and assure the Sublime Negotiant[481] that you are duly and truly prepared for his appearance.

Sign

1st, place left hand over the eyes and the first two fingers of right hand on the lips. 2nd, right knee on the floor, cross arms on the breast. 3rd, Place open hand on forehead as if to screen the eyes, thumb in square. These three signs are required when scrying this point and meeting the Negotiant.

Additional Materials

Three passwords–MEUNITH, TZDIKIM, ABRAHAM (answer) BRAHMA, SARAH (answer) SARIS-SATI.[482]

Jewel—a luminous triangle[483]

† † †

---

[481] The specific entity of this Degree

[482] This is a reference to Saraswati, the Hindu goddess of music and the arts, knowledge, nature and wisdom. She is linked here with Abraham's wife, Sarah from the Old testament, which is curious as Saraswati is one of the "help mates" of the Trinity of Brahma, Vishnu, & Shiva.

[483] If this Jewel is drawn in black ink upon a white ground, the scrying image will be precisely a luminous triangle. This simple optical trick lends itself well to beginning the scrying session which quickly goes beyond visual hallucinations or auras.

Synopsis

In this Degree, the Officer called *President* states "You understand now our Mysteries, our Science, our Altar, and our God; it is with the idea of Unity that the luminous triangle unites all our symbols. In investing you with the Habit, I invite you to let it cover forever the darkness of error and prejudice.[484]" We find the luminous triangle in the East in all French Lodges who espouse the lofty ideals of *liberty, fraternity and equality*. In those Lodges, a true sense of tolerance and openness to all religious faiths, philosophical platforms and revelations is embodied and the focus of mastery of the self becomes the goal and purpose of Initiation[485].

A brief perusal of the Words of this Degree displays the comparative religious nature of the work, and the unity that the President speaks of. *MEUNITH* is a minor tribe of uncertain origin on the eastern border of Edom, just southeast of the Dead Sea. Both the Essenes and certain Gnostic sects once inhabited this region. *TZDIKIM* translates to "righteous one" in Hebrew and is used for rabbis as well as Holy Elders and spiritual masters. *ABRAHAM* and *SARAH* are the husband and wife team of the Old Testament, Abraham being the first of the three great Patriarchs of Israel and Sarah being his wife who miraculously bore a son, Isaac, at the age of 90[486]. *BRAHMA* and *SARIS-WATI* are the Hindu gods who are each a part of a Trinity and who are husband and wife. And finally we find, *JEHOVAH*, most accurately styled, YHVH.

This Degree is formed of three grades, answering again to our Three-fold path. They are *Believer, Elect* and *Perfect*. These are directly analogous to the Three-fold path of prayer of Dionysius the Areopagite and along with the "Habit" mentioned in the quote, we find a reference to Christian monasticism and mysticism. There is a section of the Degree that quotes the Koran concerning star worship. We can find a Rosicrucian analogy in the same quote in the motto, *Astra Inclinant non Necessitant* (the stars incline, they do not compel). The Astrology of the Babylonians is mentioned as well as purification of the four elements, which is an Alchemical and Ceremonial magic reference. In one Degree we find Jewish, Christian, and Hindu suggestions; alongside Islamic, Astrological and Alchemical details. Far from being a vague syncretism, this Degree is an exposition of the perennial philosophy–the universal truths found scattered widely across the globe and in diverse regions and subjects of study–which the *Spirit Builder* must gather together and extract the Primitive Doctrine from, and which is symbolized by the luminous triangle.

---

[484] As with the majority of the "Secrets" of each grade, this quote comes from Yarker's work as compiled by T Allen Greenfield in his, *Compleat Rite of Memphis*, 1999, p. 102.

[485] Several recent attempts have been made to establish "regular" French Lodges in America, under American rule. There are multiple French Lodges, particularly in the D.C. area that are still linked to the Grand Orient of France, but a few experiments have developed on American soil—namely the *Grand Orient of the United States of America*, and the Brazil derived, *Modern Rite in North America and the Caribbean*. The latter has recently developed and extended its working and influence, and fully embodies this notion of *mastery of the Self* in its working of the Modern, or French Rite. Additionally, mention must be made of the authentic and deep work of Le Droit Humain, American Federation, and its sister, American Co-Masonry, as well as the Lodges of the George Washington Union-- who are recognized by the Grand Orient of France as well as CLIPSAS.

[486] Genesis 21:2

The points chaud empowerment of this Degree puts the Initiate in contact with the Sublime Negotiant of all religious doctrines. This is the perennial philosophy personified. This spirit is the grand negotiator of all seemingly disparate dogmas. His more personal name can be discovered through the Advanced Scrying method, utilizing any of the Holy Books which are connected with this Degree.

37th Degree

Knight of the Shota or Sage of Truth

Invocation of La Sirene

37th *degree,*
Knight of Shota (Sage of Truth).

Battery of Knocks

Eleven even knocks. **X X X X X X X X X X X**

Points-chaud

Lower right thigh

Sacred Word

EDUL-PEN-CAGIL (Do that thou wishest should be done unto thee) Answer, TRUTH.

Grip

Master Mason's Grip, Facilitator says MO, reverse hands and Initiate says HA, again reverse, Facilitator says, BON. The Initiate finishes, saying; MO HA BON (Remembrance of the dead).

Signs

1st, point upwards with right forefinger. Answer, form a triangle with the thumb and index finger before the stomach. 2nd, clasp the hands palms outwards, above the head, saying: "To me the children of the Widow." 3rd, right hand supported on the hip.

Additional Materials

Password–KEKATHITES (One who knows the written law)

Jewel–A triangle with the letter M in the center.

Synopsis

If at all possible, this Degree should be given outdoors near a body of water. The Degree may be given after the performance of a sacred dance, as the name, Shota, refers to an Albanian dance. One may want to wear blue, bring sweet treats and champagne, gin or white rum. This is the first Degree to *directly* invoke a Lwa of Haitian Vodou, even though *all* of the Degrees potentially draw from the spirits, Saints, Lwa and energies.

This Degree has three Signs. The Signs are directly related to the Voudon+Gnostic experience that accompanies the points chaud empowerment. The first sign is composed of two parts. First, you point upwards with your right forefinger. The second part of the first sign is the answer, which is forming a triangle with the thumb and index finger before the stomach. This is a downward facing, water triangle. The second sign is made by clasping the hands, palms outward above the head and saying, "To me the children of the Widow." The third Sign is the right hand supported on the hip. All three signs seal the point within the body, which is on the lower right thigh. This point puts the Initiate in contact with a great Lwa of Haitian Vodou, *Mambo La Sirène*.[487] The Signs of the Degree create a metaphysical *veve*[488] with the body, as the Initiate imitates La Sirène by directing the gaze upwards (to Bondye, the Absolute) and then back to her source, the water triangle and then in welcome to all Freemasons, (sons & daughters of the Widow) and finally with characteristic femininity, right hand on hip.

La Sirène is a very rich Lwa and has a direct message for the Initiate through the Sacred Word, EDUL-PEN-CAGIL. It is by doing unto others what we wished would be done to us that we obtain the true riches of this life. The number of knocks is the number of magick, eleven. This battery begins her invocation.

---

[487] La Sirène often accompanies a *trial by Water*, but keep in mind that we are moving into relationship with the entities and energies in this set. There will be an accompanying trial, but the point empowerment begins a sort of courtship with this Queen of the waters that was alluded to and begun in the 26th Degree.

[488] Veves in traditional Haitian Vodou, are a sort of visual landing strip for the Lwa. According to Kenaz Filan, they are a "glyph that expresses the spirit's nature and forms a doorway by which the lwa can be brought to earth" (*The Haitian Vodou Handbook*, 40-41).

38th Degree
Sublime Elect of Truth, or the Red Eagle
Invocation of Erzulie La Flambeau

38th degree,
Sublime Elect of Truth (The Red Eagle).

Battery of Knocks

Five X X X X X

Points-chaud

Left genital

Sacred Word

ZURISHODOAI (God is my strongest rock)

Grip

Press five times on the palm of each other's right hand with the second finger. Facilitator begins.

Sign

Military salute with magickal sword. Answer, make a fire triangle on the forehead with thumb and index finger.

Additional Materials

Password–HORI (Celestial Day), answer, ACHMONEYN (Name of a tomb).

Jewel–A silver key crossed with a cubit rule

Synopsis

If at all possible, this Degree should be performed outside with a brazier of fire using pure spirits. This represents the sacred fire of ancient initiations. The Initiate may want to be hoodwinked for a moment while she considers the eternal contest of Light and Darkness, before the Battery of Knocks invokes the spirit.

This Degree continues working with the Lwa of Haitian Vodou in a direct and invoking manner. Whereas, La Sirene represented water and all of the currents associated with the receptive, dream-like, and sometimes illusory realms, this Degree of the Red Eagle represents fire and all of the warrior like, active, and passionate realms related to such. It is an invocation of *Erzulie la Flambeau*. The Invocation begins with the simple action of kindling the fire. When the Battery of Knocks commences, Erzulie is called from her realms into the location of the body where the points chaud resides. The specific aspect of Erzulie that arrives depends upon numerous factors; the personality type of the Initiate, the "cleanliness" of the Initiate, the offerings presented (fire), the emotional state of the recipient, etc.

This Degree requires of the Initiate, circumspection and examination of conscience, before reception, as Erzulie la Flambeau sometimes appears as a jealous lover and such an invocation can cause excitation due to the location of the point and the nature of this goddess like Lwa. Care and watchfulness should be maintained at all times and in all places that this powerful Degree is worked.

The Jewel of the silver key that is drawn as a sigil for scrying the point represents how Erzulie will reveal herself to the Initiate as either the key to love and harmony, or the key to victory. Either way, it is crossed by a cubit rule which, as Masonry oft does, suggests to the Initiate to maintain a life of balance and justice. This Jewel should be shown to any females (particularly those of a provocative nature) that arise in the scrying session. This has been discovered to be the same for both male and female recipients of this Degree.[489]

---

[489] The Lwa are in general, irrespective of gender. Oft times, a male will be fully taken over by a female Lwa, or the Ghuede in their rambunctiousness will make lude gestures to either gender. Additionally, in the case of an individual "marrying" a Lwa, gender is again, a non-issue. It appears that we, on Malkuth, have much to learn from the spirits. See Maya Deren's, *The Divine Horsemen*.

Part Three – Chapter Four: Hermetic, Gnostic, & Kabalistic Degrees

39th Degree

Grand Elect of the Aeons

Invocation of the Second Ray of Christ

39th *degree,*
Grand Elect of the Aeons.

Battery of Knocks

Three. X X X

Points-chaud

Right genital

Sacred Word

AIUS-LOCUTIUS (The Word, the Lord)

Grip

Facilitator places the left hand on the heart of the Initiate

Sign

Place the two fingers of the left hand on the mouth, and the right hand over the heart.

Additional Materials

Passwords–1st, Amara, 2nd, Archimage, 3rd, ANAGOGIE, answer, DOUNNOUN.

Signs–1st, right hand on the brow, 3rd, join the two hands, flex the left knee and fix the eyes on heaven. (The 2nd is the Sign demonstrated during the point)

Jewel–a star with a central point.

Synopsis

This is a Gnostic Degree that at once introduces the Initiate to the Primordial currents, the essences behind the energies of spirits, Lwa, and elemental forces, while also presenting the Initiate with a clean sensation of the "virgin simplicity of natural laws.[490]" To approach the former, the Initiate must continuously sharpen his inner instruments, so as to see clearly in the Ontic sphere, or magickal imagination. It is to the points-chaud empowerment that we must look to accomplish the opening of this inner eye to the Higher realms. The more abstract the Deity, the more the representation becomes pure symbol, and so we come to the hidden nature of Freemasonry altogether. One key aspect of the Primitive Doctrine of Freemasonry is the realization of entities lying latent within pure symbols.

---

[490] *Compleat Rite of Memphis*, p. 103

Upon reception of this point, the Initiate will be given a symbol within the Ontic sphere. It may be only a hint of some lines formed in light or the impression of an image that the Initiate then converts into a drawn symbol. This typically happens immediately after reception of the point, but may be derived through scrying afterward. Whereas the Jewel of the Degree is worn as a sigil and protective amulet during scrying, the symbol derived from this points-chaud empowerment is meant to be a condenser for the Aeon, the Primordial current of old–the Avatar, or direct Emanation of Deity–to inhabit. Once this is accomplished, the Initiate should place the hand drawn symbol in an Atua,[491] or house of the spirits, made from wood and consecrated for the work with anointing oils and Holy water.

The Words of this Degree directly relate to the new duties of the Spirit Builder. He or she is now an *Archimage*–a great magician or wizard. With the reception of this point and the relationship born from the pure symbol that condenses the Primordial current, comes the gift of *Anagogie*[492]–the ability to discern the hidden meanings of Sacred writ.[493] This gift may come in the form of unique interpretations of Scriptures, or in the understanding of obscure texts, or in the ability to make links amongst vast topics.[494] The Psalms–Sacred to all Hoodooists–are a wonderful collection to test one's new gifts. *Amara* means eternal in Greek and is the password given right after the Grip of placing the left hand on the heart of the Facilitator. This reflects the nature of Aeons, their continuity and the eternal movement of the cosmos. The Initiate must keep her heart pure and eternally present while working these deeply mystical Degrees. One Aeon that Martinists utilize for this relates directly to this Degree, as it is "the Word, the Lord," which our words, *AIUS-LOCUTIUS*[495] mean. It is THIS Lord of the Second Ray that is invoked by this mystical grade.

---

[491] See the *Voudon Gnostic Workbook*, p. 36.
[492] Anagogie also refers to the process of ascent hidden in this degree title and point, which carries the initiate upwards into the 3rd echelon, or cosmic/æonic Masonry
[493] Should this gift lie latent for even a single day, it will move into dormition. This Holy discernment is not to be paraded about, but utilized in Bibliomancy, and in treating the needs of the Community.
[494] --which is essentially a hallmark of *critical thinking*.
[495] Here we refer to the *Repairer*, *La Chose*, the *Unknown Agent*—even sometimes referred to as, *Elias Artista*.

Spirit Builders

40th Degree

Sage Savaiste, or Perfect Sage

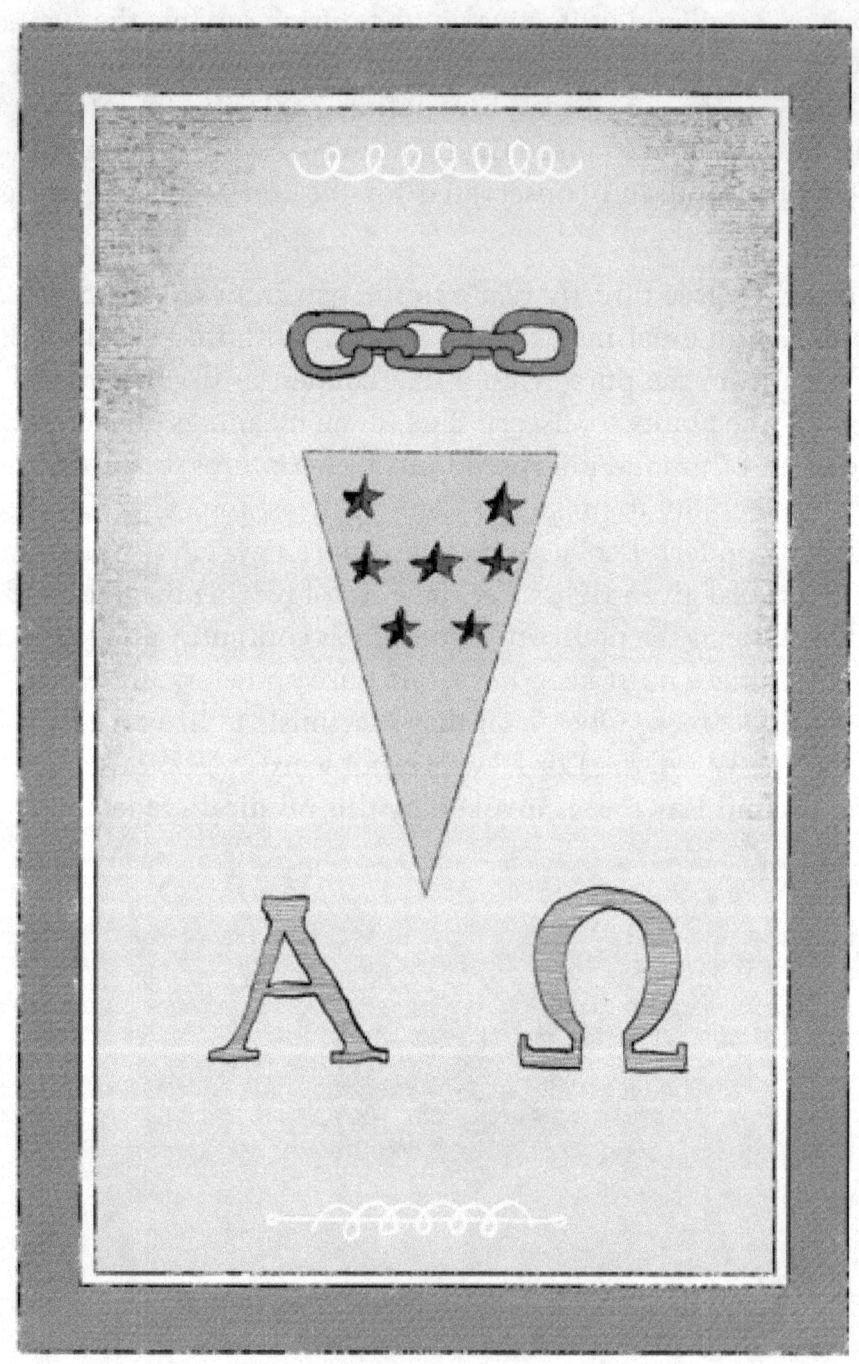

40th *degree,*
Sage Savaiste (Perfect Sage).

Part Three – Chapter Four: Hermetic, Gnostic, & Kabalistic Degrees

Battery of knocks

Seven knocks, 2 by 3 by 2.   **XX   XXX   XX**

Points-chaud

Left inside thigh

Sacred Word

KEKATHITES (One who knows the written law)

Grip

Link the two index fingers.

Sign

Point to heaven with the index of the right hand.

Additional Materials

*Password–*KARAELITES

*Jewel–*a Triangle with seven stars placed, 2, 3 and 2.

† † †

Synopsis

This is a mystical Degree. It more properly concerns the sort of apophatic knowledge that we endeavor upon in the Administrative set of Degrees, however, is given here as a necessary balance to the magickal Degrees[496] that the Initiate has been bombarded with. The primary focus in this Degree is upon the "existence of a God, who draws us to himself by eternal chains, whose links are the love of goodness.[497]" In French, the name of this Degree, Savais tu, means, *if you knew*. This knowledge is transformative. The Jewel, a triangle with seven stars, hints at the nature of this God and the eternal hypostasis of his persons. It is a continuing lesson on Emanationism as the clearest representation of the *luminious principle.*[498] Freemasonry, in its Gnostic sense, is a direct means to engage with this Light.

---

[496] In this sense, it is imperative to recall the words of Bertiaux in the VGW; *"this power is both complex and subject to an ever-developing process, and it is mysteriously identified with the Rite of Memphis-Misraim, which, in our system, is a structure within the Gnostic Church,"* p. 176.
[497] *Compleat Rite of Memphis*, p. 104.
[498] Rev. George Oliver's, *The Theocratic Philosophy of Freemasonry*, 1855, p. 3.

Spirit Builders

41ˢᵗ **Degree**

Knight of the Arch of Seven Colors

Call to the Masters of the Seven Rays

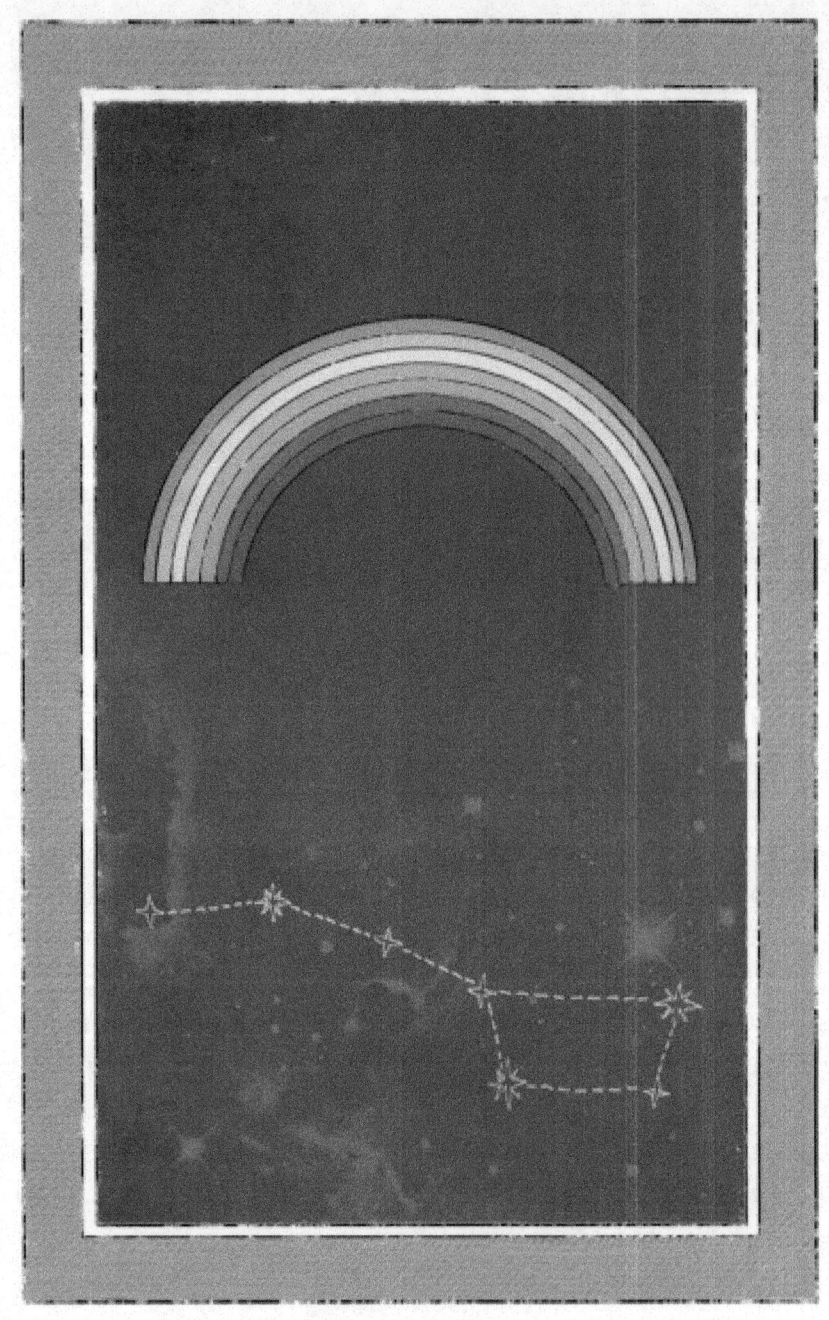

41ˢᵗ *degree,*
Knight of the Arch of Seven Colours.

Battery of knocks

Seven.   X X X X X X X

Points-chaud

Lower left inside thigh[499]

Sacred Word

UR (Light)

Grip

Facilitator places right hand upon the Initiate's outer left thigh where the guard of a sword would be. The Grip seals the point, and balances it in the upper left leg.

Sign

Draw the sword[500] and plant it on the Earth. Recover sword, and place self on guard as if for combat. Answer, Salute to right, to left, and in front.

Additional Materials

Password–TSEDAKAH (Justice)

Jewel–A rainbow

†††

Synopsis

Seven is a Holy number. It has a balancing agent in the center, flanked on either side by trinities. When seven objects are laid out in such a way, it suggests balance, a menorah and an arch. The Password for this Degree means *justice*, the Sacred Word means *light* and the emblem is an arch of color, the *rainbow*.

Light becomes the focus once again in the next few Degrees. Of the Holy Sun, Yarker writes that: "All nations have bowed down and kissed their hands to this grand symbol of universal life.[501]" Indeed, a form of solar worship has been found on every continent. The sun is described as a "well of beneficence" in this Degree and we are told that "we believe in those sublime, divine, and supernatural principles which are above our intelligence, because the second causes of these impressions strike our Senses, and demonstrate the existence of a superior force.[502]" Immediately from the meditation upon the sun, we move into the musing upon entities, intelligences, and other forces that vibrate at a different

---

[499] Note that this point on the diagram is a bit confusing. As with all of these point empowerments, the gnostic pressure must be applied using the inner vision. The diagram is a very rough outline of the vicinity of the empowerments.
[500] Again, may be a "magickal" sword.
[501] *Compleat Rite of Memphis*, p. 104.
[502] Ibid., p. 105.

frequency than we do. In this we find a down pouring of celestial energy from the sun, passing through other mediaries and making contact with our senses.

On Consecration rock on the Holy Arabia Mountain, the sky opens wide where the points and other empowerments are given. Some days in July it gets to 100 degrees or greater and on blustery days, when there are few trees to protect from the wind, the chill can be biting. Yet in choosing to work outside, in a geographical sacred *marma*, exciting the physiological marmas[503] upon the sacred human form, we are aligning with the Ancients—the Druids of old in their Sacred Groves, the Holy authors of the Vedas in the Iranian Mountains, the open air schools such as the Lyceum of the Greeks—we are practicing the Primitive Doctrine.

The points-chaud empowerment of this Degree is best received out of doors, lying on one's back in what is commonly known in yoga circles as the corpse pose[504] and with an open sky above. As the point is administered and the Sacred Word, *UR* (Light) vibrated, while the gnostic pressure awakens and stimulates the energies and entities within the body into action, open your eyes and gaze upwards at the sky and the glory of Light, color, and the dome of the atmosphere. The visualization of a rainbow often follows the closing of the eyes after the point empowerment. The Initiate should go into this band of light[505] and begin to communicate with the colors, for each color is a power and a current. Each color current has Archangels, angels, spirits, elementals and neutral forces of all sorts aligned with it.

The practice of color breathing[506] is suggested here. Visualize clearly the color you want to invoke, along with its correspondences as found in books such as Dion Fortune's *Mystical Qaballah*. Inhale the vivid *color tinted air* through the nostrils and then exhale the same. Feel the subtle vibration of the color and sense the entities that are attracted to it. Once this practice becomes second nature, it can be used in healing others, for each color has therapeutic uses as well. This can be done with each color in succession, to receive a direct blessing from the Seven Rays[507]. This process mirrors, in fractal form, the experience that accompanies the 95° in the 3rd echelon, with its "dazzling light" which contains all of the colors.

---

[503] "The gnostic body becomes a perfect map or network of the ideal and perfect or abstract and logical worlds of being. These worlds come and are present in the body and in the processes, which enable the body to function in every way, from the exoteric to the most esoteric, because the spirits of these very high or remote worlds are totally in the field of the body, present really in the incarnation of the physical substance, and awaiting the magickal awakening of their true essence." ~Michael Bertiaux, *VGW*, p. 167.

[504] Consider also, A. O. Spare's teachings on the **Death Posture**.

[505] For *some*, this Degree is a direct entrance into the Monastery of the Seven Rays, as it exists upon a hyper-spatial plane. "Its structures, cloisters…its scriptorium and workshops, Chapels and shrines, are accessible through the means of the diaphanous regions which can be traversed through something akin to auto-suggestive trance states." *Syzygy, Reflections on the Monastery of the Seven Rays*, p. 21.

[506] This classic occult technique is nowhere more plainly described than in John Michael Greer's, *The Druidry Handbook: Spiritual Practice Rooted in the Living Earth*, 2006.

[507] There are inherent connections between this Degree, the 22nd Degree, and the VII Degree of the **OTOA**, *Knight of the Rainbow*. In fact, the latter is a summation of the Degrees from 6th-41st, according to the work of *The Monastery of the Seven Rays*, Year II Curriculum.

42nd Degree

Prince of Light

Conjuration of the Spirits of Air

42th degree, Prince of Light.

This Degree is one of the few in the Haut Grades that includes readings. Both the Facilitator and the Initiate are enjoined to enter this Grade in a particularly prayerful state and to be aware that the spirits of Air are being called upon and will attend the Initiation.

Battery of Knocks

Five and two. X X X X X   X X

Reading

Initiate, in the Ancient working of this Degree, the Facilitator charged the recipient to adjust his gaze upwards. I ask you now to stand firmly upon this earth in the sign of the sovereignty of Will, the sacred pentagram, look to the skies and listen to the charge and Sacred Conjuration of the Spirit of Air.

Charge—Consult the heavens, the greatest and most beautiful of all books, written by the hand of God himself!

Conjuration of the Spirit of Air—"Spirit of Light, Spirit of Wisdom, Whose breath gives and takes away the form of all things; Thou before Whom the life of every being is a shadow which transforms and a vapor which passes away; Thou who ascendest upon the clouds and dost fly upon the wings of the wind; Thou who breathest forth and the limitless immensities are peopled; Thou who drawest in and all which came forth from Thee unto Thee returneth: endless movement in the eternal stability, be Thou blessed forever! We praise Thee, we bless Thee in the fleeting empire of created light, of shadows, reflections and images; and we aspire without ceasing towards Thine immutable and imperishable splendor. May the ray of Thine intelligence and the warmth of Thy love descend on us: that which is volatile shall be fixed, the shadow shall become body, the spirit of the air shall receive a soul, and dream be thought. We shall be swept away no more before the tempest, but shall bridle the winged steeds of the morning and guide the course of the evening winds, that we may flee into Thy presence. O Spirit of Spirits, O eternal Soul of Souls, O imperishable Breath of Life, O Creative Sigh, O Mouth which dost breathe forth and withdraw the life of all beings in the ebb and flow of Thine eternal speech, which is the divine ocean of movement and of truth! Amen."[508]

---

[508] Eliphas Levi, *Transcendental Magic*, p. 229-230.

Points-chaud

Right inside thigh

Sacred Word

JAH

Grip

Facilitator takes the hand of the Initiate and points her index finger upwards towards the Pole Star.

Sign

With index finger of right hand trace the stars; holding a magickal instrument with the left hand.[509]

Additional Materials

Password–ORION

Jewel–Upon a Triangle, a broken Star.

† † †

Synopsis

The Receiver of this points-chaud empowerment listens to two readings in this Degree. This is in contradistinction with the previous Degrees and most afterward, but this Degree is designed to begin a conjuration of the Spirit of air, as well as acting as an entrance into the nature of the occult Astrology of the Middle Ages. Several book suggestions are in order, as they will assist the Initiate as she begins to integrate this new series of Degrees and the energy derived from them. The Initiate would do well to obtain Eliphas Levi's, *Transcendental Magic*, Cornelius Agrippa's, *Three Books of Occult Philosophy* and the *Picatrix*.[510] More could be said concerning the accompanying experiences involved in the Conjuration and the point empowerment, but this is best left to experimentation as each must interpret these emblems for herself. Suffice it to say, that when taken as a pack of three points empowerments, the 42nd, 43rd and 44th Degrees open the Initiate to the vast field of inquiry known anciently as Astrology[511]. It is here again that we recognize the palpable difference between the Degrees of the prior two series' and the sublime nature of the Hermetic, Gnostic

---

[509] The nature of this particular instrument will be revealed in the scrying session.
[510] 2010,2011, Liber Atratus Edition, trans, John Michael Greer & Christopher Warnock.
[511] The persevering Initiate will see within this body of Degrees, a complete and harmonious tradition within the Western Mysteries.

and Kabalistic Grades. We are working directly with *Spirit Building* and are at labor upon a full scale investigation and research into the deepest mysteries of occultism.

Q. What did the ancient nations think upon astrology?

A. ...From these observations they drew the deduction that each star held its particular influence on some part of the earth, and that God had set the stars in the heavens to regulate all things, and over each of the stars a ruling angel was placed, who had dominion over that part of the world in which the particular star had the greatest influence; and as **man was a world in miniature they mapped out the various parts of his body in a similar way.**[512]

---

[512] *Lectures of a Chapter, Senate & Council*, 1882, p. 82, bold added. This quote clearly describes the incredibly subtle link between the vast field of ancient astrology and that of the psycho-spiritual circuitry of the points-chauds empowerments mapped upon the body.

43rd Degree

Sublime Hermetic Sage, or Hermetic[513] Philosopher

The Descension of the Temple at Karnak

43rd degree,
Sublime Hermetic Sage (Hermetic Philosopher).

---

[513] Many books are extant concerning the vast study of *Hermeticism*, but the Initiate is directed to the original, *Corpus Hermeticum*, to divine this foundation of the Western Esoteric Tradition.

Battery of Knocks

Five, two and Five. XXXXX XX XXXXX

Points-chaud

Right inside, lower thigh

Sacred Word

KARNAK, Answer, HERMES

Grip

Make the Hermetic cross; Facilitator's left hand palm down, Initiate covers with her left, same with the right.

Sign

Point upwards with the right thumb and say TACENDO (silence). Answer, place right hand flat on the heart, thumb forming a square, and say SPRENDO (Hope).

Additional Materials

Passwords—1st, ABOT (the East), answer, HELIOS (the sun), MENE (the Moon), TETRAGRAMMATON (Sacred name of God.) 2nd, if challenged further in the scrying session, vibrate the sacred INRI (en-rye). If the Temple, KARNAK, still does not appear with its living columns, vibrate, THOIMOSIS.

Jewel—On a Triangle, seven stars—4 and 3.[514]

† † †

Synopsis

This Degree is related to the one before it and the one after. It is therefore perfectly appropriate for the Node, Lodge or Chapel to administer all three at a given meeting. If such is the case, the order number of the Degrees should be followed, as the Conjuration of the Spirit of Air assists the workings of this grade as well as the one following it. All three grades invoke the presence of Sylphs, spirits of air. All three grades will stimulate the intelligence of the Initiate, possibly sending her into abstract realms hitherto untapped. The Initiate must beware of the changeable qualities of these Air grades, however, and balance them with more earthy experience if the focus gets out of equilibrium.

Hermeticism is an expansive arena of study. It comprises Astrology, Alchemy and Theurgy, (god working) as well as entering into the later developments of Rosicrucianism

---

[514] This is in reference again to the sacred constellation, Ursa Major.

and Ceremonial Magick. Hermeticism has, as its foundation, the well known and simple core doctrine from the Emerald Tablet which states, "as above, so below." In this Degree, the Initiate is called upon to work directly with the spirits above and to learn to birth them hear below, direct their energies into Holy objects, and divinize the mundane. In the Degree instructions we are told that the Initiate passes through the twelve houses of the sun (the Zodiac) and is found, as in the 2nd Degree, in between two columns once again. This place of balance where the Initiate *becomes* the Middle Pillar is the place between life and death, our field of inquiry being—this life. She is taught that within this workshop of the living is to be found the hidden-treasure house. One thinks of the "Treasure House of Images[515]" of Crowley. The instruction goes onto say that the nature of Hermeticism is threefold and comprises religious, philosophic, and scientific notions. It is suggested as the religion of Initiates for all times and climes. The Initiate is directed to Egypt, to the study of Alchemy and to the great authors of early Alchemical writings: Raymond Lully, Paracelsus and Nicholas Flamel.

The points-chaud empowerment of this Degree occurs within a hyper-spatial location known as Karnak (also the Sacred Word of the Degree). This is the great Temple complex of ancient Egypt. The Temple itself is *brought down* into the Chapel or Lodge immediately upon invoking through the Battery of Knocks. The sensation of this vast Temple is likened to being aware of living columns on all sides of the Initiate and Facilitator[516]. These living columns are teachers of the Hermetic Secrets of this grade and may be contacted further through scrying after point reception. Their teaching is that the celestial influences above can be harnessed upon this plane and utilized for a variety of purposes.

---

[515] The Initiate is directed to this Class B document which bears much light upon the mystical study of Astrology. Particular emphasis is placed on the appended note, which is a Class A (Holy Book) document, *A Note on DCCCCLXII*. This succinct item of instruction is a power packed teaching that can be applied to the entire science and art of magick.

[516] Frequent building up of this image of Karnak will strengthen the Mystic Temple altogether. Should a certain number of columns appear to the mind's eye, the Lodge or Chapel may want to acquire that number of tapers to burn while working this Degree further, as they become *living effigies* as in the work of the Elus Coëns. See the frontspiece in *The Hidden Life in Freemasonry*, by C. W. Leadbeater.

44th Degree
Prince of the Zodiac
Conjuration of the Alchemist Jabir ibn Hayyan

44th *degree,*
Prince of the Zodiac.

Battery of Knocks

Twelve equal raps. X X X X X X X X X X X X

Points-chaud

Front perineum

Sacred Word

ADONAI (Lord)

Grip

Mutually join right and left hands to seal the point.

Sign

Take the magickal sword in the right hand and hold it vertically. Make a complete, 360° circumambulation of the floor.

Additional Materials

Password–GEBER

Jewel–A book of which is Twelve stars and the letters J.H.

†††

Synopsis

Here again we have the combination of Alchemy and Astrology, two of the three main branches of study in Hermeticism. For all intents and purposes, the third branch, Theurgy (god working) is what we undertake every time we intend to awaken the spirit, Lwa, or elemental force connected with the points chauds empowerments. That field of study requires will, imagination ,and perseverance. As Zoroaster says in the Chaldean Oracles, "unto the persevering mortal, the blessed Immortals are swift." The Degree that follows is Theurgical and completes the Trinitarian nature of Hermeticism.

But the twin studies of Alchemy and Astrology that keep surfacing include a very practical side. For instance, one of the main applications of Alchemy is turning lead into gold. Astrology, likewise, includes the casting of Horary Charts and divining the future. Neither of these processes is delineated in any *practical* detail in the work, however, because we are focusing on the spiritual nature of these sciences. The student of these operative sciences is enjoined to intermingle the spirit & the science.

In this Degree, we find the Prince of the Zodiac entering a Hermetic allegory, undergoing severe tests and proofs for complete initiation, experiencing a specific trial of the planet Mercury (also connected to Hermes), enduring a new loss of some sort (reminding one of the frequent loss of the Word of a Mason throughout many Degrees) and beginning the formation of a new man—born from labor—and within this new man, a distinct truth discovered.

Where do we go to find the details of this experience? What book shall we explore? To this Degree, the Initiate is sent to the Oratory, to persevere in the practices of scrying (advanced and otherwise) to discover for himself the meaning of Alchemy and Astrology as pertaining to this Degree and to engage in spirit work with the Twelve living Signs of the Zodiac, as well as the seven planets of the ancients. Also, we find the Password GEBER, pointing to the 8th Century Arabian Alchemist, Jabir ibn Hayyan, who is also available on the diaphanous plane, for further instruction. And finally, the Sacred Word points to the next set of Degrees which focus on both the Holy Guardian Angel and other forms of Angelic magick.

45th Degree

Sublime Sage of the Mysteries

45th degree,
Sublime Sage of the Mysteries.

Battery of Knocks
Three and Three.   XXX   XXX

Points-chaud
Perineum

Sacred Word
SOLIMY (Princes of the Pre-Adamite Pitris, or Genii, and an Assyrian Divinity)

Grip
Grasp the fingers of each other's right hand with the left.

Sign
Grasp the chin or beard with the right hand.

Additional Materials
Password–FIDES (Faith)

Jewel–Triangle with an eye in the center

†††

Synopsis

This is a deeply Theurgical Degree. More can be said about Degrees that call upon forces and have the potential to invoke spirits, but those that directly place the Initiate in the presence of those same forces are of a different nature and draw from a distinct form of epistemology. The Theurgical Degrees open the Ontic Sphere of the Initiate in profound ways, and allow for the direct influx of gnosis and contact with intermediary beings.[517]

A direct quotation of Yarker's notes for this Degree should suffice to reveal the nature of the points-chaud empowerment. He says;

> *Second life of man- means of setting out from darkness- continuation of the erection of a symbolic edifice. The purified man is led by a child- First intelligence of intermediary beings that form a chain which unites us to divinity.*
>
> *Reflections upon the Number 3; the White, green, blue- the messenger indicates the gates- Rendered worthy of Initiation in the Sanctuary.*[518]

---

[517] Thus, the Jewel of a triangle with an eye in the center.
[518] *Compleat Rite of Memphis*, p. 106.

This listing of experiences aligned with this Degree/point provides much to work from upon reception of the secrets of the grade. The Initiate is being placed in a spiritual furnace in this Degree, where he is led *by a child*[519] into the *Mystic Temple* where a number of intermediary beings await. These are to be discovered in scrying the point, however, even in the Lodge working and reception of the Degree—their presence will be made known. Symbols such as the number three, the colors white, green and blue and the triangle with the eye in the center will be guide stones along these travels. Once in the Mystic Temple, the Initiate will have the option of entering a number of gates[520], which will open up Zothyrian spaces and multi-verses. This Degree is not for the chronic dabbler in mystical subjects. It is for the Theurgist.

---

[519] Consider, mystically, Cagliostro's use of a "dove," or child for divination. Also, consider Matthew 18:3; "Truly I say to you, unless you change and become like little children..." NIV And additionally, from the Gnostic, *Gospel of Truth*, "After all these came also the little children, those who posses the knowledge of the Father...they were glorified and they gave glory. In their heart, the living book of the living was manifest..." (*The Other Bible*, 291).

[520] *Gates* are referred to in Esoteric Voudon, the Necronimicon, the Typhonion Trilogies, etc., and are considered inter-dimensional portals.

46th Degree

Sublime Pastor of the Huts

Experience of the Black Sun

46th *degree*,
Sublime Pastor of the Huts.

Battery of Knocks

Two, three and two. **XX XXX XX**

Points-chaud

Anus

Sacred Word

DEUS (God)

Grip

Place the right hand on the heart, and the left on each other's right shoulder.

Sign

Place reciprocally the left hand on each other's right shoulder, and the right hand on each other's head.

Additional Materials

Password–LUX (Light)

Jewel–On a circular plate, seven tents arranged as the Knocks, two, three and two.

† † †

Synopsis

The esoteric key to this Degree is in the simple mention of the "Neophyte encounter with the green lion-labor of the Great Work.[521]" We re-enter a study of Alchemy in its most spiritualized form in this Degree and with its accompanying points chaud empowerment.

The Green Lion in alchemical symbolism is seen devouring the sun. This is what forms the *sol niger,* or Black Sun in the first stage of Alchemy called, *nigredo*. In plant alchemy the Green Lion is the chlorophyll which is derived from sunlight and present in plant matter. In many other instances, it becomes a part of vitriol, various acids which assist in the breaking down process of the constituent parts. All of this, in spiritual language, points to the breaking down of complexes, blocks, and taboos which prevent the Initiate from piercing deeply into the mysteries of nature.[522] When considered in relation to the physical

---

[521] *Compleat Rite of Memphis*, p. 107.

[522] "…the body is the matrix of the psyche and also because the body holds within itself the memories of the past as neuromuscular connections and energy points. Thus, the gnostic must use those therapies which release the blocked energies in these points, if the initiate is to be freed from the past karma of his body. Consequently, experimental theology moves into bodywork and the stimulation of the deepest roots of the psyche by association tests and gnostic pressures, in order to massage the transcendental id, and in order to reach the bedrock of the transcendental self and thereby initiate our inner and divine principle" (Bertiaux, *VGW*, 164-165).

location of the point, all is made clear. Far from being an opportunity for invasiveness, perversions or sexual stimulation, this empowerment holds within it the truths of psychology when rightly understood by the light of magick. What we renounce, we are eternally bound to. The complexes and taboos that we have built up are the very walls that enclose our Oratories[523], when we could have free reign in the Zothyrian landscapes of the mind. When particular channels are open and spiritual circuitry allowed to flow freely, the Initiate becomes capable of swift advancement upon the way.

In Yarker's notes we also find reference to the allegory of the fig-tree as a symbol of truth. Figs have long been a symbol of initiation. We find reference to the ancient Egyptian Priests eating them at their consecration ceremonies. Later on, in the same regions, we find the desert Fathers & Mothers living upon them. The many seeds in the fig are supposed to signify unity and the universality of true understanding, knowledge and faith. The fig tree is sacred in Asia. Buddha's *Banyan* was a fig-tree. Fig trees were believed to be inhabited by Djinn. Ultimately, the Eastern understanding of the fig tree was that it stood for *knowledge born of meditation.*

When considered together, the Green Lion devouring the sun, the points-chaud empowerment, and the symbolism of the fig tree all teach the same message concerning the truths of this Degree. Do not expect a series of spirits or entities to be attached to this Degree, though they may be stimulated into activity, but expect pure REVELATION. This mystical Degree will reveal itself to be heavily therapeutic and attuning in nature[524].

---

[523] Obvious connection can be made to the Thelemic current here, but at least in the West, it goes back to certain esoteric sects of the Gnostics, who turned "sin" into a way of salvation in their libertinistic tendencies. We find doctrinal significance of this line of thinking, in combination with the doctrine of the transmigration of souls, in the writings of Carpocrates. See, *The Gnostic Religion*, by Hans Jonas, 1958, p. 274. There is a psychologically healthy way to understand this mystery that can be divined through the third source of spiritual truth for Anglicans, along with Tradition and Scripture—that of *Common Sense*.

[524] This Degree also refers to the XI *Templar Noir* Degree of the **OTOA**. When combined with the training of Mastery in the Inner Knights Templar work of the Freres d'Orient, a magickal synthesis ensues that gathers that which has been scattered for millennia.

47th Degree

Knight of the Seven Stars

Introduction to the Seven Archangels

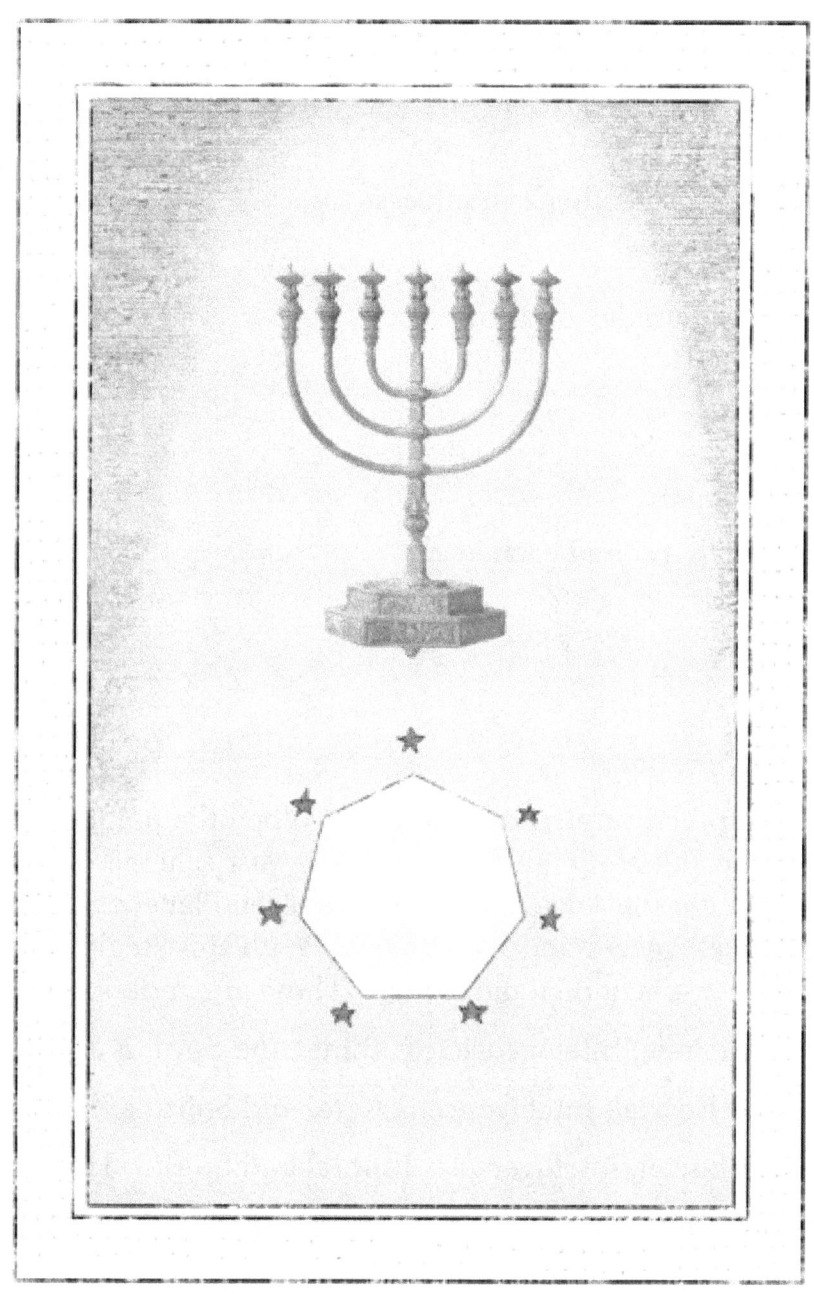

47th degree,
Knight of the Seven Stars.

Battery of Knocks

    One, two and four knocks.   **X   XX   XXXX**

Points-chaud

    Coccyx

Sacred Word

    VIGILO (Watch)

Grip

    With both hands seize each other's shoulders.

Sign

    Incline head, place right index on brow.

Additional Materials

    Password–SPERO (Hope)

    Jewel–A Heptagon with a star at each angle

† † †

Synopsis

We return to the number Seven in this Degree. When the points-chaud empowerment of this Degree *takes*, the Initiate is introduced to the vast schema of intermediary beings attached to the Planets. For the Ancients, there were seven Planets. Attached to these seven planets were spirits, intelligences and Archangels. With this single empowerment comes the introduction to twenty-one individual beings. These are understood thusly:

    Sun–Archangel is **Michael**, Intelligence is **Nakhiel** and Spirit is **Sorath**.

    Saturn–Archangel is **Kassiel**, Intelligence is **Agiel** and Spirit is **Zazel**.

    Jupiter–Archangel is **Saciel**, Intelligence is **Iophiel** and Spirit is **Hismael**.

    Mars–Archangel is **Zamael**, Intelligence is **Graphiel** and Spirit is **Bartzabel**.

    Venus–Archangel is **Anael**, Intelligence is **Hagiel** and Spirit is **Qedemel**.

    Mercury–Archangel is **Raphael**, Intelligence is **Tiriel** and Spirit is **Taphthartharath**.

    Moon–Archangel is **Gabriel**, Intelligence is **Shelachel** and Spirit is **Chasmodai**.

Additional correspondences to this Degree, as suggested by Yarker include the Seven Stars of Ursa Major, the symbol of the Fylfot Cross[525], the seven mysterious Ristus and their consorts in the Pleiades, the flaming star as light upon the path, the passage through an obscure vault, the seven-branched candlestick and the spiritual influences of the Zodiac[526]. The following Degree exposes the Initiate to the Archangels of the Zodiac. All angelic activity is heightened in the Degrees of the *Arcana Arcanorum*, but the introduction of such forces and anthropomorphized symbols occurs in this set.

When re-awakening this point and scrying further into it, it is crucial to understand the nature of the Sacred Word. VIGILO is the key to accessing the twenty-one beings of the Planets. One must keep vigil with this Degree to experience its fullness. If the Initiate is accustomed to the use of the Magickal Novena[527], this is an appropriate setting for such. The experience is simply an introduction and sense of these entities and may not result in the interaction and relations with them. For true relationship with the entities, one must cultivate devotion and treat each in the same way that one would treat a lover or the dearest of friends. Once introduced, especially when scrying the point, these spirits, archangels and intelligences become agencies to interact with on a daily basis. Then, the Initiate will be attracted to charts and data that give the specific times and dates of a planet's closeness to the earth, and conjunction with other planetary forces. With these astronomical occurrences, we may find these various entities in conversation with us, as well as with each other. An entire world of exploration opens up through intercourse with these twenty-one entities.

---

[525] A symbol found frequently in Hermetic Orders, and, of course, pre-dating its bastardization by the Nazis. One Order in particular, mystically aligned with the work of Free Illuminists through T Allen Greenfield, made use of the emblem—the H. B. of L, or Hermetic Brotherhood of Light/Luxor.

[526] MUCH of the symbolism and field of study in this Degree is found in the *Zelator Grade* of the Classical Golden Dawn system of magic.

[527] See the forthcoming, *Revelations on the Tree of Life*, by +Palamas, as well as, *The Magical Power of the Saints*, by Rev. Ray T. Malbrough.

Spirit Builders

48th Degree

Sublime Guardian of the Sacred Mount

Call to the Zodiacal Archangels

48th *degree,*
Sublime Guardian of the Sacred Mount.

Battery of Knocks

Two and one.   XX   X

Points-chaud

Left lower buttock

Sacred Word

FIDELITATE (Fidelity)

Grip

With right hand, tap thrice the hilt of the magickal sword (the hip).

Sign

Make a hasty step and then recoil.

Additional Materials

Password–CONSTANTIA (Constancy)

Jewel–On a triangle, three interlaced circles.

† † †

Synopsis

No one working these Degrees within Congregational Illuminist circles would suggest that Marconis, Yarker, or the earlier framers of the Rite of Misraim, would ever know of the innovative and esoteric work occurring upon the Holy Arabia Mountain. However, this is a *living Tradition* and the Spirit blows where it will. The "Sacred Mount" of this Degree is, for us, the Holy Arabia Mountain. Upon this Mountain individuals full of integrity and following their own ingenium, summon the spirits, work the points chauds empowerments, offer ordinations and consecrations in the various Gnostic Churches, and embody the Trinitarian notion of liberty, fraternity and equality in manifold ways.

This Degree is suggestive of pilgrimage. If at all possible, the practitioner may want to make a pilgrimage to Arabia Mountain to receive this and other points. While visiting Arabia, there are numerous other sacred sites in Georgia that radiate similar energy broadcasts and which maintain a vibratory connection with Gnosticism and other Initiatory fraternities. The Scottish occultist, Peter Davidson, once worked The Hermetic Brotherhood of Light/Luxor a couple of hours away from Arabia Mountain in Loudsville. Along with the HB of L, Davidson taught a form of esoteric Christianity and continued the

Martinist school.[528] Near Davidson's grave[529] & old family farmhouse, are the Georgia Guidestones in Elbert County, a mammoth Rosicrucian monument of very curious design and astronomical significance.[530] Within an hour of each of these are Native American burial mounds and holy sites, as well as an Orthodox and Trappist Monastery. Or if such a pilgrimage to this American hotbed of Gnostic and Rosicrucian activity is not possible, one should discern the location of a sacred marma and perform this Degree in that location, especially under the dome of sky and in a natural setting. The primary reason is that this Degree, like the one before it, calls upon a number of sky entities all at once. In this case, they are Zodiacal Archangels. Upon reception of the Degree, the Initiate may lay down upon the earth or upon a consecrated rock[531] and observe the heavens above. The Facilitator may then read the names of these Archangels which the Initiate will want to record later for further research and exploration.

Aries–the Archangel **MALKHIDAEL**

Taurus–the Archangel **Asmodel**

Gemini–the Archangel **Ambriel**

Cancer–the Archangel **Muriel**

Leo–the Archangel **Verkhiel**

Virgo–the Archangel **Hamaliel**

Libra–the Archangel **Zuriel**

Scorpio–the Archangel **Barkhiel**

Sagittarius–the Archangel **Adnakhiel**

Capricorn–the Archangel **Hanael**

Aquarius–the Archangel **Kambriel**

Pisces–the Archangel **Amnitziel**

These twelve, along with the previous twenty-one planetary beings, become accessible entities peculiarly attached to these points chauds empowerments and related directly with these Memphis+Misraïm Degree secrets.

---

[528] It is of particular interest that Papus was the student of Peter Davidson, in this respect. See, *The Story of the Hermetic Brotherhood of Light*, Greenfield, p. 7.

[529] It is at Davidson's grave that most pilgrims find a sacred, geographical marma connected with this Provincial Grandmaster of the Northern and Eastern sections of the HB of L. See the history and an informative and entertaining video journey of two Freemasons to the sacred site at, http://tausirhasirim.livejournal.com/138222.html

[530] The Georgia Guidestones had been utilized as the previously mentioned *Gates* by certain Rose+Croix Initiates until their unfortunate destruction by vandals in July of 2022.

[531] Or grave, or Guidestone…

49th Degree

Sublime Sage of the Pyramids

Arrival of the Patron Saint

49th *degree,*
Sublime Sage of the Pyramids.

Battery of Knocks

Seven. X X X X X X X

Points-chaud

Left center buttock

Sacred Word

ALETHE[532] (referring to the river, Lethe)

Grip

Grasp each other by the two first fingers and give three shakes.

Sign

1st–raise right index finger to heaven. 2nd–Place thumb of left hand on the breast to form the letter, "L."

Additional Materials

Password–SIGE

Jewel–a square design with a Mason's square. From the angle issues a serpent[533].

†††

Synopsis

This Degree and the one following it begin and complete the invocation of the Spirit of Water. This Degree has a complete ceremonial in the Yarker version, and which is suggested as a "break" in the *communication* of the Degrees that precede it back to the 34th. This highlights the distinction of our methodology, which is a continuation and extension of the Jean-Maine lineage which envisioned the Degrees of Memphis-Misraïm as a structure of the Gnostic Church, and that of some of the practicing, traditional Bodies of Memphis-Misraïm. None of the Degrees of the Ecclesiastical Revision are "communicated," as all are considered Gnostic empowerments, and are therefore conferred in full–though often with a simple gesture, such as the gnostic pressure upon the body.

---

[532] As the work suggests, this does refer to one of the rivers of Hades, however, it is also related to Eleleth, "the Great Angel, who stands in the presence of the Holy Spirit," who is "one of the Four Light-givers" (*The Hypostasis of the Archons*, 79, from, *The Other Bible*). Additionally, this degree, on the cosmic scale, furthers the 3rd echelon work by calling to the XIVth ÆONIC Syzygy: Aletheia & Nous.

[533] Note, if during the scrying session the Initiate is asked to produce a ring, it is this symbol. Such can be fashioned into a ring for the scrying adventure if preferred, but the same can be accomplished upon the inner plane.

In this Degree, there are not specific entities invoked or evoked. Instead, there is a hint at the *Visages of the Sages* which we have alluded to within the Mystic Temple. When one discovers the hyperspatial locale of the Mystic Temple, she begins to observe more closely the living columns as they are formed about the marma. These visages are "evoked by a career full of ardent researches in science and in virtue.[534]" Within this Degree and its subsequent point empowerment are lodged the secrets of entering the Mystic Temple. It is within the organization of the Degree itself that we find these keys.

Within this Degree order, we discover a completely scaffolded scrying session, that is somewhere between our general and advanced methods of scrying, and our approach to pathworking. The first emblem we are presented with is the hoodwink, which is placed upon the candidate in the dramatic working. The world of "things" can be a blinder to our spirit. We must discipline the mind and be free from distraction if we are to enter this Sacred Temple. Next, we are guided by a spirit contact[535]. He gives the Battery of Knocks which opens the gates of the spirit realm for the Initiate during scrying. Next, twenty-one Patriarchs dressed in black tunics appear. These are the previous twenty-one planetary forces invoked in the 47th Degree. A labyrinth of crypts is presented, evoking the Egyptian mysteries of the pyramids. The Initiate descends ever further into the realm of Hades, there after being presented with the mystic ladder and the inner Robe of Glory, she is offered the draught of forgetfulness[536] from the river Lethe.

The spiritual experience allied with this Degree is the forgetting of one's failures and regrets. Along with the breaking down of complexes that occurs in many of the empowerments, this Degree furthers this explosive opening of the psyche by moving the Initiate beyond the past. The waters of forgetfulness are not only hypnotic here, but are liberating and exalting of the sovereignty of the human Will. This Degree accomplishes this liberation and prepares the Initiate for the conjuration of the Spirit of Water. The negative end of this draught of forgetfulness, however, is that the Initiate may take too long a drink. Such leads to *agnosia* in the most negative sense. The best use of the draught is as a form of *forgiveness*.

---

[534] *Compleat Rite of Memphis*, p. 109.
[535] For some, this will be the trustworthy *Patron Saint* of the Initiate. See p. 165 of *Syzygy*.
[536] Much is made of the curse of *forgetfulness* in the Gnostic, *Gospel of Truth*. It is forgetfulness that prevents Gnosis in this beautiful work of the Valentinan school.

50th Degree
Sublime Philosopher of Samothrace
Conjuration of the Spirits of Water

50th *degree,*
Sublime Philosopher of Samothrace.

Battery of Knocks

Seven equal knocks.   X X X X X X X

Reading

Hear, O Brother (Sister) the Conjuration of the Spirit of Water[537]!

Conjuration–"Dread king of the Sea, Who has the keys of the floodgates of heaven and dost confine the waters of the underworld in the caverns of earth; King of the deluge and the floods of the springtime; Thou Who dost unseal the sources of rivers and fountains; Thou Who dost ordain moisture, which is like the blood of earth, to become the sap of plants: Thee we adore and Thee we invoke! Speak unto us, Thine inconstant and unstable creatures, in the great tumults of the sea, and we shall tremble before Thee; speak unto us also in the murmur of limpid waters, and we shall yearn for Thy love! O Immensity into which flows all rivers of life, to be continually reborn in Thee! O ocean of infinite perfections! Height which reflects Thee in the depth, depth which exhales Thee to the height, lead us unto true life by intelligence and love! Lead us to immortality by sacrifice that we may be found worthy one day to offer Thee water, blood and tears, for the remission of sins! Amen.[538]"

Points-chaud

Left upper buttocks

Sacred Word

SADYK (The Just, father of the Cabiri[539])

Grip

Join right hands and balance nine times (in a similar way as the Royal Arch).

Sign

Place right hand on the heart and say, *Faith*.

Additional Materials

Password–CABIRIC (Cabiric 7 Gods)

Jewel–The square and compasses, interlaced with an even balance.

† † †

---

[537] We find these sacred conjurations utilized in many initiatory fraternities, such as the H B of L. See, *The Hermetic Brotherhood of Luxor*, by Godwin, Chanel, and Deveney, pgs. 111-117.
[538] Eliphas Levi, *Transcendental Magic*, p. 231
[539] Detailed study of the *Kabiri* is undertaken in the Practicus Grade of the Hermetic Order of the Golden Dawn.

Synopsis

The Samothracian Mysteries are described in many tomes of the Western Esoteric Tradition. Though their mysteries are not relegated to one element, there is a primacy of the element of water in their workings. In this Degree, as in many, the sacred number is seven as there are seven main gods of this chthonic system. This mystery cult explored the purification of candidates by water and blood, which finds an analogue in at least one branch of the current Gnostic Church's Rite of baptism (blood being replaced by wine). Again, we find the river Lethe and the draught of forgetfulness, but with the addition of the goddess of memory, Mnemosyne, who restores the Initiate with the magickal memory.[540]

This Degree, like the 42nd, includes one of the *Conjuration of the Four* from Eliphas Levi. When this Degree is performed near water, the Initiate will experience an influx of psychic powers, a flood of subconscious memories, enhanced divinatory skills, and a general receptivity to the spirit realm, hitherto unexplored. It is best to face the West when conferring this Degree, as the West is often associated with the Archangel Gabriel, the Cup and the element of Water.

---

[540] See the *Art of Memory*, by Dame Frances Yates.

51st Degree

Sublime Titan of the Caucasus

Conjuration of the Spirits of Fire

51st *degree,*
Sublime Titan of the Caucasus.

Battery of Knocks

Three and Four. X X X   X X X X

Reading

Conjuration of the Spirit of Fire–"Immortal, eternal, ineffable and uncreated Father of all things, Who art borne upon the ever-rolling chariot of worlds which revolve unceasingly; Lord of ethereal immensities, where the throne of Thy power is exalted, from which height Thy terrible eyes discern all things and Thy holy and beautiful ears unto all things hearken, hear Thou Thy children, whom Thou didst love before the ages began. For Thy golden, Thy grand, Thine eternal majesty shines above the world and the heaven of stars! Thou art exalted over them, O glittering fire! There dost thou shine, there dost Thou commune with Thyself in Thine own splendor, and inexhaustible streams of light pour from Thine essence for the nourishment of Thine Infinite Spirit, which itself doth nourish all things, and forms that inexhaustible treasure of substance ever ready for the generation which adapts it and appropriates the forms Thou has impressed on it from the beginning! From this Spirit the three most holy kings, who surround Thy throne and constitute Thy court, derive also their origin, O universal Father! O sole and only Father of blessed mortals and immortals! In particular Thou has created powers which are marvelously like unto Thine eternal thought and Thine adorable essence; Thou hast established them higher than the angels, who proclaim Thy will to the world; finally, Thou hast created us third in rank within our elementary empire. There our unceasing exercise is to praise Thee and adore Thy good pleasure; there we burn continually in our aspiration to possess Thee. O Father! O Mother, most tender of all mothers! O admirable archetype of maternity and of pure love! O Son, flower of sons! O form of all forms, soul, spirit, harmony and number of all things! Amen.[541]"

Points-chaud

Right lower buttock

Sacred Word

SISIT (The Chaldean Enoch)

Grip

Grip arms mutually, advance length of the arm, and press thereon seven times.

Sign

Raise eyes to Heaven and say, *Hope*.

---

[541] *Transcendental Magic*, p. 232.

Additional Materials

Password–SIGE, answer ALETHE (*XIV*th *and XVI*th *ÆONs in 3*rd *echelon*)

Jewel–A ladder of seven steps and above it a star

††††

Synopsis

This Degree completes the Classical, *Conjuration of the Four*, by calling upon the Spirit of Fire. In these Hermetic, Kabalistic and Gnostic Degrees, the Initiate is being placed within the context of the magickal traditions of Western Esotericism. It may be that she would prefer to simplify her work and not explore the appendant studies mentioned within these Synopses. This is perfectly fine, as the points-chaud empowerment makes direct contact with the specific spirits and energies of the Degree and no further work, research, conjuring, or magickal operations are necessary. The Synopsis is a pointer towards further exploration and Light with the Degree. But as the Degrees enter into the nature of these mysteries– Zodiacal intelligences, planetary angels, and the like– are provided for further study and experimentation. Using the Jewel[542] of the Degree and following the Three-fold Path, the Initiate remains protected from negative entities forces and maintains her workings *within* the Light.

The Spirits of Earth, Water, Air and Fire, however, are a completion of the work of the 1st Degree, where the Candidate is purified by these same forces. Once the purification is complete, then the Candidate—now, *Initiate*—may move on to visualizing these forces personified and even calling upon their presence, blessing and assistance. That is the reasoning for including the Conjuration of the Four in the actual Degree working, as opposed to making it optional material only in the Synopsis.

As Spirit Builders, we become like Prometheus in this Degree, that sublime Titan who stole Fire for the progress, enlightenment and intellectual striving of others. Our Esoteric research via the points chauds empowerments and their connections with these occult Masonic Degrees is analogous to the brave Prometheus–by the Initiate turning around and giving freely of this knowledge, light, and initiation to others *In Free Communion*. Fire is the element present in the following two Degrees and so it is appropriate to work all three in the same meeting.[543]

---

[542] As a reminder, the Jewel of each Degree functions as a sigil *and* as a protective talisman. Additionally, when all 97 Jewels are drawn upon parchment, they can be used in a divinatory manner to decide which points an Initiate should receive during a consultation. After reception of all 97 Degrees, Initates can use these cards to divine what scrying journeys should be further explored. In this way, the Jewel becomes the visual gateway of the Degree—much like the action of the veve to the Lwa in Vodou.

[543] If, for instance, the consultation method is being employed to decide what point/Degree to receive—the Initiate whose selection ends up being one of these three Degrees would be suggested to receive all three for the sake of balance and the completion of the fiery Initiation.

Spirit Builders

52nd Degree
Sage of the Labyrinth

52nd *degree,*
Sage of the Labyrinth.

Battery of knocks

Three, five and four. XXX   XXXXX   XXXX

Points-chaud

Right center buttock

Sacred Word

AMOUN (Be discreet)

Grip

Jointly, right hand on forehead, bow the head, place left hand on breast. Meaning—intelligence, humility and fidelity.

Sign

Join right and left hands, as if walking together

Additional Materials

Password–SIGE

Jewel–A palm tree

†††

Synopsis

This Hermetic Degree puts the Initiate in contact with the great Alchemists of the ages who attend the Degree at the call of the Battery of Knocks. The Degree continues the invocation of the Spirit of Fire as well. We find mention of the Initiate showing his mantle which has been reduced to ashes. He is made to give a proof of blood to enter the sacred alchemical laboratory before him and is given a lesson concerning the nefarious ways of the charlatan. Symbols are presented; the Palm of the Valley of Oddy that supposedly had 365 properties and produced one branch a month, the Mystic rose of Khab, the principles of the lingam and yoni, the alchemical colors and processes of black, green and white, and the sacred red tincture[544]. All of these, the Initiate is enjoined to study to see not only the practical alchemical correlations, but those of the spirit as well.

If the Initiate wants to pursue further work as an Alchemist, she is encouraged to begin with plant spagyrics[545]. If she goes through the production of making these sacred salts of

---

[544] The sacred lunation kalas are sometimes ascribed to this red tincture, especially in relation to the principles of the lingam and yoni which are present in the Degree also. Holy Eucharist is typified in the red tincture as well, in its various aspects.

[545] Practical alchemy has made a return to the fore. The current Grandmaster of a particular branch of Martinism is one such expert and scientist.

plant alchemy, she can be assured of the presence of the ancients. The basic steps[546] of plant alchemy include;

1. Harvesting the plant, according to the day that relates to the planet of invocation.
2. Desiccation and pulveration.
3. Maceration
4. Maceration and Circulation
5. Filtration
6. Calcination—this produce gray-white ash that may be used in tinctures.

The points-chauds empowerment of this Degree will stimulate active, fire energies. The forces within this empowerment are manifold and are to be discerned by the Initiate through scrying the point.

One final note, the Initiate will make an immediate connection with this Degree and *our* understanding of the mystic ladder of the 2nd Degree. Here, the labyrinth goes further inward into the basic stuff of the organism, the *prima materia* of the alchemists, to unfold the pure spirits and essences that compose the whole.

---

[546] There are many great sources for this science, but these most simplified steps are taken from, *The Book of Alchemy*, by Francis Melville.

53rd Degree
Knight or Sage of the Phoenix
Invocation of Oannes

53th *degree,*
Knight or Sage of the Phoenix.

Battery of Knocks

One, two, six and one.   X XX XXXXXX X

Points-chaud

Right upper buttocks

Sacred Word

PHOENIX (Symbol of Sothis)

Grip

Join left hands and point to Sirius, or Sothis, with right index finger.

Sign

Represent examination, as if through telescope.

Additional Materials

Password–SIGE

Jewel–A triangle on which is a Phoenix.

Synopsis

This Degree is one of the most mysterious in our collection of Hermetic, Gnostic and Kabalistic empowerments. Though the points-chaud has its own energy and entity which must be discovered and developed by the Initiate himself, scrying the point has the unique property of invoking a very specific mythical being—*Oannes*, the Babylonian deity and teacher of wisdom to mankind[547]. When performing the basic scrying of the point, utilizing the Sign, Token, Jewel and Words of the Degree, the Initiate is conducted to an outdoor Temple where she will be introduced to *Oannes*. He may appear as a Bishop of the Church. In this is an even deeper mystery, as we find his fish-head to mirror precisely the Bishop's mitre. In this manner, this Degree connects to the 66th Degree of Grand Consecrator.

The nature of this connection of *Oannes*, a spiritual type of St. John, with the third of our fire Degrees is in the correlation with the Phoenix and the Star Sirius. The Phoenix rises from the ashes of the previously mentioned *Calcination* stage born from the work of spagyric Alchemy. Spiritually, the Phoenix will rise in the newness of life born from deeply understanding and practicing our first stage of the Three-fold path, *Katharismos*, Purification. The Phoenix is a symbol of Sirius and our token is pointing to the star above. With the eyes purified, the Initiate will begin to see the rarefied quality of our alchemical labors.

Finally, there is a deep connection between Oannes and Sirius, the star that is naked to the human eye but which was discovered by the Dogon people according to certain authors. Though the details of the discovery of Sirius B (the white dwarf star) by the Dogon may not be 100% accurate, there most assuredly was a deep understanding of constellations and a powerful cosmology amongst this tribe that continues today. Oannes (whom St. Jerome called *Dagon*), as their sea God and a *type* of John[548] as well as related being to the Episcopacy, can be invoked under Sirius during the *Sothis Days* of the Summer, while activating this points-chaud empowerment. He may offer a sort of *baptism* upon entrance, which will take the degree work from Purification directly into Illumination.

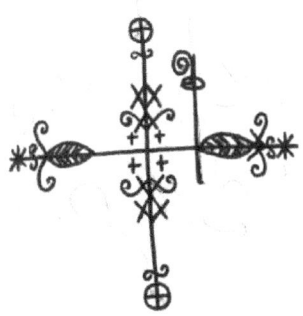

---

[547] The history of this god is complex and begins in Mesopotamia as a fertility god, but moves into Canaan becoming the father of BAAL. See: I Samuel 5:1-8 (I Kingdoms 5:1-8 in the Septuagint).
[548] The *Baptizer...Joannes*, whose Festival happens to land on the ancient Feast of Tammuz, who returns after death as *Oannes*, amongst other names. See Chapter III, Section III, in *The Two Babylons*, by Rev. Alexander Hislop. Though this is from an extremist angle, the scholarship is accurate.

54th Degree
Sublime Scalde

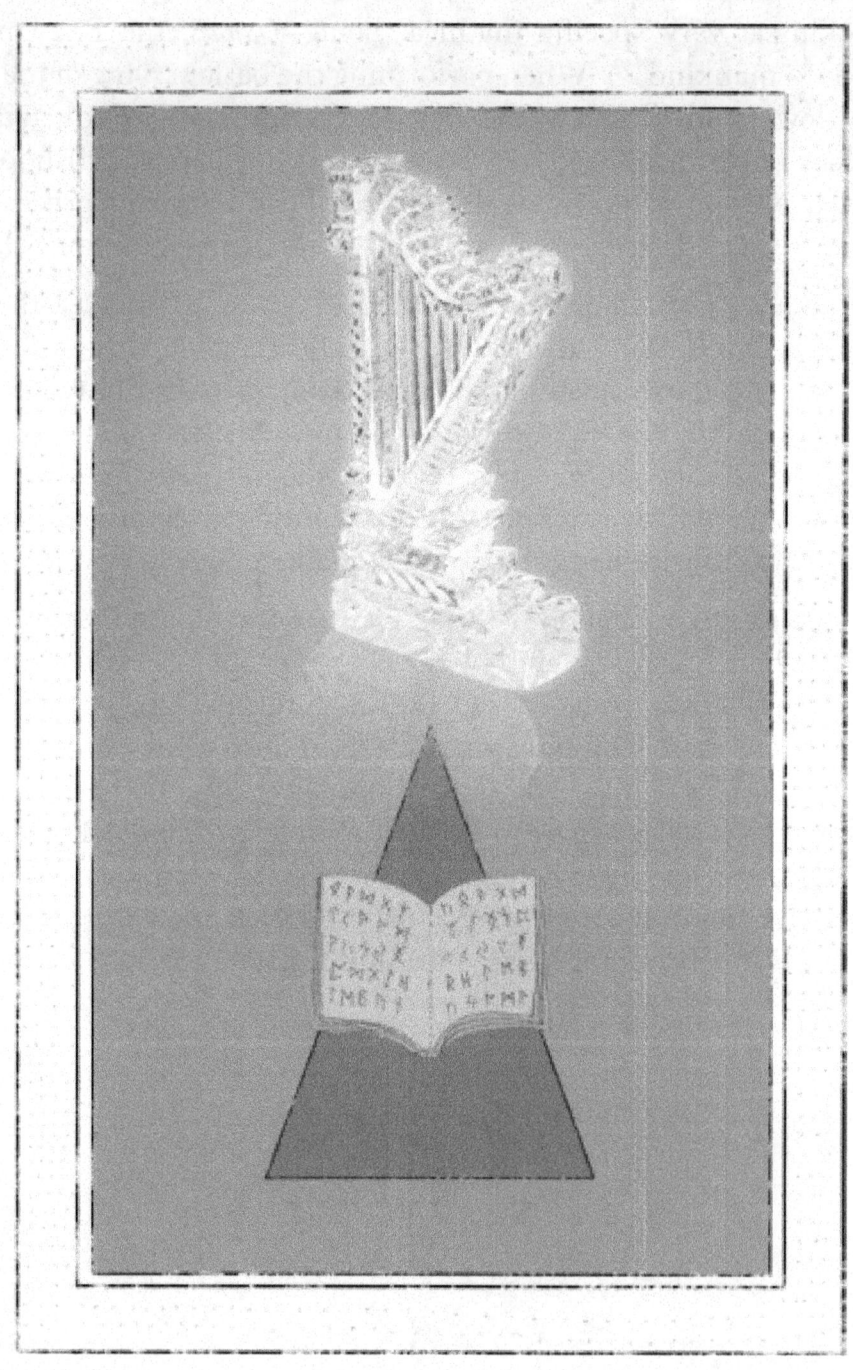

54th *degree,*
Sublime Scalde.

Battery of Knocks

One, two and two.   X   XX   XX

Points-chaud

Left lower back

Sacred Word

BALDER (A Norse Sun God).

Grip

Each takes hold of a side of an imagined book with the right hand, left hand on each other's left shoulder.

Sign

Take the magickal book and appear to be reading. In scrying, this will call upon the Wisdom spirits lodged within the book of Psalms, as well as being representative of the "living book" suggested in the Gnostic, *Gospel of Truth*.

Additional Materials

Password–SIGE

Jewel–On a triangle, a book

†††

Synopsis

This Degree has a host of attributions and fields of study. Each of these Higher Degrees has lodged within them entire sections and compartments of the Western Mystery Tradition. This Degree opens up the subjects of the Bard Grade of Druidry, the study of the spiritual gifts of the second son of Odin, Balder, the divinatory method of Bibliomancy, the use of Wisdom literature for the Initiate, the powers of mantra and drumming, and the Music of the Spheres of Pythagoras.

As with all of the Degrees, there is an individual application of the energies and entities that accompany the points chaud empowerment. Also we recall that the points chauds operate in four distinct ways, *attunement, initiation, empowerment* and *therapy*. These four channels of each Degree are unique to every recipient and these operations trump the follow-up studies listed in these *Synopses*.

Yet sometimes, as in this Degree, we see the connections deeply between these four operations of the points chauds and the nature of the Masonic Degree. For instance, in terms of attunement, we may consider the Music or Harmony of the Spheres of Pythagoras.

It is a form of mystical attunement to recognize the energies and vibratory rates of celestial bodies as a form of musical tones and sounds[549]. This recognition of the divine proportion of forms is found in studies relating to sacred geometry as well, such as the Fibonacci sequence and the Golden Mean found in nature and replicated in architecture. We also find a connection with the Bard Grade of Druidry[550] and further attunement with the arts, music and even storytelling being brought into harmony with the Druid's magic and ecological outlook.

In terms of empowerment, both contacting Balder, the son of Odin, and the practice of Bibliomancy, become methods for developing the Initiate to her fullest potential. Working with Balder strengthens the Initiate and passes on some of his qualities of radiance and light. Practicing Bibliomancy, simply by allowing a book to speak directly to the reader as an Oracle from beyond, empowers the Initiate in his divinatory skills and ability to read the pages of the spirits upon the events and objects of the daily.

In terms of Initiation, we find the mention of mantra and sacred drumming to be key. Both techniques are used in traditional Vodou. When contacting one of the lwa, the Vodouisant uses many techniques to get the attention of the lwa and to put him or herself in the receptive mode to experience full on possession by the spirit. Two of the primary methods for this are mantric singing (songs with litanies and repetitious lines) and rhythmic drumming. Mantras are also given to chelas in various systems for meditation purposes and are prominent in Crowley's discourses on union of mysticism and magic.[551] The "primitive source" as the Degree calls it, for these methods is believed by many to be India or at least in the Indus Valley.[552]

Finally, as a therapy, this Degree teaches of the beauty and Wisdom of Sacred Literature such as the Holy books of Proverbs and Psalms. The Psalms in particular have a long history of being used for healing which was codified in a piece of the practical Kabala entitled, *Sepher Shimmush Tehillim, from the Sixth and Seventh Books of Moses. When scrying the point of this Degree, it is particularly useful to chant or read Psalms prior to the experiment, or to use the Psalms in the Advanced Scrying Method.*

Beyond the Psalms, and the writings of others altogether, we find the Gospel of Truth teaching of a "living book" which acts as an inner teacher. This living book relates to our personal Ontic Spheres, and the direct instructions and learning we receive from within.

---

[549] Many Orders work with sound attunements in Initiation, such as the Builders of the Adytum (BOTA). We find teachings concerning the averse side of the Tree of Life and certain musical notes and harmonies being aligned with the inner paths in Grant's *Nightside of Eden* work as well.

[550] See both the curriculums of of the OBOD as well as the American, AODA.

[551] See Book 4, Liber ABA.

[552] See Pike's suggestion of the source of the Primitive Doctrine being the Vedas, in *Lecture on Masonic Symbolism and A Second Lecture on Symbolism: The Omkara and Other Ineffable Words.* 2006 edition.

55th Degree

Sublime Orphic Doctor

Invocation of Orpheus

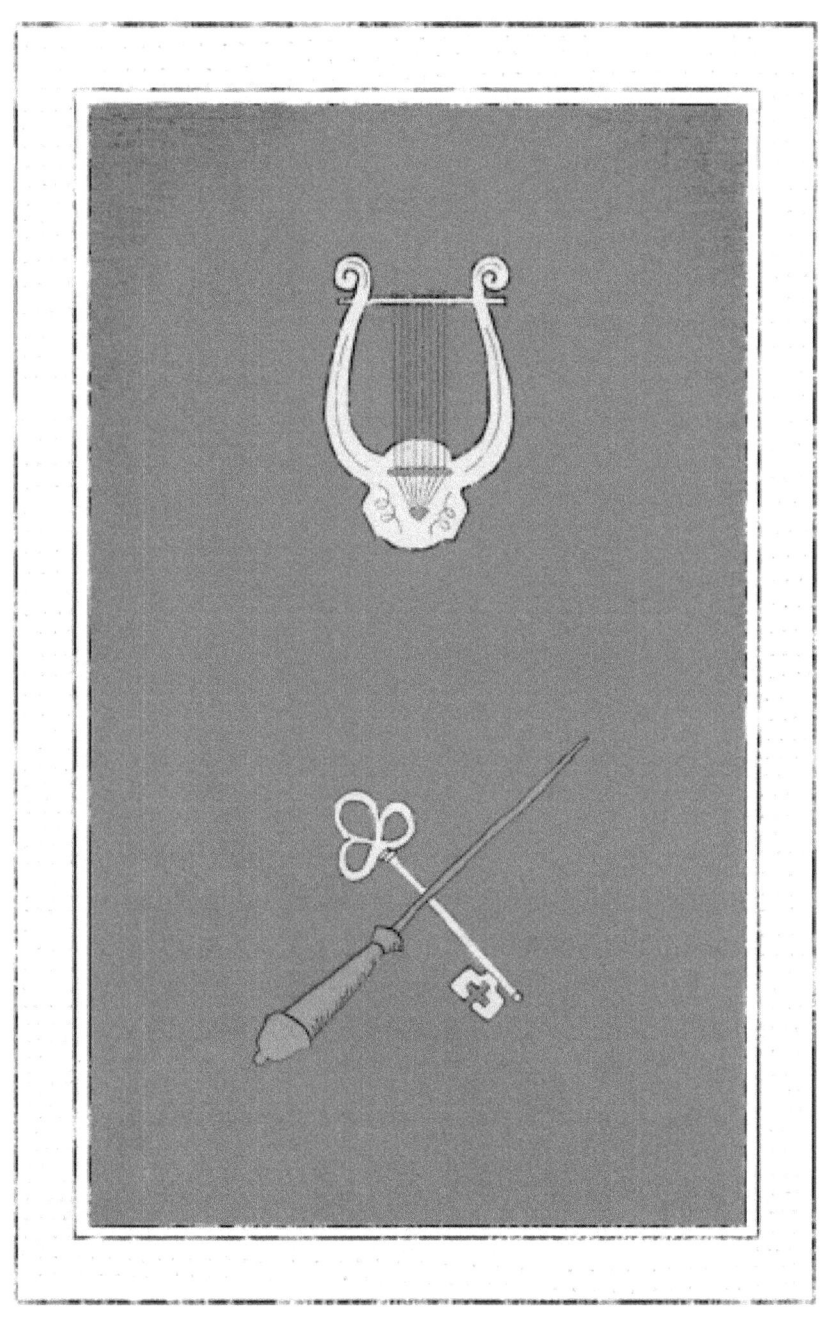

55th *degree,*
Sublime Orphic Doctor.

Battery of Knocks

  Seven.   X X X X X X X

Points-chaud

  Left back above the buttocks

Sacred Word

  ORPHEUS

Grip

  Touch each other's left side with the right hand.

Sign

  Cross arms below stomach, and stand as if musing.

Additional Materials

  Password–SIGE (Silence)

  Jewel–A key crossed with a wand

†††

Synopsis

This Degree, in its utter simplicity, is an invocation to the Greek Theurgist, Orpheus. The Sign, Sacred Word, Password, Battery and Jewel are all indicative of a singular purpose, which is to put the Initiate in contact with this Orphic Doctor upon the Inner Planes. While scrying the point of this Degree, the Initiate may be taken on a journey to Ancient Greece. He may be guided by an unseen hand who takes the Initiate to several of the sacred sites that contain the relics of Orpheus. Each of these are living Oracles in the vision. The end of the journey is often a high mountain side, overlooking a beautiful and tranquil sea, where the god Orpheus will be found singing and playing his lyre in front of an abundance of creatures and standing stones, all of which he is charming and enchanting into sentience. As Yarker states, his "magical knowledge of the Spiritual *Forces*" in these beings is now for the Initiate to partake of or at least learn from. If he makes eye contact with you, use the Sign of the Degree as a show of your Grade. He will greet the Initiate with the Token which is mutually exchanged.

The Initiate must be on guard before commencing this journey with the Unseen Guide. In the Orphic Rites, the Initiate was given a strict program of asceticism and lessons concerning metempsychosis.[553] Particular attention should be paid to the stage of *Purification* before this scrying journey. Some of the hazards along the way are the same that the wife of Orpheus, Eurydice, dealt with and which led to her death. There are hidden Satyrs along the way who are sometimes near the Sirens and Nymphs that the Initiate encounters. There are also pits of vipers covered over and hidden amongst tall grasses. Utmost care should be taken while scrying this point and Degree.

The particular energies and entities related to the points-chaud empowerment concern oracular vision and enchantment. This is a mystical Degree and nothing more need be said.

---

[553] The Transmigration of Souls is a theology found in every culture, and though most popularized in Eastern Cultures, was particularly developed by the Sethian Gnostics.

Spirit Builders

56th Degree
Pontiff, or Sage of Cadmia

56th *degree,*
Pontiff, of Sage of Cadmia.

Battery of Knocks

One, two and two. X XX XX

Points-chaud

Lower right, back

Sacred Word

CADMUS

Grip

Take each other's right and left hand, and loose them three times.

Sign

Cross arms, let fall to the side, repeat twice.

Additional Materials

Password–SIGE (Silence continues to be the key to the realms of these Degrees as it relates directly to the quality necessary to pierce into the spirit vision in scrying.)

Jewel–A triangle upon which is a heart in flames

††††

Synopsis

This Degree description begins with a beautiful phrase that is completely consistent with the scrying experience aligned to the point. It says, "This grade is a School of Wisdom which treats on the Sublime aim of the Great Work; the rehabilitation of man in divine perception.[554]" This grade is mystically aligned to the Degree of the Unknown Philosopher, directly related to the theology and mysticism of Martinez de Pasqually and his successor, Louis Claude de St. Martin. Our studies move from practical Alchemy to spiritual Alchemy, and this process involves the reintegration of the human into her original and primitive state of purity. A direct correlation here is made to the quiet and simple search for and practice of, the Primitive Doctrine that *Spirit Builders* engage in.

For one Degree to be an entire *School of Wisdom*[555] may seem strange to the observer of initiator grades, but for Masons and members of various branches of the Western Esoteric

---

[554] *Compleat Rite of Memphis*, p. 117.
[555] There are many esoteric schools of wisdom and instruction within the Western Mystery Tradition. Some schools are more comprehension and analysis oriented, while others bridge into synthesis and creative thought. The latter, of which the *Monastery of the Seven of the Seven Rays* and the method of *Free Illuminism* partake of, incorporate higher order, critical, divergent thinking. Within these schools we find gnostic and ontic knowledge developed.

Tradition, this makes perfect sense. There are often not simply singular events and lessons per Degree, but entire palaces of occult knowledge—esoteric laboratories and museums of data with closets of deeper initiations wherein dwell the spirit conductors and intelligences who take the Initiate into their hermitages, Chapels, and encampments. Such is the nature of this Degree.

The 19th Degree had the word, *Pontiff* in the title as does this Degree. This is not to suggest a Catholic Pope, but rather the height of responsibility that is attached to Degrees at various turning points. The turning point of this Degree is in relation to the darker nature of the Great Work, a semblance of which is presented in the Degree material. In the Degree we find a lesson concerning the Mythology of Cadmus, who after roaming and wandering in his personal quest, came upon the Oracle at Delphi. The divinatory message was bizarre and involved following a sacred cow with a moon upon its back (later dedicated to Serene and Hathor) who would lead Cadmus to the land he would eventually inhabit (future Thebes). We see a direct connection between this Greek myth and related imagery from the Egyptian catacombs. But when he sent his crew to the nearby spring before sacrificing the cow, the companions stirred up the seven-headed hydra that protected the spring. Take note that in the Degree are mentioned the seven musical tones, seven colors, and the seven vowels of the Greek language, the latter of which Cadmus is credited with bringing to the people.

Cadmus, like the followers of Martinez de Pasqually, is directed to slay the Dragon. His further instruction is to extract the teeth of the dragon and to plant them. This is Ceremonial Magic of the Highest form. From these plantings spring an army who warred with each other. These are the devils that the Elect Coëns must fight with in order to allow more Light into the earth's Aura[556]. Cadmus must turn and slay this army—all save five, who become his workers and build the city of Cadmia. In the Ceremonial workings of the Élus Coëns, the dark forces are called forth for the specific purpose of slaying them, yet some are revealed to be instructive and may be worked with safely by the thoroughly purified priest.[557] In the same way that T Allen Greenfield suggests ordination into Gnostic Holy Orders for safely working all of the points-chauds empowerments, by the 4th Degree in the Élus Coëns the Initiate receives a form of Ordination.

As the points-chauds of these several Degrees work along the back of the Initiate, we are beginning to explore what Voudon+Gnostics term, *the backside of the Tree of Life*.[558] As the human is fundamentally good and the body is the Temple of the Holy Spirit, the *backside* is not inherently evil; however, darker forces are often summoned in the process of complete reintegration of the whole person. It becomes increasingly important that Initiates receiving

---

[556] The major work of the Elect Coëns occurs on the two principal Feast Days of Memphis-Misraïm, the Feast of the Awakening of Nature (Vernal Equinox) and the Feast of the Renewal of Nature (Autumnal Equinox).

[557] We find this same sort of irony in the work of the *Sacred Magic of Abramelin the Mage*, where after the strenuous and light bearing operation of the Knowledge and Conversation with one's Holy Guardian Angel, the Initiate must call up a host of demonic forces.

[558] See also, the *Nightside of Eden*, by Kenneth Grant.

these Degrees have a dependable and traditional regimen for purification and banishing. The unbalanced soul dabbling with these grades could stir up obsessive and negative energies that can plague the mind and lead to madness. The built-in protections of a three-degree system, with the initial focus upon purification can safeguard the Initiate's journey, but it should be noted that this is ultimately an Ecclesiastical path, and certain functions of the body of light will be limited to those with certain consecrations. Any individual with Episcopal Consecration, or having completed an Operation for invoking the Knowledge & Conversation of the Holy Guardian Angel, should be prepared for the challenges of this Degree.

57th Degree
Sublime Magus

57th *degree*,
Sublime Magus.

Battery of Knocks

Five, five times.   XXXXX XXXXX XXXXX XXXXX XXXXX

Points-chaud

Lower right, back

Sacred Word

SAPHENATH (Spiritual Temple, this is identical to the aforementioned ideal Egyptian Temple, *Karnak*)

Grip

Right hand on each other's heart and look upwards

Sign

Touch forehead, and say, "To thee belongeth;" left shoulder, and say "Glory"; right shoulder, "Power"; stomach, "Wisdom"; heart, "The Kingdom."

Additional Materials

Password–SIGE

Jewel–A sun upon which is the double triangle

† † †

Synopsis

The term, *Magus* can be traced to the Medes and Persians and probably referred to Zoroastrian priests of the 6th Century, BCE. We find two curious bits of instruction with this Degree, but it is in the points-chaud that we discover the mystery of becoming a Magus—the sort that one finds in the second key of the Tarot.

The first portion of instruction returns to the mysteries of plant Alchemy, or spagyrics. This pre-cursor to modern day pharmacology has applications in herbal medicines and remedies as well as in mystical potions and liquid enchantments. Though the use and cultivation of entheogens[559] is certainly related to this science, it is not to be misconstrued by the Initiate that such is the point of plant alchemy, as the proper creation of planetary salts and tinctures becomes sacramental, after a manner, and the ingestion of these holy

---

[559] For most spiritual work with entheogens in the West, it is clear that there are greater risks to the dependency on such than to working in a purist manner. For the traditional shaman the same risks do not apply, but the urban shaman is plagued with so many daily cares, concerns, and stresses, that working with such comes with a host of damaging potentials. Sometimes the Initiate whose inner eye remains closed, can utilize a sacred plant for opening up the Ontic Sphere—but after such, he should consider the advice of Alan Watts concerning psychedelics, "once you get the message, hang up the phone."

medicines can both bring spiritual energies into the body and collate disparate forces within the mind. It is enjoined upon the Initiate who wishes to rightly claim the title of Sublime Magus for himself, to master plant alchemy and take thorough notes concerning the intimate connection between the physical processes and the spiritual realizations aligned with them. As this Degree suggests, the "Key to all allegories [is]-spirit and matter-God in nature."[560]

The second bit of instruction that the Magus will need in his scrying of the point involves the Sign of the Degree, which is a direct teaching of the Kabalistic Cross used by Initiates of many paths. The casual reader may simply find the last few words of the common *Our Father* prayer, but within this prayer is a deep mystery and a powerful sign of protection on the inner planes. Most groups utilize this format and visualize a cross of Light forming upon the body as they make these gestures:

- Vibrate, ATAH (suggesting "Thine") and touch the forehead
- MALKUTH (Kingdom) and touch the genital area
- Ve-GEBURAH (Power) and touch the right shoulder
- Ve-GEDULAH (the Glory) and touch the left shoulder
- Le-OLAM (Forever) and put your hands in the prayer posture at your heart.
- AMEN

The work for this Degree suggests a different pattern which forms an upward triangle upon the body from the forehead to left and right shoulder and back to the heart. This is suggestive of the fiery quality of this Degree and scrying journey. While scrying, it is up to the Initiate to discern which approach is cogent to the experience at hand. For the most powerful protection, the above scaffolding is used. For an invoking of a protective force of a martial nature, the triangular Sign of the Degree is utilized.

---

[560] *Compleat Rite of Memphis*, p. 118, brackets added.

58th Degree

Sage, or Prince Brahmin

Experience of the Trimurti

58th degree,
Sage, or Prince Brahmine.

Battery of Knocks

Seven, seven times. XXXXXXX XXXXXXX XXXXXXX XXXXXXX XXXXXXX XXXXXXX XXXXXXX

Points-chaud

Lower back, center

Sacred Word

AUM

Grip

Fingers clasped, bring palms together and vibrate the Sacred Word again, AUM.

Sign

Clasp fingers and bring back of hand to the brow.

Additional Materials

Password–SIGE

Jewel–A circle within which is a star

† † †

Synopsis

This Degree reflects on the Trinitarian nature of Deity—*Creator, Preserver, Destroyer*—the Trimurti of Hinduism formed of Brahma, Vishnu and Shiva. In Masonic circles, this notion is first introduced in the 32nd Degree, where a statue of the Trimurti reflects these three principles and suggests a creative, supporting and renovating motion of eternal and boundless energy. From this divine center are emanated outward, the various energies and essences that work within nature through the mineral, vegetable and animal kingdoms, constructing the known world. All works for all in one grand harmony. We are as much a part of the cosmos as it is a part of us. The particles and molecules about us can be traced back to the supernova of stars in such a way that it is not at all amiss to say that we are made of stars.

As we near the Degree of *Unknown Philosopher*, less can be spoken of the direct experience of the Initiate, for we are traversing the path of the Gnostic. All must be spoken of in terms of pointers, guide stones—fingers aiming towards the moon, but not the moon itself. We must revert to symbolic language for it is through symbols that we interact with the supersensual. And so, in terms of the Trimurti and this Degree with its accompanying points-chaud empowerment, no path can be traced for the Initiate. This will require the labors and effort of the Initiate herself, armed with the knowledge, skill and experience of the past and awakened by the mindfulness and awareness of the present. As this point is given in a central location on the lower back, the forces will be activated through the Middle Pillar. Take recourse to our 3rd Degree Middle Pillar practice and much may be gleamed from this Degree.

Spirit Builders

59th Degree

Sublime Sage, or Grand Pontiff of Ogygia

Invocation of Chenu

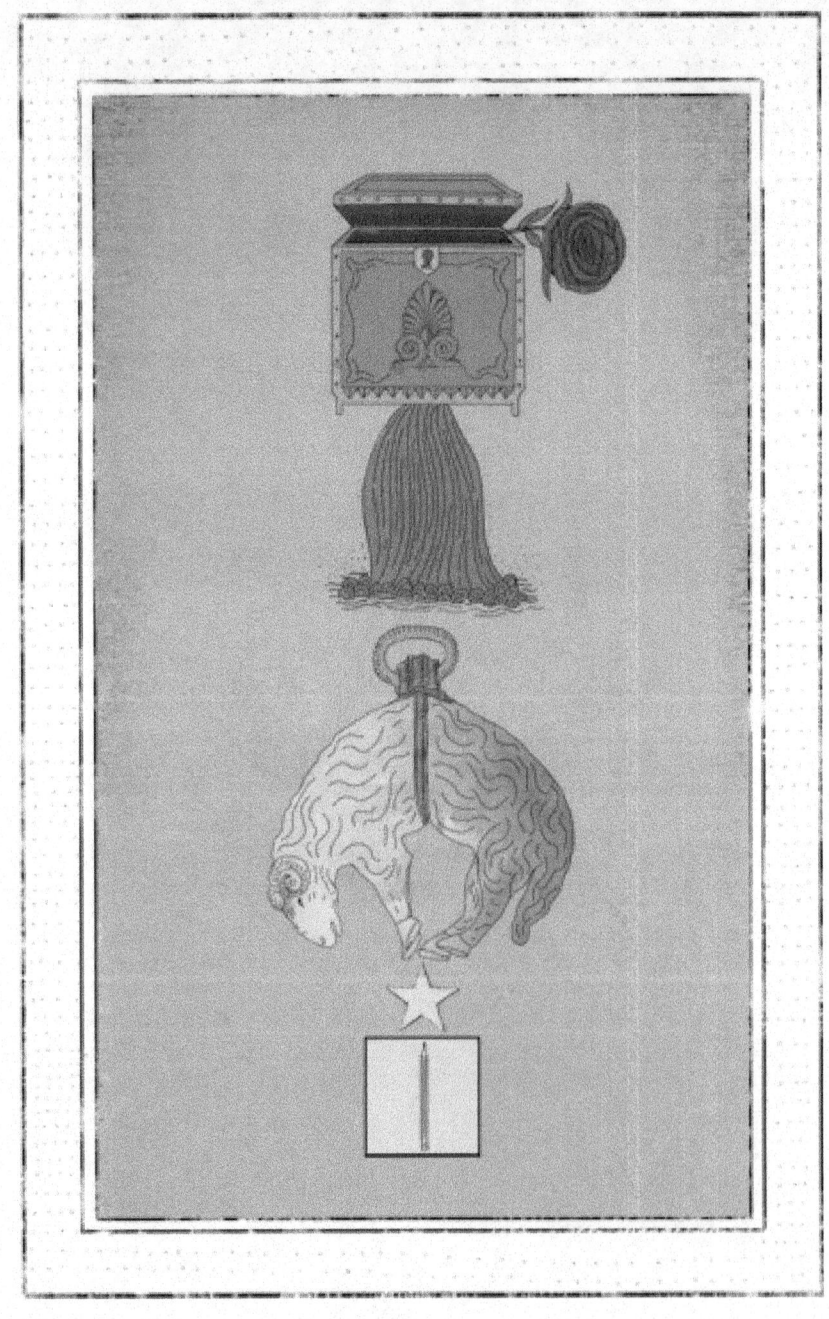

59th *degree*,
Sublime Sage, or Grand Pontiff of Ogygia.

Battery of Knocks

Three equal knocks. X X X

Points-chaud

Lower back, center

Sacred Word

OGYGIA

Grip

Left hand where a sword guard would be, right hand on each other's right shoulder

Sign

Place open right hand below the eyes, thumb erect and forming a square upon the temple.

Additional Materials

Password–SIGE

Jewel–A Square, on which is a pen and above which is a star.

†††

Synopsis

In this grade, we find another Degree concerning personal responsibility before the *Unknown Philosopher* and *Grand Consecrator* Degrees. In our system, the term *Pontiff* means just that…added responsibility. It also suggests that the mystical working of this Degree will require a heavy ascesis[561] if the Initiate hopes to gain entry into all of its mental palaces and rooms. The Initiate's Ontic sphere is caressed into activity with the gnostic pressure tied to this points-chaud empowerment. When this sphere of the magickal imagination opens, multiple paths and journeys are available, each with particular lessons, gifts for the Initiate to partake of, and entities to contact and build relationships with. This Degree takes the Initiate once again into the Grecian mysteries, this time upon the island of Ogygia where

---

[561] Asceticism, the voluntarily giving up of things or abstaining from something pleasurable, is an integral part of Christian mysticism. However, we often find that the sense of morality attached to the thing being given up (smoking, for instance) becomes an excuse for self-congratulations and dismisses the point of ascesis—rooting out the devil of pride. Here is where the Christian ascetic could learn from the mystical text, LIBER III, VEL JVGORVM, by Aleister Crowley. This simple text outlines a method that removes the notion of morality from ascesis, bridging the gap between the pure desert ascesis of the first few centuries of Christianity, and the latter—influenced by Puritanical doctrines and moralism. Not only does LIBER III deliver the Initiate from spiritual pride, but it trains the mind in one-pointedness, by selecting things to give up that are almost random—such as saying the word, "I." The student here trains the mind to not say the word, and gives himself small punishment for every break.

Calypso resides, with four main focal points that show up in differing degrees, no matter which path the Initiate takes during scrying.

1. Again we are reminded of the heavy burdens of the Élus Coëns, established by Martinez de Pasqually in the mid 1700's, which sought to not only bring its Candidates and Initiates into the presence of true essences and even, *La Chose*, the divine Repairer, but who also placed his Initiates into the furnace of qliphotic workings by laboring to remove and cast out the evil principles of the world and to lift the dark aura of demonic activity upon the earth, alleviating the suffering of many. This is symbolized in this Degree by the story of Pandora's Box.

2. The second focal point in this Degree relates to magickal potions and failed magickal arts. This is a lesson in the necessity of prayer and meditation to pierce the Cloud of Unknowing and experience the Beatific Vision. In this exalted form of mysticism, no words, images, or visionary experiences are helpful or sought after, as the *ne plus ultra* is Union.

3. The third focal point involves the use of oaths and sacrifice in spirit working. We see the vacillating nature of the Hermeticist as she moves from exorcism, to pure meditation, to making contracts and swearing oaths to the Hoo and the Doo spirits as well as offering sacrifices (of food, drink, etc.) to the Lwa and Saints. This occurs as surely in the Spirit Vision as it does within the Magic Circle and Oratory.

4. The final focus is upon the Grecian and Egyptian three-fold mythological qualities of human, cosmogonical and spiritual. This is discovered and explored through the art of Alchemy, both in practical and in spiritual terms, and is perfected in the 3rd echelon working of rising through the 16 ÆONs into the Treasury of Lights, via the 87-90°, and 95°.

A marked characteristic of this Degree working upon the Initiate is a strengthening of the Will and a resolve to accomplish the Great Work, complete transmutation. There is a secret invocation that accompanies this grade as well, which is alluded to in this synopsis. It is the invocation of Chenu, the Old Master. Contact can be made with this ancient one through Theurgical means, by calling upon him inwardly, while re-activating the points-chaud empowerment. The spirit of Chenu is nearby when working this Degree, and contact and communion with him is by virtue of attunement[562].

---

[562] p. 11, *Cosmic Meditation*, Michael Bertiaux. For an exploration in the Ordre Martinèsiste de Chenu (OMd'C), see *Lux Occulta*, 2024.

Spirit Builders

60th Degree
Sublime Guardian of the Three Fires

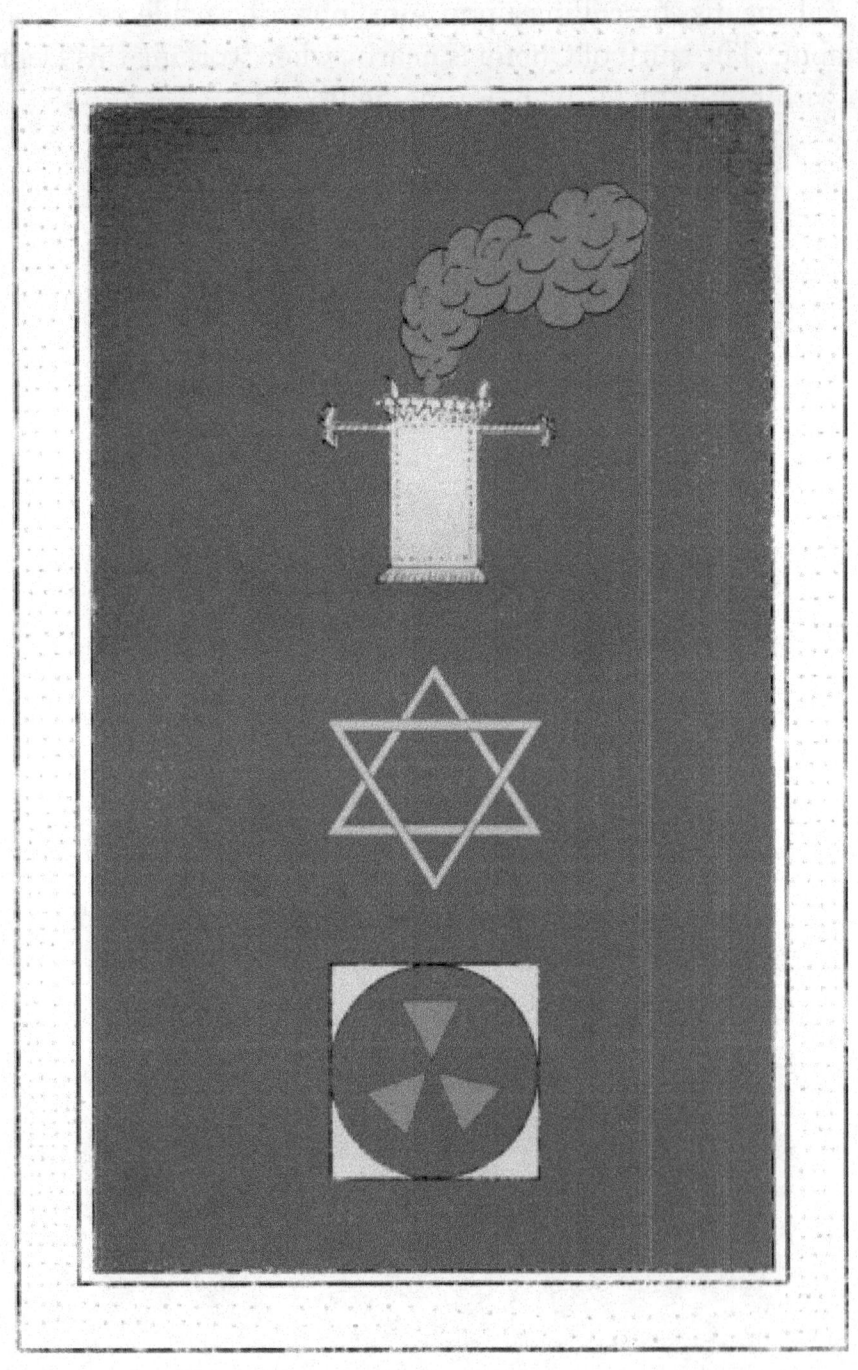

60th *degree,*
Sublime Guardian of the Three Fires.

Battery of Knocks

One, one and one.   X   X   X

Points-chaud

Center lower back

Sacred Word

ISAIC (Relating to Isis)

Grip

Join hands in a friendly way and say, "Be vigilant."

Sign

Join fingers of both hands and raise them above the head.

Additional Materials

Password–SIGE

Jewel–A square containing a circle, with three triangles united at the points.

†††

Synopsis

This Degree is one of the last with the mystical Password, SIGE, which we have seen consecutively since the 49th Degree, with the exception of the 50th. This creates eleven Degrees of *Silence*, leading up to the *Sublime Unknown Philosopher* Degree. The Degrees as Yarker and Marconis compiled them are often self-referential when it comes to word meanings. In the work, SIGE is said to mean, *silence*. Etymologically, sige would be Proto-Germanic and refer to victory and triumph. As we consider that eleven is the number of magick, and the word can both suggest silence and triumph, we begin to feel a sense of completion and success with this Degree, if worked chronologically. This is due to the fact that this is the first Degree to specifically call upon an Egyptian god, whose presence is most acutely felt and perceived with the aligned points-chaud empowerment along the base of the spine. The Initiate is now purified enough for this august order of Higher beings.

A string of correspondences are made with the point empowerment of this Degree, the gesture of the hand that is giving the point and the goddess, Isis. Firstly, we return to the procedure of giving the points and the position of the thumb between the index finger and the medius~

This is the figa hand gesture, anciently used in Rome to ward off evil spirits and the evil eye. Even prior to this it was used as a fertility gesture in reference to Astarte. Some of the oldest versions are in ivory from around 8,000 years ago. There are Russian versions of the same gesture that have sexual connotations both of the male penis and the female clitoris. The German folk use of the same amulet is for good fortune. Our gesture and method of awakening the points within the body works in these three capacities; as a banishing of evil in or around the hot point, as stimulating of the powerful magickal currents within the body that are often associated with sexual energy in the manner of the Taoist sages of sexual alchemy and their "Golden Light Body[563]," and as an amulet to bring the good fortune of awakening the hot point and its corresponding energies and entities. Finally, this gesture is also employed during Episcopal Consecrations where a powerful transfer of energy and light is required, such as when the priest's hands are anointed by this gesture.[564] Leadbeater instructs us that this gesture is utilized during a *pugnal pass* in Mesmerism, as well as for opening certain centres during Consecration, Baptism and Confirmation. Those familiar with Crowley's Gnostic Mass will recognize the gesture in that context as well.

The relationship with Isis and this gesture is twofold. First, Isis and Astarte are often conflated; we see the two goddesses both being summoned in fertility rites and both being related to the moon. Secondly, the mystical *knot of Isis* has visual similarities with the figa hand as well as consistent suggested meanings.

The knot of Isis was often used as a funerary amulet. Though its specific meanings are unknown, it is referred to as the *blood of Isis* in several places throughout history, and many reference it to the 186th Chapter of the Egyptian Book of the Dead. This blood of Isis refers to the menstrual fluids and the banishing and protecting nature of these fluids when used in Egyptian talismanic magic. Menstrual blood, for Alchemists, was symbolic of the gold

---

[563] In the cosmic working of our Rites, we labor to create the fully integrated AKH which is a form of Osirification and accomplished on the Awakening of Nature, or Vernal Equinox.
[564] See Leadbeater's, *Science of the Sacraments*, p. 132.

transmuting solvent, the menstruum. They believed that this was the grand secret to life[565], transmuting sperm to embryo. We find the very nature of the point empowerment relating to all of the energies of Isis Magic and transmuting the science and art of Egyptian Masonry in one single hand gesture.

In the Degree notes we find more clues to the High Magic and the nature of the entities and energies allied with this grade. The *Three Fires*[566], relate to the tripartite nature of humans—body, soul and spirit, which are all effected by this Degree. Further we find the nature of fire as the electric and diaphanous, *Translucid* or Astral plane. When the Initiate is purified by the regenerating fires of our occult science, the veil of the Translucid is rent and the "rays of Adamic force, confounding human reason, and humiliating before the power of God...a phenomena of the Prophetic Order[567]" rains down upon the Initiate and the *Scintillating body* is born in the *Mystic Temple*. Herein is opened, the "forgotten intelligence of the world of light and truth[568]" and the finite Initiate is joined with the Infinite.

---

[565] The very same conclusion is made with Kenneth Grant concerning the sacred kalas found in the secretions (secret-ions) of the female during menstruation.
[566] See p. 411 in Sympatheia (2023), to explore an esoteric Stoic understanding and history of the "three fires" or triple flame.
[567] *Compleat Rite of Memphis*, p. 120.
[568] Ibid.

61st Degree
Sublime Unknown Philosopher
Call to Louis-Claude de St. Martin

61th *degree*,
Sublime Unknown Philosopher.

"There have always been Spirit-Guides in the universe and each person should try to have one. My own may be Louis-Claude de Saint Martin…Saint Martin is teaching transcendental ontology and ontologism to other spirit beings, and they are teaching me."

Michael-Paul Bertiaux[569]

Battery of Knocks

Six, twelve times[570]. XXXXXX XXXXXX XXXXXX XXXXXX XXXXXX XXXXXX XXXXXX XXXXXX XXXXXX XXXXXX XXXXXX XXXXX

The Initiation of *philosophe inconnu*

The Facilitator stands in front of the Initiate after the Battery of Knocks and looks into the eyes of the Initiate intently. Then, closing the eyes, the Facilitator lays his hands[571] upon the head of the Initiate, right thumb laced over left thumb and index finger to index finger--creating a fire triangle–and blows three times on the head within this geometrical figure.

Points-chaud

Lower back, right

Sacred Word

The Pentagrammaton, **YHSHVH**[572], pronounced, Yeh,Heh,Shu,Vah

Grip

Join the insides of left foot, knees touching.

Sign

Carry the three fingers of the right hand to the mouth

Additional Materials

Password–CHEMIA

Jewel–A delta upon which is a branch having six leaves on each side.

† † †

---

[569] p. 33, *Cosmic Meditation*
[570] Here, the "twelve" represents not only the Zodiacal potencies, but the twelve disciples of Christ as a presence.
[571] "The Initiation TRANSITTED by Saint-Martin to his disciples <u>was not simply a ceremony consisting of giving out signs, words and grips</u>. It was not even the saying of a consecrating formula with imposition of marks made by a sword or a mallet. <u>It was more particularly the transmission of a spiritual influence by a word, a breath and the imposition of hands, such as the Initiator himself received.</u>" From the private Martinist papers of the author, for the Degree of Superieur Inconnu.
[572] This Sacred Word holds within it all four elements, with the addition of spirit—composing a complete and harmonious whole. It is the unutterable Tetragrammaton of the Old Testament, with the decent of the dove (the letter, Shin) in the center. This Word is used in mantric prayer while working this Grade.

Synopsis

This Degree, in sum, has little or nothing to do with the scant materials presented by Marconis and Yarker. It is, in truth, the most *mystical*[573] thus far of the entire Series and presents the Initiate with the principle means of carrying on our Sacred Tradition unto the Ages. This Degree is the primitive and pre-Papus Martinism of Louis Claude de St. Martin & Jacob Boehme[574]. In his St. Martin's own words, this is THE INITIATION and it consists of pure mystery.

> *INITIATION! Extraordinary, power of the Divine Afflatus which radiates from the hands, creates Priest or Adept and communicates the understanding and potential possession of the Sciences! Magical virtue situated on the extreme borderline of the natural and supernatural! Miraculous and impalpable agent that is given without dividing, that passes from person to person without losingits potency and preserves intact its action which remains infallible, but which develops its full power only in the mind ready to nurture it! Subtle current of avital fluid which animates the member of the spiritual body*[575]*!*

In essence, this is the nature of our entire spiritual edifice. We are *transmission* centric in many ways. Our mysteries cannot be attained only through dreams or via mail. These Degrees cannot be simply "communicated" by virtue of past labors or translated to another in honorary fashion. The points-chaud empowerments *require* person to person, physical transmission from one set of hands to another's body. Along with this transmission, in this Degree we begin the INNER WAY, which is only perfected in the final Series of Degrees, 91-97th.

But in particular, this Degree is a summation of our approach. As St. Martin says, the Initiation is *potential* and could create Priests and Adepts, cause miraculous occurrences, and thrust the Initiate into the subtle currents of the diaphanous regions. Martinist Orders the world over practice a set of three Degrees, but all will admit to their being only ONE Initiation, that of the S∴I∴. These practice the work developed and disseminated by Gerard Encausse, otherwise known as Papus, who gave to the Initiation a Masonic scaffolding,

---

[573] While this Degree is at this stage the most "mystical" of this Series, we must keep in mind that Memphis+Misraim comprises the whole of the Western Esoteric Tradition, and therefore is mystical *and* magickal.

[574] In a private letter from Michael Bertiaux on the subject, he says, "The genius of L.C. St Martin was to have a special mysticism (rather close to Quakerism than to High Mass at the Vatican, etc.). However, those who had been entrusted with Martinism in the 19th Century thought otherwise." Bertiaux here is suggesting a hearkening back to the purist ideals of Martinism, the "initiation of Jacob Boehme" as he calls it. He goes on further to say that "original Martinism, as taught by L.C. (on a one-to-one basis and never in groups) was Boehmism in the esoteric garb of Quietism."

[575] The words of Louis Claude de St. Martin, from private Martinist papers.

much like we are doing with our work as *Spirit Builders*. But the Initiation itself is one, immutable and irrevocable. Cagliostro was of the same school, as we find in his Egyptian Freemasonry the practice of breathing upon the Candidate in every Degree. In our own praxis, the 3rd Degree outlined in Book Two utilizes the very same *Divine Afflatus* and is brought full circle in this 61st Degree.

It is true, however, that the Initiation does not always take for every person. Is it then a wasted energy upon the ethers, is it null and vacuous and of no purpose whatsoever? Let us listen again to the words of the original *philosophe inconnu*, Louis Claude de St. Martin,

> *IF the Power of Initiation does not give visible results, it nevertheless works infallibly as a preventative and prepares the shell of him who remains pure to receive salutary impressions when the Spirit deems it advisable.*[576] And so the Facilitator must not over concern herself with the Initation's taking or not, as it will accomplish the Will of the Grand Initiator in a way most mysterious.

Our Battery of Knocks for this Degree relates directly to the spiritual experience that accompanies this singular Initiation. It is the number six[577] repeated twelve times, which far from being an evil number relates to the Sun and to Tiphareth on the Tree of Life. It is repeated twelve times to represent a state of completion through the twelve signs of the Zodiac. Six, on the Tree of Life, is in the place of the heart and if this Degree is an entry point to anything of purpose it is an entry point to the *Way of the Heart*[578]. Such a cardiac path is not only for the audacious who would storm the Temple, nor is it only for the seeker of presentiments and visual delights, as this is the way of mysticism.

The experience of Tiphareth is the Beatific Vision, it is the vision of the harmony of all things and the mysteries of the death and resurrection of Christ. Access to this divine realm affords the Initiate what Dion Fortune, in her book, *The Mystical Qabalah* calls, "Devotion to the Great Work" which we know to be the complete transmutation of the rough ashlar of the *Man of the Stream* to the perfect ashlar of the human that has gained full mastery of himself and returned to his primitive simplicity and unity with the All. This is the Path of Re-integration.

---

[576] Louis Claude de St. Martin, private papers of the author.
[577] It is of note that the Martinist symbol is a six-sided figure with the six-pointed star within it.
[578] See the essay of the same name by Papus that concludes with these words of wisdom, "There is nothing easier and nothing harder than to follow this path. It is open to all men of goodwill and no other man is worthy of it."

The points-chaud of this Degree, on the lower right backside should be prefaced by the simple instruction given after the Battery of Knocks. This action is vital for the transmission to be complete and is one of the few that deviate from our extraordinarily economical working. It is completely appropriate to confer this Degree alongside Holy Orders, should the Initiate be drawn to the Mysteries in such a manner. This is not the Degree that works with the energies of Episcopal Consecration, however, as that is relegated to the 66th.

62nd Degree
Sublime Sage of Eleusis

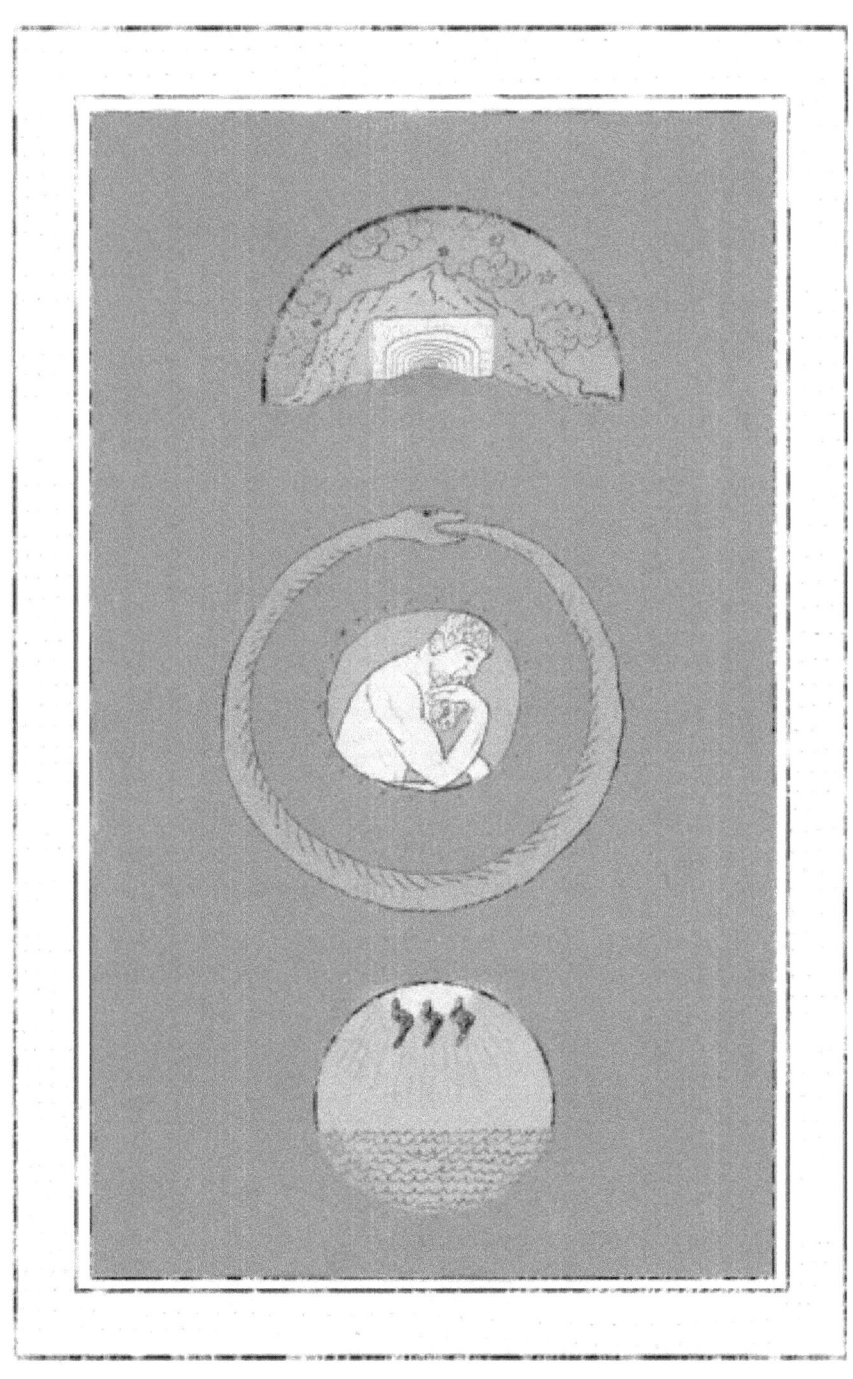

62nd degree,
Sublime Sage of Eleusis.

Battery of Knocks

Four, four times; and three, three times.   XXXX XXXX XXXX XXXX   XXX XXX XXX

Points-chaud

Lower right back, above buttocks.

Sacred Word

ELEUSIS, answer, KONX OM PAX[579]

Grip

Join the inside of the right feet and let the knees touch

Sign

Look up to heaven, then downward to earth.

Additional Materials

Password–SIGE (the Initiate returns to Silence for this sacred scrying session)

Jewel–A Sun on which are three yods[580]

Oath–The Dweller on the Threshold may ask of the Initiate an Oath. This may be composed by the Initiate, or the Oath from the Degree work can be used.

> *I_____, do solemnly declare that in seeking advancement here, I am actuated by no unworthy motive, and I sacredly pledge myself to keep inviolably secret, from the whole world, the mysteries of or belonging to this Degree, should the Hierophant (Dweller) see fit to entrust me with the same, and may the Great Dispenser of Life and Light deal with me as I keep my pledge.*

†††

---

[579] Familiar to many initiates, yet the actual meaning is unknown. MacGregor Mathers attributed its meaning to the Egyptian, *Khabs Am Pecht*, while others have suggested various meanings and sources, including Atlantean origin.

[580] This is a continuing reference to the Holy letter, Shin ש

Synopsis

The Sublime Sage of Eleusis is a Gnostic Degree. Following the veritable *ordination* of the 61st Degree, this Grade reveals the mystery of the Word, the Logos, which is born within the Mind[581] as the Divine Poimandres of Hermes suggests. This creative Word is discovered to have been present always and to have not undergone any disintegration over time. As the Degree says, "Mind, first matter and space, quantity of matter always the same" which is to say that this Word is both married to the concepts of mind (nous), the prima materia, the Void and the very particles that compose our reality. Scientists teach that the particles that are present in our world have been here since the birth of our galaxy and beyond, and that it was the explosion of a star that produced the nebula that was the womb of our galaxy and thousands of stars and solar systems.

This Word is deeply Incarnational. Often in Gnostic literature we find the notion of the body and the earth as a prison, and such is the case for those who lack integration. But the prison is our very sense of separateness, what the Vedantists call *Maya*, or the *illusion of separateness.* **We must not confuse *Incarnation* with *incarceration*.** It is a miracle that the spirit moves the flesh and that the two are so commingled that no division can be found. We should find that we are present in the garden of delights already, had we the cleansed perception of the mystics. This Word is within us, it IS us. It is a glorious thing to have "put on flesh" and incarnated to this present state. This Degree reveals the inner Word[582] which will come to us and offer counsel, the same way as the dragon[583] came to Hermes. In this encounter we find that Mind is a continuum and is eternal and is linked to a sort of prima material—the Word—which is all mixed up in matter. This is the divinizing and sacralizing of the ordinary and the mundane. It is the lifting of the Initiate out of the quagmire of everydayness and into the Holy City of mindfulness. The Word has the power to both *raise* the Initiate to new heights and to *exalt* the Initiate into the realms of living truth.

This Degree enters into the mysteries of Eleusis as well. We find the Work advancing the Candidate upon a journey with a necessary lustration, an oath and a sacred touch. The lustration is indicative of the Initiate's constant need of Purification, the oath is for the spirit realm only, and the sacred touch is a pointer to our efficient system of points chauds empowerments. The second section of the Degree is rather Christian in scope and continues the principle ideas of the Eleusinian initiation with reference to the transformative text of the New Testament, the Book of Revelations. This mystical book of twenty-two chapters (Kabalists and Tarot practitioners will recognize the significance of this number, as will

---

[581] In this sense, Mind is used to represent *Nous* which comprises the mind and the intuition on a very deep level. In Eastern Orthodoxy it signifies the mind of the heart, an additional *organ*, as it were, which comprises the soul and makes it intelligible in a super-sensual way.

[582] This Word, may in fact be a NAME. Those who receive gnosis, receive a "certain name" according to the *Gospel of Truth*, from *The Other Bible*, p. 292.

[583] This dragon, Pymander or more correctly, Poimandres, is further identified as *Agathos Daimon* in Book 12:1, *Hermes to Tat*. This "shadowy divinity" shares qualities with the dragon of the Typhonian tradition as well. See, *The Way of Hermes*, 2000, Salaman, Oyen, Wharton, & Mahe, pgs. 58 and 79.

Martinists who practice the Divine Names) is suggested study for this Degree as it is initiatory in scope and opens many doors within the Ontic Sphere.[584]

As the Eleusinian Initiations were split into the Lesser and the Greater Mysteries, it is important to note that the scrying of this point will yield results in both respects. Mention is made in the Degree to the *Dweller on the Threshold*[585]. In the materials, it is the Candidate who takes this role, however in scrying, the Dweller is a very powerful entity that the Initiate will meet. As a suggestion for protection, the Initiate should build up a powerful spirit structure from which to meet the Dweller in safety in the beginning. We find Wilmshurst speaking of this spirit structure which he says "must be perfect in all its parts and so be honorable to the builder.[586]" This structure built up from psychic energy and fed by the Ontic Sphere of the Initiate will envelop the body in a way that will be clear upon meditation. In short, it is a fully constructed *spiritual body* "capable of functioning in the 'air' or more tenuous and ethereal worlds.[587]" This body is perfected in the cosmic working of the 3rd echelon, as the holy AKH.

The mystical phrase, KONX OM PAX will be familiar to many Hermetic students. Though it is a Greek phrase that does not cleanly translate in that language, it has long carried with it the twin notions of *Light in Extension* and *Light rushing out in a single Ray*. It is to the latter that the Initiate is directed as the Word, which is also Light, may be immediately experienced in the rushing of a single ray throughout the body during the points-chaud empowerment.

---

[584] For further exploration of working the Book of Revelations as an initiatory path, see the forthcoming, *Revelations on the Tree of Life*, by +Palamas.
[585] Also identified with *Agathos Daimon*, Poimandres himself.
[586] *The Masonic Initiation*, Wilmshurst, p. 65.
[587] *The Masonic Initiation*, Wilmshurst, p. 63.

63rd Degree
Sublime Kawi

Battery of Knocks

Three equal knocks for the three paths to bliss—Liberty, Equality, and Fraternity.

X X X

Points-chaud

Lower left back

Sacred Word

KRISHNA

Grip

Upon a magical book, join open hands, one on the other

Sign

Touch the forehead, lips and heart with the right hand

Additional Materials

Password–SIGE

Jewel–A delta with a central point

† † †

Synopsis

This Degree is not specifically Hermetic, Gnostic or Kabalistic; it is devotional. The object of the Initiate's devotion in this Degree is her very own Genius. In many occult circles it is thought that each Mage has an attending Genius. This Genius is typically syncretized with one's Holy Guardian Angel, of which we will deal more in the *Arcana Arcanorum*. The Initiate can show devotion to her highest Self in a variety of ways, but this Degree specifically points to creativity and its role in the gnostic unfoldment of the true Self, for "the Gnostic artist is a conduit for angelic creativity.[588]"

Kawi means a poet. Yarker makes the correspondence with the Kawi and the Bards of Druidic lore. The points-chaud empowerment in the lower left back has the tendency to stimulate the Gnostic Artist into activity. Regardless of the medium selected by the Initiate, a drawing near to various Fine Arts accompanies this Degree.

---

[588] *Syzygy*, p. 37.

The more the Initiate mingles with the Divine, the more she will feel compelled to create something in response to such mystic embraces.

It is for the Initiate to probe and research what particular form of expression is her soul's necessity and in what manner it will show devotion to her Genius. Through study and meditation, scrying the point and experimentation, the Initiate of this Degree will discover the particular means to reveal the diaphanous to the world and show honor and praise to her Genius.

Spirit Builders

64th Degree

Sage of Mithras

Call to Mithras & Ormuzd

64th *degree,* Sage of Mythras.

Battery of Knocks

Seven, seven times   XXXXXXX   XXXXXXX   XXXXXXX   XXXXXXX   XXXXXXX   XXXXXXX   XXXXXXX

Points-chaud

Lower left back

Sacred Word

LAO-TZU

Grip

Join left hands, release them, join the right

Sign

Place right hand upon the heart, then look to right, to left, and raise right hand and the eyes to heaven.

Additional Materials

Password–SIGE

Jewel–A delta, in the middle of which is a parallelogram with seven points.

Practice–Pranayamic breathing and mantric chant. I-A-O[589] is an appropriate mantra for this Degree.

Proclamation–To be used as a "call" to Mithras and to Ormuzd:

> *To the Glory of The Supreme Architect of the Universe, and in the name of the Greatly Honored Sublime Master of Light, I proclaim, for the present and for always, myself to be a Member of the Grand Consistory of Sages of Mithras and a Thrice Illustrious Brother/Sister and request the spirits and guides to recognize me as such in this capacity and to aid and protect me in my further Initiations.*

Then give the Sign and the Battery of Knocks.

† † †

---

[589] We find this name sacred in many Gnostic texts, and amongst various Gnostic sects. The Valentinians used it as a divine name, as well as the Sethian author of the *Coptic Gospel of the Egyptians*. In the latter, we have a powerful chant of the vowels of I-A-O.

Synopsis

This Gnostic Degree is highly detailed with many significant events, yet one single lesson and aim is contained within the work—that of the *Regeneration of Man*. The important title of *Child of Earth and of the Star-filled Heavens*, bestowed upon all practitioners of this grade, is a clue to the Primitive Doctrine and the method of regeneration that this Degree stimulates within the body. Rather than point to a life of pure spirit, our working directs its Initiates to the various envelopes of reality about us and within us. These layers interpenetrate each other as never ending centers of depth. The points-chaud empowerment ignites the spiritual circuitry within the psycho-physiological being that opens countless doors to Otherwhere, each of which contains its own landscapes, entities, and natural laws. The only way for the Initiate to fully experience the Gnostic Regeneration of these Degrees is by being grounded as a "child of earth," knowing full well that this earth and our bodies are blessed and Holy, and by exploring the realm of the spirits, being born of the "star-filled heavens." The Regeneration is a bathing in light, creating the *scintillating body*, and a divinization of our Ontic Spheres, birthing the *Mystic Temple* upon the ethers. On this plane, the effects noticed by others include a lightness and deep sincerity of purpose, a specialized and heightened intuition, healing powers, profound mindfulness and awareness, and a specific mission to make the world a better place through service to others.[590]

This Degree is a treat for the Masonic student who is not familiar with Memphis+Misraïm. It is a fully worked grade based upon historic documents revealed in the late 1800's. Upon investigation it becomes clear that the Mithraic Mysteries were some of the most profound Initiations found on the globe and that we have inherited *much* in terms of worship, liturgy, initiatory rites and the like, here in the West and in the religion of Christianity in particular. A careful reading and study of both this Degree work and the Mithraic papyri are suggested for the Initiate of this grade as even the simple act of reading some of the liturgical work (with special emphasis on the "barbarous words" with heavy vowels) is initiatory in the pathworking sense.

We find in these mysteries and in this Degree, the source of the cave of birth on December 25th, the notion of the lion and the serpent conjoined, the source for the use of the mirror in our workings, an early Eucharistic Liturgy, the use of pranayama and sacred "breathings," notions concerning rehabilitation and reintegration into our primitive estate, the triumph of light over darkness, the sanctuary of spirits (Ontic Sphere) and the reward of new life from our Celestial labors. It would seem highly incongruous that the Sacred Word of this Degree would be Lao-Tzu, the great Chinese sage, but we must recall that his name means, "old boy." Our Regeneration is of this nature and brings us back to the pristine simplicity of the Ancients, which Taoism and Lao-Tzu, in particular, elucidate even to this day[591].

---

[590] See the extention of this degree in Lux Occulta, pp. 208-223.

[591] "After all these came also the little children, those who possess the knowledge of the Father," *The Gospel of Truth*, from *The Other Bible*.

The receiver of this Degree and its accompanying points-chaud empowerment can expect an onslaught of subsequent Initiations during scrying and in dreamtime. This Degree has the tendency to try the Initiate by all of the planets in one sitting, which can be both strenuous and invigorating. The practitioner of this grade should spend as much time in Pranayamic breathing and mantric prayer as possible to get the highest yields from this mystical, Gnostic school of Initiation. I-A-O is suggested here as the Divine Name to use to invoke the electrifying presence that will stimulate these initiations.

It is also of the utmost importance that the Initiate proclaim his grade when scrying this point and Degree. The *Proclamation* is found after the Jewel description. The same style proclamation can be used at any time during subsequent initiatory dreams or scryings, where the entities demand of the Initiate more proof of advancement. Simply change the wording to fit the Degree title and use the appropriate Signs and Batteries of Knocks.

65th Degree

Guardian of Sanctuary, Grand Installator

Opening the Brass Vessel of 72 Spirits

65th *degree,*
Guardian of Sanctuary - Grand Installator.

Battery of Knocks

Three, three times.   XXX   XXX   XXX

Points-chaud

Left waist, back

Sacred Word

PTAH

Grip

The first, or man's grip, symbol of reason (the EA grip). When this Grip is given to seal in the hot point, the Facilitator should perform a visualization of the human face of the Sphinx. The Facilitator may sense the brass vessel within the body of the Initiate while locating the point. It is crucial that the Grip be given swiftly so that the Initiate is in control of how and when the Goetic energies and entities are brought to light.[592]

Sign

Place the right hand on the heart, raise the eyes to heaven, carry hand to pocket area of shirt and then extend horizontally. This gesture implies, Faith, Hope and Charity.

Additional Materials

Password–SIGE

Jewel–Winged egg, three circles within a triangle

† † †

Synopsis

In Mainstream Masonry, ceremonies of *Installation* are full of pomp and circumstance and are often open to the public. These are practical grades that move individuals up through the lines of Deacons, Wardens, Masters and Grand Officers. In some Orients and Grand Lodges, the Mason spends a number of years working his way up to the highest office of Worshipful Master of the local Lodge, yet in others, the offices are appointed based solely upon merit. Still, in others, particular offices are *ad vitam*, for life. All of these are a colorful and significant part of the history and practice of regular Freemasonry all across the globe, but what have such to do with spiritual Freemasonry, with *spirit building*?

After so many mystical Degrees, including the highly spiritual grade of *Unknown Philosopher*, and before the Degree of *Grand Consecrator*, which, for all intents and purposes completes the

---

[592] This relates to the notion of *Benedicamus*, in *Syzygy*, 2013.

61st Degree, the Initiate might find it strange to discover yet another reference to Ceremonial Magic here in this formal working. It is to Goetia in particular, that this Degree directs the Initiate and the reasons are direct and simple.

The points-chaud empowerment of this Degree upon the back along the left waist, when activated with the Sacred Word of Ancient Egypt, PTAH, stimulates currents within the Initiate that can, with a directed will and fine tuned Ontic Sphere, open the brass vessel of King Solomon and release the 72 spirits of the Goetia for the service of the Initiate.

The way that this works is that it is the *body itself* that is the brass vessel of Solomon, and the proper locating of this points-chaud, with the vibrated word of the Egyptian Demiurge, PTAH (builder), is the method of opening the vessel and thereby creating a line of communication with the 72 spirits. A careful reading of Crowley's introduction to the *Goetia* gives a hint to the nature of the spirits being within as he artfully skirts around admitting to the *separate* and independent existence of these spirits in the external world. We find him saying, "I am not concerned to deny the objective reality of all 'magical' phenomena; if they are illusions, they are at least as real as many unquestioned facts of daily life.[593]" Crowley continues even more sternly, saying, "The spirits of the Goetia are portions of the human brain.[594]" The portion of the brain in which they reside is our subconscious. It is here that the point empowerment comes in, for the gentle gnostic pressure of this Degree, precisely located upon the waist, awakens the slumbering consciousness and vivifies the magickal beings into form. The nature of the Sacred Word should be evident, as it is the *Initiate himself* who becomes the great fashioner, the Demiurge of his own Universe, as he births forth the spirits of the Goetia from his own body and substance. What he must not do, is fall prey to the same power play and despotism that the Demiurge of Classical Gnosticism, IALDABAOTH did. For being the Architect of oneself is a sacred injunction and is due

---

[593] Crowley, *The Initiated Interpretation of Ceremonial Magic*, from *The Goetia, the Lesser Key of Solomon the King*, 1995, p. 15.
[594] *Ibid*, p. 17.

preparation for vocation into Holy Orders, which require humility and psychological balance.

The direct relationship with this Degree is further cemented by the concept of Installing Officers. The 72 spirits of the Goetia become working partners for the Initiate, yet they must be installed into their proper office and given their proper role in relation to the life of the Mage. The Jewel worn during scrying the point is a winged egg—the KNEPH, a reoccurring emblem in our Memphis+Misraïm rituals, with three circles within a triangle in the center. Some meditation upon the possible meanings of this symbol in relation to Solomon's vessel and our Goetic spirits within the body is cogent to the further research and exploration of this Degree. Much can be gleamed from book study, but the meditative and receptive mind, made supple through pranayama and mantric prayer, will discover the inner meanings of our Degrees.

Spirit Builders

66th Degree

Grand Architect of the Mysterious City / Patriarch Grand Consecrator

Episcopal Consecration

66th *degree,*
Grand Architect of the
Mysterious City — Grand Consecrator.

Battery of Knocks

Three, three times. XXX   XXX   XXX

Points-chauds

This point balances the last. Directly across from the 65th Degree point, right lower back of the waist.

Sacred Word

Ye-Ho-Ha (or AUM)

Grip

The second (Fellowcraft) or Eagle's grip, symbol of prevision and intelligence. While sealing the point, the Facilitator visualizes the wings of the Sphinx.

If performing actual Episcopal Consecration, begin traditional Liturgical working here and give further instructions concerning the other qualities of the grade after the Ceremony. The work should be followed by a mystic repast or interpolate the work entirely within the Mass as demonstrated in the Appendix. Do not forget to utilize the figa hand gesture in anointing the hands of the one being Consecrated.

Sign

Uplift both hands as in invocation and then lower them by three equal acts, inhaling and exhaling mentally a breath. Say the Sacred Word at the same time.

Additional Materials

Password—KNEPH

Jewel—Winged egg, on which is a circle, within which are three stars, 1 and 2.

Synopsis

There are many beautiful passages from the texts discovered in Egypt in the city of Nag Hammadi. One of the more complete texts which, though not of great length, carries on the literary ideal of Gnosis, is the mystical piece called, Thunder, Perfect Mind. This selection was read during my own Episcopal Consecration on Arabia Mountain in 2012:

THUNDER, FLASH, ILLUMINATE, I DECLARE YOU ILLUMINATUS

Initiator anoints forehead and continues:

I was sent forth from the power,
and I have come to those who reflect upon me,
and I have been found among those who seek after me.
Look upon me, you who reflect upon me,
and you hearers, hear me.

You who are waiting for me, take me to yourselves.
And do not banish me from your sight.

And do not make your voice hate me, nor your hearing.
Do not be ignorant of me anywhere or any time. Be on your guard!

Do not be ignorant of me.
For I am the one who alone exists,
and I have no one who will judge me.

For many are the pleasant forms which exist in numerous sins,
and incontinences,
and disgraceful passions,
and fleeting pleasures,
which (men) embrace until they become sober.

And so we come to the Patriarch Grand Consecrator Degree and its holy placement in this series of mysterious and Hermetic grades. As a complement to the work undertaken in the 61st Degree of Unknown Philosopher, this degree functions, more or less, as a virtual Consecration. No individual working this grade is given immediate Episcopal powers in any of the varied Gnostic Churches; however, the seed and germ of such an Office may be planted and cultivated with this degree, and the alignment of this degree with such a consecration (for those who are called to Holy Orders) is a powerful and potent experience. Other recipients of the grade will experience resonation and relationship with the Passed Masters which far surpasses the vague impressions of these Holy Ones in previous workings. And still others, who have already received the orders of Subdeacon, Deacon, Exorcist (among other Minor Orders practiced by some which include Cleric, Porter, etc.) and the Priesthood, will see this opportunity as the moment for consideration of Episcopal Consecration.

I happened to receive this point and my initial Consecration on the same day upon the Holy Arabia Mountain, and so can attest to the wisdom, strength and beauty of such an august alignment. There is nothing to compare with this arrangement and no words would suffice to describe it. Such would be putting legs on a snake.

How then, does this degree with its accompanying point, act as a virtual Consecration for the typical Spirit Builder? It is in essence, the same concept as the "Past Master" Degree worked in American Lodges. Once upon a time, it was required of Masons to have sat in the East as a Master of the Lodge before he could move up into the Higher Degrees of the York Rite, the Holy Royal Arch in particular. All Worshipful Masters receive the Degree of "Past Master." As the York Rite grew in popularity, the requirement of being an actual Past Master of a Lodge was lifted and a degree that was considered a virtual Past Master was introduced into the line-up of grades. Though a simple ceremony, many find the degree of Past Master to easily slip into a pathworking state where they literally receive the essence of the degree, even in such a virtual modality. Such is not an entitlement; it is an attunement to the nature of the work.

For the Patriarch Grand Consecrator degree, we simply have to take note of the Secret Work to realize its deep connection with Episcopal Consecration. In the work it says that the Sign is made by uplifting both hands as in invocation and then lowering them by three equal acts, inhaling and exhaling mentally a breath while saying, Ye-Ho-Ha. Additionally, our Password is KNEPH, which among other things means the Spirit or breath. We also have the Battery of Knocks being three, three times. Finally, the Jewel is the winged egg with a circle and three stars within it—one over two.

For all Episcopal Consecrations, there are at least three Bishops attending the ceremony. There is one Principal Consecrator and two attending Bishops who also lay hands upon the Neophyte of this Order. We see this arrangement in the stars within the Jewel of the degree. The circle around the stars is the accompanying spiritual intelligences witnessing the administration. We find in Episcopal Consecrations the twin means of passing on the spiritual transmission and the Apostolic succession via the laying on of hands and (at least in Gnostic circles) the divine breath. There is also a moment when the Principal Consecrator has his hands over the Candidate while saying a prayer. It is in this moment that Consecrators in our line take the mudra of the ancient High Priesthoods of Israel, which continues the mysterious line of Melchizedek. This Holy hand posture figures the fiery Hebrew letter of the spirit, shin, which resembles the symbol of the dove descending. Finally, before investing the future Bishop with the regalia of this Order, which includes the Miter (from the previously mentioned, Mithras), the Pastoral Staff, and the ring, we find the Consecrator anointing the Candidate with the Holy chrism. This act is directly related to the fire of the Holy Spirit and its further descent into the heart of the Candidate.

In Conclusion, when this degree takes, the Initiate will experience a compounding effect. In one manner, she will feel an added responsibility and call to service towards others. This is the pastoral nature of Consecration settling into the body, mind, and spirit of the Initiate. Another effect will be the sensing of the down pouring (epiclesis) of Holy Spirit that accompanies Consecration. It is crucial that the distinction be made between the Holy Spirit and spirits here, as this degree does not have entities(s) aligned with it, only the Holy dove of the Spirit. This is felt as a fiery energy within which acts as a springboard for further work and exploration. The Initiate will also feel her body vitalized in a way that the points-chaud thus received appears to light up vibrantly, the scintillating body is further invigorated and nurtured by this grade. This may spurn the desire to give away some of the Light thus received. The call to offer healing to others in various ways may be born from this. Those interested in the sacerdotal arts may want to analyze the Mass within which is situated the extended, Honorary version of this degree found in the Appendix. Lastly, the Initiate may sense an overall change of outlook and worldview after this Degree. For my own part, after Episcopal Consecration (which was again, aligned with points empowerments via the APRM+M) I received profound clarity concerning my own path and a clear vision of how my Chapel would work with the Degrees and points. In fact, this book and the arranging of the Secrets of the Degrees with the points, along with the use of these Secrets in scrying, were immediately realized after the reception of this Holy Order. Philosophically this is interesting, as the Western Mystery Tradition appears on the surface to suggest Enlightenment by degrees, while the East often suggests immediate realization. With the proper reception of this degree, this dichotomy becomes yet another, either/or fallacy. One may attain Enlightenment by degrees, or instantaneously in one crucial moment of realization. A lifelong follower of this way comprehends that at some points on the path it is realization by degrees while at other times, it is earth shattering, mountain-top moments of immediate divine realization.

Part Three – Chapter Four: Hermetic, Gnostic, & Kabalistic Degrees

67th Degree

Guardian of the Incommunicable Name / Grand Eulogist

Lodge of Sorrow

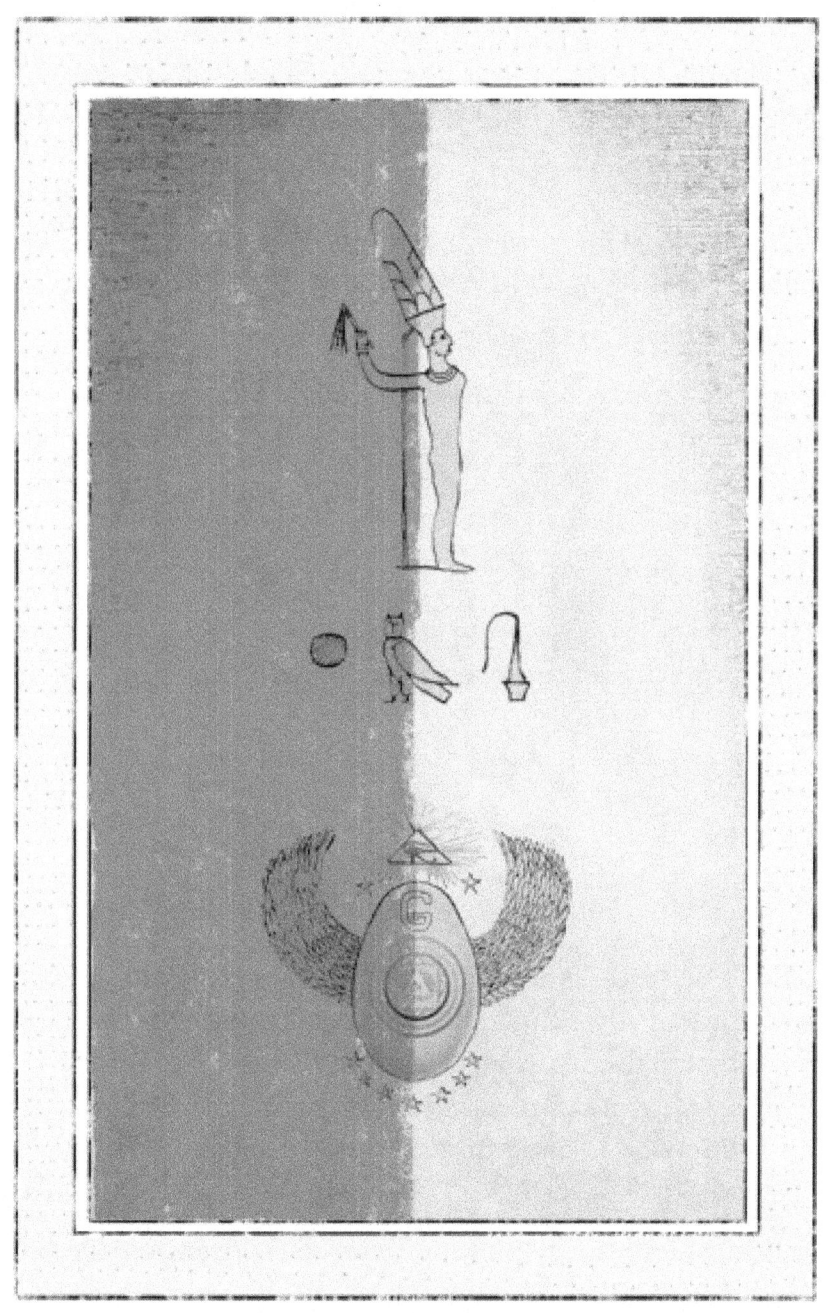

67th degree,
Guardian of the Incommunicable
Name - Grand Eulogist.

Battery of Knocks

Three, three times.   XXX   XXX   XXX

Points-chaud

Lower mid back, right

Sacred Word

There is no Sacred Word for this Degree as it should be given in absolute silence, symbolic of the tomb that the Initiate will visit in the scrying procedure.

Grip

The third, or lion's grip, symbol of Divine strength and truth. The Facilitator is to complete the visualization of the sphinx by adding in the *lion-body*.

Sign

Make a sign of horror, stroke hand over forehead, and then interlace the fingers and bring the backs of the hands to the brow; then extend the arms upwards.

Additional Materials

Password–KHEM

Jewel–Winged egg upon which is a ray-ed triangle with the letter "G" in the center.

† † †

Synopsis

If the Chapel, Lodge or Node is working the Degrees chronologically, this Degree may seem strangely placed directly after the grade of virtual consecration. However, this Degree is deeply meditative and signals a further extension of the 3rd Degree of Freemasonry, that of Master Mason. In this way, it is precisely aligned with the Grand Consecrator, as a *new life* is begun by the Initiate who is enlightened in that Degree. This new life is symbolized by Khem, who the Degree work describes as "The Son, 'whose manifestation is his birth.[595]'"

The 65th Degree returned to the grip of the Entered Apprentice, the 66th—the Fellowcraft grip, and now this Degree gives us the completion with the strong grip of the lion's paw of the Tribe of Judah, the Master's grip. Each of these had accompanying visualizations for the Facilitator as she was building up the image of the Sphinx with every points-chaud empowerment. The visualizations began with the human face, move to the wings and now are completed with the lion's body. Further meditation on the brilliance of this schema and

---

[595] *Compleat Rite of Memphis*, p. 133.

its return to the principal Degrees of Masonry at this specific stage of the Hermetic, Kabalistic, and Gnostic Series will reveal a *guiding hand* throughout the Rites of Memphis+Misraïm.

As a Eulogist is the speaker who praises the life of the deceased at a funeral, we begin to see the further parallels to the story of the Master's Degree in this grade. However, the tables are turned, and rather than the death of Hiram Abiff being acted out by the Candidate, it is the Initiate of our Rite *witnessing* a Lodge of Sorrow being enacted. But for whom is this funeral Rite being conducted? If we extend our study to the nature of our Password, KHEM, then we will build another layer into the story. Khem is the masculine fertility god of Egypt and along with the Jewel—a winged egg on which is a triangle with the letter, "G" (for Gnosis) in the center, is a consistent correspondence with the resurrection theme of the Masters Degree, accomplished by the lion's paw or Grip. The Degree, then, like the 3rd is both funereal and transmutative. But again, who is it that has died?

The suggestion for scrying this Degree and point empowerment is rather distinct from those thus far. In this procedure, it is suggested that the Initiate research various "Lodges of Sorrow" as they have been conducted in the prominent Orients and Grand Lodges around the world. Each one is distinct, but many include the use of an empty chair which will remind the Martinist of the chair of the Passed Masters in their workings. No matter which ritual is utilized by the Initiate, it is suggested that the empty chair be employed, with emblems of the Initiate's own Masonic or Initiatory journey. It may be her apron, gloves, regalia or jewels that are placed upon the chair—these and an accompanying solitary candle are all that are necessary for the work to begin. The Initiate then proceeds to conduct an entire Lodge of Sorrow for herself! The transformative nature of this undertaking is profound. The Initiate is attending a visage of her own funeral, a simulacrum of one's own Lodge of Sorrow. Then the Initiate performs the basic scrying method by re-activating the point along with the mantric chanting of the Sacred Word *Khem*. Upon this journey, she will endeavor upon the super-celestial realms that accompany the Afterlife.

It is upon this journey that she will meet a guide. This guide is the literal, "Grand Eulogist" who, when given the Sign of the Degree will provide the Initiate with a Word. It is from the Grand Eulogist (often experienced in the form of the virile, KHEM), that the Initiate will receive the "Incommunicable Name" which she then becomes the sole Guardian of[596]. After this Word[597] is received, the Initiate is to perform Gematria with the Word, either with the use of the English Qaballah or another such as Crowley's 777, depending upon the derivation of the Word. This Word has particular significance for the Initiate.

---

[596] Refer again to the gnostic, *Gospel of Truth*, and the notion of receiving a divine name. The distinguishing nature between this and utilizing others' Divine Names should be apparent.
[597] This practice differs from the basic and the Advanced scrying methods, in that a Word is researched—but no Holy Book is utilized. The Initiate is looking within the within for the sacred Word.

Spirit Builders

68th Degree

Patriarch of Truth

Stimulation of the Inmost Light

68th *degree,*
Patriarch of Truth.

Battery of Knocks

Three, four and two. XXX   XXXX   XX

Points-chaud

Right midpoint of the back

Sacred Word

SHCETA

Grip

With the right thumb, Facilitator and Initiate balance three times; palm to palm, balance five times; long index finger to index finger, balance twice.

Sign

Point to Heaven with right thumb; carry the open hand to the forehead; then point with the index finger to the earth. (Signifying, God, Intelligence, Futurity.)

Additional Materials

Password–KAB

Jewel–On a winged egg, a square from which proceeds four rays in the middle of the sides; in the center a delta upon the center of which is a Star (symbolic of the inmost Light).

† † †

Synopsis

This Degree is simple in that it points directly to one sole doctrine. This doctrine is shared with sages the world over, but was given particular voice by the author of the Book of the Law. In this mystical and Holy treatise, we read, "8. The Khabs is in the Khu, not the Khu in the Khabs. 9. Worship then the Khabs, and behold my light shed over you![598]" This text appears obscure until we read in other pieces by Crowley, how he defined the "Khu" and the "Khabs."

In our Work, Kab is said to refer to a mystical section of Memphis where a symbolic palm tree was found. This is the same palm that we will explore further in the 83rd Degree. This is significant to note when viewed in light of Crowley's definition of Khab. For him, the Khab is the "Inmost Light" or the "star" within each individual. It is extremely unique and original and is, "our one sole Truth.[599]" The Password for this Degree, then, is none

---

[598] *The Book of the Law*, 1:8-9, p. 25, 26, 2009, Weiser edition.
[599] *The Law is for All*, Crowley, pgs. 32-33.

other than our own inner Self. This is a Word in the sense of Logos, rather than a pointer to something else. It may be that the Incommunicable Name discovered in the previous Degree is symbolic of this Word or *is* this Word. For most, however, it will be silence, which is the reason for the continuous use of SIGE as the Password for the Higher Degrees.

The points-chaud empowerment of this Degree will stimulate the "inmost Light" within us. The entity related to this point is generally one's very own secret and abiding Center. The energy that is stirred within our spiritual circuitry is the search for our "one sole Truth." Each of us have a particular purpose to fulfill, our sacred duty that was pointed at in the Philosophical Series. This Degree will massage this duty into further action and establish its place of priority within the life of the Initiate.

Scrying the point of this Degree will place the Initiate into the Holy land of Egypt. He will be led into Kab, the mystic section of Memphis where the sacred Palm is found, a palm which confers 365 distinct properties. The Initiate will then be led into the mystic valley, Shcheta, where all of the Patriarchs of Truth assemble. In the distance will be seen the ephemeral Temple at Karnak.

69th Degree

Knight or Sage of the Golden Branch of Eleusis
Compline of the Misraïm

69th degree,
Knight or Sage of the Golden Branch of Eleusis.

Battery of Knocks

One. X

Points-chaud

Right, mid back

Sacred Word

ENDYMION

Grip

Facilitator places the right hand on the Initiate's head and instructs the Initiate to do likewise to him.

Sign

Draw the magickal sword and extend horizontally, raise it to the height of the head and return to the scabbard.

Additional Materials

Password–SIGE

Jewel–Winged egg, with a circle in which is the Y branch

Office of Compline of the Misraïm–

Spend some moments in quiet meditation with all lights out. Kindle the incense and visualize the column of smoke as the poteau mitan of your Oratory. Proceed to light a single candle and call inwardly upon the attending spirits and Passed Masters of the Misraïm. Visualize the great gods of Egypt in attendance as well as the Communion of Saints of the Egyptian Coptic Churches, all in harmony and at peace at this sacred time. Sense their willingness to accompany you on your soul journey as you pass into sleep after the Office. Begin with the Kabalistic Cross, chanting[600]:

> *O God, come to my assistance, Lord make haste to help me...*
>
> *+Glory to the Father and to the Son and to the Holy Spirit.*

Chant Psalm 4 with solemnity:

> *Answer me when I call to you, my righteous God*
> *Give me relief from my distress;*
> *have mercy on me and hear my prayer.*

---

[600] "It has been my understanding that because in Vŭdŭ the way of chant is so close to a type of trance; the Loa come over to us by many forms of music- particularly I have noticed in elements of automatic singing (chant) and even speaking- a set to music- or incantation." Michael Bertiaux, *Vudu Cartography*, p. 14.

How long will you people turn my glory into shame?
How long will you love delusions and seek false gods?
Know that the Lord has set apart his faithful servant for himself;
the Lord hears when I call to him.
Tremble and do not sin;
when you are on your beds,
search your hearts and be silent.
Offer the sacrifices of the righteous
and trust in the Lord.
Many, Lord, are asking, "Who will bring us prosperity?"
Let the light of your face shine on us.
Fill my heart with joy
when their grain and new wine abound.
In peace I will lie down and sleep,
for you alone, Lord,
make me dwell in safety.

+Glory to the Father, and to the Son and to the Holy Spirit, both now and ever and unto the ages of ages. Amen.

Spend a few moments building up the image of the Temple of Karnak, the *Sovereign Sanctuary* of the Ontic Sphere. Proceed to Psalm 91:

He that dwelleth in the secret place of the most High shall abide under the shadow of the Almighty.

I will say of the Lord, He is my refuge and my fortress: my God; in him will I trust.

Surely he shall deliver thee from the snare of the fowler, and from the noisome pestilence.

He shall cover thee with his feathers, and under his wings shalt thou trust: his truth shall be thy shield and buckler.

Thou shalt not be afraid for the terror by night; nor for the arrow that flieth by day;

Nor for the pestilence that walketh in darkness; nor for the destruction that wasteth at noonday.

A thousand shall fall at thy side, and ten thousand at thy right hand;

but it shall not come nigh thee.

Only with thine eyes shalt thou behold and see the reward of the wicked.

Because thou hast made the Lord, which is my refuge, even the most high, thy habitation;

There shall no evil befall thee, neither shall any plague come nigh thy dwelling.

For he shall give his angels charge over thee, to keep thee in all thy ways.

They shall bear thee up in their hands, lest thou dash thy foot against a stone.

Thou shalt tread upon the lion and adder: the young lion and the dragon shalt thou trample under feet.

Because he hath set his love upon me, therefore will I deliver him: I will set him on high, because he hath known my name.

He shall call upon me, and I will answer him: I will be with him in trouble; I will deliver him, and honor him.

With long life will I satisfy him, and show him my salvation.

+Glory to the Father and to the Son and to the Holy Spirit. Amen.

Continue with Psalm 134:

Behold, bless ye the Lord, all ye servants of the Lord, which by night stand in the house of the Lord.
Lift up your hands in the sanctuary, and bless the Lord.
The Lord that made heaven and earth Bless thee out of Zion.

+Glory to the Father and to the Son and to the Holy Spirit. Amen.

End your Prayers with the *Nunc Dimittis*, the dismissal Canticle of Simeon:

Lord, now lettest thou thy servant depart in peace : according to thy word.
For mine eyes have seen: thy salvation,
Which thou hast prepared: before the face of all people;
To be a light to lighten the Gentiles: and to be the glory of thy people Israel.

Take Holy, or blessed Water and sprinkle in the four directions and upon yourself, saying;

May the divine assistance of the spirits, the Saints and the Lwa be with us always, and with our loved ones everywhere.

+Blessed be our God, now and always and unto the ages of ages. Amen.

After this round of prayers, the following should be said to oneself and in a meditative manner before snuffing out the candle;

Holy guides of the spirit, attend to my nightly journey.

Lead me to the fields of Elysium wherein your treasures lie and your teachings await.

Show me the spirit map of the Rite of Memphis+Misraïm.

Reveal to me your divine plans of constructing the Holy City and the Scintillating body.

Assist our intimate Community of Spirit Builders!

I ask for your protection and your guidance on this journey, through the Holy Name of La Chose, YHSHVH, and under the Divine Protection of the Gran Erzulie, the ever Virgin Mother and spirit filled one,

More honorable than the cherubim and more glorious than the seraphim.

+AMEN

†††

Synopsis

This is the first of six Degrees which all open up the Initiate to the system of Memphis+Misraïm as a divine plan and spirit map. The spiritist perspective of Degrees and Initiations is presented in these grades, beginning with this mystical and Gnostic empowerment. A host of Voudon+Gnostic multi-verses are laid open for the Initiate as he develops further and deeper connections with the points chauds empowerments and the system of Memphis+Misraïm.

This Degree begins, as all others, with the Battery of Knocks. This time the knock is singular, however, which alludes to the path that the Initiate must decide upon at this point of the journey. The emblem of the letter Y is presented as symbolizing the split in this journey, where the Initiate may take the common and easy route which leads to Tartarus or the narrow and difficult route of Elysium. Allusions are made to the Golden Branch of Eleusis, the Ivy of Heliopolis, the Papyra of India and the Acacia of Freemasonry. All of these, according to the work, point out this dual path and the choice presented to the Initiate. If the Initiate chooses the singular path of Elysium, then she may proceed further to the distinct journey of this grade.

Before scrying the point of this Degree, the Initiate who chooses the life-long path to Elysium is enjoined to perform the *Office of Compline of the Misraïm* provided in the "Additional Materials." It is this meditation and practice that will reveal the spiritist workings of Memphis+Misraïm, and the overarching plan and spirit maps of various Degree systems to the Initiate. The inhabitants of the various spirit worlds found in dream-time will acknowledge the Initiate's grade and will make themselves known through dream transmissions from this point onward, if they have not done so before thus Degree. The wording of this *Office of Compline* is Mystical in the Judeo-Christian sense. One must remember the continuity of ideas, culture, and structure that has come down to us from the deserts of Egypt. These very Psalms were chanted by those survivors of Egyptian Magic, the Coptic Monks and Desert Fathers who preserved the tradition. By joining with them in the continuum of prayer and through our common spiritual lineage, we engage in true spiritist exploration and esoteric relations with these beings of light.

The blessing that is bestowed as the "Grip" of this Degree ensures the safety and protection of the Initiate as he traverses these mystical realms in sleep. Additionally, the Sacred Psalms selected are those that mystics the world over chant before retiring for the night. They have been divinized through frequency and have a particular vibration consistent with the energies and entities of the night. It is important that the Initiate go directly to bed after the Office, even if sleep does not come immediately. He may call upon Endymion, the personification of sleep, to assist in his travels. Particular note should be taken of the so-called Old Ones who may appear in the dream, as well as any signs of antediluvian landscapes and African deities.

70th Degree

Prince of Light / Patriarch of the Planispheres
Call to Adonai

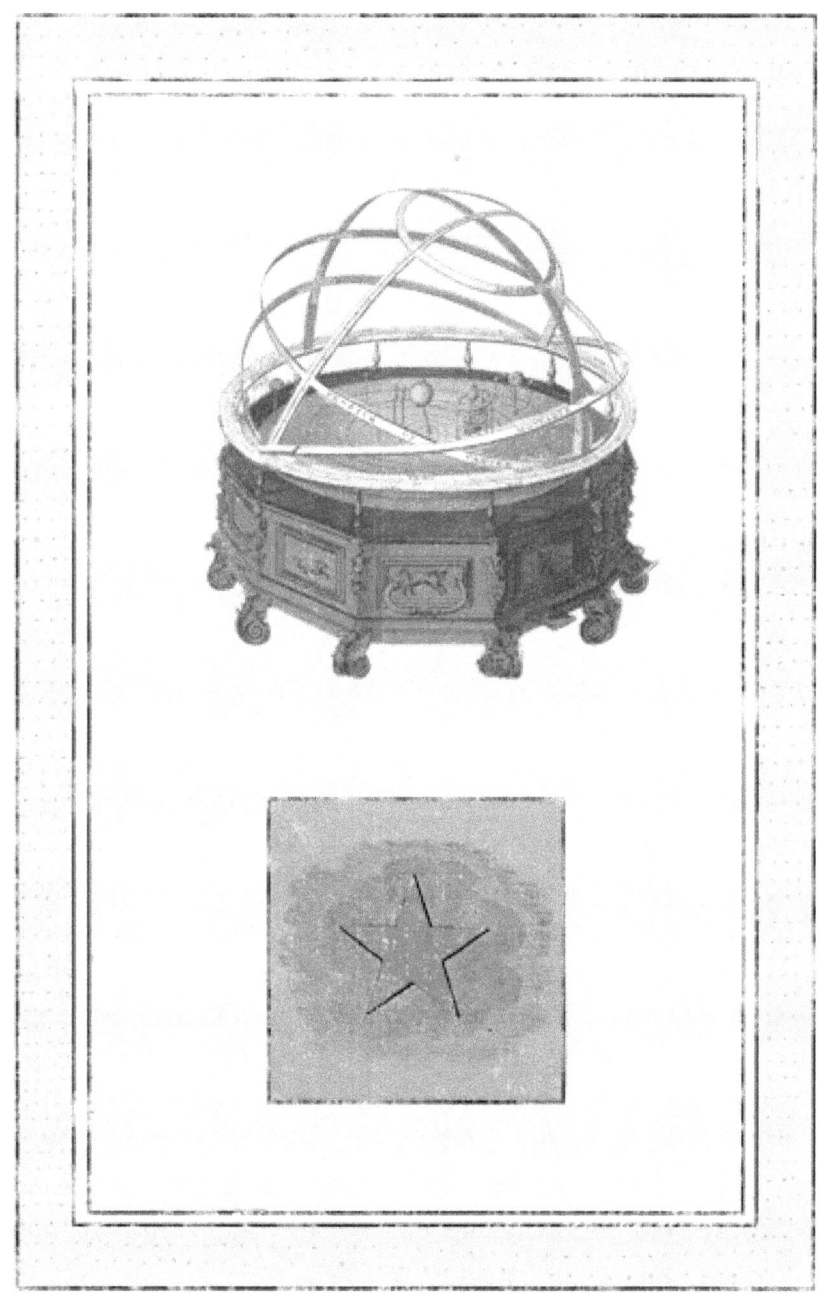

70th degree,
Prince of Light or Patriarch of the Planispheres.

Battery of Knocks

Three, four and two.   XXX   XXXX   XX

Points-chaud

Right, upper mid back.

Sacred Word

DOUNNOUN (abode of the Lord)

Grip

Place the right hand upon each other's head.

Sign

Point with magickal sword towards the Orient, the East.

Additional Materials

Password–SIGE

Jewel–A star within a square

† † †

Synopsis

In the previous Degree, the Initiate was given a great key to unlock many doors in our grand system. This key was the recognition of the Ecclesiastical Revision of the Antient & Primitive Rite of Memphis+Misraïm as a spirit map, a chart of the heavenly spheres, each Degree and corresponding point empowerment relating directly to an otherworldly realm and spirit beings residing in these regions. It was suggested that African Deities (of which West African Vodun is a descendent), more ancient than Egypt may arise within the psyche of the Initiate and that antediluvian landscapes may open forth in dream time. These and other identifiable changes suggest the shift in the texture of these Degrees and the high nature of their import. The Initiate is being presented with the magickal Universe which is becoming more and more real and tangible with every point empowerment.

With this Degree comes the mystical *abode of the Lord*. The particular nature and location of this abode is not revealed, nor is the secret name of this "Lord." This research is reserved for the *Arcana Arcanorum*, however, this Degree begins to develop the body and mind for the coming relationship with this Lord who is sometimes styled, *Adonai*. It is the *Nous* of the Initiate that is beginning to awaken at this stage.

Part Three – Chapter Four: Hermetic, Gnostic, & Kabalistic Degrees

The relationship between the abode of the Lord and the Prince of Light/Patriarch of the Planispheres is clearly discovered through scrying the point of this Degree. A great Patriarch is present in this region who will begin to reveal to the Initiate the secrets of the spirits of esoteric Voudon. He will introduce the Initiate to these spirits and then leave the Initiate to do his own further exploration with them. These same Lwa will attend the Initiate and assist in bringing forth the *Lord* at the appropriate time. It must be understood that the Lwa of our *Esoteric* Voudon are considerate spirits who will reveal themselves in ways that are specific to the Initiate. For instance, a Catholic practitioner will most likely have visions of specific Saints who are syncretized with the appropriate Lwa. A practitioner who does not subscribe to any particular tradition may have a more abstract experience of the spirits, even to the extent of visualizing vivified Euclidean and non-Euclidean[601] designs.

The entire Zodiac can be explored through this one Degree and point empowerment. In essence, it is an ancient form of primitive astrology. In the old forms of astrology, the constellations were beings of mythology—spirits and demigods of old. The Patriarch will guide the Initiate through the twelve stations of the planisphere if asked to do so, but the Initiate must be *duly and truly prepared* for the ordeals and trials of each station. Each constellation is its own gnostic space with a hierarchy of beings and a superstructure of diverse energies. As always, purification is required before embarking upon such work. For this Degree, the Initiate is sent back to the Sacred Book of the Psalms and suggested to chant a round of eight of these Holy hymns before scrying the point.

---

[601] A curious side venture of this Degree could be the study of the bizarre geometry present in the fearful dreams of the Cthulhu Mythos of H.P. Lovecraft.

Spirit Builders

71st Degree

Patriarch of the Sacred Vedas

Invocation of Erzulie Freda

71st *degree,*
Patriarch of the Sacred Vedas.

Battery of Knocks

Three, four and two. **XXX XXXX XX**

Points-chaud

Center, mid back

Sacred Word

AUM

Grip

Place the right hand on each other's head, as in last several showing a blessing and spiritual transmission.

Sign

Point to Heaven with right finger

Additional Materials

Password–SIGE, answer, ALETHE

Jewel–A crescent with a center square

† † †

Synopsis

From Egypt we inherit an entire corpus of ceremonial magic, whether from the continuity of ideas as preserved in their papyri or by virtue of passed down traditions through the Gnostic and Coptic Orthodox Churches. The Indo-Aryan regions provide us with their own magic, via the Religion and subsequent cults of Zoroastrianism, Mithraism, and a plethora of Middle Eastern Gnostic sects. In this Degree, the Initiate is directed back to the *Rigveda, the Yajurveda, the Samaveda* and the *Atharaveda*. These are amongst the oldest continuously used Holy Texts in the world. What is their relationship to our Egyptian magic as worked in the APRM+M? The relationship is in the nature of gates[602].

From the beginning of this Series, we have explored ceremonial magic, Hermeticism, working with Hellenistic gods, and spiritist endeavors. All of these have been the opening of various gates. The visionary experiences that have accompanied the scrying of these points and the immediate realization that often follows the reception of the points leads to

---

[602] See too the Sumerian, Babylonian, and Assyrian rites of Mesopotamia as well. Several Initiates, for instance, have had visions of Inanna and Marduk with this points-chaud empowerment.

the self-creative Mind which penetrates the unknown and transcends all barriers.[603] The Initiate finds herself standing in the center of the Universe, with endless directions to travel in and endless worlds to traverse. These are the multitude of gates open unto the practitioner of these mysteries. Once the *Nous,* or the Mind's eye is open to these mysteries, no longer does one see in terms of Egyptian, Indian, or Persian and Hellenistic. There is simply the great *Polyarchy of Being*, in limitless extension outwards, and in every direction from the Initiate and within the Initiate.

The particular gates that this Degree and its point empowerment open are Indian in derivation, but enter into Hermetic practice and god-names. The points-chaud of this Degree is the first upon the center of the back and stimulates balanced energies and entities within the soul of the Initiate. This center of equipoise is the proper juncture to begin the scrying extension that accompanies this Degree.

We find the Jewel of this Degree to be one of the Tattwas of Indian philosophy, with a sub-element within it. The Jewel is a crescent with a center square. This is the *Earth of Water* Tattwa, as utilized in the Hermetic Order of the Golden Dawn. As Mathers developed his system of scrying these emblems, he attributed various corresponding colors, directions, God names and angels to the symbols based upon the four elements. This creates a transcultural meditation device and introduces the Initiate to scrying a visual stimulus in addition to the previously instructed point/word method.

As an example of the string of correspondences and the interdependent nature of such visual scrying apparatus, the Initiate would do well to begin to investigate this one particular Tattwa with its sub-element and research its relationship to the points-chaud empowerment and the Degree itself.

The attributes and names of this Jewel are:

- Prithivi~Earth~**Square**
- Apas~Water~**Crescent**

The Sephirotic correspondences are:

- Square~Malkuth
- Crescent~Netzach

The cardinal directions are:

- Earth~North
- Water~West

The God-names are:

---

[603] Bertiaux states, "Remember that the basic law of magickal realism is that whatever can be conceived can also be explored astrally...thus we will now be able to induct the contents of any world..."(*VGW*, 251).

- Earth~Adonai-Ha Aretz
- Water~Elohim Tzabaoth

The Archangels are:

- Earth~Uriel
- Water~Gabriel

The angels are:

- Earth~Phorlach
- Water~Talihad

Each of the Tattwas of the Eastern School includes all of these correspondences and in fact, more if coordinated with books such as Crowley's *777*.[604] This example is presented to the Initiate to exhibit the string of influences and the way that they interpenetrate each other to provide the details of the scrying experience. The specific method utilized by Free Illuminists the world over is much simpler and direct, but when used in conjunction with these Hermetic methods yields further avenues of exploration and study.

Each of the Tattwas and sub elements also include landscapes and beings in the same manner that our standard practice of scrying does. The Initiate is encouraged to work with all 36 of these and make cards with the appropriate colored symbols for future study[605]. The Tattwa of this Degree will open up a region upon our spirit map that is protected and watched over by one of the primary Lwa of Esoteric Voudon. She is Erzulie Freda, a very powerful and jealous spirit of the Rada family who is related to this Tattwa in conjunction with its Sephirotic correspondence of Netzach. The points chauds empowerment will immediately stimulate her activity within the sphere of sensation of the Initiate and can be sensed by an increase of love and desire.

---

[604] Or the compendious volume, *7761/2*, by Jim Eshelman, 2010.
[605] See Israel Regardie's, *The Golden Dawn*, or Chic and Tabatha Cicero's, *Self Initiation into the Golden Dawn System of Magic*.

Spirit Builders

72nd Degree

Sublime Master of Wisdom

Encounter with the Dweller on the Threshold

72nd *degree,*
Sublime Master of Wisdom.

Battery of Knocks

Three and four. XXX XXXX

Points-chaud

Center mid back

Sacred Word

MACROCOSMOS, answer, MICROCOSMOS

Grip

Grasp the blade of each other's sword[606]

Sign

Raise sword, and place flat on forehead, then salute three times in front and place sword twice on the left shoulder and twice on the right. This is the completing action of the *Unknown Philosopher* Degree[607].

Additional Materials

Password–SIGE, answer, ALETHE

Jewel–A pyramid over which is a sun

† † †

Synopsis

This Degree is philosophical in its work. It directly explains the nature of our non-dual Gnosis and how it is that we come to find the divine, through the within. In the Neo-Platonic schools the student is called to look upon all things, no matter their size, and to see them as a reflection of the whole. Whether the portion is sub-atomic, or whether it is the earth itself, each is a mirror of the cosmos altogether. It is in this light that we treat the body as a spirit map of the universe. We chart the 97 points, primarily upon the central pillar, yet we recognize that this is no original concept. We easily share ideas and even doctrines with the system of nadis and chakras of the Hindus, the movement of *chi* through the various palaces of the body in Taoist Alchemy, or even the notion of the Hebrew Sephirah superimposed upon the body as spheres of light. All of these speak to the same reality of the microcosm

---

[606] Both the sign and grip of this Degree require a dagger or sword.

[607] This Degree inherits the *knighting* of Willermoz and his *Knights Beneficent of the Holy City*. See also the CBCS Squire Novice and Knight of the Temple degrees at the end of *Degrees of Wisdom* (Triad Press, 2025).

being a reflection of the macrocosm, and such specifically through the human body. Our 97 points are specific and particular, in so much as they relate to this mystical branch of Freemasonry through the Ecclesiastical Revision of the APRM+M, but they are not an isolated discovery operating within a vacuum.

As we further explore the nature of the points empowerments, we begin to see subtle connections between points. This gives rise to a clearer understanding of the suggestion of *packs* of Degrees. In almost all cases, the points/Degrees can be safely worked with in groups of three. This ensures both equipoise, as the points often fall upon the left center or right center, as well as ensuring a thorough grounding in the energies and entities that relate to each other in a given set. With further exploration and research–via scrying the point, the advanced method, along with the facilitating of points for others–the Initiate will discover additional correspondences and connections between the points. Once these connections are made, the realization of each point as a universe in miniature is easily grasped and that same universe is swiftly accessible and traversed.

We find the number seven again in this Degree. It arises in the Battery of Knocks, in the symbol of the pyramid in the Jewel (which has three sides and a square of four sides for its base) and in the Sign of the Degree as well as in the brief wording provided by Yarker. There are seven separate spirits allied with the points-chaud of this Degree, who answer to the Primitive Doctrine and relate back to the ancient Rites and their split between the Lesser and Greater Mysteries. Three spirits are attached to the Lesser Mysteries and four to the Greater. As this split of the Mysteries is alluded to often in Masonic texts, it is important to recognize here that there are entities overseeing each of these seven grades.

Whether the Initiate has fully made contact with these seven along the way or not, this Degree presents her with their Wisdom. When scrying the point of this Degree, the Initiate is taken into seven separate chambers, there to meet the spirit of each and to be tried by the same. Many do not move beyond the first three. This should not be a point of contention or stress, however, as it simply suggests that the Initiate is not quite prepared for what the final four chambers hold. Upon entry into the fourth chamber, the Initiate will once again be faced with the Dweller on the Threshold, but this time he will appear not too unlike that experienced in *Zanoni*, by Bulwer-Lytton. Another example of this Dweller is the divine Poimandres of Hermes Trismegistus. A careful reading of the first few chapters of Book 1 of the *Corpus Hermeticum* will jumpstart the entry into the seven chambered mountain of the Rosicrucians.

Part Three – Chapter Four: Hermetic, Gnostic, & Kabalistic Degrees

73rd Degree

Patriarch, or Doctor of the Sacred Fire

Awakening AZOTH

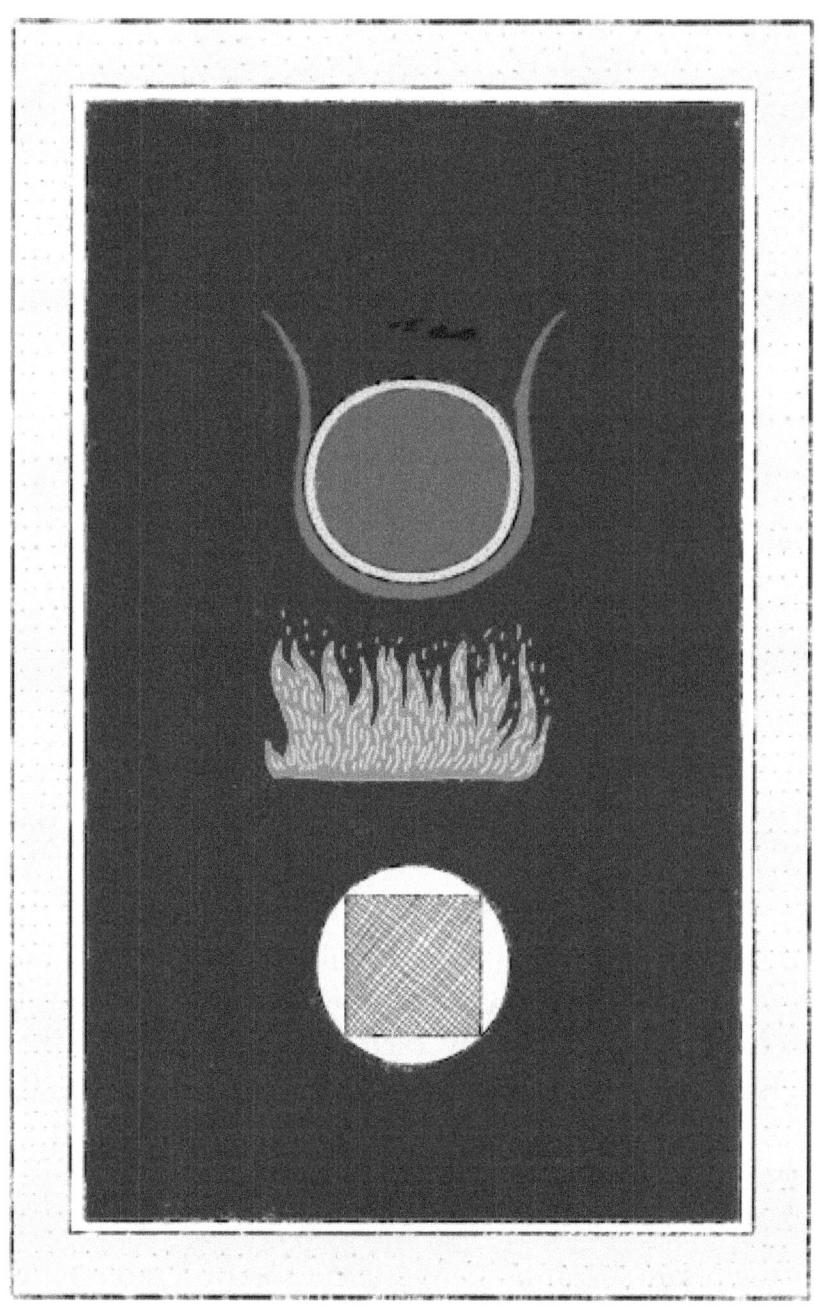

73rd *degree,*
Patriarch, or Doctor of the Sacred Fire.

Battery of Knocks

Seven, seven times. Each set of seven equals one of the seven seals.

XXXXXXX XXXXXXX XXXXXXX XXXXXXX XXXXXXX XXXXXXX XXXXXXX

Points-chaud

Center mid-back

Sacred Word

AZOTH

Grip

Grasp each other's left hand and press seven times for the seven seals.

Sign

Elevate both hands and bow thrice to the East.

Additional Materials

Password–SIGE, answer ALETHE

Jewel–Circle enclosing a square

† † †

Synopsis

The next several Degrees in this Series open multiple gates and trans-cosmic marmas of the Initiate. The initiatory experiences of the points empowerments comport with the specific elements of the Degrees that are worked in our primitive methodology and relate directly to the centers of the body in which the Degrees are enacted. The *Doctor of the Sacred Fire*[608], for instance, refers to the rise of the occult fire from the base of the spine– the serpent energy called, *kundalini*[609]. We receive a mystical understanding of the actions and uses of this occult fire when referenced with the Sacred Word of this Degree.

There are many important words in the Western Esoteric Tradition. Some are words of power, used to invoke specific entities and forces, while others are anagrams of various words and still others form a string of correspondences via the art of Gematria and their numerological significances. In Masonic circles, there are Lost Words, True Words, Sacred

---

[608] This also refers to Paracelsus, the "Doctor" who achieved AZOTH.
[609] Here kundalini is allied with AZOTH, as the regenerating fire, the creative and animating force or energy of evolution both within physical, sentient beings and within the mind itself.

Words and a panorama of passwords, utilized to enter Lodges and signifying various inner developments of the Candidate.

The word AZOTH[610], our Sacred Word in this Degree, comes full-freighted with a number of meanings and powers. In one sense, the Word forms a call to the network of powerzones, the points chauds empowerments within the body, stimulating them to activity and vivifying the Body of Light for its coming journeys that are of an intensity that requires a substantial and nourished light body. This activating of the other points in the body prepares the organism for the lightening flash of the occult fire from the base of the spine that accompanies meditation on this Degree/point. Our Masonic Middle Pillar becomes a living practice when the occult fire is fully sensed and enlivened with this work. But AZOTH is more than this, for AZOTH stimulates the sleeping dragon, symbolized by Mercury (another name for Azoth) and the caduceus, as a specific entity. The sexual nature of this entity is overt and not to be toyed with, lest the soul be dashed to pieces by his very own libido. This AZOTH becomes a focal point for meditative work and enters the realm of devotion when properly understood. As the last Degree mentions a certain dragon-type entity that Hermes encounters as *Poimandres*, this Degree extends the understanding and directs the attention to the Dragon's lair at the base of the spine. It takes intensive soul work to direct the AZOTH up and down the middle pillar at will. But of what purpose to the world at large is such auto-suggestive trance stimulation? It is this, that when the Initiate masters the AZOTH, becoming a *Doctor of the Sacred Fire,* the secret Mercury within, it may then be directed outwards into the sphere of sensation and released from the hands[611] to offer healing, light, and initiation to others. THIS is the key to realizing AZOTH for oneself. The individual is realized as a reflection of the ALL; this realization is a treasure we in turn, share with others.

AZOTH has other meanings as well. In the points-chaud empowerment of this Degree, the Initiate is given a particular attunement. The attunement is to a sort of realized eschatology, where the Initiate senses the trans-historical nature of our work and its unification with all times. It is common to experience a sort of atavistic resurgence in this Degree, where old primitive gods and goddesses, primeval currents and primal urges, evolutionary forces and ancestral residue arises—where the old Degrees and their references to Hindu gods or Greek myths become living agents in the Initiate's sphere, and where all of the pantheons lay open as one grand scheme of theosophy. This gorgeous and kaleidoscopic realization, this sacred attunement to the Divine that enshrouds the daily brings the beginning and the end of things together in one point-event of *inbetweenness*. Hermeticists will recognize the hint here, as AZOTH, when analyzed, refers to the first and the last in all of its parts—Alpha and Omega, Aleph and Tav, A and Z—the beginning and the end, the Sacred Ouroboros devouring its tail. This AZOTH is within the Initiate, curled

---

[610] A Compendium of this Degree could be the paper, "Wherein does Sexual Magic Occur?" from the 2nd Year Course, Introductory paper or Letter I, *The Monastery of the Seven Rays*.
[611] --which become the "tubes of Light" that Bertiaux describes.

at the base of the spine[612] and waiting in eternal potentiality for the moment when the Magus decides to utilize his supra-physical and non-spatial powers within the worlds. The atavisms that accompany this Degree are indeed ancient and are the lifeblood of all Rites and Initiations the world over. *This* is the Primitive Doctrine of old, *this* is Spirit Building.

There is another aspect of this Degree that differs in quality and intensity from the others. It is in the Battery of Knocks of which there are, again, seven. Seven has recurred over and over again, but in this Battery, we connect with the realized eschatology of the Holy Book of Revelations. Seven here refers to the seven seals. When the Battery is made, the seven seals are opened for the individual. This is contradistinguished from the "end of times" understanding of this Kabalistic book. Appeal must be made to the mystic writings of Kenneth Grant for the deeper understandings of the next few Degrees, as we have mentioned one of his pet doctrines already—along with A.O. Spare who developed it further—that of *atavistic resurgence*[613]. Of the mystical Battery of Knocks he says they are:

> *...a primitive mode of knocking on the door of the spirit world and of arousing the subconscious entities and evoking ancient atavisms which manifest in the mirror of dream, otherwise clairvoyant vision. In later times, the bell was the most usual means of attracting the attention of the spirits, and this was based upon the vibrations heard or experienced by sensitives during trance.*[614]

What we have skirted around thus far, we now face head on and develop with the courage and audacity of true Initiates. The seven seals that are opened through the Battery, especially prior to scrying the point, open wide the doors of the spirit realm. As mentioned early on, a gong is one of the more powerful media for the Battery of Knocks and Grant elucidates the reasons that go beyond the aesthetic when he says that they attract the attention of the spirits, based upon the vibrations they create.

Finally, Yarker adds other elements of study for the Initiate of this grade. These include the twin nature of the Chinese *yin* and *yang* and its relation to the occult fire. Animal magnetism and electricity are studied as aspects of the Creative Logos. Additionally, attention is directed to the physical Sun that is the source of the solar-phallic quality of this occult fire.

---

[612] This regards our points being centrally located on the Masonic Middle Pillar and the energies entailed in ÆONic, 3rd echelon work.
[613] Reference can be made to the use of this phrase in the Social Darwinism of philosophers such as Herbert Spencer.
[614] *Cults of the Shadow*, 2013, p. 42.

Part Three – Chapter Four: Hermetic, Gnostic, & Kabalistic Degrees

74th Degree

Sublime Master of the Stoka (Shloka)

Intonation of the Astral Bells

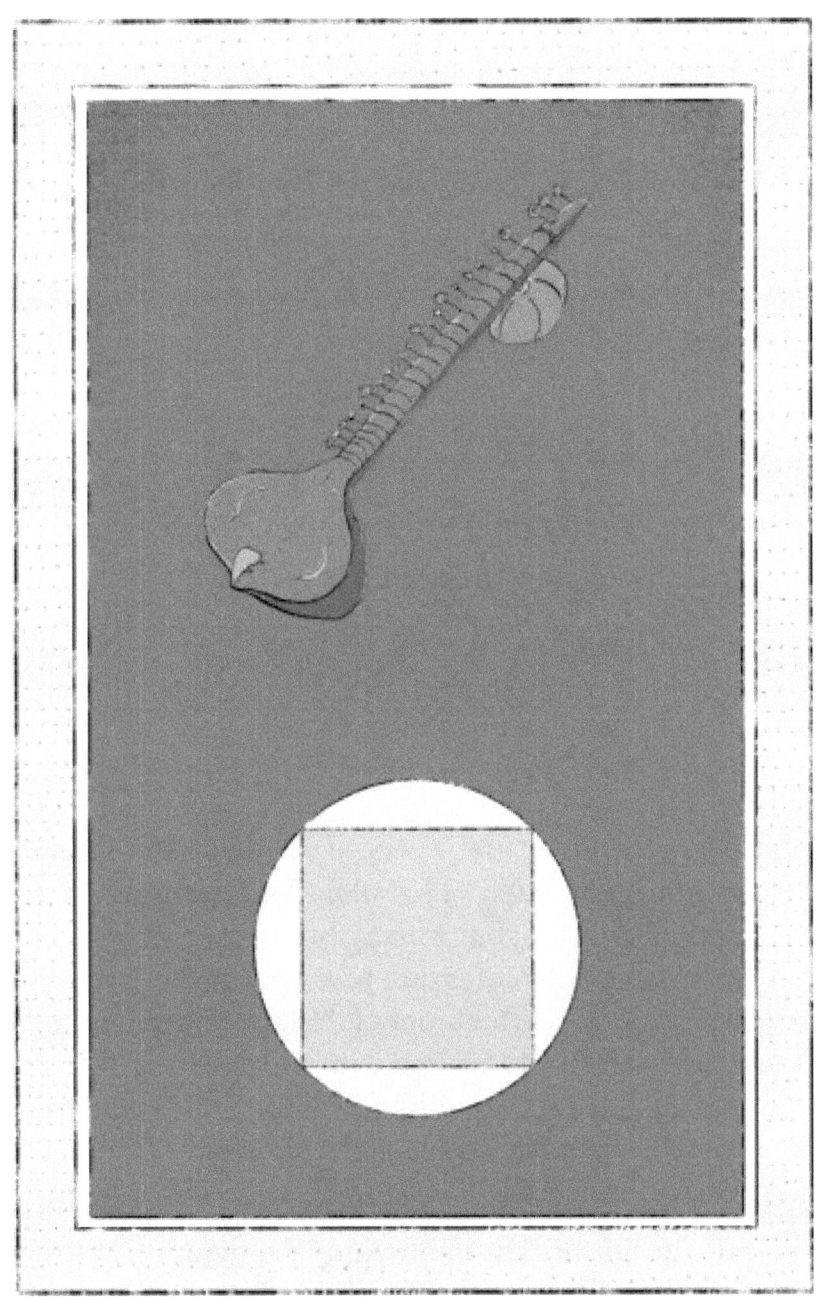

74th *degree,*
Sublime Master of the Stoka.

Battery of Knocks

Four, four times. One. Seven, seven times. One. Two, two times, One.

XXXX XXXX XXXX XXXX X XXXXXXX XXXXXXX XXXXXXX XXXXXXX XXXXXXX XXXXXXX XXXXXXX X XX XX X

Points-chaud

Center mid-back

Sacred Word

MAHABOD (the Great Wisdom as found by the Buddha sitting under the Bodhi Tree.)

Grip & Sign

The Grip and Sign are used interchangeably in this Degree. Hold the left hand elevated (for the Tantric path of Kali) and grasp right hands.

Additional Materials

Password–SIGE, answer, ALETHE

Jewel–A circle containing a square with a central point.

† † †

Synopsis

We find in the Kaula Tantric literature, a very secret mantra of fifteen letters that causes the expression of a sixteenth silent letter. This silent letter creates a *kala*, which is literally related to time in the Hindu Tradition, but which also suggests death, blackness and a fixed destiny. The Degree work directs the attention to a *Shloka* (the term, Stoka is erroneously used) containing sixteen syllables of which only a "Master" knows the construction. The occult property of these numbers is synthesized with the power of "Music in composing the Mind, and in healing of bodily disease by aiding its efflux.[615]" This final term, *efflux* is very selective and suggests the out *flowing* or expiring of a substance or thing.

The Initiate may be inspired to study the Vama Marga to increase the understanding of the sixteen *kalas* worked with in this left hand path (see Sign of the Degree) Tantra. The work has many applications and brings to light much of the sun and moon symbolism of Classical Freemasonry. Dedicated as it is to *Kali*, it often appears "dark[616]," yet this linear

---

[615] *Compleat Rite of Memphis*, p. 135.

[616] We find, upon inner research, that all phenomena have their source in the noumenal (Grant, *Outside the Circles of* Time, 84). The work of magick comprises the whole being, "all magick is colourful" says the artistic mage, A.O. Spare (ibid, 24). The source of this noumenal realm is explored in the *Administrative Grades* through a form of *agnosia*, as contradistinguished with our current work of *gnosis*.

thinking is of little use for the spiritual cosmonaut. The spirit realms that are traversed by high Initiates of all systems move beyond the one-dimensional morals, codes and mores of civilization. The form of true *Caritas* hinted at in *Syzygy*[617] is one of the operative modes of Tantric meditation for Western Esotericists. The sixteen syllable mantra and sixteen syllable verse or Shloka relate back to the Voudon Kabala of the *Monastery of the Seven Rays* and its insistence on the mystical number sixteen[618]—sixteen Degrees, sixteen kalas, sixteen Magical Axioms, sixteen Lwa, sixteen gods of Ifa, sixteen powers of the High priesthood, etc. It is here that we locate the intense nature of the atavisms engendered by this Degree. But their method of arousal is singular.

Again, we refer back to the wording of Yarker concerning, *the power of Music in composing the Mind, and in healing of bodily disease.* To give birth to the various powers, forces and entities of the number sixteen, as a *Sublime Master of the Shloka*, the Initiate must *chant*[619] the forces into being. These same forces then act upon other bodies by virtue of a subtle *efflux* from the Initiate. What are referenced here are the sixteen principal healing Psalms of Hoodoo practitioners. These, along with their specific uses and a powerful Rosicrucian prayer are found in Part II of *Syzygy*, yet their use comes full circle when aligned with this particular Degree of the Memphis+Misraïm cycle and the points-chaud empowerment connected to it along the central pillar of the spine.

The AZOTH worked with in the previous Degree becomes the mode of moving the current up and down the spine. When allied with the Masonic Middle Pillar, the wheels of the Sephira begin to vibrate and spin within the Initiate. This cosmic stirring of energy within the body can then be directed outward and through touch, offer healing and initiation to others. When aligned with one of these sixteen sacred Psalms, the specific entity will aid and guide the blind energy released from the hands. These Psalms are worked for numerous needs, from physical healing, to psychological healing, to banishing evil elements and spirits, to psychic self defense. The appropriate Psalm for the condition is selected and chanted, then allied with physical touch to bring about this composing of mind and healing of body that Yarker speaks of.

The extensive Battery of Knocks relate to the sounds of the *astral bell* heard by many Initiates during meditation. The large number of knells have a hypnotic effect and when meditated upon frequently, surface again in scrying this point, but as astral bells. They equal seventy two strikes, which relates to the 72 lettered name of God, the *Shem ha-Mephorash*. The source of most Healing uses of the Psalms is the same Grimoire in which we find a powerful and divine Seal for the Shem-ha-Mephorash. It is from the mystical *Sixth and Seventh Books of Moses* which typically includes the additional piece on the Psalms called, *the Sefer Shimmush Tehillim.*

---

[617] Beginning on p. 156 in *Syzygy*, 3rd edition. This work reaches its conclusion in the liturgy of cosmic Masonry, 87-90, 95°.
[618] See p. 142, *The Voudon Gnostic Workbook*.
[619] "a subtle sorcery of sonorous sounds; of spells potent to evoke an ineffable and magical mystery" (*Outside the Circles of Time*, 34).

Spirit Builders

75th Degree
Knight Commander of the Lybic Chain
Call to All Passed & Present Masters

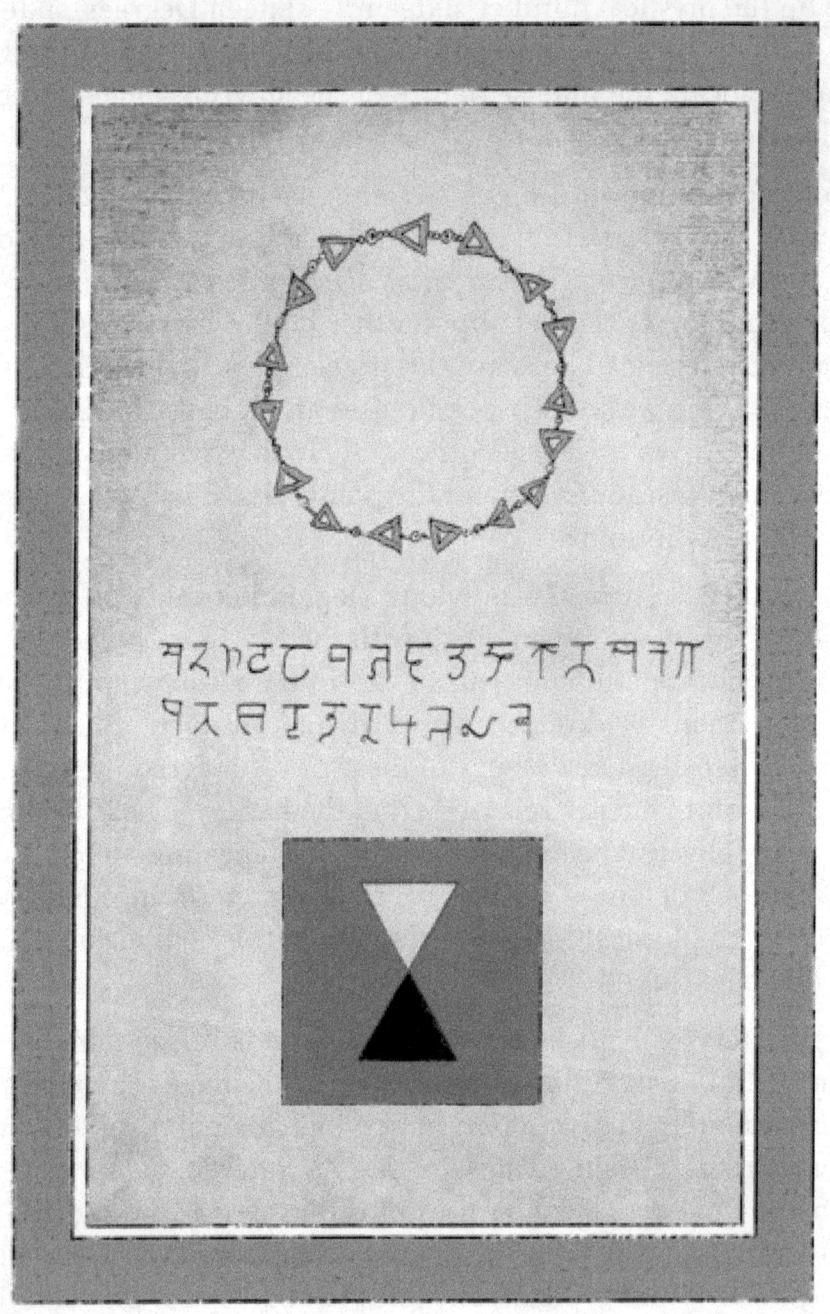

75th *degree,*
Knight Commandel of the Lybic Chain.

Battery of Knocks

Three, three times. XXX   XXX   XXX

Points-chaud

Left, mid-back.

Sacred Word

LYBIA

Grip

Keep the left hand on side, grasp the right hand.

Sign

Place the left and right hand triangularly in the fire symbol and kiss the magickal sword at the waist of the Initiate thrice.[620]

Additional Materials

Password–SIGE, answer, ALETHE

Jewel–A square containing two deltas, point to point.

Formation of the Lybic Chain–

Let the Initiate draw the Jewel, consisting of a square containing two deltas point to point, upon virgin parchment or upon a card. This symbol may be colored in golds and yellows as the Initiate is pleased.

Perform the Battery of Knocks with a gong or bell. Put yourself into spiritual communion with all of your Brothers and Sisters, Adepts and Neophytes alike, across the globe.

At the 9th Hour of the 9th Day, meditate upon the Jewel for 9 consecutive minutes.

This may be performed four times a year, on the 9th Day before the Solstices and Equinoxes.

This may seem like a simple task, but Initiates with experience in meditation will attest to the difficulties of maintaining one-pointedness even for 30 seconds. A timer is suggested for this operation.

† † †

Synopsis

The Lybic Chain is a royal inheritance of all esoteric Masons. It is, simply put, the *Chain of Union* realized at particular points of the year and *In Free Communion* with other Brothers and Sisters. It is *preparatory* in nature, which Yarker points out by discussing the nature of the Degree as decorative in the closing of the Consistory. This signals the last time that the

---

[620] This sign alludes to the intimacy between the Knight Commander and those connected by the Lybic chain.

Password of this Series, *SIGE*, with its answer, *ALETHE* will be used, as we are moving into deeper and deeper operations of the spirit which require further purifications and communications with higher beings. This is the place in the Degrees where the study of the *assumption of godforms*[621] begins, with a special emphasis on the classical gods and goddesses of Egypt.

But before such work is undertaken, the Initiate is enjoined to form the *Lybic Chain* with other Brothers and Sisters throughout the globe. We find something of the nature of monastic unification in this process. Monastics the world over unite at various times of the day and night to chant the Offices of the Church. These Hours, performed in union create a hyperspatial fabric that strengthens the monks and nuns for their difficult ascetic endeavors and vigils. For Spirit Builders, forming the *Lybic Chain* strengthens the physical body of scintillating points, coalesces the Body of Light and unites Brothers and Sisters in the common goals of birthing more Light into this world, initiating and healing others and fashioning the Mystic Temple in the Ontic Sphere.

The method of forming the *Lybic Chain*, in alignment with our Primitive Doctrine, is an efficient and simple procedure. The Initiate is to align with other Brothers and Sisters on the 9th day of the month prior to one of the principle festivals of Freemasons—the Solstices and Equinoxes.[622] For example, on December the 9th, Spirit Builders will labor with this simple working tool before their particular operations on Winter Solstice, the 21st or 22nd. It consists of meditating deeply upon the Jewel of the Degree at 9 pm. The number 9 is utilized as it relates directly to the Battery of three sets of three knocks. The specifics of the procedure are further developed in the "Additional Materials" section of the Degree.

The points-chaud empowerment of the Degree upon the right side of the back has the wonderful benefit of stimulating communion upon the Inner Planes with other *living* Brothers and Sisters of the Gnosis. Rather than awakening entities and otherworldly beings, this Degree is *chain* related and labors to form deep bonds *In Free Communion* with other Illuminists, Masons and Esotericists living upon the globe. This is symbolized in the Degree work by the delta formed between the cities of Memphis[623], Thebes and Heliopolis, and the juncture of the two deltas in the Jewel that is meditated upon.

---

[621] According to the *Monastery of the Seven Rays*, the return to the animal symbolism of Egypt is essential in the Inner Retreat. This provides a deep meaning to the concepts of were-wolf and were-cat related to Voudon-Gnosis.
[622] The classical terms for the Equinoxes of Memphis-Misraïm are the *Awakening of Nature* (Vernal Equinox) and the *Renewal of Nature* (Autumnal Equinox). These equinoxes become increasingly important in the 3rd echelon workings.
[623] These are symbolic of *powerzones*, sacred geographical marmas found all over the earth. Such can be discovered in the writings of H.P. Lovecraft, as well as in Druid literature and other earth-based spiritualities.

76th Degree

Interpreter of Hieroglyphics, or Patriarch of Isis

Introduction to the True Sovereign Sanctuary

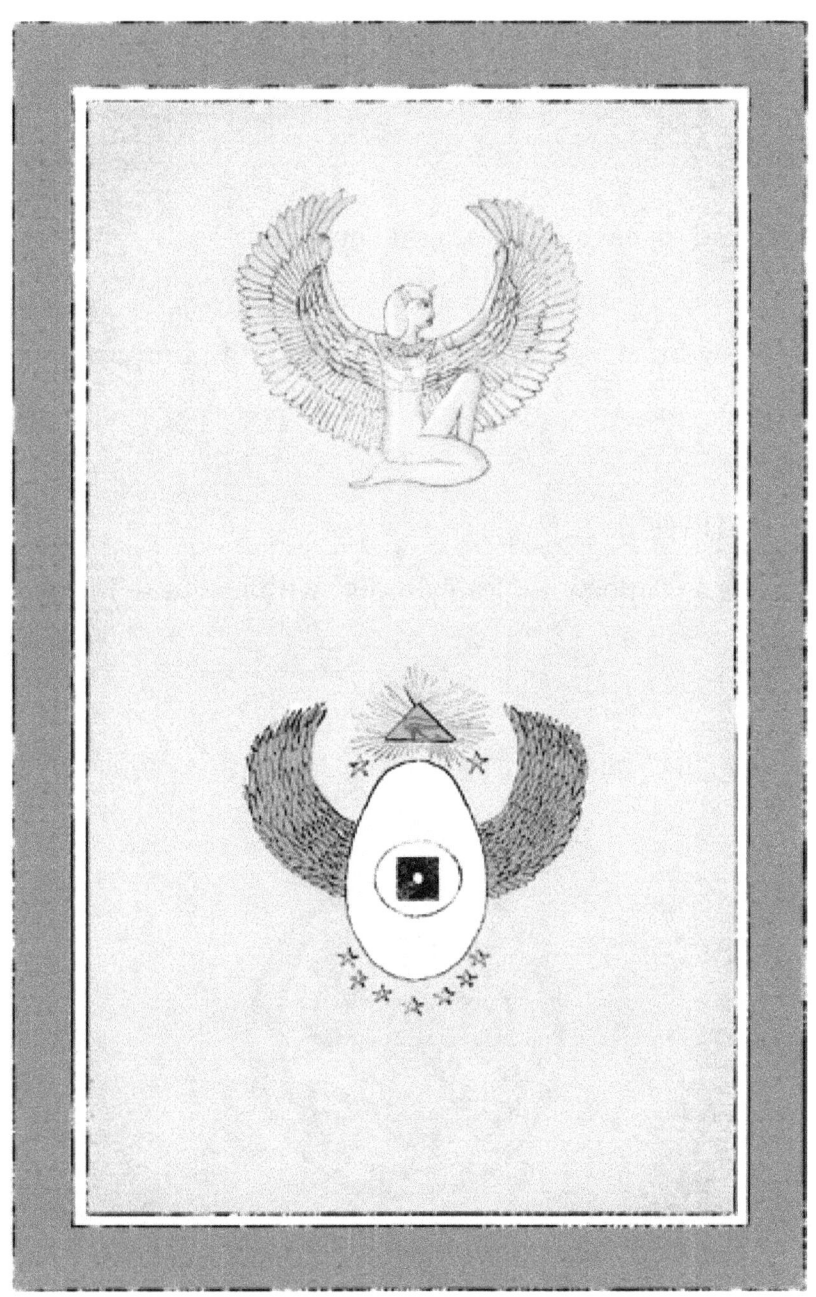

76th *degree,*
Interpreter of Hieroglyphics, of Patriarch of Isis.

Battery of Knocks

Three, three times. Four, four times. XXX XXX XXX XXXX XXXX XXXX XXXX

Points-chaud

Left, mid-back

Sacred Word(s)

STELLA, SEDET, SALI

Grip

Mutually place a hand on each other's right shoulder.

Sign

Draw the magickal sword across the neck and then point it upwards.[624]

Additional Materials

Password–HOFF OMPHET

Jewel–The winged egg. A portion of a cylinder, with a square in the center and a point in the middle.

---

[624] Consider both the similarity and the differences between this sign and that of the 1st Degree.

Synopsis

In Isidora Forrest's, *Isis Magic*, she suggests that the original working of this Degree took the Candidate upon a journey down the Nile wherein a death-Rite was conducted. From this experience, the Candidate was given a "glimpse of paradise, and finally had the mysteries of the degree symbols revealed to him. Among the mysteries that were revealed was that Isis is the symbol of 'teeming Nature' and that the Moon (Isis) is the Divine Regeneratrix.[625]" This Degree further incorporates Egyptian themes with the Jewel; the winged egg, the principal emblem of the APRM+M.

The *Password* of this Degree, one of the significators of the switch in thematic study and quality of Initiation in the following degrees, is mysterious indeed. It relates to two energies, both connected with the high nature of this degree. First, we are introduced to *Hoff Omphet* in the 49th Degree of *Sage of the Pyramids*. The Initiate is reminded of the mysterious phrase, *Bahlasti! Ompehda!* from the *Book of the Law*, 3:54. The nature of the word in this Degree is distinct, however. The pyramids are emblematic of the sacred oratory that becomes a super-sensual space craft for the pharaohs and high Initiates to traverse the worlds. The words are said to mean, *watch and be pure*. The experience and the entity related to this Degree are mystical in nature, as opposed to purely magickal. The requirements are vigilance (watchfulness) and katharismos (purification). The other connection with the Password, is the *omphalos*, hollow stones found in various parts of the world—Greece, Jerusalem, England, etc.—believed to act as Oracles and to signify the "navel of the world."

The Sacred Word(s) of the Degree are STELLA, SEDET and SALI (also seen as Stella, Sedet and Soli in Jeremy Cross's *Templar Chart* and other late 1800's Masonic texts. The usage of the words in the pre-Pike Scottish Rite are found in the 28th Degree, Knight of the Sun. Here it says, "The three S∴S∴S∴ represent the *Stellato, Sedeck, Solo,* or the residence of the Sovereign Master of all things.[626]" All of these ideas lead to the energy and entity of the Degree and the points-chaud which makes of the Initiate, a *Patriarch of Isis*. The reception of the points-chaud opens and begins the process that is only completed by prayer and vigils, along with our basic method of scrying the point. We have spoken of the *Mystic Temple* which is our very own creation. More often than not, this will be created in a sacred marma or powerzone that we have established for our working. Such may be indoors like our Chapel of the Gnosis, or outdoors like the Holy Arabia Mountain. Yet, we build *Mystic Temples* within our Ontic Spheres as well. These are mental palaces wherein we receive further instruction, initiation and Light. But there is another hyper-spatial locale that is above all others. It is not populated by magickal beings or approached through the artifice of magick. It is a Holy place that is the abode of the *Sovereign Master of All Things*, as our Sacred Word suggests. It is the *Sovereign Sanctuary*, of which the Temple at Karnak is but a *type*.

The experience of the Sovereign Sanctuary and the felt sense of the Sovereign Master's presence is not of the nature of magick, it is pure mysticism. The soul, like the winged egg

---

[625] p. 211.
[626] DeHoyos, *Masonic Formulas and Rituals*, p. 501.

symbolized in our Rite and in this Degree, flies upward to this Sanctuary with only one thought in mind, *theosis*. This is the process of becoming one with the Divine, the Absolute, the very Ground of All Being. One resides already within the bosom of this Sanctuary; the realizing of its presence is akin to Samadhi. The Initiate is enjoined to amp up her efforts of one-pointedness into a laser beam of direct union with the One[627].

This Degree lifts the Initiate into the higher echelons of experience. Rising on the Planes the Initiate moves in an arrow directly upwards upon the Tree of Life through Yesod and into upper Tiphareth, wherein the Beatific Vision is accomplished through *theoria*. She can see the Abyss in the distance, guarded as it is by the demon Choronzon, who, while accompanied by very harsh ordeals and trials, is the very guardian, the living Pylon, of the highest levels of experience. Prepare to leave the known Universe and enter the transmundane.

---

[627] Further instruction in this arena will be found in the Administrative Grades.

Part Three – Chapter Four: Hermetic, Gnostic, & Kabalistic Degrees

77th Degree

Sublime Knight or Sage Theosopher

Presentation of the Illuminists of Old

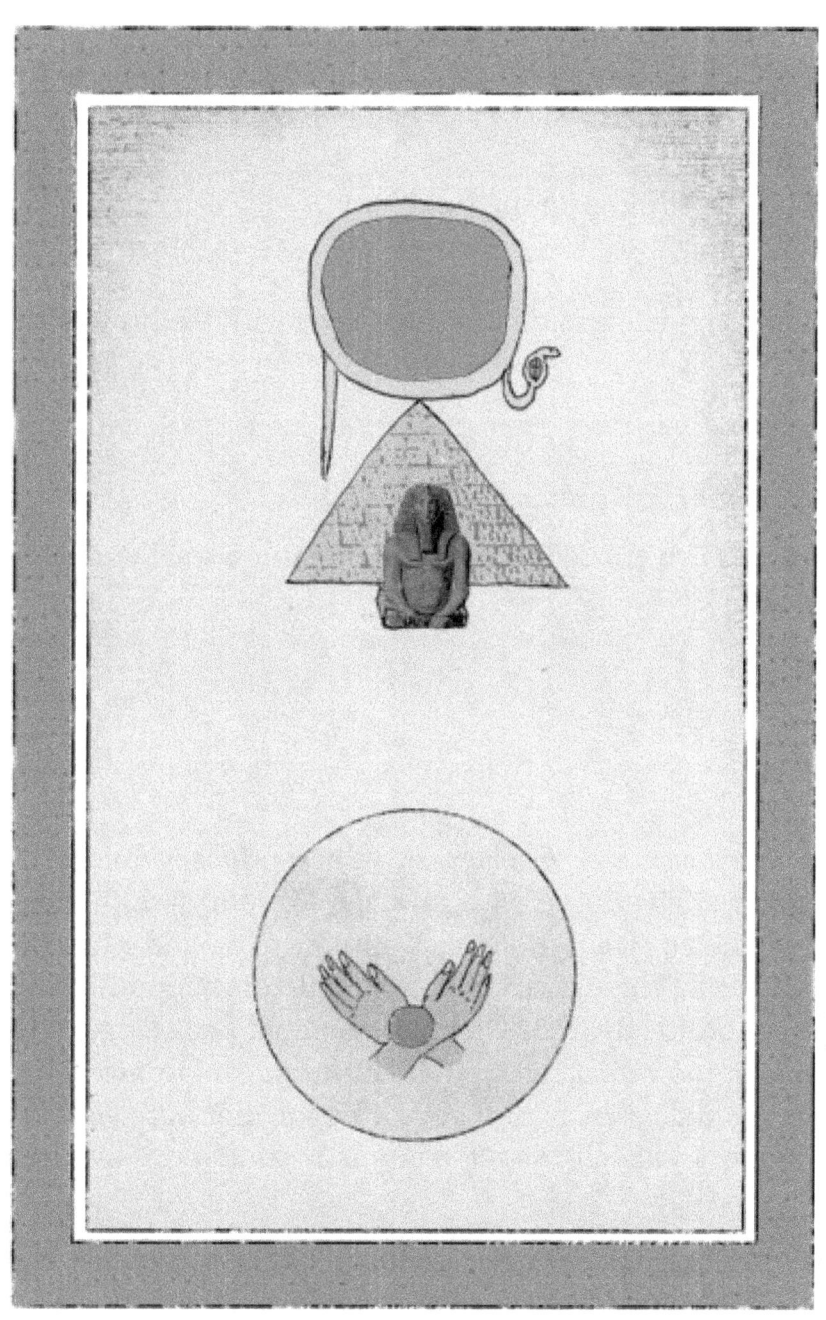

77th *degree,*
Prince of Memphis, or Grand Administrator.

Battery of Knocks

Three, three times. One. **XXX   XXX   XXX   X**

Points-chaud

Upper left, mid back

Sacred Word

SOPHIA *(First feminine ÆON in 3rd echelon with syzygetic partner, THELETOS).*

Grip

Touch each other's forehead with the right hand.

Sign

Rest magickal sword on left arm, then raise it level with the brow with the right hand.

Additional Materials

Password–HOFF OMPHET (watch and be pure)

Jewel–A circle having two crossed hands, in the center a smaller circle.

† † †

Synopsis

In his colossal, *Encyclopedia of Freemasonry*, Albert Mackey informs us that the most important theosophists having to do with mystical Masonry are the likes of Swedenborg, Louis Claude de St. Martin, Jacob Bohme, Dom Pernetty, and Martinez de Pasqually.[628] The re-occurring themes of these theosophists include the supposition that they possessed supernatural inspiration directly from Divinity, obtained knowledge of the regeneration of humans, held a faith in the Kabala as a pure Tradition containing the mysteries, energies and entities of Heaven, had a penchant for Apocalyptic literature viewed symbolically, and considered all of these as having direct relation to Initiation, and that of Masonry in particular.

Yarker's words concerning this Degree are that it "develops the Mystic and transcendent parts of Masonry, including those historic dogmas that have an eternal germ of perpetuity.[629]" We are working with what Aldous Huxley and others have deemed the *perennial philosophy* in this Degree. These are the *universals* realized amongst *particulars* within all traditions. This Degree, more than any other, opens the Initiate up to the mystical nature

---

[628] p. 926.
[629] *Compleat Rite of Memphis*, p. 136.

of Universal Freemasonry,[630] the concept of which is typically restricted to the fraternity being opened to humans of all faiths. This Degree goes one step further and suggests that it is not only *open* to all faiths, but in fact, by virtue of the Primitive Doctrine, *partakes* of the perennial truths, divine potencies, and qualities of all faiths.

It is telling that the Sacred Word of this Degree is, *SOPHIA*[631]. Sophia literally translates to "wisdom," however, Gnostics and mystical Christians know Sophia to be a female entity related to the Theotokos, yet on a Higher arc. The single entity related to this Degree is in fact this Holy Sophia who is accessible to all men and women who seek her. The single energy accompanying this degree is theosophical, which in this case is an action, analogous to the Holy Sophia's "moist light" which she gave to Adam and Eve in the Ophite Tradition. The action of theosophy in the life of the Initiate of our system is a unique ability to perceive the mystic and transcendent parts of all philosophies and religions, to read symbolically all works of Apocalyptic & Gnostic literature, and to relate and commune with the deities of all climes and times. These sublime qualities can be realized by the Initiate of the 77th Degree with meditation upon the points-chaud of the Degree and through the invocation of Holy Sophia. The Battery of Knocks equals ten, the number of completion which by Kabalistic metathesis brings the Initiate back to Omniety. 10=1+0=1.

---

[630] Two of the most outspoken living proponents of Universal Freemasonry in America, are Bros. Eoghan Ballard and John Slifko, who both hold office in the *Modern Rite in North America and the Caribbean*.
[631] Note, in particular, Sophia's role as illustrated in the Gnostic texts, *The Sethian-Ophites* and *The Second Treatise of the Great Seth*.

Spirit Builders

78th Degree

Grand Pontiff of the Thebaid

Vision of the Egyptian Trinity, Assumption of Osiris

78th *degree*,
Grand Pontiff of the Thebiad.

Battery of Knocks

One, One, One.　X　X　X

Points-chaud

Upper left, mid back.

Sacred Word

BYTIS (Early Theban Priest – and XI ÆON, 3rd echelon.)

Grip & Sign of Ordination

(Grip) Join right hands, and place left hands on right shoulder. Then release and place left hand on the heart, right on forehead and bow thrice **(Sign)**.

Additional Materials

Password–HOFF OMPHET

Jewel–Two concentric circles within a square.

† † †

Synopsis

The term, *Pontiff*, in its exclusive sense signifies the Pope. But in Roman antiquity, we find entire Colleges of Pontiffs. It is in this sense that we approach the Holy Office of Grand Pontiff of the Thebaid, for this Degree is an Ordination.

We find the entire time span of this sacred section of the Egyptian desert represented in this Degree. Not only are the ancient Egyptian priests of the Thebaid, the originators of "Sacrifices, divine worship and religious festivals and solemn Assemblies" celebrated in this grade, but those Coptic hermits and cenobites—monks and nuns of the Thebaid are a portion of this inheritance. Each priest of each generation maintained a sacred Trinity—whether that of Osiris, Isis and Horus, or the Father, Son and Holy Spirit. Each priest of each generation maintained the secrets of communion with the Divine and each considered a canopy of lesser Deities above, either through the endless gods and goddesses of Ancient Egypt, or the living beings within the constellations of the night sky, or through the Communion of the Saints.

This powerful line of priests is continued on in this Degree/Ordination, introducing the Initiate to the never ending College of Pontiffs, to which he or she now formally belongs. Through the actions of the Grip and Sign of this grade, the Initiate is made one with the Orders of Priesthood of the Thebaid.

The spiritual experience that accompanies scrying the point of this Degree is a vision of the Trinity of Egypt; Isis, Osiris and Horus. Following the vision of these three, the Initiate is encouraged to identify most especially with Osiris in this working. Horus is worked closely with in the 81st Degree, while Isis is dedicated to the 90th. To identify closely with the Father god of ancient Egypt, the Initiate assumes the godform of Osiris. With the Ordination as a Theban Priest, this technique comes more easily to the Initiate than if simply dabbled with amongst a vague collection of other magickal methods and means. Consistent with the rest of our Primitive Doctrine, the method of *assumption of godforms* in Spirit Building is concise and efficient. It is suggested that the Initiate not accustomed to Hermetic work of this nature, study the various descriptions and processes of this technique in the works of the Golden Dawn. The specific reasoning for our process is discussed in the 81st Degree Synopsis. For our current purposes, the succinct method which has proven efficacious for our Initiates is as follows:

Put yourself in the Prophet Asana as in Scrying the Point. Call inwardly upon the god of your choice until an image of the same arises in your mind's eye. Repeat his or her name in mantric form until the appearance crystallizes. With the mind, step into the god's image and sense the blending of your consciousness with its. In the beginning this feels like putting on the mask of the god, but this same feeling is intensified with the sense of expansion and exaltation. You are now a living manifestation of the god and may perform further rituals and journeys as such.

Once you achieve the assumption of the godform of Osiris, you may move about freely in the *astral* Thebaid. Here, you will discover the further mysteries of this Degree and make sense of the curious statement of Yarker, "the seven first and primitive orders of Gods, developed 12 Cosmogonical powers, and these seven humanized deities.[632]" End the technique by the sign of silence, right forefinger upon the lips and bring your consciousness back to the ground you are upon.

---

[632] *Compleat Rite of Memphis*, p. 137.

79th Degree
Sage of the Redoubtable Sada
Reception of the Name

79th *degree*,
Knight, or Sage of the Redoubtable Sada.

Battery of Knocks

Four, four times. Three, three times.   XXXX   XXXX   XXXX   XXXX   XXX   XXX   XXX

Points-chaud

Upper left back

Sacred Word

SADA

Grip

Join right hands, cover these by gripping with left hands and repeat the Sacred Word.

Sign

Right hand upon magickal sword, draw it back, look at blade, pass it to the left hand[633]. This is a sign upon the plane of inquiry, that you are thenceforth and forevermore, a *Sage of the Redoubtable Sada.*

Additional Materials

Password–HOFF OMPHET

Jewel–Three points, 1 and 2, over a crescent enclosing a square.

† † †

Synopsis

This Degree, placed in the midst of intense initiatory work, is a follow-up to the ordination of the previous grade. If worked in packs of three, the 77th, 78th and 79th go together wonderfully. The 77th introduces the Initiate to the perennial philosophy as developed by specific theosophists. The 78th Degree ordains the Initiate to the labors of the Theban priest and reveals the nature of the Egyptian Trinity as well as identifying the Initiate with Osiris through the practice of the assumption of godforms. This Degree completes the ordination by giving the Theban priest a specific *name*, which is a practice in all priesthoods, orders and Rosicrucian branches.

The meaning of the name of the ordinand of the Theban priesthood, *Redoubtable Sada*, suggests two main ideas. The first is that the member of this College of Pontiffs is to remain constant and to continually persist and persevere in the Great Work, which is the transmutation of the whole Self and the extension of this transmutation into the world

---

[633] The passing of the sword from the right to the left hand is a mystical gesture in Martinism.

around us. We think of Crowley's motto in the Golden Dawn, *Perdurabo*, which meant that he would endure unto the very end. This is assuredly what he did and the Initiate would do well to study this Master's thorough exploration of consciousness and his adept blending of Magic and Mysticism. But *his* way is not necessarily the Initiate's way. The difficult portion of true initiation is that no one can trod the path for you. It is yours and yours alone to traverse. The battles, ordeals, and trials cannot be surmounted by another—they are for the Initiate to take upon herself. This constancy and persistence cannot suffice alone, the Initiate needs power—not the power over others, but the power that is involved in mastery of the Self.

The *Redoubtable Sada* is a formidable presence upon the astral. Persisting as he does until the end, he knows that he is emboldened and strengthened through the points chauds empowerments and the constant nourishing of the Light body through scrying the points and frequent Eucharist. He also energizes himself through the telluric and solar currents by seeking out sacred marmas to meditate in or to practice our Primitive Doctrine.

The points-chaud of this Degree begins the powerful set of empowerments in the upper back, below and between the shoulder blades. These complete the Series of Hermetic, Gnostic and Kabalistic grades and strengthen the back-side of the central column more than any other set.

The Grip of this Degree should be accompanied by a repetition of the Sacred Word that was vibrated with the points empowerment. Once the left hands cover the right hands, the Word is vibrated once more and the Theban priest becomes, thenceforth and forever more, *Sage of the Redoubtable Sada*.

Spirit Builders

80th Degree
Sublime Elect of the Sanctuary of Mazias

80th *degree*,
Sublime Elect of the Sanctuary of Mazias.

Battery of Knocks

Four, four times. Three, three times. **XXXX XXXX XXXX XXXX XXX XXX XXX**

Points-chaud

Upper back, left.

Sacred Word

MINI NINICHARON MONACH (I count the days of Anger)

Grip

Each grasp arm above elbow, press 7 times.

Sign

Cross arms on breast and bend 7 times before the Altar.

Additional Materials

Password–HOFF OMPHET

Jewel–A square with 3 points.

††††

Synopsis

This mystical Degree is begun in the Chapel or Lodge, but completed upon the Inner Planes. The Sacred Word introduces the Initiate to one of the aspects of the god of the following Degree, Horus. In conjunction with the Kadosh Grades of the Philosophical Series and its *Nekam Adonai*, we find Horus described as the avenger of his Father's death. This righteous vengeance points to the necessity of the right arm of strength, Geburah, and its utility in the integrated life of the Initiate. In this way, the Sacred Word or phrase, MINI NINICHARON MONACH (I count the days of Anger) becomes a mantra when the assumption of the godform of Horus is accomplished (81st Degree) and the astral battle commences. This hyperspatial war is fought not only upon the tenuous planes of the diaphanous, but also in the realm of form. The enemies of fanaticism, ignorance, and tyranny ever pose a threat to the free thinking individual and it is our divine right to fight against them.

Scrying the point of this Degree places the Initiate into a supersensual Chapel. He is approached by numerous Brothers and Sisters, clothed in long white robes, who will test his fitness in all arenas. Within this trans-cosmic Chapel, the Initiate is challenged and questioned concerning his understanding of the perennial philosophies of the East and West, the dogmas of the Vedas and the Hermetic doctrines, and he is tested in his efficiency with the occult and regenerative fire of AZOTH. He will now be expected to perform an instant Masonic Middle Pillar (in the form of a lightening bolt) within the Ontic Sphere or magickal imagination, and be able to project his Ojas—or radioactive energy generated from the dragon at the base of the spine—outward, in this case for defense and protection. Within the Ontic Sphere his now scintillating body of vivified hot points and powerzones becomes a shield and buttress against psychic and interstellar attacks. Additionally, his projection of Ojas can be used to slay opponents within the within.

After proofs are given of the Initiate's fitness in mind and body, he is to give the Sign of the Degree (crossing arms upon the breast, right over left as a Rose+Croix, and bowing seven times towards the white clothed challengers and the Chapel altar) and return to the Prophet Asana and the meditative chanting of the Sacred Word, MINI NINICHARON MONACH. This Degree and point empowerment is easily worked with the following Degree and prepares the Initiate for assuming the mighty form of Horus.

81st Degree

Intendent Regulator or Patriarch of Memphis

Assumption of Horus

81st *degree,*
Intendent Regulator, or Patriarch of Memphis.

Battery of Knocks (This battery equals 29, which is 2+9=11, the number of magick)

Three, three times. Four, four times. Two, two times. **XXX XXX XXX XXXX XXXX XXXX XXXX XX XX**

Points-chaud

Upper back, left, between shoulder blades

Sacred Word

HESERI

Grip

Seize each other's arms with both hands.

Sign

Draw the magickal sword across the neck, breast, hips[634] and then point thrice to Heaven.

Additional Materials

Password–HORUS

Jewel–Circle with hexagram, and star in center.

Assumption of godform Horus:

Put yourself in the Prophet Asana as in Scrying the Point. Call inwardly upon the god Horus until an image of the Hawk-headed one arises in your mind's eye. Repeat his name in mantric form until the appearance crystallizes. With the mind, step into the god's image and sense the blending of your consciousness with its. In the beginning this feels like putting on the mask of the god, but this same feeling is intensified with the sense of expansion and exaltation. You are now a living manifestation of the god and may perform further rituals and journeys as such.

†††

Synopsis

The Egyptian god, Horus has a number of different aspects. He is a sky god and an avenger, but he is also known in his child form of Harpocrates. He is a protective god and has been uniquely attributed to our age through the writings and work of Aleister Crowley. As the child of Osiris and his sister wife, Isis, Horus contains within himself both the sun and the moon. He is, therefore, the primary example of integration and the progeny from

---

[634] Daath, Tiphareth, and Yesod.

such. In discussing the Egyptian Trinity, Frank C Higgins[635] illustrated the Forty-seventh Problem of Euclid with Osiris being the vertical side, Isis being the base and Horus the hypotenuse. Horus equals the combination of his mother and father as disclosed mathematically; the vertical side equals 3^2, the base equals 4^2 and the hypotenuse equals 5^2. The Pythagorean Theorem[636]($3^2 + 4^2 = 5^2$) can then be used to represent the integration of mother and father within the son. As HORUS is the password of this Degree, it is he that is the specific entity allied to the points-chaud and the godform that is assumed in scrying the point.

The power that accompanies this is mind energy, the actualization of the *Nous*. Up until this point, there has been discussion of the Body of Light without a detailed exploration of what we mean by it as non-dual Gnostic Spirit Builders. For us, it is a function of the *Nous*[637], which means much more than simply "mind."

The presence of the Nous in Greek writings pre-dates Socrates, shows up in the Hermetic tracts of 1st Century Alexandria, was utilized by Gnostics and is in current usage in Orthodox Churches. Homer used the term in reference to a particular type of mind that was uninfluenced by the emotive sense. It was an exalted form that both gods and humans possessed. Throughout history, the Nous as accumulated an abundance of meanings suggesting its connections to the intuition, to a form of cosmic creative intelligence, to the image of God within humans, to the mind's eye and to pure conscious light. The Valentinian Gnostics attributed NOUS to one of the primary ÆONs (XIV), consort or syzygy of ALETHEIA, or Truth which was the precious response to the Password of the Consistory, *Alethe*. The Eastern Orthodox Churches consider the Nous to be the eye or mind of the heart, which requires purification before it can attain to theoria where it may witness for itself, the Uncreated Light of the divine. There is a sense in most of these definitions of Nous that it can be *developed*. It is in this sense that we work with the Nous in Spirit Building. From this Degree onward, the Nous is energized and developed to open the Ontic Sphere (magickal imagination) of the Initiate in deeper ways. We find that through the simple act of a gnostic pressure to our powerzones, the Nous is actuated immediately and an inner realm is revealed—complete with its life forms, landscapes and scientific laws. The Zothyrian Universe described by Bertiaux is accessible in a similar manner through Esoteric Engineering and magickal machines. These are often as simple as a piece of Euclidean geometry which transports the Initiate through meditation.[638] The Rites of Memphis-Misraïm themselves are a superb form of intuitional machines.

The theories and processes concerning the Body of Light and activities of this Body such as the Assumption of godforms comprise a huge portion of the Western Mysteries. Pages and pages have been composed upon the subject and tried and true methods and means

---

[635] *Hermetic Masonry*, 1916, Pyramid Publishing, p. 32.
[636] In some jurisdictions, this symbol is the Jewel of the Past Master.
[637] See the papers on LA NOETIQUE, from the IVth Degree, 1st Year which continues into the 3rd & 4th year papers, *The Monastery of the Seven Rays*.
[638] See the 3rd Year, Part IV, Lesson 13, *The Monastery of the Seven Rays*.

have been developed in Hermetic, Thelemic, and Rosicrucian Orders. As the Lodges, Chapels and Nodes of Congregational Illuminism are in fact, *Research Lodges,* The Chapel of the Gnosis has dedicated itself to researching the Primitive Doctrine in all of its forms. Its discoveries concerning these subjects are strangely consistent with traditional ideas of the Nous and with a portion of the Mystical Theology of the Eastern Orthodox Church. Primarily, we have maintained a steadfast commitment to non-dual Gnosis, which has elucidated certain tenants concerning the Body of Light. As we do *not* understand the body to be a prison or to be evil, while the separate mind or spirit is supreme, neither do we conceive of the Body of Light as a separate being from the individual. It is more akin to an effluvia[639], in our workings—a projection of our *isness* into the outer spaces around us.

The labors of Spirit Building—creating the scintillating *physical* body through points empowerments, establishing the Mystical Temple through repeated working within sacred geographical marmas, and scrying the Degrees for individual Light and meaning—form a spring board into the Aethers and greatly simplify all procedures. Experiments have revealed a fundamental paradigm shift in our practitioners from the classical idea of the Body of Light as an animation of an etheric simulacrum, to undertaking all journeys available while in the scintillating body through the action of the Nous, and the aforementioned effluvia. The efforts expended in forming a separate Light body are conserved and focused upon the physical organism itself, vibrating as it is from the points empowerments along the central column and powered by the AZOTH from the base of the spine which projects a portion of itself as the Body of Light![640] The journey shifts in direction from the traditional outward and upward movements and visions through the eyes of the self-created Doppelganger, to an inward movement of the Nous, the Hermetic eye of the mind and heart.

Let us recall that the Ecclesiastical Revision of the APRM+M of 1921-22 took on a peculiarly Gnostic tone and that the Degrees became more like ordinations and empowerments than dramatic enactments. As in every Ecclesia, the Gnostic Church has for its primary function, the celebration of the Eucharist in varied forms. From the writings of Crowley and others, it becomes apparent that the Body of Light is nourished through *god eating*, or the Eucharistic sacrifice. For these reasons, our Chapel and Lodge are unified in the Misraïm Chapel Rite, and the primary means of initiation and points chauds working for us is within the Liturgy. It is the Temple of the Holy Spirit, the physical body, enlivened by the awakened powerzones and nourished by god-eating that becomes the enlightened vehicle to Otherwhere, through the Nous. The integrated mind and body work together in our practice. Where the body may be settled and quiet in its asana, it is still coursing the necessary blood, oxygen and vital energies to the central nervous system for the Nous to move inward. This inextricable relationship forms a single process that honors both the

---

[639] This is in the sense of a vapor or gas, emitting from the Initiate as an emanation of her Nous. In all technicality, it is a form of Ontic Broadcasting. See Bertiaux's, *VGW*, p. 615.

[640] Here, we share in the Orthodox theology of the Nous being located in the center of the organism, rather than simply in the head. This is the "mind" in terms of the whole being and the inherent intelligence of each part.

divinity of the body and the expansive capabilities of the Mind. Where others may say upward, higher and higher—we say inward, deeper and deeper. But this is simply a semantics game, because the further we go inward, the higher we move upward.

In his writings against the heresies, St. Irenaeus describes the ÆONic outflowing of divinities from God, beginning with BYTHOS (Sacred word of the 78°) which signifies the Deep, with its syzygetic partner, SIGE (Password in most of the degrees of this Series) which means Silence, and these two give birth to NOUS down the line. These relate to the XVI and XIV ÆONs in the 3rd echelon working, as described in the Preface. Within the mind of the Initiate exists all three. We enter the Deep (Bythos) in scrying the point. From this, a penetrating Silence is born (Sige) and the two combined stir the inner workings of the mind (Nous) into life and activity. The Nous then becomes the opener of the Ontic Sphere that we traverse in an inward direction; spiraling into the depths of our soul.

Before discussing further our method of assuming the godform, let us look at the Sign and Jewel of this Degree for additional instruction. The Sign is very telling to the mainstream Mason. It is made by drawing the sword across the neck, breast, hips and then pointing three times towards Heaven. This Sign is emblematic of the first three penal signs of the Symbolic Degrees along with the Grand Hailing Sign of Distress. When giving this Sign in the scrying journey of this Degree, the Initiate will be opening the entire scintillating body (thus far) on the Inner Planes as well as with the physical body. The points-chauds, as has been said, are primarily upon the central pillar. But they are also mostly relegated to the sections of the body that are housed within the penal signs of the three primary Degrees of all Freemasonry; the head (throat in the Sign), the chest and below the navel in the groin region. These portions of the body are not arbitrary, as we find their significance developed in Kabalistic as well as Hindu literature. When the Tree of Life is superimposed upon the body, the three Sephirah that are activated with this Sign are Daath (a dark or non-Sephirah at the throat), Tiphareth (the heart) and Yesod (the groin). These Sephirah open the astral realm to the Initiate (Yesod), initiate the Beatific Vision of theoria (Tiphareth) and lead the Initiate to the brink of the super-celestial realms through the Gnostic and penetrating experience of Daath. Daath becomes the great Gateway unto the Abyss which takes the Initiate into the Nightside, or backside of the Tree of Life[641]. In Hindu metaphysics, the three chakras that are stimulated through the action of the magickal sword in this Sign are; Vishuddhi which is growth, expression and dream related, Anahata which is the heart-mind, and Muladhara which is life oriented.

The Jewel of this Degree relates directly to the Sign as both in Hindu metaphysics and in Kabalistic thought, the heart center is symbolized with a hexagram in a circle. The star in the center of the symbol is the soul of the Initiate.

---

[641] In rounding out his discussion of the Voudon Cabala and the safety of working along the backside of the Tree of Life for those who do not follow the dualisms of Manichean and Augustinian doctrines, Bertiaux says, "In other words, the exploration of the Divine Mind is a helpful and spiritually vitalizing experience, which you should look forward to without any anxiety." *Cosmic Meditation*, p. 55.

Spirit Builders

When assuming the godform of Horus, it is important to visualize the putting on of a hawk-headed mask. Images of the god in Egyptian books assist this greatly. In fact, the Egyptian pantheon is so perfectly suited for the assumption of godforms that it almost seems as if the teaching is a re-awakening of an ancient practice. The Nous of the Initiate enters into a sort of theoria with the Archetype. From here, when the mask is put on, when we transfer our consciousness into the image that is within ourselves, identification through devotion develops[642]. The assumption will not be complete without the three levels that are exhibited in the Sign of the Degree—through the throat (points chauds 12-19) which signifies the inner gateway of Daath, through devotion to the god in the heart (points 28-24) and the essential life of the body (points 34-44) where the life-force resides and the AZOTH is stirred into wakefulness. With the vivified effluvia of the Light Body, the entire consciousness need not be projected *outward* to a vivified chimera of the godform; instead, he is taken upon oneself inwardly through the Nous. "Up" and "down" no longer fitly describe our travels, for all occurs within the within. The stepping into the godform, the putting on of the mask of the god, is the inner realization that *That Art Thou*, Tat Tvam Asi.

---

[642] This process is developed organically by Bertiaux in his teachings on Lycanthropy.

Part Three – Chapter Four: Hermetic, Gnostic, & Kabalistic Degrees

82nd Degree

Grand Elect of the Temple of Midgard

Vision of the Sovereign Sanctuary

82nd *degree,*
Grand Elect of the Temple of Midgard.

Battery of Knocks

Seven, seven times. Two, two times. XXXXXXX XXXXXXX XXXXXXX XXXXXXX XXXXXXX XXXXXXXX XXXXXXX XX XX

Points-chaud

Upper right back, below the shoulder blade.

Sacred Word

MIDGARD (Elevated Sanctuary)

Grip

Hold position of point empowerment momentarily, then move around front and join hands, pressing nine times. (Battery is of 7s and 2s, 7+2=9)

Sign

Draw magickal sword, rest left hand upon it. Look upwards.

Additional Materials

Password–HORUS

Jewel–A circle intersected by three horizontal and three perpendicular lines.

† † †

Synopsis

As we near the end of the Hermetic, Kabalistic and Gnostic Series, we return to the beginning with reference back to the 34th Degree, Knight of Scandinavia. The primary reason for this is the wisdom lodged within the Sacred Word of the Degree, MIDGARD, which means, *elevated Sanctuary*.

Much has been spoken of in terms of the Ontic Sphere, the *Mystic Temple* and the *Sovereign Sanctuary* on high, but it is in this grade that some of these secrets are spoken of more clearly and the instruction becomes more practical concerning entrance into these august Holy Places.

The Ontic Sphere has been defined as the magickal imagination. This is the term and definition used by Michael-Paul Bertiaux in his *Voudon Gnostic Workbook*.[643] At a glance, it is indistinguishable from the normal imagination, yet the Ontic Sphere has the singular quality of continuance that sets it apart from a space simply dreamt up on an isolated

---

[643] p. 615.

occasion. With the continuous efforts of the Initiate, the Ontic Sphere is built up as an etheric cloud within the Nous, which is fed and drawn from by the will of the Initiate as well as by others either purposefully or not. It is a constant reservoir of stored energy, bubble and cloudlike in formation. One of the reasons why T Allen and others suggest Holy Orders for those working with the points-chauds empowerments is that the priest's Ontic Sphere is fed continuously by way and virtue of Apostolic and Gnostic Succession. For many, this is literally experienced as *ray-ing* from the very SOURCE existing on a plane more tenuous than ours. In this way, the Ontic Sphere is never depleted and becomes a dependable reservoir of energy and healing for the priest of the Gnosis. Within the Ontic Sphere reside beings of a different nature than our own, whom we invite to inspire our work and who are assisting members of our Chapels and Lodges; called upon as "Passed Masters" in the work. The Ontic Sphere also has the capacity of revealing various gates and entryways into further spheres and planes of development. But the mystery, in sum, is that it *continues*—acts as a *reservoir*—and is *close* at hand at all times. We may dip from this sacred well at will. It is the first room in the inner Chapels that are explored in scrying. It is familiar and hallowed by repeated excursions as well as by frequent nurturance and Spirit Building.

The Mystic Temple, referred to in the administrative texts of the Antient and Primitive Rite of 33 Degrees by Yarker, is for us, what is clairvoyantly seen in our Holy place of working.[644] When we select, for instance, a geographical marma—discovered by means of those sensitive to such subtle vibratory shifts, or hallowed by time, nature or ancient peoples—and begin to work our form of the APRM+M in this place, with the points chauds empowerments, then a Mystic Temple begins to settle upon the place. Great pylons and columns are sensed, forming a square about the powerzone. Glimpses of white clothed beings may be seen passing in and out of the four gates of the cardinal directions, offering obeisance to the Initiates in waiting or towards the table of elements (in the Elemental Mass of the Misraïm). Openings from above are perceived, ray-ing down yellow and golden solar currents into the hot spot where the Eucharist, initiations, and healings are conferred. From below bubble forth green and earth-toned telluric currents, vivifying creatures of salt, chalk, charcoal and clay, making of the primitive elements involved a divinized ground of the laborer's working tools and blessing the proceedings from the earth's inner resources. This Mystic Temple alone is enough reason to pursue a course of study and research into the nature of our working, as it is one of the most profound experiences gifted to the Seer.

But the Sovereign Sanctuary, the *MIDGARD*, elevated above all forever, is not drawn out clearly for Initiates, as it is pure mystery. What do the word and the Degree work teach us concerning it? Firstly, that it is a "Temple not made with hands, eternal in the heavens, that of Brahma, Krishna, Buddha, Odin, Christ, in Egypt Osiris, and Thoth or Hermes.[645]" So it is a common place where the perennial philosophies come together without admixture. They are still recognized as "Buddha" or "Christ," yet they are in a state of concord. This

---

[644] See Leadbeater's, *The Hidden Life in Freemasonry*.
[645] *Compleat Rite of Memphis*, p. 138.

is the spiritualized *Universal Freemasonry* spoken of previously, that is far beyond a sense of tolerance. It moves into the realm of understanding and further, into the state of identification and non-duality.[646] It is also, "not made with hands." This is not a human creation, it does not partake of the same nature as either the Mystic Temple or the Ontic Sphere. Additionally, it is said to be "eternal in the heavens" and an "Elevated Sanctuary." It does not suffer corruption or dissolution and is located in the heavens. But here is the deepest aspect of the mystery, for we are not referring here to "Heaven" with a capital, *H*. The mystery is in the word that is used for the Sovereign Sanctuary, *Midgard*. Midgard is none other than the *known world*, identical in meaning to the Greek, *oikoumene*, or the portion of the universe that is known—the phenomenal. In other words, we are somehow *within* this Sovereign Sanctuary already, and this world too is amongst the stars[647] (heavens). It is a pointer to the everlasting quality of the essences within the known world, the energy and matter which is neither created nor destroyed over time—simply changed. But our phenomenal Universe is filled with dark matter—with the noumenal, the "tails" side of the quarter. It is a subtle lesson in looking too fondly on things that are "heavenly" and forgetting the mystery beneath one's feet, and the darkness above. It is a principle concerning the SOURCE of All that is beautiful, good, Holy and harmonious—containing the dark and the light– and where it is that we are to look for that Source. The original Norse usage of the word suggested something akin to middle earth, which was surrounded by an ocean inhabited by a gigantic sea-serpent resembling the sacred Ouroboros. This myth will elucidate further meanings and qualities to the eternal Sanctuary, elevated above, yet more nearer ourselves than "I."

The points-chaud of this Degree is accompanied by a vision of the Sovereign Sanctuary and further communications with the Sovereign Commander of this sphere.

---

[646] What the Vedantists call, *Advaita*.
[647] A beloved phrase of Albert Pike.

Part Three – Chapter Four: Hermetic, Gnostic, & Kabalistic Degrees

83rd Degree

Sublime Elect of the Valley of Oddy

Invocation of the Ancient Hierophant

83th *degree,*
Sublime Elect of the Valley of Oddy.

Battery of Knocks

Two sets of six. X X X X X X   X X X X X X

Points-chaud

Upper right back, between shoulder blades

Sacred Word

SASYCHIS (Ancient Hierophant)

Grip

Grasp each other's wrist with right hand.

Sign

Rest the magickal sword over right shoulder, eyes on heaven.

Additional Materials

Password–HORUS

Jewel–A circle with 12 points

† † †

Synopsis

It is common to find Egyptian style palms, fronds and branches, mingled into Masonic motifs, columns, certificates and the like. Our Degree speaks of two trees at once, the symbolic palm of the Valley of Oddy (could be a mis-translation of Wadi), dedicated to the Sun and having 365 properties. This mystical tree[648] produced one branch each month, or 12 annually. Both numerical correspondences suggest completion of the year and with the addition of the "properties" of the palm, abundance. The palm tree is often considered an emblem of the productive phallus. Symbolized in this light, the 365[649] properties may allude to anything from consecrating talismans, to creating the sacred Elixir, to the production of curses and hexes. Overall, the emblem indicates the productive nature and the cyclical quality of this mysterious tree and its equal production of branches along the year.

---

[648] A very interesting connection to this tree is made in *The GNOSTICS According to St. Epiphanius of Salamis, Against Heresies*, Chapters 25-26, "I beheld a tree bearing twelve crops per year, and he said to me, 'This is the tree of life' they interpret the passage allegorically as referring to the woman's monthly emissions." This is derived from p. 207 in Bentley Layton's, *The Gnostic Scriptures, Ancient Wisdom for the New Age*. If related to the sacred kalas of Grant's *Typhonion Trilogies*, much can be gleamed from this emblem.

[649] The Gnostic ABRAXAS has a relationship with this as well, as the name adds to 365 in Greek Gematria, and he was considered the ruler of 365 gods.

Yarker then goes on to discuss a Sycamore, sacred to Isis and found near Heliopolis. This tree, known as the *ished*, was not only sacred to Isis, but also to Nut and Hathor. This tree was sacred to the sun and was thought to offer food and other victuals for the dead. Funeral coffins were made from the sycamore. It had a particular draw to the goddesses and is found often with one of the Ba's of the gods within it.

The Egyptian conception of the afterlife is truly rather brilliant. It is an elaborate and intricate scheme based upon the needs and journeys of *this* life, but with the added bonus of no real limitations. The *Ba* of a person, for instance is able to fly about freely after death. It may move in and out of this life and even in and out of other life forms. It is consistent with many notions of the Soul.

The *Ka* is what is often considered the Body of Light. In fact, many in the Western Tradition have used this singular Egyptian concept to support the notion of the *separate* Body of Light. However, if one analyzes the glyphs where we find the Ka, it is typically shown right near the King or Pharaoh, acting as a sort of guardian—like our notion of the effluvia from the Nous. The Ka was understood to be present in other things, such as statues and reliefs. But it isn't necessarily that the Ka was projected outward as a separate identity from the priesthood and into the statues. Our notion is consistent with the writings attributed to Hermes Trismegistus. In the 17th Book of these small tracts, we find the statement, "That is why you should worship the statues, because they contain the forms of the mind of the cosmos.[650]" Look at the wording however, as it is the *nous* of the cosmos that is invigorating and vivifying the statues, not that of the man. It is in the same way that the Eastern Orthodox consider their sacred art of Icon painting. The Icons of Jesus and Mary and the Saints are considered to be *windows* into the eternal. The parishioner doesn't project a portion of *his own nous* into the Icon, the Icon, *by way of sympathy and magickal attraction*, draws in the essences from the cosmos and reflects the same to the sensitive viewer. Again, we find the same notion in the veves of Haitian Vodou drawn with cornmeal upon the ground and acting as landing strips for the gods and Lwa, as well as in the iconography of our Tracing Boards. All of this is not too unlike the method of Ceremonial Magicians and the use of sigils. A well made sigil need not be impregnated by the nous of the Mage, it will vibrate of its own accord. The *Ka* then, may not necessarily be the Body of Light. Could it refer to something else? We find it guarding Kings and Pharaohs in the paintings and glyphs. All humans are said to posses one and the gods may have more than one. The research of the Chapel of the Gnosis suggests that the Ka is intimately connected with the *Holy Guardian Angel* of Sacred Magick. This will be explored further in the *Arcana Arcanorum*. It is understood to be the vital essence[651] of the human that, at its purest state, IS the higher Self.

The *Akh*[652] is a notion less discussed in magick circles, but connected with this Degree. The Akh is the blessed or transmuted soul who has passed through the ordeal of the weighing of the heart. When our Degrees have the title, *Elect*, such as the current one, it refers to the *Akh*. The Akh becomes a star, as it were, upon death. In the commentary on the *Book of Going Forth by Day*, it is said that, "an *akh* of the deceased was truly transfigured, in an essentially incorporeal state, having become a stellar or solar being.[653]" In other words, the Akh is no longer in an insatiable state of wandering, he has gone beyond the wheel of samsara and realized his unity with the All. He is free from the transmigration of souls, of Pythagoras. He is a sort of Bodhisattva or Saint.

The *ished* then, seen upon the astral, will be a sacred tree feeding the Ba's of gods and mortals and overseen by the goddesses. Its production of one leaf per month and its 365 properties are for the souls of the dead, those that wander in the shades[654] and seek relief as they work out their karma and complete their True Wills. In this way, those who do not attain the Akh, are still cared for and have hope for achieving their highest state. Interestingly enough, the symbolism of the sacred sycamore continues in Egypt today, yet

---

[650] *The Way of Hermes*, p. 78.
[651] In Edmund Meltzer's Introduction to "Old Coptic Texts of Ritual Power," he defines the ka as, "vital essence." *Ancient Christian Magic, Coptic Texts of Ritual Power*, p. 15.
[652] See Preface.
[653] Goelet, *The Egyptian Book of the Dead, the Book of Going Forth By Day*, p. 152, 1998.
[654] Reference again could be made to the Kaula cults and their work in cremation grounds and with the lunar kalas.

it is dedicated to the Theotokos, the Mother of God–the Virgin Mary. The patronage of the goddess continues in another form in this sacred land, and the secrets of the Egyptians are passed down to the next generation under the cloak of Christianity[655].

The final way that the sacred tree is utilized in this Degree is in reference to our Primitive Doctrine. Yarker says, "The primitive Initiations were under the shadow of trees.[656]" Our approach to the Rites does not require elaborate Temples and buildings. Those Free Illuminists who are capable, make a pilgrimage to the Holy Arabia Mountain as oft as possible, there to gather with other Magi, Adepts and Priests to worship, initiate, and consecrate under the shadow of trees and atop the rough hewn, *Consecration Rock*. As Initiates hike up the Martian-like monodknock, they may spy T Allen Greenfield or others purveying the temporary pools that form on the crater like surface after the rains. Performing a type of hydromancy prior to the order of work, he will receive a word or an injunction for all involved from these passing sources of divination. Those of the Primitive Doctrine see *this* world as revelatory and the dome of sky to be the proper roof for our ceremonials. Even if one's primary marma is located inside, such as our Chapel of the Gnosis, the practitioner of the Primitive Doctrine will be drawn to the outdoor altar on a regular basis and will thereby connect with the ancients. Within a few paces from our Chapel is located a clearing with a stone altar dedicated to Our Lady. It is a natural circular spot with a second powerzone directly in the center of the space. Nature developed this Holy Place and our members are drawn to it in a particular way during the Equinoxes and Solstices.

The Sacred Word, SASYCHIS, refers to ASCHIS an Egyptian King and Lawgiver. The Battery of Knocks equaling twelve, refers to the continuity of the *ised* and its ever productiveness. This is further indicated by the Jewel of a circle with twelve points, all directing the mind to the eternal qualities of this sacred tree upon the astral. The points-chaud empowerment puts the Initiate in contact with an "Ancient Hierophant" as Yarker describes SASYCHIS, however this Hierophant is not SASYCHIS. He responds to this Sacred Word when meditated upon, but he has another name which he will tell the Initiate.

---

[655] In the same manner that Cagliostro passed on Egyptian Masonry through Christian emblems.
[656] *Compleat Rite of Memphis*, p. 138.

Spirit Builders

84th Degree

Patriarch or Doctor of the Izeds

Beginnings of Angel Magic

84th *degree,*
Patriarch or Doctor of the Izeds.

Battery of Knocks

Four, four times. XXXX XXXX XXXX XXXX

Points-chaud

Right, upper back between the shoulder blades

Sacred Word

IBIS

Grip

Form St. Andrew's cross by placing hands on each other's shoulders.

Sign

Cross the arms within the sleeve of the robe.

Additional Materials

Password–HORUS
Jewel–Three concentric circles, with a single point in the center.

† † †

Synopsis

In this Degree, we return to the idea of Emanationism, so prevalent in all of our mysteries. From the Aeons of Gnosticism, to the Sephirah of the Kabala, we find this notion of Light, Deities, angels, and forces descending from a singular source. With the Zoroastrians it is the same. We have Ahura Mazda (Ormuzd) from whom all of the Amesha Spenta (worded Amaschpands in the Degree work) descend. Among these are the Izeds[657] to whom this Degree is dedicated. These Devas govern the calendar of the year which is pointed to by the repetition of the number 30 in reference to the Izeds. Pike connects this back to the 30 Aeons of the Valentinian Gnostics[658] and one could follow this line of thinking to no end. Mitra is one of the angelic Deities born from this eternal dividing of gods into parts who govern particular functions of the known world. Mitra then became, for the Romans, a sun God and the focus of the Mithraic mysteries.

As a Doctor of the Izeds, the Initiate has a simple role to fulfill. She is to look inside of herself and see the various parts that create what we call, "I." This is explored further in the next Degree, but for the meditations upon the points-chaud of this Degree and the

---

[657] Some will see the similarity in Izeds to the Yezidis. These two names certainly have the same Persian source.
[658] See the diagram of the Treasury of Light from GRS Mead in the Preface.

subsequent scryings of the point, the Initiate must look inward to see if the *Nous* truly contains all that we suggest it may, and if so, what does such emanationism from within the Nous mean? Of what use to the world then, is this concept that we have an infinite number of spirit contacts, angels, devas, etc., at our immediate disposal when we learn the secret of their interior nature? The answer is in the Jewel of the Degree and the point empowerment.

There is a danger within the entire Western Esoteric Tradition, of falling into pure abstraction. This danger is multiplied sevenfold when the Initiate first experiences presentiments, or passes or showings of the other realm to the senses. Suddenly *that* world becomes the preeminent domain and physicality is either hated, damned with faint praise, or simply forgotten. As we near the *Arcana Arcanorum*, we must be more cautious in our excursions into the deep and realize that life is whole and unified. All of these inner realms are of no purpose whatsoever if they do not bless, sanctify, and make more Holy, the outer realm—for it is simply two sides of the same coin. Ahriman and Ahura Mazda need each other in the same way that front needs back, male needs female and inner needs outer. To attribute too much importance to one is to atrophy the other. Our Jewel is a simple symbol of three concentric circles, with a point in the center. This is suggestive of our holistic Self, its unity of inner and outer and the secret center that retains the gnosis of integration. If the Initiate is standing in the sign of human sovereignty, the sign of the pentagram, and given the points-chaud empowerment between the shoulder blades, upon the right side of the back, she will experience an immediate tingling of the limbs and slight light-heatedness. This is the integration happening within the body, carried by the vital fluids and unifying the organism.

As the Devas, Izeds and others of Zoroastrianism are some of the first versions of winged angels in sacred literature we cannot help but think of the angelic hierarchies. Speaking on the 14th Major Arcana *Temperance*, Valentin Tomberg says, "If the law of wings is the love of God, that of arms is the love of neighbor. And the law of legs is the love of terrestrial

Nature.⁶⁵⁹" Here, he is using the Angel as a rational, yet spiritual being of Light—emanated from God—whose wings are emblematic of his love of God, and comparing this with our arms and legs. This is a work of initiated genius when analyzed. We are moving from the study of an abstract form back to the body and our personal calling on this earth—to love the earth and our neighbor. He goes on in the same letter to describe precisely the physical experience related to this points-chaud empowerment, saying;

*For just as there exists a system of physical circulation, so also there exists a system of vital and astral circulation, which in its turn is simply a reflection of the system of circulation comprising spirit, soul and body—the threefold body—as living unity...it is the mission of the guardian Angel to see to it that the total system of circulation functions in as healthy way as possible.*⁶⁶⁰

It is this physico-spiritual circulatory system that we are working with in our Primitive Doctrine. The body and the Nous are inseparable while on this plane and it is in gross error to raise one above the other. What the next life brings is its own, while we are a complete unity it is for us to bring about the entire renovation of our selves. The *Scintillating Body* in turn, blesses and brings life to the *Mystic Temple* which then welcomes with open arms, the community working *In Free Communion*. Physicality and spirituality are mutually dependent in our workings.

The Sacred Word of our Degree is IBIS, which refers to Thoth—the Egyptian Hermes. His wife is the goddess of the balance, Ma'at. Thoth is often considered the mediating power and his unity with Hermes is best understood by the Hermetic dictum, "as above, so below." THIS is the key to our science; that which is divine, celestial and otherworldly is strangely found within! The Doctor of the Izeds is Master of the forces within, knowing them to full well be in concert with the forces without.

---

⁶⁵⁹ *Meditations on the Tarot*, p 385.
⁶⁶⁰ Ibid, p. 385.

Spirit Builders

85th Degree

Sublime Sage, or Knight of Kneph

Knowledge of the KA

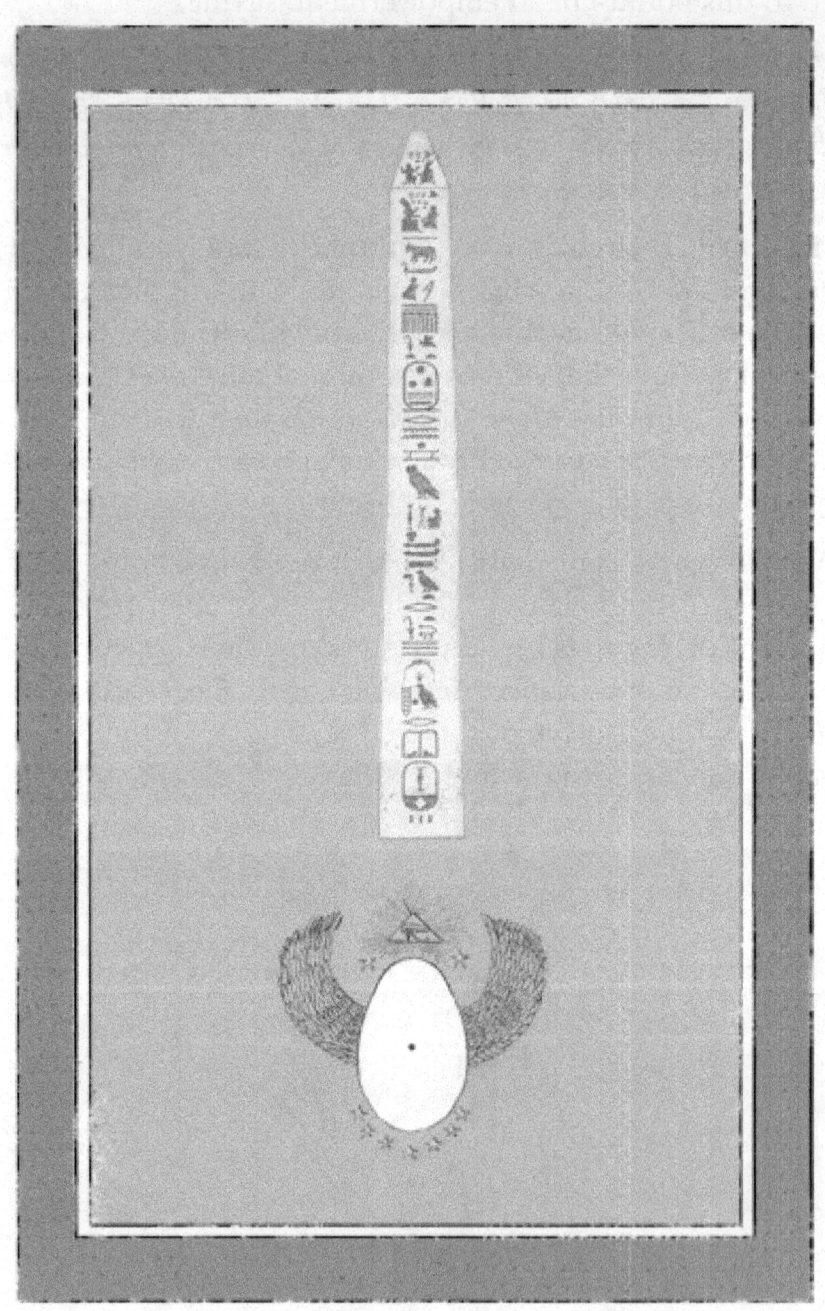

85th *degree,*
Sublime Sage, or Knight of Kneph.

Battery of Knocks

Three and four. **XXX XXXX** (symbolizing the seven principles of the spirit becoming four and three, or the square and the triangle)

Points-chaud

Upper left shoulder, back

Sacred Word

KNEPH, answer JOA (two natures united[661])

Grip

Join hands, and touch each other's palms with the fingers.

Sign

Represent the Kneph by making an oval with the thumb and forefingers and spreading out the remaining fingers as the wings. This is a powerful sign upon the Inner Planes and suggests to the super-celestial beings that the Initiate is aware of his Ka[662]. The sign should not be given lightly, nor by the Initiate in scrying who does not yet sense the presence of the Ka. In such case, the Sign of a Master Mason will suffice for entrance into the Chapel related to this Degree, whereas the Sanctuary requires knowledge of the Ka. Transmission of the KA occurs in the 3° with the exchange on the five points of Fellowship. Such begins the end, as this same KA comes into play in the 3rd echelon working of the Grand Rite of Osirification.

Additional Materials

Password–HORUS

Jewel–An oval with a central point.

†††

Synopsis

This Degree is preparatory to the *Arcana Arcanorum*. We return to the Egyptian idea of the *Ka* which we have seen as more descriptive of the Holy Guardian Angel of Ceremonial Magic than of the astral double, or separate and *ensouled* Body of Light. In earlier works, the Ka is defined as the "double" but in the most recent scholarship we find that the Ka is

---

[661] Continuing the theme of the former Degree.
[662] We are using *Ka* in the sense of the HGA here, from research undertaken in our Chapel. It is still a fitting emblem for the Body of Light, so long as that body is not understood to be literally "separate" from the individual.

more closely connected with the soul and yet often symbolized as being near to the King, or as a pair of arms above the head of him.

The most crucial understanding of the Ka here is that we each have one. This Ka can move about us and is in some sense, *loosely* attached to us. As the HGA, it appears loosely attached simply because it is un-realized by the average person. This is one's truest Self— the ultimate divine that is who we are, our vital essence. We identify with our persona, or the mask that is what we project of ourselves to others. When the mask is stripped away, through purification, then the Sol Philosophorum—the living spirit of gold– of Alchemy is revealed. This mystery is developed more fully in the Arcana Arcanorum.

The energy and entity allied with this empowerment of are of one nature. A dissolution is sensed within the Initiate, which is a sign of the rising nature of the Ka. The immortal and universal spirit acting within primordial matter and signified by the winged egg or Kneph is indicative of the ceaseless and boundless creativity of the Universe and the realization of the creative Ka as the secret Center. The Knowledge and Conversation afforded by this Ka may have already begun for the Initiate.

This Degree and the next, complete the Hermetic, Gnostic, and Kabalistic Series and they also complete the points-chauds working upon the back. The remaining points are upon the head and face. The points upon the back have stimulated the spiritual circuitry of the Initiate in such a way as to prepare and pave the way for the deepest conceptions of the spiritual life related in the final Degrees of our Rite.

Part Three – Chapter Four: Hermetic, Gnostic, & Kabalistic Degrees

86th Degree
Sublime Philosopher of the Valley of Kab

86th degree,
Sublime Philosopher of the Valley of Kab.

Battery of Knocks

Three and seven. XXX   XXXXXXX

Points-chaud

Upper right shoulder on the back.

Sacred Word

KAB

Grip

Press each other's hand thrice and give the Sacred Word.

Sign

Bend the head, and appear to be smelling a flower.

Additional Materials

Password–HORUS

Jewel–A large square, containing two concentric squares with three points in the center, 1 over two.

†††

Synopsis

The Kab is described by Yarker as the mystical location of Memphis where the Holy Rose was found. This Holy Rose is none other than the sacred Lotus blossom which is indicative of the entire nature of the *Arcana Arcanorum*. The Lotus is the symbol of the *Sahasrara chakra,* the thousand-petalled Lotus at the crown of the head which opens and flowers in the state of Samadhi. It is the Kether of the Tree of Life. As our points-chauds empowerments move their way to the head of the body, this flowering of the mind, this state of pure and unfiltered consciousness draws nearer and nearer. It is attainable in each step along the way. Every Degree has, built within it, a secret door to this Samadhi. Every points-chaud is a powerzone which can open the Lotus immediately. We often *realize* by degrees, but we may *attain* in an instant. The experience of this Degree and its point empowerment is perfectly described by Yarker. In speaking of the Lotus, he says that it is "consecrated to the Sun, and is an emblem of the same nature as Kneph, for bursting its seed vessel over the waters it propagates itself.[663]" The sense of this is felt intimately in the proper working of the Masonic Middle Pillar, when the AZOTH is brought forth from the base of the spine

---

[663] *Compleat Rite of Memphis*, p. 139.

and drawn upwards with the breath to the crown of the head, bursting forth in a shower of infinite light which rains down upon the body, tingling inside from the dazzling sparks.

This Degree is the culmination of all of the work of the Series. We have courted all aspects of the Western Mystery Tradition—astrology, alchemy, Ceremonial Magick, Gnosis, spiritism, traversing the planes, divination—all leading to a fundamental flowering of this source of infinite light and knowledge within the body. One gnostic pressure–balancing the pressure from the 85th Degree– upon the upper right shoulder and our hairs stand on end. In the Zohar we find an intimation of what our physical head contains with the speech on the Greater Countenance:

> *Its intimate thoughts are hidden, but its exterior, creative thoughts shine forth like a head of hair. White hair without shadow and whose strands are never tangled. Each strand is a thread of light attached to millions of worlds.*[664]

All of our spirit workings converge in the knowledge that pure consciousness, pure unity, pure Advaita is available in a moment's notice with any of our diverse workings. The prerequisite is simply a unified mind/body. Our creation of the *Scintillating Body* working within the *Mystic Temple, in Free Communion* with others, is simply the offering of 97 opportunities of oneness. This is the Primitive Doctrine in action. This sense of completion is further demonstrated by our Battery of Knocks which equal ten, the sum total of the Sephirah, the basis of our numerical system, the number of our fingers! 10=1+0=1.

---

[664] Eliphas Levi, *The Book of Splendours*, p. 25.

Suggested Reading for the Hermetic, Gnostic and Kabalistic Series

This listing may seem extravagant, but there are numerous seminal texts that help to develop the Spirit Builder working this Series of Degrees. So many subjects are covered in these Degrees that an exhaustive list is nearly impossible. But these tomes are worthy of study to the interested Initiate working this path. They form a University style curriculum in Hermeticism and Ceremonial Magick. The sections are not water-tight compartments and much overlap exists in multiple books. For those beginning the magickal path, choosing one per section might be helpful in the beginning.

Masonic and related books

- *96th Degree Rite of Memphis,* Calvin C Burt
- *The Alchemical Keys to Masonic Ritual,* Timothy Hogan
- *The Arcane Schools,* John Yarker
- *The Baylot Manuscript in Translation,* Sar Phosphoros (trans.)
- *The Compleat Rite of Memphis,* T Allen Greenfield
- *Degrees of Wisdom: A Compendium of Rituals from the Rites of Memphis and Misraïm,* Tau Phosphoros (trans., ed.)
- *The Egyptian Masonic History of the Original and Unabridged Ancient and Freemasonry and its Ancient Mystic Rites,* C. W. Leadbeater
- *La Franc-maçonnerie Égyptienne de Memphis-Misraïm,* Serge Caillet
- *Freemasonry,* Mark Stavish
- *Freemasonry, Foundation of the Western Esoteric Tradition,* Angel Millar
- *Freemasonry: A French View,* Roger Dachez & Alain Bauer
- *The French Rite: Enlightenment Culture,* Cécile Révauger
- *Lectures of a Chapter, Senate & Council: According to the Forms of the Antient and Primitive Rite, but Embracing All Systems of High Grade Masonry,* John Yarker
- *The Masonic Magician,* Faulks and Cooper
- *Masonic Orthodoxy: Followed by Occult Masonry and Hermetic Initiation,* J.-M. Ragon
- *Mystic Masonry,* J.D. Buck
- *Quest for a Lost Rite: The Origins, High Degrees, and Spiritual Practices of Traditional Egyptian Masonry,* Mathieu Ravignat
- *Rituels Secrets des Hauts-Grades de la Franc-maçonnerie Égyptienne,* Joël Duez
- *The Royal Masonic Cyclopedia,* Kenneth Mackenzie
- *Sacred Geometry,* Robert Lawlor
- *The Sanctuary of Memphis,* E.J. Marconis
- *The Secret Science of Masonic Initiation,* Robert Lomas
- *The Secret Tradition in Freemasonry,* A.E. Waite

Ceremonial Magick

- *776 ½,* Jim Eschelman
- *Abrahadabra,* Orpheus
- *Aurum Solis,* Osborne Phillips
- *Between the Gates,* Mark Stavish
- *The Book of Ceremonial Magic,* A. E. Waite
- *Circles of Power,* John Michael Greer
- *The Complete Mystical Records of Dr. John Dee* (Vol. 1-3), Kevin Klein (ed.)
- *The Goetia, the Lesser Keys of Solomon the King,* Mathers and Crowley
- *The Hermetic Brotherhood of Luxor,* Godwin, Chanel and Deveney
- *The History of Magic,* Eliphas Levi
- *Initiation in the Aeon of the Child,* J Gunther
- *Isis Magic,* M. Isidora Forrest
- *The Key of Solomon the King,* translated and edited by Mathers
- *The Key to the Mysteries,* Eliphas Levi
- *Magick, Book IV, Liber ABA,* Aleister Crowley
- *The Magus,* Francis Barret
- *The Picatrix,* John Michael Greer and Christopher Warnock
- *The Ritual Magic of the Golden Dawn,* Francis King
- *Secret Rituals of the O.T.O.,* Francis King (ed.)
- *Secrets of the Magickal Grimoires,* Aaron Leitch
- *Self Initiation into the Golden Dawn System of Magic,* Chic and Tabatha Cicero
- *The Sixth and Seventh Books of Moses,* ed. Joseph Peterson
- *Taboo: Sex, Religion and Magick,* Hyatt and Duquette
- *Three Books of Occult Philosophy,* Cornelius Agrippa
- *Transcendental Magic,* Eliphas Levi

Hermeticism, Egyptian and related subjects

- *Ancient Christian Magic, Coptic Texts of Ritual Power,* Meyer and Smith
- *The Art of Memory,* Frances A Yates
- *Collectanea Hermetica* William Wynn Westcott
- *The Egyptian Book of the Dead, the Book of Going Forth by Day,* Wasserman (ed.)
- *Egyptian Magic,* Florence Farr
- *Golden Shrine, Goddess Queen: Egypt's Anointing Mysteries,* Alison Roberts
- *The Great Secret,* Eliphas Levi
- *The Greek Magical Papyri in Translation,* Hans Dieter Betz
- *Hermetica,* Brian P. Copenhaver
- *Kybalion,* by Three Initiates

- *Meditations on the Tarot*, Anonymous (Valentin Tomberg)
- *My Heart, My Mother: Death and Rebirth in Ancient Egypt*, Alison Roberts
- *The Mysteries of Isis: Her Worship and Magick*, DeTraci Regula
- *Paradoxes of the Highest Science*, Eliphas Levi
- *Sacred Science: The King of Pharaonic Theocracy*, R.A. Schwaller de Lubicz
- *The Unknown Philosopher, Louis Claude de St. Martin*, A.E. Waite
- *The Way of Hermes*, Clement Salaman, Dornine Van Oven, William D. Wharton, and Jean-Pierre Mahe (translators)
- *What a Master Mason Ought to Know*, Papus

Vodou/Voudon and related

- *Cosmic Meditation*, Michael Bertiaux
- *The Divine Horsemen*, Maya Deren
- *Faces of the Gods: Vodou and Roman Catholicism in Haiti*, Leslie G. Desmangles
- *Haitian Vodou Handbook*, Kenaz Filan
- *Powers of the Psalms*, Anna Riva
- *Secrets of Voodoo*, Milo Rigaud
- *Syzygy, Reflections on the Monastery of the Seven Rays*, +Palamas
- *The Typhonian Trilogies*, Kenneth Grant (newly revised and typeset by Starfire Publications)
- *The Vodou Quantum Leap*, Dr. Reginald Crosley
- *Vodou Visions*, Sallie Ann Glassman
- *The Voudon Gnostic Workbook*, Michael Bertiaux
- *Vudu Cartography*, Michael Bertiaux

Gnostic & Martinist

- *B.M.G. Ms. 4123: Extract of what is contained in the Grades of the Ordre of the Élus Coëns*, Ordre Martinistes Souverains
- *Echoes from the Gnosis*, G.R.S. Mead
- *Exegesis of the Soul* (3 work compilation), Papus
- *Gnosis, the Nature and History of Gnosticism*, Kurt Randolf
- *Gnosticism*, Stephen Hoeller
- *The Gnostic Religion*, Hans Jonas
- *The Gnostic Scriptures*, Bentley Layton
- *The Gnostic Tree*, Tau Synésius
- *Grand Marvelous Secrets*, Abbé Julio
- *Liturgical Prayers*, Abbé Julio
- *Lux Occulta*, PALAMAS

- *The Nag Hammadi Scriptures: International Edition*, Marvin Meyer (ed.)
- *Occultist Freemasonry in the 18th Century and the Order of Élus Coëns*, René Le Forestier
- *The Original High Degress and Theurgical System of the Masonic Elect Cohen Knights of the Universe*, Mathieu G. Ravignat
- *Martinezism, Willermozism, Martinism and Freemasonry*, Papus
- *The Martinist Libers*, ICES, Barbados West Indies
- *The Martinist Tradition*, ICES, Barbados West Indies
- *Mask, Cloak, Silence: Martinism as a Way of Awakening*, Rémi Boyer
- *The Secret Book of John: The Gnostic Gospel Annotated & Explained*, Stevan Davies
- *Treatise on the Reintegration of Beings*, Martinès de Pasqually

Kabalistic, Alchemical and other

- *Alchemy and Mysticism*, by Alexander Roob
- *The Book of Alchemy*, Francis Melville
- *The Book of Lies*, Aleister Crowley
- *The Book of Splendours*, Eliphas Levi
- *The Chaldean Oracles*, Ruth Majercik
- *Christ and the Master Therion*, T Allen Greenfield & Frater Achad
- *The Cloud Upon the Sanctuary*, Eckartshausen
- *The Druidry Handbook*, John Michael Greer
- *Egregores: The Occult Entities that Watch Over Human Destiny*, Mark Stavish
- *The Great Secret*, Eliphas Levi
- *Liber Aleph*, Aleister Crowley
- *Magick Without Tears*, Aleister Crowley
- *The Middle Pillar*, Israel Regardie
- *The Mystical Qabalah*, Dion Fortune
- *The Roots of Modern Magick*, T Allen Greenfield
- *Sepher Yetzirah*, Aryeh Kaplan (trans., ed.)
- *Spagyrics: The Alchemical Preparation of Medicinal Essences, Tinctures, and Elixirs*, Manfred M. Junius
- *The Story of the Hermetic Brotherhood of Light*, T Allen Greenfield
- *Tarot of the Magicians*, Oswald Wirth
- *The Tree of Life*, Israel Regardie

Chapter Five
Arcana Arcanorum[665]

87th-90th Degrees

"From this it results that the magnum opus propounded in this work is: by purity and self-denial to obtain the knowledge of and conversation with one's Guardian Angel.

Mathers, *xxvi*,
Introduction to, The Book of the Sacred Magic of Abramelin the Mage

As we near the end of our particular working of the Antient & Primitive Rite of Memphis+Misraïm, our focus becomes more clear and our work more unified. What in the previous Series was mere *contact* becomes deep *relationship* in this Series. What was an introduction to the nature of the spirit realm in the previous Grades, becomes pure experience of the *blessed Immortals* in these Degrees. We are moving from exposure and interaction with spirits, otherworldly beings and landscapes, to direct communion with angels and Archangels in this Series. Though only comprised of four Degrees, these four points-chauds, their secret work, and the follow up labor and synopsis comprise a lifetime of study and development. From research we move into praxis. From practical magic we move into prayer and *sacred* magic.

This Series consists of four unique, powerful, and complete rituals.

There are three main operations in our working of the Arcana Arcanorum. These are: sacred magic with two Grimoires that establish deep contact with the Archangels, Enochian Magick with regards to scrying the 30 Æthyrs, and the pursuit of the Knowledge and

---

[665] For many groups, the A-A will constitute what is known as the **Hieros Gamos**. For the present working, this is not explored, as this is more closely connected to a secret branch of French Rosicrucianism that is beyond the scope of the present work. However, *that* A-A and the one presently expounded upon, are close allied on many accounts. An aspect of this work is pointed to in the Preface and entails cosmic Masonry, as found hidden in the 87-90°, 95°.

Conversation of our Holy Guardian Angel. These three Operations are not practices that are tried or attempted once and then set aside. The Grimoiric work with the Archangels opens the gates to a profound relationship with the Archangels. The Enochian studies and research are beyond a single lifetime. The work occurring currently in this vast field of study is astonishing and inspirational. Finally, if the Initiate attains to the Knowledge and Conversation of his Holy Guardian Angel, then this relationship drives the direction of the Initiate's life from thence forth onward. This culmination of the Rite constitutes relations with one's very own Ka, which is presaged by a crisis/ego-death and which is related to the Demiurge and to the Bearer of Light. If the Initiate is not interested in undergoing the alchemical transmutation of the soul that requires an ego death, then he should not delve too deeply into the 90th Degree.[666]

Two important keys to this Series are suggested in Mark Stavish's book, *Freemasonry, Rituals, Symbols & History of the Secret Society*. The first is that Freemasonry itself has not only produced its own Egregore, but it has an Angel attached to it. He says, "We often hear of the Genius of Freemasonry referred to as 'she' and discussed in anthropomorphic terms—expressing human qualities, but on a perfected or archetypal level.[667]" Here he is speaking of the Angel of Freemasonry. This Angel is joined by the "Angel of the Presence" in the fully operative 66° (Appendix B). The acquisition of the four points chauds of the Arcana Arcanorum establish within the sensitive Initiate communication with the spirit of Masonry itself. Secondly, he reveals that the aspect of Cagliostro's Arcana Arcanorum, "deals with alchemical rejuvenation, communication with the seven planetary angels, and the perfection of the human body as an alchemical vessel.[668]" The alchemical rejuvenation and perfection of the human body are achieved through the actions of the points-chauds upon the head,[669] completing the majority of the *Scintillating Body*. The Communication with the seven planetary angels begins in the 87th Degree and continues through till the 90th.

Before providing the reader with an example of how to pull together all these components of the 2nd Echelon working of the degrees of the APRMM, a reminder is in order. The points-chauds empowerments approach to these degrees is original to the Free Illuminist movement spearheaded by Michael Bertiaux's student, Allen H. Greenfield and practiced across the globe. It is an authentic approach to the noetic potentialities lodged within this mystical system of occult Masonry, but it is not the traditional conferral of the degrees. To establish the three primary means of working these degrees in our own fraternal group, Horus Lodge, we present the work in three Echelons: the traditional conferral of the degrees of the APRMM (Bertiaux Lineage) as they have come down to us lawfully as a

---

[666] In point of fact, the author, like many who undergo the Abramelin Operation, lived through massive upheaval with the coming of the HGA. This included divorce, change of jobs, and moving. Though certainly not the case for all, there **will be some sort of crisis** that accompanies such deep soul work as establishing the knowledge and conversation of one's HGA. This should simply not be toyed with if the Initiate is unprepared for true transmutation. True transmutation partakes of sacrifice, thus the frequent use of the crucifixion as a symbol for such rebirth.

[667] p. 75

[668] Ibid, p. 161.

[669] Here we return to the idea of the *Met tet*, with the HGA functioning in a similar way as the "Head Lwa" of the Voduisant.

Chartered Lodge under the umbrella of the World Association of Egyptian Obediences with Most Puissant Alexander Rybalka as the Sovereign Grand Master of Light; the points-chauds empowerments and original scrying method of the Free Illuminists as taught by Allen H. Greenfield; and, the third echelon which we have labeled, ÆONOLOGY, which utilizes the scaffolding of the degrees to ascend with the spirits unto the Treasury of Lights and Land of RA. The present tome along with the previously released Spirit Builders entails the 2nd Echelon and is the result of much labor within a Research and Philosophical Lodge originally chartered by Greenfield on December 22nd, 2011. This approach is incredibly elastic, can be utilized by any research lodge or practicing Triangle, and greatly expand one's understanding of the power of Egyptian Masonry.

There is a guiding hand at work in the Ancient and Primitive Rite. Though often failing in its leadership, internal and external consistency, and sometimes even degree coherency, the Rites of Memphis+Misraïm have a power that is unmistakable. Much of the force and energy behind this vast superstructure of degrees is lodged within the so-called Arcana Arcanorum. The Naples Regime, 1788 version of the A∴ A∴ is a carefully guarded system of four degrees / instructions of the nature of spiritual alchemy. The source of this material is argued to be the Divine Cagliostro, though others see the hand of Past Grand Master Jean Mallinger and others during the heyday of the F.U.D.O.S.I. Whatever its origin, it has, as one of its premier goals, the "re-membering" of the body of Osiris through the creation of a Light Body (the integration of the SAH, the BA, and the golden body of the AKH) that is able to traverse the inner regions through a sort of noesis. One aspect of the written A∴A∴ work is the Boule Blanche which can be understood as partaking of some of the same energy reservoirs of the body as our Masonic Middle Pillar but having a distinct modus operandi. Our 3rd Echelon workings of the APRMM actually begin with the written and Oral instructions of the 1788 Naples Regime[670], as the goal of those workings is anagogic.

† † †

The following degree presentations are the result of one Research and Philosophical Lodge's experimentation with the 2nd Echelon working of this series of degrees (87-90) composing the Arcana Arcanorum. The student of esotericism will understand the necessity of experiencing the 90th degree in this particular manner before moving forward with advanced ÆONIC workings which often require war with Archons and forces much more advanced than the average practitioner. In this way, the 2nd Echelon working of the A∴ A∴ is a prerequisite in our Lodge; it is preparatory and serves an apotropaic function for the 3rd Echelon. But beyond these prefatory considerations of the points empowerments, it will be clear to the reader that this echelon of working the Rites is a world unto itself! A

---

[670] See *Degrees of Wisdom: A Compendium of Rituals from the Rites of Memphis and Misraïm*, Triad Press, LLC, 2025, pp. 700-734.

lifetime of study, experimentation, and gnosis is contained in this approach and is yielded by this work.

The alignment of the Enochian Aires/Æthyrs with the points empowerments was worked out by Bishop Greenfield from the very beginning of his experimentation with the inner landscape of Memphis and Misraïm. It is original to our Research Lodge working In Free Communion to explore Enochian Magic altogether in the 2nd Echelon working of the Arcana Arcanorum, and to work out a procedure that is both simple and consistent with the body of research being undertaken by Free Illuminists with these empowerments. For this series of four degrees, we are moving from exposure and interaction with spirits, otherworldly beings and landscapes, to direct communion with angels and Archangels. Though only comprised of four degrees, these four points-chauds empowerments, their secret work, and the follow up labor and synopsis comprise a lifetime of study and development. From research we move into praxis. From practical magic we move into prayer and sacred magic. This Series consists of four unique, powerful, and complete rituals.

There are three main operations in our 2nd Echelon working of the Arcana Arcanorum. These are: sacred magic with two Grimoires that establish deep contact with the Archangels, Enochian Magick with regards to scrying the 30 Æthyrs, and the pursuit of the Knowledge and Conversation of our Holy Guardian Angel. These three Operations are not practices that are tried or attempted once and then set aside. The Grimoiric work with the Archangels opens the gates to a profound relationship with the Archangels. The Enochian studies and research are beyond a single lifetime. The work occurring currently in this vast field of study is astonishing and inspirational. Finally, if the Initiate attains to the Knowledge and Conversation of his Holy Guardian Angel, then this relationship drives the direction of the Initiate's life from thence forth onward. This culminating series of the points-chauds empowerments constitutes relations with one's very own KA, which is presaged by a crisis/ego-death and which is related to the Demiurge (PTAH) and to the Bearer of Light. If the Initiate is not interested in undergoing the alchemical transmutation of the soul that requires an ego death, then he should not delve too deeply into the 90th Degree.

Two important keys to this Series are suggested in Mark Stavish's book, Freemasonry, Rituals, Symbols & History of the Secret Society. The first is that Freemasonry itself has not only produced its own Egregore, but it has an Angel attached to it. He says, "We often hear of the Genius of Freemasonry referred to as 'she' and discussed in anthropomorphic terms—expressing human qualities, but on a perfected or archetypal level." Here he is speaking of the Angel of Freemasonry. The acquisition of the four points-chauds of the Arcana Arcanorum establish within the sensitive Initiate communication with the spirit of Masonry itself. Secondly, he reveals that the aspect of Cagliostro's Arcana Arcanorum, "deals with alchemical rejuvenation, communication with the seven planetary angels, and the perfection of the human body as an alchemical vessel." The alchemical rejuvenation and perfection of the human body are achieved through the actions of the points-chauds upon the head, completing the majority of the Scintillating Body. The Communication with the seven planetary angels begins in the 87th Degree and continues through till the 90th. Referring back to the points charts, the initiate will see that the points being activated at the back of the head begin, in the 87th degree, with the activation of the medulla oblongata. The 9th chakra in the yogic system, the medulla oblongata is sometimes referred to as the mouth of God, the Golden Chalice, and the seat of life wherein is found the silver cord mentioned in the Ecclesiastes of Solomon which is read aloud during the traditional working of the 3rd degree in the American or York Rite as well as in Emulation working. Truly opening and activating this hot point is akin to the Egyptian ceremony of the "Opening of the Mouth" of the mummy. One truly moves from a "dead level" to a "living perpendicular" when this empowerment takes.

As in all Sacred Magic, the Initiate will learn to *invoke the Highest* [671] before any further operations. This may seem backwards, coming as it does in the latter Degrees of the Rite, but it must be remembered firstly that our Rite is not required to be worked chronologically, and secondly that life, in our working, is deemed Holy in all of its aspects. There is little to fear in the early stages of spiritist working. It is enough to make sufficient contact with the spirit realms and to be able to stand upon one's own feet and traverse the realms through the supremacy of the human will and imagination. However, darkness may begin to surface in these latter grades. It must be remembered that the darkness that exists in this work is only present insomuch as the Light that is cast. The brighter the Light, the more intense is the shadow, and so this Series requires more of a grounding in traditional High Magic techniques and protections. All work will include a simple banishing and all work will include the invocation of the presence of the Four Major Archangels. These Four, along with the positive energies of the Solar and Telluric currents from above and below, create a powerhouse and Holy furnace of our oratories and sacred marmas.

These Degrees will differ in their scrying procedure slightly as well. Whereas previously, the Initiate was scrying the point to find the meaning and to allow whatever beings, landscapes or energies that would arise to arise, this set is more directed to singular goals and relationships. The Initiate has been protected all along by his direct spiritual transmission from Facilitator to Initiate, continuing on the Egregore of Free Illuminism, but now it is crucial that the Initiate maintain a studied focus and sharp will and awareness. The ordeals incumbent to this leg of the journey are intense and could result in profound changes upon the physical plane. These may be changes in one's everyday life that become necessary to pursue the path further. It could also be the awakening of "sleeping dogs" that lash out at the Initiate and lead to a life crisis. It may be that one begins to think deeply about the priorities in life and which ones are out of whack. All of these are directly affected

---

[671] In the years when I was working the Golden Dawn system of magic, I remember Chic Cicero using this phrase almost as a mantra to the Initiates. It was his succinct method of reminding all of us to prioritize and to not get lost in vainglory and become an astral junkie.

by this set of grades and the effects should be positive, but on occasion some barnacles require scraping off, and this can be painful.

Finally, the recognition that the Archangels and angels reside upon Golgotha, *the place of the skull,* the core of the Initiate's *Nous,* can sometimes lead to bombardment. It is suggested that these points chauds worked upon the face, back and top of the head are done in singular sessions or at the most in sets of two when one side of the face or head needs balancing by the other.

† † †

Q. Dost thou believe that there are celestial spirits who form an invisible chain between man and God, like that which exists between man and the brutes?

A. Yes; I believe that celestial intelligences avowed by the most ancient and universally spread traditions, pure spirits who are enlightened by the divine fire and burn with holy love are elevated by degrees even to the throne of His glory, and are ministers of His wishes to the intelligences of this world. All these spirits, disengaged as they are from matter, continue nevertheless, the chain of beings, and form a new one amongst themselves, such as is offered to our contemplation in this world of material beings. Over all this chain of beings presides T.S.A.O.T.U.[672]

---

[672] *Lectures of a Chapter, Senate & Council,* p. 81. Note the key to this quote is that over ALL presides the Grand Bondye, the ABSOLUTE, the Ground of All Being, **The Sovereign Architect of the Universe**.

Part Three – Chapter Five: Arcana Arcanorum

87th Degree

Sublime Prince of Masonry

Invocation of the Seven Great Archangels

87th *degree,*
Sublime Prince of Masonry.

Battery of Knocks (signifying the three-fold division of the grade)

    Three. X X X

Points-chaud

    Medulla Oblongata and the brain stem, on the nape of the neck

Sacred Word

    MENES

Grip

Place left hand on each other's right shoulder and give the Sacred Word.

Sign

Place the right hand on the left forearm, raise the hand and then let it fall on the thigh. When scrying and testing an entity to see if it is the Archangel, use this Sign which will be responded to with the Sign of silence.

Additional Materials

Password–HORUS

Jewel–A circle in which there is a standard Masonic square and compass and an angle, and beside this, an oval with a central point.

† † †

Synopsis

The *Arbatel* says, "YOU WILL RECEIVE WHATEVER YOU HAVE ASKED FOR.[673]" In brief and potent aphorism, this is the key to the Arcana Arcanorum. You must ask for what it holds within it. If you do, in earnest and from a humble heart, you *will* receive. This Degree begins the small Series of four grades that unfurl the operations of Sacred Magick to the Initiate. Up until this point, spirits, angels, intelligences, forces, entities, and blind energies have been stirred up, worked with and experienced from a place of equipoise, research and spiritual groundedness. Now that we enter upon our the search for more superior interactions upon the Inner Planes, more pure energies from the Deity, we must marry this ardent labor and profound research with humility and purity of intent, and work within the life-giving grace of the Absolute. This portion of our path is far more one-pointed and direct, yet with such singleness of purpose comes great responsibility and the need for perseverance.

---

[673] *The Arbatel, Concerning the Magic of the Ancients*, translated, edited, annotated, by Joseph H. Peterson, p. 21.

To simplify the matter, this particular Degree and points-chaud empowerment, places the Initiate upon a course of relating with the seven principal Archangels of the Western Esoteric Tradition. There are many differing groups of these Holy Seven, but our selection comes from experience with the point empowerment over a period of seven days and in alignment with the Planet for which the Archangel is the primary spirit. The points-chaud of this Degree begins when it is received and then is worked upon for seven subsequent days to invoke each Archangel and begin relations with them.

- Sunday—Michael
- Monday—Gabriel
- Tuesday—Zamael
- Wednesday—Raphael
- Thursday—Sachiel
- Friday—Anael
- Saturday—Cassiel

Though schedules for the Planetary Hours can be used in relation to contacting the Archangel of the Day, we have followed the injunction from the *Arbatel* and work the first hour after sunrise. This is best accomplished if preceded by Orations cogent to the work, such as the Liturgical Hour before or near dawn–*Matins/Lauds*.[674]

Prior to any of the follow-up work with the Degrees of the Arcana, the Initiate should invoke the protection and presence of the Four Archangels of the four directions. This is simply done in our Rite by forming an equal-armed cross (sign of the cardinal directions and emblematic of the sacrifice of our separate and isolated ego) in each direction and vibrating the name of the Angel. Towards the East, we make the large sign of the cross with our same hand gesture we use to open the points-chauds, and vibrate, RAPHAEL, to the South, MICHAEL, to the West, GABRIEL and to the North, URIEL. More than banishing outward forces, this invocation *prevents the escape* and dissipation of the powerful energies that are summoned within the sacred space created by the Initiate.

After this, the Initiate should say the following conjuration from the *Arbatel*, which though simple and austere in wording, is a powerful statement to the angelic realm of the progress made upon the path and the humble attitude that is brought to the present working.

---

[674] A simple version of Matins is provided in the Breviary of Book 2 in, *Syzygy, Reflections on the Monastery of the Seven Rays*, p. 195, 3rd edition.

O GOD ALMIGHTY AND ETERNAL, you who have established all of creation for your praise and honor and the service of mankind, I beg you to send your SPIRIT N.N (_____) of the solar order, to inform and teach me the things I have asked, but may your will, not mine be done, through JESUS CHRIST your only begotten son, OUR LORD. Amen.[675]

Once the scrying session is ended, the dismissal of the Archangel should be said,

BECAUSE YOU CAME PEACEFULLY AND QUIETLY, and answered my petitions, I give thanks TO GOD in whose name you have come, and may you go now in peace to your order, returning to me when I call you by your name, or order, or office, which is permitted by the Creator. Amen.[676]

Along with the Jewel of the Degree, the points-chaud and the method of scrying the point, the Initiate will want to procure the sigil appropriate to each Archangel. The most effective ones for this particular working have been found to be those of the *Grimoire of Armadel*. These, drawn upon virgin parchment in the appropriate colors, may be selected for the appropriate day and *pressed upon the forehead of the Initiate*[677] while scrying the point in the Prophet asana (this is directly after *re-awakening the point*). This will mean that the sigil is upon the ground. It is best to use a small space rug for this and to move into the asana and rest the forehead directly upon the sigil of the Archangel before going into the point deeply through the mantric chanting of the Sacred Word, MENES (First King of Egypt). The heart and mind must be raised to the vibratory rate of the Archangel and then he will appear in his own particular space. A thorough knowledge of the nature of the planet and Sephirah attached to the same will clarify the details of the visualization, but such is not *required* for our Primitive Doctrine.

The *Aphorisms* in the *Arbatel* will guide the Initiate further into the mysteries of this divine magick. Entire texts could be composed on the proper methods and procedures for developing this science, but in truth, as the writer of the Arbatel attests, "there is no other MEANS OF RESTORING THESE ARTS, than through the instructions of the holy spirits of God: Because true faith comes FROM HEARING.[678]" This practice is for the Initiate who has experienced and embraced the attunement, therapy, initiation, and empowerment that has accompanied each Degree. With this is born the *Scintillating Body* within the *Mystic Temple* and *in Free Communion* with others. The faith that can move mountains or invoke Archangels accompanies this labor. We must now attune in the deepest manner possible to the holy spirits and attend to their further instructions. But beyond even this, we must begin to relate to these ancient currents and birth true communion with them.

While working upon this route, we should begin to consider the work of the 90th Degree and daily pray this simple orison from the *Arbatel*,

---

[675] *The Arbatel*, p. 45.
[676] Ibid.
[677] This was a classic divinatory method of MacGregor Mathers. It has been adopted by other luminaries, not the least of which is the creative genius, A.O. Spare.
[678] *The Arbatel*, p. 23.

Grant to me therefore one of your spirits, who will teach me whatever you wish me to learn and understand, for your praise and honor, and the benefit of our neighbors. Grant to me also a heart that is easily taught, so that I may easily retain in my mind what you have taught, and I will secure them there to be brought forth, as from your inexhaustible treasures, for all necessary uses.[679]

This prayer will begin the preparations for the Great Work ahead and will ready the channels for the spirit building that accompanies Angel Magick. It must also be understood, throughout the working of the Arcana Arcanorum, that in this formula of magick, we must *not mix the planes*. This portion of magick is very studied, directed, and streamlined. As the *Arbatel* suggests, "CARE must be taken not to mix experiments, but each one should be simple and by itself. For GOD and NATURE have ordered each towards a fixed and destined end.[680]" If we remain devoted to the task of converse with the Angels, then we will attract ministering spirits who will assist in these labors.[681] Some, who have worked in earnest in this section, have experienced the presence of the Abbe Boullan, who lent his support and expertise to the working. Each Initiate will attract his or her own spirits and ministers to assist in the work. There is no need in hurrying to the next Degree, one may work with the 87th for weeks on end before he is "duly and truly prepared" to move on further. It is also a section that can be repeated over and over again, each time yielding new information on the nature of these planes and the spiritual quality of the Archangel contacted.

In the same way that the Degree work suggests that there are three divisions of the ancient Temples, this Degree has three main operative sections. The first apartment, so to speak, is when the point and Degree are first given. This points-chaud empowerment branches off into seven further Rays—the Archangels, whose converse and appearance during scrying constitute the second apartment. The third is difficult to speak of in words, for it is the private communion between the Initiate and the Archangels. The contents of this communion are as natural and spontaneous an occurrence as the first conversation between a lover and his beloved.

---

[679] Ibid, p. 27.
[680] Ibid., p. 71.
[681] Ibid. p. 95.

Spirit Builders

88th Degree

Grand Elect of the Sacred Curtain

Beginning Enochian Magick

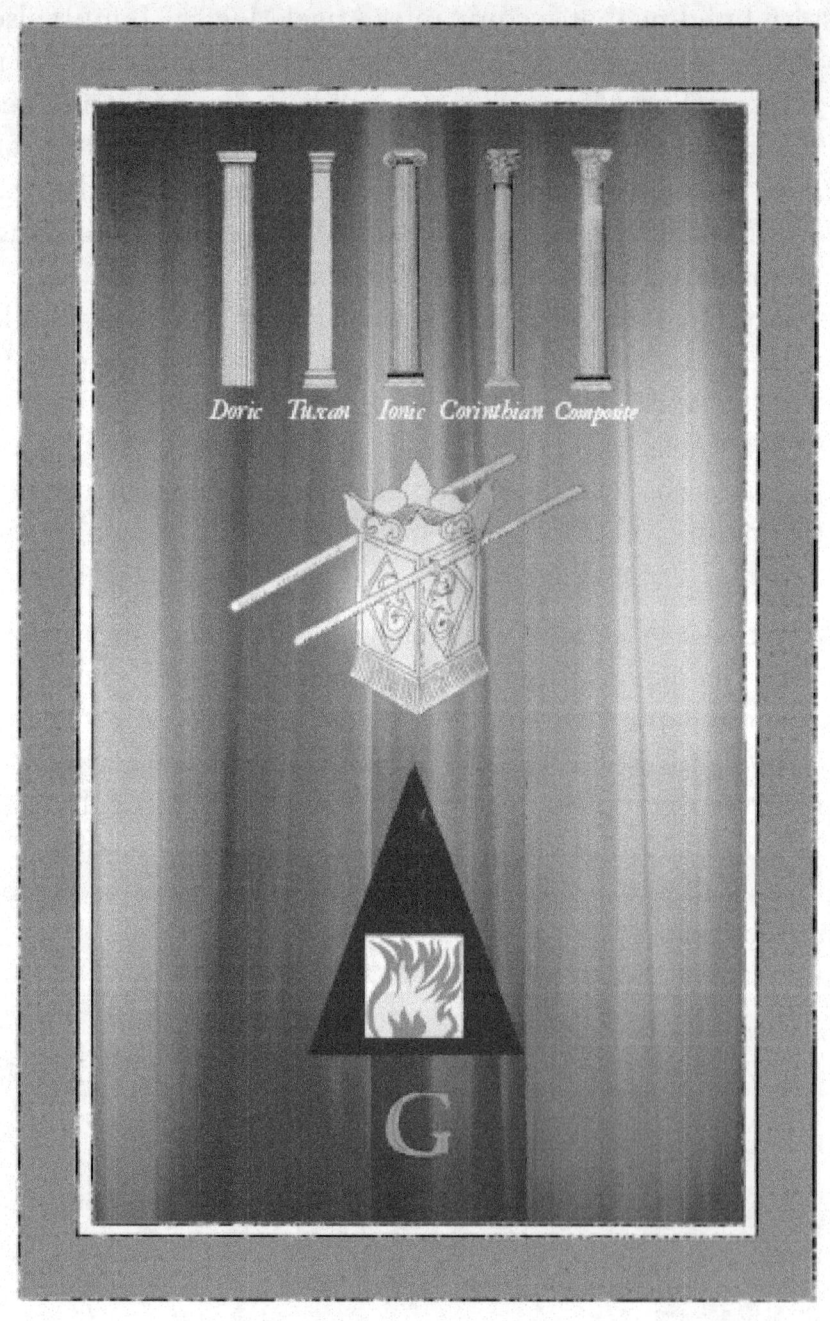

88th *degree,*
Grand Elect of the Sacred Curtain.

Battery of Knocks

Two, two times. One   XX XX X

Points-chaud

Left side, back of the head, mid-way to ear.

Sacred Word

GNOSIS

Grip

Take each other by both hands, then throw arms outward

Sign

Motion with both hands, as if opening a curtain

Additional Materials

Password–SIEGE, answer, ALETHE

Jewel–A triangle containing a ray-ed square.

† † †

Synopsis

In this grade we return to a familiar set of words. Our *answer* to the Password of this Degree, ALETHE (Truth) is the consort of NOUS (Mind), and Mind is born from our Password, SIEGE (Silence). This, according to St. Irenaeus, is the descending Aeonic emanation, all of which is born from the Deep (Bythos). We spent a great deal of time with these words in the previous Series, but we did not explore their true import in relation to Memphis+Misraïm. In this Degree and the one following it, we will delve into one of the seminal aspects of our system that has been traversed and outlined thoroughly by the first research Lodges in the Tradition. A portion of the Sacred Curtain is raised in these two grades, and the inner sanctum is revealed. The inner sanctum of the Initiate is Bythos, and it is attended to by the "Deep Ones," sometimes referred to as the "Great Old Ones." From here, we find 30 concentric circles moving inward from the epidermis[682]. These correspond to the 30 Aeons of the 84th Degree, *Patriarch of the Izeds*, but in this Degree we reveal more of

---

[682] An appropriate visual for this is Hildegard Von Bingen's *the Man in Sapphire Blue*, with waves surrounding him. The vibrations of the 30th Aethyr can be seen clairvoyantly upon the scintillating body of those working with the points-chauds. It is vibratory and wave-like in formation.

the mystery. These 30 circles are in fact, the 30 Æthyrs of Enochian Magick.[683] The Truth that is to be discovered within these Æthyrs is directly related to the spiritually expansive qualities of the Nous, which are, in turn, a product of Silence. This systematic unfolding of our Primitive Doctrine and its Source has been meted out at steady pace along the way. As our practice may have very little to do with chronologically working the Degrees, the Initiate may marvel at the progression that appears to have been laid out. The reasoning is twofold. Firstly, there will be those of the Masonic cast who choose to work these grades according to their numbering. If this is the case, the unveiling of the inner sanctum will be properly prepared for through a thorough grounding and segmented approach to the inner teachings. Secondly, we have steadily unraveled these mysteries for the reader who decides to study first and practice afterwards. This level of caution and rectitude is not to be shunned or eschewed in any way by those who seek experience above all else. The Lodge, Node, or Chapel that studies these Degrees as they are laid out, practicing in incremental ways as they go, will find much fruit to be gleamed, come Spring. There are mysteries upon mysteries within the Primitive Doctrine and a lifetime could be dedicated to gleaming the treasures of our Rite without exhaustion.

The Degree work refers to the Holy of Holies, the Inner Shrine, the Esoteric teaching, the Sanctuary and the Sacred Curtain. These are so many pointers to the elevated form of scrying that we are embarking upon. One perusal of Enochian literature reveals the system to be an immense undertaking, complex in form and function, and loaded with intricacies and abstruse language. It is not the intent of this or the next Degree to introduce the Initiate to this system, lay out its program, or to develop it on its own terms. That may come with steady progress in our method, but the Initiate is directed outwards to other texts[684] to get the groundwork of Enochian and to study its development, import, and efficacy as a program of magick on its own. With our work, we are concerned chiefly, with the scrying of the 30 Æthyrs. Applied to our points-chauds empowerments as T Allen Greenfield and others have done, our system of 97 Degrees becomes amplified tenfold with the introduction of this profound and simple approach to Enochian. Each Degree (save six, which afford further developments of the last level called TEX) becomes a conduit into a section of an Æthyr and establishes relations with one of the 91 Governors of the realm. The method used is of the utmost simplicity, but as we have learned from the writings of Bertiaux and the author of the *Arbatel*, in simplicity is great power.

Of the efficacy of our program of utilizing the Key of the Enochian Æthrys, the Nineteenth Call with the appropriate Æthyr name interpolated, Lon Milo Duquette in his, *Enochian Vision Magick,* says, "What *is* clear to me, after more than a quarter century of practical application, is the fact that the calls by themselves (with only the briefest of additional verbiage to awaken target angels and their hierarchy) serve admirably as the only

---

[683] The ÆONs of the 84° signal the advancement of the Arcana Arcanorum (88°)in the 3rd echelon working, where the number of ÆONs is reduced to our magickal number 16 and moves beyond the Æthyrs, beyond the sublunary and planetary spirits, and into the very Kósmos Noetós.
[684] See the Suggested Reading following the Arcana Arcanorum.

invocations a magician needs.[685]" The *briefest of additional verbiage* is for us, the practice of our Simple Opening with the addition of the Archangelic Invocation in the cardinal directions, the Masonic Middle Pillar, and re-awakening the point through the gnostic pressure and repetition of the Sacred Word. From here, the Initiate uses the Nineteenth Call, with the appropriate name that relates to the Degree and then immediately before assuming our familiar, Prophet asana; the Initiate makes the Sign of the 88th Degree. This is described as a *Motion with both hands, as if opening a curtain.*[686] This is a traditional "rending of the veil" sign, but particular to the APRM+M. Once the mind is settled, the Initiate may invoke the Governor of the Æthyr by vibrating the name until he appears. Consulting the books suggested will also reveal the Governors sigil which can be made in the air with the index finger during the journey. It is not to be worn or used as a talisman. After scrying the region, the Initiate immediately relays the material gathered in his magickal diary, including: words that stand out, images that are perceived and other data that can be used in research later.

It is helpful to have a dependable spirit guide to work with these energies. For this, we implore the assistance of the true *Inner Guard*.[687] We may not know our personal Guardian Angel as yet, but this should not prevent us from imploring his aid for our difficult spiritist endeavors upon the Æthyrs. This may be done by a simple inward calling out to the Guard to provide us with mutual aid and assistance in our labors. He is near us, just as the *Ka* in Egyptian relief sculptures and paintings, and he will attend when called upon.

To begin to open the Sacred Curtain upon the Mystic City within, we simply practice the Nineteenth Key using the Æthyr of LIL. If the Initiate is familiar with Crowley's excursions in these realms, she will have read his, *Vision and the Voice*, an epic tome of erudition concerning the Enochian Aires. Crowley and others suggest working from the 30th Æthyr upwards towards the first. This is based upon the notion of these Æthyrs being higher and higher on the planes. For us, they are inward journeys and so the traveling starts at the epidermis and goes inside, deeper and deeper through the layers of consciousness as we explore the subtle domains of the Self. Following the oldest glyphs of the Æthyrs, the concentric circles begin with LIL on the outermost (epidermis) and move inward towards the center of TEX. We stay in the centermost region for an extended amount of time, study and Degree work. The Administrative Degrees reveal the inner quality of these regions and their vice-regent.[688]

---

[685] p. 197.

[686] *Compleat Rite of Memphis*, p. 140.

[687] Here we find the symbolism from Book Two coming full circle, with the Inner Guard—a Masonic Office in Emulation Working, and one of the two Officers in our Violet Lodge, symbolizing the HGA. A re-reading of the Inner Guard's movements and attitude towards the Candidate, *as the HGA*, reveals interesting data about the nature of the HGA when first courting him.

[688] A paradox occurs in the center, where gnosis is no longer possible. This is the transition from katophatic knowledge, to apophatic—*agnosia*. The viceregent cannot be *known* in the casual sense, but is the Source, the Noumena of all that we encounter. He is the "Father God" of esoteric and mystical Christianity—the Uncreated Light that is more properly deemed, luminous *darkness*.

Before embarking upon a full 30 day adventure or Magickal Retirement with these points-chauds and Æthyrs, we must begin to lift the veil of Isis with this 88th Degree, its points-chaud and the Sacred Word peculiar to our developing science, GNOSIS. As a way of preparing the Nous and the body to fully engage in Enochian magick, we will do our simple opening procedures, re-activate the 88th point and chant the Nineteenth Key, awakening the energies and entities of the 30th Æthyr of LIL. At this juncture, this is all that is necessary. The Initiate is free to scry the point in the usual or the advanced manner for further meaning and light, but this is as far as we shall travel for now upon the supersensual Aires.

†††

In English, the Key to the Æthyrs, or the Nineteenth Call

O you Heavens which dwell in the *(Name the Æthyr) First Aire are mighty in the parts of the Earth, and execute the Judgment of the Highest, to you it is said, Behold the face of your God, the beginning of comfort, whose eyes are the brightness of the heavens, which provided you for the government of the Earth and her unspeakable variety, furnishing you with a power of understanding to dispose all things according to the providence of Him that sitteth on the Holy Throne, and rose up in the beginning saying: the Earth let her be governed by her parts and let there be division in her, that the glory of her may be always drunken and vexed in itself. Her course, let it run with the heavens, and as a handmaid let her serve them. One season let it confound another, and let there be no creature qualities, and let there be no creature equal with another: the reasonable Creatures of the Earth let them vex and weed out one another, and the dwelling places let them forget their names: the work of man, and his pomp, let them be defaced: his buildings let them become caves for the beasts of the field. Confound her understanding with darkness. For why? It repenteth me I made Man. One while let her be known and another while a stranger: because she is the bed of a Harlot, and the dwelling place of Him that is Fallen. O you heavens arise: the lower heavens underneath you, let them serve you! Govern those that govern: cast down such as fall! Bring forth with those that increase, and destroy the rotten! No place let it remain in one number: add and diminish until the stars be numbered! Arise, Move, and Appear before the Covenant of his mouth, which he hath sworn unto us in his Justice. Open the Mysteries of your Creation: and make us partakers of Undefiled Knowledge.

In Enochian (using the Phonetic spelling employed by the Golden Dawn and Crowley[689])

Madariatza das perifa {LIL} cahisa micaolazoda saanire caosago od fifisa balzodizodarasa Iaida. Nonuca gohulime: Micama odoianu MADA faoda beliorebe, soba ooaona cahisa luciftias peripesol, das aberaasasa nonucafe netaaibe caosaji od tilabe adapehaheta damepelozoda, tooata nonucafe jimicalazodoma larasada tofejilo marebe yareryo IDOIGO; od torezodulape yaodafe gohola, Caosaga,

---

[689] This is purely a stylistic choice. Many Adepts do not utilize this manner of pronouncing Enochian with the added vowels. I have found the chanting of the Keys in this manner to be deeply sonorous, and therefore evocative, which is the reasoning of including it here. There is nothing sacrosanct about this pronunciation format.

tabaoreda saanire, od caharisateosa yorepoila tiobela busadire, tilabe noalanu paida oresaba, od dodaremeni zodayolana. Elazodape tilaba paremeji peripesatza, od ta qurelesata booapisa. Lanibame oucaho sayomepe, od caharisateosa ajitoltorenu, mireca qo tiobela Iela. Tonu paomebeda dizodalamo asa pianu, od caharisateosa aji-latore-torenu paracahe a sayomepe. Coredazodizoda dodapala od fifalazoda, lasa manada, od faregita bamesa omaoasa. Conisabera od auauotza tonuji oresa; catabela noasami tabejesa leuitahemonuji. Vanucahi omepetilabe oresa! Bagile? Moooabe OL coredazodizoda. El capimao itzomatzipe, od cacocasabe gosaa. Bajilenu pii tianuta a babalanuda, od faoregita teloca uo uime. Madariiatza, torezodu!!! Oadariatza orocaha aboaperi! Tabaori periazoda aretabasa! Adarepanu coresata dobitza! Yolacame periazodi arecoazodiore, od quasabe qotinuji! Ripire paaotzata sagacore! Umela od perdazodare cacareji Aoiveae coremepeta! Torezodu! Zodacare od Zodameranu, asapeta sibesi butamona das surezodasa Tia balatanu. Odo cicale Qaa, od Ozodazodame pelapeli IADANAMADA!

Each of the 30 Æthyrs has 3 Governors, except for TEX which has 4

The Names of the Æthyrs and their Governors

1. **LIL**: OCCODON, PASCOMB, VALGARS
2. **ARN**: DOAGNIS, PACASNA, DIALIVA
3. **ZOM**: SAMAPHA, VIROOLI, ANDISPI
4. **PAZ**: THOTANF, AXZIARG, POTHNIR
5. **LAT**: LAZDIXI, NOCAMAL, TIARPAX
6. **MAZ**: SAXTOMP, VAVAAMP, ZIRZIRD
7. **DEO**: OBMACAS, GENADOL, ASPIAON
8. **ZID**: AMFRES, TODNAON, PRISTAC
9. **ZIP**: ODDIORG, CRALPIR, DOANZIN
10. **ZAX**: LEXARPH, COMANAN, TABITOM
11. **ICH**: MOLPAND, VANARDA, PONODOL
12. **LOE**: TAPAMAL, GEDOONS, AMBRIAL
13. **ZIM**: GECAOND, LAPARIN, DOCEPAX
14. **VTA**: TEDOOND, VIVIPOS, OOANAMB
15. **OXO**: TAHANDO, NOCIABI, TASTOXO
16. **LEA**: COCARPT, LANACON, SOCHIAL
17. **TAN**: SIGMORF, AYDROPT, TOCARZI
18. **ZEN**: NABAOMI, ZAFASAI, YALPAMB
19. **POP**: TORZOXI, ABAIOND, OMAGRAP
20. **CHR**: ZILDRON, PARZIBA, TOTOCAN

21. **ASP**: CHIRSPA, TOANTOM, VIXPALG
22. **LIN**: OZIDAIA, PARAOAN, CALZIRG
23. **TOR**: RONOAMB, ONIZIMP, ZAXANIN
24. **NIA**: ORCAMIR, CHIALPS, SOAGEEL
25. **VTI**: MIRZIND, OBUAORS, RANGLAM
26. **DES**: POPHAND, NIGRANA, BAZCHIM
27. **ZAA**: SAZIAMI, MATHVLA, ORPAMB
28. **BAG**: LABNIXP, FOCISNI, OXLOPAR
29. **RII**: VASTRIM, ODRAXTI, GOMZIAM
30. **TEX**: TAONGLA, GEMNIMB, ADVORPT, DOZINAL

The general study of the Enochian Æthyrs is given to the Initiate of the 88th Degree. His scrying of the Degree will reveal a beginning relationship with the Governors of the Æthyr, LIL (OCCODON, PASCOMB, VALGARS). The energy will be sensed as an inner opening of the gates.

89th Degree
Patriarch of the Mystic City
Scrying the Æthyrs

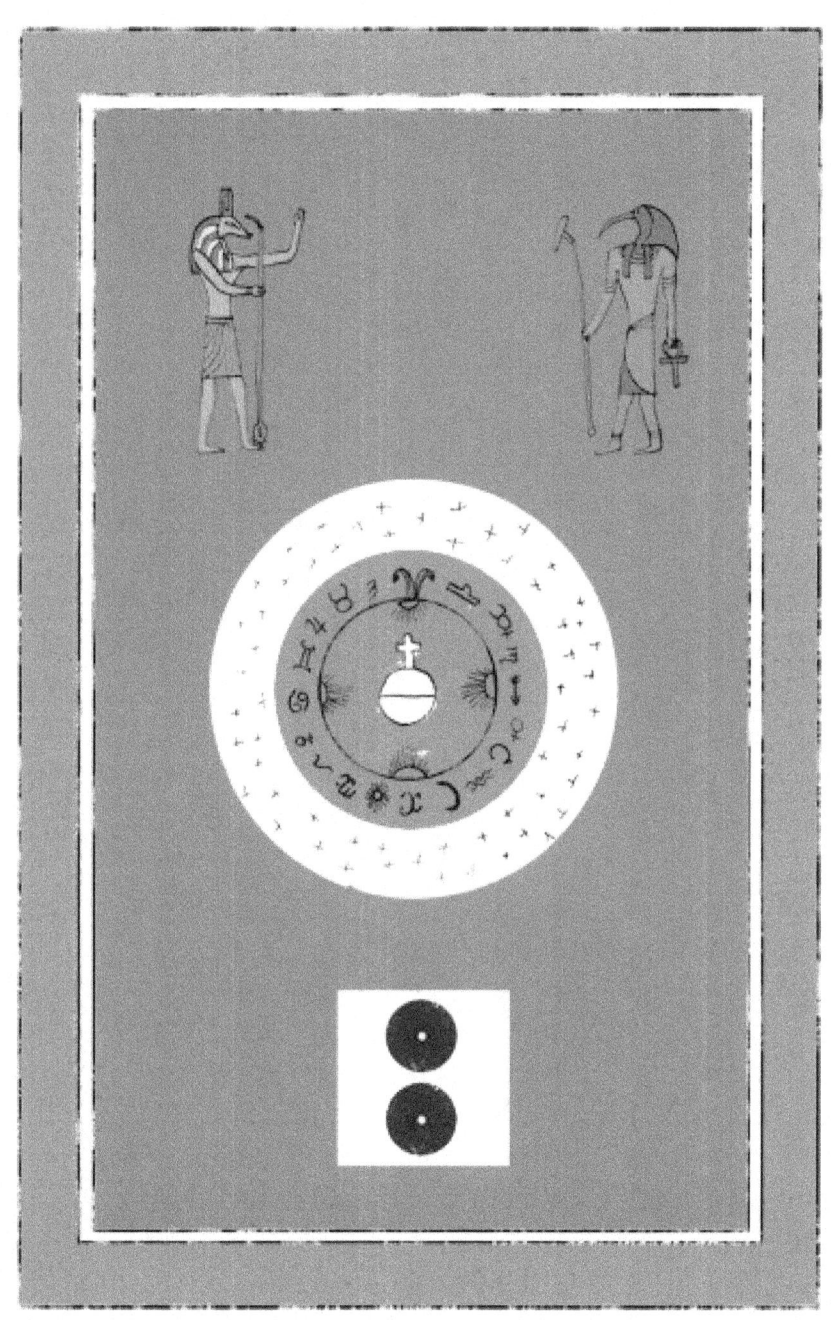

89th *degree,*
Patriarch of the Mystic City.

Battery of Knocks

Four and Seven. XXXX   XXXXXXX

Points-chaud

Back of the head, right

Sacred Word

TAUT (the Revealer; the Defender)

Grip

Four strokes of the thumb on the first finger, to which the other responds by seven.

Sign

Interlace the fingers; press them to the lips four times, then extend the hands still clenched to the Orient.

Additional Materials

Password–SET[690] (The accuser of Man)

Jewel–On a square is drawn a square board, having two circles like a figure 8 and a point in each.

† † †

Synopsis

One of our most recent Passwords has been HORUS. Horus is the god of the black soil of Egypt. The Black Ray, in the Voudon Gnostic Tradition is concerned with occult and Logos oriented energies. The Password of this Degree is HORUS's arch-nemesis, SET, who is the Lord of the red desert. The Red Ray is concerned with Eros and creativity. These two seemingly contradictory forces wrestle for dominance in the Initiate's life, but the Initiate of the 89th Degree will find the simple path of balance between the two, knowing full well when to appropriately utilize the energies of the Deities for each particular moment in life. The contending forces are more like a dance of the elements. The vibrations of each may interrupt, antagonize and even debilitate the actions of the other for a time, but the pendulum swings back in the necessary movement of adjustment.[691] Balance and a

---

[690] The Initiate is again directed to the *Typhonian Trilogies* of Kenneth Grant for further study of SET. When considered in the light of the Typhonian tradition, we find many misunderstandings of SET that lead to a deeper understanding of the nature of evil, the relationship of Typhon and SET, and the later developments of Satan.

[691] Just as Light has its reign for a time at the Summer Solstice, but then the *Renewal of Nature* (Autumnal Equinox) brings the darkness that is necessary for the circle to be complete.

thorough adjustment are necessary qualities of this grade and will open up the limitless vistas of the Æthyrs.[692]

Both the Grip and the Battery of this Degree add up to eleven. It is no secret that eleven is the number of magick. ABRAHADABRA is but one word of the present Aeon that evokes the energetic, growth centered, and occasionally avenging spontaneous vivacity of the current formula of magick. It is left to the ingenium of the Initiate to unravel the manifold meanings of the number and this particular Word, in relation to our present undertaking.

The points-chaud empowerment of this Degree is the beginning of the end of the Arcana Arcanorum. It is uniquely balanced by the previous Degree and forms a complete system of angelic working with the present Degree. These two grades form a complete whole, a spectrum of angelic and sacred magick that opens the Initiate to the infinite realms of the inner world.

The Sacred Word of this Degree is the Phoenician form of Thoth/Hermes, TAUT. We have explored the Hermetic Tradition and its connection to our Rite. In this Degree, however, we put into practice the dictum, "as above, so below" and we perform the third aspect of the Hermetic axiom, "To Know, To Will, To *Dare* and to Keep Silent." As we invoke the aid of the intellectual Hermes, the Mercurial messenger of the gods who brings all knowledge, learning and hidden arts to the mage, we endeavor upon a path of courage and of audacity as we present ourselves to the Angelic realm, and we *Dare* to plumb the depths of our souls where these divine ones reside.

As the ground plan of our Primitive Doctrine has been laid out with equity all along the way, we now come to the content of our Science that is profound, yet again, simply achieved. This is our Mystery, that we may work the most efficient, the most paired down, and the most eloquent exposition of the divine economy, yet what we perform, the energies and entities that we enliven, the Bodies of Light that we bless and empower, the Mystic Temples that we give birth to in the inner and the outer and the collective workings that we perform *In Free Communion,* are potent and preeminent in this genre. Nodes, Temples, Lodges, and Chapels have formed and are forming across the globe, in praise of our basic precepts and in awe of the efficacy of our empowerments. Let us return to the beginning and refresh ourselves at the well at which the agents of our spiritual Masonry sprang.

T Allen Greenfield originally began his ordering of the system of points-chauds to the Degrees of Memphis-Misraïm in 1988, *directly after being consecrated a Bishop* and through a flash of mystical realization via the Grimoire of Michael Bertiaux entitled, *The Voudon Gnostic Workbook.*[693] He began putting this received spirit map into practice in the early 1990's within an Esoteric Lodge where participants experimented and charted their progress and results with the use of the magickal diary. The meditation techniques and mystical *prophet*

---

[692] The Initiate would do well to study the chapter, *Aequus Animus,* starting on p. 47 in *Syzygy*, 3rd ed. Though speaking specifically about the Monastery of the Seven Rays, this chapter applies to the present work as well.
[693] Greenfield, *The Roots of Modern Magick: An Anthology*, p. 222,

asana, were developed through his correspondence with Michael Bertiaux and his work with the late W. W. Webb. Greenfield clearly visualized the Jean-Maine inspired, 1921 Ecclesiastical Revision of the APRM+M as an extension of the consecratory lineage of the Gnostic Church and selected Yarker's final definitive version of the Memphis+Misraïm system to align the points. Each of Greenfield's original students were empowered by the points, then asked to perform the advanced scrying method to obtain the particular meaning of the Degree for themselves. Utilizing his expertise in Kabala and the Hebrew language, he would follow this up with the use of the English Qabalah, 777 and other guides to unlock the secrets of the words derived from the grade. The elegance of this approach is that,

> *the process, if successful, would reveal the next step in empowerments for the individual, and was thus, in a sense, self guiding. Sometimes this led to precognitive powers, advanced travel in the body of light to other terrestrial locations and times, healing powers, et al.*[694]

He goes on to suggest that the more correspondences to the system that are discovered, the more useful it becomes. Here, Greenfield completely self identifies as a Scientific Illuminist where the motto is, *the Aim of Religion–the Method of Science*. One of these additional correspondences to the system is to the Enochian Æthyrs that were introduced in the previous Degree.

The primary example of our treatment of the Enochian Æthyrs is the method of the spiritual cosmonaut and creative genius, Aleister Crowley. His beautiful piece, *The Vision and the Voice*, is an authentic record of a Magus who has traversed the Æthyrs and experienced their trials, beauties, woes and insights–at least, the portion that was unveiled to him. His process was completely consistent with our Primitive Doctrine and we find no need to alter the basic premise, save a few points. Firstly, we scry the Æthyrs beginning at the 1st, LIL. This is unique amongst practitioners, as the message that has been passed down through the ages is to begin with the 30th. However, John Dee and Edward Kelley only penned the Calls down in reverse order so as to not *accidentally conduct Invocations* while penning down the same! From this ordering of the Æthyrs, Crowley took the track of beginning with the 30th Æthyr of TEX and going downward towards the first, LIL. We will follow the traditional organization of the Æthyrs and move from LIL to TEX. Also, for Crowley the Æthyrs were moving *outward*, and though this may seem a subtle distinction, we maintain that the movement is strikingly *inward*. Additionally, we do not require the use of a shew stone of any sort. Such may be employed, as all of the implements of the greater workings of Enochian Magick may be, but they are simply not required for the Primitive Doctrine, nor are they for many a mage. In answer to the question, "But do you need all this stuff," Lon Milo DuQuette responds, "My answer is this: In order to do this particular variety of magick you need all this stuff *inside* you. That's where the real magick takes place.[695]" For our purposes, we need only our sacred marma where we are working,

---

[694] Ibid, p. 224.
[695] *Enochian Vision Magick*, p. 85.

and the Nineteenth Call provided in the previous Degree. Our Prophet asana and meditation will unveil the mysteries of the Æthyrs.

When the Initiate tunes in to the Call of the Æthyr, and aligns himself with its vibratory rate, riding its column of energy as a trajectory into his own soul, the living spirits of the Æthyrs come forth, the landscapes peel back, and the vision is accomplished. A word of caution is in order, however, for the soul unprepared for the sheer power of Enochian vision magick. The previously mentioned balance is necessary in all aspects of the Initiate's life. She must be psychologically balanced, spiritually in a state of equipoise, and emotionally stable. In our own experience, the worst fate that befalls such ill-prepared Initiates is lack of vision and frustration of the path. Others have reported more severe results from such dabbling in territories that are not befitting of the Initiate's actual level of adepthood. In such thinking we must beware of passing judgment and we must also realize that quite often, the loudest "experts" in the field are not necessarily the most experienced. In fact, many a mage becomes downright fundamentalist when it comes to the subject of Enochiana. DuQuette responds to such by saying;

> *There is nothing particularly sacrosanct about the methods and techniques developed by the Golden Dawn, Crowley, or any other latter-day magicians. As an informed and competent magician, you are just as free as these individuals were and are to develop your own Enochian magick art form based and structured on your personal interpretation and understanding of Dee and Kelley's experiences and material.*[696]

Our transformative method of working with the 30 Æthyrs and 91 Governing spirits of Enochian Magic is incorporated into our points-chauds empowerments in this Degree. ALL of the energies and entities related to the 30 Æthyrs are attributed to this Degree and spread out amongst the entire set of 97 points. This Degree can be completed over 30 Days if the Initiate would like, receiving packs of three or more points per day, or it can be worked within the longer alignment of 91 primary days with each of the Governing spirits (genii) and 6 additional *sealing* days of points chauds, meditation, thanksgiving, and record examining. This practice only scratches the surface of the vast field of Enochian magick, but it is a veritable gold mine of spirit work for the persevering mage.

If at any point throughout these workings the vision begins to fade prematurely, the Initiate need only vibrate the God Name three times clearly and then invoke the Governor of the Æthyr again. If this does not clear up the vision and all begins to blur, the Initiate is not prepared for the experience. It may be a simple matter of adjustment or some time for spiritual maturation.

---

[696] Ibid, p. 167.

Alignment of the Degrees with the Enochian Æthyrs and Governors

The body, mind and spirit unity are symbolized by the three-fold nature of the concentric circles. There are 91 Governors of the 30 Æthyrs which are attributed to the points empowerments and Degrees of our Rite. The additional 6 Degrees are relegated to the Four sections of the center of the Initiate's consciousness. The remaining two Degrees are dedicated to Silence in all of its aspects, including that of Enochian Vision Magic.

Degree	Point-Chaud	Æthyr	Governor	God Name
1. Apprentice	Top of head	LIL	Occodon	ORO
2. Companion	Top of head	LIL	Pascomb	OIP
3. Master	Top of head	LIL	Valgars	PDOCE
4. Discreet Master	Upper Forehead	ARN	Doagnis	ARSL
5. Perfect Master	Mid-Forehead Left	ARN	Pascana	DIAL
6. Intimate Secretary	Mid-Forehead Right	ARN	Dialiua	DIAL
7. Provost and Judge	Upper Cheek Right	ZOM	Samapha	ORO
8. Intendant of the Building	Upper Cheek Left	ZOM	Virooli	PDOCE
9. Élu of the Nine	Lower Cheek Left	ZOM	Andispi	MOR
10. Élu of the Twelve	Lower Cheek Right	PAZ	Thotanp	MOR
11. Élu of the Fifteen	Chin	PAZ	Axziarg	MOR
12. Master Architect	Upper Neck Left 1	PAZ	Pothnir	MPH
13. Royal Arch of Solomon	Neck Left 2	LIT	Lazdixi	IBAH
14. Perfect Élu	Neck Left 3	LIT	Nocamal	PDOCE
15. Knight of the East, or of the Sword	Neck Left 4	LIT	Tiarpax	OIP
16. Prince of Jerusalem	Upper Neck Right 1	MAZ	Saxtomp	AOZPI
17. Knight of the East and the West	Neck Right 2	MAZ	Vauaamp	MPH
18. Knight Rose+Croix	Neck Right 3	MAZ	Zirzird	AOZPI
19. Grand Pontiff	Neck Right 4	DEO	Opmacas	ARSL
20. Master of the Symbolic Lodges	Left Upper Chest	DEO	Genadol	TEAA
21. Noachite or Prussian Knight	Right Upper Chest	DEO	Aspiaon	OIP
22. Knight of the Royal Axe	Center Chest	ZID	Zamfres	AOZPI
23. Chief of the Tabernacle	Heart	ZID	Todnaon	IBAH
24. Prince of the Tabernacle	Left Upper Abdomen 1	ZID	Pristac	ORO

Degree	Point-Chaud	Æthyr	Governor	God Name
25. Knight of the Brazen Serpent	Left Abdomen 2	ZIP	Oddiorg	TEAA
26. Prince of Mercy	Left Abdomen 3	ZIP	Cralpir	MOR
27. Knight Commander of the Temple	Left Abdomen 4 / Left Wrist Inside	ZIP	Doanzin	GAIOL
28. Knight of the Sun	Right Upper Abdomen 1	ZAX	Lexarph	OIP
29. Knight of St. Andrew	Right Abdomen 2	ZAX	Comanan	PDOCE
30. Knight Kadosh	Right Abdomen 3	ZAX	Tabitom	ORO
31. Grand Inspector Inquisitor	Right Abdomen 4 / Right Wrist Inside	ICH	Molpand	MOR
32. Master of the Royal Secret	Center Upper Groin	ICH	Vsnarda	HCTGA
33. Sovereign Grand Inspector General	Center Groin	ICH	Ponodol	TEAA
34. Knight of Scandinavia	Upper Left Thigh	LOE	Tapamal	HCTGA
35. Knight of the Temple	2 Left Thigh	LOE	Gedoons	GAIOL
36. Sublime Negociant	1 Right Thigh	LOE	Ambriol	DIAL
37. Sage of Truth	2 Right Thigh	ZIM	Gecacond	MOR
38. Sublime Elect of Truth, or the Red Eagle	Genital 1	ZIM	Laparin	IBAH
39. Grand Elect of the Aeons	Genital 2	ZIM	Docepax	PDOCE
40. Sage Savaiste	Left Inside Thigh 1	VTA	Tedoand /Tedoond	AOZPI
41. Knight of the Arch of Seven Colors	Left Inside Thigh 2	VTA	Viuipos	PDOCE
42. Prince of Light	Right Inside Thigh 1	VTA	Ooanamb	MPH
43. Sublime Hermetic Sage	Right Inside Thigh 2	OXO	Tahando	ORO
44. Prince of the Zodiac	Front Perineum	OXO	Nociabi	MOR
45. Sublime Sage of the Mysteries	Perineum	OXO	Tastoxo	MPH
46. Sublime Pastor of the Huts	Anus	LEA	Cucarpt	DIAL
47. Knight of the Seven Stars	Coccyx	LEA	Lauacon	TEAA
48. Sublime Guardian of the Sacred Mount	Left Lower Buttock	LEA	Sochial	MPH

Degree	Point-Chaud	Æthyr	Governor	God Name
49. Sublime Sage of the Pyramids	Left Center Buttock	TAN	Sigmorf	DIAL
50. Sublime Philosopher of Samothrace	Left Upper Buttock	TAN	Aydropt	IBAH
51. Sublime Titan of the Caucasus	Right Lower Buttock	TAN	Tocarzi	ORO
52. Sage of the Labyrinth	Right Center Buttock	ZEN	Nabaomi	AOZPI
53. Knight of the Phoenix	Right Upper Buttock	ZEN	Zafasai	PDOCE
54. Sublime Scalde	1 Left Lower Back	ZEN	Valpamb	MPH
55. Sublime Orphic Doctor	2 Left Back	POP	Torzaxi	MPH
56. Pontiff of Cadmia	3 Left Back	POP	Abaiond	GAIOL
57. Sublime Magus	4 Left Back	POP	Omagrap	OIP
58. Prince Brahmin	1 Lower Back Center	CHR	Zildron	AOZPI
59. Grand Pontiff of Ogygia	2 Lower Back Center	CHR	Parziba	TEAA
60. Sublime Guardian of the Three Fires	3 Left Back Center	CHR	Totocan	PDOCE
61. Sublime Unknown Philosopher	1 Left Back Right	ASP	Chirspa	MPH
62. Sublime Sage of Eleusis	2 Left Back Right	ASP	Toantom	GAIOL
63. Sublime Kawi	3 Left Back Right	ASP	Vixpalg	HCTGA
64. Sage of Mithras	4 Left Back Right	LIN	Ozidaia	MPH
65. Guardian of the Sanctuary	Left Waist	LIN	Paraoan	IBAH
66. Grand Consecrator	Right Waist	LIN	Calzirg	MPH
67. Grand Eulogist	Lower Midback 1	TOR	Ronamb	ARSL
68. Patriarch of Truth	Left Midback 2	TOR	Onizimp	MOR
69. Knight of the Golden Branch of Eleusis	Left Midback 3	TOR	Zaxanin	OIP
70. Patriarch of the Planispheres	Left Midback 4	NIA	Orcanir	ARSL
71. Patriarch of the Sacred Vedas	Center Midback 1	NIA	Chialps	MOR
72. Sublime Master of Wisdom	Center Midback 2	NIA	Soageel	OIP

Degree	Point-Chaud	Æthyr	Governor	God Name
73. Patriarch of the Sacred Fire	Center Midback 3	UTI	Mirzind	ARSL
74. Sublime Master of the Stoka	Center Midback 4	UTI	Obuaors	DIAL
75. Knight Commander of the Lybic Chain	Right Midback 1	UTI	Ranglam	MPH
76. Patriarch of Isis	Right Midback 2	DES	Pophand	MPH
77. Sage Theosopher	Right Midback 3	DES	Nigrana	GAIOL
78. Grand Pontiff of Thebaid	Right Midback 4	DES	Bazchim	MPH
79. Sage of the Redoubtable Sada	Upper Back Left 1	ZAA	Saziami	DIAL
80. Sublime Elect of the Sanctuary of Mazias	Upper Back Left 2	ZAA	Mathula	ARSL
81. Patriarch of Memphis	Upper Back Left 3	ZAA	Orpanib	AOZPI
82. Grand Elect of the Temple of Midgard	Upper Back Right 1	BAG	Labnixp	MOR
83. Sublime Elect of the Valley of Oddy	Upper Back Right 2	BAG	Focisni	ORO
84. Doctor of the Izeds,	Upper Back Right 3	BAG	Oxlopar	HCTGA
85. Knight of Kneph	Left Shoulder Back	RII	Vastrim	TEAA
86. Sublime Philospher of the Valley of Kab	Right Shoulder Back	RII	Odraxti	ARSL
87. Sublime Prince of Masonry	Medulla Oblongata	RII	Gomziam	MPH
88. Grand Elect of the Sacred Curtain	Back of Head Left	TEX	Taoagla	MPH
89. Patriarch of the Mystic City	Back of Head Right	TEX	Gemnimb	ARSL
90. Sublime Master of the Great Work	Back Top of Head Left	TEX	Advorpt	TEAA
91. Grand Defender	Back Top of Head Right	TEX	Dozinal	HCTGA
92. Grand Catechist	Ridge Above Left Eye 1-4			
93. Regulator General	Ridge Below Left Eye 1-4			

Degree	Point-Chaud	Æthyr	
94. Grand Administrator, Prince of Memphis	Ridge Above Right Eye 1-4		
95. Grand Conservator	Ridge Below Right Eye 1-4		
96. Grand and Puissant Sovereign of the Order	Left & Right Temples		Silence in the Center, beginning of *agnosia*
97. Grand Hierophant	Ajna Chakra	The 30 Æthyrs	Silence

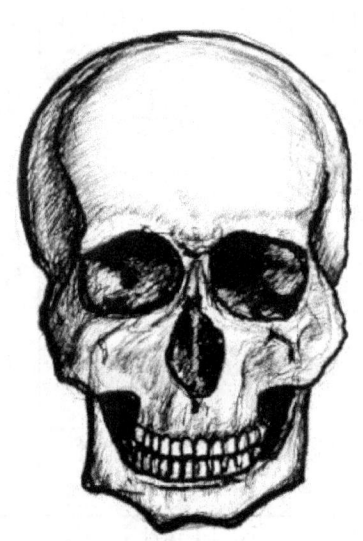

Scrying the Æthyrs

Basic Run-through for a Magickal Retirement with the Angels

The Opening

The Facilitator and the Initiate select a place for the working. It is suggested that no more than three points/Degrees are worked at a time. The only prop needed for the Degrees is a device to create the Battery of knocks. Some prefer to use a gong for this and experience will show that the energies and entities attached to the Degrees often prefer such. There is no specified regalia, though it is appropriate to where Masonic regalia if desired, as well as more formal, clerical robes and stoles, or simply "street clothes." The Opening is begun by both parties facing East with their arms in the sign of the Good Shepherd, right arm over left upon the chest. The Facilitator proclaims firmly:

> To the glory of the Sovereign Architect of the Universe! In the Name of the Sovereign Sanctuary of the Antient and Primitive Rite of Memphis+Misraïm, and under the auspices of Free Illuminism, I call upon all Passed Masters, Guardians of Freemasonry and Angelic Beings and Countenances! Come now into the magickal Temple of our bodies and bring that Initiation that descends from Antiquity and extends unto Eternity! Salutations upon all points of the Triangle! Respect to the Order!

Bow fully towards the East and then rise with the two fingers of the right hand upon the lips in the sign of the silent Horus.

Facilitator
    Let us banish from this place all powers of darkness by the Holy sign of the cross.

Standing in place, the Facilitator silently forms first a large, equal-armed cross in the East. Then, he turns to the South and does the same, then West and North and back to the East. The Initiate places herself in the form of the Vitruvian man, the sacred pentagram, symbol of the sovereignty of the human Will.

Proceed to the Middle Pillar

† † †

The Ritual

Sit in a crossed legged position or in a chair in the Pharaonic posture seen in Egyptian statuary. Maintain a straight back and practice rhythmic breathing for several minutes[697]. Then, visualizing a sphere of white light above your head and touching your 97th Degree point[698], silently invoke the Sovereign Architect of the Universe. Then move the white light down your skull towards your third eye or Ajna chakra. Here, vibrate the Sacred Word of the 4th Degree three times;

- ❖ **YOD** (the first sound of Creation)

Next, move the light downward from this point upon the forehead to the right side of the throat, the place of Daath. Vibrate the Sacred Word of the 18th Degree three times,

- ❖ **INRI** (pronounced, *in-rye* and alluding to the secret of Alchemy)

Bring the light from the throat towards the right, center chest–the place of Tiphareth and vibrate the Sacred Word of the 28th Degree three times,

- ❖ **ADONAI** (The Holy Guardian Angel within)

Move the shaft of Light from the heart center down to the genitals in Yesod and vibrate the Sacred Word of the 33rd Degree three times,

- ❖ **MICHAMICHAH BEALIM ADONAI** (who is equal to you, among the great lords?)

Finalize the beam of Light in your perineum seated upon the earth and vibrate the Sacred Word of the 45th Degree three times,

- ❖ **SOLIMY** (Princes of the Pre-Adamite Spirits or Genii)

Once you sense the beam of light from your head and down your spine to your seat, then inhale deeply and draw the light back upwards towards the cap of your skull and strongly exhale through the mouth[699] as you visualize a bursting of light from your crown and raining down upon your body and back into the earth. Draw the Light back upwards with a strong inhale and exhale again sensing the circulating currents that you will now be moving within another body in Initiation. Repeat as needed.

† † †

---

[697] The four-fold breath of the Golden Dawn is helpful in this section.
[698] See the Diagrams of the points for the specific locations upon the body.
[699] Pranayamic breathwork is helpful in this practice. The Initiate should feel the diaphragm raise and lower with these breaths and fully empty the lungs with each.

Call to the Four Archangels

Towards the East, make a large sign of the cross with our same hand gesture we use to open the points-chauds, and vibrate, **RAPHAEL**, to the South, **MICHAEL**, to the West, **GABRIEL** and to the North, **URIEL**.

† † †

Points-chaud Empowerment

- Give the Battery of Knocks for the Degree
- Vibrate strongly the Sacred Word
- Identify the points-chaud empowerment and give the gnostic pressure upon the body.
- Seal the empowerment with the Grip or Token of the Degree

† † †

19th Call, Key to the Æthyrs

Madariatza das perifa {LIL} cahisa micaolazoda saanire caosago od fifisa balzodizodarasa Iaida. Nonuca gohulime: Micama odoianu MADA faoda beliorebe, soba ooaona cahisa luciftias peripesol, das aberaasasa nonucafe netaaibe caosaji od tilabe adapehaheta damepelozoda, tooata nonucafe jimicalazodoma larasada tofejilo marebe yareryo IDOIGO; od torezodulape yaodafe gohola, Caosaga, tabaoreda saanire, od caharisateosa yorepoila tiobela busadire, tilabe noalanu paida oresaba, od dodaremeni zodayolana. Elazodape tilaba paremeji peripesatza, od ta qurelesata booapisa. Lanibame oucaho sayomepe, od caharisateosa ajitoltorenu, mireca qo tiobela Iela. Tonu paomebeda dizodalamo asa pianu, od caharisateosa aji-latore-torenu paracahe a sayomepe. Coredazodizoda dodapala od fifalazoda, lasa manada, od faregita bamesa omaoasa. Conisabera od auauotza tonuji oresa; catabela noasami tabejesa leuitahemonuji. Vanucahi omepetilabe oresa! Bagile? Moooabe OL coredazodizoda. El capimao itzomatzipe, od cacocasabe gosaa. Bajilenu pii tianuta a babalanuda, od faoregita teloca uo uime. Madariiatza, torezodu!!! Oadariatza orocaha aboaperi! Tabaori periazoda aretabasa! Adarepanu coresata dobitza! Yolacame periazodi arecoazodiore, od quasabe qotinuji! Ripire paaotzata sagacore! Umela od perdazodare cacareji Aoiveae coremepeta! Torezodu! Zodacare od Zodameranu, asapeta sibesi butamona das surezodasa Tia balatanu. Odo cicale Qaa, od Ozodazodame pelapeli IADANAMADA!

† † †

Scrying the Æthyr

Each Æthyr has an appropriate Name, Governor, and God-name. Proceed to the Prophet Asana and rather than vibrating the Sacred Word of the Degree, Vibrate the God-name and Governor's name. The Degree materials can be utilized during the visionary journey for self-defense and the general testing of spirits, but the Angels should only respond to the Æthyr's specific God-name and Governor. When utilizing this method, some have seen the Name of the Æthyr itself within the journey. This is a clear confirmation that the Initiate is in the right sphere.[700]

---

[700] One student, for instance, saw ZIM written on a boxcar of a train while in the vision for ZIM. This was followed by further confirmation when the student was stopped for a train passing some months later and one of the boxcars was indeed ZIM!

Part Three – Chapter Five: Arcana Arcanorum

DAILY EXERCISE OF THE WHITE BALL "BOULE BLANCHE"[701]

Robert AMBELAIN

We pray you to tell, sub rosa, whether we should suppress this EXERCISE of the ORDER OF THE MAGI (2nd Grade) of Clymer, very slightly modified by us, according to the indications of *La Kabbale Pratique*, page 202. We have practiced this Exercise thrice daily for over 7 years, but we find some doubts on certain opposition to our present Martinist and Cohen "training." (Prayer of the heart 2.)

Alternated breathing with concentration and visualization of the living fire.

Seated, or in the "Siddhasana" position, practice the alternated breathing: (right nostril and in-breathing, retention of the breath, left nostril and out-breathing, retention "in the void"; reversed repetition of the process), synchronized with an alternating visualization of the Living Fire descending from the top of the head to the lower extremity of the spinal column, concentration of the Fire on this point, ascension of the same Fire to the upper extremity of the head (or only to the heart), concentration on this point, and finally, rest "in the void."

1st time: IN-BREATHING. Mental mantra:

"I cause to descend the in-breathed LIVING FIRE, from the UPPER Triangle to the LOWER Triangle, to awaken VE RUACH ELOHIM…"

2nd time: RETENTION OF THE BREATH. Mental mantra:

"May I transmute into LIFE, WISDOM, LOVE" (9 times).

3rd time: OUT-BREATHING. Mental mantra:

"I bring VE RUACH ELOHIM from the LOWER Triangle to the THRONE of the HEART (or to the UPPER Triangle) to purify my thoughts and desires, and to vivify the FIRES of the SOUL on the ALTAR of the THRONE."*

4th time: RETENTION IN THE VOID. No mantra. Expectant contemplation.

---

[701] English translation by Tau Phosphoros, reprinted with permission from *Degrees of Wisdom: A Compendium of Rituals from the Rites of Memphis and Misraïm*, Triad Press, LLC, 2025, p.723.

The effects of this EXERCISE have, and will have, immediate and profound effects, but sometimes too intense and difficult to control. They lead to a "SIGNIFICATION of the ASTRAL LIGHT."

*:

If I bring the FIRE to the UPPER Triangle at the 3rd time, I say:

"I bring VE RUACH ELOHIM from the LOWER Triangle to the UPPER Triangle to purify my thoughts and desires, and to unite me to: VE RUACH HAKOBESCH."

Fire in the HEART: Emotional purification. Fire in the HEAD: Intellectual purification.

(1) DESCENT OF THE LIVING FIRE.

(2) PRAYER OF THE HEART.

(3) ASCENSIO

Part Three – Chapter Five: Arcana Arcanorum

90th Degree

Sublime Master of the Great Work[702]

The Knowledge & Conversation of One's Holy Guardian Angel

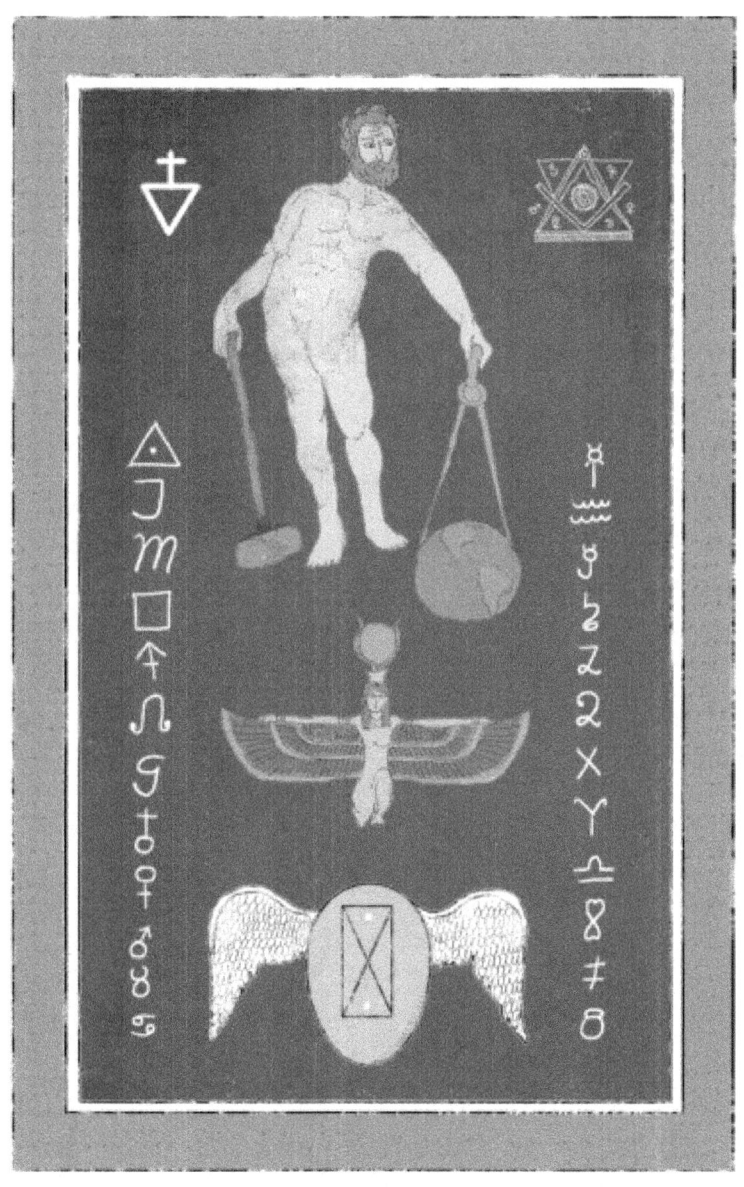

90th *degree,*
Sublime Master of the Great Work.

---

[702] This Degree may be worked alongside a traditional aspect of the A-A, the **Hieros Gamos** of the Rose+Croix d'Or. When the Initiate shares a Syzygy with another—in sacred "Caritas" (See *Syzygy*, 3rd edition, p. 156) the nature of the Demiurgos is expanded and the entire Arcana Arcanorum is worked in the most Holy Communion of souls, leading to the 3rd echelon working of ÆONic Masonry.

Battery of Knocks

Ninety knocks in *three, three times* and *nine, nine times.*

Points-chaud

Left, top of the backside of the head

Sacred Word

Given only in Council[703]

Grip

Three strokes on the first joint of the right index finger; then nine, then nine of the first joint of second finger of the right hand.

Sign

Draw the magickal sword across the breast from left to right, then make nine points to the right and nine points back to the left. On retiring, bring the sword across the breast and sheathe it. This is a sign to the Demiurge that you are going to expose the true Self, even if it means that you will open your very chest to do so.

Additional Materials

Password–ISIS

Jewel–Winged egg. A point in the center of three squares which end in a triple triangle with two points at the base.

†††

Synopsis

This Degree not only marks the end of the *Arcana Arcanorum*, but it marks a high point[704] in the career of the Mage. In fact, in the minds of many magicians, the focus of this grade–which is ultimately the *Knowledge and Conversation of one's Holy Guardian Angel*–is the primary goal of all High Magick. Crowley goes so far as to say that all else that deviates from this is black magick. Strong words. There is no "Degree" or empowerment that will provide this experience, but this grade is dedicated to the accomplishment of such and acts as a door opener and consecration to the Great Work. Listen to the words from the Council Lectures:

---

[703] This is revealed within the Synopsis and discovered through T Allen Greenfield's researches.
[704] Notice, it doesn't mark the "end of the career" of a Mage, but a high point.

Q. What is a Sublime Master of the Great Work?

A. A Mason who feels the prize of existence and seeks the means of perfecting it by the good employment of life; by observation of nature, experience, and the culture of science, and who estimates men and brethren and things in general at their true value; comprehending that which he is and that which he may make himself, and who has found, in short, the guide of real life, and the road of virtue which conducts to happiness.[705]

Happiness...not a subject frequently mused upon in occult works, yet the basis of a sane existence. The integration that follows the K & C of the HGA brings about the *Summum Bonum*, spirit-filled happiness. Along with this integration comes the recognition of the inherent symmetry of the spirit mapping of the points-chauds empowerments upon the body, aligned mystically with the degrees of the Antient & Primitive Rite of Memphis+Misraïm in an Ecclesiastical context. A MIND is revealed through the work, which far exceeds human capacity. This realization of the divine geometry and spiritual circuitry of our system brings about a profound trust and joy in the labors, and strips away the veils that hide the true Self and prevent deep and lasting happiness.

Starting with the Degree work itself, we have a series of interesting words. Firstly, we have the Password of ISIS. As we have assumed the godform of Osiris and of Horus, we are now given the opportunity to assume the form of Isis. She is the goddess of magic and this Degree is dedicated specifically to *Sacred* Magick. Assuming her godform and visiting the chthonic realms that she is free to roam is a precursor to the higher work that she will assist the Initiate in, for just as she went in search of the torn pieces of her husband Osiris, she will endeavor to assist the search of the soul who in earnest seeks converse with his Ka (Holy Guardian Angel).

The second word that is used as an additional passport in the underworld, is DEMIURGOS. The Demiurge is frequently referenced in the Gnostic scriptures such as the *Apocryphon of John*. This entity is named, Ialdabaoth, who is the Fabricator of the known world in Gnostic pantheons. As a personage *under* the Very God,[706] he is sometimes considered jealous. He was pictured as lion-faced with the head of a serpent, an emblem found on ancient gnostic coins.

It is important for the Initiate to meet this Fabricator, because he is also the creator of the *persona*, or the mask of the Self.[707] Until Ialdabaoth is dealt with, one cannot hope to meet the divine HGA within. This mask maker is something of a devil sometimes and so the Initiate must prepare for his haughty nature. In his hubris, Ialdabaoth has convinced the Initiate that the face that is worth showing the public is the face that is carefully

---

[705] Yarker, *Lectures of a Chapter, Senate & Council...*, 1882, p. 76.
[706] The "Very God" is a reference to the Nicene Creed, which states, "True God of True God," or "Very God of Very God." It is *this* Deity, and not the Demiurgos, who we dedicate the Administrative Grades to. The Very God is the super-unknown Source.
[707] The Demiurgos reveals himself as the "Shadow" in psychological terms. This can be a very daunting experience. The Initiate should maintain close ties to his tradition (religious) while working this path, and frequently offer prayers and obeisance to the Source.

constructed and crafted by the Self. The true Self, the deepest portion of our very *isness*, which was pointed at in the center of the 30 Æthyrs and which *naught but silence can express*, is the abode of the Angel. As the Ka is often shown outside of the god in Egyptian paintings, it is thought that the HGA can exist outside of the individual. It can, but it is a chimera of the reality—a corporeal similitude which can assist in our arousal of bhakti yoga,[708] but which ultimately must be eschewed for the inner nature and reality of the Angel.

The final name, the Sacred Word of the Degree, is a mystery full of further mysteries. This Word is certain to be misinterpreted by many and has created strife and confusion in the realm of religion since it was employed. The name, given only within a Council of Sublime Masters (i.e., within a Lodge or Chapel) is *Lucifer*. It is in the sense of its original Latin meaning that we utilize this word, as Lucifer simply means, "Light bearer." The conflagration of Lucifer with Satan, the serpent of Genesis, the falling star in Isaiah, and the morning star in Revelations, to name a few, is a great error in the history of the Church, but there is some evidence that the nature of all of these separate words is beginning to be understood in common publications as well as critical exegeses. For our purposes, Lucifer is precisely what the name suggests, a light bearer and bringer to the Initiate. The *Manifestation of the Light*, the completion of the search which was undertaken in the Violet Lodge of the APRM+M, is most comprehensively manifested by the Knowledge and Conversation of the HGA.

The points-chaud of this Degree, along with the 90 strikes upon the gong, creates a hypnotic atmosphere of calm and openness that begins the quiet receptivity necessary to listen to the directives of the Angel. When re-worked at the close of a 3-6 month[709] extended exploration of the HGA, via the *Sacred Magic of Abramelin the Mage* or another such Rite[710] dedicated to this Highest of sciences, this point begins to make the other points in the body vibrate, throb, and pulse with light. The Scintillating body is *duly and truly prepared* for the experience of the HGA which is born from a pious devotion to the same. These points of light within the body, this constellation of flickering points seen through *La Prise des Yeaux*, act as an invitatory Psalm to the Angel!

The Knowledge & Conversation of the HGA is intimately related to the sense of Holy Duty that was mentioned as early as the 4th Degree. This Duty is co-equal with the Thelemic understanding of True Will. The knowledge of one's True Will and the carrying out of the same is often a portion of the conversation that is held with the Angelic being. The visible

---

[708] When beginning working with the Angel, there is simply no stronger magic than that of devotion. This sentence concerning the corporeal similitude of the external Angel involves the very strength of devotion. An example is how devotees of the Christ often have external visions of him.

[709] The original undertaking, as demonstrated by the latest research of George Duhn and Steve Guth, 2006, suggests an 18 month work, but the undertaking of the K&C of the HGA is deeply personal and does not have a required time frame. As Jason Miller says in, *The Holy Guardian Angel*, Nephilim Press, "The law of sufficient time is sometimes why people fail at the six-month version of the operation…Approach the work with passion. Follow the two principles of invoking often and retreating as much as possible from the world. Realize that, spiritually speaking, different people are at different levels when they start the operation" (25).

[710] Such as Liber Samekh or one devised by the Initiate.

evidence of one in whom this important undertaking has fulfilled its purpose, is the sense of serenity and artfulness upon their personage. There is a greater honesty and complete lack of artifice in their speech. They are driven by a new purpose, a divine vocation as it were, and they will not sleep until they fulfill their calling. Yet, as Crowley suggests, they are not hung up on the "lust of result." In his Magical Diary entitled, *John St. John*, we find Crowley returning to the Sacred Magic and desirous of a *continued conversation*[711] with the Angel whom he had already contacted and begun relating with on a trek across China (all of which, it is important in our Primitive Doctrine to point out, was carried out without any equipment whatsoever, entirely within the realms of the mind). In this Diary, Crowley shows the reader how thoroughly enmeshed the life of the Mage becomes with the daily. He eats in a Yogin manner, makes love unto the Highest, and chants Holy Invocations to the gods of coffee and citron presses. This is a beautiful revelation of the complete interpenetration of the spiritual and the physical, the above and the below—so that there is simply one process remaining, one that is directed unto Adonai (the HGA), conceived of as the *highest* aspect of the Self. We read in the Lecture of the Senate;

Q. How do you name yourself?

A. Adonai.

Q. Why?

A. To show that the lowest rank may mount to the highest.[712]

It is up to the Initiate to discover the means to contact her Angel. There are many worthy pointers available, some of which can be found in the *Suggested Reading*, but we will offer some advisory material that has been helpful for the +Chapel of the Gnosis.

The parishioners of our Chapel utilize the Holy Book of the Psalms at regular intervals. These magickal hymns of antiquity have been hallowed by usage and have the capacity to create the appropriate space (The Mystic Temple) for the arrival of the Angel. The Sacred Magic of Abramelin is very dependent upon the Psalms for the orisons of the mage and we find particular mention of the *Miserere Mei* (Psalm 51) and the *De Profundis* (Psalm 129). These are the words of a struggling individual who has endured ordeals and trials and who wants nothing more than union with his Lord. Now Lord, for us, is Adonai as it often appears in the Bible, but whose significance in magick is in relation to the HGA. If the Initiate chants the Psalms with the understanding that the "Lord" is none other than her HGA, the text becomes transportative and transformative. The Psalm becomes a spiritual circuit directing the Self to the Angel within. In *Syzygy*, we find reference to a number of monastic practices that enhance the Invoking of the Angel, such as *Opus Dei, Obsculta,* and *Lectio Divina*. But there is no greater key than that of living a pious and humble life in

---

[711] Aaron Leitch and others attest to the same continued conversation. See pgs. 74-75 of *The Holy Guardian Angel*. In point of fact, this book is a continuing conversation with my own Angel.

[712] *Lecture of a Senate, Chapter & Council*, 1882, p. 48. This quote is really rather interesting. It brings up the age-old argument concerning the nature of the HGA—is it a separate entity or conterminous with the Initiate? This is for the Initiate to decide for herself. Nevertheless, the relationship is close enough to *feel* as if the HGA is simply the highest expression of the individual.

simplicity and calling upon the Angel with frequency and devotion as a lover to his beloved. This *will require* a certain amount of retirement, but as the eminently practical Aleister Crowley demonstrates, a great deal of the work can be carried out amongst others. This retirement is the very INNER RETREAT spoken of within the Monastery of the Seven Rays teachings.

For the priesthood and laity alike, there is a special program leading to Daily Mass that is often utilized as a retreat to intensify the communion with the Angel, after the initial contact and converse. For the priest or other clergy, this is simply the practice of the Holy Mass of Rome (particularly the *Tridentine* Mass) beginning twice a week and working up to daily Mass. The twist on this Holy source of sacred magick, is that the divinity that we invoke into the elements is none other than our beloved, our Angel. This manner of "god-eating" is not meant to blaspheme the common usage, it is meant to elaborate upon its intended meaning—for if as the Book of Luke says, *the kingdom of God is within you*, then this action of transmuting earthly items into divine fragments and partaking of them, is an action of Grace and ushers into the body the experience of Emmanuel, God with us. As the Initiate enters the final week, partaking of Mass every day, he begins to see the structure of the Mass as one of the most compete and occult forms of sacred magick available, as it cleanses and purifies the exterior (Katharismos), calls down the inner heavenly spheres into the earthly (Photismos), and finds its culmination in complete union with the Divine (Henosis). With the subtle shift in *intention* from the host and cup being the body and the blood of Christ or another deity, to that of the body and blood of Adonai—the HGA, which is to *feed* the Initiate from this point forth and forevermore, we find an incantation whose subtlety is unequalled in occult practice. In the same way that the Facilitator does not technically *give* the Initiate the points-chaud empowerment, but instead awakens what was already latent within, this form of Eucharist is not a one-dimensional imagining of taking the HGA into the body as a foreign substance. It is rather, a projection of the corporeal similitude,[713] for which we have grown in such deep devotion and love, into common things, only to be more fully integrated back into the physical organism.

Through this magickal use of the Eucharist, the Initiate learns to will the presence of the Angel into being. He will have other tools in his arsenal for further development with the Angel, including: the Battery of Knocks, the points-chaud empowerment with its subsequent scrying procedures, the Masonic Middle Pillar and movement of AZOTH[714] throughout the body, awakening the Angelic presence, and the side effects of such labor—*initiations on the Inner Planes with the Angel during sleep*. The Angel will teach the Initiate how

---

[713] Again, a type of effluvia, like the projection of the Body of Light.

[714] Connecting AZOTH with the Great Work, we hear Yarker quoting from the Lectures of the Senate, "The secrets of the Great Work, or search for the absolute, like all the mysteries of Magism, have a three-fold application; they are religious, philosophical and natural. Above all it is the creation of man by himself, the conquest which he makes of his future, and the perfect emancipation of his will, represented by the pentacle of Solomon. It is that law of creation which results from the accord of two forces, the development of complete power over the universal magical agent, or Azoth, and the separation of the subtle from the gross with much industry and painful labor" (*Lectures of a Chapter, Senate & Council*, 42). In a single quote we find the Three-fold path, the sign of man in which receive our points (pentacle) and the union of the Great Work with AZOTH.

to think of the points-chauds and awaken them with the mind, he will show how they pulse and warm up when concentrated upon, and he will reveal the method of enlightening all of the points at once in a full bodied spasm of light expansion.[715] These are some of the gifts that accompany the completion of the Great Work. These are the labors of Spirit Builders.

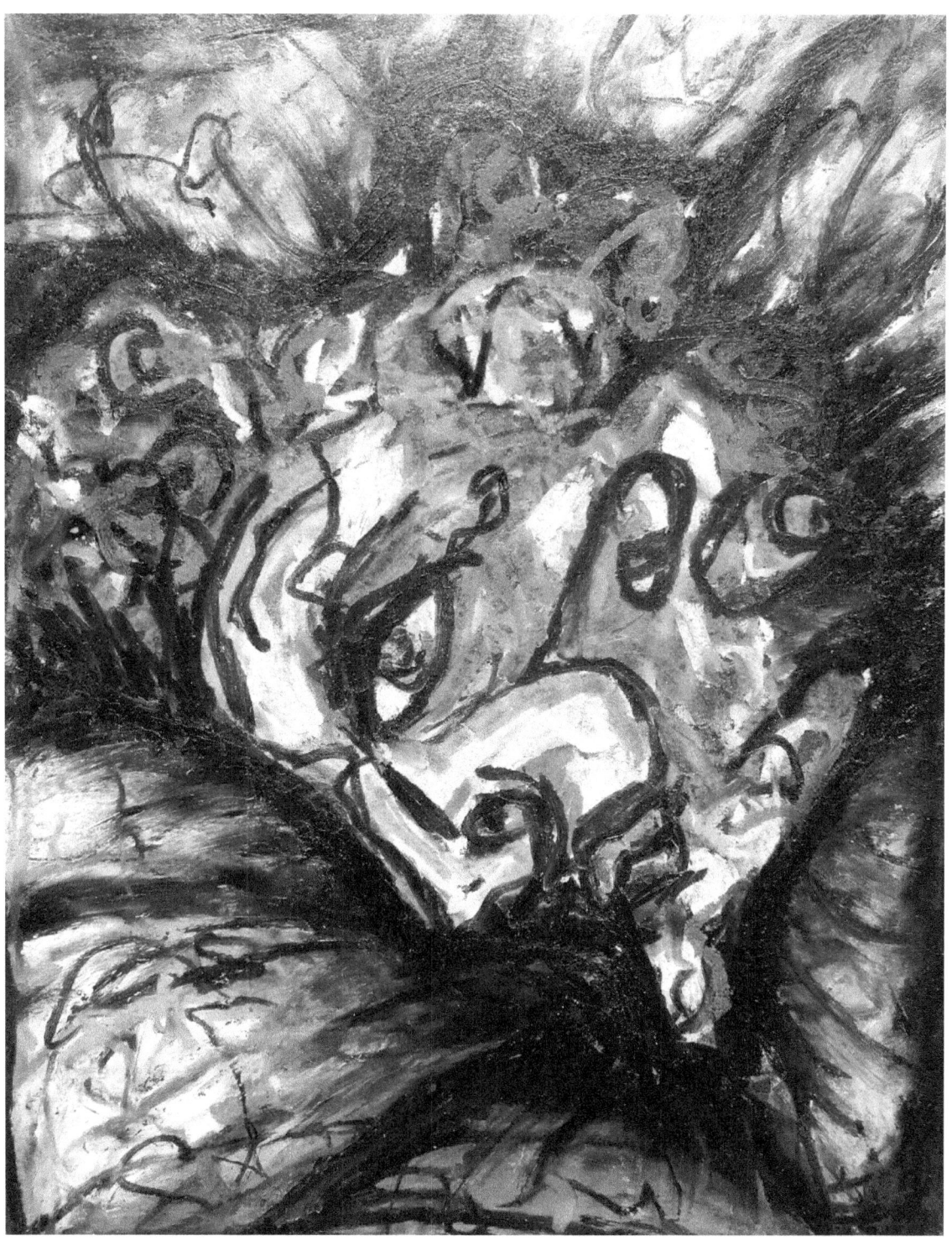

---

[715] Which can, in turn, be utilized in healing, amongst other applications—particularly in reference to the Hieros Gamos.

Suggested Reading for the Arcana Arcanorum Series

There are certainly fewer Degrees in this Series than in the previous one, and so it would seem proper that there are fewer book suggestions. But this is not the only reason we have a slim title listing. The main reason is that as we get into the final Degrees of the *Hauts Grades* we get more and more focused in our singularity of purpose. Our Sacred and Primitive Doctrines becomes more stream lined into the conduit of initiatory power that is our inheritance. The things that we are building: the Scintillating Body, the Mystical Temple and the Community of Light, become more tangible and more economized in these latter grades. The works that are suggested here are mostly primary documents—Grimoires and diaries of those that have gone before us. And though the listing could be greatly expanded upon, it is sufficient to study these several tomes and to thereafter, direct the course of study for oneself.

- *The Book of Abramelin*, by Abraham of Worms, newly translated and edited by Dehn and Guth.
- *The Book of the Sacred Magic of Abramelin the Mage*, Mathers version. Though we now have the extended and corrected version above, many of us used this version with complete success before the newly revised piece.
- *After the Angel*, by Marcus Katz
- *The Sacred Magician*, by William Bloom (George Chevalier)
- *Aleister Crowley and the Practice of the Magical Diary*, text by Crowley and Frater Achad, introduced and edited by James Wasserman.
- *The Magick of Aleister Crowley*, by Lon Milo DuQuette, an excellent introduction into the practical workings of Thelemites as well as a fantastic alternative to the classical Sacred Magic of Abramelin. Includes both Crowley's *Liber Samekh* and DuQuette's clearly organized and greatly solidified version.
- *Meditations on the Tarot*, anon, (Valentin Tomberg) This book is listed again as it is of universal import to the way of a sacred magician.
- *The Grimoire of Armadel*, Mathers
- *The Arbatel of Magic*, edited and introduced by Joseph Peterson
- *The Greek Magical Papyri in Translation*, edited by Hans Dieter Betz
- *The Holy Guardian Angel, On the Practice and Experience of the Holy Guardian Angel*, edited by Michael Cecchetelli
- *The Celestial Hierarchy*, by Dionysius the Areopagite. This is the companion volume to the *Mystical Theology* and explores the kataphatic knowledge of the angelic realms, whereas the latter explores the subjects of the Administrative Grades.
- *Enochian Vision Magick*, by Lon Milo Duquette
- *The Essential Enochian Grimoire*, by Aaron Leitch

- *The Vision and the Voice*, by Aleister Crowley
- *John Dee's Five Books of Mystery*, by Joseph H. Peterson
- *Practical Enochian Magick*, by Jason Augustus Newcomb
- *Enochian Magic for Beginners,* by Donald Tyson
- *The Golden Dawn Enochian Scrying Tarot*, by Genaw & Cicero
- *Degrees of Wisdom: A Compendium of Rituals from the Rites of Memphis and Misraïm,* pp. 700-734.
- For the *Hieros Gamos*, no text can exceed that of the **Song of Solomon** the King.

Chapter Six
Administrative Degrees

91-97th Degrees

Divine Darkness, therefore, is not the appearance of God as darkness, but the weakness of man to see the Essence of God, which is the 'unapproachable Light.

–Metropolitan of Nafpaktos, Hierotheos

Up until this point, our Primitive Doctrine has given us the means and suggestions of putting the Initiate in contact with the entities and energies of the spirit realm. We have engaged in philosophical studies and explorations into the doctrines of other cultures, climes, and times. We have delved deeply into the magickal and occasionally mystical, nature of our Degrees as they are aligned to the points-chauds and we have scryed into Otherwhere to bring back individualized meanings of the Degrees and information from the beyond. We have worked with Ceremonial Magick, Hermeticism, Gnosticism (including forms of Voudon+Gnosis) and Angel Magick. In the following Series, we bring our labors to a close and investigate the roles of *Administration* in our Spirit Building and the final portion of our Hermetic axiom, "...to Keep Silent."

As mentioned in Book One, the Congregational Illuminist manifestation of Freemasonry is rather unique. Our structures are minimal and our organizational edifice is almost non-existent. The businessman will look at our program and find it to be a complete *loss*-in terms of the bottom line–for the Facilitators and leaders in this revolutionary movement. But fortunately, we are not building on a business model, nor are we in the least bit interested in the *incorporated* versions of spiritual orders. In fact, we have found that such packaging and distribution of the Western Esoteric Tradition can be toxic to the subtle processes of the Great Work, distracting from the necessary concentration and focus of the spiritual life, and can hinder the labors of our less fortunate Brothers and Sisters. And so when we say

Administrative Grades, what we are in turn saying is, *Service* Grades, for when the Initiate of our Rites works these Degrees, he or she is entering upon a course of service to others, in the form of mutual aid and support, mentoring and guidance, and the sharing of ideas. In some cases, the mutual aid and support will be financial when we discover a Brother or Sister in need, while in other cases it may be in the form of lending prayers, good vibes and emotional support. Lodges, Nodes, and Chapels will find their own pet projects to offer service in, such as shelters for the homeless, animal rights activism, environmental programs and initiatives, and social justice/equality efforts and outreach programs, to name a few. Many Free Illuminists in the Atlanta community are involved in multiple projects of this nature and do all in the name of humanity and for the sake of humanity.

We will explore the four basic precepts of Congregational Illuminism one more time, but in the light of service mindedness in this Series. It is our conviction that these simple guidelines can revolutionize the Western Esoteric Tradition and open the gates of Initiation to those who may have previously been marginalized, or who would never knock upon the doors of the sanctuary in the first place because of social and economical inequalities. In this way, we activate the dictum, *Liberty, Equality and Fraternity* in new, inclusive, and innovative ways.

The final two Degrees of our Rite unashamedly regard a religious experience. Whereas many Orders and Rites of Freemasonry steer clear of referring to their working as being spiritual or religious, we proclaim from the outset that what we are doing is indeed spiritual. The 96th and the 97th Degrees are mystical and can be approached and fully experienced by Brothers or Sisters of any religious persuasion, though the model that we are presenting in this study is unique to our own Chapel. It is for the individual Free Illuminist or the particular Lodge to decide how best to enter this study and what books are most appropriate, as the material presented is suggestive only. The experience is One. Initiation is One. And so we do not fret about the nature of these two Degrees and their deeply spiritual quality. Whatever route that is chosen, the Initiate can scale the heights, for as the Chaldean Oracles say, "unto the persevering mortal, the blessed Immortals are swift." For the assiduous laborer in the quarries of the soul, the silent and unknown God will make himself known.

As the Administrative Grades brings the points-chauds back to the starting place of the Degrees, and wrap up the system in its entirety, we find a paradox in viewing the dark path of *agnosia* that the highest Grades suggest, as distinguished from the spiritist and magickal workings of the other Degrees. This agnosia is experienced through via one very specific gate, that of Silence. This silence attunes the human instrument to the states of high trance necessary to enter into the Uncreated Light in deep meditation.[716]

The bridge of this paradox lies within the path of *Sacred Magic*, which Tomberg[717] distinguishes rather strongly from so-called, *arbitrary magic*. We find simple admonitions in various places, such as in the Arbatel where the prerequisites for this path are simply the

---

[716] See p.39 in Bertiaux's, *Cosmic Meditation*
[717] *Meditations on the Tarot*.

right attitude and the living of a pious and charitable life.[718] This simple aphorism is consonant with Yarker's thinking in his *Grand Book of Maxims*; "105. Exact no other condition for admission amongst us than probity and knowledge; receive and instruct all honest men, whatever their belief, country, or laws—our dogmas are simply, God and virtue. 106. Purify thy heart."[719] And again in the *Arbatel*, we are told that "neither evil daemon nor ill fate can harm one whose help rests in the Most High."[720] And further that, "The true and divine magus is able to use all creatures of God,[721]" which reminds us that all shall be well if we steer the noble course and do ALL, *To the Glory of the Sublime Architect of All Worlds!*

---

[718] See the Introduction by Peterson in *Arbatel, 2009*, p. XVIII.
[719] *Lectures of a Chapter, Senate & Council*, p. 95.
[720] *Arbatel*, p. 29. This quote is aligned deeply with Psalm 91.
[721] Ibid, p. 39.

91st Degree
Grand Defender of the Rite

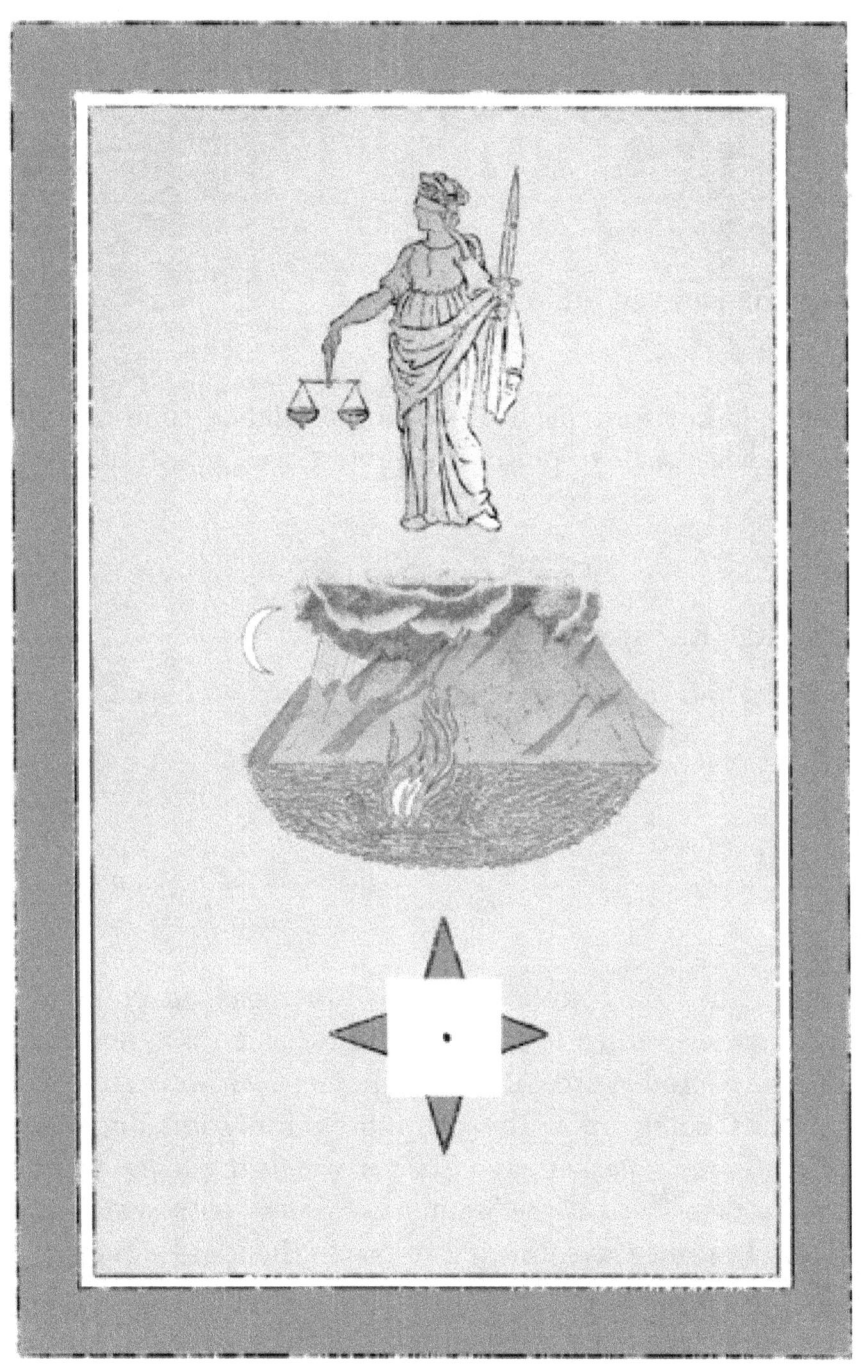

91st degree,
Grand Defender.

Battery of Knocks

Seven, seven times. XXXXXXX XXXXXXX XXXXXXX XXXXXXX XXXXXXX XXXXXXX XXXXXXX

Points-chaud

Back top of head, right side

Sacred Word

ASTREE (Justice)

Grip

Press each other's hand seven times.

Sign

Extend the right hand horizontally, as if holding a balance, then with the left hand, take, as it were, from the heaviest scale to put in the lightest, as if to establish equality.

Additional Materials

Password–MIDGARD (Elevated Sanctuary)

Jewel–A four pointed and rayed star, enclosing a square with a central point.

† † †

Synopsis

This Degree returns us to a couple of familiar themes, but enlarges upon them in a profound manner. First, we return to the idea of justice, equity, and harmony within the Yarker synopsis and the Sacred Word, ASTREE (Justice). However, the direction is moving outward–from the focus being upon the continuing initiation and development of the Initiate–to the world at large. Yarker says, "Never weigh thy fellows in one scale alone; if evil has the advantage take from it the human weakness with which it charged, and let charity do the rest.[722]" In some ways, this is a return to the ideas, concepts, and beneficence of mainstream Blue Lodge workings. However, it is extended in a precise way regarding the freedoms awarded our Initiates and the respect of the individual's unique pursuit of the spiritual. To be more specific, we regard this in light of our first Congregational Illuminist precept, **Spiritual growth is incompatible with authoritarian structure.** The heavy hand of authority has no place in our workings and the manner of justice we practice is in our very relinquishing of the notion of judgment. We take the words of the Great Initiate, *Judge*

---

[722] *Compleat Rite of Memphis*, p. 142.

not lest ye be judged rather literally and refrain from judgment in things moral as well as spiritual. One of the tell-tale signs of authoritarian structures is the utilizing of a business model. Our work would be completely stymied by the CEO/top-down superstructure and mentality. The spirits do not operate in this manner, nor do we. The process of creating the Scintillating body, building the Mystic Temple and working in Free Communion with others is incompatible with authoritarian structures and so-called, "leaders." Our very existence as a body of spirit builders *requires* us to operate in less hierarchical, less institutional, and less commercial ways; thus returning to the original mottos of the Rosicrucians who offered their healing and mystic work freely, and before them to the Sacred Groves where a man or woman's fitness for Initiation was based upon more subtle qualities than the contents of their purse. Our method of working is a free service to all who are committed to the labors it requires. It is stabilized simply by the notion of mutual aid and support based upon the basic goodness of the human species. Bad eggs tend to be rooted out early in our circles due to the expectation of real work, self-development, and self-direction, and the lack of powerful positions, seats of honor and external rewards.

The Battery of Knocks of this Degree, is seven times seven, or 49. This refers to the Biblical Jubilee Year, which follows the 49th year (or in some texts, the 50th) in which festival, slaves were set free, land and property rights were returned to their original owners, and a general restoration was celebrated after a set of 50 years. This is analogous to our sense of "justice" in this Degree, which reinvests our Initiates of that which they have been divested of. What is reinvested is the Initiate's original rights and benefits that are befitting a deity (albeit on a lesser arc). For, as St. Athanasius said, "God became man that man might become god." Or in the *Book of the Law,* 1:3, "Every man and every woman is a star." This Degree marks the realization of this mystery and its application to the sense of harmony that accompanies our Free Communion, liberated from authoritarian strictures and celebratory of each individual's unique Self.

Another familiar theme of this Degree is the *elevated Sanctuary* (the Password, MIDGARD) which was investigated in the 82nd Degree as well as the 34th, and identified with the *Sovereign Sanctuary* on high. We recall that this elevated sanctuary is paradoxical because it is given a name that suggests middle earth. Our concept of the *Sovereign Sanctuary*, an inner sanctum found within our Ontic Sphere, is continuous with the elevated sanctuary and so we come to see that it is earthly, but within the core of our being (middle earth) as we found in the Arcana Arcanorum while scrying the Æthyrs and entering the center in silence. For this Degree, MIDGARD is opened to us in a unique manner, particularly upon reception of the points-chaud empowerment. This point balances the empowerment connected with The Great Work, and thereby is a continuation of the growing relationship of the Initiate with her HGA. In the scrying of this Degree, the Initiate is given a guide into the Sovereign Sanctuary, by way of the HGA who may still only be sensed. If the experience of the Angel has not yet occurred, the Initiate may create a corporeal similitude of the angel in the form of the Egyptian Ka, and begin to strongly visualize and give personal devotion to, this attendant spirit.

As we near the completion of our Degrees, we must remember that our Rite is analogous to a pliable and supple body, trained and rigorous—yet flexible. Our work is internally self-referential and consistent. Yet this consistency does not equal an inhumane rigidity and there are many areas that allow for innovation, diversity, and variation—as well as a multitude of applications of the Degree materials and points empowerments. Even within our own *Chapel of the Gnosis* are variants to the working, particularly with regards to the mystery of the 97th Degree which some see as being most completely expressed in the magical *Lunation Mass of the Syzygy*, where the complete annihilation of the self is accomplished through the ecstatic union of a couple who share in Caritas[723].

---

[723] See pages 156-168, 3rd edition, *Syzygy*, as well as the Preface of the present work for 3rd echelon connections.

92nd Degree

Grand Catechist

Invocation of the Great Silence

92nd degree,
Grand Catechist.

Battery of Knocks

Seven equal knocks. X X X X X X X

Points-chaud

Ridge above left eye, 1-4.

Sacred Word

TRUTH

Grip

Cross left hands as in saluting, raise hat with right, or motion as if doing so.

Sign

Enter with hat on head, draw magickal sword with right hand, bring it horizontally across breast and return it.

Additional Materials

Password–ASTREA (Justice), response, SILENCE

Jewel–Within wavy lines a 4 pointed star, enclosing a central point.

† † †

Synopsis

This is a very simple Degree with a rather coherent message. There are no specific entities or energies invoked by the point, however, in practical workings in our Chapel, we have found that this Degree through the 95th encourage transdimensional traffic with otherworldly entities.[724] This may simply be due to the spiritual circuitry inherent in these points upon the face and their quick stimulatory powers within the Ontic sphere of the Initiate. Largely speaking however, there are no *specific* entities or energies allied to this point.

What is stirred up with this Degree is the nature of our 2nd precept in Congregational Illuminism which states; **Scientific Illuminism requires a non-dogmatic, experimental approach.** As this Degree is titled Grand Catechist, making of the recipient an Officer of the *Grand Liturgical College of Sublime Catechists of the Order*, it is highly suggestive that the

---

[724] This may seem odd at this juncture, but when considering the fact that we are entering upon the study of the ONE, the noumenal SOURCE, we can see how super-terrestrial beings may be attracted to this endeavor. These may not be of the wholesome variety. Again, reference is made to the Holy Order of the Élus Coëns, whose work includes battling the negative forces that attempt to penetrate the Earth's Aura.

precept allied to it concerns a **non-dogmatic, experimental approach**. In concert with the Sacred Word of this Degree, TRUTH, we have the foundation of our spiritual edifice.

Whereas the normative sense of catechesis refers to religious doctrine, education, and formulaic responses, we find the terms *non-dogmatic* and *experimental* antithetical to the common understanding of catechesis and thereby the role of a Grand Catechist as something wholly other than what tradition would suggest. It is the primary role of the Grand Catechist in our Rite to ensure that *The Method of Science, the Aim of Religion* is adhered to with accuracy and scrutiny, via the Magical Diary which holds a crucial place in our workings. In this universal phrase of Scientific Illuminism, we have the injunction to apply the Scientific method of observation, testing, and analysis (as well as replicating our experiments and working towards verifiable results) to our labors, and to thereby achieve the common goals of knowledge of the self, knowledge of the "Other," converse with the "Other," and union with the Deity(s) of the great Religions. The process is open to innovation, experimentation, and synthesis. In this way, religious *doctrine* is eschewed for the sake of verifiable religious *experience*, which is a return to our central theme of Gnosis. Additionally, rather than memorizing huge portions of a catechism and being tested upon the same, we suggest *experimentation* with what is provided and *explorations* into the supermundane realms. Our body positive and simple approach instills a sacred trust in the overall goodness, the *original blessing* as Fr. Matthew Fox calls it, of this world and its many entryways into the Unknown.

Finally, the response to the password, ASTREE is Silence. It is not a lack of response, it is the word itself spoken for the last time within the scrying session before being employed entirely in the deep meditation of the final grades. This silence carries with it the Grand Key of Rosicrucian healing. Bertiaux states,

> *The longer we spend in the silence the more it becomes for us a source of both physical and metaphysical strength. The physical body is healed and experiences repair, just as the soul of man is more and more aware of the inner powers that are his during the experience of the silence.*[725]

---

[725] p. 66, *Cosmic Meditation*

Spirit Builders

93rd Degree
Regulator General
Invocation of the 93 Current

*93*th *degree,*
Regulator General.

Battery of Knocks

Seven equal knocks. X X X X X X X

Points-chaud

Ridge below left eye, 1-4

Sacred Word

WISDOM (Sophia)

Grip

Clasp right hands, then place left on waist.

Sign

The sign of fidelity and truth in Masonry, place right hand on the heart.[726]

Additional Materials

Password–TRUE LIGHT (eras lux vera)

Jewel–Within a circle, a 4-rayed Star with a central point.

†††

Synopsis

The 92nd through 95th Degrees have points-chauds upon the front of the face over and under each eye socket. These equal four primary points, but the points have quarter-points, as it were, as is seen on the diagram. We noticed an immediate stimulation in our scrying abilities upon reception of these four points and the previously mentioned "traffic" of interdimensional entities. The way that we work with this in our Chapel is by sensing the location of the single point that is *hotter* than the other three linked to it. While in the process of writing this Synopsis, it occurred to me that there may be more to this, as it felt like all of the points were at least warm, but one point would be the most vibratory. As I have done throughout this book and throughout the years of working with and communicating with T Allen Greenfield, I sent him a quick note asking how he visualized these particular points. His additional insight hit the nail on the head. He simply described the points with these four Degrees as having quarter points and operating like something akin to Christmas lights. Voila! This simple bit of instruction, which I would liken to an *apothegm*, or compact and concise maxim delivered from an Elder, was precisely meted out by the Adept in an instant. This form of astonishing penetration into the moment and into the heart of the question,

---

[726] This sign is ubiquitous amongst the Rites, and is a sign of utmost honor and respect. The gesture is indeed, prayerful.

with brevity and wisdom, is characteristic of many wisdom teachers and is an appendage of all who *practice* the work of Spirit Building. This is one of our keys to success, for though we come together freely and have very little by way of authority in our Congregational Illuminist circles, we are a conglomerate of hard workers–our focus is primarily on the work itself, and so the inquirer finds a large number of *true practitioners* amongst our numbers, rather than a horde of degree mongers who use Orders, Rites, and Titles to prop their egos and bolster their occult status. We are the company with no boss.

For my own part, T Allen has taken on the role of a *Gerondas,* or a kind of spiritual father, or Elder. This role is one that cuts through the spiritual materialism of our times and goes directly into the nature of the work, the psychology of the human mind, and the spirit of inquiry. It is a self perpetuating role as well; for once the teaching is given then the student turns and teaches others freely. Our third Congregational Illuminist precept is cogent to this methodology. It states simply; **A free society linked in free communion should be actualized.** This is precisely the nature of the relationships that are forged in our Rites. Being and laboring *In Free Communion* with others suggests a type of advanced ecumenism that truly moves beyond all boundaries.

† † †

Now with the circuit of four quarter points below the left eye socket being stimulated comes a new clarity in scrying. In fact, when all four of these points (16^{727} in all when considered quarter points) around the eyes are awakened, attuned and empowered, the Initiate will find an increase in clarity during seership. The title of Epopt will become more operative as these points complete their internal action of seeing within the Nous. There are no specific entities or energies allied to this point, yet again—the individual Initiate will feel a sort of inner calling, messages from the Deep that the super sensual realms are teeming with life.

Though there are no specific energies or beings allied to this Degree, there is a message for the Initiate. It concerns the number of the Degree, the Password, and the Sacred Word, coupled with a bit of Gematria. For Thelemites, the number 93 is singular in numerical significance. *Thelema* itself, a word which in Greek means, "will" adds up to the number 93 when each letter is taken as a number. *Agape*, also a Greek word and meaning, "Love" adds up to 93 as well. It is for the individual to interpret further the importance of these words,

---

[727] We cannot help but note again the significance of this number. There is a secret working of these Grades that utilizes the 16 quarter hot-points with regards to the 16 kalas of the Varma Marg. The visual result has an uncanny resemblance to many of the images of the weeping Virgin, where Mary is producing blood rather than tears from her eyes. Additionally, our 97 Degrees, by Kabalistic metathesis return to 16—9+7=16.

this number and the 93 current altogether, but suffice it to say that many who receive this particular point feel drawn into the current as if by some external force.[728]

A phrase can be concocted from the secrets of this Degree commingled with the Degree number. This phrase can then be used in a mantra, or as an aphorism specific to the time spent working with this Degree. The Password is TRUE LIGHT, which in Latin reads, *eras lux vera*. The Sacred Word is WISDOM, which in Greek is *Sophia* and which adds up (using English Qaballah) to 408. The Hebrew phrase for one of the negative veils of existence beyond the Tree of Life, *Ain Soph* (limitless, or infinite) also adds up to 408 (Hebrew spelling and numbers). From the Degree number and its two primary correspondences of Thelema and Agape, and the Password and Sacred Word– along with gematric extensions of Sophia- -we could arrive at some potent statements such as;

- *True Light equals Love, Will, Infinite Wisdom*
- *Will, Love, Infinity, Wisdom-the True Light*
- *Limitless Love, Will, Wisdom of the True Light*
- *Infinite Wisdom; Love and Will are the True Light*

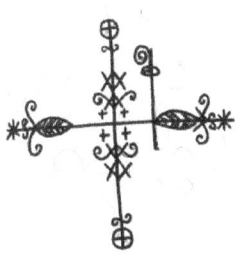

---

[728] It is of importance to note that this is a drawing towards the *current* of 93, rather than towards an Order or organization, though the latter may occur as well. On the spiritual plane, the 93 current is distinct and has very little need of Orders and organizations to accomplish its mission. Many have "ridden" this current for practical purposes and then simply let it go. Others ride it unto the Aeons.

94th Degree

Prince of Memphis or Grand Administrator

Elucidation of the Points-chauds

94th degree,
Prince of Memphis, or Grand Administrator.

Battery of Knocks

Seven, twice. **XXXXXXX XXXXXXX**

Points-chaud

Ridge above right eye, 1-4

Sacred Word

*There is no SW for this Degree

Grip

Clasp right hands; then pass the left hand round each other's waist, bringing breast to breast. (It implies *we venerate the true light which is revealed to us and sacredly treasured in our hearts*.)

Sign

Place right hand on the heart and withdraw it; then make the sign of an Apprentice. (It implies, *I promise to aid those who are in want, to be affable and to love my neighbor as myself*.)

Additional Materials

Password–ZERIGOOTHE (I have seen the true light), response, DUMAZIG (Free and Venerated Man.)

Jewel–Within a double circle, a four rayed Star with a central point.

† † †

Synopsis

This Degree and the points-chaud accompanying it have two main themes. The first, concerns the Password and its response. The Password, ZERIGOOTHE (I have seen the true Light), refers back to the previous grade and is suggestive of our Sacred Doctrine, *the Manifestation of Light*. We have observed how in the reception of the points empowerments the body becomes a scintillating, vibrating, conduit of spiritual energies and that these points become stimulators of latent forces and entities within the human organism. This *true light* is then understood to mean the Light that we possess within. When combined with the response, DUMAZIG (Free and Venerated Man), we find the deeper significance of the fourth and final precept of Congregational Illuminism, **We facilitate, we do not lead. We do the Work, we do not extract oaths or dues, or require dogmatic beliefs.** In other words, our Initiates are FREE to unearth the meanings, significances, and import of our mysteries as they see fit. No dogmatic doctrines are propounded, no oaths extracted, no dues or fees incurred. Our approach is consistent with the hero of Masonry itself, Hiram

Abiff—the Builder. We celebrate a workman because we are workers ourselves! The free exploration of the true light that our Rites offer is *facilitated* by those "venerated" or already empowered to give the Degrees/points. These are they who have direct spiritual transmission from individuals whose powerzones upon the body have been awakened, and whose geographical source is the Holy Arabia Mountain.

The points-chaud of this Degree comes with further clarity concerning the deeper understandings of our empowerments. The vision that often accompanies this opening is the interrelationship between the marmas of the body, the geographical marmas and powerzones upon the earth, and finally...the celestial powerzones intimated by the reoccurrence of Sothis/Sirius and the study of esoteric Astrology that our work endeavors upon. Each point becomes a tunnel inward, its spiritual bio-circuitry relating directly to specific powerzones on earth (eventually back to Arabia Mountain where certain ley lines converge beneath the ancient monadnock), within the body and in the constellations of the night sky. Levenda, speaking of Bertiaux's work with the points chauds puts it perfectly, stating, "These power points are located on the human body as well as at specific areas of the earth and in the cosmos, in perfect microcosm/macrocosm symmetry. It follows that if these points can be located simultaneously in the body as well as in the heavens (for instance) then physical manipulation or stimulation of those points is equivalent to opening the celestial gates.[729]" He goes on to reveal that the "*points chauds* are elements of an occult Matrix, places where one strand of the spider's web crosses another. Taken together, they form a membrane over the cranium of the magical operator like the touch screen on a computer monitor.[730]" The points-chauds of Congregational Illuminism, it is to be remembered, are unique to the work of T Allen Greenfield and others in conjunction with Bertiaux—they are not to be understood as *identical* to those used by other groups or even to those mentioned in the *Voudon Gnostic Workbook*, though they certainly continue the spiritual design of the latter. It is more accurate to say that these are speaking of the same *notion* of powerzones within the body.

There is an additional instruction concerning working with the points-chauds in this Degree as well. It is the role of the points in dreamwork. When the points are *re-awakened* before retiring to bed, they induce dream initiations and transmissions where the primordial currents and the Old Ones—those who anciently empowered our Egyptian ancestors and their magickal Rites, as well as the inner workings of the Coptic Orthodox Church, and finally the mystical Fraternity of Freemasonry—offer their nocturnal services, devotions, and enlightenment. This is the return of Freemasonry to its original state of deep initiatory power through the Primitive Doctrine, which is the divine economy of the gnostic pressures; the points-chauds. These point empowerments/Degrees, extracted from the veils often superimposed upon the essence of initiation by the dramatic ritual, emblazon the individual with pure Initiatory force and open the gates into Otherwhere.

---

[729] *The Dark Lord*, Ibis Books, 2013, p. 164.
[730] Ibid, p. 166.

The Grip/seal of this Degree exposes the heart of the Facilitator to the heart of the recipient , linking the two in the fraternal bonds of love and support. The string of four quarter points are sealed within the Initiate above the right eye-socket and the gift of seership begins to deepen and create within the Initiate a sensitive and receptive faculty for vision. The Initiate may feel compelled to create something in response to this points-chaud, as this is a way to align with the inherently creative forces of the Universe.

Spirit Builders

95th Degree
Grand Conservator

La Prise des Yeaux

95th *degree,*
Grand Conservator.

Battery of Knocks

Seven, three times.   XXXXXXX   XXXXXXX   XXXXXXX

Points-chaud

Ridge below right eye, 1-4. This is the final set of quarter points in relation to the eyes and to seership.

Sacred Word

JAIR HAVOTH (Dazzling Light).

Grip

Place the two first fingers of the right hand on each other's lips. It implies; *Preserve a prudent silence, and be not even suspected as the holder of a secret confided to thy faith.*

Sign

Carry the right hand to the forehead; then look at the celestial vault and place left hand on the heart. It implies; *God inspires me to excite in all hearts, the sacred fire of truth.*

Additional Materials

Password–ABRA (Patriarch without stain) response, AAR (Truth useful to man.)

Jewel–Within a double circle, a four pointed Star, enclosing a triangle with a central jewel.

† † †

Synopsis

The Grand Conservator is the final *normal* Degree in our system. It has a points-chaud empowerment, Battery of Knocks, Password and response, Sacred Word, Sign, Grip, and Additional Materials as the majority of our Degrees do. But as in the previous several Degrees, this Grade does not have a specific entity or energy allied to it, though it stirs a particular sentiment within the Initiate that is cogent to the duties of a Conservator of the Rite. The sentiment is hinted at in the work itself where Yarker describes the Sign as implying, "God inspires me to excite in all hearts, the sacred fire of truth.[731]" This sentiment shares nothing with the evangelical bane of our times, *Fundamentalism*, but is instead a natural zeal to give Light to all who request it.

The Responsorial to the Password *ABRA*—which literally refers to a ferry but which is also the first portion of the word Abrahadabra– is AAR, which means "Truth useful to man." AAR has a connection with AUR, or Light, here. It is in this sense that we have something

---

[731] *Compleat Rite of Memphis*, p. 143.

to share with others. We have seen our Sacred Word JAIR HAVOTH (or more correctly, Havoth-Jair, which literally refers to villages along the banks of the Jordan River), defined in the work as the "Dazzling light" the *sacred fire of truth* that we cannot help but *excite in all hearts*: for it has been given to us freely, has repeatable results revealed through the anecdotal records of the Magickal Diary, and through independent researches, and it has altered our lives in significant ways. *Spirit Building* within the open-armed movement of Congregational Illuminism, and through the points-chauds working of the Rites of Memphis+Misraïm, causes changes in these multi-dimensional spheres–beyond the individual epidermis.

- *The Ontic Sphere*—within the Initiate's own Magickal Imagination, Spirit Building enlightens and expands the faculties of the Nous. Seership is acquired *via the prize of the eyes* and the willed travelling of alternate spaces and levels of consciousness are explored.
- *The Physiological Sphere*—through the points-chauds, the Initiate's body becomes scintillating with vibratory energy. The points have precise actions of attunement, empowerment, initiation, and therapy. The body becomes a vehicle for spirit travels, each point opening up tunnels to Otherwhere and most points having specific entities attached to them.
- *The Biosphere*—the geography of the earth is positively affected by our Spirit Building as we honor and consecrate holy places, power zones and sacred marmas to the work, thereby protecting them from destruction. In fact a specific desire and drive to preserve such holy lands is a direct result of labors such as the Great Arabia Mountain Working. We also create the Mystic Temple in these zones which can be seen and enjoyed by sensitives not related to our work, but which will inspire them in other creative ways.
- *The Noosphere*—this is the collective mind sphere, the zone of human thought that is energized and stimulated by our Spirit Building. As we work upon our individual *nous*, moving it downward from the head into the heart and then back up again in ascension, aligned with the AZOTH, we achieve a form of morphic resonance with others and their mind spaces[732]. This leads to morpho-genesis and new creative outpourings in groups. Such is the nature of Congregational Illuminist bodies who work closely together with these points empowerments/Degrees.
- *The Psychic-Atmosphere*—the etheric and protective sphere that surrounds our globe and which we enrich and strengthen through Spirit Building, in concert with the *Sovereign Sanctuary* "above." This sphere receives periodic onslaughts of attack from darker forces seeking entrance into our sphere. The work of Spirit Builders, analogous to the labors of the Elus Coëns during their Equinox Workings, seeks to purify and protect the earth's subtle aura.

---

[732] This is the magical consciousness corresponding with the discovery of Noetical Being, as discussed in the Monastery of the Seven Rays, Year IV, Part I, Lesson 2.

Part Three – Chapter Six: Administrative Degrees

The Grand Conservators of our Rites– having experienced the *Manifestation of the Light* (Sacred Doctrine) through the points empowerments and subsequent scrying sessions, and who puts into practice our divine economy (the Primitive Doctrine), educating and creating their own Scintillating Bodies and sacralizing geographical marmas, birthing the Mystic Temple and working *In Free Communion* with others—will often feel the inner drive and sentiment to share all of this with others. In stark contrast with the evangelical spirit, which occult Orders are not immune from, Free Illuminists may feel this compulsion to share with others, yet it is fueled by genuine love and devotion to humankind and a purified zeal to bring healing, attunement, empowerment, and initiation to all those desirous of the same. As demonstrated here, though many of our Degrees/points elicit congress with beings, spirits or angelic forces, these are seen more as symptomatic of the greater work that we endeavor upon on multiple planes. The relationships we form with entities inside these inner worlds yield much information about ourselves and our cosmos, yet our aspirations are higher than simply data collecting. We are Spirit Builders. As is said time and again in Masonic Degrees, *of what are you in search*? More Light! And as this Light is freely given and shown to us, so we likewise freely give of it to others, and from there it spreads its tentacles of peace and blessings towards every darkened corner.[733]

---

[733] It is to be recalled that the 87-90, 95° form a gateway into the cosmic Masonry of ÆONOLOGY and Osirification. See the Preface and the following insert or "Secret and Occult Explanation of the 95th Degree" from *Degrees of Wisdom*. In this piece, there are evident parallels with the work of another well-known Memphis-Misraïm initiate and member of the British Sovereign Sanctuary, Aleister Crowley, who was conferred the 90° and 95° by John Yarker himself.

SECRET AND OCCULT EXPLANATION OF THE 95th DEGREE[734]

The following "Explanation" is given in some obediences just after the investiture of the grade. It corresponds closely with the 3rd echelon working of the grade mentioned in the Preface to Volume Two.

1. This is the secret of the Holy Graal, this is the sacred vessel of Our Lady, our Mother Isis; it is given ritually to the Grand Conservator, the Master of the Egregore of Memphis & Misraïm.

2. You shall pour out your blood, which is your life, into the golden cup of her Universal Love, for the defense of the Children of the Widow, if necessary.

3. You shall mingle your life with the universal life, and you shall not refuse even one drop.

4. Then shall your mind comprehend, and your heart shall burst with happiness, accepting a struggle for the highest ideals of Humanity, and in order to assure its vigilant defense.

5. This can only be done by the Rites of Khem and of Kudoth within and without the Pyramid; after your reception to the 66th, 94th, and 95th degrees.

6. The Patriarch Grand Conservator that you have become is the true Defender of the Order and Prince of Memphis, all the more of the Grand Hierophant, the Substitute, and the Grand Guardian who are invested therewith.

7. Now, in order for you to-be able to accomplish this ritual of the Holy Graal, divest yourself of all your useless goods, and give alms.

8. You are rich, but of a spiritual wealth which is equal to all the treasures of the world; never forget this, eternal Apprentice!

9. Furthermore, he is held as a bloodhound on a leash.

10. He has strength and great finesse. Yea, and also Victory.

11. Let the 94th degree act thus in his evocation.

12. Let him be seated and let him evoke; let him concentrate himself in this force, then let him wash, saturated and stretched; let him throw back the hood which covers his head, and let him fix his malevolent eye on the adverse forces. Then, let his force swing to and fro like a powerful Athlete of God, until the Word shoots powerfully from his throat.

13. Then let him not fall exhausted, even if he has been human ten thousand times; but what invades him is the infinite mercy of the Genitor-Genitrix of the Universe, of which he is the champion.

---

[734] Reprinted with permission from *Degrees of Wisdom: A Compendium of Rituals from the Rites of Memphis and Misraïm*, Triad Press, 2025.

14. Be not deceived. It is easy to distinguish the living force from dead matter. It is not as easy to distinguish the living serpent from the dead serpent.

15. Concerning vows. Be obstinate and be not obstinate. Understand that Good and Evil are to be judged with Severity and Mercy; judge soundly, otherwise it will be but the sound of the wind on Mount Meru.

16. How shall you worship me, I who am the Sublime Architect of the Worlds, on all the planes of Spirit, the Lord of the Creation? I am the Eye in the Triangle, the Golden Star which shines at the center of your Soul.

17. I am the Ogdoad, which is the Octuple Word destined to be equilibrated with the Three.

18. There is no act or passion which is not a hymn in my honor.

19. All things are sacred and all things are symbolic.

Spirit Builders

96th Degree
Grand and Puissant Sovereign of the Order
The Inner Retreat

96th *degree,*
Grand and Puissant Sovereign of the Order.

"The world of spirits is made One in the Presence of Absolute Truth, which is the way in which The Universal Law of Mind-Power comes to reveal itself to all spirits as Being. Everything is Mind and the manifestations of mental laws which are spiritual acts of the Absolute. Nothing exists apart from these laws, and out of these laws is built up the world as we come to know and to experience it directly, in thought and life. Spirit is all...[735]

There are no Knocks, Words, Signs, or Grips for this Grade[736]

Points-chaud—*It is suggested that these twin points be given out of doors and in a Holy place, a geographical marma with the Telluric currents beneath and the Solar and Stellar above. The Facilitator will want to bring a pad of paper and pens for the Initiate, as one of the corresponding experiences with this Degree is the reception of one's personal sigil upon activation of the points.*

Left and Right temples

Additional Material

Jewel of the 96th Degree—On one side, the cubit rule and ostrich feather, Egyptian symbols of Truth and Justice. On the backside, within a triple circle, a four pointed Star, enclosing a triangle with a central jewel.

† † †

Synopsis

In the sparse work of this Degree we find Yarker informing us that "originally these were Six *Sublime Magi*, 96th Degree, presided over by a *Grand Hierophant*, 97th Degree, and the Assembly was entitled *Grand Areopagus of the Celestial Empire of the Sublime Magi 96—Grand and Puissant Sovereigns of the Order.*[737]" Quite a lofty series of titles and appointments for such a simple grade! There is, within Congregational Illuminism, a *Grand Areopagus*[738], formed of those individuals who are committed to the work and who labor incessantly to support and encourage others interested in our working. However, the *Celestial Empire* and the literal *Grand Hierophant* are mysteries beyond human titles and territories. For, in these last two grades of our system, we are approaching the inner Sanctum of the Sovereign Sanctuary, the very heart of the Heavenly Jerusalem. In this deep mystery it is even considered idolatry

---

[735] Michael Bertiaux, *Cosmic Meditation*, p. 29.
[736] Within the Monastery of the Seven Rays, the next two grades relate to what is referred to as Universe B, the realm of non-being, where the "Dark Doctrine" of Deity is explored.
[737] *Compleat Rite of Memphis*, p. 144.
[738] http://fissaprmmus.blogspot.com/p/who-we-are-and-who-we-are-not.html

to refer to the Grand Hierophant as a *person*, for He/It is beyond such language. Additionally, the Sovereign Sanctuary cannot be considered a place or region, as such epitaphs suggest something that can be circumscribed or limited. We are entering pure Mystery.

In these Degrees, we have utilized ontic knowledge, the collected learning and experiences we have received by way of our Ontic Sphere or Magickal Imagination. We have also experienced *katophatic* knowledge—where we have had converse with spirits, angels and corporeal similitudes from the Divine. Kataphatic knowledge is affirming and uses analogy and visuals, imagery and words, to describe the spiritual realm. But we are now entering upon a journey of *apophatic* knowledge, where language and images no longer suffice. In this type of epistemology, we have to resort to negative language—suggesting what the Absolute or the Divine is *not* rather than what He/It is. We even move beyond our own Egregore with these two final Degrees. The great French mystic and invigorator of the Orders, Robert Ambelain says of Egregore that,

One gives the name egregore to a force generated by a powerful spiritual current and then nourished at regular intervals, according to a rhythm in harmony with the universal life of the cosmos, or to a union of entities united by a common characteristic nature.[739]

The Egregore with which we pass on in our spiritual transmission is therefore fed and nourished by humans. Its existence is dependent upon our working. It is, in sum, our own creation. The *Sovereign Sanctuary*, however, is not of our own making.

The simple technologies that we have made use of in our Spirit Building—our asana, spiritual transmission through points empowerments, our Sacred Words and accompanying visions, are various means for entering the super celestial spheres. These have been delivered of specific doctrinal traits and have taken on a pure methodology likened to the early Hermeticists, wherein our Initiates penetrate levels of consciousness within the human form. Our direction has been emphasized as *inward*, rather than *upward*–to distinguish our working from the dualistic thinking of spirit as being completely separate from matter—yet we find language to be limiting, suspect and deceptive altogether in these final two grades. The *Sovereign Sanctuary* that we are entering and that is entering us is likened to a *superessential darkness*, to use the words of Meister Eckhart, for all words, images and psychic archetypes are laid waste by the penetrating ecstasy of this profound union. Though darker than darkness itself, THE *Sovereign Sanctuary*, referred to as Universe B in Bertiaux's treatises, isn't evil, it is simply beyond all terms, qualities, laws, rules, and expectations concerned with the known world, or Universe A.

The inner sanctum of the Sovereign Sanctuary is inhabited by No-thing, AIN, in Kabalistic terms. AIN is beyond Light, though sometimes Light is used metaphorically to suggest its essence. This No-thing is not a person, nor a place, nor is it of the substance of an angel or archetypal energy. We must resort to negative theology to describe this

---

[739] *La Kabbale pratique*, Paris, 1951, p. 175.

luminous darkness, this Cloud of Unknowing. This same No-thing, is the venerable Source of ALL, for the Very Deity, the True God of Gnosticism, is beyond the Demiurge who must create out of some prima material; the Source of All, the No-thing creates *ex nihilo*, or "out of nothing."[740] This creation out of nothing is experienced on a lower arc with the dual points chauds empowerments of this Degree. The characteristic experience that follows this point is the reception of a unique symbol, peculiar to the Initiate, which becomes her personal emblem upon the Inner Planes. This symbol is born, "out of nothing" upon activation of the points upon the temples.

This level of working answers to the final portion of our Hermetic axiom, "To Know, To Will, To Dare and *to Keep Silent*." Nothing but Silence can be used to express this mystical experience. These final two Degrees concern the apotheosis of the human, achieved through watchfulness and inner prayer alone. This is the complete divinization of the whole person—body, mind, soul(psyche) and spirit. Watchfulness and inner silence are the only sacred practices apportioned to these two Degrees, as all other technologies are not efficient for this end of the journey. Watchfulness becomes a sword of wisdom that cuts away all that is superfluous to the task of entering the Sovereign Sanctuary.

These two grades complete the Scintillating body of points so that the physical organism may be divinized and the whole person may enter this cave of the heart, the Sovereign Sanctuary, through watchfulness and meditation.

This creative opening of the inner Sanctum often requires the aid of a Spiritual Director. In Congregational Illuminism, this is one of the functions of true Facilitators (see Appendix, *Would I make a good Facilitator?*) who become Elders through experience—what the Greeks call, *Gerondas* and the Russians deem, *Staretz*. The true significance of the Masonic term, "Past Master" is revealed by this role of the Facilitator, as through their own labors and journeys they are now able to share the penetrating words of wisdom (apothems) that project us further along the path. These words sometimes function like the Zen Koan and open the proper doors and attune the instrument of the whole person to the proper frequency, to taste of the impenetrable darkness that we are speaking of. The relationship here between Facilitator and Initiate is not only spiritual, but therapeutic, as the "blocks" within the Initiate are often easily removed by the Past Master's counsel. Here, our Craft becomes a therapeutic science, akin to that of the ancient Essene Thaumaturgists, the Rose+Croix d'Or, and others. In fact, this grade is often accompanied by healing energies that can be broadcast outward by way of the points-chauds, which become a type of spirit map and psychic technology. These points can then be transferred to anything that will conduct the heat that they are producing. Bertiaux says, "in esoteric thinking, healing is invisible, an action of contact between spirit and mortal...voyance can see it...Artists paint it everywhere...they can feel its heat. In short, it is an empowerment, and it can be hot- hot very, very hot."[741]

---

[740] The Noumena.
[741] *Vudu Cartography*, p. 136.

Additionally, the points empowerments themselves will begin to attain a sort of nurturing quality to the Initiate. An obscure visual for this sensation is the Roman sculpture of Romulus and Remus being fed by the wolf[742]. Hector F. Jean-Maine says,

> *Now, in Rome, supposedly, there is a stature of the babies, Romulus and Remus, being fed by a mother wolf, and when Hector said he saw that photo of the statue in a book, He realized that this 'feeding' is how the empowerment works and that some initiations are really giving nurture in an almost physical sense to the candidate*[743].

Of the many zoomorphic experiences of the Initiate of our Orders, the lycanthropy involving were-animals, hybrid wolves and dog-headed/Sirius related entities is the most common. These transformations occur in a number of magickal scenarios—some invited, others infused. Often, we take upon ourselves the *mask* of one of these dog-faced beings and traverse landscapes befitting divinities of Amenta. Those of the Golden Dawn persuasion will recognize this as *the Assumption of* Godforms. Jean-Maine sees these empowerments as analogous to this generous wolf-mother, saying that this "feeding is how the empowerment works and that some initiations are really giving nurture in an almost physical sense to the candidate."[744]

On other inward journeys, the morphing into a wolf form is for the express purpose of wandering the tombs and graveyards, the crematoriums and pits of darkness, in search of the Barons and of Bacaloubaka—with the intent of tracing these territories to their Source and receiving a sacred empowerment. It is the latter that our beloved Hector F. Jean-Maine refers to in the quote above. However, the experience is a profoundly moving one, and a little surprising in relation to similar workings that include these transformations.

The myth of Romulus and Remus, the foundation story of the great city of Rome, is a classic tale of destiny[745]. Aspects of the story remind one of the tale of Moses; the boys were meant to be killed by the power hungry Amulius just as the baby Moses would've been killed by the Egyptian Pharaoh,[746] Romulus and Remus were left in the river Tiber which turned out to be their salvation, just as Moses floated along the Nile River and was rescued by the Pharaoh's sister, Queen Bithia[747], and rather than suffering a tragic fate, Romulus and Remus founded the new city of Rome just as Moses composes the Torah and leads his people, becoming the most important and influential prophet of the Hebrews. But the story of Romulus and Remus maintains its indelible presence in history through the statue of the twins being fed by a mother wolf. The original statue is composite, the wolf being completed long before[748] the twins were added to highlight this compelling myth. The bestial sculpture

---

[742] See the Color Plate section.
[743] *Vudu Cartography*, p. 139.
[744] *Vudu Cartography*, p. 139.
[745] See Dionysius of Halicarnasus's, *Roman Antiquities*, 1:85.
[746] Exodus 1:10
[747] There are also some interesting correlations between the story of Moses and that of Sargon the Sumerian King.
[748] Some have suggested that the wolf is Etruscan (5th Century), but recent scholarship places the wolf and children within a couple of centuries of each other.

is jarring upon first glance, and even more curious when placed in front of the great Sienna Cathedral in Italy, yet H.F. Jean-Maine suggests a very different feeling derived from the visage—that of nourishment and nurturing.

Hector relates a dream empowerment that occurs for Damballah (Ti-Jacques) and Chango (Ti-Jean) while they were still young men, in which the oft dreaded Bacaloubaka comes to initiate the two who are brought into his realm through trance. This empowerment is the very energy that transforms the two into the Lwa that they later become. Jean-Maine, upon seeing a picture of the statue of Romulus and Remus, made a direct connection with this empowerment and proclaimed that this feeding from the she-wolf is how certain initiations work. Rather than being crisis oriented, or ordeal-centered, these empowerments are nourishing and nurturing. Further, he goes on to relate that the Black Templars of the cult of Bacaloubaka, became great healers in Haiti and secret masters behind "many cures of a miraculous nature[749]."

As we progress in our work of Spirit Building, we must persevere through the difficult trials and tribulations incumbent of all authentic initiations, and realize that after the burning away of the dross comes the healing salve of other empowerments. There are analogies that can be made with the secrets of the XI° of the **OTOA**, which is entitled, *Templier Noir* and involves certain alchemical empowerments, based upon Luciferian[750] Certain degrees of understanding act as markers and *signposts in a strange land*[751] but throughout our journey we are attended to by a heavenly host, would we but start the conversation and ask for the proper empowerment.

There is no scrying procedure, no specific asana—nay, not even a Rite of Communion in these two grades that will act as a vehicle into the Sovereign Sanctuary. It is only through silence and watchfulness that the Initiate will enter therein. The silent invocation of the Initiate's innermost being to the Center of ALL, the Ground of ALL Being, is the work of these two grades. In this inner and outer stillness, the Initiate begins to discern the distinction in quality of pure mysticism from magick, for the latter partakes of the *energies* of the Absolute, while the former approaches his very **Essence**. It is in these two Degrees that we come to realize that the Sovereign Sanctuary is identical with the "one main temple" which is the INNER RETREAT of the Monastery of the Seven Rays; while the "little temple of research for yourself" is the Mystic Temple that we birth through our occult labors.[752]

---

[749] *Vudu Cartography*, pgs 138-139.
[750] Rather than falling for St. Jerome's mistranslation of the fallen angel from Isaiah from the Latin Vulgate, let us recall that this term simply means "Light-bearing."
[751] See the non-fiction collection of the same name by Walker Percy for an inspiring set of essays exploring ethics, philosophy, death and religion in the South.
[752] Private papers of the *Monastery of the Seven Rays*, 3rd Year, Part I, Lesson 2.

Spirit Builders

97th Degree

Grand Hierophant

The Via Negativa

97th *degree,*
Deputy International Grand Master.

Part Three – Chapter Six: Administrative Degrees

99th *degree,*
Grand Hierophant.

(In the system for which Brother Rybalka created these boards, the Grand Hierophant is placed at the 99th Degree. We have therefore included both the 97º and 99º boards.)

This mist, this cloud, this darkness into which we go, transcending knowledge, is the path below which your face cannot be found except veiled; but it is that very darkness which reveals your face is there, beyond all veils.

Nicholas of Cusa

There are no Knocks, Words, Signs, Grips, or Jewels for this Degree[753]

Points-chaud

1st point–Ajna Chakra, centermost forehead, **2nd point**—the apex, or top of the head—Apprentice, 1st Degree point being only slightly forward of this point.

† † †

Synopsis

The Mysteries of this Degree are revealed through meditation alone. This meditation is not for the expert only, it is for ALL. Bertiaux says,

> *while the mind is in deep meditation, it is possible to realize many, many, of the truths of the universe, and thus by thinking deeply in any sense, one is also able to meditate deeply. The art and act of meditation, which is one reality and one total experience; these twined aspects of the same reality are common to all humans.*[754]

The reception of the final Degree and points-chaud empowerment is accompanied by a profound understanding of our entire system of working. When the Degrees are worked over time and the Initiate has ignited each of the points within the body, whether worked in order or not, then the Initiate will want to revisit the 97th Degree as it has a culminating quality. It is as if our Rite is a colossal vessel filled with the most pure water. The reception of this final dual point empowerment tips the vessel over, pouring Light into all 97 cups

---

[753] Our work has been "prepared for" by means of Theurgy and magical operations, but as is said in Year IV, Part I, Lesson 12 of the *Monastery of the Seven Rays*, "these methods only served to place one 'in the door'" of pure spiritual initiation.
[754] *Cosmic Meditation*, p. 4.

(points in the body) and enlightening the entire organism. The self organizing principle of our Rite reveals itself in this Grade and a deeper understanding of its purposes and import for the world at large is realized. The beauty, harmony, and simplicity of the points-chauds approach to initiation forms a holistic and spiritual Masonry that invigorates all channels of our daily life.

Our Rite returns Masonry to its original simplicity of form and its original occult significance. The Signs, Words, and Grips of the Degrees are no longer viewed as the "clap trap" of the system, or even damned with faint praise as a *means of recognition* in darkness as well as in light. They become the working tools of the Operative Mason in Spirit Building with the mystical points-chauds.

† † †

We have experienced the Manifestation of the light, we have built the Scintillating Body and the Mystic Temple and we have established the Primitive Doctrine through a radical efficiency and simplicity of form. Suddenly, with the reception of the 97th Degree, the Initiate sees the truly harmonious proportions and unity of our purpose. As the Initiate approaches the divine darkness of the 96th and 97th Degrees, the Wisdom, Strength, and Beauty of Egyptian Masonry unfolds.

This Degree completes the 61st Degree, in that the Unknown Philosopher is now reborn as the Unknown Servant. The silent invocation of Chenu becomes a resounding cry to all of the Masters of the Past to be present in our work and to further the Light unto Eternity.

The place where we see the most divergence from traditional Degree systems and our Congregational Illuminist model is in the understanding of Degree numbers and our non-linear approach to the Western Esoteric Tradition. One does not flaunt that he or she is such and such Degree in our Free Communion, for such would only suggest that we are working with that particular mystery and hot point. In our system, degrees are not a claim of attainment or an honor bestowed upon for years of service. It has been reiterated from the beginning that Lodges, Nodes and Chapels may work freely with these Degrees and points empowerments in whatever order that they see fit. Some will utilize the consultation method, others will discover the next Degree through scrying the previous grade, and still others may work packs of three Degrees in a chronological or semi-chronological method. This innovative approach distinguishes Congregational Illuminism from the thousands of expressions of Degree systems available. At all turns, we acknowledge that attainment can occur in the 1st Degree as much as in the 97th. Titles such as Grand Puissant or Sovereign, take on an inner significance in our work that is peculiar to the grade and to the Initiate. Typically, it is suggestive of the experience that can be expected in scrying the Degree further. Whatever the case may be, these titles and degree numbers are not in any way a certificate of attainment to be paraded.

The 97th Degree reveals this mystery further through its points-chauds empowerments in two locations upon the head. The first is at the Ajna chakra and all experiences of this chakra are allied to the non-dual experience of union with the Divine that the 96th and 97th Degrees are dedicated to. The second point however, is almost identical to the 1st Degree point of the Apprentice. Mystery of Mysteries! This stroke of brilliance, symmetry, and humility is a physical representation of the Kabalistic doctrine that *Kether is in Malkuth and Malkuth is in Kether, after another manner.* This is the true significance of the sacred serpent, the Ouroboros, for the end and the beginning are a single point-event, beyond linear time and space.

Such a circular understanding of a Degree system as this obliterates the ugliest demon of all—the bane of all religious, initiatory and fraternal systems in existence—the hideous destroyer of the spirit, megalomania. The self-conceited and the arrogant will have nothing to gain from our working and will therefore seek inflation of their lower egos elsewhere. Our focus is in no wise the display of titles, degrees or attainments. Our focus is on individual development, mastery, and attainment and collective mutual aid and support. For us, the end and the beginning are one.

The spiritual journey of the 97th Degree is one of profound silence; it is the *Via Negativa*. It is a religious silence that recognizes the ultimate of ultimates, the ABSOLUTE, as unknowable in the traditional sense. The type of knowledge that we engage in through this Degree is properly styled, *agnosia,* or unknowing. To distill even one dram of this mysterious dark nectar is to experience freedom from the known. In the profound collection entitled, *The Art of Prayer, An Orthodox Anthology*, we find instruction concerning *prelest* and warnings against appearances, presentiments, and fantasies. These warnings make little sense in our initial studies of gnosis, but are packed with wisdom when considered in our apophatic searching for the super-unknown! The experience that accompanies this *agnosia* is profound awe and humility. There is no labor in this endeavor, save watchfulness and sobriety of mind.[755]

The unknowing of this Degree is a type of *divine darkness*, as Pseudo-Dionysius calls it, and reveals hidden things in silence, which,

> *in its deepest darkness shines above the most super-brilliant, and in the altogether impalpable and invisible, fills to overflowing the eyeless minds with glories of surpassing beauty.*[756]

---

[755] See the essay, *Nepsis*, by +Palamas, in Qliphoth Journal Opus IV, Transmutation Publishing. Nepsis is this very sobriety of mind and heart, which can, in fact, be accomplished through the points-chauds empowerments themselves.
[756] *The Mystical Theology*, from *The Other Bible*, p. 721.

In this superluminous gloom, the Initiate leaves behind all images, all sights, all sounds, all oracles, all entities, and all energies to enter the shrine of hiddenness that is the Godhead. Watch and pray, are the only words of wisdom herein. As this unknowing descends from the head into the heart, a profound and limitless joy—birthed from the Uncreated Light itself—will be born within, and will be expressed in an infinite array of patterns by each unique nerve-ending of the universe, as a blissful revelation of peace and a blessing upon all of creation. This form of watchful meditation has been described by Valentin Tomberg as, *concentration without effort.*

In truth, all 97 Degrees can be apportioned to three essential stages; Katharismos, Photismos, and Henosis. We come back to our simple Three-fold Path by realizing that each Degree weaves in and out of these three stages of prayer, creating a unified whole. Unlike certain religious traditions that teach practitioners to fear the imagination, or the phantasmal realms, we enter into these fully *after* a proper purification. When we deepen the work, such as in this *Via Negativa,* we leave behind the known, the describable, and all images and intellections, for the experience of pure noetic penetration into the numinous. Each stage is compatible and preparatory for the other, but none is a water-tight compartment. Each stage enters into the next seamlessly when the Initiate quiets the mind and attains watchfulness and a deep-rooted custody of the heart.

From this esoteric and personal experience of the heart we move outward as Unknown Servants. According to scientists the heart sends more information to the brain than the brain sends to the heart. Radiating outward from the individual, the heart sends out electromagnetic waves which interact with the entire surrounding field. Indeed, no one is an island unto themselves. Non-local connections within this field are being studied by Entanglement theorists and other cutting edge scientists. [757]Random number generators across the globe are providing verifiable evidence (for the logical positivist within us all) that human feeling and emotion changes reality. When, for instance, a profound event occurs such as the attack on the Twin Towers, these so-called random number generators begin to produce astounding patterns and deviations.

We find the three main components of Spirit Building: *the Scintillating Body, the Mystic Temple,* and laboring *In Free Communion,* to reverberate these notions of the heart and service to others. The Scintillating Body, when all 97 points-chauds are vibrating and luminous, magnifies the electromagnetic waves created naturally by the heart, and can be felt by sensitives and non-sensitives alike. In other words, people become affected by our very presence when the body is enlivened in this mystical manner. The Mystic Temple not only becomes perceptible as a spiritual and holy place, but also creates an emotional field of morphic resonance from the collective of scintillating bodies that return time and time again to the sacred marma for our empowerments. This emotive force can be harnessed for specialized experiments, for the creation of magickal machines, and for inquiry into Otherwhere. But above these, it can have a healing and positive impact upon those in need

---

[757] See the profound undertakings of the Institute of Noetic Sciences @ http://noetic.org/

via the emotional field that radiates from the marma. Finally, though we recognize the truth and brilliance of scientific evolution, we as Spirit Builders also recognize the role of love within nature and along with Darwin (as opposed to Huxley and Spencer), we celebrate the dominating factor within the entire biosphere—that of ***cooperation***. It is in this exalted understanding of cooperation, rather than competition based programs, that we labor In Free Communion with others. Far from the old regime of Newtonian *parts mentality* systems, the approach of Free Illuminism embraces the reality of mutual dependence and the essential unity of all things, underlying the kaleidoscope of diversity.

Sigil received during 97th degree empowerment.

Suggested Reading for the Administrative Grades

As the Degrees from 91-97 deal with the twin concepts and practices of Service and of Mystical Union with the Divine, the *Suggested Reading* for this Series is properly one's Volume of the Sacred Law, or Holy Book(s). This may be the *Tao Te Ching* of Chinese philosophy, the *Holy Books of Thelema*, the *Holy Bible,* or any other text that is inspiring to the Initiate and which delves into these twin ideas. It could be that the combination of several books, such as *The Upanishads* and the *Bhagavad Gita*, answers to both ideas better than one sole text. Such is up to the individual. There is also the possibility that the Initiate will not be so moved by any "Holy" book as these sometimes carry the stench of dogma with them. This is also up to the individual to discern for himself. In any case, to fully integrate the secrets of these Grades it is best to lay the books aside, feed the hungry and meditate on the superessential darkness that religions sometimes call *God*.

A few pointers, however, can be found in these particular writings:

- *An Anthology of Theurgic Operations of the Rose+Croix of the Orient,* Demetrius G. Polychronis
- *The Cloud of Unknowing*
- *Cosmic Meditation*, Michael Bertiaux
- *The Philokalia*, in five volumes
- *The Sacramentary of the Rose+Croix*, Robert Ambelain
- *Theurgy,* Mouni Sadhu
- *The Writings of Abbé Julio*
- *The Writings of Jacob Boehme*
- *The Writings of Louis-Claude de St. Martin*
- *The Writings of Meister Eckhart*

While in meditation, we might consider the words in the Chapter Lecture:

Q. Where can man best find that which is necessary to his education?

A. In his own nature; he finds in his body the motive strength of his physical perfection; he finds in his soul the principle of his religious and intellectual perfection; he finds them in his faculties, morality and religion, and in his body their basis.[758]

---

[758] Yarker, *Lectures of a Chapter, Senate, & Council*, p. 17.

Afterword

REFLECTIONS AFTER TEN YEARS ON ARABIA MOUNTAIN

Having empowered perhaps a hundred or more people during the ten years of The Great Arabia Mountain Working, and having chartered many local groups worldwide, I consider this new edition of Spirit Builders incredibly timely.

The rise of congregational, but secular, free illuminism in recent years has been a phenomenon worth studying for its implications on modern society. This movement, with its focus on personal enlightenment and spiritual exploration outside of traditional religious or spiritual structures, has gained traction among individuals seeking a more individualized and flexible form of spiritual practice. The rise of secular free illuminism can be seen as a response to the rigidity and dogma of organized religion, offering a space for personal growth and intellectual inquiry that is not constrained by established belief systems. The earliest edition of Spirit Builders is quite a DIY for forming free illuminist groups, whilst the Worldwide Free Illuminist page on Facebook brings together diverse individual and groups, at midyear 2024 the membership was approaching 2000.

One of the key characteristics of congregational free illuminism is its emphasis on personal autonomy and empowerment. Unlike traditional mystical and spiritual institutions that dictate beliefs and practices, congregational free illuminism encourages individuals to explore their own spiritual paths and ideas. This emphasis on personal agency and responsibility is appealing to many in modern society who seek to break free from the constraints of traditional authoritarian bodies and find a more personal and meaningful spiritual experience.

Furthermore, congregational free illuminism provides a sense of community and support for individuals on their spiritual and life journeys. While the movement is secular in nature, it still offers individuals a space to come together, share experiences and ideas, and support one another in their quest for enlightenment. This sense of community is crucial in a world that is increasingly disconnected and isolated, providing individuals with a sense of belonging and connection that is often lacking in modern society.

Another important aspect of congregational free illuminism is its focus on intellectual inquiry and exploration. Many adherents of the movement are drawn to its emphasis on critical thinking, rationality, and evidence-based reasoning. This emphasis on intellectual rigor sets free illuminism apart from traditional occult and metaphysical configurations, which often rely on faith and authority rather than reason and evidence.

Moreover, congregational free illuminism is characterized by its openness and inclusivity. Unlike some traditional bodies that may exclude individuals based on factors such as gender, sexuality, or race, congregational free illuminism welcomes individuals from all backgrounds and identities. This inclusivity is a powerful force for social change, challenging conventional notions of spirituality and creating a more diverse and inclusive society.

The rise of congregational free illuminism also reflects broader trends in modern society, such as the decline of sectarian affiliation and the rise of individualism. As traditional institutions lose their influence and relevance, individuals are increasingly seeking alternative forms of spiritual practice and life paths that provide more flexibility and autonomy. Free illuminism fills this void by offering a space for individuals to explore their own ideas and practices in a supportive and inclusive community.

Furthermore, the rise of congregational free illuminism can be seen as a response to the growing disillusionment with top-down bodies and its role in society. As cases of corruption, abuse, and intolerance within metaphysical institutions come to light, many individuals are turning away from traditional approaches and are seeking a more authentic and ethical form of spirituality. Congregational free illuminism offers a more transparent and democratic alternative to traditional structures, allowing individuals to practice varied disciplines in a way that aligns with their values and ethics.

In conclusion, the rise of congregational free illuminism in recent years represents a significant shift in the landscape of spirituality and metaphysics. This movement, with its emphasis on personal autonomy, community, intellectual inquiry, inclusivity, and structural change, offers individuals a new way to find meaning and purpose in their lives. As congregational free illuminism continues to grow and evolve, it will be interesting to see how it shapes the future of spiritual practice and its impact on society as a whole.

T Allen Greenfield

June 25, 2024

Appendices

Appendices

History Lection

Ancient & Primitive Rite of Memphis+Misraïm

THE COMBINED RITES OF MEMPHIS AND MISRAÏM ARE AN expression of occult Freemasonry from the late 18th century which continues into the present. Though not considered "regular" by the United Grand Lodge of England, the Rites of Memphis-Misraïm are practiced around the world today with many Grand Orients viewing the work as authentic Masonry and not clandestine in the least. There are many worthwhile histories of the Rite in existence, mostly in French, but with a book of this magnitude and subject matter, it seemed cogent to present a history with the utmost brevity.

The Rite of Misraïm has its origins in Italy as early as 1738, but tradition teaches that its source is specifically in Venice in 1788 and is often traced back to the divine Cagliostro and his Egyptian Rite. The Rite was extended and fully developed by the famous Bédarride brothers of France, but its highly guarded *Arcana Arcanorum* has its source in Naples according to the Statues of 1816.

The Rite of Memphis was born in France under the direction of Marconis de Nègre, a high-grade member of the Rite of Misraïm who, after being expelled[759] twice from the Rite of Misraïm, constituted the first Lodge of the Rite of Memphis in Lyon, France in 1838. The Rite had already been in progress through the combined efforts of Samuel Honis (Cairo) and Marconis de Nègre in Montauban in 1815.

These two Rites of Memphis and Misraïm came together under the leadership of the Grand Hierophant of the World, the freedom fighter Giuseppe Garibaldi, in 1881 in Italy. Important advancements and codifications of the Rite continued under the influence of the tireless John Yarker of England, and in Belgium and France in 1934 through the Convention of the F.U.D.O.S.I,. and again in 1960 under the leadership of Robert Ambelain.

The cross pollination of the Rites continued its evolution in another vein through the Haitian-derived, *1921 Ecclesiastical Revision of the Antient and Primitive Rites of Memphis-Misraïm* under the leadership of Lucien-François Jean-Maine which spread to Spain, the French West Indies, and the United States, and which found its culmination in the enigmatic and prolific author and mage, Michael-Paul Bertiaux in Chicago (1966) when he was consecrated to the episcopacy of the Rites of Memphis-Misraïm (66° Grand Consecrator).[760] Bertiaux went on to receive all levels of the Jean-Maine lineage of magickal consecrations in in 1967. One of Bertiaux's chartered adepts and consecrated bishops is author Allen H. Greenfield who developed the points-chauds empowerments of Bertiaux's philosophy with the degrees of Memphis Misraïm and encouraged scrying the degrees for a deeper understanding of the work. His cogent contributions are noted and extended in both the second and third echelons of our working and written about extensively in Greenfield's own books and web pages.

In 1994, Michael Bertiaux separated the jurisdictions of the APRMM over Europe and French-language speaking countries, assigning the role of Grand Hierophant to Joël Duez[761] who inherited direct transmission of the Rites of Memphis-Misraïm from Ambelain's line as well, thus solidifying the French and Haitian-derived Orders into one body[762]. In 2013, Duez transmitted the Order into the highly capable hands of now Grand Hierophant of the

---

[759] The narrative of the origins of these Rites is quite a tangled web. There are several writers who attempt to navigate these waters using authentic historical means such as Serge Caillet and Milko Bogard. The reader is directed to their writings as the nature of the present text is more focused on the initiatic experience.

[760] See the Appendix by Courtney Willis (Technicians of the Sacred) in the massive, *Voudon Gnostic Workbook*, Red Wheel Weiser, 2007. Some have placed this transferal of powers to Bertiaux's time in Haiti in 1964.

[761] Early in our work in the Chapel we linked arms with Illus. Brother Joël Duez. Spiritual blessing*following the lection.

[762] See the informative website of the APRMM https://aprmm.info/archives/2955, as well as that of the WAEO https://waeo.info/

Appendix A: History Lection

World, Alexander Rybalka 99° (Israel). The energetic influx and complete endowment of authority was accomplished with Michael Bertiaux's transferal of powers to Rybalka on May 29th, 2019. The *Order of the Ancient and Primitive Rite of Memphis and Misraïm* is a part of the only global form of occult Masonry on earth, the World Association of Egyptian Obediences (WAEO), which, much like the original F.U.D.O.S.I., seeks to gather together brothers and sisters dedicated to the esoteric brotherhood in their various geographic locations in the name of Universal Freemasonry.

On May 5th, 2022, Illustrious Brother Rybalka passed to the Grand Lodge above. The position of Grand Hierophant was transferred to his successor, Fra Uraniel Aldebaran, according to Rybalka's wishes and sealed and confirmed by Patriarch Bertiaux in 2023.

Official Transferal of Powers to Sovereign Grand Hierophant Rybalka

Au nom et sous les Auspices de la Grande Loge du Rite Ancien et Primitif de Memphis-Misraim

THE APPLIED LATTICES RESEARCH INSTITUTE

RITE ANCIEN ET PRIMITIF DE MEMPHIS-MISRAIM

In this third day of the month of Psyrie of the year 3311,

And under the auspices of the Grand Sanctuary and the Supreme Counsel of the Grand Lodge of the Ancient and Primitive Rite of Memphis Misraim in the lineage of Jean Maine – Hector - Bertiaux, we confer the powers

To the T∴V∴F∴ Alexandre Rybalka 33° 90° 97°

To operate under the jurisdiction of our Bertiaux lineage of the Ancient and Primitive Rite of Memphis Misraim (A∴P∴R∴M∴M∴ - BERTIAUX LINE), and to install regular lodges in our Rites according to our customs. We also authorise him to install Grand Sovereign Masters National, members of his Supreme Counsels, or again National Hierophants, with our consent and under our counsels.

Michaël Bertiaux
33°, 90°, 97°

Signed this 29 of May 2090 E∴V∴

Conferral of powers from +Bertiaux to Rybalka

Appendix A: History Lection

Blessing of our Chapel and its labors, S.B. Mgr Joël Duez

Opening of the Violet Lodge in our Chapel of the Gnosis

Appendix B: 1° - Apprentice

Apprentice

(This ritual reprinted with permission from Degrees of Wisdom: A Compendium of Rituals from the Rites of Memphis and Misraïm. *The footnotes which follow appear in the original text.)*

Ritual and Instruction of the 1st Symbolic Degree[763]

ARRANGEMENT OF THE TEMPLE - LIST OF MATERIALS

For Normal Meetings

1 Candle for the V∴M∴, the 1st Surv∴ and the 2nd Surv∴ [764]
6 Extinguishers
1 3-branched Candlestick
3 Pillars, each with a Candle 5 single Candlesticks
The Sacred Fire
1 Incense burner, Frankincense, and charcoal
3 Mallets
1 Black Cane with a White Pommel
2 Straight Swords
1 Flaming Sword
1 Bible
2 Squares
2 Compasses
1 Ruler with 24 divisions
1 Red Sack (Widow's Trunk)
1 Black Sack (Bag of Propositions)

For Ceremonies of Reception

1 Cord with a sliding knot
1 Cup with a hawthorn infusion
1 Cup with a gentian infusion
1 Cup with some water and a napkin (2nd Surv∴)
1 Fan (1st Surv∴)

---

[763] The grades of the Symbolic Lodge or "Blue Lodge" presented here are drawn from a modern iteration of the Rite of Misraïm. The student of Egyptian Rite Freemasonry who has had the opportunity to review or experience these degrees in one or another Rite will notice some similarities with the original Misraïm grades, as well as many similarities to certain versions of the grades practiced among various obediences of the combined Rite of Memphis-Misraïm. There are also many differences to be noted, including, but not limited to, the batteries, certain words, and other ritual elements. For the most part, these similarities and differences will not be specifically mentioned in this work, as our intent is to give a glimpse into Egyptian Rite Masonry, offering English versions of degrees long in print in the French language; it is not to unduly expose the inner workings of one or another specific Egyptian Rite Obedience.

[764] In French Masonry, the Worshipful Master and the Sr. and Jr. Wardens are referred to as Venerable Master and the 1st and 2nd Surveillants. We have chosen to leave the French term "Surveillant" untranslated here, as is the custom among many English-language jurisdictions of French Obediences.

1 Dagger
1 Blazing Star
1 Mirror
1 Sterile needle
1 Rough Ashlar
1 Mallet
1 Chisel
1 Stool
1 Set of Knives and Stones for sharpening
1 Sword for each B∴
1 Black mask for each B∴

THE OATH OF THE APPRENTICE

I, *(first and last name of Candidate)*, To the Glory of the Supreme Architect of the Worlds, and of this Respectable Lodge, Assembly of Freemasons, promise and swear on my Honor as a free man (or woman), solemnly and sincerely, and without mental restriction of any kind, to never reveal any of the Mysteries and Secrets of Freemasonry which are going to be conferred on me except to a good and legitimate Brother, or, in a regularly constituted Masonic Lodge or Triangle, to never write, trace, or engrave them without the authorization of my Ultimate Superiors, nor to form any of the characters by which the Secrets of the Order may be revealed, under penalty of having my throat cut, of being dishonored and seeing my name inscribed in perpetuity upon the Column of Infamy, while my body would be buried in the sands of the sea, so that the ebb and flow carries me into an eternal forgetfulness. I promise and swear to henceforth consider all Freemasons as my Brother, to protect them, assist them, and aid them in their needs, temporal as well as spiritual. I make this Oath of Allegiance and Fidelity to the Grand Master of our Order, to the Venerable Master of the Lodge, and to all his officers, in order to preserve in my Heart the Fraternity, Mutual Aid, and Solidarity owed mutually to all the Children of the Light whose unalterable Chain I have just joined today, which binds us to the Past and Future Masters. Starting from this moment, I will spread the teachings that I will have received, so that a Light lightens the Path of Men, my Brethren, and this without distinction of social class, race, color, religion, or nationality. I will strive to be an example of all the Virtues, sacrificing beforehand every vain desire of honor, all ambitions, and all vanity. And this, not through sterile pride, but in the sole aim of inspiring in all the desire to acquire them. I will practice human Fraternity in all its extent in order to demonstrate the benefits thereof. I will be the support of the weak, the adversary of injustice, opposing myself to all unmerited violence from wherever it comes, whether towards body or soul. And in this, may the Supreme Architect of the Worlds be my aid, as well as the living Symbols that I am touching with my hand.

Appendix B: 1° - Apprentice

THE PHILOSOPHICAL TESTAMENT OF THE APPRENTICE

First question: Considering that Philosophy leads to conceiving, and observation leads to admitting, the probable existence of an intelligence at work in the Universe; intelligence whose elementary Light probably is the first tangible manifestation, and the creative agent of the Universal Matter; considering that this Universal Intelligence orders and conducts this Universe toward a finality whose remote perspectives surpass the feeble human intellect, what are, according to you, the duties of Man towards that Intelligence, that the religions call God, that the Pythagoreans specify under the name of "God who geometrizes," and that by this same, Freemasonry calls the "Supreme Architect of the worlds" or "Great Architect of the Universe"?

Second question: Considering that the ancient Hermetic Tradition and Modern Science teach that Life actually resides in the midst of the three kingdoms of Nature: mineral, vegetable, and animal, from the infinitely small to the infinitely large, considering that it is highly probable that Nature equilibrates for the best of the Universal Plan and the various finalities, the vital manifestations in view, what are, according to you, the duties of Man toward the Universe?

Third question: Considering that it is highly probable that Man is, upon the Terrestrial Globe, through his intelligence, his reason, and his undeniable material possibilities, the reflection of that universal intelligence at work in the whole Universe, and considering likewise that each human individuality is finally but the smaller reflection of the total human collectivity, called Humanity, what are, according to you, the duties of Man toward himself first of all, and then toward Humanity?

Opening of the Works in the 1st Symbolic Degree of the
RITE OF MISRAÏM

ENTRANCE INTO THE LODGE

(All the BB∴ are decorated in the Pronaos.)

(The Expert alone penetrates into the deserted temple, verifies the proper order of things, lights the sacred Pire upon the Altar of Naos, and the charcoal of the Incense Burner.)

(Do not forget to place a candle at the station of the M∴ of C∴)

M∴ of C∴
Silence, my BB∴!

We are going to enter the Temple in the following order:

First the AA∴ of the R∴L∴, then the Visiting AA∴,

Then the CC∴ of the R∴L∴, then the Visiting CC∴,

The MM∴ of the L∴, then the Visiting MM∴, The OFF∴,

Then the Visiting Venerables,

And finally, the V∴M∴ of the R∴L∴ to carry out three turns around the Temple.

(Column of Harmony, solemn music.)

(The BB∴ proceed in the inverse order of their Masonic age and Hierarchy.)

(The M∴ of C∴ is at the head of the procession that he conducts by a regular and rhythmic walk by his ebony cane with an ivory pommel.)

(The BB∴ execute this Entrance seriously and make their first circuit by the North, then a second and a third, at the conclusion of which the M∴ of C∴ announces:)

M∴ of C∴
Take your place, my BB∴!

Appendix B: 1° - Apprentice

V∴ M∴

(One strike of the Mallet) •

Salutations on all points of the Triangle! Respect to the Order!

1st Surv∴

Amen on the first and second Horizon in the Temple of Truth-Justice!

V∴ M∴

Take your place, my BB∴

(The BB∴ carry this out promptly.)

My BB∴, I invite you to leave your metals at the Door of the Temple and to make within yourself the Silent Interior.

(Pause.)

B∴ 1st Surv∴, what is the First Duty of a Surv∴ in the Temple of Wisdom which is the Second Horizon of the Temple of Truth-Justice?

1st Surv∴

V∴ M∴, it is to protect our Sacred Mysteries from any possibility of profane violation.

V∴ M∴

B∴ Tiler, please, I pray you, carry out the orders of the 1st Surv∴.

(The Tiler returns to the Parvis of the Temple while standing to Order with the Sword, closes the Door of the Temple, resumes his place, and places himself again at order with the Sword.)

Tiler

V∴ M∴, the approaches of the Temple are deserted! The echo remains silent, and no one can hear us! The inviolability of our Mysteries is assured. We are secure.

V∴ M∴

Then we are secure; stand and face the Orient, my BB∴!

(Strike of the Mallet.) •

(All the BB∴ carry this out promptly.)

Come to Order as App∴ at the passing of the BB∴ (*or* SS∴) Surveillants!

B∴ 1st and 2nd Surv∴, please accomplish the Second Duty in the Temple of Wisdom. Assure yourselves that all the BB∴ who decorate your Columns are all AA∴ Masons of the Temple of Wisdom.

(The 1st and 2nd Surv∴, armed with their Mallet across the chest, cross one another at the Occident while saluting each other with a sign of the head; they inspect the BB∴ of their Column who stand to Order as App∴ at their passage.)

(The Exp∴ stands to Order with the Sword, point in the air and guard at the height of the face.)

(The M∴ of C∴ stands to Order with the Cane.)

(The surveillants cross again at the Orient, salute one another with a sign of the head and resume their respective Stations.)

1st Surv∴

V∴M∴, all the BB∴ who decorate the Column of the South are AA∴ Masons.

2nd Surv∴

V∴M∴, all the BB∴ who decorate the Column of the North are AA∴ Masons.

(The V∴M∴ as well as the BB∴ who sit at the Orient come to Order as AA∴)

V∴M∴

I recognize the BB∴ who sit in the Orient as Masons who labor in the Temple of Wisdom and meditate in spirit in the Temple of Truth-Justice.

(Strike of the Mallet.) •

Take your place, my BB∴.

(All the BB∴ carry this out promptly.)

V∴M∴

B∴ 1st Surv∴, are you a Mason?

1st Surv∴

My Initiator has made me such after the trials by Three Steps between the Square and the Compass.

V∴M∴

B∴ 1st Surv∴, do your BB∴ recognize you as a Mason?

1st Surv∴

Yes, V∴M∴.

But in order to be a Mason, the recognition of my BB∴ is not indispensable, it is but a problem of administration. The True Initiation rests not upon the recognition of Men, even Initiates, it rests upon the true and traditional essence of a Transmission between Initiator and Initiate, validly transmitted, regularly received, approved,, and brought into its concrete form by Providence Itself, according to the designs of the Supreme Architect of the Worlds, for the Spirit blows where it will and is not subject to any judgment.

V∴M∴

Br∴ 1st Surv∴, do you know the bases of the Temple of Wisdom?

1st Surv∴

Yes, V∴M∴.

They are the sacred numbers 3, 5, and 7, which manifest the Power of the Supreme Architect of the Worlds and by means of which he has set in Order all that exists. He also manifests his Wisdom, Strength, and Beauty which comprise his sacred TRI-UNITY.

V∴M∴

My BB∴, according to the Secret Custom of the Ancient Temples, we are going to open the Gates between our Second Horizon and the First Horizon which transcends us.

Stand and to Order, my BB∴!

(Strike of the Mallet.) •

(All the BB∴ carry this out promptly.)

(The M∴ of C∴ rises, moves to the Orient, takes the candle from the V∴M∴ and lights it on the fire of the Altar of the Naos. He returns the candle to the V∴M∴ who lights, in his turn, the central Candle of the Three-Branched Candlestick.)

V∴M∴

O! Infinite Wisdom! Let the First Light be!

Opened is the First Gate!

(Strike of the Mallet.) •

(The 1st Surv∴ rises, takes his Candle and moves to the Orient. He lights his Candle on the central flame of the Three-Branched candlestick of the V∴M∴, returns to his Station and remains standing, his candle in hand.)

(The V∴M∴ then lights the Candle on the right of the Three-Branched candlestick.)

V∴ M∴

O! Omnipotent Strength! Let the Second Light be!

Opened is the Second Gate!

(Strike of the Mallet.) •

(The 2ⁿᵈ Surv∴ rises, takes his candle and goes to the Orient. He lights his candle on the central flame of the Three-Branched candlestick of the V∴M∴, returns to his Station and remains standing, his Candle in hand.)

(The V∴M∴ then lights the candle on the left of the Three-Branched Candlestick.)

V∴ M∴

O! Beauty, Sacred Fire which harmonizes the Order of the World! Let the Third Light be!

Opened is the Third Gate.

(Strike of the Mallet.) •

1ˢᵗ Surv∴

Amen!

2ⁿᵈ Surv∴

Amen!

(The V∴M∴ descends from his Station, his candle in his right hand, and places himself In the Occident, facing the Naos.)

(The 1ˢᵗ Surv∴ leaves his station, his Candle in his right hand, and places himself at the left of the V∴M∴.)

(The 2ⁿᵈ Surv∴ leaves his Station, his candle in his right hand, and places himself at the right of the V∴M∴.)

V∴ M∴

O! Supreme Architect of the Worlds! When your Supreme Pontiff Hierophant, Thoth-Hermes Trismegistus had prophesized that Egypt would become a land deprived of Initiates, abandoned by the Gods, he revealed only a part of the Truth. The Sands which would cover the Pyramidal Temple did not entirely succeed. The Great Sphinx, symbolizing the Lord of the Two Horizons, the Vanquisher of Death, Harmohaktis, which would have been buried, was done only partially.

O! Supreme Architect of the Worlds! The Pyramid that the Grand Hierophants have constructed remains unfinished. It awaits the Cornerstone,[765] and they do not see it at its summit. Since, Egypt fell to these days. But as all things have within them life upon the Earth, if they are built in Heaven, if the Hierophants place one day upon the Great Pyramid

---

[765] Here, the term seems to be describing the pyramidal capstone rather than a cornerstone in the traditional sense.

Appendix B: 1° - Apprentice

the Cornerstone as the cosmic, spiritual, and physical achievement of the Perfect Temple of the Earth, then Egypt, the Land of Initiates, will again be visited by the Gods and You, Supreme Architect of the Worlds.

The Waters engulfed the lands of Atlantis, but Egypt emerged therefrom. The Waters will attempt again to cover the Temples and Perfections extolled in stone, but if only one old Priest recognizes the Cornerstone, then Egypt will be saved, for the Cornerstone saves from the Valley of Forgetfulness.

O! Supreme Architect of the Worlds! Lord of the Two Horizons, in your Manifestations and your Epiphanies, we recognize the Cornerstone. We venerate that Stone that the True Initiates, the Sacred Builders, the Priests and Hierophants of the Eternal Egypt do not reject, but call on with all their Voices, and recognize that, without It, the Temple, every Temple of Man or Angel, must fall to the earth.

Conduct, therefore, the Truth of our labors of Edification and reveal to us, in all things, the Perfect Plans of Wisdom!

Amen.

1st Surv∴

O! Eternal TRI-UNE, who said, "I am the Source of existences and beings, I am yesterday and today, and I know tomorrow."

Hail!

2nd Surv∴

What truly lives in us, is the Word of the Eternal Master. The Master of all Initiation is manifested as the terrestrial reflection in this Ritual Assembly by the physical support of the Master of the L∴.

(The V∴M∴ lights the "Wisdom" Flambeau with his Candle.)

V∴M∴

Hail, Lord of Eternity whose Wisdom has multiple names and mysterious forms, which art THOU in manifestation.

(The V∴M∴ and the 1st Surv∴ mingle the flames of their Candles to light the "Strength" Flambeau.)

1st Surv∴

Hail to Thee, who sustains the Temple by thy Strength in the service of the only Sons of the Light.

(The V∴M∴, the 1st Surv∴, and the 2nd Surv∴ mingle the flames of their Candles to light the "Beauty" Flambeau.)

2nd Surv∴

O! Thou who can pronounce the Sacred Word, to sustain it in its Order and transmit it to the Initiates. Hail to Thee in thine Ineffable Beauty.

(The V∴M∴, the 1st Surv∴, and the 2nd Surv∴ go to the Altar of oaths.)

(The Exp∴ and the M∴ of C∴ go to the Occident, facing the Naos.)

(The V∴M∴ opens the V∴S∴L∴.)

(The 1st Surv∴ arranges the Compass on the V∴S∴L∴.)

(The 2nd Surv∴ arranges the Square upon the Compass and V∴S∴L∴.)

(The Exp∴ arranges the Compass, the Square, and the Rule with 24 divisions over the Naos.)

(The M∴ of C∴ pours the incense three times into the Incense Burner on the left side of the Altar.)

(The V∴M∴, the 1st Surv∴, the 2nd Surv∴, the Exp∴, and the M∴ of C∴ resume their respective stations and remain standing, to Order.)

V∴M∴
Take your place, my BB∴

(All the BB∴ and SS∴ carry this out promptly.)

Orator
Since every Rite is only valid if the least Obligations of the Order are scrupulously observed, at this moment has just been opened, token of our Tradition and our Regularity, the Sacred Book which speaks of the Cornerstone and upon which we have all taken Oaths at the time of our Initiations.

V∴M∴
Who, in the Temple of the Wisdom of the Oriental Freemasons, Ancient and Primitive, manifests the Mysterious Numbers and the Holy Lights of the Invisible Temple of Truth-Justice?

1st Surv∴
It is the Most Puissant Master of this R∴L∴ who possesses the Keys of Truth-Justice.

That is why he is called V∴M∴ in the R∴L∴. He is aided in his Mysterious Labors by the physical supports of the Perfect Guardians of the Temple of Truth-Justice who are, in the Temple of Wisdom, in order to accomplish the Labors of Sacred Masonry, the 1st and 2nd Surv∴.

V∴M∴
Where sits the V∴M∴, and why?

1st Surv∴
In the Orient, whence proceeds Light, Power, and Wisdom. Because all these holy things are attained here, in this place of the initiatic space that they call, traditionally and culturally, the Orient.

V∴M∴
Since all Light, all Power, and all Wisdom emanate from the Orient, the V∴M∴, who is but the support of the Eternal Word, sits in the Orient in the Temple of Wisdom in order to worthily open this R∴L∴ to enlighten the BB∴ and SS∴, to dispense the effusions of the Truth, for Love and Strength without Wisdom are naught but intolerance.

(The V∴M∴ rises.)

V∴M∴

(3 strikes of the Mallet.) • • •

I am the Orient. The Orient is mine. I manifest the Orient for the time of Labor of this R∴L∴, for the Glory of the S∴A∴O∴T∴W∴.

(The V∴M∴ takes his place.)

V∴M∴

Where sits the 1st Surv∴?

1st Surv∴

The 1st Surv∴ sits at the Corner of the Column of the North in order to give the signal for the commencement of the Labors to the BB∴, to aid the V∴M∴ in his Teaching, to replace him in case of necessity, and to develop the Occult Lights in the spirit of the BB∴ AA∴, and to lead them toward a greater comprehension of our Sacred Mysteries. He is the Support of Strength.

V∴M∴

My B∴, since you are the living Support of the Spirit of Strength, I pray you to sit as 1st Surv∴, for Love and Wisdom without Strength is naught but vain desires, without practical applications.

(The V∴M∴ rises.)

V∴M∴

(2 strikes of the Mallet.) • •

(The 1st Surv∴ rises.)

V∴M∴

B∴ 1st Surv∴, you are the North. The North is yours. You are the Manifestation of the Spirit of Strength during the Time of Labor of this R∴L∴, for the Glory of the S∴A∴O∴T∴W∴.

(The V∴M∴ and the 1st Surv∴ take their place.)

V∴M∴

Where sits the 2nd Surv∴?

2nd Surv∴

The 2nd Surv∴ sits at the Corner of the Column of the South in order to attend to the maintenance of the Order, to the perfect execution of the Labors, to transmit to the Orient all the difficulties which may arise, and to obtain solutions according to Truth-Justice.

V∴M∴

My B∴, since you are the living Support of the Spirit of Harmony and Beauty, I pray you to sit as 2nd Surv∴, for Wisdom and Strength without Beauty and Love would be naught but tyranny.

(The V∴M∴ rises.)

(Strike of the Mallet.) •

(The 2nd Surv∴ rises.)

V∴M∴

B∴ 2nd Surv∴, you are the South. The South is yours. You are the manifestation of the Spirit of Harmony during the Time of Labor of this R∴L∴, for the Glory of the S∴A∴O∴T∴W∴.

(The V∴M∴ and the 2nd Surv∴ take their place.)

V∴M∴

B∴ 1st Surv∴, how many Columns support the True Temple of Wisdom?

1st Surv∴

Nine Columns, V∴M∴.

V∴M∴

Why, B∴ 2nd Surv∴?

2nd Surv∴

In order to precipitate Alchemy in depth in this Athanor that is the Temple of Wisdom, the Sublimation of the Ennead of Egypt.

V∴M∴

Please state them my B∴.

2nd Surv∴

The V∴M∴, the 1st Surv∴, the 2nd Surv∴, the Or∴, the Sec∴, the Exp∴, the Treas∴, the Hosp∴, and the Tiler.

V∴M∴

What is necessary in order to pass to the Labors of Edification in the Temple of Wisdom?

2nd Surv∴

V∴M∴, it is necessary that all the BB∴ are the requisite age to commence the operative labor, and that the appointed hour has arrived.

V∴M∴

B∴ 2nd Surv∴, how old are you?

2nd Surv∴

I am 3 years old, V∴M∴.

V∴M∴

B∴ 1st Surv∴, what time is it?

1st Surv∴

V∴M∴, it is the hour when the physical Sun as well as the occult and eternal sun are in full zenith.

V∴M∴

It is still necessary to circulate the Secret Word, transmitted always from mouth to ear across the centuries, and which has circulated among those who are able to receive and understand it entirely.

B∴ Exp∴, please ascend to the Orient to receive the Secret Word.

(Strike of the Mallet.) •

Stand and to Order, my BB∴!

(All the BB∴ carry this out promptly.)

(The Exp∴ ascends to the Orient, to the V∴M∴ who whispers the Secret Word in his ear.)

(The Exp∴ then goes to the 2nd Surv∴ and whispers the secret word in his ear.)

(The 2nd Surv∴ goes to the 1st Surv∴ and whispers the secret Word in his ear, then resumes his Station and remains standing and to Order.)

(The 1st Surv∴ whispers the Secret Word in the ear of the Exp∴.)

(The Exp∴ returns to the Orient, transmits the Secret Word to the ear of the V∴M∴, resumes his Station and remains standing to Order.)

V∴M∴

The Temple of the Wisdom of the Oriental Masons, Ancient and Primitive, is just and perfect under the Vault of the Temple of Truth-Justice.

My BB∴, since it is the hour and we are of the age, face the Orient.

(All the BB∴ and SS∴ carry this out promptly.)

(The V∴M∴ removes his gloves, grasps the Flaming Sword in his left hand, the guard held by the Master's Claw, the Blade vertical, the Pommel resting on the Table. He holds his Mallet in the right hand.)

V∴M∴

(3 strikes of the Mallet.) • ••

1st Surv∴

(3 strikes of the Mallet.) • ••

2nd Surv∴

(3 strikes of the Mallet.) • ••

(The Exp∴ and the M∴ of C∴ go to the foot of the steps of the Orient and, feet squared, they cross the Sword and the Cane, forming a Square.)

V∴M∴

T∴T∴G∴O∴T∴S∴A∴O∴T∴W∴! Lord of the Sacred Ennead of Egypt! In the Name and under the Auspices of the Rite of Misraïm, by virtue of the powers which have been conferred upon me, I declare open the Sacred Labors of this R∴L∴, sitting at the Orient of…, under the distinctive title of …, at the secret geographical point known only to the Sons of the Light.

(The V∴M∴ lays down the Flaming sword and the Mallet, puts his gloves back on, and brings himself to order.)

(The Exp∴ and the M∴ of C∴ still cross the Sword and the Cane.)

V∴M∴

Let us unite, my BB∴, by the Sign of App∴, the Battery, and the Acclamation.

All

(Make the Sign.)

(Strike the Battery.) • ••

(Issue the Acclamation:) Alleluia! Alleluia! Alleluia!

V∴M∴

My BB∴ and SS∴, we are no longer in the exterior and profane world.

Appendix B: 1° - Apprentice

May our Labors be ever realized according to the design appointed in the Temple of Truth-Justice which transcends us. They must, without exception, serve to the Glory of the S∴A∴O∴T∴W∴ for the defense and Prosperity of the Royal Art, the True Sacerdotal and Occult Masonry, and for the good of humanity.

Take your places, my BB∴

(The Exp∴ and the M∴ of C∴ uncross the Sword and cane, resume their station, and take their place.)

(All the BB∴ and SS∴ carry this out promptly.)

1st Surv∴

My BB∴ and SS∴, the Labors are open according to the appointed designs.

V∴M∴

My BB∴ and SS∴, I pray you to pay attention to our B∴ Secretary for the reading of the Perfect Plan of the Labors of this day.

Secretary

V∴M∴ and you all my BB∴, in your Grades and Qualities…

(Gives the reading of the order of the day.)

V∴M∴

My B∴ Sec∴, please read us the Tracing Board of our Last Labors.

Secretary

(Gives the reading of the Tracing Board of the Last Labors.)

V∴M∴

(Strike of the Mallet.) •

BB∴ 1st and 2nd Surv∴, ask the BB∴ who decorate your Columns if they have any observations to formulate on the wording of the Board which has just been read to us.

1st Surv∴

BB∴ who decorate the Column of the South, the V∴M∴ invites those among you who would have an observation to formulate on the wording of the Board which has just been read to us, to offer their words.

2nd Surv∴

BB∴ who decorate the Column of the North, the V∴M∴ invites those among you who would have an observation to formulate on the wording of the Board which has just been read to us, to offer their words.

(After all the observation have been formulated…)

1st Surv∴

V∴ M∴, silence reigns over the Columns.

V∴ M∴

My BB∴, let those among you who approve the wording of the Tracing Board of our Last Labors such as it has just been read to us (or account held of the formulated observations) manifest it by raising the right hand at the strike of the Mallet.

(Strike of the Mallet.) •

(The BB∴ raise their hand.)

V∴ M∴

Opinions to the contrary?

(Strike of the Mallet.) •

(The BB∴ possibly raise their hand.)

V∴ M∴

I invite the Orator to give his conclusions.

Orator

Whereas none of the BB∴ present have formulated an observation concerning the wording of the Tracing Board of our Last Labors which has just been read to us (or taking into account the observations formulated concerning the wording of the Tracing Board of our Last Labors), may it please this R∴ L∴ to approve it.

V∴ M∴

I declare the Tracing Board of our Last Labors adopted! It will be made mention of in that of this day.

(The V∴ M∴ asks for news of the absent BB∴ He presents their excuses. If a B∴ or S∴ has been absent for several Meetings, he organizes a visit with the College.)

V∴ M∴

B∴ Tiler, please repair to the Parvis and assure yourself that there are no Visitors who request entry to the Temple.

(The Tiler carries this out and if no Visitor has present himself…)

Tiler

V∴ M∴, no B∴ Visitor has presented himself at the Entrance of the Temple.

Appendix B: 1° - Apprentice

(The V∴M∴ takes note of them and remits them to the Tiler to be transmitted to the Orator who controls the Regularity thereof.)

(The Or∴ then remits these documents to the Tiler who transmits them to the Exp∴.)

(The Tiler resumes his Station and takes his place.)

(The Exp∴ goes to the Visitors and if there is cause, receives the Words, Signs, and Tokens of the Grade.)

V∴ M∴

B∴ M∴ of C∴, please introduce the Visitors by announcing their Grades and Qualities in order to receive them with the Honors which are due to them.

(This in order to permit the V∴M∴ to honor the BB∴ that he desires to have ascend to the Orient.)

(If the Visitor has right to Masonic Honors, they are rendered to him according to the Custom. Otherwise, the M∴ of C∴ places the Visitors on the Columns.)

V∴ M∴

My BB∴, the Order of the day calls.

(The V∴M∴ may then possibly give the reading of the Correspondence.)

Ceremony of Reception to the 1ˢᵗ Symbolic Degree of the Rite of Misraïm

BEGINNING OF THE CEREMONY OF RECEPTION

V∴ M∴

B∴ Exp∴, go and confirm that the Profane has arrived.

(The Exp∴ leaves the Lodge, ascertains it and returns into the L∴, comes to Order in his Function, and says:)

Expert

V∴ M∴ the Profane awaits upon the Parvis.

V∴ M∴

B∴ Exp∴, return to the Profane and ascertain his appearance, so that he may hear nothing of what occurs around us. You will wait with him for orders from the Workshop to submit him to the trials, or to remove him at once from this place.

(The Exp∴ leaves the Lodge.)

V∴ M∴

My BB∴, the information that has come to us on the Profane N…, having been favorable to him, the conclusions of the BB∴ Investigators, those of the Orator, and the scrutiny of the ballot having been propitious, the Order of the Day calls his Reception.

Is it your opinion that we should proceed thereto?

(All the BB∴ present raise their right hand to note their approbation.)

(The V∴ M∴ then proceeds to the Reception of the Oath of the Proposer, concerning the qualities of the Candidate.)

V∴ M∴

Stand and to Order, my BB∴!

(All the BB∴ carry this out promptly.)

B∴ M∴ of C∴, please go and fetch the B∴ Proposer, and conduct him to the Altar of Oaths.

(The M∴ of C∴ conducts the Proposer to the Altar of oaths.)
(The proposer remains standing and to Order, the right hand ungloved and placed upon the V∴ S∴ L∴ as well as upon the Sword and says…)

Appendix B: 1° - Apprentice

Proposer

T∴ T∴ G∴ O∴ T∴ S∴ A∴ O∴ T∴ W∴! In the Name, and under the Auspices of the Rite of Misraïm, by virtue of the powers which have been conferred upon me, in the presence of the brilliant Lights of this R∴ L∴, I swear upon the Book of Sacred Law and upon this Sword, symbol of Honor, that the Neophyte N…, that I present for Initiation, is worthy of that Sublime Favor, and let me respond for him: Body for bodies. Soul for souls. So help me S∴ A∴ O∴ T∴ W∴.

V∴ M∴

I receive your oath in the Name of the Order.
Go, and may the God of Peace be eternally with you. Take your place, my BB∴.

(All the BB∴ carry this out promptly.)

M∴ of C∴, please accompany the Proposer to his place between the Columns and resume your Station.

B∴ 2nd Exp∴, go to the Profane and have the B∴ Exp∴ re-enter.

(The M∴ of C∴ carries out his duty, he and the Proposer take their places.)

(The 2nd Exp∴ carries out his duty; the Exp∴ and the 2nd Exp∴ enter the Temple and come to Order of their Function and resume their respective Stations.)

V∴ M∴

I invite the B∴ Exp∴ to begin the Ritual of Reception.

(The Exp∴ ritually leaves the Lodge. He wears his Apron, his Collar, as well as his Sword; he divests himself of his Decorations upon the Parvis, and goes to seek the Testament of the Neophyte.)

V∴ M∴

In order to allow our B∴ Exp∴ the time to accomplish his mission, I will give you the reading of the three questions which have been posed to the Candidate.

First question: Considering that philosophy leads to conceiving, and observation leads to admitting, the probable existence of an intelligence at work in the Universe; intelligence whose elementary Light is probably the first tangible manifestation, and the creative agent of the Universal Matter; considering that this Universal Intelligence orders and conducts this Universe toward a finality whose remote perspectives surpass the feeble human intelligence, what are, according to you, the duties of Man toward that Intelligence, that the religions call God, that the Pythagoreans specify under the name of "God who geometrizes," and that by this same, Freemasonry calls "The Great Architect of the Universe"?

Second question: Considering that the ancient Hermetic Tradition and modern science teach that Life actually resides in the midst of the three kingdoms of Nature: mineral, vegetable, and animal, from the infinitely small to the infinitely large, considering that it is highly probable that Nature equilibrates for the best of the Universal Plan and the various finalities, the vital manifestations in view, what are, according to you, the duties of Man toward the Universe?

Third question: Considering that it is highly probable that Man is, upon the Terrestrial Globe, through his intelligence, his reason, and his undeniable material possibilities, the reflection of that universal intelligence at work in the whose universe, and considering likewise that each human individuality is finally but the smaller reflection of the total human collectivity, called Humanity, what are, according to you, the duties of Man toward himself first of all, and then toward Humanity?

(The Exp∴ resumes his place in the Lodge without ceremony; he sticks the Testament of the Neophyte, folded into a Triangle, on the tip of his sword, and he brings it to the V∴M∴.)

(The Exp∴ exits, still without ceremony, to fetch the Neophyte.)

(During this lapse of time, the V∴M∴ reads the Philosophical Testament of the Neophyte.)

The Low Door.

(The Exp∴ divests the Neophyte of all his metals, and he has him undress according to the Ritual of 1786, to wit: head bare, blindfolded, in shirt-sleeves, the left arm and breast bare, the right knee bare, the left shoe removed and put on slipshod, around the neck a rough cord by which he is led gently to the Door of the Temple.)

Expert
(In a loud voice.)

Sir (*or* Madam), to be initiated was "to learn how to die" in the ancient world.

The cord that you wear from this moment around the neck ought not, in your eyes, endow you with a weak or vexatious character. It is no longer a question of a useless hazing. This symbolic cord is none other than the image of the fluidic bond tying your subtle form to the carnal envelope that material Death causes you to leave.

Leaving the Cabinet of Reflection and its funereal apparatus, you traverse, like in a bad dream, the dark "Amenti," "Hades," the Kingdom of the Dead. Guided by the subterranean "Hermes," conductor of souls into the Beyond, you go blindly towards the Ineffable Light, and this under his sole guidance.

May this let you penetrate the esoteric teaching of our Ritual. Without providential intervention, without any occult and mysterious predestination, there is little chance for the human soul, plunged into darkness, to find the Way back to his original Liberty.

Such is the formal teaching of the Gnosis!

(The Exp∴ has the Neophyte knock at the Door with the right hand several rapidly: 1, 2, 3, 4, 5, 6, 7…)

(The Tiler opens the Door of the Temple a little.)

V∴M∴
Who knocks thus at the Door of the Temple?

Expert

It is a Profane who asks to be received a Freemason.

V∴ M∴

How dare he hope this?

Expert

Because he is free and of good morals.

V∴ M∴

In that case, let him enter, but with prudence; I invite this Respectable Assembly to the customary discretionary measures.

(All the BB∴ mask themselves in black and grasp their swords.)

(The Tiler opens the Door and sets his Sword at mid-height.)

Expert

Sir (*or* Madam), before this Threshold, lower the head and bend down, for the Door is extremely low!

(The Neophyte is introduced, bent in two, into the Lodge.)

(The M∴ of C∴ accompanies the Exp∴ and the Neophyte for the entire duration of the Ceremony of Reception, and remain during the ambulations slightly behind.)

(The Exp∴ conducts the Neophyte between the Columns, facing the Orient, and has him sit upon a stool.)

(Column of Harmony, slow and gentle music.)

(Silence.)

V∴ M∴

Sir (*or* Madam), the secular Fraternity with which you have requested to be affiliated has had confidence in you up to here. But before having you undergo the rest of the Ritual of Reception, I ask you, in the name of all my BB∴ here present, as well as my own, to solemnly repeat your First Oath of Silence.

Do you swear, whatever happens, whether this Ceremony is interrupted or led to its conclusion, to never reveal to anyone, not even to a close relative, not even to a confessor, not even to a brother or a spouse, what you are going to see, undergo, or hear?

Neophyte

I swear.

(If necessary, the Exp∴ whispers the responses to the Neophyte throughout the Ceremony.)

The Water of Forgetfulness.

V∴ M∴

Sir (*or* Madam), heir of the ancient esoteric and occult Societies, Freemasonry has preserved the secret of a very ancient beverage, true philter, composed of plants cut at certain lunar periods, in order to be finally consecrated according to millenary Rites.

The beverage has for its design to depersonalize you. Some weeks after its ingestion, inoffensive as concerns your physical health, your past personality will be slowly dissolved. Imperceptibly, day after day, you will become another being. Slowly, but surely, the Egregore which animates and conducts our ancient Society will penetrate you, substituting its will for your own, and at the next anniversary of your Reception, nothing more will remain of the Man (*or* Woman) that you are presently.

You will be no more then, according to the ancient and very occult precept, but like a corpse that the hand of the washer of the dead turns and turns again at his will.

One last time Sir (*or* Madam), do you consent to die to your past life?

Neophyte

I consent.

V∴ M∴

That being the case, B∴ Exp∴, have the Candidate drink the Water of Forgetfulness.
(*The Exp∴ then places into the left hand of the Neophyte a cup containing a cold infusion of hawthorn and tells him…*)

Expert

Drink Sir (*or* Madam), drink slowly!

(*The Neophyte drinks the cup slowly, and the Exp∴ takes it back when it is empty.*)

V∴ M∴

Sir (*or* Madam), I congratulate you on your courage. Know, however, that the trials which await you, though symbolic they may be, have their double on more subtle planes, with immediate and lasting realizations… It is not to your physical courage that I appeal, but to your mental audacity.

There are thresholds which, once crossed, no longer permit one to go back. According to the popular adage "It is only the first step which counts," but you are yet unaware of the cost.

One more time Sir (*or* Madam), before continuing to endure this Ceremony, I ask you to reflect.

Do you consent to go further in this Ritual?

Neophyte

I consent.

First Voyage: Water.

V∴ M∴

In that case, B∴ Exp∴, have the Candidate accomplish his First Voyage.

(Strike of the Mallet.) •

Expert

My Son (*or* my Daughter), come with me!

(The Exp∴ conducts the Neophyte by taking him firmly by the left hand.)

(Column of Harmony, harsh, jerky, violent music.)

(All the BB∴ ring the blade of their swords, and with their feet, they imitate the rolling of a storm.)

(The Exp∴ conducts the Neophyte, departing from the Columns of the Occident. They pass by the North, then to the Orient and arrive at the south (clockwise gait). The Exp∴ periodically has the Neophyte turn around jerkily. Arriving at the south, they stop before the station of the 2nd Surv∴.)

(Column of Harmony, silence.)

(The 2nd Surv∴ rises, waits for the Neophyte before his station; he pushes him firmly 1dth his pointed Mallet upon his chest as he says in a strong voice:)

2nd Surv∴

Who goes there?

Expert

It is a Profane who asks to be received a Freemason.

2nd Surv∴

How dare he hope this?

Expert

Because he is free and of good morals.

2nd Surv∴

In that case, let him pass, and let him be purified by Water!

(The 2nd Surv∴ resumes his Station and takes his place.)

(The M∴ of C∴ grasps the right hand of the Neophyte and plunges it into a vase filled with pure water, previously prepared. He then wipes the hand with a proper napkin.)

(The Exp∴ grabs the cord around the neck of the Neophyte and leads him, accompanied by the M∴ of C∴ to his stool between the Columns, but all three remain standing.)

V∴M∴

Sir (*or* Madam), once again, I tell you, every Masonic Ceremony doubles itself, on more subtle planes, by an occult realization.

The Voyage that you have just accomplished, following your departure from the Chamber of Reflection, is symbolic of your first post-mortem contact, with the spiritual regions which immediately follow the physical plane.

The tumult, the various obstacles which have impeded your steps, are simply the reflections of the difficulties of every kind which are opposed to the attempt of liberation of the human soul, outside of the material darkness, outside of the inferior passions.

Thanks to some mysterious protections, you have crossed the First Gate, and the Arkonte which guarded it has given you access to it, after having made you undergo the first and necessary purification, that of Water!

You are henceforth MUNDUS!

Other trials, physical and mental, await you upon the second periplus. Do you feel strong enough to confront them, and do you regret nothing of what is imposed on you?

Neophyte

I persist.

Second Voyage: Air.

V∴M∴

In that case, B∴ Exp∴, have the Candidate accomplish his Second Voyage!

(Strike of the Mallet.) •

Expert

My Pupil, follow me.

(The Exp∴ resumes the conducting of the Neophyte.)

(Column of Harmony, sweet and melodious music.)

(The BB∴ and SS∴ observe silence.)

(The Exp∴ guides the Neophyte gently. They set out from the occident toward the Orient by passing through the South, then they stop at the Occident, before the 1st Surv∴ (counterclockwise movement).)

(The 1st Surv∴ rises and awaits the Neophyte before his Station; he strikes him with his Mallet upon the Chest and says in a strong voice:)

1ˢᵗ Surv∴

Who goes there?

Expert

It is a Profane who asks to be received a Freemason.

1ˢᵗ Surv∴

How dare he hope this?

Expert

Because he is free and of good morals.

1ˢᵗ Surv∴

In that case, let him pass, and let him be purified by Air!

(The 1ˢᵗ Surv∴ resumes his station and takes his place.)

(The M∴ of C∴ blows three times upon the forehead of the Neophyte. He utilizes a fan previously prepared.)

(The Exp∴ and M∴ of C∴ accompany the Neophyte again to his stool between Columns; all three remain standing.)

V∴M∴

Sir (*or* Madam), what esoteric teaching do you believe to be able to extricate from this Second Voyage?

Neophyte

(Response of the Neophyte.)

V∴M∴

Sir (*or* Madam), this Voyage continues the series of material purifications that the human soul undergoes in its flight toward the divine.

Stripping successively the subtle envelopes which enrobe that divine spark that we call Soul, you have reached the median domain, the Intermediary Kingdom where the weight of the sensual passions, symbolized by the Water, is already forgotten, but where remain the intellectual beliefs symbolized by the Air.

If the necessities of the flesh are things finally dead to us, the passions of the spirit remain, imperious and exacting.

Now, in order to become a Sage, know Sir (*or* Madam) that nothing must remain of what deceives us here below. No contingency is worth Man being, often voluntarily, subjugated to it. No belief, no opinion sufficiently approaches the Total Truth to merit such slavery!

It is here that it is necessary to make our own the words of a Great Initiate, I name Johann Wolfgang GOETHE who tells us that, "Nothing passed deserves to be revived, there is only the Eternal New which is formed from elements amplified by the Ancient, and the true and pure ardent desire ought always to be productive, to arrive at new and better creations."

This simple phrase is the whole of Masonry, the true, the traditional; the only Rule of Order of the Masters which, upon the path of the luminous: Evolution, has shown us for ages and ages, the Way of Ideal Beauty.
Your path to us Sir (*or* Madam), is still long. Other trials, I have already told you, yet await you.

Do you agree to accomplish the Third Voyage?

Neophyte
I agree.

Third Voyage: Fire.

V∴ M∴
In that case, B∴ Exp∴, have the Candidate accomplish his Third Voyage.

(Strike of the Mallet.) •

Expert
My Friend, support yourself on me!

(Column of Harmony, no music, nothing but a great silence.)

(All the BB∴ observe total silence.)

(The Exp∴ passes his left arm under the right armpit of the Neophyte, then, setting out from the Occident, they pass to the North and arrive at the Orient before the Station of the V∴ M∴ (clockwise gait).)

(The V∴ M∴ descends from his Station. He strikes the Neophyte roughly with his Mallet in the middle of the chest and asks in a strong voice:)

V∴ M∴
Who goes there?

Expert
It is a Profane who asks to be received a Freemason.

V∴ M∴
How dare he hope this?

Expert
Because he is free and of good morals.

V∴ M∴

In that case, let him pass and be purified by Fire!

(The V∴ M∴ resumes his Station.)

(The M∴ of C∴ approaches bearing a lit Flambeau that he passes three times under the right hand of the Neophyte.)

(The Exp∴ and the M∴ of C∴ lead the Neophyte back to his stool at the occident between the Columns by passing by the south; all three remain standing.)

V∴ M∴

Sir (*or* Madam), this Third Voyage has given us the character that the old liturgies denominate PURUS, pure. The Baptism of Water made us MUNDUS, cleansed. The Fire makes us PURUS, purified!

The Water may purify the body of flesh, but the purification of the Double, of the Mediator, intermediary between the corporeal Form and the Spirit, only the Air, median element in the universal energetic quartet, was in a position to realize it. It appertains solely to the Fire, superior, occult, and divine element, to realize the purification of the Soul, divine principle which animates you, imperishable reality of Being.

Your voyage has been made without any obstacle, without anything coming to trouble the inner silence of your Being. This is what you have attained, then, in the spiritual regions where all is but Beauty, Wisdom, and Harmony. In a plane where, yet blind, you have a presentiment, despite this, of the imminent clarity of the Light very near.

The Mark: The Seal

V∴ M∴

Two final trials, more serious perhaps than you have undergone, to prove to us your sincerity and your future devotion to our Order, await you.

Here they are.

Sir (*or* Madam), it is Tradition among us to mark our new BB∴ with a Seal with a hot iron upon the left arm. The esoteric paradigm which figures upon the Seal. is on one hand a discreet mark imprinted into your flesh, and on the other, an essential signature that you deposit in the very midst of the Invisible. It is the manifestation of the agreement that you bring to the constitution of a Mystical Pact with the Powers of the Unknown, animators and conductors of our Order.

In your soul as in your flesh, one last time Sir (*or* Madam), do you agree?

Neophyte

I agree!

V∴ M∴

In that case, B∴ Exp∴, please mark the Candidate on his very flesh, upon the left arm, and with the fire of the Seal of our august fraternity.

(The Exp∴ has the hot candle wax flow upon the flesh of the left arm of the Neophyte, then he presses down upon this same hot wax the flame of his Flambeau.)

V∴ M∴

Sir (*or* Madam), I congratulate you for your courage! There remains for you one final trial to surmount.

The solemn Oath that you are to take, transcribed according to ancient Custom upon vellum, must be, in order to be in a position to be projected by the Fire of the Invisible, signed in your blood.

(At this precise moment, some BB∴ pretend to sharpen knives.)

V∴ M∴

…and all Pacts, infernal or divine, were made in this manner.

Do you agree to the necessary wound which must be inflicted upon your flesh, and which will be at the same time the esoteric Promise that, if it would be necessary one far off day, you would not hesitate at all to shed it voluntarily and freely for the defense of the whole of Freemasonry?

Neophyte

I agree.

(The M∴ of C∴ goes to the Orient, takes the vellum upon which is inscribed the Oath of the Neophyte, then he returns between the Columns to rejoin the Exp∴ and the Neophyte. Here, he pricks slightly with a sterile needle the left arm of the Neophyte, just below the slight burn. He presses the small wound in order to extract a drop of blood. Then, he takes the index finger of the right hand of the Neophyte, applies it to the drop of blood, and applies this same index finger upon the vellum and affixes thereto the imprint of the Neophyte.)

V∴ M∴

Sir (*or* Madam), I congratulate you for your courage!

B∴ Exp∴, please conduct the Candidate outside of the walls and watch over him.

(The Exp∴ leaves the Lodge with the Neophyte, whom he seats upon the Parvis. He brings the Vellum into the Chamber of Reflection, and returns to wait at the Door of the Temple with the Neophyte.)

The Chastened Master

(The M∴ of C∴ prepares the L∴, he extinguishes all the lights except the Luminaries of the Order, he chooses the youngest of the AA∴ and vests them with a bloodied white shirt and a mask, then he stretches him out on the ground, a Masonic dagger across the chest, feet resting upon the first step of the Orient, arms crossed, and the head toward the Occident. He arranges two tall candelabra on either side of the head of the corpse thus represented. He arranges in a semi-circle all the BB∴, in black masks, Swords in hand, facing the Portico of the Occident. There are to be no more BB∴ upon the Columns.)

Appendix B: 1° - Apprentice

V∴ M∴

My BB∴ and SS∴, before the Candidate is introduced again into these walls, I wish to remind you that this figurative "corpse" represents not only the Chastened Master, but that, as so often in Freemasonry, it is necessary to transpose the image upon other planes. Therefore, examine what its position is.

The head is oriented toward the Occident, the arms crossed, and both feet resting upon the first step of the Orient. The corpse indicates an inverse, thus malefic, Pentacle, and may, for us, represent ADAM KADMON after his fall according to the Kabbalah.

We do not teach this second meaning to the Candidate, who will discover it at the first Ceremony of Reception in which he will assist.

B∴ Tiler, please give the sign to the B∴ Exp∴ to resume conducting the Candidate.

(The Tiler opens the Door of the Temple and gives the sign to the Exp∴ to re-enter.)

(The Exp∴ leads the Neophyte back into the Lodge, eyes still blindfolded. He places him before the Chastened Master.)

(All the BB∴ point their Swords in the direction of the Neophyte.)

V∴ M∴

(Strike of the Mallet.) •

(The Exp∴ unveils the Neophyte.)

V∴ M∴

Sir, you see right here the fatal destiny that it belongs to us to reserve to perjurers, traitors, and profaners.

(The Exp∴ re-veils the Neophyte.)

(Pause.)

V∴ M∴

If, therefore, you have decided to penetrate into our Order with any mental reservation whatsoever, we beseech you earnestly to reflect upon the gravity of the Oath that you pronounce presently, without any mental restriction.

Even if our BB∴ would forgive you, the ritual Curse, hurled in advance upon yourself, and by yourself, would not fail to set into motion the Fatal Forces, and Misfortune, Misery, Dishonor, as well as violent Death would be the sad landmarks of your terrestrial life!

Once more, Sir, reflect well upon the gravity of your promise.

B∴ Exp∴, please lead the Candidate back into the Chamber of Reflection.

Copy of the Oath

Expert

(The Exp∴ leads the Neophyte back into the Chamber of Reflection and has him write the Oath upon the Vellum.)

V∴M∴

(Strike of the Mallet.)

My BB∴, at the strike of my Mallet, the lodge is in Refreshment.

(Column of Harmony, gentle and muted music.)

(The M∴ of C∴, during this time, replaces all in order within the Lodge, and re-lights the luminaries.)

(All the BB∴ resume their places.)

The Water of Remembrance.

(The Tiler gives a sign to the V∴M∴ when the Exp∴ is ready.)

V∴M∴

(Strike of the Mallet.) •

My B∴, at the strike of my Mallet the Labors resume with Force and Vigor.

Expert

(The Exp∴ introduces the Neophyte again into the Lodge. He has him sit between the Columns, eyes still blindfolded.)

V∴M∴

Sir, since such is your will, come what may, to become a Freemason, and since it is freely that you accept the consequences of this whole esoteric Ritual upon yourself and within yourself, it appertains to you henceforth to continue your slow assimilation to the Soul of our august Fraternity.

You recently drank the Water of Forgetfulness destined to depersonalize you, to remove from you all will of your own. Here is a second cup, that of the Water of Remembrance, the Water of Mnemosyne. When you will have absorbed it, your possession will be total, absolute. The occult Soul of all Freemasonry will be passed into you. It matters not what region of the World, you will no longer make but one with all the BB∴, their affinities and their repugnances will be yours.

Just as the Water of Forgetfulness made of you a dead body and without your own will, the Water of Memory will make of you the militant Freemason, the True Child of the Widow!

Drink three times Sir (*or* Madam).

M∴ of C∴

(The M∴ of C∴ holds out a cup to the Neophyte, puts it in his right hand, and asks him to drink three times. This second cup contains an infusion of gentian.)

The Taking of the Oath

(The Exp∴ then leads the Neophyte to the Orient, facing the Altar of Oaths.)

V∴ M∴

B∴ Exp∴, I pray you, please see to it that the Candidate constantly holds his left hand armed with the ritual Dagger, the point of the blade directed upon his heart, and the right hand placed on the Compass, the Square, and the V∴ S∴ L∴, which in this R∴ L∴ is the Bible.

(Strike of the Mallet.) •

Stand and to Order, my B∴!

(All the BB∴ carry this out promptly.)

Sir, I pray you, please repeat after me, while replacing my name with your own.

I, (first and last name),[766]

In the presence of the S∴ A∴ O∴ T∴ W∴, and this Respectable Assembly of Freemasons, I promise and swear on my honor as a free man (*or* woman), solemnly and sincerely, without mental restriction of any kind, to never reveal any of the Mysteries and Secrets of Freemasonry which are going to be confided to me, except to a good and legitimate Brother, or in a regularly constituted Masonic Lodge or Triangle, to never write, trace, engrave them without the authorization of my Ultimate Superiors, nor to form any character by which the secrets of the Masonic Order may be revealed, under penalty of having my throat cut, of being dishonored, and seeing my name inscribed forever upon the Column of Infamy, while my body would be buried in the sands of the sea, so that the ebb and flow carries me into an eternal forgetfulness.

I promise and swear to henceforth consider all Freemasons as my Brothers, assist them and aid them in their needs, temporal as well as spiritual. I make this oath of Allegiance and Fidelity to the Grand Master of our Order, to the Venerable Master of the Lodge, and to all his Officers in order to preserve in my heart the Fraternity, Mutual Aid, and Solidarity owed mutually to all the Children of the Light, whose unalterable chain I have just joined today, which binds us to the Past and Future Masters. Starting from this moment, I will spread the teachings that I will have received, so that a full Light lightens the path of Men, my Brethren, and this without distinction of social class, race, color, religion, or nationality.

I will strive to be an example of all the Virtues, sacrificing beforehand every vain desire of honor, all ambitions, and all vanity. And this, not through sterile pride, but in the sole aim of inspiring in all the desire to acquire them. I will practice human Fraternity in all its extent in order to demonstrate the benefits thereof. I will be the support of the weak, the adversary of injustice, opposing myself to all unmerited violence from wherever it comes, whether towards body or soul.

And in this, may the S∴ A∴ O∴ T∴ W∴ be my aid, as well as the living Symbols that I am touching with my hand!

---

[766] The following Oath contains a few very slight differences from the one given at the beginning of the degree. I have preserved these slight variations in the translation.

(Pause.)

V∴ M∴

In the name of Universal Freemasonry, I take note of your Oath!

The Light.

(The Exp∴ conducts the Neophyte between the Columns. They remain standing.)

(The Proposer is placed discreetly behind the Neophyte.)

(The M∴ of C∴ extinguishes all the lights, with the exception of the Luminaries of the order, and places himself back at the side of the Neophyte.)

B∴ 1st Surv∴, what do you ask for the Candidate?

1st Surv∴

V∴ M∴, the Members of the Order are ready to recognize him as a B∴; they ask that the Light be given to him,

V∴ M∴

Since that is the case, let the Light be given to him at the Third Strike of my Mallet.

(3 strikes of the Mallet.) • • •

(The Proposer abruptly removes the Blindfold which covers the eyes of the Neophyte at the Third strike of the Mallet.)

(The Blazing star shines for a brief instant.)

(Column of Harmony, gentle music.)

(The M∴ of C∴, or any other B∴ charged with this duty, raises the ambient lights.)

(The M∴ of C∴ then goes to the foot of the steps of the Orient, he holds in hand the Oath as well as the Philosophical Testament of the Neophyte.)

The Projection by Fire.

V∴ M∴

My BB∴, please take your place.

(All the BB∴ carry this out promptly.)

In order for the Invisible Ether to preserve an indelible trace of the Promise made right here by the Candidate, B∴ M∴ of C∴, please project by the Fire, the Signature of the Oath and the text of his Philosophical Testament.

Indeed, the human Word fails, but what is confided to the Fire endures indefinitely!

M∴ of C∴

(The M∴ of C∴ sticks at the tip of a sword the Oath and the Philosophical Testament of the Neophyte, and enflames it at the central Candle of the Station of the Orient. He sees to it that the Oath and the Philosophical Testament are entirely consumed. Then he collects the ashes in an envelope in the name of the Neophyte.)

Expert

(The Exp∴ conducts the Neophyte before the station of the V∴ M∴, places him before the Altar of oaths, has him place his feet Squared, then has him sign the other two copies of his Oath. Then he has him raise his right hand over the Three Great Lights.)

V∴ M∴

Here are the Three Great Lights of this R∴ L∴, which have served as Sign of Support for taking your Oath.
I now give you one of the two copies of the Oath that you have just signed.

(The remaining copy will be remitted to the Secretariat of the Order.)

Investiture.

V∴ M∴

My BB∴, stand and to Order!

(All the BB∴ carry this out promptly.)

(The Exp∴ has the Neophyte kneel on the right knee.)

(The V∴ M∴ removes his gloves and takes the Flaming word in his right hand. He places it flat on the head of the Neophyte placed before the Altar of Oaths, while keeping his Mallet across his chest, and says:)

V∴ M∴

T∴ T∴ G∴ O∴ T∴ S∴ A∴ O∴ T∴ W∴! In the Name and under the Auspices of the Rite of Misraïm, by virtue of the powers which have been conferred upon me, and in the presence of this R∴ L∴ assembled of Freemasons,

(Puts the Flaming Sword upon the head of the Neophyte.)

I create, *(strike of the Mallet upon the blade of the Flaming sword.)*

Appendix B: 1° - Apprentice

(Puts the Flaming sword on the left shoulder of the Neophyte.)

Receive, *(Strike of the Mallet upon the blade of the Flaming Sword.)*

(Puts the Flaming Sword on the right shoulder of the Neophyte.)

And constitute you, *(Strike of the Mallet upon the blade of the Flaming Sword.)*

App∴ Freemason, member of this R∴L∴ assembled under the distinctive title of…, at the Orient of…

(The V∴M∴ descends from his Station and places himself, right foot to right foot, right hand on the left shoulder of the New Initiate, and gives him the Fraternal Kiss while saying:)

Receive, my B∴, this Accolade in the name of all the BB∴ here present!

(The V∴M∴ resumes his Station.)

(Pause.)

New Initiate, a short time ago you promised to reconcile yourself with your enemies, if perchance you would encounter them here.

This is the moment to carry out your promise. Behold!

(Pause.)

Our enemies are not always in front of us, they lie in wait for us, often crouched in the Darkness.

Turn around!

(At this moment the New Initiate executes the order and finds himself facing his proposer (or the M∴ of C∴ or another B∴), but he does not see the face of that one, who holds before him a mirror in which the New Initiate sees his own reflection.)

V∴M∴

Sir (*or* Madam), we have wished to make you understand that our greatest Nemesis is often within ourselves, and that it is necessary first of all to combat our own errors, prejudices, and passions.

(The Proposer then appears, and a joyous and fraternal Accolade follows.)

(The Proposer resumes his place.)

V∴M∴

Take your places, my BB∴!

(All the BB∴ carry this out promptly.)

B∴ Exp∴, please conduct our new B∴ back to the Parvis, and have him re-clothe himself, still without giving back his metals.

Expert

(The Exp∴ accompanies the new B∴ back to the Parvis, and leads him back when the latter is ready.)

(Column of Harmony, gentle music, favorable to meditation.)

(Exp∴ knocks 3 times as an Apprentice at the Door of the Temple.) • ••

V∴ M∴

Who interrupts our Labors?

Expert

(The Exp. opens the Door of the Temple a little and says:)

V∴ M∴, I come to accompany our new B∴, in order to take his place in the Temple.

V∴ M∴

Enter, my BB∴!

(The Exp∴ and the new B∴ enter the Temple.)

V∴ M∴

Halt!

B∴ Exp∴, Sir, is he really a Freemason? I see neither his Apron nor his Gloves!

Expert

Venerable Master, excuse him. It is because our new B∴ has not yet been instructed in these matters.

V∴ M∴

B∴ Expert, let our new B∴ enter, and let this fact be set always in his memory, that no one may enter into the Holy Temple who has not been purified and clothed in his Vestments of Light!

B∴ Exp∴, conduct him between the Columns, and invest him with the Apron of his Degree, and have him come to the Orient.

(The Exp∴ carries this out promptly.)

V∴ M∴

We all, we Freemasons, have an Apron. The one with which the B∴ Exp∴ has just invested you is a great symbol in itself. Its whiteness symbolizes the purity of the Initiate, purified by the Water, the Fire, and the Cup of Libations.

Appendix B: 1° - Apprentice

Why an Apron? Because a Freemason labors constantly with his Mallet and his Chisel to strip the Rough Ashlar of its unevenness in order to approach a form fitting its destination.

The bib, in the Degree of Apprentice, is raised in order to protect you from the splinters.

My B∴, it is customary in Freemasonry that those that you have just taken as BB∴ offer you two pairs of white leather Gloves.

Here are those Gloves.

One of these pairs is intended for you; your hands ought always to be clothed in Lodge in order to show the purity of your actions. The second pair you will offer to the person that you cherish the most, not for the attraction that she constitutes for your senses, but to the person who most greatly puts into concrete form, the Sister-Soul, the Ideal Person, the paragon of the Eternal Mother: the NATURA NATURANOA.

Receive also this rose, symbol of a prestigious Order, the symbolism of which is passed in our Order, in one of our High Degrees.

BB∴ Expert and M∴ of C∴, please conduct our new B∴ (or S∴) between the Columns.

(The Exp∴ and the M∴ of C∴ conducts the new B∴ between the Columns.)

V∴ M∴

B∴ 2nd Surv∴, instruct the new B∴ App∴ in the Secrets of the First Degree, and show him all this so that he may begin to labor as an App∴.

2nd Surv∴

V∴ M∴, it shall be done!

(The Exp∴ will mimic three times the Signs and Steps at the behest of the 2nd Surv∴.)

2nd Surv∴

My B∴ App∴, you see here the Mosaic Pavement, our Sacred Altar. Once I have instructed you in the Secrets of this degree, then you may carry out your First labor as App∴.

My B∴, here is the Sign of App∴ Mason.

First: to come to Order in a Lodge of App∴, is to stand upright, feet Squared, and holding the right hand flat upon the throat, the four fingers together and the thumb separated so that the right hand makes the figure of a Square.

Second: the Guttural Sign, is to come to Order, then draw back the hand horizontally with a swift gesture, as if cutting one's throat, and letting the hand fall along the body. This Sign is an allusion to the penalty of your Oath if it would come to be transgressed, and it signifies that as a Man of Honor and a Freemason, you should prefer to have your throat cut rather than reveal unduly the Secrets which have just been confided to you. Furthermore, this Guttural Sign shows that the Apprentice is not in a state to speak and that he is to respect the Sacred Law of Silence until, by his work and his obedience, his peers judge him worthy of an increase of salary and have him pass to the Grade of Comp∴. By putting his hand on his throat, thus in a Square, he stops the bubbling up of the ideas which come to him from the body, so that he may better listen, having a cool head and clear thoughts. For even a Master Mason is subject to this Sign in a Lodge of App∴, and when he addresses the Lodge, his ideas are clear, and he does not speak to say nothing!

Third: my B∴, is the Steps of the App∴. We, the V∴M∴ and your BB∴ of this R∴L∴, have allowed you to walk freely twice. There cannot be third time. You must henceforth always place yourself to Order, and always while saluting the Three Lights. This will be explained to you afterward in our Oral Tradition. However, before having you leave, you must place yourself between the Columns and make Three Small Steps, Squared, always by setting out left foot first.

Like this…

Expert
(The Exp∴ executes the steps, imitated by the new App∴.)

V∴M∴, my mission is accomplished.

V∴M∴
My B∴ Exp∴, I thank you.

My B∴ new App∴, it remains to me to instruct you on the Words and Tokens. B∴ 2nd Surv∴, please communicate to our new App∴ the Sacred Word and the Grip.

2nd Surv∴
V∴M∴, this shall be done!

(The Exp∴ conducts the new App∴ to the Station of the 2nd Surv∴.)

(The 2nd Surv∴ adds the gesture to the words.)

2nd Surv∴
My B∴ App∴, the Grip is given by pressing each other's hand with the thumb, giving three short pressures on the first phalanx of the index finger, like this…

This grip makes up part of our Tradition. Furthermore, the request of the Sacred Word also makes up part of our Oral Tradition.

B∴ new App∴, give me your hand; and you, B∴ Exp∴, whisper the responses to our new B∴.

(The 2nd Surv∴ takes the hand of the new App∴ and says:)

My B∴, please give me the Sacred Word.

App∴

My B∴, I can neither read nor write, but I will spell it willingly with you.

2ⁿᵈ Surv∴

B.

App∴

O.

2ⁿᵈ Surv∴

A.

App∴

Z.

2ⁿᵈ Surv∴

BOAZ!

App∴

BOAZ!

2ⁿᵈ Surv∴

The Sacred Word is therefore BOAZ, which corresponds to the black Column of the AA∴ of the Temple of King Solomon.

V∴ M∴, the instruction of our new App∴ is concluded.

V∴ M∴

I thank you, B∴ 2ⁿᵈ Surv∴.

B∴ Exp∴, ritually conduct the new App∴ to the Altar of Oaths, so that he may carry out his First Labor of the App∴.

(The Exp∴ leads the New App∴ to the foot of the Altar of Oaths. He has him kneel on the right knee, puts the Mallet in his right hand and the Chisel in his left. He has him strike three times upon the Rough Ashlar.)

Exp∴

V∴ M∴, the First Labor of the App∴ has been carried out by our new App∴!

(The Exp∴ has the New App∴ rise and has him come to Order.)

V∴ M∴

I thank you, B∴ Exp∴.

Now, my B∴ App∴, there is an envelope that the B∴ Exp∴ is going to give you, filled with the ashes of your Philosophical Testament and your Oath marked with your blood. These ashes will be your strength or your ruin! Your strength as a true Talisman, if you are faithful and loyal to your Oaths taken on the Three Great Lights. Your ruin if you betray yourself!

Know too, B∴ App∴, that to each Degree corresponds a symbolic Age, and that the age of the App∴ is Three Years. Three because you have been initiated into the First Three Numbers, these three points forming a Triangle. But all this will be explained to you afterward. So then…

B∴ Hosp∴, bring now the Widow's Trunk to our new B∴, so that he may deposit his obolus for the poor.

And you, our new B∴, do not forget that you are subject to the Law of Silence!

(The Hosp∴ ritually approaches the new B∴, visibly very uneasy, for he has been divested of all his metals (money) before entering the Temple.)

V∴ M∴

Why, my B∴, will you not make this small gesture?

(Expression of the App∴ visibly very uneasy.)

V∴ M∴

It is true that you have been divested of all your metals.

However, I congratulate you for the good intentions that you have just expressed. Believe truly that this trial has not at all been introduced to mock your sentiments.

Far from us is such intention! It has been conceived for three particular reasons:

First: to put your principles to the text.

Second: to demonstrate to the BB∴ that you have neither metals nor valuables on you, for if it had been otherwise, the Ceremony of Reception would have had to be repeated!

Third: as an admonishment to your Heart, so that, if you would recognize one day a B∴ in distress, and who would solicit your assistance, you would remember your Reception into Freemasonry, poor, stripped of everything, and would thus seize the opportunity to practice with regards to him this Virtue that you so admire this day that I have called Charity.

B∴ Exp∴, please accompany our new App∴ to the place which will henceforth be his, and you, B∴ Hosp∴. I thank you, you may resume your Station.

(The Exp∴ accompanies the New App∴ to the first place of the column of the North, then he resumes his Station and takes his place.)

(The Hosp∴ resumes his Station and takes his place.)

(The M∴ of C∴ resumes his Station and takes his place.)

V∴ M∴

My B∴ Orator, you have the floor!

Orator

(Gives a discourse of welcome.)

V∴ M∴

My BB∴, the Order of the day being exhausted, we are now going to ritually close our Labors and then find ourselves again upon the Parvis of the Temple in order to cement our new Fraternity by fraternal Agapes.

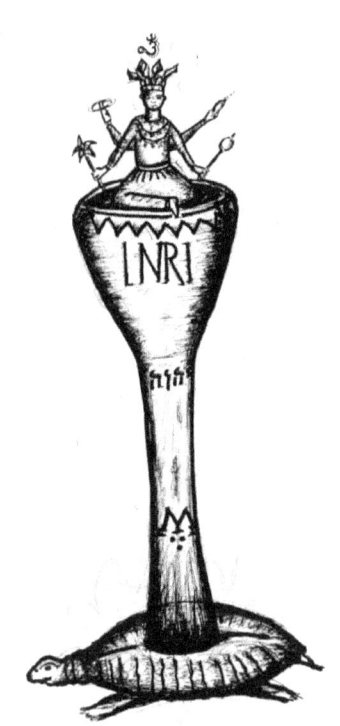

Closing of the Works in a Lodge of Apprentices of the Rite of Misraïm

V∴ M∴

Now, my BB∴, we are going to ritually close our Labors! If any B∴ who labor in this Temple of Wisdom have any propositions to make in the interest of our Venerated Order in general, or of this R∴ L∴ in particular, let them know that forthwith, they have full liberty to request the floor from their Surv∴, and that at their request, it shall be accorded to them.

(The floor is given to the BB∴ of the R∴ L∴ as well as to the Visiting BB∴.)

(If any App∴ requests the floor, the 2nd Surv∴ will be his interpreter to this end; the App∴ will have taken care to give him a written note before the Opening of the Works.)

1st Surv∴

V∴ M∴, the Columns are silent!

(If Visiting BB∴ are present…)

V∴ M∴

My BB∴ Visitors, I ask you to be willing to transmit to your V∴ M∴, to the OFF∴, and to all your BB∴ our most fraternal salutations, and to tell them how great our joy has been to receive you!

B∴ M∴ of C∴, please have circulate among the Columns, according to the traditional Order, the Bag of Proposition.

If any BB∴ desires to make a written and reserved proposition, they have the possibility of depositing it into this Bag.

(The M∴ of C∴ first presents the Bag of Propositions to the Orient. By contrast, this same Bag of Propositions is never presented to the Visiting BB∴. Once this is accomplished, the M∴ of C∴ returns between the Columns.)

M∴ of C∴

V∴ M∴, the Bag of Propositions is at your disposal between the Columns.

V∴ M∴

B∴ M∴ of C∴, please bring it to me.

(The M∴ of C∴ goes to the orient and presents the Bag of Propositions to the V∴ M∴.)

(If the Bag of Propositions returns empty, the V∴ M∴ says:)

V∴ M∴

The Bag of Propositions has returned free and without attachment.

(If the Bag of propositions returns with one or several Propositions, the Venerable Master says:)

Appendix B: 1° - Apprentice

The Bag of Propositions has returned bearing X Propositions, which will be examined later (*or* which will be read immediately to the Workshop).

B∴ Hosp∴, please take the Widow's Trunk and let each B∴ make an offering according to his possibilities for h BB∴ in difficulty.

The B∴ Exp∴ will accompany you, Sword in hand, among the Columns.

(The Hosp∴ and the Exp∴ carry out the orders of the V∴M∴, and return between the Columns.)

(The M∴ of C∴ resumes his Station.)

Hosp∴
V∴M∴, the Widow's Trunk is at your disposal between the Columns.

V∴M∴
B∴ Hosp∴, please deposit it at the Station of the B∴ Orator.

(The Hosp∴ and the Exp∴ go to the Station of the Orator, and they count together the sum total of the gifts received.)

Orator
V∴M∴, the Widow's Trunk has returned ballasted with X fragments of Osiris, to be vested in Works of Benevolence.

V∴M∴
The Orient thanks the Columns for the Fraternity expressed.

(The Hosp∴ and Exp∴ resume their stations and take their place.)

V∴M∴
B∴ Or∴, please now bring us the philosophical conclusion of the Works of Sacred Masonry that this Temple of Wisdom accomplished today, and draw therefrom suggestions for our actions when we will have emerged from this place illuminated by the S∴A∴O∴T∴W∴.

(The Or∴ rises, comes to Order, and lays out his conclusions and takes his place.)

V∴M∴
We thank the B∴ Or∴ for having thus laid out the happy Synthesis of our labors and our Amelioration.
B∴ 1st Surv∴, to what aim labors the Rite of Misraïm?

1st Surv∴
V∴M∴, they are the continuation of the Ancient Mysteries of the Sacred Builders of the Initiatic Temples of the Perfect Temple, the Great Pyramid.

Our ancient BB∴ learned to build within themselves the Ideal Temple of the Spirit-Man; Temple built in Heaven and on Earth. After which, they built the Fraternal Temple of Wisdom on Earth and the Temple of Truth-Justice in Heaven.

They followed, according to the classes of perfection, a severe asceticism which brought them to discover the Cornerstone within themselves, and within the Universal and Cosmic Work, the same Cornerstone.

They know indeed that a Master who has built within his soul the architectural image of the Temple according to the perfection and: the measures that only the S∴A∴O∴T∴W∴ suggests after much effort and prayer, would have known valiantly how to build a Sacred Temple in a traditional fashion, at the traditional point and at the traditional moment, in order to bring the Tradition to the Men of Good Will. It is still there today, our aim to safeguard the universal equilibrium.

V∴M∴
B∴ 1st Surv∴, how is this accomplished?

1st Surv∴
V∴M∴, by practicing the Cult of the S∴A∴O∴T∴W∴, through Rites and Symbols at traditional Times.

V∴M∴
BB∴ 1st and 2nd Surv∴, have we fol1lowed this today?

1st Surv∴
V∴M∴, the BB∴ who decorate the Column of the South have labored with Prudence under the Compass.

2nd Surv∴
V∴M∴, the BB∴ who decorate the Column of the North have labored with Profit under the Square.

V∴M∴
Likewise, the BB∴ who are in the Orient have labored with Wisdom under the Acacia and the Lotus.

B∴ 1st Surv∴, at what period of the daily degree of the sun do the BB∴ A∴ Freemasons labor according to the Oriental, Ancient, and Primitive Duties in the Temple of Wisdom?

1st Surv∴
From Midday to Midnight, V∴M∴!

V∴M∴
(Strike of the Mallet.)

Stand and to Order, my BB∴, facing the Orient! We are going to suspend the Labors.

Appendix B: 1° - Apprentice

(All the BB∴ carry this out promptly.)

V∴ M∴

B∴ Tiler, where stands the 2nd Surv∴?

Tiler

At the corner of the Column of the South, V∴ M∴.

V∴ M∴

Why, my B∴?

Tiler

V∴ M∴, to see good order reign, and to be certain that all has been well conducted, with order and exactitude.

V∴ M∴

B∴ Exp∴, why is the V∴ M∴ seated at the Orient?

Expert

V∴ M∴, in order to illuminate the Lodge, particularly at the time of its Closing.

V∴ M∴

B∴ 2nd Surv∴, what time is it?

2nd Surv∴

V∴ M∴, it is Midnight. The sun is at its Meridian, opposed to the Nadir of this Temple.

V∴ M∴

Since the sun is at its Meridian, opposed to the Nadir, and since it is therefore time to suspend our Labors, assist me, my BB∴ and SS∴.

(The Tiler goes to the Orient, and the V∴ M∴ gives him the Kiss of Peace, which he is then going to give to the 1st Surv∴.)

(The 1st Surv∴ places himself near the 2nd Surv∴ and transmits to him the Kiss of Peace, and resumes his Station.)

(The V∴ M∴ raises his arms in the Egyptian Rite and says:)

V∴ M∴

May the Illumination of the S∴ A∴ O∴ T∴ W∴ descend upon you my BB∴!

May physical, mental, and spiritual health descend upon you and remain within you, from the Sacred Center from where is manifested the S∴ A∴ O∴ T∴ W∴.

Amen!

Receive well, dear BB∴, my cordial and fraternal salutations! My BB∴, please now form the Chain of Sacred Union.

(All the BB∴ remove their gloves and form the Chain of Sacred Union.)

The Chain of Sacred Union.

V∴ M∴

This Chain unites us beyond Space and Time. The World of appearances holds our hearts prisoner in this Temple where our arms are enlaced. But our spirits are free beyond these walls, beyond any borders and beyond any seas. Midnight has just sounded! BB∴ visible and invisible, present in body or thought, we will keep watch together over the sleep of Men. BB∴ who hear me, you are the Guardians of a very ancient Secret which is kindled in the fraternal heart of Humanity in its cradle. There is but one Love, that of the Living and that of the Dead; that of Labor, and that of Beauty; that of Men, and that of Women; that of Nature and that of the Cosmos! In the World where reigns matter, strength, and falsehood, we take the Oath to always maintain luminous and upright the Flame of the Unique Love of the Human Spirit!

Let us leave the Chain, my BB∴; our hearts remain united.

(The BB∴ leave the Chain of Union by shaking the arms three times, they fulfill one complete circuit around the Altar of the Naos, without marking the corners, put their gloves back on, resume their respective places, and seat themselves.)

(The M∴ of C∴ goes to the Altar of the Naos and disentwines the Square, Compass, and Rule, and resumes his Station.)

(The Exp∴ goes to the Altar of Oaths, closes the V∴S∴L∴ and disentwines the Square and Compass and resumes his Station.)

V∴ M∴

Stand and to Order my BB∴, face the Orient!

(All the BB∴ carry this out promptly.)

V∴ M∴

We are going to form the Procession in order to close the Gates between the Temple of Wisdom and the Temple of Truth-Justice.

With me, BB∴ of the Orient!

With us, B∴ 1st Surv∴ and his Column! With us, B∴ 2nd Surv∴ and his Column!

(The M∴ of C∴ remains alone at the Altar of the Naos and extinguishes the Flambeaux according to the order hereafter.)

(The Procession conducted by the V∴M∴ goes to the station of the 2nd Surv∴.)

Appendix B: 1° - Apprentice

V∴ M∴

O! Invisible Powers of the Divine Light who pour forth Beauty, we bear witness for this Work accomplished in Harmony, Beauty, and Charity!

We close this Gate to the Glory of the S∴ A∴ O∴ T∴ W∴!

(The V∴ M∴, upon these final words, extinguishes the Flambeau of the station of the 2nd Surv∴.)

(The M∴ of C∴ extinguishes, at the same time as the V∴ M∴, the "Beauty" Flambeau.)

(The Procession conducted by the V∴ M∴ goes then to the station of the 1st Surv∴.)

V∴ M∴

O! Invisible Powers of the Divine Light who pour forth Strength and Energy upon those who labor in the Temple of Wisdom, we bear witness for having assisted us in this Work accomplished in Strength, Power, and Order!

We close this Gate to the Glory of the S∴ A∴ O∴ T∴ W∴!

(The V∴ M∴, upon these final words, extinguishes the Flambeau of the Station of the 1st Surv∴.)

(The M∴ of C∴ extinguishes, at the same time as the V∴ M∴, the "Strength" Flambeau.)

(The Procession conducted by the V∴ M∴ then goes to the Station of the V∴ M∴.)

V∴ M∴

O! Invisible Powers of the Divine Light who pours forth Wisdom in union with the Seat of the Supreme Wisdom, we bear witness to you for having led to a good end this Work predisposed by the Supreme Wisdom and First Love!

We close this Gate to the Glory of the S∴ A∴ O∴ T∴ W∴!

(The V∴ M∴, upon these final words, extinguishes the Flambeau of his station.)

(The M∴ of C∴ extinguishes, at the same time as the V∴ M∴, the "Wisdom" Flambeau.)

(The Procession accomplishes a third circuit in the inverse direction (counterclockwise).)

(Then all the BB∴ resume their respective places.)

(The Or∴, once at his Station, extinguishes his Flambeau.)

(The Sec∴, once at his Station, extinguishes his Flambeau.)

V∴ M∴

Take your place, my BB∴!

(All the BB∴ carry this out promptly.)

V∴M∴

B∴ 1st Surv∴, what is your Duty at this moment?

1st Surv∴

V∴M∴, it is to assure myself that all the BB∴ are ready to close this R∴L∴ of App∴.

V∴M∴

B∴ 1st Surv∴, accomplish your duty!

(The 1st Surv∴ rises and attentively examines the Columns and sits down again.)

1st Surv∴

V∴M∴, all the BB∴ and all the SS∴ are ready for the Closing of the R∴L∴.

V∴M∴

(Strike of the Mallet.) •

Stand and to Order, my BB∴, face the Orient!

(All the BB∴ carry this out promptly.)

(The V∴M∴ removes his gloves and takes up the Flaming Sword in his left hand, the cross held by the Master's Claw, the blade vertical, the pommel resting upon the table.)

V∴M∴

(Strikes of the Mallet.) • ••

1st Surv∴

(Strikes of the Mallet.) • ••

2nd Surv∴

(Strikes of the Mallet.) • ••

V∴M∴

T∴T∴G∴O∴T∴S∴A∴O∴T∴W∴!
Lord of the Sacred Ennead of Egypt!

In the Name and under the Auspices of the Rite of Misraïm; by virtue of the Powers which have been conferred upon me; I declare suspended the Labors of this R∴L∴ established under the distinct title of…, at the Orient of…, at the secret geographical point known only to the Sons of the Light!

Appendix B: 1° - Apprentice

(The V∴M∴ replaces the Flaming Sword and the Mallet. He puts his gloves back on and comes to Order.)

V∴M∴

With me, my BB∴, by the Sign, the Battery, and the Acclamation!

All

(All make the Sign.)

(All strike the Battery.) • ••

(All issue the Acclamation:) Alleluia! Alleluia! Alleluia!

(All the BB∴ come to Order.)

V∴M∴

My BB∴, the Labors are suspended!

Let us separate under the Law of Silence!

(All the BB∴ remove their gloves, salute by holding out their arms straight, and say:)

All

We swear it!

(All the BB∴ re-glove.)

(Column of Harmony, gentle music.)

(The exit is carried out in this order:
- *The V∴M∴,*
- *the BB∴ of the Orient,*
- *the 1st Surv∴,*
- *the 2nd Surv∴,*
- *the other Off∴ of the L∴ with the exception of the M∴ of C∴,*
- *the MM∴,*
- *the CC∴,*
- *the AA∴,*
- *the M∴ of C∴.)*

(The exit is carried out without coming to Order, nor with the Steps of the App∴, but while respecting the sense of rotation around the Altar of the Naos, that is to say clockwise.)

Instruction of the Apprentice in the 1st Symbolic Degree

To each Masonic grade is attached an instruction by question and response. The questions are posed in a manner to stimulate reflection.

The Brother ought to strive to respond according to logic and not to content itself with simply retaining the conventional responses.

Certain of these responses, during the tiling, must be given textually. We have written them in CAPITAL LETTERS.

CATECHISM

Q. What is there common between you and me?

A. FREEMASONRY.

Q. What is Freemasonry?

A. It is a universal alliance, humanitarian and philosophical institution, which has as its aim the intellectual and moral perfecting of humanity.

Q. Is Freemasonry a religion?

A. It is not a religion in the strict sense of the word. However, it has as its essential basis the belief in a supreme power, expressed and invoked under the name of the Sublime Architect of the Worlds (or Great Architect of the Universe).[767] By this fact, better than any other institution, it has for effect to REBIND the Beings between them, from the Latin *religare*, to rebind, in the broadest and most elevated sense of the term.

Q. Are you a Freemason of Egypt?

A. My Brothers recognize me as such.

Q. Why do you respond thus?

A. Because an Apprentice Mason ought to be suspicious of himself and fear bringing judgment before having appealed to the lights of his Brothers.

Q. What is a Mason?

A. It is a woman or a man "born free" and of good morals, equally friend of the rich and the poor if they are virtuous.

Q. What do you mean by "born Free"?

A. The Woman or Man born Free is the one who, after being dead to the prejudices of the vulgar, has seen himself reborn to the new life that Initiation confers.

Q. Why do you say that a Mason is equally a friend of the rich and the poor if they are virtuous?

A. In order to point out that individual worth ought to be appreciated by reason of moral qualities. Esteem ought to be measured only according to the steadfastness and energy that the woman or man brings to the realization of the good.

Q. What are the duties of the Mason?

A. To flee vice and practice virtue.

---

[767] The term "Sublime Architect" is, in some rituals, replace with "Supreme Architect." Sometimes the two terms seem to be used interchangeably within the same ceremony, which is likely due to the compiler of the ritual drawing from multiple sources without reconciling the one to the other.

Appendix B: 1° - Apprentice

Q. How ought a Mason practice virtue?

A. By preferring Justice and Truth to all things.

Q. Where were you received a Mason?

A. In a Lodge, just and perfect.

Q. What is necessary for a Lodge to be Just and Perfect?

A. Three direct it, five enlighten it, seven make it just and perfect.

Q. Explain this response.

A. The Three are the Venerable Master and the two Surveillants. These Officers with the Orator and the Secretary are the Five Lights of the Lodge. But it is necessary for at least seven members of the Lodge to gather to be able to proceed with regular Initiations. The Lodge alone possess the fullness of Masonic Sovereignty.

Q. How long have you been a Freemason?

A. Since I have received the light.

Q. What does this response signify?

A. That we really only become Masons beginning from the day when our spirit has been opened by study, to the intelligence of the Masonic mysteries.

Q. By what shall I recognize that you are a Mason?

A. By my signs, my words, and my tokens.

Q. How do you interpret this response?

A. A Mason is recognized by his manner of action, ever equitable and sincere (Signs); by his loyal and sincere language (Words); and finally, by the fraternal solicitude that he manifests for those to whom he is attached by the bonds of solidarity (Grips, Tokens).

Q. How are the Signs of the Masons made?

A. By the Square, the level, and the Perpendicular.

Q. Explain this response.

A. The Mason, in his actions, ought to be inspired by ideas of equity (Square), he ought to aim at levelling arbitrary inequalities (Level) and to contribute, finally, to ceaselessly elevating the social level (Perpendicular).

Q. Give me the Sign.

A. (It is given.)

Q. What does this Sign signify?

A. That I would prefer to have my throat cut rather than to reveal the secrets which have been confided to me.

Q. Does this Sign have any other significations?

A. The right hand, placed in a square upon the throat appears to contain the bubbling up of the passions which are stirred up in the chest and thus preserves the head from any feverish exaltation, susceptible to compromising our lucidity of spirit. The Sign of the Apprentice signifies this point of view: I am in possession of myself and I apply myself to judging everything with impartiality.

Q. Give me the Sacred Word.

A. I can neither read nor write, I can only spell. Tell me the first letter, I will tell you the second.

Q. Why do you say, "I can neither read nor write"? To what does your ignorance correspond?

A. To the emblematic language employed by Freemasonry. The meaning is discerned only progressively, and the Initiate, at the beginning of his career, spells with difficulty what later will be for him the object of a current lecture.

Q. B.

A. O.

Q. A.

A. Z.

(Together) BOAZ!

Q. What does this word signify?

A. The Sacred Word is therefore BOAZ, which corresponds to the Column of our AA∴ of the Temple of Solomon.

Q. What does the manner of spelling the Sacred Word indicate to you?

A. The method of teaching of Freemasonry, which solicits the intellectual efforts of each, all while avoiding the inculcation of dogmas. The Neophyte is placed upon the Path of Truth by symbolically giving him the first letter of the word, which he must find himself, then point him to the second, so that he predicts the following, and so on.

Q. What do they call SALARY in Masonry?

A. It is the recompense of the labor, the result that it produces.

Q. Have you received your salary?

A. I am satisfied!

Q. Where did you receive your salary?

A. At the Column "B"

Q. By what is the salary of the Masons conveyed?

A. By a gradual perfecting of oneself.

Q. What is the shape of your Lodge?

A. An oblong square.

Q. In what direction is its length?

A. From the Orient to the Occident.

Q. Its breadth?

A. From the South to the North.

Q. Its height?

A. From the Zenith to the Nadir.

Q. What do these dimensions mean?

A. That Freemasonry is Universal.

Q. Why is your Lodge situated from Orient to Occident?

A. It is oriented, as all the old sacred edifices of Ancient Egypt, in order to recall that Masonry indicates to its adepts the direction whence comes the Light.

Q. What do you mean by the word "Lodge"?

A. It is the NAOS which serves as shelter to the Masons in order to cover their labors.

Q. What do you mean by Naos?

A. It is the secret place of the Temples of Ancient Egypt.

Q. What is it that supports your Lodge?

A. Three Columns that we call: WISDOM, STRENGTH, and BEAUTY.

Appendix B: 1° - Apprentice

Q. How may these allegorical columns support your lodge?

A. WISDOM CONCEIVES, STRENGTH EXECUTES, and BEAUTY ADORNS.

Q. Why were you received a Freemason?

A. Because I was in darkness and I desired the Light.

Q. In what state were you when they proceeded with your Initiation?

A. NEITHER NAKED, NOR CLOTHED, but in a decent state, deprived of the use of sight and divested of all metals.

Q. Why in this state?

A. To recall that virtue has no need of adornments. The right knee bare, to indicate the sentiments of humanity which ought to preside in the pursuit of Truth. The left foot bare by respect for a place which is Holy, because we seek the truth there. Deprived of the use of sight, in order to indicate the ignorance of the Neophyte, still deprived of the Light that will bring him instruction, without which he remains plunged in darkness. Divested of all metals, as proof of disinterestedness, and to teach to deprive oneself of all that may harm our perfecting.

Q. How were you introduced in Lodge?

A. While lowering my head and bending myself over, in the sign of new birth.

Q. And after?

A. After various trials and by the consent of my Sisters and Brothers, the Master of the Lodge received me a Mason.

Q. In what consist the Secrets of the Order?

A. In the knowledge of abstract truths, of which the Masonic symbolism is the sensible translation.

Q. Where stands the V∴ M∴ ?

A. AT THE ORIENT.

Q. Where stand the Surveillants?

A. At the Occident in order to aid the Venerable Master, to pay the workers, and to discharge them.

Q. Where stand the Apprentices?

A. In the North, which represents the least enlightened region, because they have received only an elementary instruction in Masonry, and consequently, they are not in a state to withstand too much daylight.

Q. At what hour do the Masons open and close their Labors?

A. Allegorically, the labors open at midday and are closed at midnight.

Q. What do these conventional hours signify?

A. They indicate that the woman or man reaches the middle of one's career, the Midday of one's life, before being able to be useful to one's fellow men and women; but that from this instant until his last, he ought to labor relentlessly toward the common good.

Q. What does the custom of being informed of the hour before acting teach us?

A. Action is useful only if it comes at the right moment. The conquests of progress are accomplished only in their time. By showing oneself too impatient, one risks having what is on the path of preparation fail. It is necessary to know how to await the psychological moment, to act too soon or too late leads equally to failure.

Q. How old are you?

A. THREE YEARS.

Q. What does this response signify?

A. To be informed of the Masonic age of a Sister or Brother, is to ask him his grade.

Q. To what do the Apprentices labor?

A. To polish the rough ashlar, in order to strip it of its roughness and to approach a form suitable to its destination.

Q. What, then, is this rough ashlar?

A. It is the coarse product of nature, that the art must polish and transform.

Q. What are the Tools of the Apprentice?

A. The Chisel, the Mallet, and the Lever.

Q. What do they represent?

A. The Chisel represents discernment in investigation; the Mallet, the will in application; the Lever, the human intelligence which can multiply energy.

Q. What do the steps of the Apprentice signify?

A. The zeal that we are to show by walking toward the one who enlightens us.

Q. Have you any ambition?

A. Only one, I aspire to the honor of being received among the "Companions."

1° Piece of Architecture

ONE'S FIRST INITIATION INTO FREEMASONRY, NO MATTER THE Obedience, is a unique opportunity for enlightenment. Like all initiation, it is an *opportunity*, not a guarantee. Freemasonry's particular method is rather unique, however, and stands erect throughout the past few centuries as a testament to the enduring nature of the Ancient Mysteries, the continuation of a living philosophy, and the capability of men and women of various stripes to join together in a fraternal embrace of virtue. One of the single most elevating aspects of Masonry is the ideal that some branches live up to which is that of a society that does not distinguish between men or women, no matter their social class, nationality, ethnicity, race, religious persuasion, sexual orientation, or otherwise.

A key *feeling* that the initiate of Memphis+Misraïm will experience in the fully fleshed out 1st degree, is that of binding. Symbolized in some ways by how he is duly and truly prepared to receive the degrees, the new Mason senses that he is deeply bound to the brotherhood in a manner unlike any he has previously experienced. The new Mason feels himself suddenly continuous with a body made up of hundreds of thousands of members across time and space; he feels himself to be a true member of the human collectivity, operating in some mysterious way with the universal cause and intelligence inherent in reality.

It is in the symbols of Freemasonry that the apprentice finds he is truly "entered." Far beyond emblems for teaching the basics of morality, the rich symbolism of the APRM+M is a living, breathing experience of the spirit. The apprentice is presented with an array of symbols in this first degree, all of which have their *double* on the inner planes which are revealed through meditation and scrying, especially as developed in our second echelon of working. A few, however, will no doubt bring about the bridging of the conscious and subconscious mind through the initiatory process and by virtue of suspending the primary sense of modern man: the vision.

† † †

From the opening onwards, the Entered Apprentice experiences the mystery of *transmission*. Transmission is the sacred key of our work; we are transmitting the word, the grip, the token, the sign, the steps...the Tradition altogether, to the newly initiated. Being introduced and brought into the Masonic egregore is something that one may not immediately feel unless he is hypersensitive. There is a Masonic consciousness. The Rites of Memphis+Misraïm access this consciousness regularly, whether in a simple meeting of a Triangle, or in a full Lodge with scheduled initiations. A sense of something wholly "other" pervades the work of Egyptian Masonry and is inescapable from the first degree onwards.

As the candles are ceremoniously lit in conjunction with the sacred wording of old, particular gates are opened. This formula is ancient; it is a gift from the land of Khem. It may not be readily perceived in this first echelon, but it is here that it is carved into the ethers. In the Rites of M+M, the primary Officers *become* their orientations, their cardinal directions. It is through their mediation that the energies from these directions are allowed to flow. The Officer *is* the gate. The Officer *is* the spirit invoked. The Officer *is* the power, momentarily, of the "Ennead of Egypt," or one of the nine sacred gods of Heliopolis.

In M+M, the initiate begins his journey in the Kingdom of the Dead, otherwise known as Amenti in Egyptian lore, which is symbolized by the Chamber of Reflection, after he writes his Philosophical Testament. The occult light that is brought to the candidate during this *trial of earth* is a glimmer of the ineffable light. He enters the Lodge proper in a stooping manner, which far from simply being emblematic of the candidate's humility is a symbol of palingenesis—the way of return to the womb, the premier moment of rebirth.

This is a playing out of the Gnostic's remembering of his divine seed; this is the Coën's "way of Return." It also alludes, in the third echelon, to the *Grand Rite of Osirification*. The true nature of this transmutation is revealed in the grades of the *Arcana Arcanorum* (Naples Arrangement, Venice 1788), the 95°, and hinted at throughout the hermetic and Kabalistic traditions.

When the candidate partakes of the magical philter, the "draught of forgetfulness," he makes a sort of pact with the Egregore which has lasting effects. Having had many opportunities to turn back and recede into normal wake-a-day existence, he is now faced with the realities of true initiation. It will take a thorough purification, a cleansing of the outer and the inner man to complete this act in the second libation: the water of Mnemosyne. The wording that accompanies this sacrament is serious and demanding. The hoodwinked candidate can do nothing more than blindly acquiesce to the experience if he be courageous enough. It will not be the last of such serious trials.

The purification of water is a simple affair and will remind the candidate of an experience in Martinism, if he be of that persuasion, and of the Egyptian Rite of Cagliostro, if he be a student of Masonry. Yet, in its simplicity, this action again has effects on the other side. This is the first action where the candidate is said to have been given permission to proceed from the guardian of the pylon. He is given the name of Mundus in this act and encouraged to proceed to the trial of air. The three actions of purification completing the act of purification by air, again return us to the Divine Cagliostro.

The intellect is opened unto the mysteries of Masonry in the singular act of purification by air. The passions may have been the primary drivers of the chariot thus far, but now it is to the mind—and more particularly to the *nous* as the Greeks termed it—that all action will be referred. The Platonists teach of the realm of ideas; this same realm becomes tangible and relatable when this experience fully takes in the second and third echelons.

The purification of fire is the most impressive of the four elements within the Lodge setting. It is impressive, not because of the action in the rubrics but because of the *nature* of the purification. Harkening back to the Chaldean Oracles and otherwise, the purification by fire becomes more of a *consecration*, enlivening the "central axis-fire" of the Élus Coëns within the worthy candidate. It is to the divine principle within that this action is referred and the candidate who is awake to Otherwhere will sense a quickening at this moment and the subsequent actions which are not only heavy in their allusions, but which recall a time when the initiations were truly ordeals of the body, mind, and spirit.

The "seal" and the "mark" which accompany this initiation are mystical, magical operations of the highest and most exalted nature. Their actions are written upon the eternal; the sacrifices accomplished are accrued and taken account of unto the infinite. The act of transferring the mark to the oath is nothing short of a classical, grimoiric pact between the candidate and the powers invoked in the degree. The Coëns have an analogue to the seal and mark which those of the CHENU Order will recognize in their IVth and Vth degree workings.

The "chastened Master" is a macabre experience in the first degree of French Freemasonry and that of the APRM+M. It is a lived experience of the Death card of the Tarot and connects, immediately, the first degree with the third. Beyond all of the significations of the Tarot card, this experience reveals to the Apprentice (after he has studied the degree in full) a symbol of maleficence formed of the body of the chastened Master. It is a symbol of the Fall; it is a mark of the Demiurge, the jealous and angry God of the Old Testament. A ritual curse is enacted in this moment—yet another memento of the religion of the Nile.

The survival of the previous trial leads the candidate directly to the font of Mnemosyne. The three draughts of this philter transmit the entirety of the tradition, secretly, to the candidate. He is introduced to the occult soul of the Order in this sacrament: the Egregore itself. He may not perceive the power of this moment or understand the import of the operation, but the act will have its consequence.

The mystical "bringing to Light," which reveals to the Candidate for the first time the *Sacred Doctrine* arises in all of its mystique and glory and this juncture of the work. It is said that during this "mystical shock" the *blazing star shines for a moment*. This is an internal experience, as well as an external one, that will not be readily forgotten, and which connects mystically to the 95° and advanced æonology. The encounter with "The Light" will grow within the Candidate over time if he continues his labors into the second and third echelons. The previous question throughout history of whether or not Masonry is a religious practice becomes rather absurd in this moment in time, as there is no other word for the experience beyond the Latin *religare,* which literally means "to tie, or to bind."

The next moment of transmutation comes when the oath and the Philosophical Testament of the candidate are projected into the invisible. This sole action, this occult transference of word, blood, idea, and promise to the immortal flame, is of such caliber that none living may revoke its action. One may renounce his Masonry; yet he is forever a Mason. One may reject the universal brotherhood; yet he remains a member of the stream of antiquity. One may lapse into forgetfulness again; yet his soul yearns for reintegration into unity. This Projection by Fire completes the sacred doctrine brought about during the bringing to Light with the investiture and constitution of the Mason, an action that moves beyond the Chivalric to the inner dimensions of the Templar.

The enemies of the soul are aplenty. When the individual decides to take that first step into Masonry, especially into esoteric Masonry, he should expect the forces of good to fly to his side along with the beginnings of a war with the darkness. One of the primary initiatory moments is the realization of the subtlety of the enemy. The enemy will often appear as an angel of light. When the candidate is made to turn around and face this most subtle of enemies, an opportunity for quickening ensues. What we have clung to, tooth and nail, fighting for its elevation, its solidification, its crystallization, its ossification—is revealed to be ghostly, spirituous, and fleeting. The enemy that we've identified our deepest selves with must be sacrificed via kenosis.

A host of cogent, powerful symbols are jam-packed into the remaining moments of the degree when the Candidate is clothed in his Vestments of Light, receives the rose and the gloves, learns the sacred words and how to communicate them, the grip, the steps, and the sign or token. These strange anachronisms become practical to the mage as he enters the second and third echelons of working. There are more symbols and further instruction related to the degree that the Candidate is enjoined to not only study, but to allow to penetrate him to his core.

After instruction in these items, the Venerable Master hands the Candidate an envelope containing the ashes[768] of the *Projection by Fire.* No mere emblematic activity or lesson in morality, this envelope becomes for the Candidate a sacred relic of his initiation, a true talisman containing an element that forever binds him with the Craft. It should be forever treasured and kept safely wrapped in silk within the cabinet of his home temple or oratory. It will swell with force and strength as the Candidate learns the Royal and Sacerdotal art.

---

[768] The Réaux+Croix will see an analogue here as well.

As the newly made Entered Apprentice accomplishes his first "work upon the stone," the nature of spirit building is revealed. We are enjoined to erect Temples within ourselves to serve the Most High, the S.A.O.T.U.! This is the ideal Temple not made by human hands which we can enter at will. It is here that we will practice the cult of the S.A.O.T.U. which is revealed through each degree, ritual, and symbol we encounter in our work. The Coëns of Pasqually's system will recognize this language and see a sister system which works analogously with the Divine Cultus quietly as it has since the 19th century. Our spirit building becomes synonymous with the work of the true Gnostic as well, revealing in every step the means to acquire a direct, piercing experience of the divine.

The Original Scrying Method Of Allen H. Greenfield

ANCIENT AND PRIMITIVE RITE OF MEMPHIS AND MISRAÏM

ancient and primitive rite of Egyptian initiation

IV SERIES, KABBALISTIC
FRATER 171[769], 90º ADMINISTRATOR

Transcribed and annotated by PALAMAS

Au nom et sous les Auspices de la Grande Loge

du Rite Ancien et Primitif

de Memphis-Misraïm

---

[769] FRATER 171 is none other than Tau Allen Greenfield, recognized worldwide as a 97°, Past Grand Hierophant. As the following monograph was composed in 1993, it reflects his initiatory grade of that time.

Lodge of the Sons of Aaron

Under Authority of Hierophant, Conservator and Grand Master Michael Bertiaux,

Le Sanctuaire Souverain Du Rite Ancien & Primitif de Memphis-Misraïm

That rather lifeless system, which contained some rather interesting Egyptian roots, was really quite remarkable...which, at that time, as strange as it might seem to the uninitiated reader of these matters, was posing rather inconspicuously as the Egyptian Rite of Ancient Freemasonry with the name of 'Memphis-Misraim.'

Tau Michael Bertiaux

Most of the members of the Mission to Egypt who accompanied Bonaparte were Masons of old initiatic Rites: Philalethes, African Brothers, Hermetic Rite, Philadelphes, Primitive Rite, without omitting for all the Grand Orient of France. Having discovered in Cairo a gnostic-hermetic survival, then in Lebanon the Druse Masonry which Gerald de Nerval had encountered there and which went back to the operative Masonry of the Templars, the Brothers of the Mission to Egypt decided as a result to renounce their affiliation to the Grand Lodge of London, and to practice a new Rite which owed nothing to England, then enemy number one. An thus, under the direction of Samuel Honis and Marconis de Nègre was born the Rite of Memphis in 1815 in Montauban.

Robert Ambelain

Preamble

The Antient and Primitive Rite of Memphis and Misraïm (that of Egypt) derives from the earliest Masonic sources, and the Lodge of the Sons (Suns) of Aaron is authorized by the Hierophant of the Rite, Tau Ogoade Orfeo IV, to carry on in that lineage the tradition. We have close ties to the Ecclesia Gnosticæ Catholicæ (Gnostic Catholic Church, in specific the Coptic Rite) and Hermetic Brotherhood of Light as well.

Under the personal protection of the Conservator Tau Ogoade Orfeo IV. Blue Lodge or Blue Lodge Equivalent training is recognized with the proviso of participation in our Egyptian work of comparable level. The Royal Arch is also communicated under charter. In the great Egyptian tradition, this Lodge accepts members regardless of sex, race, religion, personal lifestyle, or nationality. All persons of full age and of good repute are welcome. **No oaths or declarations of fealty are extracted, no fees demanded.** Spiritual consecration and mystical ritual are observed, but no ritual initiations as such are performed. Therefore, the just sovereignty of other Orders and the obligations of their members are not infringed upon.

The European and Ancient Egyptian esoteric Masonic traditions are said to have intermeshed through the meeting of the Knights Templar and Oriental Rosicrucian Order in 1118. The Rite was introduced at Uppsala in Sweden 32 years later, and thereafter spread throughout Europe. During the Napoleonic Wars in Egypt, European Masonic bodies fused with primordial Egyptian survivals in various hermetic brotherhoods of light, notably at Cairo. Here is an abbreviated chronology, down to present Lodges.

- **Lodge of Egyptian Masonry**[770], Alexander, Count Cagliostro, Grand Kophta, 1789 (Rome)

- **Lodge of the Disciples of Memphis**, Samuel Honis of Cairo, April 30, 1815 (Montauban)

- Jacques Etienne Marconis de Nègre, July 7, 1838 (Paris)[771]

---

[770] Due to the availability of hitherto unattainable documents, we now know that Cagliostro established his Rite within the Mother Temple *La Sagesse Triomphante* in Lyon, on Christmas Eve, 1784 (See Milko Bogard's *Of Memphis and of Misraïm*, 2018, pages 48-70). As our rites are a combination of Memphis & Misraïm, it is of note that Cagliostro's occult work was called, *Secreto-Secretorum*, which gave rise to the Arcana Arcanorum of the Rite of Misraïm. The A A is understood to have been born in Naples in 1788, which fits snugly into Cagliostro's timeframe in the region.

[771] Though this list is described as brief and doesn't pretend to encapsulate the long and winding path of these rites, we would be remiss to not include the *Rite of Misraïm*, founded by Charles Lechangeur in Milan in 1804 and established in France by the Brothers Bédarride in 1814. Our Brother, Marconis, was a one-time member of the *Rite of Misraïm*, and after expulsion from

- David McClellan, November 9, 1858 {American Charter} (USA)
- Harry J. Seymour, Grand Master, 1861 (USA)[772]
- John Yarker, Grand Master, October 8, 1872 (England)
- G. Encausse (PAPUS), Grand Master, 1908 (France)
- Lucien F. Jean-Maine, Grand Master, 1910 (France-Spain-Haiti)
- Martin Ortier de Sanchez y Marraga, Grand Master, 1921 (Spain)
- Hector-François Jean-Maine, Grand Master, November 2, 1960 (Haiti)
- Michael Bertiaux, 97° Grand Master, January 18, 1966 (USA)
- Lodge of the Sons of Aaron, Frater 171=TSH 90° Mizr., Master, October, 1992

August 1, 1993

Dear Friend in the Holy Vision of the Gnosis.

This is an invitation to participate in the Highest Magick available to mortal human beings. If the statement seems flamboyant, test it. "The proof of the pudding is in the eating." It leads to the *knowledge and conversation of the Holy Guardian Angel.*

The Ancient and Primitive Rite of Memphis and Misraïm is one of the core wellsprings of modern Magick, coming up from the most ancient Coptic (Egyptian-Chaldean) traditions[773], and is available only to first-rate students of Magick. We are inextricably linked to the Ancient and Primitive Gnostic Catholic Church (Coptic Rite).

During the period 1919-1921 Tau Ogoade-Orfeo I and his successor and Vicar for Europe, Tau Ogoade-Orfeo II,

---

the same, developed the Rite of Memphis. There is growing evidence that, at the least, quite a few elements of the Rite of Misraïm were in existence before the establishment of the Order in Egyptian Masonry and in the Carbonari.

[772] Seymour would go on to work with the Grand Orient of France in an agreement to reduce the Rite to 33 degrees of development, a task that was not fully sketched out until the administrative prowess of John Yarker rose to the occasion and created the *Manual of the Degrees of the Ancient and Primitive Rite*.

[773] The classical *History* of Memphis+Misraïm typically entails the story of Ormus, a priest of Serapis, who converted to Christianity. This legend (a complete version of which can be found in T Allen Greenfield's, *A Compleat Rite of Memphis*) is consistent with the earliest surviving Coptic manuals of Christian magic. See Meyer and Smith's, *Ancient Christian Magic: Coptic Texts of Ritual Power*, Princeton University Press, 1999.

reorganized the Spanish and Haitian branches of the Rite of Memphis-Misraïm (and) gave up entirely their quasi-masonic character and become completely esoteric and Gnostic orders of magic...within the larger, totally occult and much more ecclesiastical, 'Ancient and Primitive Rite of Memphis-Misraïm.'

During the period of April 10-17, 1973, representatives of the Ancient and Primitive Rite, the QBLH Alchemist Church, Fraternitas Hermetica and numerous other esoteric gnostic bodies met in Liege, Belgium, and agreed to recognize the Grand Hierophant of the Rite of Memphis-Misraïm, Tau Ogoade-Orfeo IV "the ruling adept of each of the 16-member orders and their sub-orders[774]."

It was under his authority that the present Keneset B'nai[775] was organized under Frater 171=TSH 90° Mizr.[776] Frater 171 has been the direct student of Tau Ogoade-Orfeo IV for many years. The Keneset (Community, or Lodge) communicates the most fundamental empowerments, consecrations and authority including all 90° of the Ritus Misraïm through direct gnostic techniques, without recourse to Initiation Rites, Oaths or Obligations. Nor do we charge any fees whatsoever.

The primary method of communication is philosophical study and research, secret methods of trance and sexual gnosis, high magical ritual and consecration and recognition by demonstrated rights of accomplishment.[777]

Since no fealty is demanded, nor Initiation Rituals per se conferred, there is absolutely no infringement upon the just sovereignty and rights of any initiatory body, Masonic or otherwise.

*

* *

---

[774] It is of note that this Conference was held in Belgium, as a similar one was held in the same in 1934 by the FUDOSI. It is at this latter Convocation that the grades of Memphis & Misraïm as later established by Ambelain, took their solid form and the "required" active degrees were agreed upon.

[775] Keneset, refers to an *assembly*, while *B'nai* refers to *sons*; altogether it would signify the *Assembly of the Sons of Aaron*.

[776] It is entirely consistent to find the "Sons of Aaron" within the *Rite of Misraïm*, as history has shown that this particular Rite has been favored by Jewish communities; Ragon even referred to the Order as the "Judaic Rite." The Bédarride brothers themselves were of Jewish descent, as well as the name Misraïm—Hebrew plural for "Egyptian."

[777] One of the gems of this essay is this fundamental statement. Though the working model has altered over the years, the necessity for a "demonstration" of one's right of accomplishing the degree *spiritually* is an intelligent and balanced approach to ascending the Masonic tree.

Appendix D: Original Scrying Method of Allen H. Greenfield

Brief Instruction for Visionary Gnostic Scrying

To directly obtain the essences of each degree of the Ancient and Primitive Rite, one must have a prerequisite knowledge of (A) the scrying technique as in *The Vision and the Voice*[778], or otherwise understand scrying; (B) One must know divination by randomization as in the I-Ching, Tarot and, in specific, Bibliomancy. The latter involves selecting at random a passage from the Old or New Testaments of the Judeo-Christian Bible. (C) a general knowledge of yoga, in specific mantra and asana. (D) a general working knowledge of English Qabala[779], and general Qabalistic theory, and (E) a broad general knowledge of alchemy is helpful.

1. To obtain the essences, select the name of a degree with an alchemical title. Degrees of various systems may be obtained in Mackenzie's *Royal Masonic Cyclopedia*, Crowley's review *Waite's Wet or the Backslider's Return* (in the Equinox), or our own literature; for example, *A Companion of the Luminous Ring*."[780]

2. Via Bibliomancy, obtain a biblical verse.

3. Assume the prophet asana, and meditate upon the degree name and a Vision will appear with a word or pass.

4. Record the results.

5. Through E.Q. (English Qabala), convert the name of the degree and the word or pass into its cipher value.

6. Compare this to the values of text of *Liber AL vel Legis*, or other Class A Thelemic documents.

7. Get an independent, informed opinion as to whether the name, its value, and that of the word or pass obtained contain the essence of the degree.

8. Record and log the results.

---

[778] This selection by Aleister Crowley outlines his visionary journey of scrying into the Enochian 30 ÆTHYRs. Originally published in 1911, the Equinox edition was released by Weiser in 1999.

[779] A terrific place to begin studying this intriguing approach to English gematria, notariqon, and other aspects of Qabala can be found here: http://www.englishqabala.com/

[780] To update this list, we could add Allen Greenfield's own 2014 edition of The Compleat Rite of Memphis, or Spirit Builders, or utilize the informative website, https://www.stichtingargus.nl/vrijmetselarij/frame_en.html

For confirmation and accreditation, submit your results to the appropriate adept of the Ritus Misraïm system. If approved, you may now claim the degree by right of accomplishment.

Magick in Practice: Scrying the Degrees of the Egyptian Rite

In spiritual dealings, the Qabalah, with those secrets discovered by yourself that are only known to yourself and God, forms the grip, sign, token and password that assure you that the Lodge is properly tiled.

Aleister Crowley, "An Essay Upon Number

Abrogate are all rituals, all ordeals, all words and signs. Ra-Hoor-Khuit hath taken his seat in the East at the Equinox of the Gods...

Liber AL vel Legis I:49

Behold! the rituals of the old time are black. Let the evil ones be cast away; let the good ones be purged by the prophet! Then shall this Knowledge go aright.

Liber AL vel Legis II:5

The present Rite of Misraïm (Hebrew: Egypt) "accomplishes" the degrees within its traditional structure by a system of reclamation available to any Adept of Magick. The accomplishment of the degree, delineated elsewhere, contains a method of self-validation[781], and may safely be applied to any system of progressive illumination with and occult, Rosicrucian and alchemical basis.

The following deciphering and reclamation were accomplished with Frater 171=TSH 90° Mizr. QBLH, OAA as scryer and Soror 148, Q.B.L.H., O.A.A. acting as scribe. Soror

---

[781] It is indeed this method of self-validating, self-organizing, and self-discovery that lends this particular approach so well to a *Research and Philosophical* Lodge model.

148 was asked to select at random a degree from the Ritus Misraïm system as a "target." She picked the 24°, that is, I Series, 5th Class 24th Degree[782], Architecture.

The Magical weapons of this Operation include: A reliable copy of the Hebrew Scriptures and the New Testament, in the original, in translation: Frater Lamed's *Lexicon Cipher Program*; include *Liber AL vel Legis*, or a print copy of Liber Al with a copy of the classical English Qabalah Cipher; and a reliable reference guide to the traditional Masonic Degrees, including the higher degrees.

It is understood that the scryer, at least, has previously been given the empowerment to "accomplish" these decipherments. It should be recognized that each "accomplishment" is personal, though all true decipherings have this in common: they can be analyzed and the Word or Pass of the Degree, when deciphered through the English Qabalah and compared diligently to *Liber AL* or other Class A documents of the New Aeon, will reveal directly the aboriginal meaning of the Degree.[783]

Soror 148 selected the 24°, *Architecture*, giving only the name and number to the scryer.

Frater 171 then proceeded to perform Bibliomancy, selecting at random 1 Kings 17:2, *The word of the Lord came to him*: The context was not sought out; Frater 171 immediately entered the trance state, speaking aloud with Soror 148 recording the results.

> *I am standing on a rock, overlooking the sea, on Mr. Carmel. I see the Walls of Acre, the Crusader Fortress, up the coast. I am at the Tomb of the Bahai Prophet, and a golden angel appears to me: Gabriel, but he seems identical with the Mormon Angel. The angel opens his hand, and there is a (green) caterpillar in it. It says: Study the permutations of the word "Worm"–Great Orm, the Dragon. The innocent caterpillar can become Birth: the butterfly, which is the Soul, or the Dragon of the Apocalypse that fell from Heaven. The Word of the Degree is "ORM" and the Image is* **THE GREAT ORM OF LOCH NESS UNDULATING PAST BOLESKINE**.

After the vision was recorded, the word, ORM, was reduced by Lexicon to Cipher. **ORM**=40. Compared to the texts of Liber AL and Liber Cheth, **ORM=40=VAST**, also **HOST**, and **AS A SWORD**.

The Degree in question is part of a series of Architectural Degrees that apparently refer, in their original construction, to the erection of the enormous monuments of early Dynastic Egypt, and to Architecture as a science. The Phallic nature of that science (as in modern skyscrapers, the dual use of the term 'erection' etc.) is confirmed in **ORM=40=AS A**

---

[782] The 24° in the current Memphis+Misraïm system is in the First Series, Second Class. The degree of *Architect* in the Rite of Misraïm is distinct from the 24th degree in the *Scottish Rite* and from Yarker's, *Ancient and Primitive Rite*.

[783] Here again we discover the brilliance of this self-referential system. One's attainments are entirely contingent upon one's WORK.

SWORD. The first fruit of such endeavor was the Great Pyramid, known for its incredible vastness both as an architectural undertaking and in terms of size. It is the last surviving Wonder of the Ancient World. **ORM=40=VAST**. The inspiration for such endeavor is a form of secret communion with the infinite, thus **ORM=40=HOST**. (The word HOST, be it noted, relates to VAST).

In the monitorial reading of the Fellowcraft Degree, it is noted that,

> *geometry is the science on which Masonry is founded so that architecture is the art whence it borrows the language of symbolic instruction. Some knowledge of the art is necessary for the speculative Mason as well as the operative Mason.*

As this particular Scrying was not only to obtain the essence of the degree, but to point the way (by noting the procedure) to our fellows "the language of symbolic instruction," the Vision seen is apt, appropriate and valid.

Frater 171=TSH 90°

Admin. IV Series Ritus Misraïm

Aux. Bishop. Q.B.L.H., O.A.A.

Bish. Antient & Primitive Gnostic Church (Coptic Rite)

Episcopal Consecration

In the Rites of Memphis+Misraïm

66°

Over a period of six-to-eight months, I worked through the minor orders of the *Universal Gnostic Church*, culminating in the major order of Deacon on 10/15/11, under the tutelage of Archbishop John Gilbert, of blessed memory. Due to my background in the Episcopal Church (as both lay Eucharistic minister and Verger), I moved rather quickly through the UGC's method of seminary training and was duly ordained to the priesthood on 11/12/11 on the shores of the beautiful Lake Chatuge in the Appalachian Mountains of North Carolina. With this *awakening* on a crisp autumn afternoon, I knew my work would be forever stamped by the sacerdotal.

In my brief interim between ordination and consecration to the Episcopacy, I developed closer and closer ties with Bishops Allen H. Greenfield and Bill Zenn. We frequently discussed the purpose and power of points-chauds empowerments within the larger context of the Rites of Memphis and Misraïm, as well as what the *Ecclesiastical Revision* entailed. Bill and I had been conversing for a couple of years prior to my consecration which began my inner movements towards Arabia Mountain. I was already familiar with this huge tract of land from the sprawling monadnock, as I frequented the Trappist Monastery whose land butts right up to Arabia Mountain preserve. Arabia Mountain is a truly magical and majestic spiritual geography in the piedmont region of Georgia that intuitively instructs the sensitive in its hidden vortices, powerzones, and ley lines. I had spent some time in Sedona, Arizona while teaching at a Montessori school in Flagstaff, and had visited all of the vortex sites there a decade prior to Arabia; but oddly enough, I felt more of the full-body tingles, electrical inner currents, and anagogic "lifting" from the rock faces of Arabia Mountain than from the gorgeous red-rock vortex sites of Arizona.

Receiving points-chauds empowerments on Arabia Mountain was a turning point in my esoteric career. Having already experienced dozens and dozens of Masonic degrees, Hermetic grades of the Golden Dawn, Martinist degrees, the Élus Coëns grades, and more, there was an organic quality to the work on Arabia Mountain that completed the *awakening* at Lake Chatuge and elevated my Hermetic and Masonic work at the same time. Additionally, though I had assisted at the sacred altar and led processions in Holy Church, had experienced the joys of fraternity in my mainstream Masonic work from the previous decade, as well as having partaken of the kindness and generous R+C spirit of perfect strangers who welcomed me into their home for initiation after initiation with Chic and Tabatha Cicero, there was an extra layer of openness, something quite extraordinary, about our experiences with Free Illuminism on Arabia Mountain.

The spirit of absolute freedom of conscience (laïcité) and absolute acceptance pervaded the eclectic collective of Free and Congregational Illuminists. But this open-armed approach did not melt into some wavy-gravy, new age soup; there was a significant Tradition being embodied, enlivened, and transmitted in novel form among these individuals upon that powerzone known as *consecration rock*. Old rites were reified, egregore awakened and transmitted, and gates opened.

In his extensive experience and deep intuition, T Allen believed that individuals actually needed episcopal consecration to protect and empower them (among other reasons) and properly ground the points-chauds work our second echelon of operating the APRM+M. And why wouldn't he come to this conclusion when the form of the Rite he was working was the 1921 *Ecclesiastical* Revision of the Bertiaux line!

This was Masonry spiritualized in much the same way as Jean Bricaud (1881-1934) created his degree system of the Gnostic Church generations prior.[784] It is from Bricaud that Memphis & Misraïm became forever attached and attuned with the French Occult Synthesis (Martinism, the Gnostic Church, and allied bodies), which in addition to the Rose+Croix d'Orient and other side branches, is precisely our working as well.[785]

But Episcopal Consecration has a precise purpose, and such is not typically to protect or empower one for further initiations (such as the points work). Make no mistake, one who fully works the system of Spirit Building without proper preparation and protection (via a duly functioning three-degree system of initiation, a strictly moral and ethical discipline and lifestyle, and frequent communion through authentic Eucharistic celebrations) is headed for trouble as has been stated throughout this work. But consecration, historically, is the pleroma of the Church's Holy Orders, providing the new Bishop with Apostolic lineage and conferring upon him the powers of the Office to teach, govern, and sanctify persons, places, and things. It is understood that this consecration passes on the Holy Spirit in a discreet manner, more closely resembling that of the original Pentecost, transforming the individual into a shepherd of souls.

Whether Masonic, Gnostic, or Liturgical Christian (Orthodox, Catholic, Anglican), Episcopal Consecration is a Christian office of antiquity deeply entangled with the twin moments of Jesus' Baptism where he receives the Holy Spirit descending upon him like a dove (outlined in Matthew, Luke, and John) and the descent of the Holy Spirit at Pentecost as tongues of fire for the early Church, 50 days after Easter (Acts 2). Water and Fire. Consecration, then, marks the ongoing Presence of the Holy Spirit among us and passes on Apostolic Succession in all its fulness.

And yet, my consecration was not in a Church; it was outside upon granite, among the trees, and under the dome of sky like some pagan celebration of old. The readings were Gnostic, yet I had the traditional laying on of hands by three duly consecrated Bishops of the Gnosis. Though completely interwoven into the APRM+M working of points empowerments (some of which occurred immediately before my consecration), the Episcopal Rite itself was performed under the aegis of the *Coptic Gnostic Church,* Masonry and Ekklesia completely intertwined!

---

[784] Interestingly enough, Bricaud came to some of the same conclusions that we intuited in Horus Lodge: that of the third echelon of working the APRM+M which utilizes the ÆONIC operations and seals of the gnostic *Books of Jeu* and the *Pistis Sophia* from upper Egypt, 3rd or 4th century CE.

[785] See *Lux Occulta* for an exploration of the Martinezist incorporation of the APRM+M in the V° of the OMd'Chenu.

First homily as a consecrated Bishop, Arabia Mountain, 2012

My love and appreciation for the APRM+M is such that I honestly see it as housing, within its lodge doors, the *fullness* of the French Occult Synthesis. In other words, my ideal form of the Rite is as a complete system as well as federation of Orders. Certainly not an original idea and realized in various parts of the globe, I envision the degrees as so many keys to an overarching and grand edifice: from the 3° making one a Master Mason consistent with all Universal Masonry; minor orders of the French-Gnostic Tradition beginning with doorkeeper and the 8°; the Élus degrees of the 9-12° aligning with the further orders of Pasqually's Scottish Judges, or the Élus Coëns degrees of *Apprentice Coën, Companion Coën, Master & Élu Coëns, and* the 12° the Grand Master Coën; 13° and 14° conferring all known Royal Arch grades and traditions; continuing the alignment with Pasqually's Knight of the East and the 15° and the Commander of the East aligning with 17°; all Rose+Croix grades conferred in the 18° (including the RCO with Hieros Gamos teachings passed on to honorary members working the third echelon); both the CBCS of Willermoz and the Réaux+Croix of Pasqually given to Honorary members of the 26°; Baron de Tschoudy's Hermetic and alchemical work transmitted by the 28°; the Kadosh and Egyptian Hall of MAAT in the 30°; completion of the SR mysteries in the 32-33°; Hermetic and Kabbalistic grades of the APRM+M beginning in the 35°; the Gnostic Minor Order of Reader at the 37°; the beginnings of the third echelon workings introduced in the ÆONOLOGY of the 39°; the Gnostic Minor Order of Exorcist in the 42° as well as Acolyte in the 45°, and Major Orders of Deacon in 56° and Ordination to the Priesthood in the 57°; the combined lineages of Martinésism and Martinism in the 61°; the Mithraic Mysteries as precursor to the Christian Tradition in the 64°; Episcopal Consecration in the French Gnostic lineage in the 66°; continued Egyptian magic and grades in the higher degrees such as the 70-78°; 86° beginning study of the HGA traditions; 87-90° incorporating the *Arcana Arcanorum* in the first echelon as further teachings in spiritual alchemy, second echelon as Enochian magic and the knowledge and conversation of the HGA, and the third echelon merging with the 95° teaching advanced ÆONOLOGY leading to Osirification/Christification; and further Administrative grades conferring the Egyptian Rite of the divine Cagliostro, as well as teaching the divine mystagogy of apophatic theology.

A grand and incomplete idea, for sure, but difficult to accomplish if one only sees the outer form of the APRM+M, only knows of the physical *degrees* of the first echelon of working.[786] What the Great Arabia Mountain Workings did for the Rite was make them truly operative and functional for authentic seekers of the gnosis through the points-chauds empowerments of the second echelon.

Our own Chapel experimentation and research extended the work further, intuiting the true function of the "secrets" of the grades on the spiritual planes as defensive (apotropaic) signs, sealing the work *into the body* through the grips, testing the spirits with further words and signs, jewels and other data acting as synthemata or tokens to open gates and travel further through scrying, as well as more recently, the Tracing Boards as eidetic pylons.[787] Our experiments seem never ending, opening up the third echelon of working, identifying a method of Osirification within the work and other such research. And so, for us, the APRM+M is fully workably and functional in this sense and is a highly effective *container* for the vast traditions and transmissions of the French Occult Synthesis, with natural equivalencies such as the few mentioned above.

But what of our reworking of the *Patriarch Grand Consecrator* grade presented here? What we experienced on Arabia Mountain was assuredly *enough* in all its elegance and simplicity. We have said all of this in order to present what we feel is one of the most important, powerful, and complete grades known to the Western Mystery Tradition. It is such because of its integration of the raw power of the Arabia Mountain Working with what we have received from the Ambelain-line in terms of the 66°[788] which has all of the necessary components of true Episcopal consecration, yet owing to its development at a time of great interest in theosophy, the primitive doctrine, and the Vedas, the work in its present form is both incongruous and detached from its Mother, *the Ecclesia*. What we have endeavored to do through Horus Lodge, our Episcopal line from Arabia Mountain, our Masonic inheritance (French and English through the 96°), our French occult transmissions (Martinist, Coëns, RCO, and others), and experience in the Church is to exalt the 66° to the level of a true, coherent means of conferring the Major Order of Bishop for Honorary Masons who wish to serve, teach, sanctify, and govern in the Ecclesiastical Revision of the APRM+M.

This single Honorary degree establishes, then, by its very nature, what Bricaud put into place beginning in the early 1900's. Bricaud[789], once elevated to the Episcopate, took Doinel's

---

[786] It is important to note, once again, that the first echelon Lodge workings of the APRMM, revised by Ambelain and others (see +Phosphoros' *Degrees of Wisdom*), do not always match the titles, words, and secrets of the material provided by Greenfield in his, *Compleat Rite of Memphis* from Yarker, Cagliostro, Marconis, Burt, Kenneth MacKenzie, and others (see p. 16). The initiate is encouraged to compare and work with both sets of materials.

[787] See Preface to the second volume.

[788] Refer to the version in *Degrees of Wisdom* for reference.

[789] See Ravignat's *The French Gnostic Church Doctrinal and Liturgical Evolution*, pgs. 33-93, 2019.

simple work and infused it with elements of the Tridentine Mass, actions which completely resonate with our endeavors in our Chapel and Lodge. Our work herein hearkens back to Bricaud's original infusion of the Gnostic Church with a grade structure within a spiritualized system of Memphis and Misraïm, making the Church itself an Order of esoteric initiation. It is to Bricaud also that we turn to find the third echelon of working the APRM+M, as advanced ÆONOLOGY and initiatic physics, utilizing the Egyptian Gnostic *Books of Jeu* and the *Pistis Sophia*. And it is Bricaud who consecrates our own Lucian François Jean-Maine who created the OTOA through his French, Spanish, and Haitian hybridized lineages, which has continued the Gnostic and Apostolic lineages within the APRM+M in spiritual form through the LCN and the *Monastery of the Seven Rays*, through the august Patriarchy of Michael-Paul Bertiaux, and extended into our present tome through the reification of the Ecclesiastical Revision by way of Allen Greenfield's labors.

And so, returning to Bricaud, we have the premier Ecclesiastical grade of the APRM+M, the 66°. The work, studied and practiced by the dedicated Mason and Gnostic, speaks for itself in terms of efficacy and import, but one of the most striking features is the animated, mystical mandala shown in the first pages which is utilized world-wide in varying forms. Our version is peculiar to our Lodge being a combination of the published version of Illustrious Brother Joël Duez's mandala for the grade, with a more clearly represented Pentagrammaton and reinvested with the Trinitarian formula of Ecclesiastical tradition, returning the glyph to the Tradition it seeks to embody and make present: that of the Master Initiator, the Source of All Episcopal Consecrations, the Christos. The *Lost Word* YHVH[790] is vitalized by the descent of the Holy Spirit through the Hebrew letter shin ש, one of the premier purposes of the consecration, becoming the mysterious PENTAGRAMMATON. We see the continuing of the French Occult Synthesis in this symbol as well as with the crown of thorns, the Grail and egg/host, and the dove—all of which have Kabbalistic significations. Additionally, we have the sacred ternary repeated in the triangular shape, the three crosses, the Trinitarian formula, the three Mother letters, and the symbols. Rybalka says that our *98°, 99°, and 100° represent the 3 Mother Letters of the Hebrew Alphabet...shin is attached to the 98°, mem 99°, and aleph 100°.*[791] In this way, we see that this degree houses essential elements of the final degrees of the system in its entirety.[792]

---

[790] Discovered in the Royal Arch tradition.
[791] From p. 10 of the booklet included in Rybalka's *Egyptian Freemasonry of Count Cagliostro, Explanation of the Tracing Boards for the 100 Degrees*, Silhouette Publishing, Moscow, Russia.
[792] *Spirit Building*, proper, ends with the 97°; however, as has been shown in the Preface to Vol. 2, the third echelon operates through the 100° by virtue of the 100 words from the Gnostic *Apocryphon of John*.

98th degree, Superior Inconnu of Egyptian Freemasonry (SI98) (International Grand Master).

99th degree, Grand Hierophant.

100th degree, Sovereign Architect Of The World.

Further, Rybalka instructs us in understanding the import of the 66° in the greater context of the Rite, saying it is *one of the Key degrees in Egyptian Freemasonry. Only the holder of the 66° has the right to found a new Sanctuary.*[793]

Returning to the Lost Word in its completed form in the center of the mandala, Rybalka gives us an additional key to the mystery informing us that the symbols of the Tracing Board for this degree incorporate the Tetragrammaton *and the Holy Breath* which we know to be the Holy Spirit/Pneuma, symbolized again by the shin descending into the Tetragrammaton. Finally, the Tracing Board for the 66° refers to the sacred ternary with its three circles.

But what does the mandala *do?* What is its function? Whether we are on consecration rock on Arabia Mountain, in our private oratory, or in a traditional Lodge, this mandala becomes the central-axis fire, the *poteau-mitan*, the pillar of fire, the beacon of the god. It is a vèvè formed in chalk to briefly "contain" La Chose, it is the Triangle of Manifestation of the Master of Initiation where through the Holy Spirit, the PENTAGRAMMATON is animated and appears to those with the "prize of the eyes" and a cleansed sensorium.

And so we see that this degree can be conferred in the second echelon as explored in this volume, with its use of Vedic terms and mixed symbolism, which opens up quite interesting inner departments of inquiry in scrying to those desirous of such and who understand the "Adoptionism" of the time, which treated such Vedic terms as pre-Christian heralds of the

---

[793] Ibid., 46.

forthcoming New Law. But, to one who is *called to serve* in the capacity of Bishop, this grade operates on the first and third echelons simultaneously[794], activating the fullness of Apostolic succession and the Church's Holy Orders, and presenting a blueprint or lattice of the entire system (incorporating advanced ÆONOLOGY) of the APRM+M 1-100°, as its subtitle suggests: *Grand Architect of the Mystical City.*

This degree occurs both within the time and space of traditional Masonic Lodge settings, and mystically in the so-called *Eighth Day* of what the Gospels refer to as the *Kingdom of God* which is both *in our midst* (Luke 17:2) and *within us*, as well as being *at hand* (Matt 3:2, Mark 1:15) which is the Eighth Day experience of Now-ness, the ever-present, non-dual and eternal moment of reality we dwell in, *when fully awakened.*

Enter this Temple with awe. We begin with purification and end in mystery and communion, just as our threefold path has taught all along. It is a digest and summary of *katharismos, photismos,* and *henosis.* Linking the traditional esoteric school of Freemasonry with the traditional Holy Orders of the Ecclesia, it is, in my mind at least, the *ne plus ultra* of our labors, only to be embellished upon by grades above it in the same way that the degrees beyond the 3° are understood not to confer further rank, per se, but to deepen and make richer the Master's degree. Let us proceed, then. Let us proclaim the mystery of faith!

---

[794] For the full working of Osirification, the third echelon of advanced ÆONOLOGY, the initiate *as Osiris* must hold the fully worked 66° or other valid Episcopal consecration, for the Royal & Sacerdotal arts of those mysteries.

Spirit Builders

Patriarch Grand Consecrator

66° *Grand Architect of the Mystical City*

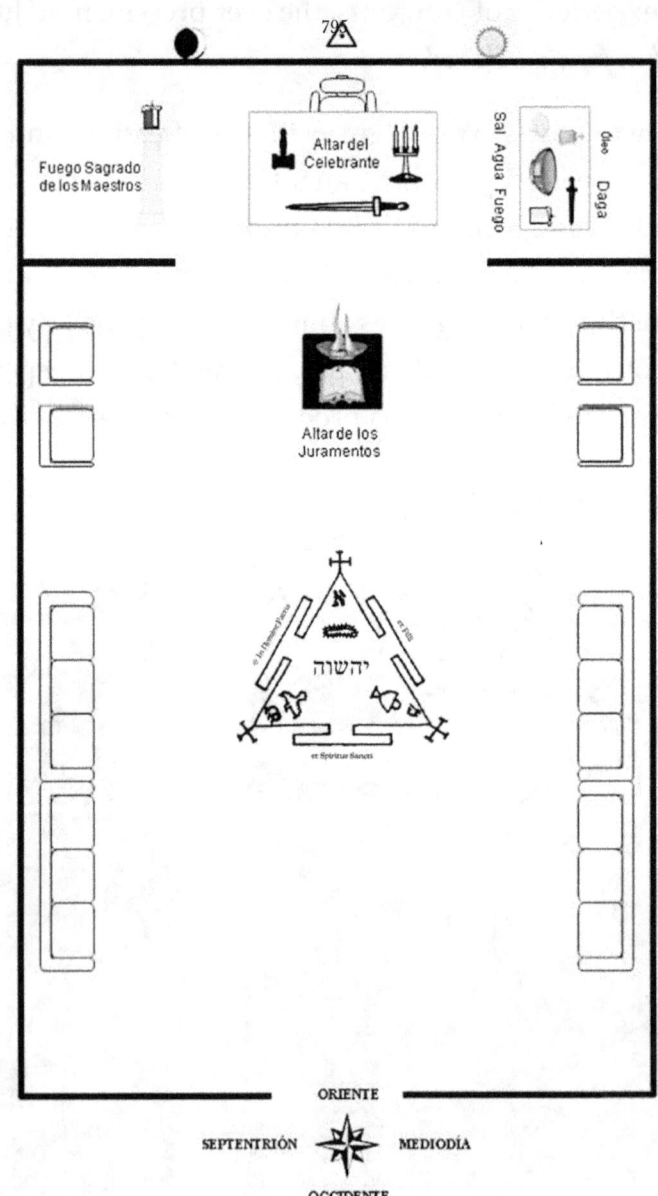

---

[795] Altar diagram created by the *Sovereign Sanctuary of Spain, Masonic Order and Egyptian Hermética Kabbalistic*, with our adjusted mystical mandala. Mandala should be drawn in blessed chalk upon the floor or ground of the Temple. The *gifts* of Holy Mass are to be housed in the Initiator/Celebrant's altar until the *Ritus Communionis*.

Appendix E: 66° - Patriarch Grand Consecrator

Templar Bishop

ANIMATED ALTAR MANDALA

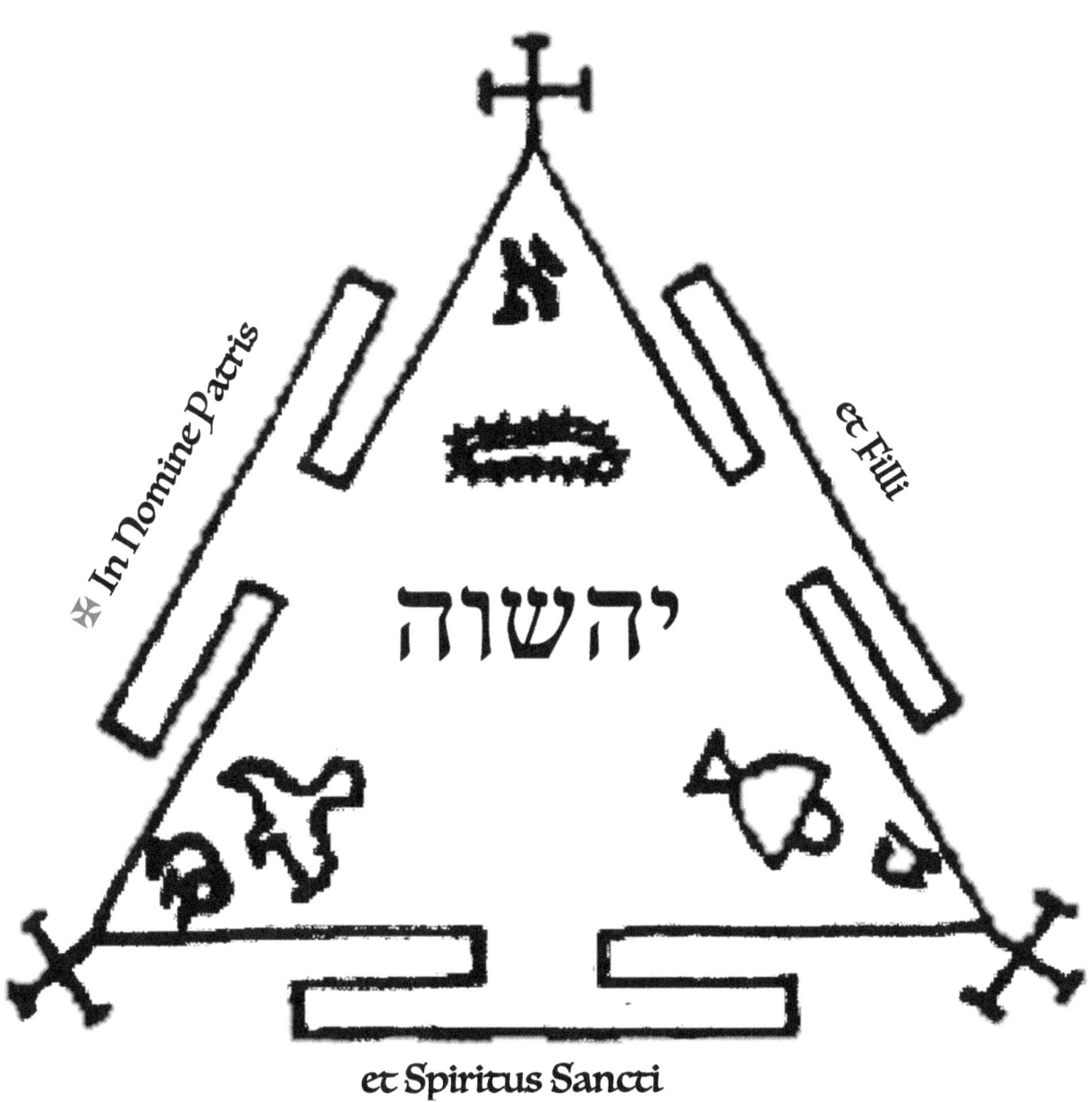

NECESSARY MATERIALS:

- The Sacred Fire or Sacristy Lamp (a red glass candle on the Altar)
- Three self-standing candlesticks with pure beeswax for the mystical mandala.
- Triple flambeaux with pure beeswax candles for the Patriarch Initiator's altar.
- Burning coals and censer placed on central altar, east of the Bible.
- Chalk to trace the mandala.
- A Board (preferably of slate or natural material) where the mandala is traced and cloth to erase the mandala during closing. The floor or ground may also be used for the mandala.
- A shroud (preferably black).
- A small water basin, *blessed salt*, and aspergil or boxwood for the Asperges.
- A white altar cloth with a red Patriarchal or Lorraine pectoral cross  for the new Bishop.
- A white rose
- Communion wafers (Catholic) on a gold paten
- Gold paten for the wafers and small glass cruets for the wine and water
- A chalice with silk napkin
- The Holy Bible
- The Sacramentary of the Rose+Croix, or *Lux Occulta*
- A small central altar on which are placed the Bible, Sacramentary, and the censer
- A flaming sword
- A mallet or scepter and gong or *sanctus* bells
- The new Bishop's stole and crozier[796]

---

[796] It is appropriate to include additional items of the Office, such as gloves, the ring, miter, etc.

Appendix E: 66° - Patriarch Grand Consecrator

CONSECRATORY ELEMENTS

- The lustral water and *blessed salt*
- The incense
- The censer
- Oil of consecration (formula by +Jon J. included in *Lux Occulta*)
- The three large candlestick holders and candles
- The triple flambeaux
- The flaming sword

COMPOSITION OF THE INCENSE[797]

- 3 parts Myrrh
- 2 parts Benzoin
- 3 parts Olibanum (Frankincense)
- 1 part powdered sugar

COMPOSITION OF THE SENATE

Denominations

- **The president:** Patriarch Initiator, 66° or higher
- **Assistant:** Acolyte, 45° or higher
- **Two assisting Bishops:** Assisting Patriarchs, 66° or higher
- **The temple:** Senate, 3° and higher are invited to attend
- **The candidate:** Neophyte, 65° or higher (as this is the Honorary form of the degree)

The Initiator sits in the Orient behind the Altar at his station, facing the mystical mandala.

Two Patriarchs are also in the Orient seated on the left and the right of the Patriarch Initiator.

Decoration of the Celebrant's altar:

The Celebrant's altar should be covered in a pure white cloth. A balustrade may be set up in the East before the Celebrant's altar, with a kneeler for the new Bishop to commune, or receive *upon the tongue*.

---

[797] An alternative to this formula (Holy Myron) is presented in *Lux Occulta* by the late +Jon Johnson.

Station of the Patriarch Initiator (eastern altar and south side altar for water and oils)

- The triple flambeaux
- The lustral water
- The consecrated oil
- Communion wafers on gold paten (inside altar until *Ritus Communionis*)
- Cruets of wine and water (inside altar until *Ritus Communionis*)
- A chalice and silk napkin (" ")
- A white rose
- The flaming sword
- The mallet

Decoration of the central altar:

- The Bible opened to Psalms 110:4 (Vulgate) and appropriate Gnostic texts, see *Alternate Readings* after the Rite.
- Closed *Sacramentary of the R+* or *Lux*
- The incense and censer

It is customary for the Neophyte to have fasted the day before his consecration and for the ceremony to be undertaken during Mass on the day of the Sun, the mystical *Eighth Day* for the Ogdoad.

The Neophyte waits in patience in the traditional *Chamber of Reflection* wearing a single black robe.

Appendix E: 66° - Patriarch Grand Consecrator

The following degree and consecration is an amalgamation of the 66° from +Phosphoros' *Degrees of Wisdom*, traditional Episcopal Consecration sources prior to Vatican II, the Liturgy from *Lux Occulta*, Bricaud's original Consecration materials, and other source material, revised, reworded, and reworked by PALAMAS & Horus Lodge.

CONSECRATING THE ELEMENTS

†

Blessing of the Water

Each gesture performed by the Patriarch Initiator is performed in tandem, to his right and to his left, by the two Assisting Patriarchs.

The Patriarch Initiator takes the container of blessed salt and brings it to the glass container of lustral water, and begins:

✠ My help is in the name of the Lord

Who made heaven and earth.

Hear my prayer, O Lord,

And let my cry ascend unto Thee.

May the Lord be with you,

And with your spirit.

I exorcise you, creature of water, ✠ in the name of God the Father All-powerful, ✠ in the name of Jesus Christ his Son Our Lord, ✠ and by the virtue of the Holy Spirit: in order that you become exorcised water which dissipates every power of the Enemy, that you are able to draw out and displant the Enemy himself with his apostate angels. Through the power of this same Jesus Christ Our Lord who must come to judge the living and the dead, and to pass the world through fire. So mote it be!

✠

Let us pray. My God, who for the salvation of men has established with the substance of water the greatest sacraments, be propitious to our prayers, and upon this element which must serve for such purifications, shed the virtue of your blessing; in order that your creature, utilized in your mysteries, serve through an effect of divine grace, to cause the demons to flee, to expel diseases, and may wherever this water shall be scattered, dwellings of the faithful or any other place be cleansed of every impurity, delivered from whatever may be able to harm. May there never reside there any pestilential suffering, any corrupted air. May every hidden trap of the Enemy be dispersed; and if it is someone or something which is able to do harm to the health or to the rest of those who inhabit them, may the sprinkling of this water dissipate it and cause it to disappear entirely. May all health requested by invoking your holy Name be to the shelter of all those attacked. Through Our Lord Jesus Christ. So mote it be!

The Initiator sprinkles a portion of the blessed salt into the water in the form of a cross three times while chanting:

May this mixture of salt and water be united together in the name ✠ of the Father, ✠ and of the Son, ✠ and of the Holy Spirit. So mote it be!

Lord, hear my prayer.

And may my cry rise unto Thee.

Let us pray. God, author of every invincible force, King of an unshakable Empire, and ever-magnificent victor; you who destroys the forces of adverse Power, who tames the fury of the roaring Enemy, who victoriously thwarts its hostile darkness: we beseech you, Lord, humbly and trembling, and we ask of you to look favorably upon this creature of salt and water, honor it with your goodness, sanctify it with the dew of your mercy; in order that everywhere it will be spread, with the invocation of your holy Name, every infestation of the unclean Spirit be repelled, the terror of the venomous Serpent be far removed, and that the presence of the Holy Spirit deigns to make itself felt everywhere and over us all, who implore your mercy. Through Our Lord Jesus Christ, who lives and reigns with you, my God, in the unity of the Holy Spirit across all the ages. So mote it be!

☦

Sanctify, Lord, this water. Give it the ability to relieve us and to expel every sickness, to put the demons to flight and to preserve us from its traps.

The Initiator then puts three drops of pure hyssop in the salted water and says:

Purge me with hyssop and I shall be made clean.

☦ In the name of the Father, and of the Son, and of the Holy Spirit. So mote it be.

☦

Blessing of the Bread and the Wine

It is, of course, by the Liturgy itself that the bread and wine become for us the body and the blood of the Christos, the Logos and Master Initiator. But before we proceed to the Liturgy, the physical materials are blessed, consecrated, and exorcised according to Tradition. Place the bread to the left and the wine to the right on the Initiator's altar, with the sacristy lamp or sacred fire on a stand or small altar to the right (north) of the Initiator.

Let us pray. Lord God, All-powerful, may blessings descend from the ☦ Father and from the ☦ Son, and from the ☦ Holy Spirit upon this creature of bread and creature of wine, in order that whomever partakes of these gifts receives health of spirit, protection of body, certitude of salvation, solidity of faith, consolation of hope, the totality of charity, the strength of perseverance and the visitation of the Holy Spirit. Through Our Lord Jesus Christ. So mote it be.

Sprinkle both the bread and the wine with the blessed and consecrated holy water. Then continue:

> Let us pray. Lord Jesus Christ, bread of the Lamb, living bread of eternal life, who is also called the true Vine, and who has called your Apostles the shoots of this same vine, ✠ bless, ✠ sanctify, and ✠ exorcise this bread and this wine in order that those who eat and drink of these creatures may work effectively against the demonic forces and participate as true sons of God in the divine life and vision of the Saints and Angels. Destroy all Satanic undertakings and works through these sanctified gifts, and let those who partake of these be protected against every snare of the Enemy. May these gifts be a salutary remedy to all those who will partake of them. And see, by the invocation of your Holy Name, that whoever tastes of it receives, by your grace, health of both soul and body.
>
> *And may the blessings of God All-Powerful, ✠ Father, ✠ Son, and ✠ Holy Spirit, descend upon these creatures of bread and wine and remain there always. So mote it be.*

Sprinkle a final time with holy water in cruciform fashion over the bread and the wine. Return the bread and wine to the inside of the Initiator's altar until the *Ritus Communionis*.

✠

Blessings of the chalk, candles, incense, oil, and dedication of the space

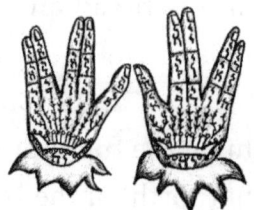

Before the initiation *proper* is performed, the space should be consecrated to the purpose through a very simple, yet powerful gesture that announces to the spirits the intentions of the Initiator and Senate members of the Lodge. The abode should have already received the formal *house blessing*, but before each 66°, the following procedure should be followed to the letter. Using the chalk[798] that is blessed in this simple ceremony, the Initiator writes upon the door of the room (or otherwise) where the Liturgy will be performed, the names of the three kings, or Magi.

> **Let us pray.** ✠ **Bless, Lord God, this creature of chalk. May it be salutary to me, and see that by the invocation of your Holy Name, whoever takes this chalk, and with it inscribes upon the doors of his house the names of your saints Gaspar, Melchior, and Balthazar, obtain, by the intercession of their merits, health of body and salvation of soul. Through Our Lord Jesus Christ. So mote it be!**

✠ The Initiator sprinkles the chalk with the blessed water. As soon as the chalk is dry, inscribe the names upon any and all doorways leading into the chamber where the Liturgy will be performed, or at the North, West, and East of the space if outdoors. Then, pray:

(Psalm CXXVII)

> **Except the Lord build the house, they labor in vain that build it: except the Lord keep the city, the watchman waketh but in vain. It is vain for you to rise up early, to sit up late, to eat the bread of sorrows: For so he giveth his beloved sleep.**

✠

(Psalm CXXV)

> **They that trust in the Lord shall be as mount Zion, which cannot be removed, but abideth forever. As the mountains are round about Jerusalem, so the Lord is round about his people from henceforth even forever.**

The Initiator completes the sacralization of the space with arms outstretched and hands in the Rabbinic gesture of the Holy letter *Shin* ש with thumbs interlaced, and cries the holy injunction:

> *Let thine eyes be upon this space, our spiritual home, both day and night, and deign to grant our prayers and bless our Operations. We ask this of you in the name of the ✠Father, and of the ✠ Son, and of the ✠ Holy Spirit.* **Amen.**

The Patriarch Initiator proceeds with the blessing of the candles.

---

[798] The chalk is also be used to inscribe the sacred mandala onto a piece of slate or other natural surface, or the floor.

> Let us pray. Lord Jesus Christ, Son of the Living God, bless these candles for use in the liturgy. Let them become for us living effigies of the spirits freed from matter, and of the Angels whose presence we deign to request. Let descend the blessing of the ✠ Father, and of ✠ the Son, and of ✠ the Holy Spirit upon these creatures of wax and may we who partake of the mysteries which these candles illuminate, be delivered from any working, binding, signature, influence, bewitchment, or illusion, and from every fear of temptation, from faint-heartedness, from all the ruses of the Demons and their ministers, and in a word, from every peril of the soul and body and from all our enemies. Through the same Jesus Christ, Our Lord. So mote it be.

Initiator sprinkles with blessed water. He then turns to all members and says:

> Brothers & Sisters, I ask our Passed Masters to help us to receive spiritual Light as, by the action I now take, I increase the physical illumination of the Temple by borrowing life from these profane but pure lights, which will now physically lighten our work, from the flame of the sacred fire.

The Initiator then takes the sacristy lamp and lights one of the candlesticks which will then light the triple flambeaux, and any other necessary vigil lamps, lectern lights, or beeswax candles.

The Initiator continues with the incense:

> Let us pray. As one of the holy gifts of the Magi, we ask that you ✠ sanctify, ✠ bless, and ✠ purify this creature of incense, for the honor of your Holy Name. May every demonic force flee from this creature; all deceit, all evil, and all of the cunning of the devil be released so that this incense may become a saving remedy to all who utilize it. May we who offer the sacrifice of incense be purified with the confidence in your divine power, and may this creature sanctify our homes, lodgings, and the persons who are delivered from the snares of the devil by its saving fragrance. Oh God, be pleased to endow with your blessing and power, this creature of incense, and may your spiritual influence descend upon these grains now in the name of the ✠ Father, and of the ✠ Son, and of the ✠ Holy Spirit. Amen.

The Patriarch Initiator sprinkles with blessed water and continues with the blessing of the oil:

> I exorcise you, creature of oil, by ✠ God the Father All-powerful, who has made the heavens and the earth, the sea, and all things found therein. May every force of the Enemy, may every army of the Devil, and may every invasion, every phantasmagoria

of Satan be drawn out and flee this creature of oil, in order that it gives, to those who use it, salvation of soul and health of body, in the name of ✠ God the Father All-Powerful, and of ✠ Jesus Christ his son Our Lord, and of the ✠ Holy Spirit Consoler, and in the love of this same Jesus Christ Our Lord, who will come to judge the living and the dead, and purify the world by fire. So mote it be!

Lord, hear my prayer.

And let my cry ascend to you.

Let us pray. Lord God All-powerful, before whom is held every army of the Angels, so known by us for the spiritual services they grant us, deign ✠ to look upon, ✠ to bless, and ✠ to sanctify this creature of oil, that we have drawn from the essence of olives and by which the sick are anointed by your commandment, in order that having recovered health, they are able to give thanks to You, the Living and True God. We beseech you, see that those who use this oil, which we ✠ (The Initiator sprinkles with blessed water) **bless in your Name, be delivered from every languor, and from every infirmity, and from every trap of the Enemy. And may all adversities be removed from your creature, that you have redeemed by the precious blood of your Son, in order that she never be harmed by the bite of the ancient Serpent. Through the same Jesus Christ Our Lord, your Son, who lives and reigns with you, my God, in the unity of the Holy Spirit unto the ages of ages. So mote it be!**

INITIATON PROPER

While lighting the first candle at the apex of the mystical and sacred mandala, the Initiator invokes the *Angel of the Presence*:

Come, *Angel of the Presence*, all angels and Archangels, ministers of flame and fire; six-winged cherubim and many-eyed seraphim; Come and "repair the break between

God and Man and restore Man to his original and divine condition prior to the Fall of the Sons of Light or The First Man."[799]

While lighting the second candle on the bottom right, the Initiator invokes the Master of Initiation, the PENTAGRAMMATON:

> Master, open this Neophyte's mind to your spiritual influence, so that he may begin to see with eyes other than those perceiving only the forms of things. May his ears hear the words and melodies of the Empyrean. May his nose perceive the aroma of holiness. And may his heart become a sanctuary for the Holy Name.

While lighting the third candle on the bottom left, the Patriarch Initiator invokes the Holy Spirit:

> [800]Come Creative Spirit, visit the hearts of your followers, fill them with the Grace from Above: these hearts which you have created. You are called the Consoling Spirit, the gift of God Almighty, the source of Living Water, the Divine Fire, the Charity, the Invisible Unction of Souls.
>
> Come then, with your Seven Precious Gifts, You who are the finger of God, You who are the Supreme Subject of the Father's Promise, You who place His Word on our lips. Light up our Spirits with your Light, embrace our hearts with Your Love and sanctify at all times our frail flesh.

The Initiator then turns to the East and proclaims with arms outstretched:

> To the Glory of the Sublime Architect of ALL Worlds. In the name and under the auspices of..., of the *Antient & Primitive Rite of Memphis+Misraïm*, I declare open the labors of this Respectable Senate, in the visible as in the invisible, of the Patriarch Grand Consecrator Templar Bishops.

The Patriarch Initiator and two Assisting Patriarchs walk around the mystical mandala three times, passing their forefinger through each of the three flames, then raise their arms, then lower them toward the mandala and strongly chant the following invocation over the sigil with the sign of the cross at each:

> ✠Blessed art Thou, O Lord, show me Thy Initiation!

---

[799] Quoted by permission of the author from the *Apprenti* grade Catechism of the *Ordre Martinèsiste de Chenu*, Michael Bertiaux, 1983.
[800] From the traditional Office of the Holy Spirit, assigned to each R+ to say daily, or at least every Thursday. It is also called the *Invocation of the Seven Spirits before the Throne*, from the Revelation of St. John the Divine.

✠Blessed art Thou, O Lord, show me Thy Initiation!

✠Blessed art Thou, O Lord, show me Thy Initiation!

The Initiator chants the Kyrie slowly and makes a deep bow towards the mandala after each, then continues with the manifesting prayers and sacred Names:

Kyrie Eleison

Christe Eleison

Kyrie Eleison

Come Holy Spirits and Saints, you Passed Masters and Patrons of the Great Ones! Be Present with us and attend this Holy Consecration. We dedicate ourselves anew to you on this day, in this holy place, and we ask that you contribute to our Neophyte some sign or shewing of your nearness and immediacy.

Through Christ Our Lord, AMEN.

And YOU, Our guide and Master of Initiation, spirit freed from the ties of matter, I pray that You will be present, and I conjure you by the Holy and Mighty Names,

✠El ✠Elohim ✠Eloah ✠Soter ✠Emmanuel ✠Sabaoth ✠AGLA ✠Tetragrammaton ✠AGIOS ✠O THEOS ✠ISCHYROS ✠ATHANATOS ✠JEHOVAH ✠ADONAI ✠SHADDAI ✠EHIEH ✠ALPHA & OMEGA ✠The One and Holy ✠YEHESHUVAH!

Initiator raises his voice to a roar, vibrating:

LET THE SYMBOLS MANIFEST THEMSELVES!

The Patriarch Initiator continues with the final words of invocation over the mandala with his hands in the Rabbinic gesture:

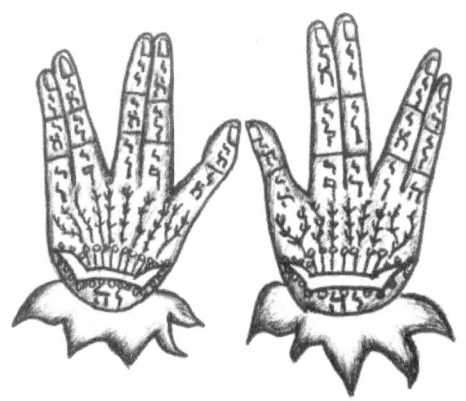

> **May the divine energies of Omneity deign at this instant to descend into this radiant center of spiritual desire and render it animated, luminous, and incorruptible.**

He reverently bows to the mystical mandala and says to his Acolyte:

> **Have enter the Respectable Copts, members of this Respectable Senate.**

The Acolyte has the Copts enter the Temple, hands over their chest in the sign of the Good Shepherd. The Copts bow and meditate before the MANDALA,[801] then take their places on either side of the altar. The Patriarch Grand Consecrator Initiator takes his place behind the altar with the two Assisting Patriarchs to his right and left. The Patriarch Initiator proclaims:

> **Respectable Copts, we are going to proceed to the divine ceremony of initiation of the 65°** *Guardian of the Sanctuary, Grand Installator* **N..., to the grade of Honorary** *Patriarch Grand Consecrator Templar Bishop* **66°.**

The Neophyte is brought in by the Acolyte and questioned before the Patriarch Initiator. Assisting Bishops witness with right hands covering their hearts, forming a triangle around the Neophyte.

Initiator:

> **Neophyte, is it your intention to be consecrated by Holy Church, in the mysterious lines of Melchizedek, and join the august society of Patriarchs of the Antient and Primitive Rite of Memphis+Misraïm?**

---

[801] The Martinist will recognize the treatment of the mandala as corelating to the chair of the "Passed Master."

Neophyte:
> It is.

Initiator:
> Do you believe in the Holy Gnosis?

Neophyte:
> I do.

Initiator:
> Will you commit to setting your mind upon things above rather than on the passions and pleasures of the world?

Neophyte:
> I will.

Initiator:
> Will you ever cherish as a sacred trust the powers now being committed to you, pledging yourself to exercise your office with care and discretion in choosing those who, in the name of the Pentagrammaton, you bestow the gift of Holy Orders?

Neophyte:
> I will.

Initiator:
> And finally, dear Brother, do you believe—according to the measure of your own faith—in the sacred Ternary herein symbolized (Patriarch Initiator and Assisting Bishops point to the sacred mandala) and commit to spreading the "Good News" of non-dual Gnosis?

Neophyte:
> I do.

The Neophyte is then made to lie prostrate on the floor in the west of the Temple, arms spread out and head facing the mystical mandala which acts as a *poteau-mitan* or central axis of the Temple wherein the Master of Initiation is invoked. The Acolyte adds grains of incense to the censer and then covers the Neophyte with a funereal shroud. The Initiator and Assisting Patriarchs then extend their arms while the Initiator says strongly,

> **Almighty and eternal God, you have called this your servant to share in the ministry of your Son, Jesus Christ, the Apostle and High Priest of the Gnosis, our Master**

Initiator and the Shepherd of our souls. Through Christ our Lord, we pray: Pour out upon N. (the bishop-elect) the power of your princely Spirit, whom you bestowed upon your beloved the Pentagrammaton, with whom he endowed the apostles, and by whom your Church is built up in every place and time.

Fill the heart of this your servant whom you have chosen to be a bishop of the gnosis and holder of the august 66°, with such love of you and of all your people, that he may faithfully feed and tend his flock, and exercise his office for the glory of your Name and the well-being of your Church; through , ✠YEHESHUVAH! who lives and reigns with you in the unity of the Holy Spirit, one God, unto the ÆONs.

The degree continues with the Asperges.[802] Each Patriarch and all members of the Senate are purified by water (in renewal of their baptism) beginning with the Initiator, & especially dousing the Neophyte, as the Initiator directs the aspergil towards all while singing in Gregorian chant:

✠ Asperges me, Domine, hyssopo et mundabor,
Lavabis me, et super nivem dealbabor.
Miserere mei, Deus, secundum magnum misericordiam tuam.

Each in attendance signs him or herself as the rays of light and holy water cascade from the wand

or sprig. When the asperges is complete, the Patriarch Initiator and assisting Patriarchs vibrate the following pronouncement strongly:

Blessed is the ✠ kingdom, and the power, and the glory, now and forever and unto ÆONs of ÆONs. Amen.

The Initiator and Assisting Patriarchs turn once again to the mystical mandala while the Initiator says in a low voice:

✠ St. Peter, Open the Gates

St. Lazarus, I am your child

Sacred Heart of Jesus, I am here

Christ of the Noonday, Master of the Crossroads, Son of the Living God and Head of the 2nd Ray, remove the barriers that we may pass beyond the pylons.

---

[802] Most priests and Bishops will have a special aspergil for this operation, but a sprig of boxwood is also appropriate.

Appendix E: 66° - Patriarch Grand Consecrator

The Initiator turns back towards the Neophyte and chants the *Litania Major* while an Acolyte rings the gong three times for each Saint:

XXX *bell* **Saint Expedite** ALL respond: ***hear us and be near us.***

St. Patrick of Ireland ALL respond: ***hear us and be near us.***

Our Lady of the Immaculate Conception ... " "

Holy St. Anne, Mother of Mary ...

Sacred Heart of Yeheshua ...

St. Joseph ...

Sts. Cosmas & Damien...

St. Gerald Majella...

St. Lazarus...

Our Lady of Czestochowa...

St. James the Greater...

Our Lady of Sorrows...

St. Isidore...

St. Philomena...

St. Claire...

All Holy Saints and Passed Masters ALL respond: ***hear us and be near us.***[803]

MENTAL & PHYSICAL PURIFICATION

The Initiator then performs the penitential rite, or *Actus Pænitentialis*. Performing his secret exorcism of the *logismoi*[804] facing the mandala, the Initiator says:

---

[803] The student of religion and our sacred Voudon+Gnosis will see the intentional selection of Saints being called to attend near the mystical mandala.
[804] The Initiator should strike his chest audibly at each red x

✕ **Mea culpa,** ✕ **Mea culpa,** ✕ **Mea máxima culpa.**

After releasing the *logismoi* to their abodes, the Initiator then turns to the Senate and proclaims:

Misereátur nostril omnípotens Deus et, dimíssis peccátis nostris, perdúcat nos ad vitam ætérnam.

The Initiator then continues with the *Litania Minor*:

> **In Peace, let us pray to Divine Wisdom[805]!**

All: *Holy Sophia, Grant Us Peace*

> For the Peace of all present and for spiritual equilibrium within us all let us pray to Divine Wisdom!

All: *Holy Sophia, Grant Us Peace*

> For the Peace of the Whole world and for the Union of all peoples, let us pray to Divine Wisdom!

All: *Holy Sophia, Grant Us Peace*

> For the Patriarchs, the Venerable Clergy, our Brothers and Sisters, and the Grand Hierophant of the *Antient and Primitive Rite of Memphis+Misraïm*, let us pray to Divine Wisdom!

All: *Holy Sophia, Grant Us Peace*

> For this City and this countryside and the Faithful that dwell therein, let us pray to Divine Wisdom!

All: *Holy Sophia, Grant Us Peace*

> For our own wholeness and dedication to a life of balance and gnosis, let us pray to Divine Wisdom!

All: *Holy Sophia, Grant Us Peace*

---

[805] This Litany doubles as an invocation to the other half of the Christos Syzygy: Sophia.

ASTRAL PURIFICATION & BARRIER

The Patriarch Grand Consecrator Initiator takes the censer which burns at the central altar and says, as he lifts the censer to the heavens:

> **Let us now purify our astrality by the sacred fire of these burning coals and the pure resins of this suffumigation.**

Swinging the censer, the Initiator walks around the Neophyte to surround him with an ASTRAL BARRIER while saying:

> **Sublime Brother (*or* Sister), I give you the ASTRAL PURIFICATION by purifying your astrality by the sacred incense of the Rose+Croix.**

He then walks around the Neophyte with the censer in a manner to surround him with an astral barrier.

> **May this sacred fire create a circle of constant protection, an ineffable barrier.**

The Initiator proceeds to cense all in attendance, starting with the altar in the east, according to tradition, and then the north, west, south, and back to the Orient. He then says:

> **And now that we have erased our faults, and consumed our final imperfections, let us ascend with joyous heart to the altar of truth.**

The Initiator now takes his place behind his altar in the far East with the Assisting Patriarchs on either side. The Neophyte is raised and conducted by the Acolyte to the Orient and caused to kneel on the other side of the altar upon the kneeler.

CONSECRATION

The Initiator and two Assisting Patriarchs rise in the East and surround the kneeling Neophyte. *Laying their hands upon the head and two shoulders* of the Neophyte, they say in unison:

> **Receive the Holy Spirit for the office and work of a Bishop of the Gnosis.**

Then, the Initiator alone says, as the three maintain their hands upon the Neophyte:

> I, elected Bishop _____, by the authority of the ÆONs and under the auspices of the Antient & Primitive Rite of Memphis+Misraïm, sanctify you, consecrate you, create you, and confirm you as a Bishop of the Gnosis.[806]

The three Patriarchs embrace the Neophyte, and the Initiator continues with the anointing of his forehead, saying:

> Receive, finally, Sublime Copt, the grand and sublime power to CONSECRATE

The Initiator anoints the brow of the Neophyte in the form of a Triple TAU.

> ...other Sublime Copts to the PRIESTHOOD on the THREE PLANES and to confer upon them validly the real powers which are the privilege thereof.

The Initiator anoints the hands of the Neophyte, saying:

> May these hands be consecrated and hallowed for the work of the High Degrees of Masonry, as well as of the pontifical Order by this anointing with holy chrism of sanctification. In the Name of the ✠ Father, and of the ✠ Son, and of the Holy ✠ Spirit.

All in attendance say, **Amen.**

The Initiator then strikes the shoulders of the neophyte with the mallet (right then left), imposes his hands upon his forehead again, forming an open triangle, and breathes on him while saying:

> Participate now in the Divine breath which transports, animates, and vivifies all that exists in the Universe.

RADIANT PRAYER

The Initiator and Assisting Patriarchs extend their hands over the new Bishop while the Initiator chants the radiant prayer:

> O Sovereign Power that we invoke under divers names and who alone rules the destinies of men and things, receive in this moment our homage, our heart, and our

---

[806] This is an amended version of the consecratory prayer utilized by Jean Bricaud from p. 29 of Ravignat's *The French Gnostic Church*, 2019.

joy. See that this new guide of men be permeated with Thy Light, transported by Thy Strength, devoured by Thy Zeal, and burned by Thy Goodness which consumes.

See that he remains ever worthy of Thee, and that he also passes worthily the Sacred Torch, which has been confided to him this day, to that one of his disciples whom he shall estimate the best, the purest, the most enlightened, the most worthy of this supreme favor.

Be blessed by the Children of the Widow and celebrated unto eternity by all the harmonies of the Spheres and the radiance of the worlds.

ADONAI, ADONAI, ADONAI. To the Glory of the Sovereign Architect of All Worlds!

Rise, Sublime Brother (*or* Sister), for you are going to don the robe of purity, the cloak of charity, the hat of perseverance, and the Shepherd's staff.

The Initiator vests him in the habits of his functions and then says as he places the double tau pectoral cross ✝ of the 66° over his head:

I now have the duty and the pleasure to communicate to you the sublime sacerdotal secrets of the Patriarch Grand Consecrator Templar Bishop.

INSTRUCTION OF THE DEGREE

The Patriarch Initiator gives to the new Patriarch Grand Consecrator Templar Bishop, the secrets of the degree, saying:[807]

Attend to and repeat the following demonstration between myself and the Assisting Bishop:

ORDER: **Cross the arms over the chest.**

SIGN: **cross the hands outwardly over the abdomen.** COUNTER-SIGN: **cross the hands outwardly over the head.**

PASSWORD: **Place the hand on the heart while saying: FAITH.**

---

[807] As in degrees derived from differing sources and traditions, the Honorary 66°, Ambelain-line, has distinct secrets from the traditional material as collected by T Allen Greenfield and Alexander Rybalka in their respective works. We include these here to further the distinction between this Honorific and the second echelon working of our materials; however, the inner work aligns naturally and coherently for the persevering. Each Bishop should engage in the work on all three echelons after consecration.

1st Response: place the hand on the forehead while saying: **HOPE**

2nd Response: open the arms while saying: **CHARITY**.

GRIP: **a light blow on the right shoulder and give one another the left hand.**

BATTERY: **(4+2+3:) ....**

MYSTERIOUS ACCLAMATION: **Adonai, Adonai, Adonai.**

AGE: **An Eternity** (for the Gnostics, this signifies a cycle of a thousand years fulfilled; this corresponds to our time of Labor, issuing from the three kingdoms of the secret fire to the Arcana and the Elixir. What they sometimes call an AEON, that is to say a period of creation, may be analogous to one of the seven "days" or a new Universe after this one).

RITUS COMMUNIONIS

The Senate and Patriarchs all applaud the newly consecrated Bishop and then return to their stations for the remainder of Holy Mass. The new Templar Bishop joins in with the consecration of the gifts, taking his place at the head of the altar facing the Orient with the three Patriarchs at each of the other sides of the altar. Still standing, the Patriarch Initiator and fellow Patriarchs hover their hands over the gifts brought out of the Initiator's altar and placed by the Acolyte, saying:

> **As we continue this Holy Service, let us pray for mindfulness and awareness as we partake of this unbloody sacrifice and imbue the gifts with our own light, energy, and personal intentions...**

Pause—all present raise their hands out in front of them and towards the Holy Altar as the Initiator chants in plain tone:

> **Let us pray to Divine Wisdom!**

All: *Holy Sophia, Grant Us Peace*

The Initiator takes the Bible from the central altar, has the new Bishop kneel once again before the Initiator's altar, and with the help of the two Assisting Patriarchs has the Holy Book opened and held above the new Bishop's head and shoulders. An Acolyte adds incense grains to the censer. The Initiator reads the first passage (Psalms 110:4):

The Lord hath sworn, and will not repent, Thou art a priest forever after the order of Melchizedek.

The Initiator then turns the Bible to the first chapter of the Gospel of John, saying strongly:

WISDOM! Let us attend! Let us hear the Holy Gospel according to St. John. Peace be unto you all!

All respond:

And with your Spirit!

Initator:

*In the beginning was the Word, and the Word was with God,
and the Word was God.
² The same was in the beginning with God.
³ All things were made by him; and without him was not
any thing made that was made.
⁴ In him was life; and the life was the light of men.
⁵ And the light shineth in darkness; and the darkness comprehended it not.*[808]

The Acolyte then assures that the items are spaced in triangular formation on the Initiator's altar, with the wine at the apex, the bread to the left, and the water to the right. Incense is added to the censer, and the Initiator censes the altar in a +cruciform pattern, as well as the participants, icons and mystical mandala. The Initiator then washes his hands with the help of the Acolyte. While washing he says,

> ✠ *Purge me with hyssop and I shall be made clean; wash me and I shall be made whiter than snow. Create in me a clean heart O God and renew a right spirit within me.*

Taking the paten of bread in his hands and raising it aloft (Assistant Patriarchs and new Bishop raising their hands in unison), the Initiator chants:

> **Blessed art Thou, Lord, God of all creation. Through your goodness we have this bread to offer, which earth has given, and human hands have made. It will become for us the bread of life.**

The Initiator makes the sign of the cross over the bread, then takes the cruet and pours a portion of the blessed water into the chalice of wine and says:

---

[808] Optional readings which were used in my consecration on Arabia Mountain provided after the ritual.

> **By the mystery of this water and wine may we come to share in the divinity of Christ, who humbled himself to share in our humanity.**

The Initiator then raises the chalice high and chants (Assisting Bishops raise hands):

> **Blessed are you, Lord, God of all creation. Through your goodness we have this wine to offer, fruit of the vine and work of human hands. It will become our spiritual drink.**

All sing slowly: **Benedíctus Deus sæcula.**

The Initiator replaces the wine upon the altar and makes the sign of the cross over its contents. With the help of the Acolyte, the Initiator then breathes the sign of the cross over the bread and the wine at the same time while inaudibly saying:

> **Angel of the Presence, descend upon these gifts and make them the living body and blood of our Lord, the Master Initiator, ✠ YEHESHUA. Direct, O God, a ray of your Love and Wisdom upon this food and drink. Mark us with the indelible mark of reconciliation and transmit to us your luminous influx.**

The Initiator takes the bread and the wine and walks it towards the mystical mandala and, holding the gifts over the apex of the Triangle (crown), he says:

> **We offer unto Thee this bloodless sacrifice, and we ask Thee, and pray Thee, and supplicate Thee: Send down Thy Holy [809]Spirit upon us and upon these gifts here offered and make this bread the living Body of the Christos. (Amen)**
>
> **And make of this spiritual drink the precious Blood of the Christos. (Amen).**
>
> **Forming the epiclesis by the Holy Spirit! (AMEN 3x).**

The Acolyte prepares to sound the bells during the *Sanctus*. The Initiator returns the gifts to the altar and with hands extended over the gifts, making the Rabbinic sign ש, thumbs interlaced, the Initiator roars:

> (bells vigorously rung)

---

[809] This portion comprises the mysterious *epiclesis* wherein the Holy Spirit is invoked within the context of the Eucharistic sacrifice. All should focus intently on the mystical mandala, as this moment is given to certain "happenings," visions, knocks, floating glyphs, etc., as a sign of the presence of the Initiator and the Holy Spirit.

Appendix E: 66° - Patriarch Grand Consecrator

HAGIOS O THEOS, HAGIOS ISCHUROS, HAGIOS ATHANATOS, ELEISON IMAS!

The Initiator makes a deep bow towards the altar and then takes the paten of bread and chalice, holds them aloft in front of the congregants and says:

Holy things are for the HOLY!

The Initiator then chants the Pater Noster with hands outstretched:

✠ Our Father, who art in Heaven, hallowed be Thy Name. Thy Kingdom come, Thy will be done on earth as it is in heaven. Give us this day our daily bread, and forgive us our trespasses, as we forgive those who trespass against us. And lead us not into temptation but deliver us from evil.

The Initiator then performs the Qabalistic Cross, saying:

✠ For the Kingdom, the Power, and the Glory are yours. Now and forever. Amen.

The Initiator then continues with the Commemoration of the Saints, the final *Litania* of the Mass:

Again and again we ask for your presence Holy Saints and Angels, and we cry unto thee with one accord,

> All: **HEAR US AND BE NEAR US**

Hear us and be near us Sts. Philomena, Expedite, Cosmas & Damian,

> All: **HEAR US AND BE NEAR US**

Hear us and be near us Sts. Isidore, James the Greater, and St. Patrick of Ireland,

> All: **HEAR US AND BE NEAR US**

Hear us and be near us Sts. Gerald Majella, Claire of Assisi, and Our Lady of Sorrows,

> All: **HEAR US AND BE NEAR US**

Hear us and be near us Sts. Brigid, Lazarus and Our Lady of Czestochowa,

> All: **HEAR US AND BE NEAR US**

> Hear us and be near us Sts. Joseph, Sacred Heart of Jesus, Anne, and Our Lady of the Immaculate Conception,

> All: **HEAR US AND BE NEAR US.**

The Initiator then takes the paten of bread and the chalice and forms an extended cross in the air towards the West of the Temple. He then turns towards the altar and does the same gesture for himself. He then turns with the gifts towards the West and pronounces the final words before administering communion:

> **The gifts of God for the people of God; happy are those who come to his table. Feast upon Him in your hearts with thanksgiving.**

Serving himself a portion of the bread and the wine, the Initiator signs himself and says inaudibly:

> ✠ **O Lord open my lips, and my mouth shall proclaim your praise.**[810]

All in attendance form a line in front of the Holy Table where they will receive communion on the tongue from the kneeler. The Initiator then takes the bread and with it makes the sign of the cross on the forehead of the kneeling new Bishop first, saying:

> **The Body of our Lord keep us unto life eternal.**

The New Bishop responds, as all who will come to commune:

> ✠ **Amen.**

The same is repeated with the wine for the new Bishop first, then all after:

> **The Blood of our Lord keep us unto life eternal.**

All respond:

> ✠ **Amen.**

Each member moves off to one side of the altar after communing until all have received.

---

[810] From Psalms 50:15 (Septuagint). This moment also should bring to mind the various ceremonies of the "Opening of the Mouth," such as *Utterance 93* from the "Pyramidal texts, spell 527," which states, *open your mouth with the eye of Horus...receive this your bread which is the eye of Horus*. In our own Chapel, we cut out small ankh-shaped bread for the 66° mystic repast, in alignment with both my dream of being fed an ankh and this gesture's coherence with the ceremonies of opening the mouth.

BENEDICTIONS & CLOSING OF THE TEMPLAR BISHOP GRADE

After all in attendance have communed under both species, the Initiator finishes the cup, whispering *it is finished* and placing a cover over the paten. Turning towards the north and the south, with outstretched hands, he completes the ritual in ancient fashion saying:

> **The Lord be with you.**

All respond:

> **And with your spirit.**
>
> **Let us lift up our hearts unto the Lord.**

All respond: **It is right to give him thanks and praise.**

The Initiator concludes the ceremony of initiation after the new Initiate has given his first benediction Urbi et Orbi. The Initiator bids the new Bishop to take his double tau pectoral cross in hand as he prays. (**Provide the following prayer to the new Bishop if needed*):

The newly consecrated Templar Bishop prays:

> May the Holy Apostles Peter and Paul, whose power and authority has been confided to us, intercede personally for us to the Lord! Amen.
>
> By the prayers and the merits of the Blessed Mary, Ever-Virgin, of the Blessed John the Baptist, and of the Saints Peter and Paul, as well as all the Saints, may God All-Powerful have mercy on you, and having remitted your sins, may Jesus Christ conduct you to life eternal! Amen.
>
> May this work be unto you an indulgence, absolution, forgiveness of all your sins, a sacred space of an authentic and fruitful penance, may you have an ever-penitent heart and engage in a correction of your life, may the grace and counsel of the Holy Spirit be with you, and give you perseverance until the end in good works: may the Lord All-Powerful and Merciful grant all this to you! Amen.

> And may the benediction of God All-Powerful, the ✠Father, ✠the Son, and the Holy ✠Spirit, descend upon you and remain there forever. Amen.

Assisting Patriarchs move to the right of the Initiator. The Acolyte conducts the new Patriarch Grand Consecrator Templar Bishop to the left of the Initiator.

The Patriarch Initiator strikes one knock of the mallet while saying:

> Illustrious B∴B∴ & S∴S∴, we are going to close the Labors of this Respectable Senate.
>
> All stand and to order, my Sublime BB∴ & S∴S∴.
>
> To the Glory of the Sublime Architect of ALL Worlds. In the name and under the auspices of…, I declare closed the mystical labors of its Sublime Senate and Council laboring at the Zenith of…
>
> By the sign… And by the countersign… And by the mysterious acclamation.
>
> ADONAI… ADONAI… ADONAI…

✠

CHAIN OF UNION

The Acolyte adds fresh grains of incense to the censer. The Patriarch Initiator continues:

My Sublime Copts, before we separate, let us form the Chain of Fraternal Union.

All rise and take their places around the mystical Mandala; the Initiator takes his place between the Flambeaux of the South and the North.

The *Chain of Union* is made long and in perfect silence, while slowly chanting the "Our Father."

All:

> Our Father, who art in Heaven, hallowed be thy name, thy kingdom come, thy will be done on earth as in heaven. Give us this day our daily bread. Forgive us our offenses, as we forgive also those who have offended us. And do not subject us to temptation, but deliver us from Evil. Amen.

The Patriarch Initiator then prays in solemn tones:

> May the Eternal God bless and keep us. May He make his Face to shine upon us and be gracious unto us. May he lift up His countenance upon us and give us peace!
>
> Our hope is in the ✠Father, our refuge the ✠Son, our shelter the Holy ✠Spirit, O Sacred Ternary, glory be to Thee.
>
> To thee do we commit our every hope, O Mother of God, guard us under thy shelter. It is truly meet to call thee blessed, the Theotokos and Mother of Our God. More honorable than the Cherubim and more glorious than the Seraphim, thee who without corruption gavest birth to God the Word, the very Theotokos, thee do we magnify.
>
> With me, my Brothers & Sisters, let us vibrate into ALL worlds, the Holy Name at which every knee shall bow and every tongue confess, the Mighty Pentagrammaton, י ה ש ו ה

ALL inhale deeply, then vibrate slowly but powerfully, on a complete exhalation at the Patriarch Initiator's prompting:

YE-HE-SHU-VAH

After a moment of silence, the Chain is ended. To quit the Chain, do not shake the hands three times (as in the Royal Arch), but let them slide gently, so that this Chain may be Fixed in Time as in Space.

All return to the Orient and wait there standing facing the mystical mandala.

Once standing at the Orient, the Initiator collects himself, followed by the Assisting Patriarchs and Acolyte who come to Order. The Initiator may then proceed to the extinction of the Flambeaux.

EXTINCTION OF THE FLAMBEAUX - ERASING OF THE MANDALA

The Initiator, mallet on the chest, descends to the mandala, passing to the south, and places himself between the candle of the south and north.

He erases the mandala and extinguishes the candle of the south.

He then passes to the north and extinguishes the candle of the north. Passing the north, he faces the candle of the east.

He extinguishes the candle of the east and returns to the central altar. He closes the Holy Bible or Holy Books and re-ascends his station.

In silence, the Initiator extinguishes the Triple Flambeaux, beginning with the candle on the right, then that on the left, and finally that of the middle.

The Initiator rests his mallet at his station; the sacred Fire or sacristy lamp on the altar remains lit if the work is held in a chapel or oratory that maintains the host for Eucharistic adoration. Otherwise, the sacristy lamp is extinguished by the Patriarch Initiator after *all* have left the Temple.

The Patriarch Initiator strikes one knock of the mallet while saying:

> **Let us all swear to keep secret the progress of our labors.**

Raising the right hand, ALL say:

> **We swear it.**

The Initiator continues, saying:

> **Sublime B∴B∴ & S∴S∴, the Meeting is suspended. May the disciples of the Lord retire in peace.**

Making a large sign of the cross towards the north, west, and south, the Patriarch Initiator says:

> **Benedícat vos omnípotens Deus, Pater, et Filius, ✠ et Spíritus Sanctus.**

ALL respond: **Amen.**

> **Ite, missa est.**

ALL respond: **Deo grátias.**

Before all exit in silence, the Patriarch Initiator pronounces the license to depart:

> **Angels and celestial spirits who have assisted us, we give thanks to Thee. May the peace of God be always between Thou and us.**

Any spirits, forms, or countenances who remain, depart; as many as who are constrained by our workings depart; let all presences depart from this our Consecration in the name of the ✠ Father, and of the ✠ Son, and of the ✠ Holy Spirit. We thank thee for thy guidance and ask that you return to us in haste when we call upon thee. By the Most Holy Name of יהשוה.

The Service is ended. All items are returned to their previous state through the Execration Formula known to the Patriarch Initiator and Assisting Patriarchs. All lights are extinguished or snuffed, rather than blown out. All holy water, ashes from the censer, or half-used charcoal should be returned to the earth, while spent candles and other items should be thrown away.

Signing & sealing of the instrument of Consecration after the Arabia Mountain Working at a Free Illuminist Gathering at the Chapel of the Gnosis and within our sacred marma.

Animating the sacred marma in the Chapel of the Gnosis by the sacred fire from the Sacristy Lamp.

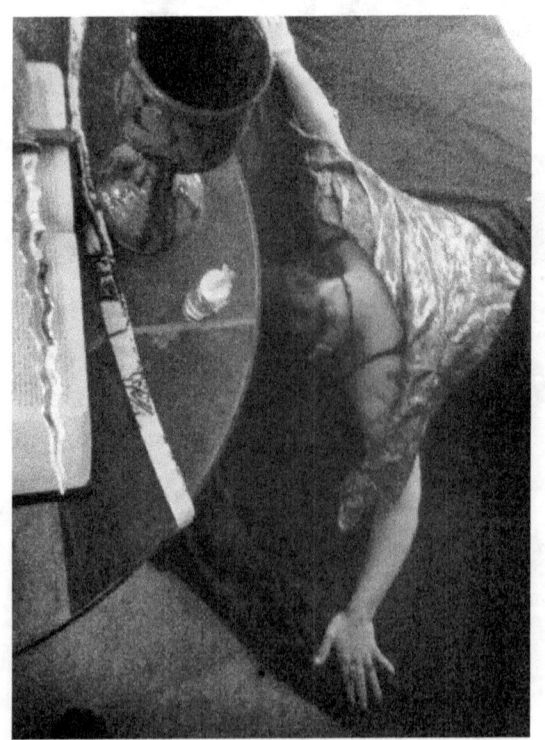

Salome during ordination.

Appendix E: 66° - Patriarch Grand Consecrator

ALTERNATE READINGS

The following readings were the ones in use when I was consecrated on Arabia Mountain. As mentioned in the Hauts Grades section of the 66°, a very simple ceremonial could be utilized–much the same way as the Free Illuminist gatherings were conducted– with these powerful readings, the material from the second echelon working of the degree, and three consecrated Bishops. Alternately, these readings could be used within the context of the grade developed above during the Liturgia Verba.

Special thanks to our Illustrious, Grand General Hierophant, T Allen H. Greenfield, 33° 90° 95° 97°100°, WAEO APRMM, for permission to use the readings from his, *Rituals for the 21st Century*, pgs. 7-11.

From Allen:

This ceremony of empowerment has been used by me well over 100 times. Although it has obvious spiritual implications, I do not regard it as sectarian in any sense. Note that it draws from Ancient Egyptian texts, the Book of Proverbs and the Gnostic Gospels. It does validly carry the egregore of the Apostolic Succession, the Gnostic Succession, the Old Roman Priesthood, the Ancient Coptic (Egyptian) Priesthood, if given by one who has these empowerments, to one seeking them.

Patriarch Initiator says:

THUNDER, FLASH, ILLUMINATE, I DECLARE YOU ILLUMINATUS

Initiator anoints forehead and continues:

I was sent forth from the power,
and I have come to those who reflect upon me,
and I have been found among those who seek after me.
Look upon me, you who reflect upon me,
and you hearers, hear me.

You who are waiting for me, take me to yourselves.
And do not banish me from your sight.

And do not make your voice hate me, nor your hearing.

Do not be ignorant of me anywhere or any time. Be on your guard!

Do not be ignorant of me.
For I am the one who alone exists,
and I have no one who will judge me.

For many are the pleasant forms which exist in numerous sins,
and incontinences,
and disgraceful passions,
and fleeting pleasures,
which (men) embrace until they become sober.

BLESSING OF THE KOHENIM (Consecrator)

May the LORD make his face shed light upon you and be gracious unto you—
May the LORD lift up his light unto you and grant you peace.

Pause. **Do You Will to Accept Consecration—that is empowerment—in the Gnostic and Apostolic Lineages Passing through Us from the Dawn of the World?**

On Affirmation: **By the Power Vested in Us from our predecessors in the Most Antient Egregore of Spiritual Power, I Consecrate—that is, fully Empower You**

EPISKOPUS forever in the Succession Apostolic and Gnostic.

ALL: **May it BE SO! IT IS SO!**

HYMN OF THE ATEN (2nd Consecrator)

When you set in western lightland,
Earth is in darkness as if in death;
One sleeps in chambers, heads covered,
One eye does not see another,
Were they robbed of their goods,
That are under their heads,
People would not remark it,

Every lion comes from its den,
All the serpents bite;
Darkness hovers, earth is silent.
As their maker rests in lightland.
Earth brightens when you dawn in lightland,
When you shine as Aten of daytime;
As you cast your rays,
The Two Lands are in festivity.
Awake they stand on their feet,
You have roused them;
Bodies cleansed, clothed,
Their arms adore your appearance.
The entire land sets out to work,
All beasts browse on their herbs;
Trees, herbs are sprouting.
Birds fly from their nests,
Their wings greeting your KA,
All flocks frisk on their feet,
All that fly up and alight,
They live when you dawn for them.
Ships fare north, fare south as well,
Roads lie open when you rise;
The fish in the river dart before you,
Your rays are in the midst of the sea.
Who makes seed grow in women,
Who creates people from sperm;
Who feeds the son in his mother's womb,
Who soothes him to still his tears.
Nurse in the womb,
Giver of breath,
To nourish all that he made,
When he comes from the womb to breathe,
On the day of his birth,
You open wide his mouth,
You supply his needs.
When the chick in the egg speaks in the shell,
You give him breath within to sustain him;

When you have made him complete,
To break out from the egg,
He comes out from the egg,
To announce his completion,
Walking on his legs he comes from it.[811]

*Illustrious Grand General Hierophant T Allen Greenfield
during the wedding of +Jon & +Skyler we performed on Arabia Mountain*

---

[811] This Hymn is also read by Isis at the close of *Osirification,* in the third echelon working of the APRM+M.

Letter from Zagreb, Croatia

The story of the Points Chauds workings was, for me, the most important factor that originally drew me toward Congregational Illuminism and the EGNU associations. I had long felt that ritual initiations, because of their human nature and the different levels of effort, skill, and enlightenment applied by initiators, could not in themselves guarantee a completely reliable line of spiritual development for every seeker. One might pass through various initiations in any tradition, but there is always the risk that at least one of them was improperly transmitted, leaving an "unsealed" segment in the spiral of magical energy.

Because of this conviction, I was eager to discover methods of initiation that could bypass the uncertainty of elaborate ceremonies. I found such a method in the Points Chauds, as taught to me in the CI/EGNU temples at Split, Croatia. Their beauty was in their simplicity and directness: the empowerment was self-sufficient, rooted in experience, and capable of standing on its own without dependency on perfect ceremonial conditions.

When the **Ma'at-Set Temple** was founded in Zagreb, this interest in Points Chauds grew quickly. Many sought the empowerments—some completely new to such workings, others having already received them from Split initiates. The empowerments became the central axis of our early initiatory activity. They electrified the student's energy system, generated enthusiasm, and awakened the capacity to participate in a wide range of other practices: EGNU, Voudon, Golden Dawn, and Thelemic rituals alike.

At the same time as this esoteric APRMM work was unfolding, another need became apparent for several experienced Rosicrucians and Gnostics: the need for a more classical form of lodge practice, one that would anchor our work in the heritage of Freemasonry. Out of this impulse was born the **"Templum Custodum Lucis Ma'at" Sovereign Gnostic Sanctuary**, formed by the work of Tau Donaticus in close alliance with the Sovereign Gnostic Sanctuary *Misi* in Vršac.

Over the decade between the first publication of *Spirit Builders* (2015) and this new edition (2025), this lodge-based current spread its wings widely. It forged strong connections with **WAEO**, facilitated pilgrimages and visits to **Bansko, Sofia, Tel Aviv–Jaffo and Jerusalem**, and brought into being several specialized bodies. Among the most notable were the **"Violet Flame" Lodge of the Order of the Arcanum of Comte de Saint Germain**, chartered by the unforgettable Hierophant **Alexander Rybalka**, and the **Order of the Balkan Voudon Gnostic Cross-Roads**, led by Tau Qadosh and me, chartered by Grand Cophta **Allen Greenfield**.

The visits themselves became milestones in our development. In **Bansko**, we encountered a wide international fellowship of APRMM, with brethren from the **USA, Canada, France, Macedonia, Albania, Bulgaria and other nations**. The gathering was more than ritual—it was a living exchange of traditions, experiences, and fraternal warmth, a reminder that our work was part of a vast global current. The journeys to **Sofia** deepened these ties, rooting us in the long-standing Balkan lineage of Memphis-Misraïm practice.

Even more profound were the visits to **Tel Aviv–Jaffo**, where we entered the mother lodge in the ancient stone heart of the city. There, within walls that had witnessed centuries of spiritual striving, we were granted the rare privilege of receiving **high lodge initiations** seldom performed in today's world. These rites, transmitted with care and reverence, became an anchor of spiritual depth for our own lodge's progress.

Tau Esau and Naakim Bey in Jaffo

Important Esoteric work was also done in Jerusalem 2017., and during visits of our brotherly Misir lodge adepts to Spain in 2024. Misir lodge work had spread to Belgrade, Novi Sad, Subotica, and far abroad.

Through all this expansion, two distinct but complementary streams emerged. On the one hand, the **Ma'at-Set Temple** pursued a path of high esoteric exploration, especially through intensive work with *Liber 231*. This line of inquiry lifted the spiritual dimension of our temple to a higher octave, opening visions and symbolic structures that reshaped our understanding of inner landscapes. On the other hand, the lodge-work of **Templum Custodum Lucis Ma'at** matured and stabilised through the classical Memphis-Misraïm rites. Where the Temple embodied esoteric innovation and daring exploration, the Lodge embodied order, continuity, and tradition. Together they formed a balance: fire and stone, vision and structure.

Our members themselves testify to the power of these experiences:

- **I.**: "The first Point was the most important for me. My life literally broke apart, but later I understood it was clearing the way for new things. I left a harmful relationship, passed through deep depression, and then felt myself reborn. After the Third Point I experienced renewal in spirit and in matter alike. I began yoga practice and cut down my consumption of alcohol. I intend to move forward step by step."

- **J.**: "The empowerments gave me clearer vision in spiritual work, and I no longer felt drained after seeing clients for tarot or astrology. Some old clients disappeared, but new ones appeared immediately. I found myself deepening my Reiki practice, and my relationship with my partner became much more harmonious."

- **V.**: "Meditation became much deeper and entry into inner states much easier. I also gained the ability to connect many small impressions into one larger pattern—finding magical meanings in the fabric of daily life."

- **D.**: "For me, the same changes happened as with V., but with an additional flow of symbols flooding my mind during the process."

- **W.**: "After the first empowerment, I experienced many extremes of mind, but with time, they calmed and settled into peace. The whole process I compare to putting on the apron and taking the oath."

Of course, not all experiences were smooth. This taught us an important lesson: initiatory fire must be tempered with rhythm, balance, and the clerical line of blessings and initiations. For this reason, we became more deliberate, pacing empowerments carefully and ensuring that students were grounded and guided.

Looking back, it is striking how much has unfolded in ten years. What began as a simple search for continuity beyond imperfect initiations has blossomed into a full tapestry of currents. The **Points Chauds** remain a living fire that fuels every other work. The **Ma'at-Set Temple** carries us into deeper symbolic explorations, while the **Templum Custodum Lucis Ma'at** offers the solid framework of Masonic tradition. The international gatherings—from Bansko to Jaffo—remind us that we are part of a brotherhood that spans continents and centuries.

Together, these experiences stand as twin pillars—esoteric ascent and ritual stability—and around them, the network of allied bodies across the Balkans, Europe, and the Near East ensures that this work is not isolated but woven into the living fabric of a wider initiatory community.

Looking ahead, we sense that these currents will continue to evolve. The inner work of *Liber 231* still contains unexplored depths, promising new visions for those who dare. The Memphis-Misraim tradition remains a vessel of stability, but also one capable of transformation when wedded to modern needs. Our alliances—from Split to Zagreb, from Bansko to Jaffo, with Vršac, Novi Sad, Belgrade and Subotica—show that the age of isolated temples is ending. A global web of lodges and temples is emerging, not to erase local character, but to interlace it with universal brotherhood. In the age of political turmoil, it is notable that the works of Tau Libero, Tau Qadosh, Tau Donaticus and me, Tau Esau – stand in balance as four elements, as noted on our charter, connecting across borders in brotherly ties.

As we cross the threshold of 2025, the Work stands at a point of maturity, but not of completion. If the past decade was about planting seeds and raising wings, the next may be about bearing fruit and building enduring structures. Spirit builds not only within the seeker but also between seekers, across borders, generations, and traditions. And it is in this broader building that our task now lies: to continue the fire, to preserve the stone, and to prepare the way for those who will come after us.

Tau Esau, 33°, 66°,98° SIEEM (WAEO), APRMM

Tau Esau and WAEO Grand Hierophant Uraniel

Letter from Puerto San Isidro, Leon, Spain

Valhalla Lodge is a mostly virtual lodge working high in the Cantabrian mountains of Spain. When we do have a full ritual working it is usually on those infrequent occasions when we have a member or potential member travelling to stay with us for a few days and whilst the work usually includes reading through some full rituals together, normally the main work is the conferral of the Points Chaud and sometimes the Gnostic Consecration (66°). Spirit Builders is completely invaluable for this work as we refer to it for the Points Chaud Charts, the sacred words, batteries and signs of each degree.

Spirit Builders is also my constant companion in my personal solitary practice. I often choose a random number between 1 and 97 and "scry the Point Chaud" for that particular degree. My usual practice is to open the Tracing Board (from The Tarot of the Egyptian Masonry of Cagliostro) on my Tablet which is placed on the altar as a visual aid, along with candles and possibly some "working tools", as well as a shamanic rattle and rum. I then tend to "tread the mill" for a couple of minutes, whilst rattling and repeating or chanting the Sacred Word and/or password of the degree. This induces a state of spiritual openness and attunement and builds power in the circle. Having read the relevant chapter in Spirit Builders I then settle down to journey with my drum, first drumming the battery of the degree before settling into a steady and usually quite fast rhythm. Over several decades I have found that the drum induces the trance state more easily for me than any other method and usually as I journey some message is bound to come through either clairvoyantly, clairaudiently or clairsentiently.

The clues Tau Palamas gives us in Spirit Builders for an "invocation" or "call" are very helpful - for example "Call to Papa Legba" (18°); "Invocation of Damballah" (25°) or "Call to Louis Claude de Saint Martin" 60° and actually, this practice of invoking the Spirits or Lwa through my shamanic scrying process became a perfect foundation for my later work with the Black Preceptory of Haiti. Any freemason could gain great insights with little effort simply by "scrying the points" using the information which Tau Palamas supplies so abundantly; but for me the whole system presented the unexpected blessing of an introduction to the magical world of the Haitian Lwa, which has been so fundamental to the whole Free Illuminist tradition. To conclude I might observe that what "Science and Health" is to the devout Christian Scientist, "Spirit Builders" is to the keen Free Illuminist, so thank you Tau Palamas for mediating this spiritual treasure to us!

Tau Blaise, 95° - Valhalla Lodge

Bibliography

Ambelain, Robert. *La Kabbale pratique*. Paris: French and European Publications Inc, 1951.

Anonymous. *Meditations on the Tarot: A Journey into Christian Hermeticism*. Rockport: Element Classic Editions, 1993.

Anonymous. *Ophiolatreia: An Account of the Rites and Mysteries Connected with the Origin, Rise, and Development of Serpent Worship in Various Parts of the World*. Citrus Heights: Transmutation Publishing, 2013.

Aquinas, Thomas. *Summa Theologica*. Vol. 12. Part II. New York: Benziger Brothers, 1912.

Artress, Lauren. *Walking A Sacred Path*. New York: Penguin, 1995.

Barnstone, William. *The Other Bible*. New York: Harper Collins Publishers, 1984.

Bernheim, Alain. "Did Early 'High' or Écossais Degrees Originate in France?" *Freemasonry in Context, History, Ritual, Controversy*. Eds. Arturo de Hoyos and S. Brent Morris. Lanham: Lexington Books, 2004. 19-41.

Bertiaux, Michael. *Cosmic Meditation*. London: Fulgur Limited, 2007.

— The Monastery of the Seven Rays. Years I-IV. Chicago, Privately published.
— *The Voudon Gnostic Workbook*. San Francisco: Red Wheel/Weiser, LLC, 2007.
— *Vudu Cartography*. London: Fulgur Limited, 2010.

Besant, Annie, and C. W. Leadbeater. *Thoughtforms*. Bradford: The Country Press, 1925.

Bogdan, Henri. *Western Esotericism and Rituals of Initiation*. Albany: State University of New York Press, 2007.

Burt, Calvin C. *Egyptian Masonic History of the Original and Unabridged Ancient and Ninety-six 96th Degree Rite of Memphis*. Montana: Kessinger Publishing, LLC., 2014.

Cecchetelli, Michael, ed. *The Holy Guardian Angel: On the Practice and Experience of the Holy Guardian Angel*. Timmonsville: Nephilim Press, 2014.

Charpentier, Louis. *Les Mystères de la cathédrale de Chartres*. Paris: Robert Laffont, 1995.

Cicero, Chic and Sandra Tabatha. *The Essential Golden Dawn: An Introduction to High Magic*. St. Paul: Llewellyn Publications, 2003.

Cicero, Chic and Sandra Tabatha. *Self Initiation into the Golden Dawn Tradition*. St. Paul: Llewellyn Publications, 2002.

Cooper, Robert L D and Philippa Faulks. *The Masonic Magician. The Life and Death of Count Cagliostro and His Egyptian Rite*. London: Watkins Publishing, 2008.

Crowley, Aleister. *Gems from the Equinox*. San Francisco: Red Wheel/Weiser, LLC., 2007.

Crowley, Aleister. *The Holy Books of Thelema*. York Beach: Weiser Publications, 1983.

Crowley, Aleister. *Magick: Liber ABA, Book 4*, parts I-IV. York Beach: Weiser Publications, 2000.

Crowley, Aleister. "The Initiated Interpretation of Ceremonial Magic." *The Goetia: The Lesser Key of Solomon the King*. Trans. Samuel Liddell MacGregor Mathers. Ed. Aleister Crowley. York Beach: Weiser Publications, 1997. 15-19.

Crowley, Aleister. *The Book of the Law, Liber Al Vel Legis*. San Francisco: Red Wheel/Weiser, LLC, 2009.

Crowley, Aleister. *The Law is for All*. Tempe: New Falcon Publications, 1996.

Damascene, Hieromonk. *Christ the Eternal Tao*. Platina: St. Herman Press, 2004.

de Hoyos, Arturo. *Albert Pike's Morals and Dogma of the Ancient and Accepted Scottish Rite of Freemasonry*. An Annotated Edition. Washington, DC: The Supreme Council, 33, Southern Jurisdiction, 2011.

de Hoyos, Arturo. *The Scottish Rite Ritual Monitor and Guide*. Washington, DC: The Supreme Council, 33, Southern Jurisdiction, 2007.

de Hoyos, Arturo. *Masonic Formulas and Rituals, Transcribed by Albert Pike in 1854 and 1855*. Washington, DC: The Scottish Rite Research Society, 2010.

Del Campo, Gerald. *New Aeon English Qabalah Revealed*. Marietta: Luxor Press Inc, 2002.

Del Campo, Gerald. *New Aeon Magick: Thelema Without Tears*. Marietta: Luxor Press Inc, 2000.

Deren, Maya. *Divine Horsemen: The Living Gods of Haiti*. Kingston: McPherson Publishing, 1983.

Desaguiliers, René and Roger Dachez. "Chinese Thought and Freemasonry in the Eighteenth Century: The Degree of Irish Master, Provost, and Judge." *Freemasonry in Context, History, Ritual, Controversy*. Eds. Arturo de Hoyos and S. Brent Morris. Lanham: Lexington Books, 2004. 144-161.

Dionysius the Areopagite. *On the Divine Names and the Mystical Theology*. New York: Macmillan, 1920.

DuQuette, Lon Milo. *Enochian Vision Magick: An Introduction and Practical Guide to the Magick of Dr. John Dee and Edward Kelley*. York Beach: Weiser Publications, 2008.

DuQuette, Lon Milo. *The Book of Ordinary Oracles*. York Beach: Weiser Publications, 2005.

Eschelman, James A. *776 ½: Tables for Practical Ceremonial*. Los Angeles: College of Thelema, 2010.

Farr, Florence. *Egyptian Magic*. Wellingborough: The Aquarian Press, 1982.

Faivre, Antoine. *Access to Western Esotericism*. Albany: State University of New York Press, 1994.

Filan, Kenaz. *The Haitian Vodou Handbook: Protocols for Riding with the Lwa*. Rochester: Destiny Books, 2007.

Forrest, Isidora M. *Isis Magic: Cultivating a Relationship with the Goddess of 10,000 Names*. St. Paul: Llewellyn Publications, 2001.

Fortune, Dion. *The Training and Work of an Initiate*. York Beach: Weiser Publications, 2000.

Fortune, Dion. *Aspects of Occultism*. York Beach: Weiser Publications, 2000.

Bibliography

Fox, Matthew. *Christian Mystics*. Novato: New World Library, 2011.

Francken, Henry Andrew. *The Francken Manuscript 1783*. Montana: Kessinger Publishing, LLC., 2010.

Godwin, Jocelyn, Chanel, Christian, and John Patrick Deveney. *The Hermetic Brotherhood of Luxor: Initiatic and Historic Documents of an Order of Practical Occultism*. York Beach: Samuel Weiser, Inc., 1995.

Golet, Dr. Ogden Jr. "Introduction." *The Egyptian Book of the Dead: The Book of Going Forth By Day*. Eds and Trans. Eva Von Dassow, et al. San Francisco: Chronicle Books LLC, 2008.

Grant, Kenneth. *Cults of the Shadow*. London: Starfire Publishing, Ltd., 2013.

Grant, Kenneth. *Nightside of Eden*. London: Starfire Publishing, Ltd., 2014.

Grant, Kenneth. *Outside the Circles of Time*. London: Starfire Publishing, Ltd., 2008.

Greenfield, Allen. *The Compleat Rite of Memphis*. Marietta: Luxor Press Inc, 1998.

Greenfield, Allen. *The Story of the Hermetic Brotherhood of Light*. Marietta: Luxor Press Inc, 1997.

Greenfield, Allen H. *The Roots of Modern Magick: Glimpses of the Authentic Tradition from 1700 to 2000*. Lulu Press, 2004.

Greer, John Michael. *The Celtic Golden Dawn: An Original & Complete Curriculum of Druidical Study*. Woodbury: Llewellyn Publications, 2013.

Greer, John Michael. *The Druidry Handbook: Spiritual Practice Rooted in the Living Earth*. York Beach: Weiser Publications, 2006.

Greer, John Michael and Christopher Warnock. *The Complete Picatrix: Liber Atratus Edition*. Lulu Press, 2011.

Hall, Manly P. *The Secret Teachings of All Ages*. Los Angeles: The Philosophical Research Society, Inc., 2000.

Hall, Manly P. *The Lost Keys of Freemasonry*. New York: Penguin, 2006.

Higgins, Frank C. *Hermetic Masonry*. Ferndale: Trismegistus Press, 1980.

Hutchens, Rex. R. *Albert Pike's Lecture on Masonic Symbolism and A Second Lecture on Symbolism: The Omkara and Other Ineffable Words*. Washington DC: The Scottish Rite Research Society, 2006.

Jacob, Margaret C. *The Origins of Freemasonry: Facts and Fictions*. Philadelphia: University of Pennsylvania Press, 2007.

Jacob, Margaret C. *Living the Enlightenment: Freemasonry and Politics in Eighteenth-Century Europe*. New York: Oxford University Press, Inc., 1991.

Jonas, Hans. *The Gnostic Religion*. Boston: Beacon Press, 1971.

Julio, Abbé. *Grand Marvelous Secrets*. Fox Lake, IL: Triad Press, LLC, 2022.

Julio, Abbé. *Liturgical Prayers*. Fox Lake, IL: Triad Press, LLC, 2025.

Julio, Abbé. *The Secret Book of Grand Exorcisms and Benedictions.* Fox Lake, IL: Triad Press, LLC, Forthcoming.

Kauffman, Stuart A. *Reinventing the Sacred: A New View of Science, Reason, and Religion.* New York: Basic Books, 2008.

Kinney, Jay. "Is Freemasonry Afraid of Its Own Shadow? Masonry's Love/Hate Relationship with Esoteric Traditions." *Heredom* Vol. 10. Ed. S. Brent Morris. Washington DC: The Scottish Rite Research Society, 2002. 139-153.

Lawlor, Robert. *Sacred Geometry: Philosophy & Practice.* London: Thames and Hudson, 1982.

Layton, Bentley. *The Gnostic Scriptures: A New Translation with Annotations and Introductions.* New York: Doubleday, 1987.

Leadbeater, C.W. *The Hidden Life in Freemasonry.* Adyar: Theosophical Publishing House, 1955.

Leadbeater, C.W. *Freemasonry and its Ancient Mystic Rites.* New York: Gramercy Books, 1998.

Le Forestier, René. *Occultist Freemasonry in the 18th Century and the Order of Élus Coëns.* Fox Lake, IL: Triad Press, LLC, 2023.

Levenda, Peter. *The Dark Lord: H.P. Lovecraft, Kenneth Grant, and the Typhonian Tradition in Magic.* Lake Worth: Ibis Press, 2013.

Levi, Eliphas. *Transcendental Magic.* York Beach: Samuel Weiser, Inc., 1968.

Levi, Eliphas. *Book of Splendours.* York Beach: Samuel Weiser, Inc., 1973.

Lomas, Robert. *The Secret Science of Freemasonry.* San Francisco: Red Wheel/Weiser LLC., 2010.

Mackey, Albert. *Encyclopedia of Freemasonry and Its Kindred Sciences.* Philadelphia: McClure Publishing Co., 1917.

MacNulty, Kirk W. *Freemasonry: Symbols, Secrets, Significance.* London: Thames and Hudson, 2006.

Macoy, Robert. *The True Masonic Guide (1854).* Montana: Kessinger Publishing, LLC., 2013.

Mahe, Jean-Pierre, et al. *The Way of Hermes.* Rochester: Inner Traditions, 2004.

Malbrough, Rev Ray T. *The Magical Power of the Saints: Evocation and Candle Rituals.* Woodbury: Llewellyn Publications, 2009.

Marconis, E.J.. *The Sanctuary of Memphis or Hermes.* Montana: Kessinger Publishing, LLC., 2010.

Mathers, S.L. MacGregor. *The Book of the Sacred Magic of Abramelin the Mage.* New York: Dover Publications, Inc., 1975.

Mathers, S. L. MacGregor. *The Grimoire of Armadel.* San Francisco: Red Wheel/Weiser, 1995.

McClenachan, Charles T. *The Book of the Ancient and Accepted Scottish Rite of Freemasonry.* New York: Macoy Publishing, 1914.

Mead, G.R.S. (trans.). *Pistis Sophia.* London: Watkins, 1921.

Melville, Francis. *The Book of Alchemy: Learn the Secrets of the Alchemists to Transform Mind, Body, and Soul.* Hauppauge: Barron's Educational Series, Inc., 2002.

Meyer, Marvin and Richard Smith. *Ancient Christian Magic: Coptic Texts of Ritual Power.* Princeton: Princeton University Press, 1994.

Nikolic, Stevan V. *Royal Art: Three Centuries of Freemasonry.* Lincoln: iUniverse, 2006.

Oliver, Rev. George. *The Theocratic Philosophy of Freemasonry (1855).* Montana: Kessinger Publishing, LLC., 2010.

PALAMAS. *Lux Occulta.* Citrus Heights: Transmutation Publishing, 2021.

Palamas, Tau. *Syzygy: Reflections on the Monastery of the Seven Rays.* France: Hadean Press, 2013.

Palamas, Tau. "Nepsis." *Qliphoth Journal, Opus IV, "Quintessence."* Ed. Edgar Kerval. Citrus Heights: Transmutation Publishing, 2014.

Papus (Dr. Gérard Encausse). *Exegesis of the Soul: Three Treatises on the Nature, Origin, & Destiny of the Human Soul.* Fox Lake, IL: Triad Press, LLC, 2022.

Papus (Dr. Gérard Encausse). *What a Master Mason Ought to Know.* Fox Lake, IL: Triad Press, LLC, 2022.

Pasqually, Martinès de. *Treatise on the Reintegration of Beings.* Fox Lake, IL: Triad Press, LLC, 2024.

Peterson, Joseph H. *Arbatel: Concerning the Magic of the Ancients.* Lake Worth: Ibis Press, 2009.

Phosphoros, Sar (trans.). *The Baylot Manuscript in Translation.* Fox Lake, IL: Triad Press, LLC, 2020.

Phosphoros, Tau (trans.). *Degrees of Wisdom: A Compendium of Rituals from the Rites of Memphis and Misraïm.* Fox Lake, IL: Triad Press, LLC, 2025.

Pike, Albert. *The Porch and the Middle Chamber: The Book of the Lodge.* Montana: Kessinger Publishing, LLC., 2003.

Pike, Albert. *The Book of the Words, Sephir H'Debarim.* Washington DC: The Scottish Rite Research Society, 1999.

Pike, Albert. *Morals and Dogma of the Ancient and Accepted Scottish Rite of Freemasonry.* Richmond: L.H. Jenkins, Inc., 1948.

Pike, Albert. *Legenda of the Lodge of Perfection.* Washington DC: The Supreme Council, 33, Southern Jurisdiction, 1956.

Pike, Albert. *Liturgy of the Ancient and Accepted Scottish Rite of Freemasonry, Part III, 15-18.* Springfield: Goetz Printing Co., 1982.

Ragon, Jean-Marie. *Masonic Orthodoxy: Followed by Occult Masonry and Hermetic Initiation.* Fox Lake, IL: Triad Press, LLC, 2023.

Rebold, Emmanuel, M.D. *A General History of Freemasonry in Europe.* Cincinnati: American Masonic Publishing Association, 1868.

Regardie, Israel. *The Middle Pillar: The Balance Between Mind and Magic*. Woodbury: Llewellyn Publications, 2002.

Regardie, Israel. *The Complete Golden Dawn System of Magic*. Tempe: Original Falcon Press, 2010.

Sellner, Edward. *The Wisdom of the Celtic Saints*. Notre Dame: Ave Maria Press, 1993.

Spare, Austin Osman. *Ethos*. Louth: I-H-O Books, 2001.

Stavish, Mark. *Between the Gates: Lucid Dreaming, Astral Projection, and the Body of Light in Western Esotericism*. San Francisco: Red Wheel/Weiser, LLC., 2008.

Stavish, Mark. *Freemasonry: Rituals, Symbols, & History of the Secret Society*. Woodbury: Llewellyn Publications, 2007.

Steiner, Rudolf. *Freemasonry and Ritual Work: The Misraim Service*. Great Barrington: Steiner Books, Anthroposophic Press, 2007.

Teder (Charles Détre). *Rituel de l'Ordre Martiniste*. Paris: Dorbon-Ainé, 1913.

Tresner, Jim. *Vested in Glory*. Washington DC: The Scottish Rite Research Society, 2000.

Tyson, Donald. *Three Books of Occult Philosophy written by Henry Cornelius Agrippa of Nettesheim*. Woodbury: Llewellyn Publications, 1993.

Vlachos, Hierotheos. *A Night in the Desert of the Holy Mountain: Discussion with a Hermit on the Jesus Prayer*. Greece: Birth of the Theotokos Monastery, 2003.

Wilmshurst, W.L. *Masonic Initiation*. Montana: Kessinger Publications LLC., 1992.

Yarker, John. *The Arcane Schools: A Review Of Their Origin and Antiquity, With a General History of Freemasonry (1909)*. Zion, IL: Triad Press, LLC., 2006.

Yarker, John. *Lectures of a Chapter, Senate and Council: According to the Forms of the Antient and Primitive Rite, But Embracing All Systems of High Grade Masonry*. Montana: Kessinger Publications, LLC., 2004.

Yarker, John. *The Secret High Degree Rituals of the Masonic Rite of Memphis*. Montana: Kessinger Publications, LLC., 1993.

Yates, Francis A. The Art of Memory. Chicago: University of Chicago Press, 2001.